Displaced

Displaced

Refugees, Trauma, and Integration Within Nations

SHAIFALI SANDHYA

OXFORD
UNIVERSITY PRESS

OXFORD
UNIVERSITY PRESS

Oxford University Press is a department of the University of Oxford. It furthers
the University's objective of excellence in research, scholarship, and education
by publishing worldwide. Oxford is a registered trade mark of Oxford University
Press in the UK and certain other countries.

Published in the United States of America by Oxford University Press
198 Madison Avenue, New York, NY 10016, United States of America.

Library of Congress Cataloging-in-Publication Data
Names: Sandhya, Shaifali, author.
Title: Displaced : refugees, trauma, and integration within nations / Shaifali Sandhya.
Description: New York, NY : Oxford University Press, [2024] |
Includes bibliographical references and index.
Identifiers: LCCN 2023038558 (print) | LCCN 2023038559 (ebook) |
ISBN 9780197579886 (hardback) | ISBN 9780197579909 (epub) |
ISBN 9780197579916
Subjects: LCSH: Refugees—Case studies.
Classification: LCC HV640 .S263 2023 (print) | LCC HV640 (ebook) |
DDC 362.87—dc23/eng/20230925
LC record available at https://lccn.loc.gov/2023038558
LC ebook record available at https://lccn.loc.gov/2023038559

DOI: 10.1093/oso/9780197579886.001.0001

Printed by Integrated Books International, United States of America

In memory of Manju and Raj,
humanitarians and my parents,
and for their unconditional love,
hope, and optimism

Contents

Acronyms	ix
Maps	xi
Preface	xvii
Acknowledgments	xxiii

1. Our Refugee Crisis: Trauma, Integration, and Resettlement — 1
2. Trauma Beyond Borders: At Sea in the World — 50
3. A White Coat or a White Heart?: The Methodology — 67
4. Queen of Proofs and the Kings of Torment: Psychological Sequelae of Torture — 78
5. Enrique Iglesias Goes German: Identity Politics and Identity Repair — 107
6. Culture and Globalization in Postconflict Trauma Care — 127
7. What's the Trouble with Mrs. Khaled?: The Mental Health of Refugee Women and Their Communities — 152
8. Family Trauma: The Psychological Legacy of War — 174
9. Mental Health and Integration: Structuring Refuge for Resettled Refugees — 200
10. Best Practices in Treating Trauma and Refugee Care: The Ecology of Trauma-Informed and Cultural Health Interventions — 232

Epilogue: The Forcibly Displaced: Looking Ahead — 268

Appendix: Quantitative Data on Anxiety and Depression Subscales — 281
Author Index — 285
Subject Index — 313

Acronyms

ACLU	American Civil Liberties Union
AfD	Alternative for Germany
AI	Amnesty International
APA	American Psychological Association
BAMF-FZ	Research Centre on Migration, Integration, and Asylum of the Federal Office of Migration and RefugeesBPtK: Federal Chamber of Psychotherapists in Germany
BTT	Brief Manual-Based Trauma Therapy
BVOR	Blended Visa-Office Referred
CAT	Convention Against Torture
CBT	Cognitive Behavioral Therapy
CIA	Central Intelligence Agency
CPT	Cognitive Processing Therapy
CPTSD	Complex Posttraumatic Stress Disorder
CRPS	Complex Regional Pain Syndrome
DHS	Department of Homeland Security
ECRE	European Council on Refugees and Exiles
EMDR	Eye Movement Desensitization and Reprocessing
FRA	European Union Agency for Fundament Rights
GAR	Canadian Government Assisted Refugee Program
HSCL	The Hopkins Symptoms Checklist
IAB	Germany Institute for Employment Research
IASC	Interagency Standing Committee
ICE	US Immigration and Customs Enforcement
IDMC	The Internal Displacement Monitoring Center
IDP	Internally Displaced Populations
IIRIRA	Illegal Immigration Reform and Immigrant Responsibility Act
IJRC	International Justice Resource Center
IRCT	International Rehabilitation Council for Torture Survivors
ISIS	Islamic State of Iraq and Syria
LGBTQ	Lesbian, Gay, Bisexual, Transgender, Queer
LGBTQI+	Lesbian, Gay, Bisexual, Transgender, and Intersex Lives
MHPSS	Mental Health and Psychosocial Support
MSF	Médecins Sans Frontières
NET	Narrative Exposure Therapy
NRC	Norwegian Refugee Council
nRS	Northern Rakhine State
OAU	The Organisation of African Unity or the OAU Refugee Convention

OIDA	Ontario International Development Agency
ORR	Office of Refugee Resettlement
PE	Prolonged Exposure
PHR	Physicians for Human Rights Research
PRM	Bureau of Population, Refugees, and Migration
PSR	Private Sponsorship of Refugees
PTSD	Posttraumatic Stress Disorder
R&P	Reception and Placement
RCT	Randomized Control Trial
SNHR	Syrian Network for Human Rights
SOA	US Army's School of the Americas
SOEP	The Socio-Economic Panel of the German Institute for Economic Research
SVGB	Sexual and Gender-Based Violence
TASSC	Torture Abolition and Survivors Support Coalition International
TBI	Traumatic Brain Injury
TCA	Tricyclic Antidepressants
TF-CBT	Trauma-Focused Cognitive Behavioral Therapy
UNDP	United Nations Development Program
UNFPA	United Nations Population Fund
UNHCR	United Nations High Commissioner for Refugees
UNICEF	United Nations Children's Fund
USCIS	US Citizenship and Immigration Services
USGAO	US Government Accountability Office
USICE	United States Immigration and Customs Enforcement
USRAP	US Refugee Admissions Program
WHO	World Health Organization

Maps

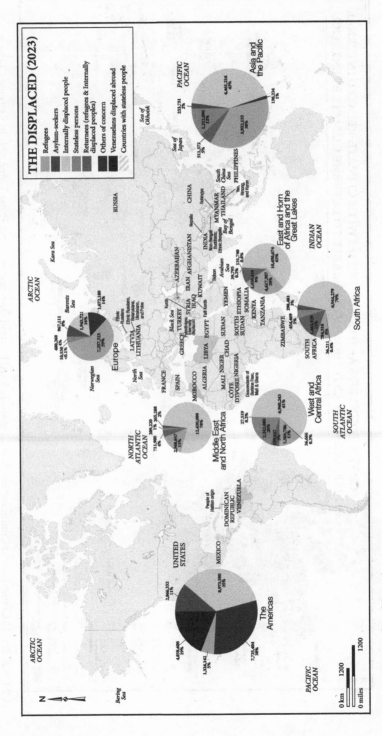

Map 1 The Displaced (2023)

Map 2 Top 10 Countries and Communities With Climate-Related Internal Displacement and Those Vulnerable to Extreme Climate Events (2023)

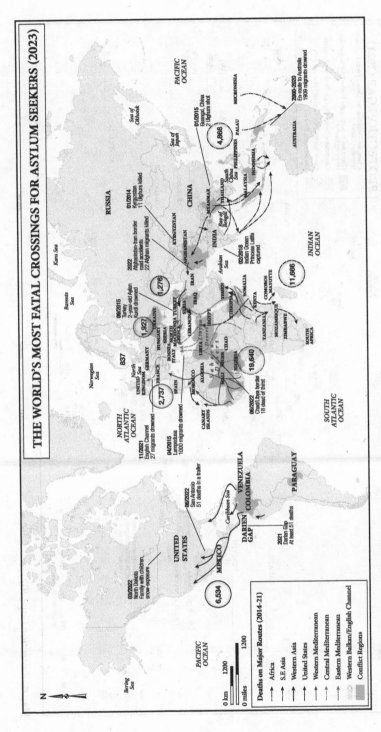

Map 3   The World's Most Fatal Crossings for Asylum-Seekers (2023)

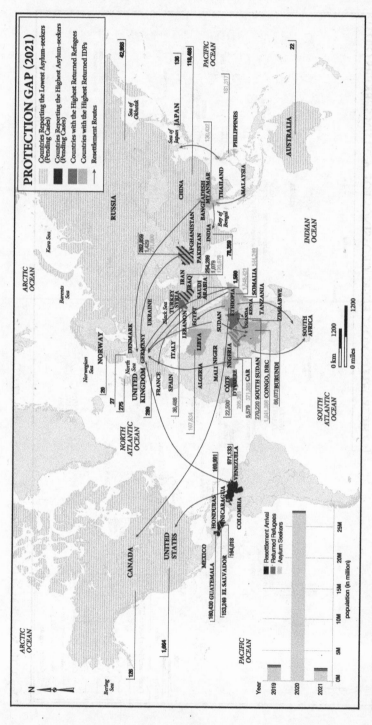

PROTECTION GAP (2021)

Countries Reporting the Lowest Asylum-seekers (Pending Cases)
Countries Reporting the Highest Asylum-seekers (Pending Cases)
Countries with the Highest Returned Refugees
Countries with the Highest Returned IDPs
→ Resettlement Routes

Map 4 Protection Gap (2021)

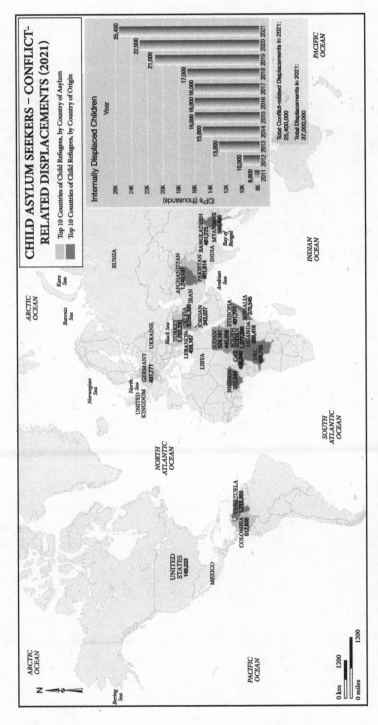

CHILD ASYLUM SEEKERS – CONFLICT-RELATED DISPLACEMENTS (2021)

Top 10 Countries of Child Refugees, by Country of Asylum
Top 10 Countries of Child Refugees, by Country of Origin

Internally Displaced Children

IDPs (thousands)

Year

2011 8,600
2012 10,000
2013 13,000
2014 15,000
2015 16,000
2016 16,000
2017 17,000
2018 21,000
2019 22,900
2020 25,400
2021 25,400

Total Conflict-related Displacements in 2021:
25,400,000

Total Displacements in 2021:
37,000,000

RUSSIA

AFGHANISTAN 1,240,137
PAKISTAN 481,775
BANGLADESH
INDIA MYANMAR 569,406
Bay of Bengal

SYRIA
1,192,853
IRAQ
TURKEY
JORDAN 343,027
LEBANON 459,167
Black Sea

UKRAINE
GERMANY 407,771
UNITED KINGDOM
North Sea
Norwegian Sea

SUDAN 524,161
CAR 465,305
SOUTH 491,771
ETHIOPIA
UGANDA 570,545
SOMALIA
888,416
DRC 400,795

NIGERIA 212,544
LIBYA

Arabian Sea

COLOMBIA 512,638
VENEZUELA 1,216,905

UNITED STATES 149,033
MEXICO

ARCTIC OCEAN
Bering Sea
Kara Sea
Barents Sea

N

PACIFIC OCEAN

NORTH ATLANTIC OCEAN

SOUTH ATLANTIC OCEAN

INDIAN OCEAN

PACIFIC OCEAN

0 km   1200
0 miles   1200

Map 5 Child Asylum-Seekers: Conflict-Related Displacements

Preface

In the hostile climate refugees faced in 2015, like others, I was transfixed by the almost 1.4 million refugees outside Europe's doors.[1] The world over, 2015 had been considered one of the worst for antiforeigner discrimination and hate crimes.[2] In my clinical practice, minority patients including Muslim ones who were American citizens, born in the United States fretted in private about how they did not belong in America. In this atmosphere of prejudice, if the mental health of minority patients who enjoyed privilege and citizenship was being severely strained, how would the forcibly displaced fleeing persecution and cruelty, and with nothing to their names, fare in their new homes?

Many countries, including the United States with its history of slavery and ongoing racism toward many of its communities, may provide physical refuge, but may also present new and different racialized, religious, or immigration-related traumas for refugees. As a native of a country with its own history of colonization and displacement and as an immigrant in many countries, I have navigated language, race, identity, allyship, and social access in cultures different from mine. Thus, some aspects of the refugee experience resonated with me, yet I remain in awe of the herculean strength required to bear losses, dispossession and indignities as a refugee.

With homes besieged by bombs and neighborhoods engulfed in deadly sarin gas, the world watched as Syrian civilians turned into refugees and walked through Austrian hamlets in worn-out shoes with their babies strapped to their chests. For each refugee that lives, many more lose their lives and many more women, children, and elders are left behind to a fate far worse than death. For Germany absorbing these groups was no small task, and it would be the equivalent of welcoming the populations of San Diego, Copenhagen, or Mombasa into its fold. Could Germany facilitate their integration in better ways than the United States has?

---

[1] Pew Research Center. (2016, August 2). *Number of refugees to Europe surges to record 1.3 million in 2015*. https://www.pewresearch.org/global/2016/08/02/number-of-refugees-to-europe-surges-to-record-1-3-million-in-2015/

[2] Elmira. R. (2016, September 16). Muslim women experience thinly veiled discrimination. *Chicago Tribune*. https://www.chicagotribune.com/opinion/commentary/ct-muslim-women-discrimination-hijab-20160916-story.html?int=lat_digitaladshouse_bx-modal_acquisition-subscriber_ngux_display-ad-interstitial_bx-bonus-story

My unique bifocal perspective is honed through education and clinical training. I earned two of Cambridge University's highest awards to gain a master's degree at Trinity College. At Cambridge, I learned the foundations of Psychology and skills of scientific rigor and critical reasoning. The Mellon scholarship, one of the United States' highest academic honors for graduate work, allowed me to conduct my doctoral research at The University of Chicago. At the Committee on Human Development, The University of Chicago, I learned the craft of interdisciplinary research and analyzing how and what people communicate using clinical, quantitative, and qualitative methods. With the rigorous skills and scientific knowledge that I have gained over the course of my education and practice, I have been able to conduct over a thousand face-to-face personal interviews with couples and families, from the Arctic to South Asia.[3,4] I have traveled to over ninety countries and lived in five, including those in the Middle East and Europe. Global travels in addition to education have imparted a dexterity in intercultural communication and a recognition of how individuals can mobilize cultural and social change.

My knowledge of culture's dynamicity, its alchemy and nuance, and respect for the influence of larger forces on one's mental health has only grown with psychological practice and teaching. As a professor at universities in the United States, I have taught doctoral students of the reciprocal and dynamic dialogues between culture, politics, family, religion, biology, gender, and our self, health, and relationships. I have learned that social-political conditions are as important as personal traits in shaping one's psychological health and happiness.

As a clinical psychologist, I have hands-on experience working with clients with complex trauma, such as survivors of childhood abuse, captivity, sexual abuse or incest, torture, terrorism, ethnic cleansing, and others. We might expect the narratives of trauma to be pristine, precise, and consistent across their retelling. After all, how could one obfuscate the horrific things one endured? But in reality, chronicles of trauma present a peculiar paradox. Survivors yearn mostly to forget that what haunts them. Terror, if the walls of silence are pierced, imparts in survivors a language of stonewalling, contradictions, chaos, and ambiguous meanings. I have had to develop the ability to parse through the trauma story and the tolerance to sit through its painful retelling.

Experiences of the vulnerable when concealed, overlooked or excluded, can be costly for human development, social cohesion, ecological balance, and

[3] Sandhya, S. (2021). *Love will follow: Making love and intimacy work in Indian couples.* https://books.apple.com/us/book/love-will-follow-making-love-and-intimacy-work-in/id1537817468

[4] Sandhya, S. (2021). The Glocal family: Exploring its international variations using a family systems framework. In K. S. Wampler, R. B. Miller, R. B. Seedall, L. M. McWey, A. J. Blow, M. Rastogi, & R. Singh (Eds.), *The handbook of systemic family therapy* (Vol. 4; pp. 49–76). Wiley.

economic progress. With my cross-cultural and clinical training, I was drawn to center the voices of those who had endured state violence, warfare, and displacement. Between 2016 and 2021, I traveled to Germany and France from the United States, taking time off from my clinical practice for multiple weeks each time to interview newly arrived refugees. I invested my personal resources, for the most part, to fund research, writing, and travel to Germany. Sponsorship from the Alexander von Humboldt Foundation and Dr. Michael Forster, codirector of the International Center for Philosophy at Bonn University, enabled me to attend academic conferences at the University of Bonn, Germany and the École Normale Supérieure, France, to share this book's seminal findings with European faculty colleagues and graduate students. These and the dialogues they encouraged lent wings to this research.

From the vantage point of 2023, 2015 was a turning point in the hatred towards the *Other*, inflamed through stereotypes and disinformation, worsening worldwide. During the Christmas of 2022 when I walked across the Polish border into Ukraine, I witnessed grandmothers and mothers braving hardships to spend Christmas with their menfolk at war with Russia. The millions of displaced Ukrainians had never imagined that they would be on the run from their country or referred to as refugees, with all the negative connotations associated with the word *refugee*. In my ongoing interviews with them, I hear a sentiment I have heard many times over, "being a refugee hurts."

We may believe that our national prosperity and protection hinges on pushbacks of refugees and making impossible or illegal their universal right to claim asylum from persecution. Consider some forms of their pushbacks by states in 2023: the capsizing of the fishing trawler drowning atleast 700 primarily South-Asian and Middle-Eastern migrants as the Greek Coast Guard looked on; the shootings of Ethiopian women and child asylum seekers by Saudi border forces[5]; asylum seekers warehoused aboard UK's *Bibby Stockholm* putting them at risk for infection, isolation, and instability; and in safe haven nations such as the US, thousands of women and children face physical and sexual abuse in government-funded detention centers and at the hands of authorities tasked with protecting them.[6] We may believe that peace in their countries of origin will engender the return of refugees. Or we may believe that permitting refugees entry within our borders and temporary cash assistance ensures their future. Such are the planks in our eye.

[5] Human Rights Watch (2023, August 21)."*They fired on us like rain:" Saudi Arabian mass killings of Ethiopian migrants at the Yemen-Saudi border*. https://www.hrw.org/report/2023/08/21/they-fired-us-rain/saudi-arabian-mass-killings-ethiopian-migrants-yemen-saudi

[6] Warsi, Z. (2023, July 21). Immensely invisible: Women fighting ICE's inaction on sexual abuses. *Futuro Investigates*. https://futuroinvestigates.org/investigative-stories/immensely-invisible/

But cruel migrant-management policies and horrific tragedies will do little to staunch the flow of those seeking refuge. From Myanmar to Cote d'Ivoire, the statelessness of many does not keep us safe. Being displaced reflects in essence, our disinclination to uphold all lives as equal and a growing disrespect of our responsibility to protect commitment towards civilians.[7]

Moreover, the hierarchy of human life through dehumanizing the sufferings of some over others is not unrelated to the unbearable costs of being the displaced. Consider the horrifying Hamas massacre of innocent civilians and the unleashing of carnage by Israel in turn, leveling Gaza's homes, places of worship, schools and critical infrastructure. In the nearly 113 days of the Israel-Gaza war, nearly 10,000 children have endured violent deaths. Many more have been maimed, orphaned, lost or trapped with nowhere to go in the deepening crisis. Fifty-thousand pregnant mothers are living in fear of what awaits them and newborns in the absence of essential obstetric care, risk premature death[8]. The world's response to the sufferings of Gaza's mothers are a far cry from the fleeing Ukrainian mothers who were received with open arms and plied with not just free diapers, hygiene products, clothes, toys[9], emergency ambulatory services but also cash and Spanish holidays for their children.[10]

In Israel-Gaza, as in the wars of Iraq, Ukraine, Syria, Bosnia and Herzegovina, Sudan, and Ethiopia, far from being accidental, targeting civilians for massive physical destruction and psychological damage is reemerging as an intentional strategy for coercing the enemy into acquiescence. Unfolding in front of our eyes is the collective punishment of civilians through their enslavement, rapes,[11] starvation, suicides of their children,[12] despair, deaths, and displacement. Innocent civilians and their future generations will pay the psychological costs of wars.

[7] United Nations (n.d.). Responsibility to protect. https://www.un.org/en/genocideprevention/about-responsibility-to-protect.shtml

[8] Relief Web (2023, October 12). *Over 37,000 pregnant women at risk of life-threatening complications in Gaza.* https://reliefweb.int/report/occupied-palestinian-territory/over-37000-pregnant-women-risk-life-threatening-complications-gaza

[9] UNICEF (n.d.). *Relief as Ukrainian mothers receive Baby Box supplies.* https://www.unicef.org/ukraine/en/stories/ukrainian-mothers-receive-baby-box-supplies

[10] Boyes, R. (2023, April 10). Spanish holidays for traumatized children of Ukraine. *The Times.* https://www.thetimes.co.uk/article/spanish-holidays-for-traumatised-children-of-ukraine-war-rhs978700

[11] The Guardian view on the war in Sudan: destruction and death are going largely unnoticed (2023, November 19). Editorial. *The Guardian.*
https://www.theguardian.com/commentisfree/2023/nov/19/the-guardian-view-on-the-war-in-sudan-destruction-and-death-are-going-largely-unnoticed

[12] Rahmani, M., Silverman, A.L., Thompson, A., & Pumariega, A. (2023). Youth suicidality in the context of disasters. *Current Psychiatry Reports,* 25(11), 587-602.

The backlash against the displaced can snowball and stoke dangerous downturns in normalizing the inhumane treatment of those seeking humanity. Consider, the contagion effect of the forcible evacuation of Gaza's 1.6 million and how it has spurred a global race to exploit and shunt refugees: Egypt sealed its border with Gaza, trapping the internally displaced Palestinians further into devolving humanitarian crises. Pakistan is expelling 1.7 million Afghans from the only home many of them have ever known. In Turkey, Erdoğan pitched plans to force the return of over a million Syrian refugees to Turkish occupied zones in northern Syria even though they remain dangerous. In many cradles of war, like regions of the Global South where armed conflicts and hostilities are raging, being displaced will become repetitive and prolonged where the plight of refugees will also remain, unfortunately, invisible.

Integrating refugees is as much about healing their psychological traumas as it is about tolerating pluralism, enforcing international protections for human beings, preserving the truths of the survivors, strengthening inter-ethnic relationships, and tackling the polarization and hatred that divides and destroys our communities.

I wanted to tell the refugee story, albeit in an inverted way, and with an insider's approach—How did they survive? How did they view their host countries? And how did they view their circumstances and their future? I wanted to share their nightmares but also their dreams. I wanted to tell their stories in their own words.

Acknowledgments

A book can be a North Star for its writer in some form or another, and I am truly grateful for the gifts of learning and purpose granted by this book. Its story is an urgent one, and it would not have been possible without the blazing energies and immeasurable support of a village of people that have anchored me and contributed to its evolution.

I owe a world of gratitude to my mother for her unconditional love and lessons—to live without fear and with the nose of an albatross, follow through on one's passions. I am thankful to my father for his cheerfulness and boundless commitment to our family. During the short 13 months of writing this book, I lost them both, although their spirit suffused the book's journey.

I am grateful to my friend Alastair King-Smith, his Majesty's Ambassador to the Republic of Albania, for opening the door to this research and putting his resources behind this labor of love. In North Rhine Westphalia, Germany, I met Felix von Gruenberg, a German politician who has dedicated his life to the cause of socioeconomically impoverished and refugees, holding weekly meetings with them for almost 5 decades. This book benefits greatly from Felix's indefatigable energy in creating connections for me with members of the state legislature, human rights organizations, and refugees and in offering a multitude of other practical assistance.

My gratitude extends to my friends Linda and Alfred Saucedo, for always caring for me through the vicissitudes of our lives and circumstances with an unfailing love that goes above and beyond. I am grateful to Alfred for his contributions in developing the proposal, for engaging in conversations, and for making time to edit several chapters. This book would not have been possible without his presence and energy.

I am thankful to Michele Davies for her assistance with the quantitative analysis of the research that elevated insight into the respondents' experiences. Her friendship, international dinners, and interesting conversations were always a welcome intrusion. And to my friend Chante DeLoach, whose sage counsel and deep friendship has always benefited me in life and profession. Chante's feedback on four chapters has afforded the book the value of astute clinical input; I am grateful to have a doppelganger in her. And to my friend Paul Julian for always making life so entertaining and batting its many fires for me with finesse, so I had the peace of mind to write.

I am lucky to find a research assistant like Ruochan Pan who was able to assist in transforming refugee trends into bold, visual depictions that, hopefully, enhance readers' ease of access to the material. I am thankful to Todd Stump, whose energy and work helped give this book its initial wings through its conceptualization. This book developed its depth through the many profound conversations blending academic research with the psychological freight of displacement, with the gifted Carrington Ward. I am also thankful to Neal Rubin who has supported me as a lifelong mentor and friend. I am also thankful to Susan Zoline who generously made herself available to discuss the development of an ethically sound research study. In Bonn, Germany, I was grateful for the generosity, knowledge, and investment of Sherihan Inalo who helped me parse complex layers of language, social categories, and history following the interviews, and her assistance greatly enriched my relationships with refugees and their communities. I am grateful for the masterful and patient translations of Sherihan and Sophie Gelep in Germany and Mahajano Tsitozoe Emile ("Emile") in Madagascar, whose help with some interviews allowed the refugee story to be accessed, along with its local expressions and community responses in a sensitive, meaningful, and intimate manner.

I am indebted to Michael Forster, codirector of the International Center for Philosophy at Bonn, for his friendship, patience, invaluable guidance, and conversations through the many shapes, versions, and dilemmas posed by this book. He has truly nurtured ideas from inception to press. I am grateful also to Chantal Winicki for her long and valued friendship, and to Mario Pezzini, former director of the Organization for Economic Cooperation and Development (OECD) and special advisor to the OECD Secretary General on Development, for his counsel on the integration chapter.

I am deeply thankful for the incredible generosity of Robert Labate and Jaime Herren from Holland, and Knight Law Firm, who, with their responsiveness and excellent counsel at several stages of the book, made me feel they were always within reach. Their strategy and thoughtfulness in planning enabled productive working relationships that enriched my journey.

A warm thanks to Nikolaos van Dam, former Dutch Ambassador to Iraq, Egypt, Syria, and Germany, for deepening my knowledge on the Middle East through conversations and his writings. I am thankful to Joost den Otter of the World Psychiatry Association's Section on Psychological Aspects of Persecution and Torture for his thoughtful observations and reading of the chapter on torture from Juba, South Sudan. Many thanks to Timothy Kelly of the Administration for Children and Families Office of Refugee Resettlement Division of Refugee Health, who shared useful resources related to the American refugee resettlement structure. Ram Das of Care USA assisted in deepening my knowledge both of the humanitarian landscape and of intergovernmental negotiations in the context of Rohingya families in Bangladesh. Kilian Kleinschmidt, CEO of IPA

SwitxBoard group, Tunisia, offered a rare, personal, and historic perspective of the evolution of camps and the treatment of the displaced within them, besides also facilitating other useful contacts.

This book and I benefit much from the ever-loving care of the Lal family, Ranjan, Sunita, Nikhil, Sohan, and Rocky. Much gratitude to the wonderful Rosenow family, especially Penny, Lindy, Laurie, and Theo, for always making everything more fun and being present with their support. I feel very fortunate to partake in several important occasions with the Rosenow family. I am grateful to be included in the fun activities of the Fenton-Kreuger family—Nina, Jens, and Annabel—whose warm embrace afforded me a home away from home. I am also thankful to the Lynch family—John, Kasia, Jake, and Sophie—for their warm welcome, and, especially, to John Lynch, for his immeasurable support in facilitating connections in Poland that benefited this book. I am also thankful to the Young Presidents' Organization Gold Chapter of Poland for their support.

Sarah Harrington, my editor shared my urgency to tell this story from the moment I met her. I feel truly fortunate for her steadying presence, support, and meticulous readings of drafts. I am thankful to the OUP team for their energy and momentum in publishing the manuscript.

I am also thankful to our Labrador, Scotch, for taking me on long walks that were always a welcome treat. However, there is no one else who has quite shared the same path and walked beside me as my sister, Shipra Sandhya. Words cannot express my gratitude for her commitment, unconditional love, and steely resolve to love me as we made it through this book and this chapter of our lives. I feel blessed to have her as my sister and this book is as much her accomplishment as it is mine.

Finally, thank you to the refugees and the other displaced for placing their trust in me and sharing their profound experiences that I hope are transformational to you, the readers.

1

Our Refugee Crisis
Trauma, Integration, and Resettlement

Johnny, Sara, and Faisal Sabri

Sara, Syrian-Kurdish and 21 years old at the time of the incident, is reluctant to remember the day she refers to as the "most calamitous day of my life." For a good part of our interview, her son Johnny, 3 years old, lay one apple-colored cheek against Sara's, and with his chubby baby arms, clasped her neck. Under a mop of brown curls in a burgundy shirt, Johnny has eyes like large opal discs. He had been in Germany for only 30 days or so as a new refugee.

In the early morning of August 21, 2013, screams filled Sara's quiet hometown. Rocket launchers and helicopters loaded with the deadly nerve and blister chemical agents, chlorine, sarin, sulfur, and mustard gas dropped on their dense neighborhood. Over microphones, religious leaders beseeched people to "move away from your windows" over the wails of her friends and neighbors. Sara recalls the beckons were urgent and insistent: "close your windows," "don't let in the poison air," "get some water to cover your nose."

It was the summer. People had slept with their windows open to let in the cool evening breeze. Sara rushed to close the windows. She had wanted to muzzle her nose with wet tissue, but there was no water in the entire region.

Outside, "it was a massacre," said Sara. "People were frothing saliva, and some choked on their vomit. Others were convulsing and writhing in pain. The entire family who lived next to them, a dad, a mother, and their three daughters, died that day. Neighbors were trying to help pull out people convulsing within cars to either line them up for ambulances, resuscitate them, pull clothes soaked in gas off them, or bury them."

Sara sobbed during her account, gulping air in between torrents of words.

"Those who had slept with their windows open were more defenseless against the incoming toxins," said Sara.

"When you are shocked by chemicals, you don't die at once," explained Sara. "Many people were alive when they were buried, for we didn't know the meaning of 'chemical'. . . . As we got to know what a chemical attack was, shocked neighbors had various warnings: 'Don't bury them before 24 hours,' 'make sure people are

Displaced. Shaifali Sandhya, Oxford University Press. © Shaifali Sandhya 2024.
DOI: 10.1093/oso/9780197579886.003.0001

not dead,' 'give them kola seeds to smell to help them wake up,' 'throw water on them, maybe they can wake up.'"

"But . . . there was no water."

"There were a lot of people who got crazy red eyes. I heard that if the eye color changed to red or if it had something blue from chemical materials, then the person had died. If your eyes turned red and blue, it was the worst. If the eyes turned blue or white, they had to be taken to emergency. But there were no ambulances, and the emergency was overflowing. People died while helping others. They did not realize it was dangerous to breathe the poisoned air."

"There were . . . rows upon rows of newly dead infants."

The nerve gas would suffocate to death over 1,400 civilians, including at least 426 children.[1] The attack aimed to inflict maximum, collective punishment on the population. Its indiscriminateness was like "draining the sea by filling the graves." Johnny was barely 3 months old at that time, but in her recall to me, Sara could not remember the date or the year of the chemical attack or even whether she was pregnant or had already delivered her baby.

The attack and, in its aftermath, widespread insecurity and starvation caused the Sabris to flee. They escaped at first to Lebanon and later to Turkey. After spending over a year in Turkey, Sara's husband Faisal left for Germany to apply for asylum and had reunited with his wife and son 30 days prior to our interview, after a gap of 1 year and 8 months. It was in a refugee accommodation in Germany that I sat face to face with the Sabris. More than 3 years later, I found them still anguished, shell shocked, and deeply unprepared for what life held for them, as they recounted to me what you read above. In their new countries, many remain cautious as they believed that "the eyes and arms of the regime are everywhere," that people sympathetic to the Syrian government had infiltrated host societies.

In a separate interview, Faisal recalled Sara's state at that time: "she went crazy, crying and screaming . . . and just wild." He spoke about the episode visibly anguished and clenching his arms, its unspoken horror escaping from a vigorously trembling left elbow. Faisal has endured torture by the Asad regime. "But," he says, "the chemical attack was the worst day of my 32 years of life." In the following weeks, he says, "Sara just stopped producing breast milk." Little Johnny wakes up with night terrors and struggles with any separation from her; they both attribute his nervousness to that day "when all the newborn babies died."

---

[1] Warrick, J. (2013, August 30). More than 1400 killed in Syrian chemical weapons attack, says US. *The Washington Post.* https://www.washingtonpost.com/world/national-security/nearly-1500-killed-in-syrian-chemical-weapons-attack-us-says/2013/08/30/b2864662-1196-11e3-85b6-d27422650fd5_story.html

The Setting

We are living through a refugee crisis of epic proportions. Conflict such as that faced by the Sabris, climate change, insecurity, poverty, and the pandemic are forcing an estimated 117.2 million people,[2,3] 1 in 68 of the global population, to abandon their homes and heritage. Some, the internally displaced or refugees, accept the slender protections for which they may qualify. But most are generally excluded from equitable economic, social, cultural, and political opportunities and alienated from their rights to food, reproductive health, education, and more.

A majority of the forcibly displaced, including 43.3 million children,[4] the highest on record, live in penury in border tents,[5] urban slums,[6] and collective centers. In all, 83% of refugees and displaced Venezuelans[7] are in low- and middle-income countries.[8] Of this group, 27%[9] reside in the least developed nations,[10]

[2] The statistic of 112.6 million captures the total displaced through the last decade until June 2023 and includes populations under UNHCR's mandate—approximately 35.3 million refugees and people in refugee-like situations (for instance, Venezuelans and Ukrainians), asylum seekers, other people who may find themselves out of their countries and in need of international protection, conflict-affected internally displaced, and returnees (refugees and internally displaced). This statistic does not include the 6.69 million registered Palestinian refugees and other persons of concern under UNRWA: UNHCR. (2023, June). *A threat to lives, dignity, and hope: The implications of underfunding UNHCR's activities in 2023*. https://reporting.unhcr.org/underfunded-report-implications-under funding-unhcr%E2%80%99s-activities-2023; IOM. (2022, May 17–23). *Ukraine—internal displacement report—general population survey round 5*. https://displacement.iom.int/reports/ukraine-inter nal-displacement-report-general-population-survey-round-5-17-may-2022-23-may

[3] Based on UNHCR's mid-year 2022 trends, the statistic of 117.2 million are projected to be forcibly displaced and stateless in 2023: UNHCR. (2023). *Global appeal 2023*. https://reporting.unhcr. org/globalappeal2023/pdf

[4] Number of displaced children reaches new high of 43.3 million. UNICEF. (2023, June 13). *UNICEF*. https://www.unicef.org/press-releases/number-displaced-children-reaches-new-high-433-mill ion#:~:text=NEW%20YORK%2C%2014%20June%202023,them%20for%20their%20entire%20ch ildhood

[5] Sherman, C. (2022, May 2). Ukrainian refugees at camp in Mexico City await US action. *AP News*. https://apnews.com/article/russia-ukraine-mexico-caribbean-united-states-europe-75b71 5dca02d61a7dfb0b08efebd7419

[6] Yousafzai, S. (2022, June 21). "Rescue us," beg Afghan refugee families as they protest their "slum life" in a Pakistani park. *CBS News*. https://www.cbsnews.com/news/afghan-refugees-pakis tan-islamabad-slum-life-protests

[7] Forced displacement is a coerced movement of individuals and communities who are compelled to escape conflict; violence; persecution; human rights abuses; disasters, including human-made ones; or development and, thus, abandon their places of habitual residence: Francis M. Deng. (1998, February 11). *Further promotion and encouragement of human rights and fundamental freedoms, including the question of the program and methods of work of the Commission: Human rights, mass exoduses and displaced persons*. United Nations Economic and Social Council. https://digitallibrary. un.org/record/251017?ln=en

[8] UNHCR. (2021). *Global trends report 2021*. https://www.unhcr.org/media/40152

[9] UNHCR. (2022, June 16). *Refugee population statistics database*. https://www.unhcr.org/refu gee-statistics/

[10] Least developed countries also include Rwanda, South Sudan, Sudan, Uganda, the United Republic of Tanzania, and Yemen. United Nations. (n.d.). *Methodology: Standard country or area codes for statistical use (M49)*. Department of Economic and Social Affairs. https://unstats.un.org/ unsd/methodology/m49/

lowest on socioeconomic development measures, such as Bangladesh, Chad, the Democratic Republic of the Congo, and Ethiopia. For another example, the stateless Rohingya,[11] known as the "world's most persecuted minority,"[12] languish in unsanitary conditions of Bangladesh's Cox Bazaar, vulnerable to calamities such as Cyclone Amphan, Covid-19, and other threats.[13] One to three million Uyghur[14,15] are spared no mercy by China. They endure forcible separation from their children,[16] interrogation, indoctrination, imprisonment, slavery, and sterilization in its internment camps, where flight and refuge are impossible.[17]

Nearly a million soon-to-be-stateless Bengalis living in Assam,[18] India, for generations, teeter on the brink of having their citizenship erased, and are spurned as "illegals." Faced with the specter of conflict and violence in the last 2 years, 700,000 Afghans, majority of them women and children,[19] abandoned their homes, villages, and cities.[20] The Russian invasion of Ukraine, the biggest land war in Europe since World War II, has displaced an estimated

[11] A stateless person is someone "who is not considered as a national by any State under the operation of its law" according to Article 1(1) of the 1954 Convention of the Status of Stateless Persons: UNHCR (1954). Convention relating to the status of the stateless person. https://www.unhcr.org/ibelong/wp-content/uploads/1954-Convention-relating-to-the-Status-of-Stateless-Persons_ENG.pdf

[12] Office of the High Commissioner for Human Rights. (2017, December 5). *Human Rights Council opens special session on the situation of human rights of the Rohingya and other minorities in Rakhine State in Myanmar.* Human Rights Council. https://www.ohchr.org/EN/NewsEvents/Pages/DisplayNews.aspx?NewsID=22491&LangID=E

[13] Khan, S., & Haque, S. (2021). Trauma, mental health, and everyday functioning among Rohingya refugee people living in short- and long-term resettlements. *Social Psychiatry & Psychiatric Epidemiology, 56*(3), 497–512.

[14] *Senate Foreign Relations Committee Subcommittee on East Asia, the Pacific, and International Cybersecurity Policy.* (2018, December 4) (testimony of Scott Busby). Senate Foreign Relations Committee Subcommittee on East Asia, the Pacific, and International Cybersecurity Policy. https://www.foreign.senate.gov/imo/media/doc/120418_Busby_Testimony.pdf

[15] Ramzy, A., & Buckley, C. (2019, November 16). "Absolutely no mercy": Leaked files expose how China organized mass detention of Muslims. *The New York Times.* https://www.nytimes.com/interactive/2019/11/16/world/asia/china-xinjiang-documents.html

[16] *The Chinese Community Party's Ongoing Uyghur Genocide.* (2023, March 23) (testimony by Nury Turkel). United States Commission on International Religious Freedom Select Committee on the Chinese Communist Party Hearing. https://www.politico.com/f/?id=00000187-0dcc-d418-a1df-7dec44bf0000

[17] Turkle, N. (2022). *No escape: The true story of China's genocide of the Uyghurs* (S. Lang, Trans.) [Audiobook]. https://www.audible.com/pd/No-Escape-Audiobook/B09R39ZYJH

[18] Wade, F. (2020). Soon to be stateless: Modi's plans for Assam. *London Review of Books, 42,* 1.

[19] UNHCR. *UNHCR Afghanistan operational update.* (2022, July 7). UN High Commissioner for Refugees. https://reliefweb.int/report/afghanistan/unhcr-afghanistan-operational-update-may-2022

[20] There are many other forcibly displaced populations not included here, such as the 900,000 from Guatemala, Honduras, and El Salvador displaced since 2015 because of violence by criminal gangs or the 113,000 Hong Kong residents who took flight in 2022 in response to China's security laws: Tung, C., Man, J., & Loi, A. (2022). Hong Kong exodus continues as rights groups pinpoint leaders' overseas property. *Radio Free Asia.* https://www.rfa.org/english/news/china/hongkong-exodus-08152022123051.html

13.9 million Ukrainians.[21] Russian men who are evading being drafted for war against Ukraine[22] and the Sudanese fleeing violence and pouring through its borders[23] are the world's newest refugees. The war also compounded the humanitarian plight of an estimated 44 million forcibly displaced Africans, 66% of whom are stranded as internally displaced within their own countries.[24] Map 1 (in the front matter) illustrates those who constitute the displaced.

Over and above the scale of the immense and global displacement today is its sheer velocity. Figure 1.1 shows the top seven countries that experienced internal displacement between 2021 and 2022. In mid-2022 alone, the displaced increased to around 105 million,[25] an increase of roughly 15 million—nearly the size of the population of Cambodia—from the year prior, and almost 2.5 times that of the decade prior.

Being forcibly displaced, in contrast to previous decades, is increasingly also driven by extreme climate events or factors associated with it.[26] Fires, floodings, famine, and droughts are making refugees of members of the 65,000-year-old indigenous cultures of Gudamalulgal Nation, Torres Strait, Australia;[27] Quejá, Guatemala,[28] and Ambovombe, Madagascar.[29,30] They are displacing Americans

[21] Ukraine emergency (n.d.). *UNHCR.* https://www.unrefugees.org/emergencies/ukraine/ (retrieved June 26, 2023)

[22] Mayne, C. (2023, April 14). Putin signs a tough new military draft law, banning conscripts from fleeing Russia. *NPR.* https://www.npr.org/2023/04/13/1169464889/russia-military-draft-ukraine-war

[23] Adeoye, A. (2023, April 24). Sudan crisis threatens to bring fresh turmoil to neighbouring Chad. *Financial Times.* https://www.ft.com/content/fa73b428-7d71-4ed8-aaeb-2e0e858004b4

[24] Global Appeal (2023). *UNHCR.* https://reporting.unhcr.org/global-appeal-2023?page=10

[25] In 2012 the displaced including the internally displaced, refugees under UNRWA's mandate, and asylum seekers were estimated to be 42.7 million. By mid-2022, UNHCR was mandated to protect and/or assist an estimated 104.5 million: Mid-year trends (2022). UNHCR. https://www.unhcr.org/sites/default/files/legacy-pdf/635a578f4.pdf

[26] IDMC & NRC (2022, May 19). *Global report on internal displacement: Children and youth in internal displacement.* https://www.internal-displacement.org/sites/default/files/publications/documents/IDMC_GRID_2022_LR.pdf

[27] Pabai Pabai & Guy Paul Kabai v. Commonwealth of Australia. (2021, October 22). Form 17 Rule 8.05(1)(a). http://climatecasechart.com/climate-change-litigation/wp-content/uploads/sites/16/non-us-case-documents/2021/20211022_14765_petition.pdf

[28] Kitroeff, N., & Volpe, D. (2020, December 4). After 2 merciless hurricanes, rising fear of a new refugee crisis. *The New York Times.* https://www.nytimes.com/2020/12/04/world/americas/guatemala-hurricanes-mudslide-migration.html

[29] Harrington, L. J., Wolski, P., Pinto, I., Ramarosandratana, A. M., Barimalala, R., Vautard, R., Philip, S., Kew, S., Singh, R., Heinrich, D., Arrighi, J., Raju, E., Thalheimer, L., Rzanakoto, T., van Aalst, M., Li, S., Bonnet, R., Yang, W., Otto, F. E. L., & van Oldenborgh, G. J. (2021). Attribution of severe low rainfall in southern Madagascar, 2019–21. *World Weather Attribution.* https://www.worldweatherattribution.org/wp-content/uploads/ScientificReport_Madagascar.pdf. Southern Madagascar's food insecurity and, consequently, forcible displacement of its population has two prominent but differing perspectives. According to the UN, it is the first climate-change-induced famine, while the World Weather Attribution Report (Harrington et al., 2021) assigns the droughts to natural climate variability of the region and poverty.

[30] Pilling, D., & Bibby, C. (2022, August 1). Why famine in Madagascar is an alarm bell for the planet. *Financial Times.* https://www.ft.com/content/8fa3596e-9c6a-4e49-871a-86c20e0d170c

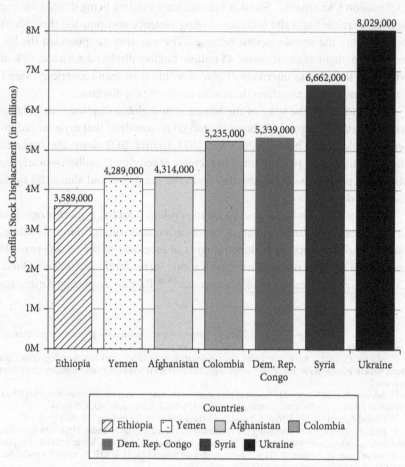

Figure 1.1 Top-Seven Countries With Conflict-Related Internal Displacement (2021–2022)
Source: iDMC, IOM.

from Lahaina, Hawaii to Montpelier, Vermont and are 24 million each year.[31,32] Figure 1.2 illustrates the countries that experienced the most disaster-related internal displacement in 2021.

---

[31] Internal Displacement Monitoring Center. (2019). Global internal displacement database. https://www.internal-displacement.org/database/displacement-data.

[32] During a period of 6 months (September 2020–February 2021), climate change migrants accounted for more displacements than those displaced by conflict, suggesting the growing pace of climate change refugees: Climate change created 10.3m refugees last year. (2021, March 18). *Shanghai Daily.*

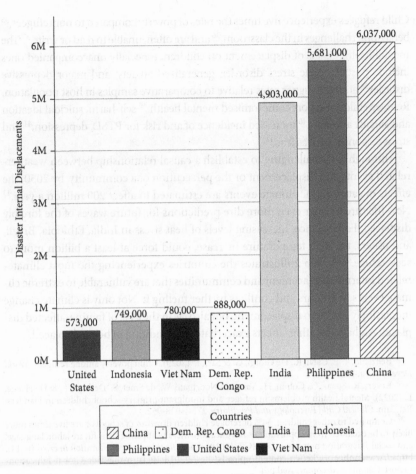

Figure 1.2 Top Seven Countries With Disaster-Related Internal Displacement (2021)
Source: https://www.internal-displacement.org/database/displacement-data

Storms, cyclones, and floods are the most common weather-related disasters and set off about 62% of global displacements.[33] At the same time, the absence of "climate refugees"[34] as a legal term and concomitant protections afforded to the displaced raises the issue of whether the cause of displacement trumps the experience of being displaced. Whether the catalyst may be climate or conflict, experiences of displacement may be similar and can include, staving off hunger, enduring daily assaults to one's safety and dignity, and living below the international poverty line.

---

[33] Disasters triggered more than 60% of global internal displacements: IDMC & NRC (2022, May 19). *Grid 2022: Children and youth in internal displacement.* https://www.internal-displacement.org/sites/default/files/publications/documents/IDMC_GRID_2022_LR.pdf

[34] Behrman, S., & Kent, A. (2018). *Climate refugees: Beyond the legal impasse?* Routledge.

Child refugees experience five times the rates of poverty compared to nonrefugees,[35] behavioral challenges in the classroom,[36] and are often, unable to read or write.[37] The mental health effects of displacement on children, especially unaccompanied ones include posttraumatic stress disorder, generalized anxiety, and major depressive disorder[38] at much higher rates relative to comparative samples in host population. Refugee children report compromised mental health,[39] self-harm, suicidal ideation and suicide attempts,[40] increased incidence of and risk for PTSD, depression,[41] and stress responses such as fear.[42]

Although it is challenging to establish a causal relationship between weather-related events and displacement or the persecution of a community, by 2050, the effects of catastrophic climate events are estimated to affect 200 million a year.[43] New life threats offer even more dire predictions for future waves of the forcibly displaced. For instance, increasing levels of heat stress in India, Ethiopia, Brazil, and others, through temperature increase, could force at least a billion more to seek refuge.[44,45] Map 2 illustrates the countries experiencing the most climate-related internal displacement and communities that are vulnerable to extreme climate events, with wars and conflicts further fueling it. Not only is climate change increasingly linked to displacement, but also, as in the case of famine-affected displaced Afghans, weather-effects exacerbate the condition of being displaced.

[35] Beltramo, T. P., Calvi, R., De Giorgi, G. & Sarr, I. (2023). Child poverty among refugees. *World Development*, 171.

[36] Kevers, R., Spaas, C., Colpin, H., Van Den Noortgate, W., de Smet, S., Derluyn, I., & De Haene, L. (2022). Mental health problems in refugee and immigrant primary school children in Flanders, Belgium. *Clinical Child Psychology and Psychiatry*, 27(4): 938-952.

[37] Compared to other children, 54% of refugee children drop out of school or are five times more likely to be excluded from opportunities in education, thereby affecting their future labor, language, and social-integration outcomes: UNHCR. (2018). *Turn the tide: Refugee education in crisis* (p. 14). https://www.unhcr.org/ke/wp-content/uploads/sites/2/2018/10/Turn-the-Tide-Global-Education-Report-Compressed-compressed.pdf

[38] Bürgin, D., Anagnostopoulos, D., Board and Policy Division of ESCAP, Vitiello, B., Sukale, T., Schmid, M., & Fegert, J. M. (2022). Impact of war and forced displacement on children's mental health—multilevel, needs-oriented, and trauma-informed approaches. *European Child and Adolescent Psychiatry*, 31(6), 845–853.

[39] Lee, A. C. K., Khaw, F. M., Lindman, A. E. S., & Juszczyk, G. (2023). Ukraine refugee crisis: Evolving needs and challenges. *Public Health*, 217, 41–45.

[40] Amarasena L., Samir, N., Sealy, L., Hu, N., Rostami, M. R., Isaacs, D., Gunasekera, H., Young, H., Agrawal, R., Levitt, D., Francis, J. R., Coleman, J., Mares, S., Larcombe, P., Cherian, S., Raman, S., Lingam, R., & Zwi, K. (2023). Offshore detention: Cross-sectional analysis of the health of children and young people seeking asylum in Australia. *Archives of Disease in Childhood*, 108(3), 185–191.

[41] Kemei, J., Salami, B., Soboka, M., Gomaa, H. I. M., Okeke-Ihejirika, P., & Lavin, T. (2023). The forms and adverse effects of insecurities among internally displaced children in Ethiopia. *BMC Public Health*, 23(1), 200.

[42] Tay, A. K. (2022). The mental health needs of displaced people exposed to armed conflict [Comment]. *Lancet*, 7(5), E-398–399.

[43] Gaynor, T. (2022, November 30). *Climate change is the defining crisis of our time and it particularly impacts the displaced.* UNHCR. https://www.unhcr.org/en-us/news/latest/2020/11/5fbf73384/climate-change-defining-crisis-time-particularly-impacts-displaced.html

[44] Madge, C. (2021, November 9). One billion face heat-stress risk from 2 °C rise. *Met Office*. https://www.metoffice.gov.uk/about-us/press-office/news/weather-and-climate/2021/2c-rise-to-put-one-in-eight-of-global-population-at-heat-stress-risk

[45] Gatrell, P. (2019). *The unsettling of Europe: How migration reshaped a continent.* Basic Books.

Coerced by different disasters, violations of their rights, and mitigating circumstances of history and geopolitics, a swelling tide of humans has spilled at nations' seams and into others. But no matter what the origins or reasons compelling people's flight, the circumstances of the forcibly displaced are, in many ways, similar: their experiences are complex; they strive for safety; and they are vulnerable, some more than others. Rather than as a humanitarian disaster, the refugee crisis has often been understood perfunctorily as a catastrophe created by a swelling number of Muslims appearing at Europe's door. The crisis must be recast as a calamity of being,[46,47] an involuntary return of refugees to their often still at-war countries of origin, and as an inadequacy of humanitarian response in the face of human rights abuses, portending an imminent change in the world's moral landscape. The posttraumatic suffering of refugees mirrors their violations[48] and our response to it must also reflect the moral imperative of human rights norms.[49]

"*Tisniy Svit*," or "the world is small," Viktoria, a 31-year-old Ukrainian refugee, tells me. She is referring to the fact that no distance is vast enough for her to reunite with her husband who serves in the Ukrainian army. Viktoria and thousands of other family members return to war zones to be reunited with their loved ones, placing their own lives at risk. The refugee crisis has far-reaching effects for family demography and cohesion,[50] regional peace,[51] sectarian balance,[52] politics,[53] security of societies,[54] religious demography,[55] development,[56]

[46] Daniel, E. V., & Knudsen, J. C. (1995). *Mistrusting refugees* (p. 1). University of California Press.

[47] Weber, M. (1915). The social psychology of world religions. In H. H. Gerth & C. Wright Mills (Eds. and Trans.), *From Max Weber: Essays in sociology* (pp. 267–301). Oxford University Press,

[48] Rees, S., Silove, D. M., Tay, K., & Kareth, M. (2013). Human rights trauma and the mental health of West Papuan refugees resettled in Australia. *Medical Journal of Australia, 199*(4), 280–283.

[49] Good, B. J., & Hinton, D. E. (2016). Introduction: Culture, trauma, and PTSD. In D. E. Hinton and B. J. Good (Eds.), *Culture and PTSD: Trauma in global and historical perspectives* (pp. 3–49). University of Pennsylvania Press.

[50] The war has thrown Ukraine's surrogacy industry into a crisis. (2022, September 9). *The Economist*. https://www.economist.com/europe/2022/09/08/the-war-has-thrown-ukraines-surrogacy-industry-into-crisis

[51] Loescher, G., Milner, J. Newman, E., & Troeller, G. (2008). Introduction. In G. Loescher, J. Milner, E. Newman, & G. Troeller (Eds.), *Protracted refugee situations: Political, human rights and security implications* (pp. 3–19). United Nations University Press.

[52] Brand, L. A. (1988). Palestinians in Syria: The politics of integration. *Middle East Journal, 42*(4), 621–637.

[53] Zoe, O. (2022, May 15). Australia election 2022: Are Australia's refugee releases an election ploy? *BBC*. https://www.bbc.com/news/world-australia-61423035

[54] Rana, M. S., & Riaz, A. (2022, March). Securitization of the Rohingya refugees in Bangladesh. *Journal of Asian and African Studies, 0*(0), 1–17.

[55] Leustean, L. N. (2022, March 3). Russia's invasion of Ukraine: The first religious war in the 21st century. *London School of Economics*.https://blogs.lse.ac.uk/religionglobalsociety/2022/03/russias-invasion-of-ukraine-the-first-religious-war-in-the-21st-century/

[56] Mattner, M. (2008). Development actors and protracted refugee situations: Progress, challenges, opportunities. In G. Loescher, J. Milner, E. Newman, & G. Troeller (Eds.), *Protracted refugee situations: Political, human rights and security implications* (pp. 108–122). United Nations University Press.

and economies[57,58,59] of host[60] and nonhost countries. There is not an aspect of modern society unaffected by the refugee crisis and not a nation where its effects are not felt. For nations, it may be tempting or expedient to dismiss the refugee problem as temporary[61] or to contextualize it as a problem so overwhelming and dire that it is unsolveable.[62] But the reality is inescapable, the refugee crisis is multifaceted, complex, global, and likely to persist. As with the unexpected creation of Ukrainian refugees, the future augurs newer crises and newer waves of refugees. Forced displacement with its multiple drivers will continue unabated in the future. The potent combination of climate-related disasters and conflict,

[57] Evans, W. N., & Fitzgerald, D. (2017, June). *The economic and social outcomes of refugees in the United States: Evidence from the ACS* (Working Paper 23498). National Bureau of Economic Research. https://www.nber.org/papers/w2349

[58] Edwards, B. (2022, June). Investing in refugees. *Finance & Development* (pp. 30–31). https://www.imf.org/en/Publications/fandd/issues/2022/06/investing-in-refugees-cafe-economics

[59] The United States has spent more than $253 million a day: Federation of American Scientists. (n.d.). *Cost of war through March 31, 2018.* https://fas.org/man/eprint/cow/fy2018q2.pdf. However, this figure is considered an underestimate and murky by some, especially considering military operations in Afghanistan, Syria, and Iraq: Cordesman, A. J. (2019, January 16). *America's military spending and the uncertain costs of its wars: The need for transparent reporting.* [Powerpoint]. Center for Strategic and International Studies. https://csis-website-prod.s3.amazonaws.com/s3fs-public/publication/190123_Cost_of_War.pdf

[60] Low- and middle-income countries like Jordan, Lebanon, Turkey, Pakistan, Liberia, Peru, and Colombia, who shelter 83% of the world's displaced, are also experiencing their share of challenges: Fabre, C. (2018). *Crisis in middle-income counties: The commitments into action series.* OECD. https://www.oecd.org/development/humanitarian-donors/docs/Crises_in_middle_Income_Countries_OECD_guideline.pdf. In low-income countries, 50% of refugee children were in primary schools, and only 9% were in secondary schools: UNHCR. (n.d.). *Left behind: Refugee education in crisis.* https://www.unhcr.org/left-behind/; Charles, S., Huang, C. Post, L., & Gough, K. (2018, November 5). *Five ways to improve the World Bank funding for refugees and hosts in low-income countries and why these dedicated resources matter more than ever.* [Commentary]. Center for Global Development. www.cg-dev.org/publication/five-ways-improve-world-bank-funding-refugees-and-hosts-low-income-countries- and-why. Two thirds of Syrian refugees in Lebanon lacked access to medical care. Johns Hopkins University Bloomberg School, Médecins du Monde, IMC, AUB, & UNHCR. (2015, July). *Syrian refugee and affected host population health access survey in Lebanon* (pp. 1–71). https://data.unhcr.org/en/documents/details/44869

[61] Bangladesh tells UN that Rohingya refugees must return to Myanmar (2022, August 17). *Aljazeera.* https://www.aljazeera.com/news/2022/8/17/rohingya-refugees-have-to-be-taken-back-bangladesh-pm-says

[62] Some historians believe to varying extents that some refugee surges may be unremitting, as the conflicts giving rise to them may be intractable. According to Nikolaos van Dam, in his book *Destroying a Nation*, although it is valid that boundaries within greater Syria may be considered artificial and imposed, earlier boundaries in the region during the rules of the Umayyads, Abbasids, Fatimids, Nizari Ismailis, Malmuks, and several other dynasties reflected their zones of power and were drawn not along ethnic lines. Van Dam also asserts that the clandestine 1916 Sykes-Picot agreement between France and Britain that carved up the Middle East with no attention to local identities, is at the root of its present-day upheavals: van Dam, N. (2016). *Destroying a nation: The civil war in Syria.* Bloomsbury. Authors like David Fromkin claim that the secret Sykes-Picot agreement between Britain and France, with Russia and Italy as assenting partners, ignored local identities, as it partitioned the Ottoman Empire in 1916 into mutually agreed upon areas of control: Fromkin, D. (1989). *A peace to end all peace: The fall of the Ottoman Empire and the creation of the modern Middle East.* Owl.

and the socioeconomic effects of dispossession, such as food insecurity, will be significant drivers forcing more to be displaced from their homes and habitats.

The Interviews

As I interviewed individuals and families in refugee camps, similar to the Sabris, I heard many firsthand reports of physical, psychological and sexual abuse, and torture. Little is known about refugees of mass trauma,[63] of the nature of their trauma and its unfolding psychological effects on their lives. With these interviews I sought to understand how trauma is expressed and experienced by refugees by utilizing the mixed methods quantitative and qualitative research with Middle Eastern refugees that forms the basis of this book; wherever possible, I have sprinkled its findings throughout the chapters. Vignettes are based in and follow real cases,[64] but I use either pseudonyms to retain interviewees' anonymity and/or alter identifying information, including village or city of origin, family, region, physical trait, profession, and tribal affiliation.

I grew consumed by refugees' stories. Between November 2016 and 2021, I interviewed over a hundred refugees from Syria, Afghanistan, Iraq, and Lebanon, who had arrived in Germany 1 to 3 years prior, and others. The duration of each interview ranged from 90 minutes to 5 hours. Chapter 3 details the study. I traveled from city to city in Germany interviewing trauma therapists, social workers, refugee shelter coordinators, researchers, public officials of various German departments,[65] and global humanitarian workers. In December 2022, I traveled to Ukraine and Poland and met with newly displaced Ukrainian families. I heard blow-by-blow accounts of the war's impact on ordinary citizens fleeing, and the accounts of those receiving them in host nations through from a US state official, mayors of border towns, Ukrainian officials, and humanitarian agency heads, all first responders. Many of these officials are still sifting through the crisis and its ongoing consequences. In their accounts I found that their roles converged; they spoke not only as public officials but also as parents, children, and citizens, intersecting often with emotions of panic, uncertainty, inadequacy, and overwhelm. Although a complete study of Ukrainian refugees was out of scope for this book, I have referenced some of these urgent conversations here.

---

[63] Steel, J. L., Dunlavy, A. C., Harding, C. E., & Theorell, T. (2017). The psychological consequences of pre-emigration trauma and post-migration stress in refugees and immigrants from Africa. *Journal of Immigrant Minority Health, 19*(3), 523–532.

[64] Refugee stories are polished for linguistic accuracy and clarity.

[65] Public officials at municipal and state levels from the state of North Rhine Westphalia involved in refugee affairs pertaining to employment, integration, and social affairs; family, health, and law; housing; and integration were interviewed.

I wanted to know the nature and trajectory of posttraumatic stress by looking at refugee experiences through four lenses: personal, interpersonal, intracultural, and intercultural. I wanted to uncover a wide-angled and multifaceted view of how posttraumatic suffering manifested in refugee populations, across domains. In looking within the lives of forcibly displaced war-affected refugees of mass trauma, I hope to deepen our understanding of trauma and integration. On the one hand, the various conditions driving forcible displacement can disproportionately affect the mental health of the displaced, the resettled, families, and their communities. Yet, on the other, host nations do not always associate refugees' psychological well-being with their future self-sufficiency, and humanitarian organizations seldom inquire into the policy levers that will lead refugees to improved outcomes.[66] Positive mental health, instrumental in living a meaningful life and perceived as the right to the highest standard of health established under many human rights instruments,[67] must also be included in nations' integration initiatives.

The world is entering a period during which mental health services may become more out of reach for many more,[68,69,70,71] even as rising mental health burdens exert greater tolls on disability-adjusted life years.[72] Investigating the critical role of mental health for the inclusive integration of refugees affords a glimpse into civic society's moral obligation in supporting refugee health and suggests a stepped-up role for citizens, governments, financial institutions, development agencies, the private sector, and local providers.

---

[66] Betts, A. (2021). *The wealth of refugees: How displaced people can build economies.* Oxford University Press.

[67] 1946 Constitution of the World Health Organization; Article 25 of the 1948 Universal Declaration of Human Rights; 1966 International Covenant on Economic, Social and Cultural Rights.

[68] Fifteen million more health workers are needed by 2030, according to the World Health Organization: World Health Organization. (n.d.). *Health workforce.* https://www.who.int/health-topics/health-workforce#tab_1

[69] Rathod, S., Pinninti, N., Irfan, M., Gorczynski, P. Rathod, P., Gega, L., & Naeem, F. (2017). Mental health service provision in low- and middle-income countries. *Health Services Insight*, 10, 1–7.

[70] Freeman, M. (2022). Investing for population mental health in low and middle income countries—where and why? *International Journal of Mental Health Systems*, 16, 38.

[71] Weiner, S. (2022, August 9). A growing psychiatrist shortage and an enormous demand for mental health services. *The Washington Post.* https://www.aamc.org/news-insights/growing-psychiatrist-shortage-enormous-demand-mental-health-services

[72] The 2019 Global Burden of Diseases, Injuries, and Risk Factors Study shows mental disorders to be among one of the top ten leading causes of burden. There has been no reduction in the burden since 1990: Ferrari, A. J., Santomauro, D. F., Herrera, A. M. M., Shadid, J., Ashbaugh, C., Erskine, H. E., Charlson, F. J., Degenhardt, L., Scott, J. G., McGrath, J. J., Allebeck, P., Benjet, C., Breitborde, N. J. K., Brugha, T., Dai, X., Dandona, L., Dandona, R., Fischer, F., Haagsma, J. A., Haro, J. M. . . . Whiteford, H. A. (2022). Global, regional, and national burden of 12 mental disorders in 204 countries and territories, 1990–2019: A systematic analysis for the Global Burden of Disease Study 2019. *Lancet*, 9(2), 137–150.

Refugees, Protection Gap, and Protracted Displacement

Of the forcibly displaced, more than two-thirds of all refugees are from just eight nations:[73] Sudan, Democratic Republic of Congo, Myanmar, South Sudan, Afghanistan, Syria, Venezuela, and Ukraine. Approximately 13 million Syrians,[74] two-thirds of the population, fled their homes as the Syrian Civil War, termed one of the "deadliest wars of the twenty-first century,"[75] erupted. With other conflicts erupting in Afghanistan, Iraq, Libya, and Yemen, other masses[76] joined the Syrians, mostly in Europe, either in ramshackle boats or by walking.[77] Some families in Syria were uprooted up to 25 times over 6 years[78] of armed conflict. Recently, the displaced Palestinians of the 1948 Arab-Israeli war were pushed once again into newer camps in Jordan and Lebanon and became "double refugees."[79] Amid geopolitical complexity nations can fluctuate in their ability to create refugees, and Figure 1.3 depicts the top refugee-producing nations in 2021-early 2022. In 2024, displacement continues marching at its rapid and relentless pace with asylum seekers from Ukraine, Venezuela, Palestine, and many parts of Africa.

Refugees, unlike those displaced internally within their countries' borders, are people forced to flee their nations. They seek sanctuary for themselves and their families[80] because of a "well-founded fear of persecution for reasons of race, religion, nationality, political opinion or membership in a particular social group."[81]

---

[73] UNHCR. (2021, June 18). *UNCHR Global trends: Forced displacement in 2019.* https://www.unhcr.org/5ee200e37.pdf

[74] Schneider, T., & Lütkefun, T. (2019). *Nowhere to hide: The logic of chemical weapons use in Syria.* Global Public Policy Institute.

[75] Ray, M. (n.d.) *8 Deadliest wars of the 21st century. Encyclopedia Britannica.* https://www.britannica.com/list/8-deadliest-wars-of-the-21st-century

[76] Since the 1970s, protracted conflict has destabilized Afghanistan. Previously displaced 97,000 Afghan families exposed to war and tragedy with the Battle of Kunduz in 2015, for instance, fled their nation again.

[77] In 2015, the International Organization for Migration (IOM) estimated that more than 1,011,700 migrants arrived by sea in 2015 and almost 34,900 by land: IOM. (2015, December 22). *Irregular migrant, refugee arrivals in Europe top one million in 2015.* https://www.iom.int/news/irregular-migrant-refugee-arrivals-europe-top-one-million-2015-iom

[78] Handicap International. *Qasef: Escaping the bombing.* (2016). https://d3n8a8pro7vhmx.cloudfront.net/handicapinternational/pages/2303/attachments/original/1475080189/Study_EWIPA-Syria-2016_Web_final.pdf?1475080189

[79] Fraihat, I. (2014, February 25). *What about the Palestinian double refugees?* Brookings Institute. https://www.brookings.edu/opinions/what-about-the-palestinian-double-refugees/

[80] Inability to cross international boundaries by an overwhelming number of internally displaced does not imply that they are without legal rights or may not suffer from many of the same issues as refugees. For more information on the rights of the internally displaced, please review: The Guiding Principles on Internal Displacement (1998). Unlike refugees, internally displaced persons do not enjoy a special status in international law with rights specific to their situation, are reliant on the nations where they are located, and there is no international agency leading the protection and assistance of the internally displaced.

[81] UNHCR. (n.d.). *What is a refugee?* https://www.unhcr.org/en-us/what-is-a-refugee.html

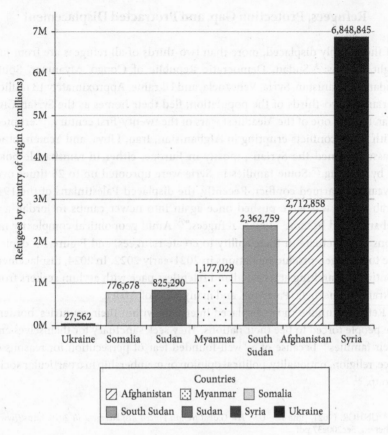

Figure 1.3 Refugees by Country of Origin (2021)
Source: https://data.worldbank.org/indicator/sm.pop.refg.org

Nations' refugee protectorate, suggests the *Handbook on Procedures and Criteria for Determining Refugee Status and Guidelines on International Protection*, are those asylum-seekers within its borders who are unable to return to their home country or are afraid to do so. Says the *Handbook* of the asylum-seeker, "Recognition of his refugee status does not therefore make him a refugee but declares him to be one. He does not become a refugee because of recognition but is recognized because he is a refugee."[82] A refugee then, becomes a refugee not as soon as or whether a State recognizes his status as a refugee but "as soon as he fulfills the criteria contained in the

[82] UNHCR. (2019, February). *Handbook on procedures and criteria for determining refugee status and guidelines on international protection* (p. 17). https://www.unhcr.org/media/handbook-procedures-and-criteria-determining-refugee-status-under-1951-convention-and-1967

definition." There is a long history of international refugee law with its regional versions[83],[84],[85] and regional human rights instruments to protect refugees.[86]

In practice, however, asylum-seekers face many impossible hurdles and pro- tection gaps as they attempt to become refugees. In the absence of any legal protections, the 71.1 million internally displaced[87] are adrift within their conflict-torn countries. Special populations within them, including girls and young women, the elderly,[88] physically disabled,[89],[90] and lesbian, gay, bisexual, trans-gender, and queer individuals,[91] face unique problems.[92] The poor, for instance, are at higher risk for mental disorders[93] compared to the economically well-off as they may be less successful in articulating their needs effectively to obtain as-sistance, or unable to fill our requisite forms.[94] The more vulnerable in inegali-tarian societies often become the most persecuted, the first to be displaced as they

[83] The 1951 Convention relating to the Status of Refugees (hereby referred to as the "Convention") and the Geneva Convention of July 28, 1951, serve as the foundation of international refugee law and are key legal documents of the United Nations that set forth a definition of the refugee and her rights as well as the responsibilities of nations that grant asylum. Unlike the Refugee Convention of 1951 that places temporal and geographic limits on the refugee definition, the 1967 Protocol is inde-pendent of time and place constraints.

[84] The Organisation of African Unity (OAU) Convention Governing the Specific Aspects of Refugee Problems in Africa, also called the OAU Refugee Convention or the 1969 Refugee Convention, is a regional legal instrument governing refugee protection in Africa. It reaffirms the centrality of the Convention and expands it.

[85] The Cartagena Declaration is a nonbinding agreement for the protection of refugees. It reaffirms the centrality of the Convention and expands it. It was adopted in 1984 by delegates from 10 Latin-American countries: Belize, Venezuela, Mexico, Colombia, Costa Rica, Honduras, El Salvador, Guatemala, and Nicaragua: Colloquium on the International Protection of Refugees in Central America, Mexico and Panama. (1984, November 22). *Cartagena Declaration on Refugees, colloquium on the international protection of refugees in Central America, Mexico and Panama* (pp. 1–6). https://www.oas.org/dil/1984_cartagena_declaration_on_refugees.pdf

[86] According to the principle of nonrefoulement, nations are legally obligated to protecting all refugees (including those who may not have been formally recognized as such) by not returning them to the country where they face threats to their well-being: UN General Assembly. (2016). *New York Declaration for Refugees and Migrants* (Resolution 71/1).

[87] IDMC. (2024). *Global report on internal displacement.* https://www.iom.int/sites/g/files/tmzbdl486/files/appeals/iom-global-appeal-2024_final.pdf

[88] Okenwa-Emegwa, L., Tinghög, P., Vaez, M., & Saboonchi, F. (2021). Exposure to violence among Syrian refugee women preflight and during flight: A population-based cross-sectional study in Sweden. *SAGE Open, 11*(3). https://doi.org/10.1177/21582440211031555

[89] Little is known about the incidence and nature of disability among the displaced given the lack of extensive work in the area of the disabled in displacement.

[90] Crock, M., Ernst, C., & McCallum, R. (2012). Where disability and displacement intersect: Asylum seekers and refugees with disabilities, *International Journal of Refugee Law, 24*(4), 735–764.

[91] Bassetti, E. (2019). Integration challenges faced by transgender refugees in Italy. In A. Güler, M. Shevtsova, & D. Venturi (Eds.), *LGBTI asylum seekers and refugees from a legal and political per-spective: Persecution, asylum and integration* (pp. 337–348). Springer.

[92] Unlike refugees, the internally displaced are at the mercy of host nations. The Kampala Convention, adopted in 2009 is the African Union's treaty and is the first regional instrument related to the assistance and protection of the internally displaced.

[93] Rathod, S., Pinninti, N., Irfan, M., Gorczynski, P., Rathod, P., Gega, L., & Naeem, F. (2017). Mental health service provision in low- and middle-income countries. *Health Services Insight, 10*, 1–7.

[94] Aptekar, L. (1990). A comparison of the bicoastal disasters of 1989. *Behavior Science Research, 24*(1–4), 73–104.

cannot sustain themselves through persistent and prolonged crises. Paradoxically, they are also those who are unable to seek asylum or are denied it: for instance, the *khwaja siras* or the transgender women of Pakistan.[95] Throughout this book the term *refugee* will be used broadly to refer to all of these categories, given that specific legal definitions are used in different ways in practice.

We often think of refugee flights as taking place immediately, without delay following the slightest sign of trouble and occurring alike for all refugees. In reality, not every person who flees will be able to secure safety, enjoy good health, or access education for their children. Only a tiny proportion will be able to ever access the wealthiest and best-resourced nations.[96,97,98] Circumstances do not always dictate who flees, where to, and whether they can stay in a safe sanctuary.[99,100] Even among those who have undergone horrific atrocities like torture, only 42% will be able to escape.[101]

Impoverished families from insecure countries generally demonstrate a preference for securing the flight of their sons over daughters, even if it means entrusting their fate to traffickers. Map 3 illustrates some of the most dangerous routes to refuge of asylum-seekers worldwide. In these fatal crossings, sometimes across the Mediterranean, in boats referred to as convoys of death, in flimsy vessels referred to as floating coffins;[102,103] across the Sahara Desert, or

[95] Munir, L. P. (2019). Fleeing gender: Reasons for displacement in Pakistan's transgender community: Persecution, asylum and integration. In A. Güler, M. Shevtsova, & D. Venturi (Eds.), *LGBTI asylum seekers and refugees from a legal and political perspective: Persecution, asylum and integration* (pp. 49–69). Springer.

[96] Pew Research Center. (2016, August 2). *Syrian asylum-seekers to Europe constituted about one-tenth of a percentage of its population.* https://www.pewresearch.org/global/2016/08/02/number-of-refugees-to-europe-surges-to-record-1-3-million-in-2015/

[97] By 2018, less than 5% or 0.2% of the global refugee population, under the protection of UNHCR were resettled: Baldoumas, A., van Roemburg, E., & Truscott, M. (2019, December 11). *Welcome, support, pledge, resettle: Responsibility sharing in the global compact on refugees.* Oxfam International. https://policy-practice.oxfam.org/resources/welcome-support-pledge-resettle-responsibility-sharing-in-the-global-compact-on-620923/

[98] Less than 1% of refugees are resettled to third countries: UNHCR. *Resettlement.* https://www.unhcr.org/resettlement (retrieved on May 10, 2023).

[99] Men and boys with disabilities also face heightened risk of sexual violence: Women's Refugee Commission and International Rescue Committee. (2015, May). *"I see that it is possible": Building capacity for disability inclusion in gender-based violence programming in humanitarian settings.* https://www.womensrefugeecommission.org/wp-content/uploads/2020/04/Disability-Inclusion-in-GBV-English.pdf

[100] Older refugees are mostly unable to flee due to the arduous nature of the journeys: Kofman, E. (2019). Gendered mobilities and vulnerabilities: Refugee journeys to and in Europe. *Journal of Ethnic and Migration Studies, Open Access, 45*(12), 2185–2199.

[101] Ozaltin, D., Shakir, F., & Loizides, N. (2020). Why do people flee? Revisiting forced migration in post-Saddam Baghdad, *Journal of International Migration and Integration, 21*(2), 587–610.

[102] Fraihat, I. (2014, February 25). *What about the Palestinian double refugees?* Brookings Institute. https://www.brookings.edu/opinions/what-about-the-palestinian-double-refugees/

[103] Lui, K. (2017, September 5). A Mediterranean rescue ship is relocating to Asia to help the Rohingya flee Myanmar. *Time Magazine.* https://time.com/4926670/myanmar-rohingya-mediterranean-rescue-ship-phoenix-moas

the Darien Gap,[104] countless have perished.[105] Some as stowaways have huddled onto departing planes and dropped to their deaths from the skies[106] onto the gardens of London.[107] Others have drowned in the English Channel[108] in a bid to secure asylum. Displaced women and children are trafficked for labor and prostitution[109] by community members and armed groups in exchange for food, money, and being smuggled across borders.[110]

A successful refugee flight is one that culminates in survival. In 2022 only 114,300 refugees (0.32% of the global refugee population) were resettled but almost three times as many were returned to their countries of origin.[111] [112] Only about 8.1% of registered refugees who were in need of protection in 2022 were relocated for protection to a new country. The United States admitted only 10,000 refugees in 2022, its lowest in almost half a century. Map 4 illustrates this protection gap when there are high rejections of asylum-seekers' applications and their forced returns to their home countries are more colossal than admission rates to host nations. Overall, there is much flouting of international humanitarian laws that can result in impossible dilemmas for the asylum seekers: accepting "voluntary return" or being stranded at borders,[113] differential treatment based on their methods of arrival and routes taken,[114] and forcible return of unaccompanied

[104] Roy, D., & Baumgartner, S. (2022, June 22). Crossing the Darien Gap: Migrants risk death on the journey to the U.S. *Council on Foreign Relations*. https://www.cfr.org/article/crossing-darien-gap-migrants-risk-death-journey-us

[105] Could virus see Rohingya "floating coffins" crisis return to ASEAN? (2020, April 20). *VOA News*. https://www.voanews.com/a/east-asia-pacific_could-virus-see-rohingya-floating-coffins-crisis-return-asean/6187845.html

[106] Cooper, H., & Schmitt, E. (2021, August 17). Body parts found in landing gear of flight from Kabul, officials say. *The New York Times*. https://www.nytimes.com/2021/08/17/us/politics/afghans-deaths-us-plane.html

[107] Veselinovic, M., & John, T. (2019, July 2). Stowaway falls into London garden from Kenya Airways plane. *CNN*. https://www.cnn.com/2019/07/01/uk/kenya-airways-airplane-death-intl

[108] Gross, A., & Wright, R. (2021, November 27). Migration crisis: "We believed we were going to die out there." *Financial Times*. https://www.ft.com/content/2aa6e111-54f7-4ac7-a399-a528a9fe4b07

[109] Bauer-Babef, C. (2022, November 30). Trafficking and sexual exploitation of Ukrainian refugees on the rise. *Euraactiv*. Retrieved on May 10, 2023, from https://www.euractiv.com/section/europe-s-east/news/trafficking-and-sexual-exploitation-of-ukrainian-refugees-on-the-rise/

[110] US Department of State. (2022). *Trafficking in Persons Report: Syria*. https://www.state.gov/reports/2022-trafficking-in-persons-report/syria/

[111] UNHCR (n.d.) *Refugee data finder*. https://www.unhcr.org/refugee-statistics/#:~:text=Between%202018%20and%202022%2C%20an,born%20as%20refugees%20per%20year.&text=Some%20339%2C300%20refugees%20returned%20to,with%20or%20without%20UNHCR's%20assistance (retrieved June 26, 2023)

[112] The statistic of 114,300 was 0.07% of the projected global resettlement needs in 2022: UNHCR (2022). Resettlement fact sheet 2022. https://www.unhcr.org/media/resettlement-fact-sheet-2022

[113] Amnesty International. (2022). *Latvia: Refugees and migrants arbitrarily detained, tortured, and forced to 'voluntarily' return to their countries*. https://www.amnesty.org/en/latest/news/2022/10/latvia-refugees-and-migrants-arbitrarily-detained-tortured-and-forced-to-voluntarily-return-to-their-countries/

[114] Castle, S. (2022, December 13). Britain's leader unveils tough plans to tackle illegal crossings by migrant boats. *The New York Times*. https://www.nytimes.com/2022/12/13/world/europe/uk-migration.html

children to their countries of origin,[115] arbitrary detention of asylum-seekers while their claims are in process,[116] and transfer of asylum-seekers to a third processing country.

Most often, flight likely results in one subsisting among millions under tarpaulin shacks in sprawling shanty-towns of the world's most poor and unstable countries.[117] Or in settlements alongside the borders of its wealthy neighbors, such as the Rio Grande/US border or the Belarus-Poland borders in subzero temperatures. Ongoing civil strife including disagreement over whether a certain people are in fact asylum-seekers can also affect the length and nature of their protracted displacement.[118] Examples of the latter include the Palestinian case, which can be considered multigenerational displacement,[119] with its fifth generation of descendants now being born. It would also include the ethnic Buddhist Chakmas from East Pakistan (now Bangladesh), unrecognized as citizens by both their native Bangladesh and India, where they had sought refuge 50 years ago.[120]

The vastness of the transatlantic exodus of a complex population comprising different nationalities[121] is only surpassed by their warehousing in large numbers in such camps, often in conditions likened to a "gigantic Auschwitz."[122] Map 5 shows the large presence of forcibly displaced children in deplorable conditions in developing countries. In these "zones of anguish,"[123] there is largely little or no access to running water, sanitation, lifesaving medications, or medical treatment. Three out of four asylum-seekers can wait to be processed as refugees for more than 5 years[124] in the face of declining health, hope, and fortune. Pressing burdens

[115] Child migrants: Massive drop in children held by border officials. (2021, May 5). *BBC News*. https://www.bbc.com/news/world-us-canada-56405009

[116] Mao, F. (2021, May 10). Biloela family: Locked up by Australia for three years. *BBC News*. https://www.bbc.com/news/world-australia-56768529

[117] Loescher, G., Milner, J. Newman, E., & Troeller, G. (2008). Introduction. In G. Loescher, J. Milner, E. Newman, & G. Troeller (Eds.), *Protracted refugee situations: Political, human rights and security implications* (pp. 3–19).United Nations University Press.

[118] Protracted refugee situations are those in which at least 25,000 refugees from the same country have been living in exile for more than 5 consecutive years: UNHCR. (2019). *Protracted refugee situations explained*. https://www.unrefugees.org/news/protracted-refugee-situations-explained/

[119] Dumper, M. (2008). Palestinian refugees. In G. Loescher, J. Milner, E. Newman, & G. Troeller (Eds.), *Protracted refugee situations: Political, human rights and security implications* (pp. 189–213). United Nations University Press.

[120] Singh, D. K. (2010). *Stateless in South Asia: The Chakmas between Bangladesh and India*. Sage.

[121] The same year, compared to 2014, the number of Syrians (362,800) seeking international protection doubled, the number of Afghans (178,200) quadrupled, and the number of fleeing Iraqis (121,500) soared sevenfold.

[122] Omar al-Bashir charged with Darfur genocide (2010, July 12). *The Guardian*. https://www.theguardian.com/world/2010/jul/12/bashir-charged-with-darfur-genocide

[123] Whittaker, D. (2005). *Asylum seekers and refugees in the contemporary world: Making of the contemporary world* (p. 1). Routledge.

[124] World Bank. *Forced displacement: Refugees, internally displaced, and host communities* (2022, September 30). https://www.worldbank.org/en/topic/forced-displacement

of infectious diseases such as tuberculosis,[125,126] malaria[127] cholera, various skin conditions[128] (e.g., varicella, scabies,[129] lice, and xerosis cutis), leishmaniasis,[130] and the more expensive to treat, noncommunicable diseases[131] such as human immunodeficiency virus, diabetes, hypertension, and cancer, can worsen in the absence of medical assistance. Longer wait times for asylum in turn, can have a negative effect on asylum-seekers' psychological health,[132,133,134] and with some exceptions,[135] its effects are worse for women compared to men.[136]

Refugee Mental Health

Geopolitical insecurity, the soaring cost of living, high unemployment, and Covid-19, have brought to its zenith an urgency to attend to refugee mental

[125] Proença, R., Souza, F. M., Bastos, M. L., Caetano, R., Braga, J. U., Faerstein, E., & Trajman, A. (2020). Active and latent tuberculosis in refugees and asylum seekers: A systematic review and meta-analysis. BMC Public Health, 20, 838.

[126] Holt, E. (2022). Growing concern over Ukrainian refugee health. Lancet, 399(10331), 1213–1214.

[127] Correa-Salazar, C., & Amon, J. J. (2020). Cross-border COVID-19 spread amidst malaria re-emergence in Venezuela: A human rights analysis. Global Health, 16, 118.

[128] Knapp, A., Rehmus, W., & Chang, A. (2020). Skin diseases in displaced populations: A review of contributing factors, challenges, and approaches to care. International Journal of Dermatology, 59(11), 1299–1311.

[129] Manfredi, L., Sciannameo, V., Destefanis, C., Prisecaru, M. Cossu, G., Gnavi, R. Macciotta, A., Catalano, A. Pepe, R. R., Sacerdote, C., & Ricceri, F. (2022). Health status assessment of a population of asylum seekers in Northern Italy. Global Health, 18(1), 57. https://doi.org/10.1186/s12 992-022-00846-0

[130] Lindner, A. K., Richter, J., Gertler, M., Nikolaus, M., Equihua Martinez, G., Müller, K., & Harms, G. (2020). Cutaneous leishmaniasis in refugees from Syria: Complex cases in Berlin 2015–2020. Journal of Travel Medicine, 27, 7.

[131] Amara, A. H., & Aljunid, S. M. (2014). Noncommunicable diseases among urban refugees and asylum-seekers in developing countries: A neglected health care need. Global Health, 10, 24.

[132] Suhaiban, H. A., Grasser, L. R., & Javanbakht, A. (2019). Mental health of refugees and torture survivors: A critical review of prevalence, predictors, and integrated care. International Journal of Environmental Research and Public Health, 16(13), 2309.

[133] Hvidtfeldt, C., Petersen, J. H., & Norredam, M. (2020). Prolonged periods of waiting for an asylum decision and the risk of psychiatric diagnoses: A 22-year longitudinal cohort study from Denmark. International Journal of Epidemiology, 49(2), 400–409.

[134] Staehr, M. A., & Munk-Andersen, E. (2006). Suicide and suicidal behavior among asylum seekers in Denmark during the period 2001–2003: A retrospective study. Ugeskr Laeger, 168(17), 1650–1653.

[135] In the case of suicide, higher rates of suicide have been reported among men compared to women, in asylum reception and detention centers: Goosen, S., Kunst, A. E., Stronks, K., van Oostrum, I. E. A., Uitenbroek, D. G., & Kerkhof, A. J. (2011). Suicide death and hospital treated suicidal behaviour in asylum seekers in the Netherlands: A national registry-based study. BMC Public Health, 11, 484. ; Van Oostrum, I. E. A., Goosen, S., Uitenbroek, D. G., Koppenaal, H., & Stronks, K. (2011). Mortality and causes of death among asylum seekers in the Netherlands, 2002–2005. Journal of Epidemiology and Community Health, 65, 376–383.

[136] Phillimore, J., & Cheung, S. Y. (2021). The violence of uncertainty: Empirical evidence on how asylum waiting time undermines refugee health. Social Science & Medicine, 282, 114154. https://doi.org/10.1016/j.socscimed.2021.114154

health.[137] Covid-19 pushed many refugee families in countries such as Pakistan, Iran, Jordan,[138,139] and the United States into greater economic misery. For at least five reasons, mental health in general, among diverse refugees,[140] is unreported[141] and an unexplored area.[142,143,144] For one, their poor physical health such as somatic symptoms may camouflage the urgency of addressing refugees' mental health.[145] Two, research on refugee families generally utilizes homogenous samples,[146] is circumscribed to Western host nations and ethnicities of convenience, and, barring some exceptions,[147,148,149] does not extend to refugees of poor income countries or in the Global South.[150] Three, it may not focus on trauma's role in shaping dynamics within families or, conversely, on the role of

[137] World Bank. (2022, June 30). *Refugees, internally displaced, and host communities.* https://www.worldbank.org/en/topic/forced-displacement

[138] Ghufran, N. (2006). Afghan refugees in Pakistan: Current situation and future scenario. *Policy Perspectives, 3*(2), 83–104.

[139] Khalil, S. A. (2021, March 17). *Covid-19 recovery and the next stage of the Syrian refugee response after ten years* [Webinar]. Migration Policy Institute. https://www.migrationpolicy.org/events/covid-19-recovery-and-next-stage-syrian-refugee-response-after-ten-years

[140] Richa, S., Herdane, M., Dwaf, A., Bou Khalil, R., Haddad, F., El Khoury, R., Zarzour, M., Kassab, A., Dagher, R., Brunet, A., & El-Hage, W. (2020). Trauma exposure and PTSD prevalence among Yazidi, Christian and Muslim asylum seekers and refugees displaced to Iraqi Kurdistan. *PLOS One, 15*(6), E0233681.

[141] Vijayakumar, L., John, S., & Jotheeswaran, A. T. (2021). Suicide among refugees: The silent story. In D. Bhugra (Ed.), *The Oxford book of migrant psychiatry* (pp. 543–552). Oxford University Press.

[142] Alemi, Q., James, S., & Montgomery, S. (2016). Contextualizing Afghan refugee views of depression through narratives of trauma, resettlement stress, and coping. *Transcultural Psychiatry, 53*(5), 630–653.

[143] Steel, J. L., Dunlavy, A. C., Harding, C. E., & Theorell, T. (2017). The psychological consequences of pre-emigration trauma and post-migration stress in refugees and immigrants from Africa. *Journal of Immigrant Minority Health, 19*(3), 523–532.

[144] Zipfel, S., Pfaltz, M. C., & Schnyder, U. (2019). Editorial: Refugee mental health. *Frontiers in Psychiatry, 10*, 72.

[145] Bhugra, D., Gupta, S., Bhui, K., Craig, T., Dogra, N., Ingleby, J. D., Kirkbride, J., Moussaoui, D., Nazroo, J., Qureshi, A., Stompe, T., & Tribe, R. (2011). WPA guidance on mental health and mental health care in migrants. *World Psychiatry, 10*(1), 2–10.

[146] Keller, A., Lhewa, D., Rosenfeld, B., Sachs, E., Aladjem, A., Cohen, I., Smith, H., & Porterfield, K. (2006). Traumatic experiences and psychological distress in an urban refugee population seeking treatment services. *Journal of Nervous Mental Disorders, 194*, 188–194.

[147] Mollica, R., McInnes, K., Sarajlic, N., Lavelle, J., Sarajlic, I., & Massagli, M. P. (1999). Disability associated with psychiatric comorbidity and health status in Bosnian refugees living in Croatia. *JAMA, 282*, 433–439.

[148] Naeem, F., Muftim, K. A., Aub, M., Harioon, A., Saifi, F., Dagawal, S., & Kingdom, D. (2005). Psychiatric morbidity among Afghan refugees in Peshawar, Pakistan. *Journal of Ayub Medical College, 17*(2), 23–25.

[149] Terheggen, M. A., Stroebe, M. S., & Kleber, R. J. (2001). Western conceptualizations and Eastern experience: A cross-cultural study of traumatic stress reactions among Tibetan refugees in India. *Journal of Trauma Stress, 14*, 391–403.

[150] Richa, S., Herdane, M., Dwaf, A., Bou Khalil, R., Haddad, F., El Khoury, R., Zarzour, M., Kassab, A., Dagher, R., Brunet, A., & El-Hage, W. (2020). Trauma exposure and PTSD prevalence among Yazidi, Christian and Muslim asylum seekers and refugees displaced to Iraqi Kurdistan. *PLOS ONE, 15*, 6.

positive relationships in alleviating it.[151] Four, emerging data reveals that from neuroimaging studies reveals that the underlying PTSD may function differently in refugees relative to other trauma-affected groups. Finally, refugees face a high burden of lifetime trauma and posttraumatic stress symptoms that, although some research contradicts this, may increase with time.[152,153]

We are witnesses, post-2013, to a bewildering and devastating scenario confronting asylum-seekers and refugees. On the one hand, refugee families, such as those affected by war,[154] comprise one of the most vulnerable categories of families. Their pattern of triple trauma,[155] especially in refugees who have endured torture, is unique. Many of them will face acute stressors premigration, during their long flight(s) and while seeking asylum in the host nation, and in the long tail of complex trauma in their lives. In the midst of unexpected conflicts and disasters, an unprecedented mass exodus[156] of some of the most vulnerable across fatal routes around the globe is taking place.

But also unfolding are some nations' retaliatory responses in either weaponizing refugees in hybrid wars,[157] capitalizing on people's fear of refugees, enacting racist abuse and retraumatization of some groups of refugees over others,[158] coercing refugees to return to their violent nations, or warehousing them in offshore isles of detention, like Nauru, Manus Island, and Papua New Guinea.[159]

We stand thus, at the crossroads of a tragic situation but a tremendous opportunity—that of transforming refugee resettlement in host nations through how we envision and implement refugee access to better health, inclusion, and belonging.

[151] Exceptions include: Rosenheck, R., & Fontana, A. (1998). Transgenerational effects of abusive violence on the children of Vietnam combat veterans. *Journal of Traumatic Stress*, *11*(4), 732–741.

[152] Mollica, R. F., Sarajlic, N., Chernoff, M., Lavelle, J., Sarajlic, I. V., & Massagli, M. P. (2001). Longitudinal study of psychiatric symptoms, disability, mortality, and emigration among Bosnian refugees. *JAMA*, *286*(5), 546–554.

[153] Lie, B. (2002). A 3-year follow-up study of psychosocial functioning and general symptoms in settled refugees. *Acta Psychiatry Scandinavia*, *106*(6), 415–425; Pew Research Center. (2016, August 2). *Number of refugees to Europe surges to record 1.3 million in 2015*. https://www.pewresearch.org/glo bal/2016/08/02/number-of-refugees-to-europe-surges-to-record-1-3-million-in-2015/

[154] Bogic, M., Njoku, A., & Priebe, S. (2015). Long-term mental health of war-refugees: A systematic literature review. *BMC International Health and Human Rights*, *15*, 29.

[155] Baker, R. (1992). Psychosocial consequences for tortured refugees seeking asylum and refugee status in Europe. In M. Basoglu (Ed.), *Torture and its consequences: Current treatment approaches* (pp. 83–106). Cambridge University Press.

[156] Morland, P. (2021, August 22). A world on the move. *The Sunday Times*, p. 25. London.

[157] Higgins, A., & Santora, M. (2021, November 16). Cold and marooned in a police state as desperation takes hold. *The New York Times*. https://www.nytimes.com/2021/11/16/world/europe/pol and-belarus-border-crisis.html

[158] Amnesty International (2022, April 11). *Poland: Racist pushbacks at Belarus border are "in stark contrast" to welcome for Ukrainian refugees—new evidence* [Press release]. https://www.amnesty.org.uk/press-releases/poland-racist-pushbacks-belarus-border-are-stark-contrast-welcome-ukrainian-refugees

[159] In such detention centers, often plagued by human rights abuses, their children languish in the "grip of a mental health crisis." Doherty, B. (2016, August 9). A short history of Nauru, Australia's dumping grounds. *The Guardian*. https://www.theguardian.com/world/2016/aug/10/a-short-hist ory-of-nauru-australias-dumping-ground-for-refugees

The Book

This book will provide a systems-informed roadmap for multicultural societies to address the mental health issues of its economically disenfranchised, vulnerable, and marginalized refugee families by building multisectoral partnerships in a culturally competent manner to enhance their capacity and commitment.

This book relates firsthand accounts and draws upon international and interdisciplinary research in its systemic response to and care of refugees. It will reference specific countries' policy wherever possible, to draw out some relevant attributes of asylum structures and/or practices in general, as they impact its refugees. Even though refugee groups can differ based on characteristics such as cohort, age, geography, national history, and other factors, knowledge of nations' integration strategies can aid other countries in responding to refugees by fostering mutually beneficial growth opportunities for both their displaced populations and host communities. But although it can be valuable to compare and contrast country policies, in the absence of complete data, and with varying refugee populations, their unique experiences, and future needs, it can be a futile and exhaustive process. "There is no single or best integration model," says the Organization for Economic Cooperation and Development (OECD),[160] and, thus, the primary purpose of referencing a country's integration practice or asylum policy is to understand the impact of its context for all of its refugees' equally and their health, inclusivity, and thriving.

Readership

The audience for this book can be practitioners such as social workers, psychologists, physicians, immigration attorneys, judges, prison wardens, and psychiatrists interested in gaining knowledge on the cultural influences on trauma or trauma-informed assessment and treatment in clinics, camps, polyclinics, outpatient hospital settings, and other tertiary settings like prisons, veterans' affairs mental health, and intensive care units in emergency health care, worldwide. The challenge of broaching a difficult topic such as trauma also underscores the importance of cultural competence with respect to trauma. Culturally informed trauma treatment is a dynamic and developmental process that requires clinicians and systems to: acknowledge and incorporate the importance of culture; invest time and resource; commit to learning the skills,

[160] Cerna, L. (2019, May 13). *Refugee education: Integration models and practices in OECD countries* (Working Paper, 203, p. 23). OECD. https://one.oecd.org/document/EDU/WKP(2019)11/En/pdf

knowledge, and attitudes for service delivery to culturally diverse patient groups; and, put practices and policies in place for responsive and tailored treatment.[161]

Mental health services for diverse refugees and asylum-seekers is a specialized field; a large number of mental health professionals feel untrained or helpless or possess limited knowledge in this area.[162] I hope to address this need, at least partially, with this book. International students, educators, and health professionals who work with trauma in different populations may find the book useful to build on their knowledge of trauma through refugee experiences. To provide effective treatment, services, and advocacy to refugees, it is imperative that practitioners, policymakers, human rights workers, and educators have a comprehensive understanding of how refugees may express and experience trauma, its precursors, and sequelae in their different contexts. The audience can also be agency, institutional, and State Department heads in the United States or abroad, interested in understanding the precursors of refugee mental health for aiding their taskforces coordinating rapid response with local and international partnerships in more linked-up manner.

In those who routinely confront stories of horrific atrocities, the cumulation of the "unspeakable,"[163] can in turn, challenge and diminish their story. For the refugees this can symbolize a re-enactment of the torture experience, and for the professionals who may work within the asylum process, it can lead to burnout and high attrition.[164] For humanitarian actors, doctors, nurse practitioners, therapists, and asylum attorneys who tend to be first responders or listen to first-hand accounts, this book explores issues of secondary trauma and vicarious traumatization[165] during and after "life in the compound."

This resource will engage humanitarian professionals, agency heads, and clinical directors of international refugee organizations, through a better

[161] U.S. Department of Health and Human Services. (2003). *Developing cultural competence in disaster mental health programs: Guiding principles and recommendations* (DHHS Pub. No. SMA 3828). Center for Mental Health Services, Substance Abuse and Mental Health Services Administration. https://www.eird.org/isdr-biblio/PDF/Developing%20cultural%20competence.pdf

[162] Duden, G. S., & Martins-Borges, L. (2021). Psychotherapy with refugees: Supportive and hindering elements. *Psychotherapy Research*, 31(3), 386–401.

[163] Graessner, S. Ahmad, S., & Merkord, F. (2001). Everything forgotten! Memory disorders among refugees who have been tortured. In S. Graessner, N. Gurris, & C. Pross (Eds.), *At the side of torture survivors treating a terrible assault on human dignity* (p. 187, pp. 184–197) (J. M. Reimer, Trans.) Johns Hopkins University Press.

[164] Harris, L. M., & Mellinger, H. (2021). Asylum attorney burnout and secondary trauma. *Wake Forest Law Review*, 56, 733.

[165] Other terms used to describe the trauma caused by indirect exposure to trauma include *trauma transmission, unconscious, secondary,* or *empathic traumatization*: Nagata, D. K. (1990). The Japanese American internment: Exploring the transgenerational consequences of traumatic stress. *Journal of Traumatic Stress*, 3(1), 47–69; Major, E. F. (1996). The impact of the Holocaust on the second generation: Norwegian Jewish Holocaust survivors and their children. *Journal of Traumatic Stress*, 9(3), 441–454; Baranowsky, A. B., Young, M., Johnson-Douglas, S., Williams-Keeler, L., & McCarrey, M. (1998). PTSD transmission: A review of secondary traumatization in Holocaust survivors' families. *Canadian Psychology—Psychologie Canadienne*, 39(4), 247–256.

understanding of culture, gender, family, and national systems when organizing intersectors services, providing psychosocial support, and coordinating treatment in postconflict communities to elevate public health. The book takes a broad look at refugee health by drawing out best practices on treatments and approaches for positive refugee mental health, globally. Although the book focuses primarily on refugees resettled in Western nations, it also explores scaling-up opportunities for affordable and effective mental health in low- and middle-income countries.

In the following sections of the chapter, I discuss some widescale displacements in history. Following this, I explore some effects of untreated trauma and its long-term consequences for refugees in postconflict and resettled communities. I conceptualize complex trauma to gain insights on core obstacles contributing to the silence around refugee trauma. Finally, I reflect on the significance of the refugee's voice and the influence of untreated trauma on integration within host nations. I conclude with an overview of the remaining chapters of the book, as well as a brief plea for more recognition of the contribution refugees can make to their host societies when properly supported and integrated.

Forced Displacement in History

The contemporary global refugee crisis of the twenty-first century, apart from the India-Pakistan Partition and expulsions of people from Europe during World War II in the century prior, is the most widescale mobilization uprooting humans in modern history. We may perceive the influx of asylum seekers as irregular,[166] distinctive of present times, and arriving in massive proportions from Third-World countries to seek the unconditional largesse of Western nations. However, large-scale forced displacements and the refugee condition seen from a historical lens can afford valuable clues to repair some misassumptions. Consider the deportations during the First Persian Empire[167] (550–330 BC) to the deportations of prisoners of war in ancient Syria and Mesopotamia under the rule of the Iranian King Khosrow (r. 531–579). Or population movements generated by the Aztec empire in Mesoamerica.

Some examples in more recent history include escaping Protestants sailing aboard the Mayflower who had fled religious persecution and were the first

---

[166] "Irregular" generally relates to those people who lack legal documentation, such as visas, for border entry.

[167] Sanahuja, M. M. (2018). Deportations in the first Persian empire: Affinities and differences in comparison with the Neo-Assyrian and Neo-Babylonian periods. In F. Puell de la Villa & D. G. Hernán (Eds.), *War and population displacement: Lessons of history* (pp. 10–31). Sussex Academic Press.

British settlers of North American colonies in 1620; the ejection of women, children, the old, and the sick as far as a thousand kilometers into the Syrian desert[168] during the genocide of the Armenian people within Turkey; the large-scale emigration of Jews from Nazi Germany to other parts of the world (including Israel); the expulsion of 700,000 Palestinians—95% of the total Arab population in the area—to the neighboring countries of Jordan, Lebanon, and Iraq[169] following the creation of Israel in 1948 and the partition of Palestine. Nearly 100,000 Lhotshampa, an ethnic group with Nepali origins, were evicted in 1992 by Bhutan into Nepal. Sudden migratory movements of masses of people have arisen due to colonial legacies, ethnic cleansing, religious persecution, territorial expansion, environmental crises, militarization of poorly governed societies, or development. Asylum seekers sought sanctuary in places where they have shared commonalities and aspirations.

Refugees' stories may be unspoken and unshared but asylum seekers as *hijrah*,[170] *atithi*,[171] *ibn-sabeel*,[172] *muhajir*,[173] and *réfugiés* are as old as history.

Nor is the story true that some countries may tell themselves—that refugees only flee *to* their countries rather than *from* them. One has to turn back some pages of time in the United States to remember the tremendous violence endured by its ancient people, the Nez Percé of the Pacific Northwest, forced to be refugees and seek shelter in Canada. Seeking sanctuary and the granting of refuge have roots in both Eastern and Western religions.[174,175]

The word *refugee* first applied to the Protestant Huguenots who fled religious persecution by King Louis XIV in France to Britain following the revocation of the 1598 Edict of Nantes.[176] The word derives from the old French language *refuge* or "those who seek shelter." We are no strangers to refugees. Indeed, some may argue that many of us, as descendants of refugees, are ourselves part refugee.

[168] Üngör, U. Ü. (2012). *The Armenian genocide, 1915* (p. 54, pp. 45–62). NIOD Institute for War, Holocaust and Genocide Studies. https://web.archive.org/web/20210508050001/https://www.niod.nl/sites/niod.nl/files/Armenian%20genocide.pdf

[169] Alferez, M. G. (2018). Palestinian refugees: Between integration and return. In F. Puell de la Villa & D. G. Hernán (Eds.), *War and population displacement: Lessons of history* (pp. 194–212). Sussex Academic Press.

[170] *Hijrah*, migration or emigration (transliterated *Hegira*), of Prophet Mohammed's flight from Medina to Mecca marks the beginning of the Muslim calendar.

[171] *Atithi Devo Bhava*, derived from Sanskrit, means "the guest is equivalent to God."

[172] *Ibn-Sabeel*, variously meaning "wayfarer" has been referred to in the Quran, the holy text of Muslims, as a traveler or "son of the road."

[173] Muslim immigrants and their descendants who migrated from India to Pakistan post-Partition.

[174] Chetty, D. (2013). Refugees, exiles, and other forced migrants in the late Ottoman Empire. *Refugee Survey Quarterly*, 32(2), 35–52.

[175] Chetty, D. & Marfleet, P. (2013). Conceptual problems in forced migration. *Refugee Survey Quarterly*, 32(2), 1–13.

[176] Stanwood, O. (2019). *The global refuge: Huguenots in an age of empire.* Oxford University Press.

The Conflict-Affected and Their Untreated Trauma

Massive Trauma: A Systems View

The word *trauma,* originally from the Greek, refers to an injury inflicted on the body. In scientific literature, it is, however, more than the physical wound or its pathology. It is an unexpected breach in the mind's experience wounding its sense of time, self, and the world.[177]

Trauma is a natural response in the wake of violence—however, the trauma borne by refugees is no ordinary trauma." Extreme circumstances of traumatization"[178,179] are referred to as "massive trauma" in scientific literature.[180] Massive trauma is distinguished by its severity, multiple morbidities, multiple stressors, recurrent nature, and the ability of its negative psychological symptoms or dynamics to affect families and subsequent generations. The World Health Organization uses the term *complex posttraumatic stress disorder* (CPTSD[181]), and its International Classification of Diseases (ICD-11) captures more complex traumatic presentations or massive trauma. It is not well appreciated that a better approach needs to account for and effectively address the broad nature of trauma in refugee populations and develop an evidence base of interventions for their adequate care.

In this book, using existing scholarship,[182] we situate posttraumatic distress and healing in a systems framework. Within its multiple and dynamic systems such as gender, family, biology,[183] religion, community, economic,

[177] Caruth, C. (1996). *Unclaimed experience: Trauma, narrative and violence.*Johns Hopkins University Press..

[178] Krystal, H. (1968). Patterns of psychological damage. In H. Krystal (Ed.), *Massive psychic trauma* (pp. 1–7). International Universities Press.

[179] Danieli, Y., & Engdahl, B. (2018). In multigenerational legacies of trauma. In C. B. Nemeroff & C. Marmar (Eds.), *Post-traumatic stress disorder* (pp. 497–512). Oxford University Press.

[180] Kinzie, J. D., Sack, W. H., Angell, R. H., Manson, S. M., & Rath, B. (1986). The psychiatric effects of massive trauma on Cambodian children: I. The children. *Journal of the American Academy of Child Psychiatry, 25*(3), 370–376.

[181] CPTSD is typically associated with sustained, repeated, and multiple forms of trauma or polyvictimization (e.g., in childhood sexual abuse, genocide, domestic violence, torture, or slavery); individuals with such experiences report more severe impairment and unique sequelae such as dissociation.

[182] Drozdek, B. (2015). Challenges in treatment of post-traumatic stress disorder in refugees: Towards integration of evidence-based treatments with contextual and culture-sensitive perspectives. *European Journal of Psychotraumatology*, 6, 24750. https://doi.org/10.3402/ejpt. v6.24750

[183] PTSD also has biological bases although it is not the focus of this book. The biological network underpinning PTSD can include the amygdala, locus coeruleus, hippocampus, noradrenergic system and the hypothalamic-pituitary-adrenal (HPA) axis. Individuals with PTSD demonstrate increases in inflammatory markers such as interleukin 6, cortisol, c-reactive protein,and tumor necrosis factor. Source: Peruzzolo, T.L., Pinto, J.V., Roza, T.H., Shintani, A.O., Anzolin, A.P., Gnielka, V.,

political,[184] cultural and national forces, and the international, the self evolves through reciprocal dialogs.[185,186,187] This matrix of experiences and networks of relationships suffuses our psyche, relationships, and identities and has been variously referred to as social-ecological,[188,189] psychic skin,[190] "traumascape,"[191] and eco-social.[192,193] Aspects of the social-ecological matrix can include the cultural subsystem of the surrounding society (i.e., signs, symbols, meanings, practices, and institutions);[194] social representations, such as the refugee as a criminal or anonymized "Other";[195] religious practices;[196] ethnic, biological, racial,[197] historical, and political contexts;[198] and the protest activities of its community advocates,[199,200] can shape trauma's incidence, symptoms, suffering, and healing.

Kohmann, A.M., Marin, A.S., Lorenzon, V.R., Brunoni, A.R., Kapczinski, F., & Passos, I.C. (2022). Inflammatory and oxidative stress markers in post-traumatic stress disorder: A systematic review and meta-analysis (2022). *Molecular Psychiatry, 27*(8), 3150–3163.

[184] Farmer, P. (1999). Pathologies of power: Rethinking health and human rights. *American Journal of Public Health, 89*(10), 1486–1496.

[185] Archibald, H. C., Long, D. M., Miller, C., & Tuddenham, R. D. (1962). Gross stress reaction in combat—a 15-year follow-up. *American Journal of Psychiatry, 119*, 317–322.

[186] Dekel, R., & Goldblatt, H. (2008). Is there intergenerational transmission of trauma? The case of combat veterans' children. *American Journal of Orthopsychiatry, 78*(3), 281–289.

[187] Engel, G. L. (1977). The need for a new medical model: A challenge for biomedicine. *Science, 196*, 129–136.

[188] Kirmayer, L. (2021, September 14–18). *Landscapes of trauma: A social-ecological approach to cultural diversity* [Conference session]. 21st Australasian Conference on Traumatic Stress, virtual conference.

[189] Miller, K., & Rasmussen, A. (2017). The mental health of civilians displaced by armed conflict: An ecological model of refugee distress. *Epidemiology and Psychiatric Sciences, 26*(2), 129–138.

[190] Luci, M. (2020). *Journal of Analytical Psychology, 65*(2), 260–280.

[191] De Jong, J. V. T. M., & Hinton, D. (2007). Traumascape: An ecological–cultural–historical model for extreme stress. In D. Bhugra and K. Bhui (Eds.), *Textbook of cultural psychiatry* (2nd ed., pp. 363–392). Cambridge University Press.

[192] Kirmayer, L. J. (2015). Re-visioning psychiatry: Toward an ecology of mind in health and illness. In L. J. Kirmayer, R. Lemelson, & C. A. Cummings (Eds.), *Re-visioning psychiatry: Cultural phenomenology, critical neuroscience and global mental health* (pp. 622–660). Cambridge University Press.

[193] Kirmayer, L. J. (2015). Wrestling with the angels of history: Memory, symptom, and intervention. In D. E. Hinton & A. L. Hinton (Eds.), *Genocide and mass violence: Memory, symptom, and recovery* (pp. 388–420). Cambridge University Press.

[194] Castillo, R. (1996). *Culture and mental illness: A client-centered approach.* Brooks/Cole.

[195] Donnelly, F. (2017). Migration and displacement. *International Review of the Red Cross, 99*(1), 241–261.

[196] Fernando, G., & Berger, D. (2017). The role of religion in youth exposed to disasters in Sri Lanka. *Journal of Prevention & Intervention in the Community, 45*(4), 238–249.

[197] Pole, N. (2019). Race and ethnicity. In C. B. Nemeroff & C. R. Marmar (Eds.), *Post-traumatic stress disorder* (pp. 537–559). Oxford University Press.

[198] Ball, T., & O'Nell, T. D. (2016). Historical trauma in two Native American communities. In D. E. Hinton & B. J. Good (Eds.), *Culture and PTSD: Trauma in global and historical perspectives* (pp. 334–358). University of Pennsylvania Press.

[199] Ohmar, K., & O'Kane, M. (2008). The other side of political trauma: Protest, empowerment and transformation. In K .Allden & N. Murakami (Eds.), *Trauma and recovery on war's border: A guide for global health workers* (pp. 285–310). Dartmouth College Press.

[200] Edkins, J. (2003). *Trauma and the memory of politics.* Cambridge University Press (pp. 1–19).

Within this web of relationships and meanings, trauma creates a fracture or "fixity,"[201] disrupting the ongoing self-experience through their dysfunctional posttraumatic interactions. The meaning of the trauma,[202] its timing, duration, or extent, says the traumatologist Yael Danieli, can determine how severe the rupture will be for the individual. Thus, trauma can also be interpreted in terms of positive circular feedback loop between intersecting contexts where its effects can be cumulative and magnified. Although there are a multitude of other ways in which trauma can be studied, within the social-ecological framework, trauma can be conceptualized as a response affected by systems of power, privilege, persecution, and oppression. It can be considered a response-constellation such as displacement in the self,[203] discontinuity in experiences of the self,[204] prolonged grief, suicidality, chronic pain, appraisals of moral injury, anger, guilt, shame, and traumatogenic relations.[205]

A wide-angle systems approach[206] conceptualizing and assessing trauma's effects in refugees' interpersonal, family, and social contexts, however, is, with some exceptions, rare.[207] The proposed ecological approach would also bridge the individual traumatology field with systemic family therapy.[208] Adopting a multidimensional, multidisciplinary, longitudinal, and integrative framework for designing long-term refugee well-being, mental health interventions, and prevention programs should be a significant clinical, research, and policy goal for low- and high-income nations.

---

[201] Danieli, Y., & Engdahl, B. (2018). Multigenerational legacies of trauma. In C. B. Nemeroff & C. Marmar (Eds.), *Post-traumatic stress disorder* (pp. 7–28). Oxford University Press..

[202] Ibid.

[203] According to Luci, the "consequences of trauma, especially of massive relational traumas that have a particular impact on the self, can be described as a 'displacement in the self.'" Luci, M. (2020). Displacement as trauma and trauma as displacement in the experience of refugees. *Journal of Analytical Psychology*, 65, 260–280. https://doi.org/10.1111/1468-5922.12590.

[204] Van der Kolk, B. A., & van der Hart, O. (1991). The intrusive past: The flexibility of memory and the engraving of trauma. *American Imago*, 48(4), 425–454.

[205] Trauma is a consequence of the dehumanizing and oppressive social relations that brought about situations like civil wars, and it is misleading in the implication that its experience is individual, according to Martin-Baro: Martin-Baro, I. (1994). War and the psychosocial trauma of the Salvadoran children (A. Wallace, Trans.). In A. Aron & S. Corne (Eds.), *Writings on a liberation psychology* (pp. 122–135). Harvard University Press.

[206] Goff, B. S. N., Ruhlmann, L. M., Dekel, R., & Huxman, S. A. J. (2020). Trauma, post-traumatic stress, and family systems. In K. S. Wampler, R. B. Miller, R. B. Seedall, L. M. McWey, A. J. Blow, M. Rastogi, & R. Singh (Eds.), *The handbook of systemic family therapy* (Vol. 4, pp. 267–296). Wiley.

[207] Exceptions: Goff, B. S. N., Ruhlmann, L., Dekel, R., & Huxman, S. A. J. (2020). Trauma, post-traumatic stress, and family systems. In K. S. Wampler, R. B. Miller, R. B. Seedall, L. M. McWey, A. J. Blow, M. Rastogi, & R. Singh (Eds.), *The handbook of systemic family therapy* (Vol. 4, pp. 267–296). Wiley; Coulter, S. (2013). Systemic psychotherapy as an intervention for post-traumatic stress responses: An introduction, theoretical rationale and overview of developments in an emerging field of interest. *Journal of Family Therapy*, 35(4), 381–406.

[208] Goff, B. S. N., Ruhlmann, L. M., Dekel, R., & Huxman, S. A. J. (2020). Trauma, post-traumatic stress, and family systems. In K. S. Wampler, R. B. Miller, R. B. Seedall, L. M. McWey, A. J. Blow, M. Rastogi, & R. Singh (Eds.), *The handbook of systemic family therapy* (Vol. 4, pp. 267–296). Wiley.

Trauma in Postconflict and Resettled Communities

The mental health effects of untreated trauma can extend to resettled refugee, postconflict, and internally displaced communities and can be devastating.[209] A typical Syrian refugee's experience before escaping their country, for example, can be marked by aerial bombardment of bombs, missiles, and shootings; confinement in subhuman conditions; rape and sexual violence during detentions;[210] executions of family, neighbors, and loved ones; and kidnapping, either their own or of their loved ones. Their trauma is compounded by the government-sanctioned imprisonment and torture[211] of an estimated 19.5%–40% of Syrian refugees;[212] enslavement, starvation,[213] and conscripted service in paramilitary factions.[214]

Beyond its impact on individuals, conflicts in insecure societies have other far-reaching, lingering, and broad social repercussions for its vulnerable members. Wars can inflict disproportionate violence on women,[215,216] the disabled,[217] and children. Scores of Syrian children committed suicide rather than

[209] The terms postconflict settings and complex human emergencies sometimes are used interchangeably. They are those which may exhibit ongoing armed violence, high insecurity, and competition for resources with an enhanced risk for protracted displacement or reverting to another mass conflict. Resettled communities are formed from the transfer of refugees from an asylum country to another that has extended legal stay to them.

[210] Lawyers and Doctors for Human Rights. (2017). *Voices in the dark: Torture and sexual violence against women in Assad's detention centers.* https://ldhrights.org/en/wp-content/uploads/2017/07/Voices-from-the-Dark.pdf

[211] International Rehabilitation Council for Torture Victims. (2007, June 26). *26 June—International Day against torture: The fight against torture; a key priority for the EU.* European Commission. https://ec.europa.eu/commission/presscorner/detail/en/MEMO_07_254. These figures do not account for recent Syrian refugees.

[212] A UNHCR study investigated that 19.5%–27% of male survey respondents in Jordan, the Kurdistan area of Iraq, and Lebanon reported sexual harassment or unwanted sexual contact as boys. One focus group of refugee women in Jordan confirmed that 30%–40% of adult men in their community had experienced sexual violence while in detention in Syria: UNHCR. (2017, October). *"We keep it in our heart": Sexual violence against men and boys in the Syria crisis.* https://www.refworld.org/docid/5a128e814.html

[213] Independent International Commission of Inquiry on the Syrian Arab Republic. (2016. February 3). *Out of sight, out of mind: Deaths in detention in the Syrian Arab Republic.* United Nations. https://digitallibrary.un.org/record/823747?ln=en

[214] Shultz, J. M., Garfin, D. R., Espinel, Z., Araya, R., Oquendo, M. A., Wainberg, M. L., Chaskel, R., Gaviria, S. L., Ordóñez, A. E., Espinola, M., Wilson, F. E., Muñoz García, N., Gómez Ceballos, A. M., Garcia-Barcena, Y., Verdeli, H., & Neria, Y. (2014). Internally displaced "victims of armed conflict" in Colombia: The trajectory and trauma signature of forced migration. *Current Psychiatry Reports*, *16*(10), 475. https://doi.org/10.1007/s11920-014-0475-7

[215] Dannon, Z., & Collins, S. R. (2020, November 27). *Women in the Middle East and North Africa: Issues for Congress. Congressional Research Service.* https://sgp.fas.org/crs/mideast/R46423.pdf

[216] This awareness led to the adoption of the U.N. Security Council Resolution 1325 on women, peace, and security and nine subsequent resolutions, including Resolution 2493 (2019). Office of the Special Adviser on Gender Issues and Advancement of Women. (n.d.). *Landmark resolution on women, peace and security* [Press release]. https://www.un.org/womenwatch/osagi/wps/

[217] Motz, A. (2020). *The refugee status of persons with disabilities.* Brill Nijhoff.

face their bleak future.[218] In Iraqi Kurdistan faced with the prospect of abuse, more than 1,000 women chose to set themselves on fire.[219] In the event of war-related disabilities, the families of disabled in Afghanistan report stigma. At least one in five families[220] face discrimination when they seek what ought to be life's ordinary pursuits: marriage, education, and employment. Wars increase the risk of harm for the disabled by making it harder for them to flee and to access health or basic services.

When wars erupt, some families or religious groups can coax young girls into fake conjugal contracts, instead of protecting them.[221] Patriarchy, with its duplicitous cultural messages, can ensnare young women into enslavement, prostitution, or forced marriage. Through systemic gender-based abuses,[222] the moral and sexual exploitation of women through sexual attacks (and thereby of their men), and the low probability of prosecuting offenders,[223] conflicts erode the resilience of family and society. If they are sexual violence survivors, refugee girls also face barriers in accessing safe and hygienic menstrual products, prenatal and pregnancy care, ritual and cultural knowledge of womanhood, protection from domestic violence, and treatment for sexually transmitted infections. Social scientists[224] examining institutions of Chile, Argentina, El Salvador, Rwanda, and other countries reveal the fraught nature of the post-conflict social fabric in the form of complex intergroup dynamics,[225] lingering feelings of "shame, sadness, and distrust,"[226] and other long-term harms on community ties. But mental health care in complex humanitarian settings tends to be either

[218] Save the Children. (2021, April 29). *Northwest Syria: High number of suicide attempts and death, with children accounting for one in five cases.* https://www.savethechildren.net/news/north-west-syria-number-suicide-attempts-and-deaths-rise-sharply

[219] Self-immolation continues against Iraqi Kurdish women. (2013, June 12). *Al-Monitor.* https://www.al-monitor.com/originals/2013/06/self-immolation-kurdish-iraqi-women.html

[220] Human Rights Watch. (2020, April 28). *"Disability is not weakness": Discrimination and barriers facing women and girls with disabilities in Afghanistan.* https://www.hrw.org/report/2020/04/28/disability-not-weakness/discrimination-and-barriers-facing-women-and-girls

[221] Dauvergne, C., & Millbank, J. (2010). Forced marriage as a harm in domestic and international law. *Modern Law Review, 73*(1), 57–88.

[222] United Nations Secretary-General. (2015, March 23). *Conflict-related sexual violence.* UN Doc. S/2015/203. https://www.un.org/sexualviolenceinconflict/wp-content/uploads/report/s2015203-23-march-2015/SG-Report-2015.pdf

[223] Oosterveld, V. (2018). Forced marriage during conflict and mass atrocity. In F. Ní Aoláin, N. Cahn, D. F. Haynes, & N. Valji (Eds.), *The Oxford handbook of gender and conflict* (pp. 240–252). Oxford University Press.

[224] Martín-Baró, I. (1994). War and mental health (A. Wallace, Trans.). In A. Baron and S. Corne (Eds.), *Writings for a liberation psychology* (pp. 108–121). Harvard University Press.

[225] Páez, D., Basabe, N., & Gonzalez, J. L. (1997). Social processes and collective memory: A cross-cultural approach to remembering political events. In J. W. Pennebaker, D. Páez, & B. Rimé (Eds.), *Collective memory of political events. Social psychological perspectives* (pp. 147–174). Psychology Press.

[226] Kanyangara, P., Rimé, B., Philippot, P., & Yzerbyt, V. (2007). Collective rituals, emotional climate and intergroup perception: Participation in Gaçaca tribunals and the assimilation of the Rwandan genocide. *Journal of Social Issues, 63*(2), 273–288.

overwhelmed, evidences gaps in service provision,[227] excludes the involvement of affected communities, and ignores the utility of clinical intervention using health services.[228]

Despite their long stay in host countries, resettled refugee communities continue to be one of the main disadvantaged groups.[229,230,231,232,233] Compared with comparable immigrant, migrant, or age-matched general communities of host nations,[234] resettled refugees are 10 times[235] more likely to suffer from posttraumatic stress and other psychopathology.[236] For instance, among predominantly sub-Saharan refugees resettled in Sweden, a greater number of traumatic events are associated with both the severity of posttraumatic symptoms[237] and an eightfold risk of a mental health disorder.[238,239,240] Compared to other migrants, refugees are vulnerable[241] on parameters such as

[227] Kane, J. C., Ventevogel, P., Spiegel, P., Bass, J. K., van Ommeren, M., & Tol, W. A. (2014). Mental, neurological, and substance use problems among refugees in primary health care: Analysis of the health information system in 90 refugee camps. *BMC Medicine, 12*(1), 228. https://doi.org/10.1186/s12916-014-0228-9

[228] Vivalya, B. M. N., Vagheni, M. M., Kitoko, G. M. B., Vutegha, J. M., Kalume, A. K., Piripiri, A. L., Masika, Y. D., & Mbeva, J. K. (2022). Developing mental health services during and in the aftermath of the Ebola virus disease outbreak in armed conflict settings: A scoping review. *Globalization and Health, 18*, 71.

[229] Sole-Auro, A., & Crimmins, E. M. (2008). Health of immigrants in European countries. *International Migration Review, 42*(4), 861–876.

[230] Patel, N. (1999). Black and minority ethnic elderly: Perspectives on long-term care. In *With respect to old age: Long term care—rights and responsibilities.* Royal Commission on Long Term Care (Cm 4192-II/1, 38, pp. 257–304). http://www.archive.official-documents.co.uk/document/cm41/4192/4192.htm

[231] Songur, W. (2021). Older migrants' use of elderly care in Sweden: Family affects choice between home help services and special housing. *European Journal of Social Work, 24*(3), 481–491.

[232] Ruspini, P. (2009). *Elderly migrants in Europe: An overview of trends, policies and practices.* University of Lugano (pp. 4–5).

[233] Directorate General Home Affairs. (2011, May). *Migrant integration aggregate report.* Qualitative Eurobarometer. http://ec.europa.eu/public_opinion/archives/quali/ql_5969_migrant_en.pdf

[234] Fazel, M., Wheeler, J., & Danesh, J. (2005). Prevalence of serious mental disorder in 7000 refugees resettled in Western countries: A systematic review. *Lancet, 365*(9467), 1309–1314.

[235] Ibid.

[236] Refugees, in general, may be roughly up to 14-times more likely to have depression and 15-times more likely to suffer from post-traumatic stress.

[237] Steel, J. L., Dunlavy, A. C., Harding, C. E., & Theorell, T. (2017). The psychological consequences of pre-emigration trauma and post-migration stress in refugees and immigrants from Africa. *Journal of Immigrant and Minority Health, 19*(3), 523–532.

[238] Silove, D., Steel, Z., & Bauman, A. (2007). Mass psychological trauma and PTSD: Epidemic or cultural illusion? In J. P. Wilson & C. S.-K. Tang (Eds.), *International and cultural psychology: Cross-cultural assessment of psychological trauma and PTSD* (pp. 319–336). Springer Science & Business Media.

[239] Steel, J. L., Dunlavy, A. C., Harding, C. E., & Theorell, T. (2017). The psychological consequences of pre-emigration trauma and post-migration stress in refugees and immigrants from Africa. *Journal of Immigrant and Minority Health, 19*(3), 523–532.

[240] Ibid.

[241] Bhugra, D., Gupta, S., Bhui, K., Craig, T., Dogra, N., Ingleby, J. D., Kirkbride, J., Moussaoui, D., Nazroo, J., Qureshi, A., Stompe, T., & Tribe, R. (2011). WPA guidance on mental health and mental health care in migrants. *World Psychiatry: Official Journal of the World Psychiatric Association, 10*(1), 2–10.

health and well-being, social participation, and socioeconomic domains. In the UK, besides posttraumatic stress, older refugees face critical health and socio-economic challenges,[242] and compared to other immigrant groups in the UK and Europe,[243] lower rates of access to social services and higher depression, anxiety,[244] and loneliness.[245]

In the United States, one-third of refugees who had arrived between 1980 and 1989 stayed in the low-income group 20–30 years after their arrival.[246] Resettled Iraqis in the United States cannot secure sustainable employment or support themselves or their families and some become homeless. Sixty-two per-cent of resettled Cambodians in the United States continue to suffer psychiatric disorders 20 years after their arrival.[247,248,249,250,251] Vietnamese refugees show how trauma continues to be a powerful predictor of poor mental health,[252] 11 years after resettlement. Although global rates of refugee suicide are unavail-able, not only is seeking asylum related to self-harm, but refugees also evidence higher incidences of suicide rates compared to the respective national popu-lation.[253,254] Among the Bhutanese communities resettled in Texas, Arizona, Georgia, New York, and Ohio, the prevalence of suicidal ideation has ranged

[242] Oglak, S., & Hussein, S. (2016). Active aging: Social and cultural integration of older Turkish Alevi refugees in London. *Journal of Muslim Minority Affairs*, 36(1), 74–87.

[243] Ehrkamp, P. (2005). Placing identities: Transnational practices and local attachments of Turkish immigrants in Germany. *Journal of Ethnic and Migration Studies*, 31(2), 345–364.

[244] Peconga, E. K., & Høgh, T. M. (2020). Post-traumatic stress disorder, depression, and anxiety in adult Syrian refugees: What do we know? *Scandinavian Journal of Public Health*, 48(7), 677–687.

[245] Aragona, M., Castaldo, M., Cristina Tumiati, M., Schillirò, C., Dal Secco, A., Agrò, F., Forese, A., Tosi, M., Baglio, G., & Mirisola, C. (2020). Influence of post-migration living difficulties on post-traumatic symptoms in Chinese asylum seekers resettled in Italy. *International Journal of Social Psychiatry*, 66(2), 129–135.

[246] Capps, R., Newland, K., Fratzke, S., Groves, S., Auclair, G., Fix, M., & McHugh, M. (2015). *The integration outcomes of U.S. refugees: Successes and challenges*. Migration Policy Institute.

[247] Marshall, G. N., Schell, T. L., Elliott, M. N., Berthold, S. M., & Chun, C. A. (2005). Mental health of Cambodian refugees 2 decades after resettlement in the United States. *JAMA*, 294(5), 571–579.

[248] Refugee parents are more likely than nonrefugee parents to perceive their child's behavior (e.g., showing disrespect or noisy behaviors, having troubles in school or not complying with agreements) as problematic.

[249] Zannettino, L. (2012). ". . . There is no war here; it is only the relationship that makes us scared": Factors having an impact on domestic violence in Liberian refugee communities in South Australia. *Violence Against Women*, 18(7), 807–828.

[250] Ibid.

[251] Spencer, J. H., & Le, T. N. (2006). Parent refugee status, immigration stressors, and Southeast Asian youth violence. *Journal of Immigrant Minority Health*, 8(4), 359–368.

[252] Silove, D., Steel, Z., Bauman, A., Chey, T., & McFarlane, A. (2007). Trauma, PTSD and the longer-term mental health burden amongst Vietnamese refugees: A comparison with the Australian-born population. *Social Psychiatry and Psychiatric Epidemiology*, 42(6), 467–476.

[253] Centers for Disease Control and Prevention. (2013, July 5). Suicide and suicidal ideation among Bhutanese refugees in the United States, 2009–2012. *Morbidity and Mortality Weekly Report*, 62(26), 533–536.

[254] Arieli, A., Gilat, I., & Aycheh, S. (1996). Suicide among Ethiopian Jews: A survey conducted by means of a psychological autopsy. *Journal of Nervous and Mental Disease*, 184, 317–319.

from 3% to 6%,[255] an underestimate, as they are considered "hidden ideators"[256] in light of their elevated suicide rates.[257] Some of the factors contributing to increased risk in asylum-seekers and refugees include uncertain visa status, trauma exposure, time in detention, and social isolation[258] leading to lethal hopelessness.[259]

Although there have been advances in global mental health, in many low-income and developed countries, access to mental health care in general faces obstacles such as its lack of integration with nations' primary health care systems and community-based services;[260] affordability and accessibility; policies not aligned with human rights conventions,[261] and/or lack of legislation to guide mental health programs;[262] paucity of trained mental health professionals;[263] uneven distribution of mental health resources; lag in mental health care delivery;[264] and, nonexistent research prioritization of evolving needs.[265] During complex humanitarian emergencies, such chasms can become more profound for refugee mental health.

Nevertheless, these cracks can provide us with insight to strengthen and empower proactively social capital and social cohesion through public mental

[255] Adhikari, S. B., Daniulaityte, R., & Bhatta, D. N. (2021). Demographic and psychosocial factors associated with suicidal ideation among resettled Bhutanese refugees. *Journal of Immigrant and Minority Health, 23*, 511–518.

[256] Morrison, L. L., & Downey, D. L. (2000). Racial differences in self-disclosure of suicidal ideation and reasons for living: Implications for training. *Cultural Diversity and Ethnic Minority Psychology, 6*(4), 374–386.

[257] Meyerhoff, J., Rohan, K. J., & Fondacaro, K. M. (2018). Suicide and suicide-related behavior among Bhutanese refugees resettled in the United States. *Asian American Journal of Psychology, 9*(4), 270–283.

[258] Ingram, J., Lyford, B., McAtamney, A., & Fitzpatrick, S. (2022). Preventing suicide in refugees and asylum seekers: A rapid literature review examining the role of suicide prevention training for health and support staff. *International Journal of Mental Health Systems, 16*, 24.

[259] Procter, N. (2019). Preventing refugee and asylum seeker suicide. *Australian Nursing and Midwifery Journal, 26*(6), 58.

[260] WHO. (2018, June 6). *Mental health: Massive scale-up of resources needed if global targets are to be met.* https://www.who.int/news/item/06-06-2018-mental-health-massive-scale-up-of-resources-needed-if-global-targets-are-to-be-met

[261] Ibid.

[262] Saxena, S., Saraceno, B., & Granstein, J. (2013). Scaling up mental healthcare in resource poor settings. In G. Thornicroft, M. Ruggeri, & D. Goldberg (Eds.), *Improving mental health care: The global challenge* (pp. 12–24). Wiley-Blackwell.

[263] Kopinak, J. K. (2015). Mental health in developing countries: Challenges and opportunities in introducing Western mental health system in Uganda. *International Journal of Maternal and Child Health and AIDS, 3*(1), 22–30.

[264] Rojas, G., Martínez, V., Martínez, P., Franco, P., & Jiménez-Molina, A. (2019). Improving mental health care in developing countries through digital technologies: A mini narrative review of the Chilean case. *Frontiers in Public Health, 7*. https:doi.org/10.3389/fpubh.2019.00391

[265] Baingana, F. (2011). Developing mental health programmes in low- and middle-income countries. In R. Parker & M. Sommer (Eds.), *Routledge handbook for global health* (pp. 402–410). Routledge.

health and community programs.[266],[267] For nations worldwide, there is great potential utility and strength in mobilizing understandings of complex trauma in their reception of refugees in different contexts and in rebuilding their capacity for refugee mental health. So, it is not an exaggeration to suggest that a country's success in integrating refugee populations depends on its ability to strive toward equitable health through eliminating well-documented health disparities of race and social status to effectively address the traumas its refugee population has suffered. Humanitarian emergencies ought to be regarded as opportunities to build sustainable mental health systems for all people in need.[268] To mobilize refugees' well-being, the symptoms and meanings of complex trauma must be regarded in-context and with continuity throughout refugees' displacement and resettlement.

Straitjacketing Refugees' Experiences: Social Exclusion and Integration

In the next section, we discuss how the violence reverberating in the refugees' life may not always be discernible to those around them. Traumas incurred by refugees are dismissed at different points within the system—in the community, country's resettlement framework, and humanitarian emergencies and, sometimes, by the refugees themselves.

Limitations of Refugee Mental Health Care in Humanitarian Settings

Humanitarian emergencies can cause high rates and prevalence of posttraumatic stress, but trauma-informed treatment among the displaced remains challenging, controversial, and, for the most part, inadequate.[269] An overwhelming number of refugees especially in low-income nations who need treatment remain either at arms' length from it. Among the treated refugees, a large proportion,

[266] Kienzler, H. (2019). Mental health system reform in contexts of humanitarian emergencies: Toward a theory of "practice-based evidence." *Culture, Medicine, and Psychiatry, 43*(4), 636–662.

[267] Patel, P. P., Russell, J., Allden, K., Betancourt, T. S., Bolton, P., Galappatti, A., Hijazi, Z., Johnson, K., Jones, L., Kadis, L., & Leary, K. 2011. Transitioning mental health and psychosocial support: From short-term emergency to sustainable post-disaster development. *Prehospital and Disaster Medicine, 26*(6), 470–481.

[268] WHO. (2022, March 16). *Mental health in emergencies.* https://www.who.int/news-room/fact-sheets/detail/mental-health-in-emergencies

[269] Im, H., Rodriguez, C., & Grumbine, J. M. (2021). A multitier model of refugee mental health and psychosocial support in resettlement: Toward trauma-informed and culture-informed systems of care. *Psychological Services, 18*(3), 345–364.

18-54% show no response to treatment. Psychosocial measures, extensively employed in humanitarian settings, carry benefits[270] of fostering community engagement and health, social and cultural adaptation, and self-help, and reviving fragmented social networks. But substitutes for mental health treatments are found to be wanting in ameliorating stress, and as evidence shows, they don't always reduce posttraumatic stress.[271] In the absence of trauma-informed specialized supports, psychosocial assistance may even delay the timely detection of and early intervention[272] for mental health concerns.

Further, in complex humanitarian emergencies, data collection methods generally employ rapid assessments such as focus groups and participatory ranking techniques. This poses inherent limitations[273] for key stakeholders,[274] such as ignoring differences between people,[275] neglecting research on mental health needs in humanitarian settings, and failing to link documentation through resettlement phases. The absence of a cohesive and transcultural mental health infrastructure between nations, according to researchers, prevents relay and consolidation of torture-related and other information to stakeholders in host nations where they may resettle.[276] In focus groups, the mental health needs of the affected population can be represented by dominant figures who may generally tend to be men in high-status social positions. As a result, they become "resource brokers"[277] or interpreters to aid workers or health professionals, further marginalizing the needs of minorities such as young women. Assessment tools in complex humanitarian settings are specifically designed not to gather or elaborate on harrowing details even if participants may wish to speak about them.[278] Although new research is indicating that the more protracted the displacement, the more harmful it is, the impact on a refugee's mental health of lack of avenues

[270] Silove, D., Ventevogel, P., & Rees, S. (2017). The contemporary refugee crisis: An overview of mental health challenges. *World Psychiatry, 2,* 130–139.

[271] Neuner, F. (2010). Assisting war-torn populations—should we prioritize reducing daily stressors to improve mental health? *Social Science and Medicine, 71,* 1381–1384.

[272] Im, H., Rodriguez, C., & Grumbine, J. M. (2021). A multitier model of refugee mental health and psychosocial support in resettlement: Toward trauma-informed and culture-informed systems of care. *Psychological Services, 18*(3), 345–364.

[273] Ventevogel, P. (2016). *Borderlands of mental health: Explorations in medical anthropology, psychiatric epidemiology and health systems research in Afghanistan and Burundi.* [Doctoral dissertation, University of Amsterdam].

[274] WHO & UNHCR. (2012). *Assessing mental health and psychosocial needs and resources: Toolkit for humanitarian settings.* https://apps.who.int/iris/bitstream/handle/10665/76796/9789241548 533_eng.pdf?sequence=1&isAllowed=y

[275] Pool, R., & Geissler, W. (2005). *Medical anthropology.* Open University Press.

[276] Suhaiban, H. A., Grasser, L. R., & Javanbakht, A. (2019). A mental health of refugees and torture survivors: A critical review of prevalence, predictors, and integrated care. *International Journal of Environmental Research and Public Health, 16*(13), 2309.

[277] McSpadden, L. A., & MacArthur, J. R. (2009). Human rights and complex emergencies. In U. Linke & D. T. Smith (Eds.), *Cultures of fear: A critical reader* (pp. 84–100). Pluto Press.

[278] WHO & UNHCR. (2012). *Assessing mental health and psychosocial needs and resources: Toolkit for humanitarian settings* (p. 36). https://apps.who.int/iris/bitstream/handle/10665/76796/978924 1548533_eng.pdf?sequence=1&isAllowed=y

for sharing trauma and the absence of early trauma-informed care also needs to be explored.

The "One-Size-Fits-All" National Resettlement Framework

A nation's resettlement system with its labyrinth of agencies and providers is the central site for recognizing refugees' capacities and addressing vulnerabilities for facilitating local integration. Using the case example of the US Refugee Admissions Program (USRAP), as depicted in Figure 1.4, we illustrate how its organizational structure and functioning within its agencies can be barriers in the recognition, assessment, and timely treatment of refugees' mental health concerns.

In the United States, there are three major categories of groups involved in handling refugees and displaced persons: federal and other government agencies, humanitarian groups, and resettlement or voluntary agencies. Let us examine three limitations in the USRAP that obstruct its intentions for the local integration of some of its refugee populations.[279] Highlighting the case of Iraqi refugees, the Human Rights Institute reports that the United States is either "simply forgetting about them after they arrive" or they may be "abandoned upon arrival."[280] The case of Burmese refugees in America highlights the prevailing one-size-fits-all thinking affording a homogenous instead of tailored planning and provision of social services for the affected population.[281,282] The coordination between USRAP's different actors (i.e., the Bureau of Population, Refugees, and Migration; Reception and Placement; Office of Refugee Resettlement, and the various resettlement agencies) can be a critical element in designing tailor-made mental health services for its particular ethnic groups. Prioritizing strategic planning that envisions a more robust, routine, and comprehensive trauma-informed service provision can also better serve refugees' postresettlement needs and inform the blueprint for their care in overseas processing centers. However, information-sharing between the agencies has often been reported as unstructured or unsystematic. Refugee integration in the United States, in contrast to nations like Canada, is referred to as either one of self-sufficiency or "paper

[279] Human Rights Institute. (2009). Refugee crisis in America: Iraqis and their resettlement experience. *HRI Papers & Reports*, 4. https://scholarship.law.georgetown.edu/hri_papers/4

[280] Committee on Foreign Relations. *Abandoned upon arrival: Implications for refugees and local communities burdened by a U.S. resettlement system that is not working.* (2010, July 21). S. Rep. No. 111-52. https://www.gpo.gov/fdsys/pkg/CPRT-111SPRT57483/pdf/CPRT-111SPRT57483.pdf

[281] Brown, A., & Scribner, T. (2014). Unfulfilled promises, future possibilities: The refugee resettlement system in the United States. *Journal on Migration and Human Security, 2*(2), 101–120.

[282] Kerwin, D. (2018). The US refugee resettlement program: A return to first principles. How refugees help to define, strengthen, and revitalize the United States. *Journal on Migration and Human Security, 6*(3), 205–225.

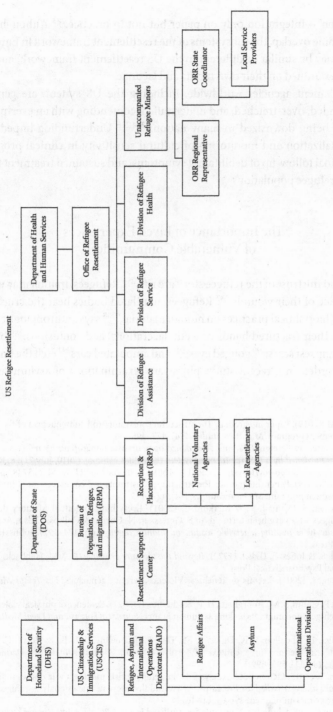

Figure 1.4 The US Resettlement System

integration"—integration only on paper but not in practice.[283] Although there may be some overlap, the subsystems of the resettlement framework in European nations may be similar or different to the US resettlement framework, and they must be examined on their own merits and lacunae.

Resettlement agencies worldwide, including the US system, are generally underfunded, overstretched, and understaffed, contending with an ever-present threat of being downsized in many nations.[284,285] Underfunding impedes the conceptualization and monitoring of cultural sensitivity in clinical programs, longitudinal follow-up of debilitating symptoms, and sustained treatment for respective refugee populations.

The Importance of Lived Experiences of Vulnerable Communities

Doubt and mistrust of the refugee story are rife.[286] Refugees' trauma may well lie in the voice of their wounds.[287] Refugees' mutilated bodies bear the cruel testimony of "biopolitical practices on human material,"[288] says anthropologist Jackie Assayag. Their fractured hands or teeth; lacerations, and contusions;[289] burned skin; palimpsest scars;[290] gouged eyes;[291] and amputated ears[292] etch the imposed political order. In a recent study, physicians' examinations of asylum-seekers'

[283] Fee, M. (2019). Paper integration: The structural constraints and consequences of the US refugee resettlement program. *Migration Studies, 7*(4), 477–495.

[284] Committee on Foreign Relations. *Abandoned upon arrival: Implications for refugees and local communities burdened by a U.S. resettlement system that is not working.* (2010, July 21). S. Rep. No. 111–52. https://www.gpo.gov/fdsys/pkg/CPRT-111SPRT57483/pdf/CPRT-111SPRT57483.pdf

[285] Fee, M. (2019). Paper integration: The structural constraints and consequences of the US refugee resettlement program. *Migration Studies, 7*(4), 477–495.

[286] Graessner, S., Ahmad, S., & Merkord, F. (2001). Everything forgotten! Memory disorders among refugees who have been tortured. In S. Graessner, N. Gurris, & C. Pross (Eds.), *At the side of torture survivors treating a terrible assault on human dignity* (pp. 184–197). Johns Hopkins University Press.

[287] Freud, S. & Jones, E. (Eds.). (1922). *Beyond the pleasure principle* (C. J. M. Hubback, Trans.). International Psychoanalytical Press.

[288] Assayag, J. (2004). Leçons de ténèbres: Violence, terreur, génocides. *Les Temps Modernes, 1*(626), 275–304.

[289] Deps, P., Collin, S. M., Aborghetti, H. P., & Charlier, P. (2021). Evidence of physical violence and torture in refugees and migrants seeking asylum in France. *Journal of Forensic and Legal Medicine, 77,* 102104.

[290] Charlier, P., Abdallah, F. B., Dulac, Y. M., Deo, S., Jacqueline, S. L. B., & Hervé, C. (2017). "Palimpsest scar" lesions in a context of torture (Darfur, Sudan). *Annales de Dermatologie Venereologie, 144*(11), 696–699.

[291] Rollin, T. (2015, October 26). Analysis: Is the refugee crisis making a war crimes indictment on Syria more likely? *Middle East Eye.* https://www.middleeasteye.net/news/analysis-refugee-crisis-making-war-crimes-indictment-syria-more-likely

[292] Hawley, C. (2004, June 10). New hope for mutilated Iraqis. *BBC News.* http://news.bbc.co.uk/2/hi/middle_east/3795785.stm

scars corroborated their accounts of torture by the police and military: 93% had endured violence through being cut, stabbed, beaten, burned, or assaulted.[293] Equally, many of the tortured, although brutally so, will carry no scars.[294,295,296] For every rare torture victim[297,298] who is still alive and whose scars we might confront, there will be many more whose scars will have faded and who worry they will be disbelieved.

When I met Gulnaz, a survivor of torture, I asked why he had not shared his experience with anyone else. Fourteen years had elapsed, he said, and yet he continued to worry: "People won't believe me. They will say to me, 'Why didn't they kill you? Why are *you* the only one who escaped?' They will be suspicious of me, 'Why did they keep you (in detention) only for 3 months, why not 10 months?'" Gulnaz's story is like many other torture survivors. Although the long-forgotten past can exert its distressing sway on present-day awareness[299] at various stages

[293] Deps, P., Collin, S. M., Aborghetti, H. P., & Charlier, P. Evidence of physical violence and torture in refugees and migrants seeking asylum in France. *Journal of Forensic and Legal Medicine, 77*, 102104.

[294] Moisander, P. A., & Edston, E. (2003). Torture and its sequel: A comparison between victims from six countries. *Forensic Science International, 137*, 133–140.

[295] Prevalence and method of torture can vary with gender, period of history, and country of origin. Garoff, F., Skogberg, N., Klemettilä, A., Lilja, E., Omar, A. A. H., Snellman, O., & Castaneda, A. E. (2021). Mental health and traumatization of newly arrived asylum seeker adults in Finland: A population-based study. *International Journal of Environmental Research and Public Health, 18*(13), 7160.

[296] The country where torture has occurred can affect the physical and psychological sequelae of torture. Moisander, P. A., & Edston, E. (2003). Torture and its sequel: A comparison between victims from six countries. *Forensic Science International, 137*, 133–140.

[297] Generally, refugees of complex trauma are referred to as *survivors*. However, I struggled with how our language for refugees can reflect the complexities of suffering, enduring, surviving, and sometimes, succumbing. The term *survivor* can reflect several biases: our steadfast belief in the endurance of human spirit despite our recognition that sometimes those who endure complex trauma can be the living dead who may barely make it from 1 hour to the next. In essence, hard times are not welcomed but rather endured. Our reliance on the term *survivor* may be based on our discomfort and unwillingness to contend with the lived realities and sufferings of others. A lot of traumatized folks may also be uncomfortable with the discomfort of others and their own. For the "survivor," the term can cloak implicit assumptions that their life ought to go back to normal after 6 months following the traumatic event or that the traumatic events are in the past, and the inevitable path from suffering to trauma is resilience. In reality, refugees' lack of choice, agency, support, and resources provided to them are victims of a political order (s). Given their tenuous survival and, often times, survival despite exigent circumstances, and in accordance with some international documents, I gravitated toward referring to them as *victims*. Finally, I adopted the strengths-based perspective that contends that refugees and others dealing with trauma are more than their trauma: Levi, P. (1959). *If this is a man*. Orion Press; Convention against torture and other cruel, inhuman or degrading treatment or punishment (General Comment No. 3, p.1), December 13, 2012, https://www.refworld.org/docid/5437cc274.html

[298] The General Comment No. 3 of the Convention Against Torture defines *victims* as "persons who have individually or collectively suffered harm . . . through acts or omissions that constitute violations of the Convention. Victims include immediate family or dependents of the victim": Ibid.

[299] Winter, J. (2010). Thinking about silence. In E. Ben-Ze'ev, R. Ginio, & J. Winter (Eds.), *Shadows of war: A social history of silence in the twentieth century* (pp. 3–31). Cambridge University Press.

of displacement and for different reasons, the trauma story of refugees is one that is bracketed or cast aside.[300]

History is rife with many kinds of mass trauma survivors who have been silent about their traumas. For instance, consider an estimated 860,000 German women[301] raped in masses at the end of World War II by Western Allied soldiers from Britain, America, Belgium, and France, and many from the Soviet-occupied zone and Eastern Germany, whose trauma has not been documented[302] and who have never been recognized as victims.[303] Self-censorship through withdrawal or cutting off oneself from its reality may also be a path to seek merciful protection from trauma's horrors[304,305,306] Psychology's retreat from exploration of subjectivities and within the contours of clinical space has also affected the neglect of refugees' lived experiences.[307]

As a result, refugee voices remain underrepresented in research,[308] with consequences such as:

- Invisibility of their experiences[309] and misassumptions of refugees
- Delayed treatment[310] affects restitution to survivors and enhances their risk[311]

[300] Ibid.

[301] Gebhardt, M. (2016). *Crimes unspoken: The rape of German women at the end of Second World War.* (N. Somers, Trans.) Polity Press.

[302] Exceptions include: Gebhardt, M. (2016). *Crimes unspoken: The rape of German women at the end of Second World War* (N. Somers, Trans.) Polity Press; Grossmann, A. (1997). A question of silence: The rape of German women by occupation soldiers. In R. G. Moeller (Ed.), *West Germany under construction: Politics, society, and culture in the Adenauer era* (pp. 33–52). University of Michigan Press.

[303] German grandmothers and mothers, the Trümmerfrau, or Germany's "rubble women," raped on a large-scale at the end of World War II, hid their accounts of sexual violence from future generations: Sander, H. (1995). Remembering/forgetting (S. Liebman, Trans.). *October, 72,* 15–26. https://doi.org/10.2307/778924

[304] Luci, M., & Kahn, M. (2021). Analytic therapy with refugees: Between silence and embodied narratives. *Psychoanalytic Inquiry, 41*(2), 103–114.

[305] McKinney, K. (2007). "Breaking the conspiracy of silence": Testimony, traumatic memory, and psychotherapy with survivors of political violence. *Ethos, 35*(3), 265–299.

[306] Ekström, E., Andersson, A. C., & Börjesson, U. (2022). "I've got many stories you know": Problematizing silence among unaccompanied migrant girls. *Journal of International Migration & Integration, 23,* 797–814.

[307] "Approaches to subjective experience flowing from descriptive psychopathology and classificatory psychiatry have not provided an adequate basis to understand the pervasive, alternating, or transformative aspects of schizophrenia.": Jenkins, J. H., & Barrett, R. J. (Eds.), Schizophrenia, culture, and subjectivity: The edge of experience. *Cambridge Studies in Medical Anthropology, 11,* 7.

[308] Lau, L. S., & Rodgers, G. (2021). Cultural competence in refugee service settings: A scoping review. *Health Equity, 5*(1), 124–134.

[309] Rajaram, P. (2002). Humanitarianism and representations of the refugee. *Journal of Refugee Studies, 15*(3), 247–264.

[310] Bhattacharyya, P., Songose, L., & Wilkinson, L. (2021). How sexual and gender-based violence affects the settlement experiences among Yazidi refugee women in Canada. *Frontiers in Human Dynamics, 3.* https://doi.org/10.3389/fhumd.2021.644846

[311] Delayed treatment enhances the risk for continuation of torture or punitive treatment to their family members in their birth countries, along with the declining likelihood of formulating

- Impoverishment and social exclusion[312]
- Myopia in designing treatment strategies[313]
- Entrapment of communities in collective suffering[314]

For traumatized communities then, this subterranean space of suffering is a socially and institutionally constructed space of silence, an expression of trauma. Forced migration and the psychological after-effects of complex trauma can be a barrier in the secure and successful integration of vulnerable and marginalized refugee families in both Western and non-Western nations.[315] Host nations do not associate psychological well-being with long-term self-sufficiency and integration. Research is now burgeoning on the impact of the postmigratory environment on the mental health of the displaced.[316,317,318,319,320,321] However, scholarly literature is lacking in how premigratory trauma links to postmigratory stressors.[322] Although

complaints against their offenders, and prosecution of human rights violators: Koopman, C. (1997). Political psychology as a lens for viewing traumatic events. *Political Psychology*, *18*(4), 830–847.

[312] Narayan, D., Patel, R. Schafft, K. Rademacher, A., & Koch-Schulte, S. (2000). *Voices of the poor? Can anyone hear us?* Oxford University Press.

[313] In contrast, exploring "historizing condition (s) that helped to produce a particular political subjectivity," in refugees can also help us expand our interventions: Malkki, L. H. (1996). Speechless emissaries: Refugees, humanitarianism, and dehistoricization. *Cultural Anthropology*, *11*(3), 377–404.

[314] Instead, unraveling truths in the form of testimonies, such as those of the forcibly taken Indigenous children within Church-run Canadian residential schools, could be the first step in helping them heal from their genocide. Cecco, L. (2021, June 27). Canada must reveal "undiscovered truths" of residential schools to heal. *The Guardian*. https://www.theguardian.com/global-developm ent/2021/jun/27/canada-must-reveal-undiscovered-truths-of-residential-schools-to-heal

[315] Sabin, M., Lopes Cardozo, B., Nackerud, L., Kaiser, R., & Varese, L. (2003). Factors associated with poor mental health among Guatemalan refugees living in Mexico 20 years after civil conflict. *JAMA*, *290*(5), 635–642.

[316] Robjant, K., Hassan, R., & Katona, C. (2004). Mental health implications of detaining asylum seekers: Systematic review. *British Journal of Psychiatry*, *194*(4), 306–312.

[317] Silove, D., Steel, Z., & Watters, C. P. (2000). Policies of deterrence and the mental health of asylum seekers. *JAMA*, *284*(5), 604–611.

[318] Steel, Z., Silove, D., Phan, T., & Bauman, A. (2002). Long-term effect of psychological trauma on the mental health of Vietnamese refugees resettled in Australia: A population-based study. *Lancet*, *360*(9339), 1056–1062.

[319] Momartin, S., Silove, D., & Manicavasagar, V. & Steel, Z. (2003). Dimensions of trauma associated with posttraumatic stress disorder (PTSD) caseness, severity, and functional impairment: A study of Bosnian refugees resettled in Australia. *Social Science and Medicine*, *57*(5), 775–781.

[320] Steel, Z., Silove, D., Brooks, R., Momartin, S., Alzuhairi, B., Susljik, I. (2006). Impact of immigration detention and temporary protection on the mental health of refugees. *British Journal of Psychiatry*, *194*(4), 306–312.

[321] Schweitzer, R., Melville, F., Steel, Z. & Lacherez, P. (2006). Trauma, post-migration living difficulties, and social support as predictors of psychological adjustment in resettled Sudanese refugees. *Australian & New Zealand Journal of Psychiatry*, *40*, 179–188.

[322] Saadi, A., Al-Rousan, T., & AlHeresh, R. (2021). Refugee mental health—an urgent call for research and Action. *JAMA Network Open*, *4*(3), E212543. https://doi.org/10.1001/jamanetworko pen.2021.2543.

economists[323] and social scientists have urged focusing attention on nonmarket social interactions[324] and cultural norms as significant indicators of the socioeconomic integration of immigrants, such variables have not been fully explored. Prior histories of trauma and mental health struggles can affect individuals' economic integration, earnings relative to the host population, or *economic assimilation*, in host societies.

Albeit conspicuously underrepresented in research[325] refugee voices can reveal the cultural processes, interpersonal, and social arrangements that heighten or assuage trauma's effects. Their voices can reveal the experiences of those they left behind and who could not afford the luxury of safety or escape. Expanding the conceptual, clinical, and methodological rigor to examine experiences of refugee families can be better achieved through incorporating qualitative, quantitative yet descriptive,[326] and longitudinal studies, and not through reliance on outcome research alone. When refugees may be overlooked in research, policymaking, and international aid, they create an empathy gap between the asylum-seeker and the world and reinforce a "*them*" and an "*us*."

The Benefits of Social Inclusion of Refugees

Successful integration can help promote social inclusion, strengthen human capacity, boost development and create more equal societies.[327]

Some of the most successful modern societies continue to build their success on refugees' entrepreneurialism and grit. The economic performance of refugees and migrants can be gained from the steepest declines of remittances to their low- and middle-income native countries projected during the pandemic.[328] That it largely remained resilient to the effects of the pandemic also shows the grit of refugees in sustaining lifelines of support for their families. Turkey further evidences how refugees can play a fundamental role in fostering international trade and investment with Syrians establishing approximately 10,000 businesses

[323] Algan, Y., Bisin, A., & Verdier, T. Integration of immigrants. In Y. Algan, A. Bisin, A. Manning, & T. Verdier (Eds.), *Cultural integration of immigrants in Europe* (pp. 1–48). Oxford University Press.
[324] Algan, Y., Bisin, A., & Verdier, T. Integration of immigrants. In Y. Algan, A. Bisin, A. Manning, & T. Verdier (Eds.), *Cultural integration of immigrants in Europe* (pp. 1–48). Oxford University Press.
[325] Lau, L. S., & Rodgers, G. (2021). Cultural competence in refugee service settings: A scoping review. *Health Equity, 5*, 124–134.
[326] Cernovsky, Z. Z. (1990). Escape stress, sleep disorders, and assimilation of refugees. *Social Behavior and Personality: An International Journal, 18*(2), 287–298.
[327] OECD. (2019). *Ready to help? Improving resilience of integration systems for refugees and other vulnerable migrants.* http://dx.doi.org/10.1787/9789264311312-en
[328] Ratha, D., De, S., Kim, E., Plaza, S., Seshan, G., & Yameogo, N.D. (2020, October). *Phase II: Covid-19 crisis through a migration lens* (Migration and Development Brief 33). KNOMAD & World Bank. https://www.knomad.org/sites/default/files/2020-11/Migration%20%26%20Development_Brief%2033.pdf

that provide livelihood for 250,000 other Syrians.[329] Improving the labor integration outcomes for refugee cohorts in Europe is estimated to create a GDP contribution of about €60 billion to €70 billion annually. [330] Refugees' higher fertility rates are estimated to drive a demographic advantage for host nations. There are real, larger social benefits to tolerance, integration, and assimilation of refugees into the larger society.

Slower rates of integration of refugees may suggest cohort effects and/or untreated mental health disorders.[331,332] In Germany, older waves of refugees have taken 20 years to integrate into the labor market, and integration has seemed more expedient for newer refugees.[333] Refugees in Sweden, relative to the native-born and other Europeans, have lower levels of employment.[334] After 1–2 years of integration programs in Sweden, only 22% of newly arrived refugee men and 8% of women[335] were employed. Of the refugees that arrived in Sweden from 1997 to 1999,[336] only 30% had a job after 2 years of residence, and 65% of these refugees had a job after 10 years of residence. New research however, suggests that the systematic development gap between refugees and their hosts,[337,338]

[329] Güven, S., Kenanoğlu, M., Kadkoy, O., & Kurt, T. (2018). Syrian entrepreneurship and refugee start-ups in Turkey: Leveraging the Turkish experience. *Tepav and European Bank for Reconstruction and Development.* https://www.tepav.org.tr/upload/files/1566830992-6.TEPAV_and_EBRD___Syrian_Entrepreneurship_and_Refugee_Start_ups_in_Turkey_Lever....pdf

[330] McKinsey Global Institute. (2016, December 1). *Europe's new refugees: A road map for better integration outcomes.* https://www.mckinsey.com/~/media/mckinsey/featured%20insights/employment%20and%20growth/a%20road%20map%20for%20integrating%20europes%20refugees/a-road-map-for-integrating-europes-refugees.pdf

[331] Walther, L., Rayes, D., Amann, J., Flick, U., Ta, T. M. T., Hahn, E., & Bajbouj, M. (2021). Mental health and integration: A qualitative study on the struggles of recently arrived refugees in Germany. *Frontiers in Public Health, 4*(9), 1–17.

[332] Harris, S. M., Sandal, G. M., Bye, H. H., Palinkas, L. A., & Binder, P. (2021). Integration is correlated with mental health help-seeking from the general practitioner: Syrian refugees' preferences and perceived barriers. *Frontiers in Public Health, 9,* 777582. https://doi.org/10.3389/fpubh.2021.777582

[333] Juran, S., & Broer, P. N. (2017). A profile of Germany's refugee populations. *Population and Development Review, 43*(1), 149–157.

[334] Lindgren, K., Nicholson, M., & Oskarsson, S. (2022). Immigrant political representation and local ethnic concentration: Evidence from a Swedish refugee placement program. *British Journal of Political Science, 52*(3), 997–1012.

[335] Bevelander, P., & Irastorza, P. (2017, July 27). The labor market integration of refugees in Sweden. *Nordregio News.* https://nordregio.org/nordregio-magazine/issues/migration-and-integration/the-labour-market-integration-of-refugees-in-sweden/

[336] Robinson, L., & Käppeli, A. (2018, November 15). *Policies, outcomes, and populism: The integration of migrants in Sweden.* Center for Global Development. https://www.cgdev.org/blog/policies-outcomes-and-populism-integration-migrants-sweden

[337] Betts, A. (2021). *The wealth of refugees: How displaced people can build economies* (p. 82). Oxford University Press.

[338] Some studies suggest the presence of cohort effects in refugee's socioeconomic integration: Kerwin, D. (2018). The US refugee resettlement program—a return to first principles: How refugees help to define, strengthen, and revitalize the United States. *Journal on Migration and Human Security, 6*(3), 205–225.

likely, stems from shortcomings within the national asylum rubric that fails to build upon their human capital.[339]

Emerging science from developing nations reveals that refugee presence has a positive impact on the welfare of local communities of developing nations.[340] The massive refugee surge in Jordan during 1990–1991 and refugees' concomitant ability to exercise their rights to work, live, and invest in the economy upon arrival was the main mechanism underscoring Jordan's economic boom.[341] Research among resettled refugee women in America (between 2002 and 2016) highlights their efforts toward adaptation and integration in the economy: over time, refugee women outpace employment rates even after controlling for education, English proficiency, and home country, of the native-born and other immigrant women.[342,343] Even though newer waves of refugees in Germany arrived with disadvantages in health and education, a longitudinal study finds,[344] they are making strident progress in language, education, training, and employment.[345] Creative models for refugee assistance, such as multiagency collaborations to improve the conditions of refugees and hosts[346] implemented in the Kalobeyei Settlement, Kenya, are showing early signs of refugees' greater social inclusion.[347]

We stand at the crossroads of an astonishing opportunity—an emboldened network of philanthropists, citizens, private donors, and international organizations united for the refugee cause on one hand, and on the other, a sprawling populace displaced in ennui often for generations, with the passage of time atrophying their capacities, dwindling their assets, and debilitating their children's future

[339] Gowayed, H. (2022). *Refuge: How the state shapes human potential*. Princeton University Press.

[340] Maystadt, J., & Duranton, G. (2019). The development push of refugees: Evidence from Tanzania. *Journal of Economic Geography*, *19*(2), 299–334.

[341] Nowrasteh, A., Forrester, A. C., & Blondin, C. (2019). *How mass immigration affects countries with weak economic institutions: A natural experiment in Jordan* (Policy Research Working Paper, 8817). World Bank.https://documents1.worldbank.org/curated/en/944551555006432470/pdf/How-Mass-Immigration-Affects-Countries-with-Weak-Economic-Institutions-A-Natural-Experiment-in-Jordan.pdf

[342] Vijaya, R. (2020). Comparing labor market trajectories of refugee women to other immigrant and native-born women in the United States. *Feminist Economics*, *26*(4), 149–177.

[343] D'Albis, H., Boubtane, E., & Coulibaly, D. (2018). Macroeconomic evidence suggests that asylum seekers are not a "burden" for Western European countries. *Science Advances*, *4*(6). https://doi.org/10.1126/sciadv.aaq0883

[344] The longitudinal study is a collaboration between Germany's Institute for Employment Research (IAB), the Socio-Economic Panel (SOEP) at the German Institute for Economic Research (DIW Berlin), and the Research Centre on Migration, Integration, and Asylum of the Federal Office of Migration and Refugees (BAMF-FZ).

[345] Brücker, H., Croisier, J., Kosyakova, Y., Kröger, H., Pietrantuono, G., Rother, N., & Schupp, J. (2019, March). *Second wave of the IAB-BAMF-SOEP survey: Refugees are making progress in language and employment*. IAB. https://ideas.repec.org/p/iab/iabkbe/201903(en).html

[346] UNHCR. (n.d.). *Kalobeyei settlement*. https://www.unhcr.org/ke/kalobeyei-settlement

[347] Betts, A. (2021). *The wealth of refugees: How displaced people can build economies*. Oxford University Press.

prospects. Only building solidarity with the refugees economically and socially can aid in establishing greater social cohesion, trust, peace,[348,349] and human potential across generations. With timely and strategic investments in their mental health, refugees are likelier to become stronger nation-building partners.

Chapters Outline

The following chapters explore the relationship between refugees' well-being and complex trauma symptoms and whether complex trauma impedes refugees' ability to integrate into their host nations. Addressing refugees' mental health issues with knowledge, flexibility, and empathy can be a crucial part of enabling them to resettle and participate productively in their new society. Understanding the global and local drivers that give rise to and maintain refugee trauma at different stages of displacement and their impact on refugee health disparities is paramount for multicultural societies.

What are the many different manifestations of trauma? Is an understanding of trauma included in integration initiatives? If so, does addressing trauma in integration initiatives of host nations contribute to the positive mental health of refugees? Chapters 2 and 3 of the book focus on how host cultures and expelling States impose an identity (e.g., pariah, victim, supplicant, and patient) on the refugee as the Other.[350] Using Germany as a case study, Chapter 2 locates the nature of trauma in both refugees' premigratory lives and their dangerous journeys out of conflict zones and examines the importance of a society's resettlement climate for the representation of the refugee. Through interviews with State officials, members of relief organizations, and mental health professionals, the chapter illustrates key integration themes in the German national asylum frameworks that may serve as barriers in addressing refugees' complex trauma.

Chapter 3 details the systematic study of newly arrived refugees from the Middle East conducted in 2016–2021 in Germany. It describes the participant population, interview setting, the measures used, and interview themes. Learning from the experiences of refugee respondents, this chapter highlights empathy and cultural knowledge as core competencies in the methodology used

---

[348] D'Albis, H., & Boubtane, E., & Coulibaly, D. (2018). Macroeconomic evidence suggests that asylum seekers are not a "burden" for Western European countries. *Science Advances*, 4(6). https://doi.org/10.1126/sciadv.aaq0883

[349] Fajth, V., Bilgili, Ö., Loschmann, C. & Siegel, M. (2019). How do refugees affect social life in host communities? The case of Congolese refugees in Rwanda. *Comparative Migration Studies 7*, 33.

[350] Given the religion of the research participants, the *Other* may be described as Muslims and "otherness" referred to as white European, although depending on the context, these terms can include other categories of people and can also be interchangeable with each other.

to access refugees' lived experiences and for inviting their collaboration to structure their healing.

Chapters 4 through 8 discuss the structural factors that affect how refugees generate and struggle with obstacles in developing an adaptive identity from within. These chapters will adopt a macro lens, examining the influence of structures such as gender, ethnicity, culture, and family, and focus on them to examine their influence on posttraumatic stress and its sequelae.

"The screams of the torture chambers," goes the saying, "echo in the streets." Chapter 4 urges our attention to any complicity created through the apparatuses of torture in the form of insidious institutional practices and efforts to co-opt the support of physicians, pharmacists, nurses, and psychologists.[351] It draws out its debilitating sequelae for survivors: somatic overload, memory impairment, dissociation, chronic pain, substance abuse, insomnia, social persecution, and feelings of shame. A collaborative understanding of torture among stakeholders in the asylum process may set in motion comprehensive, systemic, and effective rehabilitative efforts for the survivors. Conversely, the failure of accommodating their experiences in national asylum processes impacts their meaningful protection and care and has long-term ramifications for societies.

Chapter 6 explores how culture, or the normative ways of relating, behaving, and believing by a particular group of people, can shape the trauma experience,[352,353,354] expression,[355] and engagement. In this chapter, we identify the five frames of experience affected by culture, as described by Hallowell, that can also undergird the experience of trauma; identify cultural precursors shaping trauma symptoms, meanings, and treatment, using multidisciplinary research; and illustrate the meaning of psychological distress in Middle Eastern refugees by using qualitative and qualitative methods. We will also explore the implications of posttraumatic stress for the typical Arab family, framed along with the psychosocial dynamics of connectivity, patriarchy, and kinship.

Chapter 7 looks at the role of gender in the development or maintenance of complex trauma, which deserves more attention. Exposure to traumatic stress in

[351] Lifton, R. J. (2005, July 29). Doctors and torture. *New England Journal of Medicine, 351*, 415–416.

[352] Obeyesekere, G. (1985). Symbolic foods: Pregnancy cravings and the envious female. *International Journal of Psychology, 20*(4–5), 637–662.

[353] Littlewood, J. (1992). The denial of death and rites of passage in contemporary societies. *Sociological Review, 40*(1, Suppl.), 69–84.

[354] Weiss, M. G., & Kleinman, A. (1988). Depression in cross-cultural perspective: Developing a culturally informed model. In P. R. Dasen, J. W. Berry, & N. Sartorius (Eds.), Health and cross-cultural psychology: Toward applications (pp. 179–206). Sage.

[355] Rasmussen, A., Ventevogel, P., Sancilio, A., Eggerman, M., & Panter-Brick, C. (2014). Comparing the validity of the self-reporting questionnaire and the Afghan symptom checklist: Dysphoria, aggression, and gender in transcultural assessment of mental health. *BMC Psychiatry, 14*, 206.

community samples of women shows that trauma can have an enduring effect on refugee women's lives. This chapter discusses how gender constitutes one of the main dimensions of discrimination and violence[356] for female refugees and the ways in which traumatic events affect women's lives across their lifespans and in different resettlement stages.

In Chapter 8 I discuss the experience of growing up in a family suffering from war trauma and how children's experience of the violence of war may impact their parents. Family functioning is the primary mechanism by which trauma is transmitted across generations, veterans' posttraumatic stress research illustrates, and researchers of postconflict communities urge greater investment in exploring the subtle interactions of trauma transmission within families.

Chapter 9 discusses the role of host countries' integration policies in health, language, employment, education, social life, and provision of treatment for refugees.

Refugees' successful integration boosts their well-being[357,358,359] and benefits their hosts. Conversely, lack of integration among communities in the UK for instance, costs it £6 billion[360] each year, through long-term unemployment, stalling in career progression, and poor health, including suicide, cardiovascular diseases, isolation, and loneliness. Chapter 9 explores the role of receiving nations in designing better opportunities for access and belonging for their refugee communities. Toward this purpose, this chapter proposes a comprehensive definition of integration and one that has the scope to include refugee experiences within multicultural societies. It also explores the role of factors such as refugee's untreated mental illness and their race, religion, and ethnicity, along with host nations' reactions to refugees and resettlement systems. Using different national resettlement frameworks, this chapter also explores how its integration processes or the economic, legal, social, cultural, educational, and political aspects of

[356] Fiddian-Qasmiyeh, E. (2014). Gender and forced migration. In E. Fiddian-Qasmiyeh, G. Loescher, K. Long, & N. Sigona (Eds.), *The Oxford handbook of refugee and forced migration studies* (pp. 395–408). Oxford University Press.

[357] Schick, M., Zumwald, A., Knöpfli, B., Nickerson, A., Bryant, R. A., Schnyder, U., Müller, J., & Morina, N. (2016). Challenging future, challenging past: The relationship of social integration and psychological impairment in traumatized refugees. *European Journal of Psychotraumatology*, 7, 28057.

[358] Bhui, K. S., Lenguerrand, E., Maynard, M. J., Stansfeld, S. A., & Harding, S. (2012). Does cultural integration explain a mental health advantage for adolescents? *International Journal of Epidemiology*, 41(3), 791–802.

[359] De Vroome, T., & van Tubergen, F. (2010). The employment experience of refugees in the Netherlands. *International Migration Review*, 44(2), 376–403.

[360] Casey, D. L. (2016, December 1). *The Casey Review: A review into integration and opportunity* (p. 20). UK Ministry of Housing Department for Communities and Local Government. https://www.gov.uk/government/publications/the-casey-review-a-review-into-opportunity-and-integration

policies[361] affect refugees' participation, self-sufficiency, and empowerment in host societies.

Contexts where refugees find themselves are volatile, under-resourced, overstretched, and imbued with feelings of hopelessness and helplessness, both of the displaced and their health professionals. Chapter 10 begins by discussing two axes, often at a disconnect with each other—culture and evidence-based research—to design clinically relevant, culturally sensitive, and sustainable interventions for refugee intervention science. This chapter draws out the best practices in various intervention domains for refugees' mental health. It focuses on some primary interventions for refugee care, such as psychopharmacological, psychotherapeutic, social-environmental, trauma-informed community, and somatic. Included in this chapter are interviews around the status of mental health in humanitarian settings from government officials, agency directors, and managers of refugee camps.

In concluding, the book reaffirms the need to address posttraumatic stress consciously and proactively in refugee populations to build human capacity, improve outcomes at all levels, maximize the impact of public health resources, and encourage stability and prosperity for all.

Let us revisit the Sabris, whose story we heard at the start of this chapter, after their escape from the Ghouta chemical attack:

> *The Ghouta chemical attack was the tipping point for the Sabris. Overnight, they packed essentials and attempted to leave their hometown, which was strewn with thousands of dead bodies. But it was not to be. Leaving town for any man younger than 50 years old who may have miraculously survived the attacks was a crime punishable by the government's forces.*
>
> *Faisal arranged for his wife and son to stay with distant relatives while he found ways to hide. It was compulsory for Syrian men between the ages of 18 to 42 to serve in the military under Syrian law. Younger men like himself were being rounded up daily, and those who evaded military service faced imprisonment and forcible conscription. To escape being conscripted, Faisal hid himself in one water cistern after another, located in the roofs of different homes. Each day he wondered if it was going to be his last day. Following the attack there was a chronic shortage of food as, "the price of tomatoes had gone up from 7 liras to 3,000 liras, and eight pieces of bread that had previously cost 10 liras were now costing 1,700 liras." In desperation, says Faisal, the besieged and famished people of Ghouta's*

[361] Wamara, C. K., Muchacha, M., Ogwok, B., & Dudzai, C. (2002). Refugee integration and globalization: Ugandan and Zimbabwean perspectives. *Journal of Human Rights and Social Work, 7,* 168–177.

countryside *"were forced to eat whatever was available—even the moss off rocks and even cats, dogs, and donkeys."*[362]

After a year, the Sabris escaped to Lebanon, Turkey, and then to Germany, where they found safe haven. As for the horrific day when they witnessed the Ghouta chemical attack, and anguished, they promised each other, "We will never again talk about that day."

---

[362] Thomas, E. (2013, October 16). Syria: Dead cats, dogs & donkeys to be eaten to avoid starvation. *BBC News.* https://www.bbc.com/news/world-middle-east-24532793

2

Trauma Beyond Borders

At Sea in the World

One of the first refugees I interviewed was Arbaz, a 23-year-old Afghan man from a village in the mountainous valleys of Kapisa. Even before he turned seventeen, all of Arbaz's five siblings had either disappeared or died. One brother Arbaz has never met for he disappeared more than two decades ago, when he was around 2 years old. The second brother was a casualty in a Taliban bombing. A third brother died after excessive blood loss following a bombing. When Arbaz turned sixteen, his fourth sibling was lost to a Taliban attack. His last sibling did not survive after militants sawed off his left arm and right leg. Grief-stricken, shortly afterwards, his parents died of shock. Arbaz decided to flee his country when he saw "people were being flagellated, strung up like chicken with their flesh torn up and little children take pictures of corpses" in his village.

Arbaz walked out of his generational home one evening, never to return. He left its lights still burning in order not to raise the alarm among his neighbors, many of whom were Taliban supporters. He traversed thousands of miles on foot, a treacherous journey through mountains, deserts, forests, and underground tunnels. He was robbed multiple times before he arrived in Germany.

Fatal Journeys: Refugees in Host Nations

The year was 2015 when Arbaz arrived in Germany, and there were many other refugees like him. Historic, but not without precedent,[1] the year witnessed 1.3 million people seeking asylum in Europe.[2] Many others had survived dangerous

[1] In Yugoslavia 3.3 million were displaced: Wren, C. S. (1995). Resettling refugees: U.N. facing new burden. *The New York Times.* https://www.nytimes.com/1995/11/24/world/resettling-refugees-un-facing-new-burden.html Mass migrations to Europe have been ongoing since the 1800s: Hatton, T. J., & Williamson, J. G. (1994). What drove the mass migrations from Europe in the late nineteenth century? *Population and Development Review, 20*(3), 533–559.

[2] Pew Research Center. (2016, August 2). *Number of refugees to Europe surges to record 1.3 million in 2015.* https://www.pewresearch.org/global/2016/08/02/number-of-refugees-to-europe-surges-to-record-1-3-million-in-2015/

Displaced. Shaifali Sandhya, Oxford University Press. © Shaifali Sandhya 2024.
DOI: 10.1093/oso/9780197579886.003.0002

passages on the seas, walking through Balkan states and showing up at the bus and train stations of Bavaria and Munich, in Germany, to Molnal in Sweden, and Riace in Italy. The same year, compared to 2014, the number of Syrians (362,800) seeking international protection doubled; the number of Afghans (178,200) quadrupled; and the number of fleeing Iraqis (121,500) soared sevenfold.[3]

Many refugees lose their lives on hazardous journeys out of conflict zones, attempting to make their way into safe-haven countries. Those who survive report being packed into unseaworthy vessels, taped to the bottom of lorries, stuffed in fuel tanks,[4] and confined to small spaces in overland exchanges in trucks or wheel-wells, and the cargo bins of planes. Like Arbaz, they struggle to sustain themselves in mountains and forests riddled with predators, landmines, wild animals, and other hazards. They report plodding through landmines and barren no man's lands, contending with terror and panic as they traverse deadly seas in small crafts that range from small wooden boats to converted fishing boats to inflatable rubber dinghies.

The absence of safe and legal routes pushes asylum seekers into hostile territories, increases their need to rely on human smugglers and traffickers to take more dangerous routes to avoid detection, increasing human and financial costs. Women and children in particular, face heightened risks for abductions, sex work, being trafficked into begging, sexual slavery, forced marriage, and other sexual abuse[5,6,7] although displacement in general, increases the risk of involuntary servitude and slavery.[8] Undaunted by brutal seas, restrictive immigration policies, or surges in border militarization, illegal border crossings rose exponentially in Europe, [9,10]

[3] Ibid.

[4] 24 hours in a fuel tank. (2015, April 2). *BBC News.* https://www.bbc.com/news/magazine-32152670

[5] Office to Monitor and Combat Trafficking in Persons. (2020). *2020 Trafficking in persons report: Syria.* U.S. Department of State. https://www.state.gov/reports/2020-trafficking-in-persons-report/syria/

[6] UN Office on Drugs and Crime. (2017). *Trafficking of women and girls within Central America* https://www.unodc.org/documents/toc/Reports/TOCTASouthAmerica/English/TOCTA_CACaribb_trafficking_womengirls_within_CAmerica.pdf

[7] Giammarinaro, M. G. (2016, June 14). *Statement by the Special Rapporteur on Trafficking in persons, especially women and children, Maria Grazia Giammarinaro at the Human Rights Council—32nd session.* OHCHR. https://www.ohchr.org/en/statements/2016/07/statement-special-rapporteur-trafficking-persons-especially-women-and-children

[8] Bharadwaj, B., Bishop, D., Hazra, S., Pufaa, E., & Annan, J.K. (2021). *Climate-induced migration and modern slavery.* International Institute for Environment and Development. https://www.iied.org/sites/default/files/pdfs/2021-09/20441G.pdf

[9] There were about 978,300 detections of illegal border-crossings between border crossing points (BCPs) in the fourth quarter of 2015: Frontex. (2016, October 3). *FRAN Quarterly—number of illegal border-crossings at record high in Q4.* https://frontex.europa.eu/media-centre/news/news-release/fran-quarterly-number-of-illegal-border-crossings-at-record-high-in-q4-tRfbnB#:~:text=The%20number%20of%20illegal%20border-crossings%20in%20the%20area,in%20any%20other%20fourth%20quarter%20in%20the%20past

[10] In 2015, there was a 6-fold increase in illegal border crossings and a 17-fold increase when compared to 2013: European Parliament Research Service. (n.d.). *Migration and asylum.* Retrieved

US,[11] and Australia,[12] and other nations. Indeed, the number of missing migrants between 2014 and 2021 was 55,716[13] and upwards,[14] most likely an underestimate. Despite high risks and low survival rates what sustains such desperate journeys is that they are a prolonged hustle to reach or get their children to safety.

What reception greets the refugees when they arrive in safe-haven countries? In this chapter, we discuss the reception of refugees worldwide by taking a deep dive into the climate around refugees in Europe and how it shapes refugee representation, particularly Muslim refugees. Second, we explore tenets of integration at the grassroots level in Germany, through the frameworks of *Aufgeschlossenheit* or a sense of mutuality to integration, "*Selbsthilfe*" or "self-help," and "*Sittenverständnis*," "the need to bridge differences in understanding morals and values." We use the case of Germany to then probe how a nation's past traumas may affect integration efforts and the way it deals with contemporary refugee trauma. A host nation's recognition of refugees' complex trauma is of the utmost significance, as it aids professionals in assisting them better, prevents the development of later chronicity, aids in their access to collective experiences,[15] and consequently, whether refugees will integrate.

Reception by Host Countries: Framing the Refugee as a Pariah, Parasite or Patient

On the night of April 3, 2017, in Paris, a 65-year-old mother of three children, retired Jewish physician Sarah Halimi climbed into bed in a white nightgown with a floral pattern. Little did she realize that her life would soon end violently. Her neighbor, 27-year-old Kobili Troare, climbed up to her apartment using the fire escape, and upon entering her bedroom battered her and then threw her blood-soaked body into the street. Troare was from Mali, a migrant in France and a

June 24, 2023, https://www.europarl.europa.eu/thinktank/infographics/migration/public/index.html?page=intro

[11] Massey, D. S., Durand, J., & Pren, K. A. (2016). Why border enforcement backfired. *American Journal of Sociology*, *121*(5), 1557–1600.
[12] Philips, J. (2015, March 2). *Asylum seekers and refugees: what are the facts?* Parliament of Australia. https://www.aph.gov.au/about_parliament/parliamentary_departments/parliamentary_library/pubs/rp/rp1415/asylumfacts
[13] Missing Migrants Project. 55,716 missing migrants since 2014. (n.d.). International Organization for Migration. Retrieved on May 7, 2023, https://missingmigrants.iom.int/
[14] Volunteers and staff at United for Intercultural Action update the data annually, spending 6 months at a time verifying reports, categorizing deaths, and entering them into the database. They began collecting data in 1992, and the entries stretch back to 1989, but the first year with a significant number of records and when the published list begins is 1993.
[15] Barash, J. A. (2016). *Collective memory and the historical past*. University of Chicago Press.

drug dealer and user. "I killed the shaitan!" he yelled from the balcony. Shaitan is an Arabic word for "devil." Neighbors heard him repeatedly chant "Allahu Akbar" or God is Great. Four years after Halimi's death, France's highest court ruled that Traore was in the throes of an acute mental delirium brought on by his consumption of cannabis. Unable to understand what he was doing, he was deemed "criminally irresponsible." The verdict was met by incomprehension and outrage.[16]

In a world that views the refugee as a parasitic and a subversive Other, it may be more expedient to pin Troare's crime on his migrant status rather than his substance-induced mental status. The verdict fueled fears of how undeserving migrants might take advantage of the French judicial system in the future and abuse drugs before committing a crime.

The fear of the Other, people different from us, undergirds movements such as Brexit in the UK, the yellow jacket in France, the rise of the Hindu nationalist party in India, concerns of the sprawl of "ghettos" and "ghetto children"[17] in Denmark, Italy's turning away of all migrant boats, and the increasing polarization of politics in the United States. The dispossessed seeking refuge tend to be heterogeneous in ethnicity, religion, and culture from previous immigrant waves and from the dominant populations. Their different cultural behaviors, such as the wearing of the Islamic veil or the burqa, have amplified concerns of a waning of "European identity," of "hungry mouths," "foreign squatters" who are taking advantage of the Western welfare state, and "creeping Islamization of our land." This has galvanized a worldwide antirefugee sentiment and a backlash against the foreigner in general.

Interestingly, when it comes to refugees, the absence of religious differences does not deter the creation of an Other. Consider the case of approximately 1.3 Palestinian refugees, mostly Sunni Muslims, similar to most Jordanians, who despite being provided citizenship in 1948, were as refugees still subjected to an assimilation process referred to as "Jordanization." The word *Palestine* was prohibited in any government documents of Jordan and in "the names of the youth or community groups."[18] They faced restrictions on where they could live and work, whether they could participate in unions or have equal access to

---

[16] Cohen, R. (April 17, 2021). Highest French court rules killer of Jewish woman cannot stand trial. *The New York Times.* https://www.nytimes.com/2021/04/17/world/europe/sarah-halimi-murder-trial.html

[17] Barry, E., & Sorensen, M. S. (2018, July 1). In Denmark, harsh new laws for immigrant "ghettos." *The New York Times.* https://www.nytimes.com/2018/07/01/world/europe/denmark-immigrant-ghettos.html

[18] Brand, L. A. (1988). Palestinians in Syria: The politics of integration. *Middle East Journal, 42*(4), 621–637

government and educational service (although there are exceptions, as in the case of Syria's embrace of Palestinian refugees in 1948).[19]

Economic giants like India and China[20] with substantial refugee populations, in the absence of uniform refugee laws and being non-signatories to the Refugee Convention[21,22] treat refugees on an ad-hoc and arbitrary basis perpetuating their social exclusion and poor mental health.[23]

The High Social Cost of Stereotyping Refugees

There are at least four wide-ranging consequences of this pervasive negative social construction of the refugee:

1. It obscures their rights to humanitarian and legal categories[24] and thus their "refugeeness (is) discredited before (it is) even articulated."[25] Constructing the refugee in a "depoliticized space (as) an ahistorical universal humanitarian subject," Malkki argues, is also to depoliticize the refugee category.

2. Fear of foreign others can snowball to produce adverse labor market outcomes and also undermine the public's support of the welfare state and of the sustainability of public welfare. When this might occur, economists Algan et al., caution that reduced support for welfare policies could end up altering the design and political economy of public policies[26] through redistributing wealth vertically across social classes rather than correcting for horizontal inequities. In turn, it can heighten the existing economic marginalization of groups like immigrant and refugee minorities and a further failure of their effective engagement and integration.

[19] Ibid.

[20] Austin, K. (2014). *Human rights in China: Selected examinations.* Nova Publishers.

[21] UNHCR. (2020, January 31). *Fact sheet: India.* https://reporting.unhcr.org/sites/default/files/UNHCR%20India%20factsheet%20-%20January%202020.pdf

[22] Hussain, Z. (2019, January 3). India deports second Rohingya group to Myanmar, more expulsions likely. *Reuters.* https://www.reuters.com/article/us-%20myanmar-rohingya-india/india-deports-%20second-rohingya-group-to-myanmar-%20more-expulsions-likely-idUSKCN1OX0FE

[23] Albert, L. (2020). Refugee perspectives on living in India and the Global Compact on Refugees. In J. Field & S. Burra (Eds.), *The Global Compact on Refugees: Indian perspectives and experiences* (pp. 209–221). Academicians Working Group & UNHCR India

[24] Story, B. (2005). *Politics as usual: The criminalization of asylum seekers in the United States* (Refugee Studies Center Working Paper No. 26, p. 20). University of Oxford.

[25] Ibid.

[26] Algan, Y., Bisin, A., & Verdier, T. (2012). Integration of immigrants. In Y. Algan, A. Bisin, A. Manning, & T. Verdier (Eds.), *Cultural integration of immigrants in Europe* (pp. 1–48). Oxford University Press.

3. The (mis) interpretation of the refugee can also make it hard to access their lived experiences.[27] The complaints of the traumatized refugee are not well understood, says Herman,[28] and as a result, "chronically traumatized people suffer in silence." Violence impacts the extent to which refugees will remember or fail to recall. Only 3% of those exposed to political violence had reported their experiences to a clinician after moving to the United States.[29] Silence in the face of armed conflict is common, say Espinosa and colleagues citing the example of Peruvians following 20 years of armed conflicts and is rooted in the desire to forget painful memories and cultural attitudes.[30] In areas heavily affected by internal armed conflict in Peru, for instance, 64% of respondents were in favor of forgetting their trauma[31] versus in areas that were less affected (46.2%).

4. For desperate and displaced families, as the distinction between being refugees or illegal migrants crumbles in practice, and their right to refuge becomes increasingly interlinked with criminality, the smugglers' promise—to deliver their loved ones to safety—becomes the most hopeful one. Thus, more families will continue to entrust their children's safety to smugglers, thereby risking their lives. For younger asylum-seekers, this means that when they make it to safe havens, they may be living with complex trauma symptoms for more extended periods, often without the support systems of their families.

Linking asylum policies with securitization can frame refugees as the morally suspect other, often without substance.[32] In contrast to the perception that refugees are largely criminals, crimes *against* refugees have increased.[33,34] Germany has

[27] Rajaram, P. (2002). Humanitarianism and representations of the refugee. *Journal of Refugee Studies, 15*(3), 247–264.

[28] Ibid, p. 118.

[29] Eisenman, D. P., Gelberg, L., Liu, H., & Shapiro, M. F. (2003). Mental health and health-related quality of life among adult Latino primary care patients living in the United States with previous exposure to political violence. *JAMA, 290*(5), 627–634.

[30] Espinosa, A., Páez, D., Velázquez, T., Cueto, R. M., Seminario, E., Sandoval, S., Reátegui, F., & Jave, I. (2017). Between remembering and forgetting the years of political violence: Psychosocial impact of the Truth and Reconciliation Commission in Peru. *Political Psychology, 38*(5), 701–904.

[31] Sulmont, D. (2007). Las distancias del recuerdo. *Memoria: Revista Sobre Cultura, Democracia y Derechos Humanos, 2*, 9–28. http://idehpucp.pucp.edu.pe/images/publicaciones/revista_memoria_2.pdf.

[32] German refugees, relative to the population increase, have had a low impact on crime. Although the refugee numbers soared by 440% between 2014 and 2015, crimes committed by them increased by 79%. Studies by Germany's Federal Criminal Police have found no substantive connections between refugee-inflows and refugee-related crimes: Brady, K. (2016, February 17). Rise in refugee related crimes in Germany less than influx. *DW News*. http://www.dw.com/en/report-refugee-related-crimes-in-germany-increase-less-than-influx-of-asylum-seekers/a-19053227

[33] Hock, A. (2016, March 30). 199 attacks, hardly any convictions. *Correctiv*. https://correctiv.org/aktuelles/neue-rechte/2016/03/30/199-uebergriffe-kaum-verurteilungen/

[34] Some German studies have shown a slight increase in crimes by refugees, but their evidence is either too limited or provisional to form firm conclusions: Dehos, F. T. (2017). The refugee wave

seen a rise in violence against refugees:[35] In 2019, there were 1,200 such attacks, an 8% increase in eastern Germany.[36] This has led some researchers to hypothesize on the link between exposure to migrants and stronger nationalist identity[37,38] underscoring antirefugee sentiments. With the pandemic, racist and xenophobic incidents against national or ethnic minorities have escalated. They are spreading, according to the European Union Agency for Fundament Rights (in 2020) to include people perceived to be Others, such as those of Asian, Roma, Muslim, and Jewish origins, through online hate speech, physical attacks, and hate crimes on social media.[39] Linking refugee resettlement to increased crime rates in the United States, according to Masterson and Yasenov, is also without merit.[40]

The Refugee Population in Germany

Compared to native Germans, psychological well-being is considerably lower in the newly arrived asylum-seeker population in Germany.[41,42] Half of the refugees

to Germany and its impact on crime [Technical Report]. *Ruhr Economic Papers*. https://www.rwi-essen.de/media/content/pages/publikationen/ruhr-economic-papers/rep_17_737.pdf; Lange, M., & Katrin, S. (2018). *Causal effects of immigration on crime: Quasi-experimental evidence from a large inflow of asylum seekers* (Working Paper). https://conference.iza.org/conference_files/transatlantic_2018/sommerfeld_k6116.pdf

[35] Pensioner rearrested after stabbing three refugees in "politically motivated" attack. (2018, February 22). *The Local*. https://www.thelocal.de/20180222/pensioner-rearrested-after-stabbing-three-refugees-in-politically-motivated-attack

[36] Over 1,200 violent far-right attacks reported in eastern Germany. (2019, April 4). *Daily Sabah News*. https://www.dailysabah.com/europe/2019/04/04/over-1200-violent-far-right-attacks-reported-in-eastern-germany

[37] Coenders, M. T. L., & Scheepers, P. L. H. (2004). Associations between nationalist attitudes and exclusionist reactions in 22 countries. In M. I. L. Gijsberts, A. J. M. W. Hagendoorn, & P. L. H. Scheepers (Eds.), *Nationalism and exclusion of migrants: Cross-national comparisons* (pp. 187–208). Ashgate.

[38] Davidov, E., & Semyonov, M. (2017). Attitudes towards immigrants in European societies. *International Journal of Comparative Sociology, 58*(5), 359–366.

[39] European Union Agency for Fundamental Rights. *Coronavirus pandemic in the EU—fundamental rights implications* (p. 11). (2020, June 30). https://fra.europa.eu/sites/default/files/fra_uploads/fra-2020-coronavirus-pandemic-eu-bulletin-july_en.pdf

[40] Masterson and Yasenov's 2021 study focused on a sample of 18,172 local law enforcement agencies in the United States that reported violent crime and property crime in the period 2010–2018 and found no difference between the reduction in refugee arrival and changes in crime rate. Masterson, D., & Yasenov, V. (2021). Does halting refugee resettlement reduce crime? Evidence from the US refugee ban. *American Political Science Review, 115*(3), 1066–1073.

[41] Brücker, H., Rother, N., Schupp, J., Gostomski, C., Böhm, A., Fendel, T., Friedrich, M., Giesselmann, M., Holst, E., Kosyakova, Y., Kroh, M., Liebau, E., Richter, D., Romiti, A., Schacht, D., Scheible, J. A., Schmelzer, P., Siegert, M., Sirries, S., Trübswetter, P., & Vallizadeh, E. (2016). *IAB-BAMF–SOEP Befragung von Geflüchteten: Flucht, ankunft in Deutschland und erste schritte der integration* [IAB–BAMF–SOEP survey of refugees: Flight, arrival in Germany and first steps towards integration]. Institut für Arbeitsmarkt- und Berufsforschung der Bundesagentur für Arbeit. http://doku.iab.de/kurzber/2016/kb2416.pdf

[42] Bohm, A., Brenzel, H., Brücker, H., Jacobsen, J., Jaworski, J., Kosyakova, Y., Kroh, M., Kühne, S., Liebau, E., Pagel, L., Richter, D., Rother, N., Schacht, D., Scheible, J. A., Schupp, J., Siegert, M., &

who entered Germany report psychological problems such as posttraumatic stress disorder (PTSD) or depression, according to the Federal Chamber of Psychotherapists in Germany (BPtK).[43] One in five refugee children suffer from PTSD.[44] Recent arrivals report higher levels of depression and PTSD,[45] both of which are disproportionately higher among females and individuals aged older than 40 years.[46]

Between 2013 and 2016, 87% of Germany's forcibly displaced refugees[47] came from Syria, Afghanistan, Iraq, Eritrea, and Iran; they had fled war, persecution, or forced labor.[48] The refugee population was disproportionately young and male, with 75% of adult males[49] and 65% of adult females being aged 35 years or younger in 2017, compared to 25%–28% of the adult population in Germany, respectively.[50] About 51% of men were single, while 61% of female refugees lived with a spouse, and more than two-thirds of the women had children.

Drawing on my interviews with German mental health workers and integration officials, in the following sections of this chapter, I explore whether refugee

Trübswetter, P. (2017). In H. Brücker, N., Rother, & J. Schupp (Eds.), *IAB–BAMF–SOEP Befragung von Geflüchteten 2016: Studiendesign, Feldergebnisse sowie Analysen zu Schulischer wie beruflicher Qualifikation, Sprachkenntnissen sowie kognitiven Potenzialen* [IAB–BAMF–SOEP survey of refugees 2016: Study design, field results and analyzes of school and professional qualifications, language skills and cognitive potential]. BAMF. https://www.bamf.de/SharedDocs/Anlagen/DE/Forsch ung/Forschungsberichte/fb30-iab-bamf-soep-befragung-gefluechtete-2016.pdf?__blob=publicat ionFile&v=14

[43] BPtK is a professional organization of approximately 34,500 psychologists and child and youth psychotherapists.
[44] Bundespsychotherapeutenkammer. (2015). *BPtK-Standpunkt: "Psychische Erkrankungen bei Flüchtlingen"* [BPtK position: "Mental ilnesses in refugees"]. http://www.bptk.de/aktuell/einzelseite/
[45] Brücker, H., Jaschke, P., & Kosyakova, Y. (2019, December). *Integrating refugees and asylum seekers into the German economy and society: Empirical evidence and policy objectives.* Migration Policy Institute. https://www.migrationpolicy.org/research/integrating-refugees-asylum-seekers-germany
[46] Ibid, p. 8.
[47] This piece details the integration of refugees that arrived from 2013 to 2016.
[48] Brücker, H., Jaschke, P., & Kosyakova, Y. (2019, December). *Integrating refugees and asylum seekers into the German economy and society: Empirical evidence and policy objectives.* Migration Policy Institute. https://www.migrationpolicy.org/research/integrating-refugees-asylum-seekers-germany
[49] Brücker, H., Croisier, J., Kosyakova, Y., Hannes. K., Pietrantuono, G., Rother, N., & Schupp, J. (2019). *Second wave of the IAB–BAMF–SOEP Survey: Language skills and employment rate of refugees improving with time.* SSOAR: Social Science Open Access Repository. https://www.ssoar.info/ssoar/handle/document/77905
[50] The figures for the refugee population have been taken from the IAB–BAMF–SOEP Refugee Survey (weighted values); the figures for the German population are averaged from microcensus data and consider those aged 15 to 34 years as a share of those aged 15 years and older: Destatis Statistisches Bundesamt. (n.d.). *Bevölkerung, Erwerbstätige, Erwerbslose, Erwerbspersonen, Nichterwerbspersonen aus Hauptwohnsitzhaush.: Deutschland, Jahre, Geschlecht, Größenkl. persönl. monatl. Nettoeinkommen* [Population, employed, unemployed, economically inactive, inactive persons from primary residence: Germany, age, sex, size category of personal monthly net income] (Table 12211-0003). https://www-genesis.destatis.de/genesis//online?operation=table&code=12211-0003&byp ass=true&levelindex=0&levelid=1686510162758#abreadcrumb

trauma is taken into account in German integration practices. I also explore trauma-informed services within mental health available to refugees and their families.

A Sense of *Aufgeschlossenheit*

In Germany, I gained an understanding of integration as a relationship of mutuality between the refugee and host society. I met Christoph Blessin, the Managing Director of the German Red Cross in the city of Bonn, who had assisted in setting up accommodations for refugees during the first massive wave of emigrations to the border towns of Alfter and Bonn in 2015. Said Blessin:

People arrived from the border by bus. They were from Afghanistan, Iraq, and Syria. In Alfter, Germany (a western border town of North-Rhine Westphalia), we saw some families, but the most typical refugee was the lone man between 18 and 26 years of age. In Alfter, doctors checked them to see any obvious health issues and then we had vaccinations for polio, measles, tetanus. They got the X-rays for tuberculosis and then they just waited.

Blessin was born and raised in a quiet village of 1,400 people of North-Rhine Westphalia. He described the German stance and philosophy toward refugees he was witnessing:

For me, the Red Cross and for the most people of Germany, it is the sense of Aufgeschlossenheit—being open-minded and respectful of each other that pervades our interaction with refugees. In this region around the Rhine, there is a saying, "We are the most easygoing people in Germany. We are famous for laughing, and good humor. Our kind of Cologne Constitution, is to love and let live."

Today, we have both professionals and nonprofessional social workers who show the refugees how to live—Begleiten—take their hand and show them how to live together under a roof where 6–7 nations co-exist. It is not easy for the people. Sometimes you have someone in the room you don't know. Sometimes you have someone in your room you don't understand.

We learn from the people who come to Germany, and they learn how to live here. We have to learn from each other. I don't think only one side will share their whole life. That could not work. We have to learn from these people, and they have to learn from us.

The German focus is also on *Selbsthilfe* ("self-help"), as I learned from Blessin. "In Germany we call it *hilf uns dir zu helfen*. We help the refugees help themselves." Social workers in Germany in 2016 were both paid professionals and nonprofessionals, and from many different countries.

Blessin's favorable sentiments of egalitarian sharing of knowledge or practices were echoed by others I interviewed. Well-intentioned integration systems may wish to take into account refugees' mental health but fail to grasp how their emphasis on mutuality may not factor in how exposure to trauma can affect reciprocity, collaboration, and cooperation. Or how self-help, a person's ability to maintain an inner sense of well-being, can be distorted by stressful events. By emphasizing the significant need for mutuality[51,52] and equality in refugees' participation with the native population,[53,54,55] integration strategies presume normal functionality and self-sufficiency of refugees, neglect the importance of facilitative social connections and capital[56] or the power disadvantage faced by foreign-born newcomers to societies, and the specialized mental health needs of the refugee population.

Emerging Issues: Substance Abuse

With the arrival of refugees, Blessin describes the emerging issue of substance abuse for German society and resettlement workers:

> *The biggest problem for many is alcoholism. Most of them are Muslims who have not had any alcohol in their life. They come to Germany and Europe, and you get alcohol everywhere and it is normal to drink. And that's a very, very big problem.*
>
> *In Alfter there was a father with three children. They came from Syria. One of their children was a three-day-old baby. Mom had to go to the hospital, so she took*

[51] Castles, S., Korac, M., Vasta, E., & Vertovec, S. (2002). *Integration: Mapping the field* (Home Office Online Report 29/03).

[52] IOM. (2018, July 13). *The responsibilities and obligations of migrants towards host nations: Global compact thematic paper*. Retrieved on May 7, 2023, https://www.iom.int/sites/g/files/tmzbdl486/files/our_work/ODG/GCM/IOM-Thematic-Paper-Responsibilities-and-obligations-of-migrants.pdf

[53] Ager, A., & Strang, A. (2008). Understanding integration: A conceptual framework. *Journal of Refugee Studies, 21*(2), 166–191.

[54] Hynie, M., Korn, A., & Tao, D. (2016). Social context and social integration for Government Assisted Refugees in Ontario, Canada. In M. Poteet & S. Nourpanah (Eds.), *After the flight: The dynamics of refugee settlement and integration* (pp. 183–227). Cambridge Scholars.

[55] Phillimore, J., & Goodson, L. (2008). Making a place in the global city: The relevance of indicators of integration. *Journal of Refugee Studies, 21*(3), 305–325.

[56] Ager, A., & Strang, A. (2008). Understanding integration: A conceptual framework. *Journal of Refugee Studies, 21*(2), 166–191. https://doi.org/10.1093/jrs/fen016

the baby with her. And the father, who had never before been alone with his other children, had a great problem with alcohol. Now he was alone with his other children. He started to drink. He was very fortunate to be in Alfter where we were to support and help him.

Alcohol can become a big problem for these young men as they are waiting and waiting. They start to drink because they are bored. I think alcohol is one factor, but it is complex. We have a Sittenverständnis, a different understanding of norms and values and a different understanding of being together of having a party and celebrating in a group.

For the most part, the German health system is primarily invested in refugees' urgent and preventive health care needs like vaccinations, inpatient hospitalizations, alcohol detoxification, and interfacing with the police when issues of addiction or mental health spilled over. The framework of *Sittenverständnis*, or "the need to bridge differences in understanding morals and values" is broadly utilized. "We explain the rules in Germany," said Blessin, "But we also think people are grown up." It is similar to the adage, *Don't give them the fish. Teach them how to fish.* In its underscoring of self-sufficiency, the integration system may not invest requisite resources in understanding how exposure to trauma can deleteriously impact motivation, mutuality, and self-sufficiency, or how PTSD may manifest itself as substance abuse. Recognizing PTSD does not mean that it may be addressed and treated in its various manifestations in the labyrinthian German bureaucratic machinery. The section below elaborates on this.

"Everyone Says He Is Traumatized"

Does the complex trauma of refugees play a role in their integration? I asked Annette Windgasse, Director of the Psychosocial Center for Refugees in Düsseldorf (PSZ). The 30-year-old PSZ is Windgasse's brainchild. Windgasse did not have to think too hard about this, and she replied instantly: "Past traumatic experiences underscore *everything* in daily life, in refugees' perspectives to stay in Germany, and in their capacity to give proper asylum interviews."

"Positive mental health is the basis of every other step. If somebody is very depressed or dissociative then he cannot concentrate on learning the language," said Windgasse. Support for trauma-related disorders is a priority for refugees. Psychosocial centers have successfully established trauma as the basis for protection, "but it is a bit of a boomerang," says Windgasse. "Because the reason to be politically persecuted is not taken seriously anymore. The authorities now say, 'Everyone says he is traumatized.'" As a result, it is more and more difficult to persuade authorities that this person needs protection because of his trauma. Under new laws, only medical doctors in many cases write an expert opinion. The German asylum authorities do not want to accept psychological expert opinions anymore. Moreover, in practice, refugees' traumatic encounters are underplayed for as Windgasse says, "is traumatized," and "*Everything* is going to this trauma level." As deportations of asylum-seekers to their violent home-nations increase, over and beyond deportation's psychosocial impact on families left behind are two rarely studied areas are its effects on communities and on the deported individuals.[57] Ironically, as complex trauma becomes commonplace, its presence within life histories, which is meant to indicate persecution, vulnerability, and high risk for the asylum-seeker, is instead associated with the decision-makers fatigue and their skepticism of and indifference to it. Applications that require a consideration of an asylum-seeker's trauma face a greater likelihood of being tossed out of the window.

However, the underlying reason for not according trauma its due stridency and voice may have to do with the German nation's reckoning with the Holocaust, according to political theorists like Arendt,[58] and others.[59] The end of WW II in Germany was a period of immense trauma for the German nation, a low point often referred to as their zero hour.[60,61] In addition to the estimated six million murdered Jews, between 1944 and 1949,[62] an estimated 860,000[63] to two million females[64] displaced by war were mass raped by the Western Allied and Red Army soldiers, respectively. It is estimated that some women were raped as many as 60 to 70 times.[65] The barbaric violence of the Holocaust was responsible

---

[57] Ojeda, V. D., Magana, C., Burgos, J. L., & Vargas-Ojeda, A. C. (2020). Deported men's and father's perspective: The impacts of family separation on children and families in the U.S. *Frontiers in Psychiatry, 11,* 148.

[58] "But nowhere is this nightmare of destruction and horror less felt and less talked about than in Germany itself." Arendt, H. (1950). The aftermath of Nazi rule: Report from Germany. *Commentary, 10,* 342–353. https://www.commentary.org/articles/hannah-arendt/the-aftermath-of-nazi-rulerep ort-from-germany/

[59] Giesen, B. (2004). The trauma of perpetrators: The Holocaust as the traumatic reference of German national identity. In J. C. Alexander, R. Eyerman, B. Giesen, N. J. Smelser, & P. Sztompska (Eds.), *Cultural trauma and collective identity* (pp. 112–154). University of California Press.

[60] Brockmann, S. (1996). *German culture at "zero hour"* [Paper presentation] (pp. 8–36). Carnegie Mellon University Research Showcase @ CMU.

[61] Miriam Gebhardt, a German historian, German cities lay in shambles: devastated by bombing with rampant inflation, food shortage, damaged housing and electricity, gas and water supplies, brimming with large numbers of the displaced who faced chronic malnutrition, disease, and illness. The Holocaust cast a dark shadow over Germany, heralding its plunge from respect as a *Kulturnation,* a civilized nation-state of high culture and thought into a dark abyss.

[62] Teo, H.-M. (1996). The continuum of sexual violence in occupied Germany, 1945–49. *Women's History Review, 5*(2), 191–218.

[63] Gebhardt, M. (2016). *Crimes unspoken: The rape of German women at the end of Second World War* (N. Somers, Trans.). Polity Press.

[64] Naimark, N. M. (1995). *The Russians in Germany: A history of the Soviet zone of occupation, 1945–1949* (pp. 132–133). Belknap Press.

[65] Hitchcock, W. (2004). *The struggle for Europe: The turbulent history of a divided continent, 1945 to the present.* Anchor Books.

for the mass extermination of the Jewish people and others such as the Slavs, the Roma, the disabled, and homosexuals. This period can overshadow the suffering endured by ethnic Germans.[66,67,68] There are still men and women today, says Miriam Gebhardt, a German historian, "living in old people's homes who remain haunted by their painful memories."

Despite the German nation's great sufferings, researchers such as the German sociologist Bernhard Giesen[69] have spoken to the many reasons underlying its long "postwar coalition of silence" surrounding Judeocide and sexual violence extending two generations. German grandmothers and mothers were expected to hide their stories of the sexual violence inflicted against them from future generations.[70] Depending on the atrocity, their reasons for their silence could range from moral numbness, sexual prejudices that would be directed against them, and suspicion of female sexuality. The "*Trümmerfrau*," "Germany's 'rubble woman,' 'was expected to put aside their trauma' to prioritize reconstructing Germany," in turn affecting the cultural prototype of how trauma, in general, is treated. The silence of dealing with their own past trauma may be reflected in the reticence of delving into refugees' trauma. In being susceptible to national narratives that deny refugee trauma for various reasons, we fortify the silence in their lives and stand to lose the opportunity of repairing their mental health.

However, generational conflicts of young Germans, historic movements, and events,[71] have affected their desire to penetrate the wall of silence around the trauma of the Holocaust. Young Germans, not wishing to be treated as typical Germans or to carry the shame of perpetrators, according to Giesen, are

[66] Millions of ethnic Germans had been purged from their homes in Czechoslovakia, Poland, and other Eastern European countries: McDougall, A. (2004). *Youth politics in East Germany: The free German youth movement 1946–1968* (p. 40). Clarendon Press.

[67] Further, between 1949 and 1990, as the Soviets annexed Germany's eastern territory, the German Democratic Republic (GDR or East Germany), the heavily fortified Inner German Border made it impossible for East Germans to cross into West Germany. While GDR was a member of the Warsaw Pact, the Federal Republic of Germany was a member of NATO or the western military. Over a 100,000 citizens of the GDR attempted escape across the inner-German border or the Berlin Wall between 1961 and 1988, and over a 1,000 died during their escape: Ibid.

[68] In its vortex of trauma when millions lost their lives on battlefields, families were separated for decades, and many were subjected to mass rapes or had to endure living in a Stasi state of surveillance: Bailey, C. (2019, November 9). The lingering trauma of Stasi surveillance. *The Atlantic.* https://www.theatlantic.com/international/archive/2019/11/lingering-trauma-east-german-police-state/601669/

[69] Giesen, B. (2004). The trauma of perpetrators: The Holocaust as the traumatic reference of German national identity. In J. C. Alexander, R. Eyerman, B. Giesen, N. J. Smelser, & P. Sztompska (Eds.), *Cultural trauma and collective identity* (pp. 112–154). University of California Press.

[70] Sander, H. (1995). Remembering/forgetting (S. Liebman, Trans.). *October, 72,* 15–26. https://doi.org/10.2307/778924

[71] An iconic image of Willy Brandt, German Chancellor, kneeling in silence as he visited a memorial for survivors of the Holocaust resonated with Germans and globally: Hille, P., Romaniec, R., & Bosen, R. (2020, December 6). 50 years since Willy Brandt's historic gesture in Poland. *DW News.* https://www.dw.com/en/germany-poland-reconciliation-willy-brandt/a-55828523

questioning their parents.[72] Such events have contributed to a rewriting of trauma, and the circle of perpetrators has increased to include an entire nation bearing the stigma of shame, necessitating ritual admission and collective responsibility, and this has played a role in the identity of modern Germany: that innocent individuals can bear the burden of collective guilt.

At the same time, in many parts of Germany, an overwhelming number of ordinary German citizens rose to welcome refugee strangers with a steely determination, perhaps as an opportunity for redemption of their collective guilt and as a mirror for their combined unspoken historical trauma.

I Need the "Paper"

Beyond the German philosophy of help conceptualized as *self-help or mutuality* are other bureaucratic hurdles. Health professionals can provide asylum-seekers with a form for their physicians to fill out in support of their asylum applications; the expert's examination and the statement would serve to substantiate asylum-seekers' traumas. Says Windgasse:

> . . . But the problem is, it is challenging to find doctors to do this, and health
> professionals often feel instrumentalized when people come and say, "I need
> a paper." They tend to think, "He is just here because he just needs this paper."
> Another difficulty is that asylum authorities have started to imitate this. So if
> someone comes from an asylum interview and says, "Oh I have been tortured
> and I am having such pains, and I can't sleep," he gets this paper in the mail from
> the asylum authorities that says, "You should bring us a medical expert opinion
> within four weeks." Now imagine the challenges of someone who may speak Tamil
> and living in a remote village here of finding a doctor who would write an attesta-
> tion about his torture within four weeks? It is just not possible.

Evidence of trauma as a basis to prevent deportations is used in Germany, as it is in the United States and other countries. However, in practice, at the level of immigration across nations, there is resistance to implementing it to determine the status of an asylum-seeker's stay in a nation. Further, when the long-term fate of the asylum-seeker is uncertain, his possible deportation places a significant strain on clinicians and all those invested in the refugee's well-being. Windgasse elaborates on this point by illustrating a case:

---

[72] For a great exposition into the issues of collective trauma in Germany, an important source is Giesen, B. (2004). The trauma of perpetrators: The Holocaust as the traumatic reference of German national identity. In J. C. Alexander, R. Eyerman, B. Giesen, N. J. Smelser, & P. Sztompska (Eds.), *Cultural trauma and collective identity* (pp. 112–154). University of California Press.

"There was an Iranian asylum-seeker who was going to be deported from Germany to Norway," says Windgasse. "What can we do?" the case manager asked of Windgasse. "We can write that he is anxious and disturbed by the fear of being deported to Norway but if he did not have this prior condition that could worsen with deportation that would mean his asylum application would be denied." Such situations place case workers in a quandary, as deportations to unsafe countries likely seal the fate of refugees to more dire harms. The Iranian asylum-seeker offered the option of deportation to Norway asked himself, "OK, what's wrong with Norway?" Finding nothing amiss he agreed to be deported there. "But his asylum application was rejected in Norway and he faces deportation to Iran. He is distraught now."

The clamor to cater to demands of the present (versus past traumas), such as residency status of refugee families amid the chronic shortage of clinicians, might be a critical barrier in diverting focus and resources away from refugees' mental health concerns within the German integration system. Says Blessin, "Social workers are a shortage, and it is a big problem. In the last year, we have needed so many of them." Although many nonprofit agencies are providing low-level psychosocial support and mental health information to refugees, regular psychotherapeutic treatment for those who are severely mentally ill is not readily available. As with other nations, in Germany psychotherapeutic care has long waiting periods and insufficient numbers of interpreters, who are of critical importance.[73] A sample of German asylum-seekers, 39% of whom engaged in self-harm or suicidal ideation, reported lengthier wait times than other patients, and were forced to wait for an average of 50 weeks for psychotherapy to commence.[74] Refugees' mental health, although considered important, is subsumed by the pressing demands of language competence and integration.

Additional barriers to incorporating trauma into the integration infrastructure more comprehensively could also include the fact that refugee families vary across different cultures. Inability to recognize cultural themes and weave them into the therapeutic context can limit the disclosure of past traumas. The Middle-Eastern family and regional family customs can organize gender relations and family processes differently from that of a nuclear family in the West. Although some scholars have emphasized "the Arab family," given the vast differences in region, rural or urban, religion, and women's status, as well as in personal status

[73] How Europe fails to treat mental health issues. (2021, October 3). *DW News.* https://www.dw.com/en/pay-up-or-put-it-off-europe-fails-to-treat-mental-health/a-56812344

[74] Trohl, U., Wagner, K., Kalfa, V., Negash, S., Wienke, A., & Führer, A. (2021). Sick and tired—sociodemographic and psychosocial characteristics of asylum seekers awaiting an appointment for psychotherapy. *International Journal of Environmental Research and Public Health, 18,* 11850.

laws and courts,[75] it is perhaps of no more or no less utility to speak of a universal "American family."

Investing early in the specialized mental health needs of asylum seekers during their resettlement by host societies can strengthen refugees' economic and social capital, improve the likelihood of local integration, and of success in reintegrating in their countries of origin. Traumatic events are consistent risk factors for a psychotic disorder,[76] and refugees are especially vulnerable to developing non-affective psychoses, as compared with native and migrant populations in host countries.[77] The early resettlement years, especially the first 2 years postmigration[78,79] witness high symptom levels for refugees and asylum-seekers.[80,81,82,83] Problems manifested by vulnerable populations, such as refugee women, predict later symptoms and chronicity, thus highlighting the importance of early psychological screening and monitoring for up to 18 months post-resettlement.[84] For the forcibly displaced who may be struggling with debts, losses, erosion of skills from lost work or education, improved mental health can also mean better utilization of humanitarian and development opportunities.

However, resettlement programs are "founded upon unequal power and authority rather than on integration and equal worth."[85] They may not prioritize how the forcibly displaced will fare over the long-term or may preferentially

[75] Van Eijk, E. (2016). *Family law in Syria patriarchy, pluralism and personal status codes.* I. B. Tauris.

[76] Gibson, L. E., Alloy, L. B., & Ellman, L. M. (2016). Trauma and the psychosis spectrum: A review of symptom specificity and explanatory mechanisms. *Clinical Psychology Review, 49,* 92–105.

[77] Brandt, L., Henssler, J., Müller, M., Wall, S., Gabel, D., & Heinz, A. (2019). Risk of psychosis among refugees: A systematic review and meta-analysis. *JAMA Psychiatry, 76*(11), 1133–1140.

[78] Westermeyer, J. (1988). DSM-III psychiatric disorders among Hmong refugees in the United States: A point prevalence study. *American Journal of Psychiatry, 145*(2), 197–202.

[79] Chung, R. C., & Kagawa, S. (1993). Predictors of psychological distress among Southeast Asian refugees. *Social Science Medicine, 36*(5), 631–639.

[80] Beiser, M. (1988). Influences of time, ethnicity and attachment on depression in Southeast Asian refugees. *Journal of the American Medical Association Psychiatry, 145*(1), 46–51.

[81] Lie, B. (2002). A 3-year follow-up study of psychosocial function and general symptoms in resettled refugees. *Acta Psychiatrica Scandinavica, 106*(6), 415–425.

[82] Laban, C. J., Gernaat, H., Komproe, I. H., Schreuders, B. A., & De Jong, J. T. V. M. (2004). Impact of a long asylum procedure on the prevalence of psychiatric disorders in Iraqi asylum seekers in The Netherlands. *Journal of Nervous and Mental Disease, 192*(12), 843–851.

[83] Some other studies suggest symptoms first increase, then decrease: Weine, S. M., Vojvoda, D., Becker, D. F., McGlashan, T. H., Hodzic, E., Laub D., Hyman, L., Sawyer, M., & Lazrove, S. (1998). PTSD symptoms in Bosnian refugees 1 year after resettlement in the United States. *American Journal of Psychiatry, 155*(4), 562–564.

[84] Vromans, L., Schweitzer, R. D., Brough, M., Asic Kobe, M., Correa-Velez, I., Farrell, L., Murray, K., Lenette, C., & Sagar, V. (2021). Persistent psychological distress in resettled refugee women-at-risk at one-year follow-up: Contributions of trauma, post-migration problems, loss, and trust. *Transcult Psychiatry, 58*(2), 157–171.

[85] Knudsen, J. C. (1991). Therapeutic strategies and strategies for refugee coping. *Journal of Refugee Studies, 4*(1), 21–38.

treat certain groups accelerating their integration over others, as in the case of Ukrainian refugees in Poland. Although bias for instance, of the hardworking immigrant can benefit some, it can mandate the host nation's responsibility only toward productive and skilled immigrants who seamlessly acquire their language or compensate for labor shortages and not those who may experience acute needs or are perceived to lack integration utility. Preferential treatment of specific attributes can perpetuate the myth of a refugee as unidimensional and the price of preferential treatment of some groups is borne by other less privileged groups who bear the risks of exclusion such as falling into poverty, being pushed into the informal economy, deprived of integration supports, and the attrition of their human capital.

Arbaz, the 22-year-old Afghan man who had fled the Taliban, had related his life story to me as though he was reading a telegram. He spoke in short declarative sentences that ended abruptly, delivering horrifying details, one after another. Arbaz looked impassive, with eyes that looked not at me but beyond me. After 11 months as a refugee in Germany, our interview was the first time he had opened up about the trauma he had experienced in his home and during his journey. Left out of Arbaz's retelling of his life story was any description of his horror at having witnessed such events, the terror he must have felt under constant threat of death, and the heartbreak of witnessing his parents die of shock.

When I expressed my own horror at the number of tragedies Arbaz had encountered, his face registered a flicker of surprise that was uncharacteristic. He replied matter-of-factly, "When I would tell people at home, they'd treat it as an ordinary thing. Nobody knows my heart is crying."

Only a detached sensibility toward patients, many practitioners believe, lends objectivity. But in the face of such intimate sufferings, my next respondent, Arwa, helped hone the clinical methodology used to access refugees' traumatic experiences.

3

A White Coat or a White Heart?

The Methodology

Arwa's Story

Arwa's entered the room giggling and hand-in-hand with a man. Following Arwa's interview with me, I learned that she and Aboo, 30 years old and her fiancé, were headed for their wedding. Arwa wanted Aboo to be present during her interview. Four of us sat in a triangle; Aboo perpendicular to Arwa and me and the interpreter beside me. She and Aboo met each other at a social event in Germany. As our conversation progressed, it seemed that she was an eternal romantic, hopeful that love was just around the corner. But "I suffered a lot," says Arwa. Hopes for love had led Arwa to a string of disappointments and broken engagements in each of the three countries she had stayed in as a refugee: Saudi Arabia, Turkey, and Holland. "I have been engaged three times, and I met many bastards. They were a bunch of deadbeats," shared Arwa without hesitation.

Arwa and Aboo were an hour at best away from their wedding ceremony. In many Islamic societies, dating is not encouraged, and it is not common for individuals to date before marriage. Virtues like virginity are considered paramount for women's reputations and determine whether they will secure wedding proposals and the quality of their married life. Also, I did not know how much of her romantic past Aboo knew or not. Given the potential for this topic to become contentious, I gingerly approached the follow-up, asking her to elaborate.

Arwa giggled. "The first Saudi one . . ." she thought out loud, "So how do I explain it? His brain was just like a stone. If you say something, he will not be at all flexible. He will simply not understand you. He also lied a lot. He was also ill. His illness although, was not a big deal. The problem was that he lied to me. He just wanted a wife to marry, put her in a home and close the door on her and say, 'That's my wife. No one can do anything with her.' The second one was a Turkish man who was stingy and nervous. He did not trust me. The third (Dutch) one, he lied a lot. The word in Syria is 'he comes and goes.' I could not fathom what he was up to. Ever."

Displaced. Shaifali Sandhya, Oxford University Press. © Shaifali Sandhya 2024.
DOI: 10.1093/oso/9780197579886.003.0003

I was curious to know about women's experiences in war, and eventually, our discussion touched upon the presence of any lingering troubles from her hardships from war. Arwa's upbeat manner turned dark.

"I remember one thing," said Arwa quickly to me. "But I don't want to share it in front of Aboo." There was a long pause that followed. Her eyes had turned somber. I felt sorrowful at encroaching on her comfort.

It's uncomfortable and taboo for any Middle Eastern woman to broach love, romance, or sexuality in front of her future husband. In some parts of the Western world, we may believe it's normal to speak freely and honestly about past relationships. However, such candor may affect even partners who live in the West if they have not at first addressed it between themselves. Indeed, even in the most permissive of societies, talk of one's exes with one's spouse-to-be is not appropriate moments before one's wedding.

Before I could speak, Arwa broke our pause to share her life's cruelest blow. "I was in love with a soldier," she said, and she shared her love story with a soldier called Dilawar. It was a chance encounter with him, Arwa said when in her hunt for a new home, she mistakenly crossed over enemy lines into a conflict zone. The soldier who belonged to the Syrian government's army was an enemy combatant at war with the military group that controlled her neighborhood. Neighborhoods and regions in Syria had been demarcated to belong to armies with loyalties to various military groups. In the year that followed, the couple would meet secretly, undeterred by the storm of artillery shells, grenades, gun powder roasting the air, smoke, and snipers.

In the embattled conflict zone, they exchanged vows of love, honor, and duty. "We loved each other." One day Dilawar got her a beautiful fuchsia Damask rose, a rare commodity in war. It smelled of gun powder, but to Arwa that Damask rose with its 58 petals she hand-counted, was her most treasured possession. He told her that he wanted to marry her. "We planned that the following week he will seek my hand in marriage from my family. A week later . . . Dilawar died," said Arwa slowly. "I did not see his body again. I couldn't believe he died."

For a long time, Arwa searched for his body in vain. His disappearance in the absence of anything concrete about his death made her mourning eternal. I am sorry," I said to Arwa. "I asked you a lot of personal questions."

"There is no problem," she replied, "I trust Aboo as if we are one."

Aboo had been quiet all this time as Arwa and I were speaking, although he had observed our facial interchanges and interaction from his vantage point.

He replied in English, "white heart."

At this, Arwa giggled.

I asked, "Whose white heart?"

Aboo replied, "I'm talking about the trust she gave to you and what happened here . . . The trust in each other that was exchanged here that's what white heart is."

Curious, I asked, "From you to me and me to you?"
Aboo affirmed. "Yes. Kal elopiat [white] Albak abyad [heart]."

Confronted by displaced peoples' traumas and brutal wounds, how do physicians and health professionals not reel with terror and horror? Although emotional socialization is an important skill for physicians in caring for patients, medical training implicitly teaches them not to feel[1] or to have their guard up against "feeling too much" so as to reduce the risk of secondary traumatization. Some helping fields like medicine and psychiatry prize clinical detachment; conversely, the presence of empathy can imply deficiency in objectivity. If there were a "typical" refugee (there isn't), Arwa, a 29-year-old Syrian-Kurdish woman, defied it: she did not look or feel like one. But it was Aboo, her fiancée and an unwitting bystander, who revealed how critical the role of empathy was for drawing out her trauma story and its empowering influence for the researcher-client interaction, just as for a therapeutic relationship.

In observing Arwa's instinct to share more deeply as a result of her assessment of authentic caring on my part, Aboo affirmed findings from clinical literature: a patient's perception of a therapist's empathy is the most consistent predictor of a good treatment outcome.[2,3,4] According to Donna Orange, as the clinical psychologist jointly creates an experiential world, both therapist and patient are allowed the safety to "open questions that had felt too dangerous."[5] It takes two to self-disclose. But in the scientific literature, although there seems to be a great deal of research about client traits, race, and ethnicity,[6] there is not enough research on therapist factors in affecting relationship-building[7] and creating safety. Empathy is an intuitive understanding of the patient's central emotional experiences, and the capacity to tolerate what patients cannot tolerate within themselves.[8] An empathic stance can contribute to self-awareness of one's own emotional reactions, enable participation in deeply arousing experiences, deepen a researcher's repertoire of responses in the foreignness of her patient's experiences, while maintaining a professional and warm demeanor. Social

[1] Underman, K., & Hirshfield, L. E. (2016). Detached concern? Emotional socialization in twenty-first century medical education. *Social Science & Medicine, 160*, 94–101.

[2] Waugaman, R. M., & Korn, M. (2021). Empowering empathy. *Psychiatry, 84*, 223–227.

[3] Luborsky, L., McLellan, A. T., Woody, G. E., O'Brien, C. P., & Auerbach, A. (1985). Therapist success and its determinants. *Archives of General Psychiatry, 42*(6), 602–611.

[4] Elliott, R., Bohart, A. C., Watson, J. C., & Greenber, L. S. (2011). Empathy. In J. Norcross (Ed.), *Psychotherapy relationships that works* (2nd ed., pp. 132–152). Oxford University Press.

[5] Orange, D. M. (2002). There is no outside: Empathy and authenticity in the psychoanalytic process. *Psychoanalytic Psychology, 19*(4), 686–700.

[6] Dean, K. E. (2022). Treatment seeking for anxiety and depression among Black adults: A multilevel and empirically informed psycho-sociocultural model. *Behavior Therapy, 53*(6), 1077–1091.

[7] Roberts, J. (2005). Transparency and self-disclosure in family therapy: Dangers and possibilities. *Family Process, 44*(1), 45–63.

[8] Kernberg, O. (1975). *Borderline conditions and pathological narcissism.* Jason Aronson.

identities of the researcher, her race, sexual orientation, gender, or class, whether correctly or incorrectly assumed by others, influence a respondent's disclosure. In this case, my visible identities as a Brown person, woman, and an immigrant might have provided a sense of safety for Arwa, and for the many of the refugees I interviewed.

The interviews that follow reflect the importance of adopting a White Heart (empathic) approach over a White Coat (detached) one with refugees. It is important to acknowledge at the same time that although listening actively is one form of crucial support, there are other forms of support that can contribute to recipients' thriving (e.g., medical, advocacy, funding, research, and humanitarian support). Also, while openness, honesty, and frankness are valued during psychotherapy, such safe spaces may not be readily available in displacement settings. The act of listening to the refugee may conjure in the passive recipient a sense of white benevolence, the problematic perception that indigenous people require rescuing. However, not only do refugees' stories underscore their self-reliance and autonomy, but also engaging in psychotherapy is increasingly seen as self-agency, enabling refugees to gain more effective control over their lives.

The Study: 2016–2021

The 16 German federal states are individually responsible for the housing and care of asylum-seekers. States commission humanitarian organizations, such as the Red Cross and others, to manage facilities for asylum-seekers. In 2016, state and district-level officials across many departments conferred with local officials, such as camp administrators and community leaders, to review my study's proposal to access the refugees they served.

It took several months for the research proposal to make it through the various arteries of the German state and district system, and it was examined well by those who received it. Officials would reference sections of my proposal during their interviews. Going through multiple levels of scrutiny also served as a review and examination of the research methodology, equivalent to an American Institutional Review Board (IRB) designed to protect research subjects.[9] Following this, officials coordinated with nongovernmental agencies, such as the Red Cross, who were managing the refugee shelters and had daily contact

[9] The German state's review was equivalent to an American IRB, and this was verified by an attorney of the Trust, a malpractice carrier offering counsel for psychologists. I also sought legal counsel with an international law firm to ensure clarity on my responsibilities and to address all possible risks in conducting the study in the absence of a formalized IRB review in Germany. In addition to taking regular trainings in research ethics, I studied the Nuremberg Code (1947), the Declaration of Helsinki (1975), and the Belmont Protocol (1978) to ensure that the rights, integrity, and confidentiality of human subjects were protected.

with the refugees and secured access for the interviews. By and large German officials were receptive, welcoming, and invested in learning more about how they could improve refugees' situations, and they went out of their way to facilitate introductions in a calibrated and thoughtful way that made data collection smooth.

The interviews I conducted in an ambience of emotional safety reflect the active agency of refugees in crafting their own stories and new identities in their interactions with others, including this researcher. Refugee respondents from Syria, Afghanistan, Iraq, and Lebanon were interviewed in English or in their local dialect with a female multilingual translator also well-versed in German. A majority of my interviews took place in safe and secure refugee resettlement settings. Interviews were either conducted in refugees' rooms, a reserved community room in the refugee shelter, or in an office-like space located in an easily accessible part of the city. The refugees learned of the opportunity to participate in the study initially through their counselors, community leaders, fellow community members, and refugee shelter managers. Refugees were told that the study's goal was to understand how they became refugees, their experiences before and after their arrival in Germany, and their present health status.

The respondents were assured that the interviews would be confidential, any identifying information would be changed, and any audio/video recording would be conducted based on their comfort level and consent. The interpreter, whenever used, also pledged to maintain the confidentiality of the respondents. They were informed that their participation was voluntary with no compensation or financial or material incentives and that they could withdraw at any point and decline to respond to any item that might make them uncomfortable. The informed consent was broken down into simple language in their local dialect and with participants who might have experienced challenges owing to illiteracy, age, cognitive impairment, or preconceptions about clinical research. Respondents had access to mental health professionals through social workers of the agency serving them, and in case of any possible retraumatization, as per the German government's protocol, refugees were advised to contact the social workers assigned to them. The refugees were informed that their records would be kept strictly confidential in a locked file, and all electronic information would be coded and secured.

Participants understood the risk of re-exposure to trauma in their retelling. It seemed they were only too aware of this as they would sometimes referenced this risk themselves during the interviews, saying, "I'm opening old wounds," or "I prefer not to remember . . . but I have no sleep. I keep thinking, 'what shall I do?' But there's no way out (other than by sharing)."

Among refugee communities though, equally significant as it is to restrict harm to the participants is to incorporate a collaborative, participatory, and human-rights oriented approach that is mindful of participants' well-being and the progress of their community.[10] In this study refugees believed that their participation would be beneficial to them and their families. It would reflect their agency and offer them a platform to share the plight of their community. I learned that although sharing continued to be painful for many refugees, they were sharing their experiences with me because, in one respondent's words, "You're writing a book. I want to share the truths because us people, never wanted war. We did not choose what's happening to us."

Despite the measures taken to create a safe space, it is essential to remember that war was (and is) ongoing in many parts of the Middle East. Many of the refugees' family members lived in violent nations with ongoing wars and were subject to ongoing persecutions, the very persecutions that had caused the respondents to flee. Some participants had reported an atmosphere of paranoia and suspicion in their countries of origin, where neighbors could turn on neighbors and friends on friends under duress by authorities. In their new countries, initially some had been circumspect and confided sparingly. As noted earlier, in this book I use either pseudonyms or first names only. I avoided the use of last names, region, ethnicity, a tribal affiliations. These interviewees' participation was an act of courage, trust, and, in some cases, advocacy for those they had left behind or those unable to voice their sufferings. This is why identifying details used in case studies[11] were substituted or are composites created to retain anonymity.

In total, 54 people participated: Syrian (72%; $n = 39$); Afghan (11%; $n = 6$); Iraqi (13%; $n = 7$); Moroccan (2%; $n = 1$), and Lebanese (2%; $n = 1$). They were Arab (37%; $n=20$), Kurdish (59%; $n=32$), and Yazidi (4%; $n = 2$), and 46% ($n = 25$) were women and 54% ($n = 29$) men. All participants were newly arrived or had been in Germany for approximately 1–3 years at the time of the study. My research was conducted in two phases in five different cities of Germany that had experienced a significant influx of asylum-seekers over the prior few years. In the first (pilot) phase, 20 refugees responded to items in the Hopkins Checklist (HSCL-25) in

---

[10] Bullock, M., & Zakowski, S. G. (2020). Conducting psychological research across borders: Maintaining scientific rigor and safeguarding human rights. In N. S. Rubin & R. L. Flores (Eds.), *The Cambridge handbook of psychology and human rights* (pp. 490–503). Cambridge University Press. https://doi.org/10.1017/9781108348607.034

[11] Vignettes or case studies are based on qualitative interviews with primary sources. They have been scrubbed for syntax and for semantic clarity but bear the integrity of the speaker's own words. Although the case studies may demonstrate flow, in many instances and as is common with clients of trauma, information was painstakingly pieced together through follow-up questions in the interview to derive a measure of depth or sequence. Whenever the interpreter was used, they were instructed not to summarize but to use the exact words, phrases, and route taken in the narration by the respondent as well as by the interviewer. In four instances, secondary sources for vignettes have been used, and their sources are credited. Chapter 10 contains two case studies that are a composite of sources.

their local language, and this was followed by qualitative interviews. Participants included Syrian (65%; $n = 13$), Afghan (20%; $n = 4$); Iraqi 10%; $n = 2$), and Lebanese (5%; $n = 1$) persons, respectively. They were Arab (60%; $n = 12$) and Kurdish (40%; $n = 8$). There were 13 men and seven women. A translated version of the HSCL-25 was placed in front of them so they could follow the symptoms and report accordingly. This pilot phase helped establish the appropriateness of age, culture, linguistic suitability, and current health status for a future larger-scale study by including psychometric measures such as the Hopkins Checklist (HSCL-25).[12] The HSCL-25 is a symptom inventory and a quantitative tool to measures symptoms of anxiety and depression.

Almost all the participants, the pilot phase revealed, had experienced several traumatic events over a prolonged period. Arbaz (whose story appears in Chapter 2) had endured at least 23 severely traumatic events, and some of them multiple times. A cutoff score of 1.75 was used to identify clinically significant symptoms per the HSCL-25 Anxiety and Depression subscales: 75% of the participants reported clinically significant symptoms of anxiety, and 80% reported those of depression.[13] Having established the presence of past traumatic events and posttraumatic symptoms both in the quantitative and qualitative parts of the pilot phase for every refugee participant, the second phase of the study employed only detailed qualitative interviews[14,15] for 34 participants

[12] The HSCL is a widely used measure of depression and anxiety screening measure. The HSCL-25 has 10 items for anxiety symptoms and 15 items for depression symptoms. The scale for each question includes four categories of response ("not at all," "a little," "quite a bit," and "extremely," rated 1 to 4, respectively). On this basis, two scores are calculated, and the total score is the average of all 25 items. The total depression score for each individual has been found to correlate with major depression as defined by the *Diagnostic and Statistical Manual of the American Psychiatric Association Fourth Edition* (DSM-IV). It has been translated for use among Bosnian, Cambodian, Croatian, Japanese, Laotian, Vietnamese, and other populations: Kleijn, W. C., Hovens, J. E., & Rodenburg, J. J. (2001). Posttraumatic stress symptoms in refugees. *American Journal of Psychiatry, 3*, 343–351.
[13] For a list of symptoms of the HSCL-25, please refer to Appendix, Table A.1.
[14] There were at least three other important reasons for employing the qualitative methodology: (i) Information on levels of distress could not accurately describe the traumatic events during the war, ongoing economic and social upheavals created by war, and traumatic events incurred during their journeys, in transit countries, refugee camps, or resettlement countries. (ii) The symptom checklists were unable to map what was culturally unique to the Middle Eastern refugees. (iii) Soliciting responses using a finite number of items stands the risk of infusing refugees' worldview with a semantic framework of trauma rather than understanding their local expressions of distress in their own language.
[15] This stance has been validated by qualitative inquiries such as those of Jenkins and Hass, who studied 47 adolescent boys living in a psychiatric residential facility of the Southwest, mainly New Mexico. The stressors in the youths' lives ranged from experiencing parental neglect, witnessing deaths of their loved ones, attempting suicide, committing violent acts, abusing drugs, and either being abused or engaging in physical or sexual abuse. The trauma experienced by the adolescent boys, of whom three-fourths were hospitalized multiple times, far exceeds the circumscribed description of trauma in the diagnostic categories. Although some researchers might take the stance that psychiatric diagnostic categories are, generally, a good starting point for mental illness and that 28% of the adolescents in Jenkins and Haas's study met the full criteria for PTSD, clinical categories fail to elucidate the full extent and effect of their trauma in communities such as this Southwest one, which is rife with violence at many levels. Situating their trauma within the clusters of a diagnostic category could

in Germany. Wherever relevant the case studies and findings of the quantitative analyses are interspersed throughout the book.

The qualitative interview was designed to gather data on a variety of relevant topics, including migration and demographic history, acculturation in the host country, refugees' impressions of the German society in general, aspirations, expectations, attitudes toward the host society and of their host society toward them, social engagement, kinship, family life, networks of social relations and challenges in obtaining social services in their host country. The interviews employed a variety of question formats—open-ended, forced-choice, and the miracle technique.[16] The questionnaire's nonthreatening face validity was established through a review of its items by my professional colleagues and community members. Interviews were taped, transcribed, and coded. Interviews, questionnaires, and field notes were stored under lock and key in my office.

Affect and Language

Like Arbaz, many refugees demonstrated affect incongruent with their accounts of trauma. Some tittered and others punctuated brutal accounts with small laughs. I met a young woman who had witnessed two suicide attempts by other asylum-seekers at a refugee camp as a 14 year old. As she recalled the time she spent at that particular camp, she remembered being very scared on the night her friend's father cut his hand off:

> It was the night when the father cut open his wrist [laughs] . . . Fellow passengers had told us that "The refugee camp was uncomfortable," and "There are so many people who are drunk and scary." "Just take care because you are all women" [shrieking laugh].
>
> And then when we went there it was really scary [shrill laugh]. We thought we would get a room, but it was like a big playground. [There was no] privacy. When I would go to sleep, there would be a strange man sleeping next to my mattress.

carry the twin danger of situating it within the individual and reducing the complexity of their lived experience. Exclusive reliance on questionnaires may perpetuate what has been referred to as the "Americanization of suffering" instead of an accurate representation of distress experienced by them. Sources: Jenkins, J. H., & Haas, B. M. (2016). Trauma in the lifeworlds of adolescents: Hard luck and trouble in the land of enchantment. In D. E. Hinton & B. J. Good (Eds.), *Culture and PTSD: Trauma in global and historical perspectives* (pp. 179–201). University of Pennsylvania Press; Good, B. (1994). Culture and psychopathology: Directions for psychiatric anthropology. In T. Schwart, G. White, & C. Lutz (Eds.), *New directions in psychological anthropology* (pp. 181–205). Cambridge University Press); Watters, E. (2011). *Crazy like us: The globalization of the American psyche.* Free Press.

[16] The miracle method of interviewing is one where the therapist can invite the client to describe something in an imaginary scenario or in the presence of an imaginary person.

I couldn't take off my headscarf . . . I hated that place so much [laughs]. Fights broke out daily because someone stole some stuff from another person, or someone did not know how to use a Western toilet [laughs].

The purpose of the laughter may be multifold. It could serve as a self-soothing gesture for the participant or as a means of protecting the interviewer and others with no experiences of these kinds of traumas. Laughter could serve as a mechanism to observe the reactions of the observer—would they drop it? or could they handle it? How others would judge the episode would determine future disclosures by the participant. Underplaying traumatic events through their choice of words and emotions expressed could also indicate efforts to protect families and communities from further violence. Nonetheless, to those without knowledge of complex trauma or lacking a deep understanding of the respondent, the picture can appear one of resilience and stoicism, rather than as efforts to underplay experiences of violence and terror.

Focusing entirely on the narratives of the second phase of the research allowed me to home in on the language interviewees employed to describe their emotional lives. "Arabic is a rich language with many synonyms," said an 18-year-old woman fluent in English and Arabic who was learning German. In the vignette below, she describes how emotions can carry different meanings in the British (English-speaking), German, and Syrian world. In addition, she demonstrates that people can use metaphors in contrasting ways to suit their inclinations and their growing flexibility with another language.

Respondent: My mother was a very calm person but [after our journey with traffickers] she's nervous now.
Interviewer: How is she nervous?
Respondent: When you are just shouting and speaking out aloud . . .
Interviewer: Do you mean, angry?
Respondent: When you are like, "I'm nervous—Oh, I don't know what to do" . . . "Oh, don't go out," and "Oh don't do this and don't do that." [In Arabic] we have different words we have qalak *[meaning scared nervous] or* mutatawatur *[meaning uptight and restless] or* 'asby *[meaning irritable].*

Qalak, mutatawatur, and *'asby* imply different kinds of emotions than one would have inferred from the respondent's initial reference to nervousness. Focusing only on "loudness" might have caused some from a different cultural background to infer anxiety or anger in the respondent's mother, which would not be entirely accurate. Looking from within the culture, references to nervousness also exclude any suggestion of heavier feelings of *gadab* (meaning *anger*), *gadban* (being an angry person), or *huzn* (meaning *sadness*). This is most likely because feelings such as sadness are not typically culturally sanctioned because of their negative connotation. Her mother, for instance, uses several descriptors for one emotion, the respondent says, and employs different understandings for the same proverb. Respondents can use proverbs in contrasting ways to reflect sociocultural, linguistic, and generational influences. Providing an example of a proverb, one respondent said:

> For instance, my mother would say to me, "Do a task faster" or "A good task should also be completed quickly." But if I don't want to feel rushed, I can say to her in English, "Haste makes waste." And in German, I can correct her, "Eile mit weile"[or haste will delay]. They're all opposites. The three languages are using the proverb differently.

In Arabic, the proverb means: patience leads to safety, and haste to regret. The Arabic proverb may appear at face value as advocating passivity, although it can equally imply doing something with care and intentionality. The English proverb *Haste makes waste* is a warning suggesting that being rushed will waste time and effort. Proverbs can illustrate how language is entwined with culture and meaning-making.[17] The use of narratives in different cultural groups can broaden their expressions of emotional experiences, more than questionnaires alone would.

Arwa's story highlights the many influences on and levels of self-disclosure in both psychotherapy and research with refugees. The "how-can-I-trust-you" dynamic manifests itself in a dance between the interviewer and the respondent within the interview itself. We may assume that the "right" question can tilt this dance evoking a turning point in interviews; however, the wrong person asking the right question can elicit different data. In working with populations evidencing a trauma response, empathy and asking what may seem to be the right questions may not be enough; creating emotional safety as part of the process and methodology are essential to the clinical interview.

Arwa's story also highlights the critical role of splintered and suspended relationships in maintaining the trauma of refugees. Western traumatologists believe that posttraumatic stress disorder results from a distress that fragments one's social world. But the reverse was proving to be likelier, as I saw through accounts such as Arwa's, that their suspended or upended social relationships and roles were contributing to their posttraumatic stress.[18] In line with this observation, reuniting with family members, refugees report, also positively affects

[17] Essam, M., & Fahmi, E. (2016). A cross-cultural study of some selected Arabic proverbs and their English translation equivalents: A contrastive approach. *International Journal of Comparative Literature & Translation Studies*, 4(2), 51–57.

[18] Given the small sample, this trend needs to be corroborated with a larger sample.

their mental health;[19] both findings suggest the buffering role of positive inter-personal relationships in mental health. Through their posttraumatic distress, resettled refugees may also be grieving the loss of their former selves and roles. Deprived of closure in the absence of her lover's dead body, what may appear as Arwa's zest for falling in love can be reinterpreted as a search for corrective emotional experience(s) through hopes of rebuilding other intimate relationships. Efforts to repair one's former self or one's relationship with it can manifest in the refugees' need to push for family reunification, to marry Germans instead of individuals within their community, to maintain their family connections in their countries of origin, and to continue their life-tasks in their host countries. The case of Hamza exemplifies this in Chapter 5.

Along with being emotionally fraught, the telling of a traumatic event is messy, chaotic, and haphazard: the chronology may be absent, the beginning buried, and the most important details may present reluctantly toward the end. And throughout, the overwhelmed patient, breathless or confused, may either smile as though their main task is to entertain and distract the listener from its sordid details or may apologize profusely as though they are overwhelming the listener.

Take the case of Gulnaz, who told me toward the end of our interview, a trifle regretfully, "I forgot to tell you I was electrocuted." Read his story next.

[19] Löbel, L., & Jacobsen, J. (2021). Waiting for kin: A longitudinal study of family reunification and refugee mental health in Germany. *Journal of Ethnic and Migration Studies, 47*(13), 2916–2937.

4

Queen of Proofs and the Kings of Torment

Psychological Sequelae of Torture

Breakfast for 60 Boys

"Breakfast!"

"Breakfast . . . !" boomed the familiar voice.

A wave of panic ran through his body when he heard the words. It was March 2007, and Gulnaz had just turned 16 years old. Then, he would hear the familiar clang of lock and keys and the thud of approaching boots. Yanked by his hair, he would be dragged across the gutters and through the sludge to the torture chambers. In early predawn hours, he would be inflicted with heinous cruelty that Assad's regime ironically called "breakfast."

"Breakfast" meant electrocuting his body with jolts of high-voltage electric current. Electrodes would be clipped at the veins behind his ears. They would be placed in the soft spaces between his fingers for maximal impact. His veins would pulsate with currents roiling his body until fully saturated with electricity; he lay like a rag doll. Somewhere deep below in Aleppo's bowels, he was held in the squalid dungeons of its waterways swimming with vermin and cockroaches. Gulnaz was subjected to low-voltage electrocution three times a day. Just above the sewer and the drainage, life continued in its normal humdrum way, its residents unaware of the horrors that lurked 20 feet under. The torture would go on for 3 months and 3 nights.

There were other boys like him: 59 others covered in blood, urine, vomit, and diarrhea. Some of them wailed louder; others could not muster any motion, let alone a sound. Gulnaz was held in an individual cell, approximately 6–9 feet with about six other individuals; the group cell held mostly young people with "lots of broken parts in their bodies." Male survivors suffered anal fistulae and fissures that led to ongoing pain and fecal leakage.

His own body felt limp, crumpled against the same spot, half slumped against the wall, as it had been the previous night. "We will never grow up to be men," he recalls thinking. "We will never see life again." Gulnaz's voice dropped to a barely audible level, and he whispered, "90% of those 60 boys were never seen alive again by anyone."

Displaced. Shaifali Sandhya, Oxford University Press. © Shaifali Sandhya 2024.
DOI: 10.1093/oso/9780197579886.003.0004

Gulnaz is 30 years old and Syrian-Kurdish, and when we met in May 2015 in Bonn, he recounted to me the horrific period when he was 16 and subjected to protracted sexual torture.[1,2] Gulnaz with a ceaseless handshake is stocky with thick jet-black hair swept back on a flat hairline baring protruding temples. He had been training to be a teacher at the University of Afrin, Syria, when he had to flee.

If you met Gulnaz on the street, you might view him as an ordinary, hardworking young teacher in training. As I did, you might not entirely register the unsteadiness in his left leg. Gulnaz tries to ignore the chronic pain that still plagues him and attempts to push his way through life in a genial manner despite believing, as his village doctor told him, "bad things that happened to him still reside in my body." Several months after his torture, when the tremors and the pain had failed to subside, Gulnaz approached his local physician in Syria. Upon assessing Gulnaz's injuries, although the physician knew what had occurred, Gulnaz suspects, he likened his crippling pain to that of a 70 year old with arthritis. Since then, although Gulnaz is still quite young, he explains away the pain tremors that splice his body as the "shivers of aging."

Torture

The deliberate infliction of bodily pain at close quarters distinguishes torture from other kinds of trauma. The UN Convention Against Torture and Other Cruel, Inhuman or Degrading Treatment or Punishment (henceforth referred to as the "Convention") defines *torture*[3] as an act by which severe pain or suffering, whether physical or mental, is intentionally inflicted on a person for such purposes as obtaining from him, or a third person, information or a confession; punishing

[1] Male sexual violence and torture is a taboo topic but widely prevalent among boys as young as 10 years old and elderly men in their 80s; it takes many forms, has perpetrators that can include one's own community members, and occurs in different kinds of settings: Chynoweth, S. (2017). *"We have to keep in our hearts": Sexual violence among men and boys in the Syria crisis.* UNHCR, p. 7.

[2] The term *conflict-related sexual violence* refers to "rape, sexual slavery, forced prostitution, forced pregnancy, enforced sterilization, and other forms of sexual violence of comparable gravity perpetrated against women, men, girls or boys that is linked, directly or indirectly (temporally, geographically, or causally) to a conflict. This link may be evident in the profile of the perpetrator; the profile of the victim; in a climate of impunity or State collapse; in the cross-border dimensions; and/or in violations of the terms of a ceasefire agreement": UN Security Council. *Conflict-related sexual violence: Report of the Secretary-General.* (S/2015/203, para. 2). (2015, March 23). https://unama. unmissions.org/sites/default/files/wps-sg_report_crsv_-march_2015_0.pdf

[3] Other definitions of *torture* different from the Convention also exist, such as the more broad and inclusive World Medical Association's (WMA) definition in its Declaration of Tokyo: ". . . torture is defined as the deliberate, systematic or wanton infliction of physical or mental suffering by one or more persons acting alone or on the orders of any authority, to force another person to yield information, to make a confession, or for any other reason": WMA. (1975, October). *WMA Declaration of Tokyo guidelines for physicians concerning torture and other cruel inhuman or degrading treatment or punishment in relation to detention and imprisonment.* https://www.wma.net/policies-post/

him for an act that he or a third person has committed or is suspected of having committed; or intimidating or coercing him or a third person; or for any reason based on discrimination of any kind, when such pain or suffering is inflicted by or at the instigation of a public officer acting in an official capacity. Beyond the Convention, torture is completely banned under any circumstance globally.[4] The right to be free from torture is also present in many international treaties.[5,6] For nations who choose not to ratify the Convention, the prohibition against torture is a *jus cogens*, an accepted global custom of international human rights law. Its ratification is nonetheless significant as it offers a framework for the rehabilitation and protection of the rights of refugee survivors, among other benefits.[7]

In this chapter we discuss the mental health ramifications of extreme assaults such as torture, and outline their psychological, cognitive, neurological, and sexual sequelae. I examine existing scientific literature and one case study to highlight torture survivors' needs.[8] Although Gulnaz's is only one story, personal stories of torture can have a good validity[9] with clinical determination as defined by the Tokyo Declaration.[10] The biography of a refugee can elucidate the experience of torture, as well as the embedded contexts of history, race, ethnicity, culture, and politics. On the one hand, such socio-structural variables influence the trajectory of the survivor's suffering and treatment implications, and, on the other,

wma-declaration-of-tokyo-guidelines-for-physicians-concerning-torture-and-other-cruel-inhu man-or-degrading-treatment-or-punishment-in-relation-to-detention-and-imprisonment/

[4] Under Article 2, "no exceptional circumstances whatsoever, whether a state of war or a threat of war, internal political instability or any other public emergency, may be invoked as a justification of torture. An order from a superior officer or a public authority may not be invoked as a justification of torture": Convention against torture and other cruel, inhuman or degrading treatment or punishment (G.A. res.39/46, Annex, 39 UN GAOR Supp., No. 51, p. 197, UN Doc. A/39/51, art.2). (1984, December 10). https://www.ohchr.org/en/professionalinterest/pages/cat.aspx

[5] Among the most important of these instruments are the Universal Declaration of Human Rights, the International Covenant on Civil and Political Rights, the Standard Minimum Rules for the Treatment of Prisoners, Declaration on the Protection of All Persons from Being Subjected to Torture and Other Cruel, Inhuman or Degrading Treatment or Punishment (Declaration on the Protection against Torture) the Code of Conduct on Law Enforcement, the Principles of Medical Ethics Relevant to the Role of Health Personnel Particularly Physicians, in the Protection of Prisoners and Detainees against Torture and Other Cruel Inhuman or Degrading Treatment or Punishment, and so forth.

[6] International covenant on civil and political rights (Article 7), March 23, 1976; Convention against torture and other cruel, inhuman or degrading treatment or punishment, June 26, 1987;Universal Declaration of Human Rights (Article 5), December 10, 1948.

[7] Edwards, A. (2020, June 24). *The UNCAT and India: Perspectives on ratification* [Webinar]. Commonwealth Human Rights Initiative and the Organisation Mondiale Contre la Torture. https:// cti2024.org/wp-content/uploads/2021/03/India-webinar-24-June-2020_Edwards-presentation.pdf

[8] UNHCR. (2004). *Istanbul protocol: Manual on the effective investigation and documentation of torture and other cruel, inhuman or degrading treatment or punishment* (Professional training series No. 8, Rev. 1). https://www.ohchr.org/sites/default/files/Documents/Publications/training8Rev1en.pdf

[9] Montgomery, E., & Foldspang, A. (1994). Criterion-related validity of screening for exposure to torture. *Danish Medical Bulletin, 41*, 588–591.

[10] The Tokyo Declaration stipulates that a doctor shall not condone or participate in any act of torture, cruel, inhuman, or degrading procedures whatever offence the victim is suspected, accused, or guilty of and whatever the victim's beliefs or motives, and in all situations, including armed conflict

they can facilitate and abet torture. A history of torture thus alerts us to the complicit nature not only of individuals but also of institutions in creating conditions engendering refugees' permanent and disabling harm. Further, the absence of a mental health infrastructure within asylum systems compounds torture-related harms to refugees. Chapter 10 offers more treatment-related considerations to systematically repair the ones who have endured unspeakable atrocities.

Torture and Its Prevalence

Close to 4 decades after the Convention was implemented to abolish torture, almost 75%[11] of countries have practiced torture in at least the previous 5 years; the offending countries include those that are also signatories to the Convention, such as the United States. In 2021, Majid Khan, known as the al-Qaida courier, reported being sexually assaulted through forcibly administered enemas, suspended naked for long periods, doused with ice water, and starved in the overseas secret prisons of the Central Intelligence Agency (CIA) over the course of 3 years.[12] In Iraq after 2007, detention policies that permit "enhanced interrogation"[13] affected an estimated 51,000 people, including juveniles, in clandestine sites run by the CIA.[14] Within the United States and abroad, many populations have endured torture throughout history and continue to experience its longterm ramifications. These include survivors of police brutality in the United States,[15] Kashmiris' human rights violations in Indian administered Kashmir through waterboarding, sleep deprivations, and sexualized torture,[16] and Indigenous women's historical abuse and forced sterilization in Canada.[17]

and civil strife: WMA. (2016, October). *WMA Declaration of Tokyo—guidelines for physicians concerning torture and other cruel, inhuman or degrading treatment or punishment in relation to detention and imprisonment.* https://www.wma.net/policies-post/wma-declaration-of-tokyo-guideli nes-for-physicians-concerning-torture-and-other-cruel-inhuman-or-degrading-treatment-or-pun ishment-in-relation-to-detention-and-imprisonment/

[11] Amnesty International. (n.d.). *Torture: A global crisis.* https://www.amnesty.org/en/get-invol ved/stop-torture/#:~:text=Torture%3A%20A%20global%20crisis&text=Over%20the%20last%20f ive%20years,torture%20survivors%20to%20get%20justice

[12] Guantánamo prisoner details torture for first time: "I thought I was going to die." (2021, October 29). *The Guardian.* https://www.theguardian.com/us-news/2021/oct/29/going-die-guantanamo-prisoner-torture-testimony

[13] Hajjar, L. (2009). American torture: The price paid, the lessons learned; Pakistan under pressure. *Middle East Report, 251,* 14–19.

[14] Ibid., p. 15.

[15] After 30 years, accountability for police torture in Chicago (2015, April 15). *Amnesty International.* https://www.amnestyusa.org/after-30-years-accountability-for-police-torture-in-chicago/

[16] Wallen, J. (2021, July 27). Detainees held without trial in Kashmir accuse police of widespread abuse. The Telegraph. https:// www.telegr aph.co.uk/ glo bal-

[17] Forced sterilization of Indigenous women in Canada (n.d.). *International Justice Resource Center.* https://ijrcenter.org/forced-sterilization-of-indigenous-women-in-canada/

Canadians,[18] Vietnam-era repatriated prisoners of war,[19] incarcerated individuals who suffered solitary confinement,[20] and political prisoners from Nepal,[21] El Salvador,[22] and Sri Lanka,[23] among others. Many other nations, such as France, Britain, Chile, Turkey, Syria, Saudi Arabia, China, India, and others, for myriad reasons have either perpetuated in the past or continue to perpetrate human rights violations and sanction torture.

"It is the system that produces this violence," believes the refugee Behrouz Boochani,[24] highlighting the insidious apparatus of torture. In the United States, for instance, prominent members of the American Psychological Association (APA)[25] colluded with the CIA and the Department of Defense to enable the torture of detainees through rectal rehydration (rectal feeding without medical necessity, a form of rape), "waterboarding," "wallings (slamming detainees against walls),"[26] and other methods shielding the US torture program.[27,28] In addition, thousands of Muslim prisoners of war were also held in

[18]   Sutton, T. (2021, June 29). Canada has lost its halo: We must confront our Indigenous genocide. *The Guardian*. https://www.theguardian.com/global-development/commentisfree/2021/jun/29/canada-has-lost-its-halo-we-must-confront-our-indigenous-genocide

[19]   Park, C. L., Kaiser, A. P., Spiro, A., King, D. W., & King, L. A. (2012). Does wartime captivity affect late-life mental health? A study of Vietnam-era repatriated prisoners of war. *Research in Human Development, 9*(3), 191–209.

[20]   UNHCR. (2020, February 28). *United States: Prolonged solitary confinement amounts to psychological torture.* https://www.ohchr.org/EN/NewsEvents/Pages/DisplayNews.aspx?NewsID=25633

[21]   Kienzler, H., & Sapkota, R. P. (2020). The long-term mental health consequences of torture, loss, and insecurity: A qualitative study among survivors of armed conflict in the Dang district of Nepal. *Frontiers in Psychiatry, 10*, 941.

[22]   El Salvador massacre: A 30-year fight for justice. Amnesty International. (2011, December 12). Amnesty International. https://www.amnesty.org/en/latest/news/2011/12/el-salvador-massacre-year-fight-justice/

[23]   Human Rights Watch. (2022, February 7). *"In a legal black hole": Sri Lanka's failure to reform the Prevention of Terrorism Act.* https://www.hrw.org/report/2022/02/07/legal-black-hole/sri-lankas-failure-reform-prevention-terrorism-act

[24]   Bhatia, M., & Bruce-Jones, E. (2021). Time, torture and Manus Island: An interview with Behrouz Boochani and Omid Tofighian. *Institute of Race Relations, 62*(3), 77–87.

[25]   "The APA is the largest . . . professional organization of psychologists . . . , with over 146,000 members" who are "scientists, clinicians, consultants, and" researchers in the United States, and many others around the world: American Psychological Association. (2023, June 7). In *Wikipedia*. https://en.wikipedia.org/wiki/American_Psychological_Association. Sources for the APA's role in collusion: Chappell, B. (2017, August 17). Psychologists behind CIA "enhanced interrogation" program settle detainees' lawsuit. *NPR*. https://www.npr.org/sections/thetwo-way/2017/08/17/544183178/psychologists-behind-cia-enhanced-interrogation-program-settle-detainees-lawsuit; Risen, J. (2015). American Psychological Association bolstered the CIA torture program, report says. *The New York Times*. https://www.nytimes.com/2015/05/01/us/report-says-american-psychological-association-collaborated-on-torture-justification.html

[26]   S. Rep. No. 113-288 (2013–2014, p. 2). https://www.congress.gov/113/crpt/srpt288/CRPT-113srpt288.pdf

[27]   Hoffman, D., Carter, D. J., Lopez, C. R. V., Benzmiller, H. L., Guo, A. V. Esq., Latifi, S. Y., & Craig, D. C. (2015, September 4). *Report to the special committee of the board of directors of the American Psychological Association: Independent review relating to APA ethics guidelines, national security interrogations, and torture.* https://www.apa.org/independent-review/revised-report.pdf.

[28]   Torture of detainees both abroad and in the United States was conducted by the psychologists of the APA and other government officials. "The APA is the largest . . . professional organization of psychologists . . . , with over 146,000 members" who are "scientists, clinicians, consultants, and"

detention by the US military in foreign detention centers including some women and boys where they were subject to physical and psychological abuse.[29,30,31] The APA had strong reasons to suspect abusive interrogations had occurred and would likely continue to occur, according to David Hoffman, a Chicago-based lawyer who led the investigation. Reporting on APA's extensive collaboration with the government Hoffman reported that the APA had "strategically avoided taking steps to learn information to confirm those suspicions." The report also revealed how the APA shielded those psychologists involved from censure. Boochani, who was held for 4 years in the Australian-run Manus Island detention center in Papua New Guinea, underscored the complicities of practitioners in perpetuating torture:[32]

And another thing I think is very important is the role of medical practitioners which is a major part of this systematic torture. So then, we can talk about the security companies and the guards, you know. But people who look at us from outside, they think when we talk about torture, they imagine physical torture that comes from the guards and security. But I think the main torture first comes from the doctors and nurses and the psychologists who were working there.

From Boochani's perspective, it isn't only the APA's deliberate strategy of being willfully ignorant that was harmful to the public, scientific community, and its members. It was not also that its collusion flaunted the Association's human rights obligations to the Convention, nor that it sidestepped scientific literature and failed to provide evidence for the effectiveness of harsh interrogation tactics. Rather, in outlining a hierarchical structure of power and authority by those who are looked up to as "experts," Boochani alluded to the important role played by a

researchers in the United States, and many others around the world: American Psychological Association. (2023, June 7). In *Wikipedia.* https://en.wikipedia.org/wiki/American_Psychological_Association. Source for the Hoffman Report: Hoffman, D., Carter, D. J., Lopez, C. R. V., Benzmiller, H. L., Guo, A. V. Esq., Latifi, S. Y., & Craig, D. C. (2015, September 4). *Report to the special committee of the board of directors of the American Psychological Association: Independent review relating to APA ethics guidelines, national security interrogations, and torture.* https://www.apa.org/independent-review/revised-report.pdf.

29 Higham, S., & Stephens, J. (2004, May 21). New details of prison abuse emerge. *Washington Post.* https://www.washingtonpost.com/archive/politics/2004/05/21/new-details-of-prison-abuse-emerge/7346e4cb-47f8-42ab-8897-38a021a1bd0c/
30 Iraqi women raped at Abu Ghraib: Reports. (2013, August 22). *SBS News.* https://www.sbs.com.au/news/iraqi-women-raped-at-abu-ghraib-reports
31 Frank, T. (2018, March 23). Fatima Boudchar was bound, gagged and photographed naked: John McCain wants to know if Gina Haspel's okay with that. *Buzzfeed News.* https://www.buzzfeednews.com/article/thomasfrank/fatima-bouchar-was-bound-gagged-and-photographed-naked-john
32 Bhatia, M., & Bruce-Jones, E. (2021). Time, torture and Manus Island: An interview with Behrouz Boochani and Omid Tofighian. *Institute of Race Relations, 62*(3), 77–87.

society's institutions to strive for a balance of power in its interactions within and treatment of those it serves.

Although it has been over 7 years since the release of the Hoffman Report, the APA has not acknowledged the result of its actions nor the harms to the diverse populations it serves, including Muslims and other minorities with whom its clinicians painstakingly worked to build trust. Our commitment to refugee mental health can be bolstered with greater insight into the structure of our institutions and their entrenched internal hierarchies of power. Espousing human rights at the levels of teaching, training, and practice will help reinstate these rights, demonstrate that not "all suffering is equal,"[33] and remind us not to conflate poor mental health with cultural differences alone.

For world citizens and clinicians alike, there is value in understanding, as Paul Freire[34] said, how the subjugated can internalize the guidelines, image, and consciousness of their oppressor. Many communities, especially those of color, can have unique and marked histories of oppression. As a result, the subjugated can carry the deeply embedded beliefs and guidelines instilled by the oppressor that can remain unquestioned even when upheld in institutional practices. A collaborative understanding of torture with its physical and psychological sequelae can support comprehensive, expedient, and systemic repair and rehabilitative efforts for survivors. Their right to redress, including physical and psychological healing, is internationally recognized under the Convention Against Torture[35] (Article 14, General Comment 3[36]), and other human rights treaties. Specialized health care for torture survivors is our universal duty according to General Comment 3, regardless of where they were tortured, who tortured them, or whether they have filed formal legal complaints.[37]

[33] Farmer, P. (2009). On suffering and structural violence: A view from below. *Race/Ethnicity: Multidisciplinary Global Contexts, 3*(1), 11–28.

[34] Freire, P. (1973). *Pedagogy of the oppressed.* Seabury Press.

[35] Office of the United Nations High Commissioner of Human Rights. General Assembly resolution 39/46. Convention against torture and other cruel, inhuman or degrading treatment or punishment (G.A. res.39/46, art.14). (1984, December 10). https://www.ohchr.org/en/professionalinterest/pages/cat.aspx

[36] Grossman, C. M., Sveaass, N., & Gaer, F. (2018). *Rehabilitation in Article 14 of the Convention against torture and other cruel, inhuman, or degrading treatment or punishment.* https://digitalcommons.wcl.american.edu/facsch_lawrev/576/

[37] Villalba, C. S. (2009, December). *Rehabilitation as a form of reparation under international law* (pp. 58–63) [Paper]. The Redress Trust. https://www.refworld.org/pdfid/4c46c5972.pdf

Refugees and Torture: The Disappeared, the Dead, and the Detained

Being a refugee is the leading risk factor[38] for torture. It is estimated that 5%–35%[39,40,41,42,43] of the world's refugees are tortured; more recent studies peg it between 29%[44] and 35%.[45] But, by its nature, torture is often secret, likely resulting in underestimation of these figures.

Dramatically increasing the odds of torture are membership in a minority group, being in detention, and ongoing societal unrest[46] that can heighten opacity in the treatment of specific type of people. Three other factors can contribute to underestimating the prevalence of torture:

1. Definitions of *torture*, including the Convention's, can be circumscribed, excluding the sexually torturous violence women endure[47] as well as the range of sexual torture of men.[48] Although sexual violence is frequently employed as a weapon of war, men as survivors of sexual and gender-based violence are marginalized in counts, policy and practice;[49] and violence toward women constitutes torture only when state actors perpetrate it.[50]

[38] Başoğlu, M. (1992). *Torture and its consequences: Current treatment approaches*. Cambridge University Press.

[39] Baker, R. (1992). Psychosocial consequences for tortured refugees seeking asylum and refugee status in Europe. In M. Basoglu (Ed.), *Torture and its consequences: Current treatment approaches* (pp. 83–106). Cambridge University Press.

[40] Montgomery, E., & Foldspang, A. (1994). Criterion-related validity of screening for exposure to torture. *Danish Medical Bulletin, 41*, 588–591.

[41] Eisenman, D. P., Keller, A. S., & Kim, G. (2000). Survivors of torture in a general medical setting. *Western Journal of Medicine, 172*, 301–304.

[42] Jaranson, J. M., Butcher, J., Halcon, L., Johnson, D. R., Robertson, C., Savik, K., Spring, M., & Westermeyer, J. (2004). Somali and Oromo refugees: Correlates of torture and trauma history. *American Journal of Public Health, 94*(4), 591–598.

[43] Kinzie, J. D., Kinzie, J. M., Sedighi, B., Woticha, A., Mohamed, H., & Riley, C. (2012). Prospective one-year treatment outcomes of tortured refugees: A psychiatric approach. *Torture, 22*(1), 1–10.

[44] Ostergaard, L. S., Wallach-Kildemoes, H., Thøgersen, M. H., Dragsted, U. B., Oxholm, A., Hartling, O., & Norredam, M. (2020). Prevalence of torture and trauma history among immigrants in primary care in Denmark: Do general practitioners ask? *European Journal of Public Health, 30*(6), 1163–1168.

[45] Baker, R. (1992). Psychosocial consequences for tortured refugees seeking asylum and refugee status in Europe. In M. Basoglu (Ed.), *Torture and its consequences* (pp. 83–106). Cambridge University Press.

[46] Weinstein, H., Dansky, L., & Iacopino, V. (1996). Torture and war trauma survivors in primary care. *Western Journal of Medicine, 165*, 112–118.

[47] Canning, V. (2016). Unsilencing sexual torture: Responses to refugees and asylum seekers in Denmark. *British Journal of Criminology, 56*(3), 438–455.

[48] Carlson, E. S. (2006). The hidden prevalence of male sexual assault during war: Observations on blunt trauma to the male genitals. *British Journal of Criminology, 46*(1), 16–25.

[49] Edström, J., & Dolan, C. (2019). Breaking the spell of silence: Collective healing as activism amongst refugee male survivors of sexual violence in Uganda. *Journal of Refugee Studies, 32*(2), 175–196. https://doi.org/10.1093/jrs/fey022

[50] Canning, V. (2016). Unsilencing sexual torture: Responses to refugees and asylum seekers in Denmark. *British Journal of Criminology, 56*(3), 438–455.

2. The prevalence rates of reported torture vary[51] based on the heterogeneity of torture survivors;[52] survivors are affected by geographies and country of origin,[53] gender, and clinical profiles.[54,55]

3. Many asylum-seekers or detainees routinely die in detention[56] or during transportation to detention sites,[57] and the absence of witnesses can make it impossible to document their experiences. For instance, consider the controversial death of the Black detainee Oscar Lucky Okwurime, who died in the UK's Harmondsworth detention center, with the key witnesses deported by the government.[58]

Studies of displaced refugees from the Middle East estimate the prevalence of torture to be higher compared to refugees originating from other geographical locations, affecting 56%[59] of refugees and possibly as high as 76%.[60] Between 2011 and 2019, an estimated 14,298 Syrians died[61] as a result of torture they endured by any one or a combination of 72 torture methods as evidenced by over 55,000 photos taken by a Syrian military police photographer-archivist known as Caesar.[62,63] Caesar was tasked with photographing the remains of dead detainees

[51] Sigvardsdotter, E., Vaez, M., Hedman, A. R., & Saboonchi, F. (2016). Prevalence of torture and other war related traumatic events in forced migrants: A systematic review. *Torture*, 26(2), 41–73.

[52] Moreno, A., & Grodin, M. (2002). Torture and its neurological sequelae. *Spinal Cord*, 40, 213–223.

[53] Bianchi, I., Focardi, M., Bugelli, M., Pradella, F., Giolli, C., Friani, F., Pinchi, V. (2021). Tortures alleged by migrants in Italy: Compatibility and other medicolegal challenges. *International Journal of Legal Medicine*, 135, 2489–2499. https://doi.org/10.1007/s00414-021-02646-4

[54] Hougen, H. P., Kelstrup, J., Petersen, H. D., & Rasmussen, O. V. (1998). Sequelae to torture. A controlled study of torture victims living in exile. *Forensic Science International*, 36, 153–160.

[55] Rasmussen, O. V., & Lunde, I. (1980). Evaluation of investigation of 200 torture victims. *Danish Medical Bulletin*, 27, 241–243.

[56] UN condemns killings in Libyan detention center [International edition]. (2021, October 11). *China Daily*.

[57] Mackay, N. (2002, June 16). Did the US massacre Taliban. *Sunday Herald*. Retrieved on November 30, 2021, from https://web.archive.org/web/20021205095435/http://www.sundayherald.com/25520

[58] Townsend, M. (2021, April 17). Witnesses to death "deliberately" deported from the UK. *The Guardian*.

[59] Willard, C. L., Rabin, M., & Lawless, M. (2014). The prevalence of torture and associated symptoms in United States Iraqi refugees. *Journal of Immigrant and Minority Health*, 16(6), 1069–1076.

[60] Sigvardsdotter, E., Vaez, M., Rydholm Hedman, A. M., & Saboonchi, F. (2016). Prevalence of torture and other war related traumatic events in forced migrants: A systematic review. *Torture*, 26(2), 41–73.

[61] Syrian Network for Human Rights. (2021, October 20). *Documentation of 72 torture methods the Syrian regime continues to practice in its detention centers and military hospitals*. Retrieved on October 20, 2021, from https://sn4hr.org/wp-content/pdf/english/

[62] Safi, M. (2019, October 23). Syrian regime inflicts 72 forms of torture on prisoners, report finds. *The Guardian*. https://www.theguardian.com/world/2019/oct/23/syrian-regime-inflicts-72-forms-of-torture-on-prisoners-report-finds

[63] Syrian Network for Human Rights. (2021, October 20). *Documentation of 72 torture methods the Syrian regime continues to practice in its detention centers and military hospitals*. Retrieved on October 20, 2021, from https://sn4hr.org/wp-content/pdf/english/

in a military hospital in Damascus. The photos provide visual proof of torture methods such as using the back of a grenade to smash the teeth of a 15-year-old child detainee and spraying insecticide all over his body, scalding him with boiling hot water, using garden shears to sever body parts and to rape, and other forms of sexual violence. Cesar turned defector after downloading thousands of his high-resolution photographs, which he smuggled out of the country. Caesar was removed from Syria by an extraction team, hidden in a truck bed, and moved across the Jordanian border with the incriminating evidence on thumb drives hidden in his shoes.

According to Paulo Pinheiro,[64] UN Commission of Inquiry on Syria Chair, 1.2 million Syrians have been arrested or detained at some point, and "nearly every surviving detainee has emerged from custody having suffered unimaginable abuses." Caesar's documentations served to provide evidence of the torture perpetrated against those who were detained, or who disappeared, and how military hospitals served as dumping grounds for the disposal of tortured bodies.

Next, the trauma generated by torture in comparison to other traumatic events is much greater.[65] Let us review the sequelae of torture.

The High Voltage of Torture: Torture as a Chronic Condition

Across cultures,[66] the presence of torture in one's history can skyrocket survivors' posttraumatic stress to rates as high as 67%[67,68] (versus 20% for conflict-zone

---

[64] OHCHR. (2016, February 8). *Syrian civilians suffering large-scale and widespread executions and deaths in detention centres on all sides of the conflict.* https://www.ohchr.org/en/NewsEvents/Pages/DisplayNews.aspx?NewsID=17020

[65] In an analysis of 181 surveys comprising of 81,866 refugees and conflict-affected people from 40 countries, researchers Steel et al. found that when torture was reported by respondents, it resulted in the highest likelihood of posttraumatic stress syndrome, more so than the combined effect of other traumatic events. At the same time and somewhat misleadingly, high rates of posttraumatic stress can cause torture to be conflated with it or inversely, not meeting the criteria of posttraumatic stress does not imply the absence of torture: Steel, Z., Chey, T., Silove, D., Marnane, C., Bryant, R. A., van Ommeren, M. (2009). Association of torture and other potentially traumatic events with mental health outcomes among populations exposed to mass conflict and displacement: A systematic review and meta-analysis. *JAMA, 302*(5), 537–549. https://doi.org/10.1001/jama.2009.1132

[66] Van Ommeren, M., Sharma, B., Sharma, G. K., Komproe, I., Cardeña, E., & De Jong, J. T. V. M. (2002). The relationship between somatic and PTSD symptoms among Bhutanese refugee torture survivors: Examination of comorbidity with anxiety and depression. *Journal of Traumatic Stress, 15*(5), 415–421.

[67] Westermeyer, J., & Williams, M. (1998). Three categories of victimization among refugees in a psychiatric clinic. In J. Jarason & M. Popkin (Eds.), *Caring for victims of torture* (pp. 61–88). American Psychiatric Press.

[68] McNally, R. (1992). Psychopathology of post-traumatic stress disorder: Boundaries of the syndrome. In M. Basoglu (Ed.), *Torture and its consequences: Current treatment approaches* (pp. 229–252). Cambridge University Press.

refugees who do not experience torture) and 88.3%.[69] Moisander and Edston,[70] in their study of 160 refugees from six different nations with a history of torture in their homelands, found that posttraumatic stress rates ranged from 69% to 92%. Additionally, there are other[71] psychological conditions in the aureole of posttraumatic stress, including major depression, anxiety disorder, psychosis or brief psychotic reactions, sexual dysfunction, substance abuse, chronic organic brain syndrome, and attentional and cognitive difficulties. War-affected survivors of torture appear to be at high risk for neurological and cognitive impairments, chronic pain, unexplained somatization, and substance abuse. Some of the most common pain sequelae are chronic headache (often accompanied by poor quality of sleep),[72] low back pain, and joint pain.[73]

Described as a silent epidemic sweeping the world,[74] torture's lethal effects can punctuate survivors' daily lives and affect entire communities. For many forcibly displaced populations, history of torture and complex trauma can predict wide-ranging debilitating mental and physical ailments, negatively impacting their relationships and later years.

Years after exposure in tortured refugees,[75] psychiatric symptoms can be obdurate, suggesting an additional loss of ability to cope with aging. Torture is also a risk factor for chronic illness. Among war-injured refugees (including those who had been tortured) newly arrived in Sweden, 73% reported chronic pain of considerable intensity localized to body regions affected by war injuries; the prevalence of PTSD varies with pain location and was most prevalent in persons with widespread pain (versus localized pain such as orofacial pain or migraine).[76] Two years after arrival in Sweden, only 6% of refugees reported a reduction in pain.[77]

[69] Schubert, C. C., & Punamäki, R. L. (2011). Mental health among torture survivors: Cultural background, refugee status and gender. *Nordic Journal of Psychiatry, 65*, 175–182.

[70] Moisander, P. A., & Edston, E. (2003). Torture and its sequel—a comparison between victims from six countries *Forensic Science International, 137*(2–3), 133–140.

[71] Weinstein, H., Dansky, L., & Iacopino, V. (1996). Torture and war trauma survivors in primary care. *Western Journal of Medicine, 165*, 112–118.

[72] Ashina, H., Al-Khazali, H.M., Iljazi, A., Ashina, S., Amin, F. M., Lipton, R. B., & Schytz, H. W. (2021). Psychiatric and cognitive comorbidities of persistent post-traumatic headache attributed to mild traumatic brain injury. *Journal of Headache and Pain, 22*, 83.

[73] Moisander, P. A., & Edston, E. (2003). Torture and its sequel—a comparison between victims from six countries *Forensic Science International, 137*(2–3), 133–140.

[74] Weinstein, H., Dansky, L., & Iacopino, V. (1996). Torture and war trauma survivors in primary care. *Western Journal of Medicine, 165*, 112–118.

[75] Carlsson, J. M., Olsen, D. R., Mortensen, E. L., & Kastrup, M. (2006). Mental health and health-related quality of life: A 10-year follow-up of tortured refugees. *Journal of Nervous and Mental Disease, 194*(10), 725–731.

[76] Siqveland, J., Hussain, A., Lindström, J. C., Torleif, R., & Hauff, E. (2017). Prevalence of posttraumatic stress disorder in persons with chronic pain: A meta-analysis. *Frontiers in Psychiatry, 14*(8), 164. https://doi.org/10.3389/fpsyt.2017.00164

[77] Hermansson, A. C., Thyberg, M., Timka, T., & Gerdle, B. (2001). Survival with pain: An eight-year follow-up of war-wounded refugees. *Medicine, Conflict and Survival, 17*(2), 102–111.

Torture's effects make it increasingly likely that medical providers and therapists in a range of settings will likely encounter survivors of torture. But key personal and systemic factors often prevent torture survivors' experiences[78] from being considered in national asylum processes. For one, male survivors of sexual trauma may wait years before revealing sexual trauma. Gulnaz says, "Every time I want to share, I want to cry."

Tortured refugees are a high-risk group[79] with a chronic condition(s) that can affect their personalities,[80] quality of life, and integration.[81] Some additional factors that can cause torture survivors to fall between the cracks are failure to consider torture within a cultural framework, gaps in medical and legislative systems, and the absence of specialized mental health professionals trained in the effects of torture employed in the asylum process.

Somatic Maelstrom: Bad Things Reside in My Body

"When I was electrocuted," shares Gulnaz, "its sheer force thrust me against the wall, but my body kept on thrashing. After such shocks, I could not remember what had happened. My tongue would be paralyzed. I could not talk. I could not walk. Anything I would hold my tongue or my hands would fall." A disquiet in the forms of nerves that quiver, pulsate, and ache have invaded his body. Many other torture survivors also describe its after-effects as an internal level of agitation.[82] For an extraordinary savage event, its effects can be profound for the survivor and, yet can exist as soundless sufferings for those who love him. When his nerves tremble, he tells himself, "it is not happening to you."

Electrocution inflicts powerful effects on disability and morbidity. Even when mortality may be low, it has a short-term and long-term impacts.[83] Some of its

---

[78] Harris, L. M. (2019, May 6). Withholding protection. *50.3 Columbia Human Rights Law Review*, 1. SSRN. https://ssrn.com/abstract=3383646

[79] Song, S. J., Subica, A., Kaplan, C., Tol, W., & de Jong, J. (2018). Predicting the mental health and functioning of torture survivors. *Journal of Nervous and Mental Disease, 206*(1), 33–39.

[80] Luban, D., & Newell, K. S. (2019). Personality disruption as mental torture: The CIA, interrogational abuse, and the U.S. Torture Act. *Georgetown Law Faculty Publications and Other Works*, 2214.

[81] Jesuthasan, J., Sönmez, E., Abels, I., Kurmeyer, C., Gutermann, J., Kimbel, R., Krüger, A., Nikewski, G., Stangier, U., Wollny, A. Zier, U. Oertelt-Prigione, A., & Shouler-Ocak, M. (2018). Near-death experiences, attacks by family members, and absence of health care in their home countries affect the quality of life of refugee women in Germany: A multi-region, cross-sectional, gender-sensitive study, *BMC Medicine, 16*(1), 15.

[82] Haenel, F. (2001). Foreign bodies in the soul. In S. Graessner, N. Gurris, & C. Pross (Eds.), *At the side of torture survivors treating a terrible assault on human dignity* (pp. 1–28). Johns Hopkins University Press.

[83] In particular, the nature of electric current and electrocution, frequency, and variability, discuss the physicians Wesner and Hickie, affect future psychological symptoms: personality changes,

effects can have a delayed onset of 1–5 years.[84] The trembling reported by Gulnaz is most likely due to damaged proprioceptive nerves, most prone to injury with direct electrocution.[85] Under ordinary circumstances, proprioceptive nerves are considered by some to be our sixth sense[86] or our "muscular sense." This system plays an integral role in our reflexes and sense of physical self. It helps us feel our touch, maintain our balance in the dark, control the tone in our voice, and learn new dance steps.

The kind of torture inflicted, some research suggests, can affect the nature of injuries. For instance, physical torture is associated with posttraumatic stress and insomnia,[87] and sexual torture with depression, insomnia, and somatization.

Torture's physical effects can include, among other complex injuries, benign depigmented[88] and diffuse scars[89] from burnings; headaches and injuries[90]

difficulty with verbal memory and attention, emotional issues such as irritability and anger, and cognitive ones such as verbal memory, executive functioning, and attention in those who did not have such prior issues. Gulnaz reports being knocked away and being unconscious by electric shocks force; both are correlated with depression and posttraumatic stress. The full details of the nature of electrocution and of torture are beyond the scope of the interview, and additionally, Gulnaz is also not able to access the full extent of his memory of the episode. When instead of being knocked away, involuntary muscular contractions cause victims to stick to the current, their bodies can exhibit a "no-let-go" response, locking them into prolonged shock and exacerbating the injury's extent. The effects of electrical injury in industrial workers and electricians whose hazardous injuries occurred at work, say Wesner and Hickie are subtle, pervasive, and powerful despite the lapse of time. An overwhelming proportion (78%) of electric injury victims who are nonrefugees and nontortured go on to develop a psychiatric diagnosis. According to recent work by the neurologist Yiannopoulou and colleagues, electrical injuries cause complications in the central and peripheral nervous systems, including myelopathy at the spinal cord level, strokes, cerebral syndromes and edema, epileptic seizures, movement disorders, Charcot's paralysis, complex regional pain syndrome (CRPS), and urinary and erectile dysfunctions. Source for long-term sequelae: Wesner, M. L. & Hickie, J. (2013). Long-term sequelae of electrical injury. *Canadian Family Physician, 59*(9), 935–939. Source for a "no-let-go" response: Kelly, K. M., Tkachenko, T. A., Pliskin, N. H., Fink, J. W., & Lee, R.C. (1999). Life after electrical injury: Risk factors for psychiatric sequelae. *Annals of the New York Academy of Sciences, 888*, 356–363. Source for long-term impact of electric injury: Ratnayake, B., Emmanuel, E. R., & Walker, C. C. (1996). Neurological sequelae following a high voltage electrical burn. *Burns, 22*(7), 574–577. Source for electric injury impact on central and peripheral nervous systems: Yiannopoulou, K. G., Papagiannis, G. I., Triantafyllou, A. I., Koulouvaris, P., Anastasiou, A. I., Kontoangelos, K., & Anastasiou, I. P. (2021). Neurological and neurourological complications of electrical injuries. *Polish Journal of Neurology and Neurosurgery, 55*(1), 12–23.

[84] Wesner, M. L., & Hickie, J. (2013). Long-term sequelae of electrical injury. *Canadian Family Physician, 59*(9), 935–939.
[85] Ibid.
[86] Wade, N. J. (2003). The search for a sixth sense: The cases for vestibular, muscle, and temperature senses. *Journal of the History of the Neurosciences, 12*, 175–202.
[87] Tamblyn, J. M., Calderon, A. J., Combs, S., & O'Brien, M. M. (2011). Patients from abroad becoming patients in everyday practice: Torture survivors in primary care. *Journal of Immigrant and Minority Health, 13*, 798–801.
[88] Danielsen, L. (1992). Skin changes after torture. *Torture, 2*(1, Suppl.), 27–28.
[89] Rasmussen, O. V. (1990). Medical aspects of torture. *Danish Medical Bulletin, 37*(1, Suppl.), 1–88.
[90] Mollica, R. F., Donelan, K., Tor, S., Lavelle, J., Elias, C., Frankel, M., & Blendon, R. J. (1993). The effect of trauma and confinement on functional health and mental health status of Cambodians living in Thailand-Cambodia border camps. *JAMA, 70*(5), 581–586.

from blows to head; bitten lips due to the application of electricity; rattling sound of the tongue-bone from beatings to the neck; sexual dysfunction from genito-urinal insertions; muscle-pains[91] from being suspended; eye injuries and vision loss caused by violent shaking;[92] and loss of consciousness, seizures, and incontinence[93] as a result of suffocation.[94] Although tortured refugees bear both psychological and physical injuries, the psychological can often be the most grave.[95]

Chronic Pain Syndrome

Unexplained somatization is higher across the lifespan in refugees[96] than in the general Western population. Somatic complaints manifesting as chronic pain syndromes[97] are especially common among some cultural populations. Among German resettled female Yazidis who witnessed 2.5% of their population killed within days and who endured sexual and physical torture for at least 7 months on average, pain is the most frequent somatic complaint, followed by feelings of suffocation and movement disorders.[98] Given the greater degree of somatization including pain among Yazidi female refugees (who have also experienced severe and collective trauma as a community) versus other tortured female refugees such as Syrian-Kurdish[99] and Rwandans,[100] Caroline Rometsch

[91] Rasmussen, O. V. (1990). Medical aspects of torture. *Danish Medical Bulletin, 37*(1, Suppl.), 1–88.

[92] Derrick, P. (1997). Shaken adult syndrome. *American Journal of Forensic Medicine and Pathology, 18*, 321–324.

[93] Moreno, A., & Grodin, M. (2002). Torture and its neurological sequelae. *Spinal Cord, 40*, 213–223.

[94] Berryman, P. (1993). Chile: *Comisión Nacional de Verdad y Reconciliación* [Report of the Chilean National Commission on Truth and Reconciliation]. University of Notre Dame Press. https://www.usip.org/sites/default/files/resources/collections/truth_commissions/Chile90-Report/Chile90-Report.pdf

[95] Haenel, F. (2001). Foreign bodies in the soul. In S. Graessner, N. Gurris, & C. Pross (Eds.), *At the side of torture survivors treating a terrible assault on human dignity* (pp. 1–28). Johns Hopkins University Press.

[96] Rohlof, H. G., Knipscheer, J. W., & Kleber, R .J. (2014). Somatization in refugees: A review. *Social Psychiatry and Psychiatric Epidemiology, 49*(11), 1793–1804.

[97] Thomsen, A., Eriksen, J., & Smidt-Nielsen, K. (2000). Chronic pain in torture survivors. *Forensic Science International, 108*, 155–163.

[98] Rometsch, C., Denkinger, J. K., Engelhardt, M., Windthorst, P., Graf, J., Gibbons, N., Pham, P., Zipfel, S., & Junne, F. (2020). Pain, somatic complaints, and subjective concepts of illness in traumatized female refugees who experienced extreme violence by the "Islamic State" (IS). *Journal of Psychosomatic Research, 130*, 109931.

[99] Ibrahim, H., & Hassan, C. Q. (2017). Post-traumatic stress disorder symptoms resulting from torture and other traumatic events among Syrian Kurdish refugees in Kurdistan Region, Iraq, *Frontiers in Psychology, 8*, 241.

[100] Pham, P. N. Weinstein, H. M., & Longman, T. (2004). Trauma and PTSD symptoms in Rwanda: Implications for attitudes toward justice and reconciliation. *JAMA, 292*(5), 602–612.

and colleagues[101] underscore the need to consider factors such as collective identification within communities, religious beliefs, historical trauma,[102] and transgenerational traumatization. The presence of pain explains the almost 33% variance in the subjective well-being of Islamic State of Iraq and Syria survivors.[103] Chronic pain as a barometer of feelings of wellness, and the reverse, psychological functioning[104] and its bidirectional relationship with pain,[105] must be taken into account.

Headaches are also common,[106,107] with as many as 93% of survivors[108] reporting them; these could be the result of head or brain injury caused by torture. In Rasmussen's[109] research, 73% of subjects suffered a beating to the head, and 64% complained of headaches at the time of the interview and recalled experiencing headaches during torture. As a result of the widespread belief that all non-Western populations may express distress in physical ways, many doctors treat surface symptoms such as physical pain or fatigue and may never get to the root of psychological causes of the pain. Instead, neurological and psychosomatic symptomatology can illustrate the role of indirect pathways from torture to mental health.

[101] Rometsch, C., Denkinger, J. K., Engelhardt, M., Windthorst, P., Graf, J., Gibbons, N., Pham, P., Zipfel, S., & Junne, F. (2020). Pain, somatic complaints, and subjective concepts of illness in traumatized female refugees who experienced extreme violence by the "Islamic State" (IS). *Journal of Psychosomatic Research*, *130*, 109931.

[102] Kizilhan, J. I., & Noll-Hussong, M. (2017). Individual, collective, and transgenerational traumatization in the Yazidi. *BMC Medicine*, *15*, 198.

[103] Rometsch, C., Denkinger, J. K., Engelhardt, M., Windthorst, P., Graf, J., Gibbons, N., Pham, P., Zipfel, S., & Junne, F. (2020). Pain, somatic complaints, and subjective concepts of illness in traumatized female refugees who experienced extreme violence by the "Islamic State" (IS). *Journal of Psychosomatic Research*, *130*, 109931.

[104] Burke, A. L., Mathias, J. L., & Denson, L. A. (2015). Psychological functioning of people living with chronic pain: A meta-analytic review. *British Journal of Clinical Psychology*, *54*(3), 345–360.

[105] Campanini, M. Z., González, A. D., Andrade, S. M., Girotto, E., Cabrera, M. A. S., Guidoni, C. M., Araujo, P. C. A., & Mesas, A. E. (2022). Bidirectional associations between chronic low back pain and sleep quality: A cohort study with schoolteachers. *Physiology & Behavior*, *254*, 113880. https://doi.org/10.1016/j.physbeh.2022.113880

[106] Riquelme, H. U. (1995). *Entre la obediencia y la oposición: Los médicos y la ética profesional bajo la dictadura militar* [Between obedience and opposition: The practice of medicine under a totalitarian regime]. Nueva Sociedad.

[107] Mollica, R., Donelan, K., Tors, S., Lavell, J., Elias, C., Frankel, M., & Blendon, R. J. (1993). The effect of trauma and confinement on functional health and mental health status of Cambodians living in Thailand-Cambodia border camps. *JAMA*, *270*(5), 581–586.

[108] Williams, A. C. de C., & Amris, K. (2007). Pain from torture. *Pain*, *133*(1), 5–8.

[109] Rasmussen, O. (1990). Medical aspects of torture. *Danish Medical Bulletin*, *37*(1, Suppl.), 1–88.

Trauma and Memory: "You've Forgotten Your Memories, Forget University!"

"I lost my memory after the prison," shares Gulnaz. "Some time passed, but my veins did not stop shivering. Some days I could not get out of bed. So, I went to see a doctor in Aleppo. The doctor said, 'You have very bad things in your body.' I told the doctor I wanted to keep studying. At this, he looked at me and said, 'You are very strange. You've forgotten your memories. How can you complete the University? Forget your University.' The good doctor gave me a medicine called Valpakine. He said that 'it will help you with the shiver of aging.'"
I asked Gulnaz if the doctor knew why he had the shiver of aging, and Gulnaz said, "although nothing was explicitly discussed, from the sympathetic look the doctor gave me it seemed like the doctor, who was also Kurdish, knew what had happened with me."

One might imagine that remembering one's life is an uncomplicated thing. Although research is inconclusive on determining which memories are more likely to be impaired among refugees,[110,111] the nature of prior trauma,[112] postmigration stressors, and demographic factors such as gender and age[113] affect the nature of autobiographical memory recall in refugees. Refugees who suffer from posttraumatic stress or depression, or who have endured aversive experiences such as detention, are challenged in their ability to recall events of their own lives.[114] Further, traumatic memories, encoded by olfactory, auditory, and visual cues,[115] can be involuntarily triggered[116] and may revive unpleasant

[110] Barry, T. J., Lenaert, B., Hermans, D., Raes, F., & Griffith, J. W. (2018). Meta-analysis of the association between autobiographical memory specificity and exposure to trauma. *Journal of Traumatic Stress, 31,* 35–46.

[111] Brown, A. D., Root, J. C., Romano, T. A., Chang, L. J., Bryant, R. A., & Hirst, W. (2013). Overgeneralized autobiographical memory and future thinking in combat veterans with posttraumatic stress disorder. *Journal of Behavior Therapy and Experimental Psychiatry, 44,* 129.

[112] Khan, S., & Haq, S. (2021). Autobiographical memory impairment among Rohingya refugee people: Roles of direct and indirect trauma exposures and PTSD symptom severity. *Cognition and Emotion, 35*(8), 1573–1587.

[113] Khan, S., Kuhn, S. K., & Haque, S. (2021). A systematic review of autobiographical memory and mental health research on refugees and asylum seekers. *Frontiers in Psychiatry, 12,* 658700.

[114] Barry, T. J., Lenaert, B., Hermans, D., Raes, F., & Griffith, J. W. (2018). Meta-analysis of the association between autobiographical memory specificity and exposure to trauma. *Journal of Traumatic Stress, 31,* 35–46; Brown, A. D., Root, J. C., Romano, T. A., Chang, L. J., Bryant, R. A., & Hirst, W. (2013). Overgeneralized autobiographical memory and future thinking in combat veterans with posttraumatic stress disorder. *Journal of Behavior Therapy and Experimental Psychiatry, 44,* 129.

[115] Van der Kolk, B. A. (1996). The body keeps the score: Approaches to the psychobiology of posttraumatic stress disorder. In B. A. van der Kolk, C. McFaralane, & L. Wisaeth (Eds.), *Traumatic stress: The effects of overwhelming experience on mind, body, and society* (pp. 214–244). Guilford Press.

[116] Herlihy, J., & Turner, S. (2009). The psychology of seeking protection. *International Journal of Refugee Law, 21*(2), 171–192.

impressions of smells such as the odor of burning flesh,[117] sensations, and images, such as severed limbs, evisceration, or spilled blood.[118]

These cognitive challenges are associated with trauma: selective recall or a bias in recall of negative memories,[119] recall of incomplete versus specific memories,[120] presentation through a clear chronology, avoidance, and persistent short-term memory loss.[121] However, recent scientific research among unaccompanied minors has found that prior experiences of trauma increased vividness of recall.[122] Nevertheless, increased intensity of posttraumatic symptoms greatly decreased the specificity of biographical memory recall.[123] Survivors of torture suffer from cognitive impairments,[124] contradictions and inconsistencies of memory,[125] and challenges in recollecting[126] things that have happened to them. Asylum-seekers with a sexual assault history can experience memory losses.[127]

[117] Langer, L. (1991). *Holocaust testimonies: The ruins of memory.* Yale University Press.

[118] Hinton, D., Pich, V., Chhean, D., & Pollack, M. Olfactory-triggered panic attacks among Khmer refugees: A contextual approach. (2004). *Transcult Psychiatry, 41*(2), 155–199.

[119] Herlihy, J., Scragg, P., & Turner, S. (2002). Discrepancies in autobiographical memories—implications for the assessment of asylum seekers: Repeated interviews study. *BMJ, 324,* 324–327.

[120] Williams, J. M., Barnhofer, T., Crane, C., Herman, D., Raes, F., Watkins, E., & Dalgleish, T. (2007). Autobiographical memory specificity and emotional disorder. *Psychological Bulletin, 133*(1), 122–148.

[121] Saadi, A., Hampton, K., de Assis, M. V., Mishori, R., Habbach, H., & Haar, R. J. (2021). Associations between memory loss and trauma in US asylum seekers: A retrospective review of medico-legal affidavits. *PLOS One, 16*(3), E0247033.

[122] Skardalsmo Bjorgo, E. M., & Jensen, T. K. (2015). Unaccompanied refugee minors' early life narratives of physical abuse from caregivers and teachers in their home countries. *Child Abuse and Neglect, 48,* 148–159; Wylegała, A. (2015). Child migrants and deportees from Poland and Ukraine after the Second World War: Experience and memory. *European Review of History, 22,* 292–309.

[123] Moradi, A. R., Herlihy, J., Yasseri, G., Shahraray, M., Turner, S. W., & Dalgleish, T. (2008). Specificity of episodic and semantic aspects of autobiographical memory in relation to symptoms of posttraumatic stress disorder (PTSD). *Acta Psychology, 127*(3), 645–653.

[124] Taylor, T. (1992). Opening statement of the prosecution–December 9, 1946. In G. J. Annas & M. Grodin (Eds.), *The Nazi doctors and the Nuremberg Code* (pp. 67–93). Oxford University Press.

[125] Migrationsverket [Swedish Migration Board]. (2001, March 28). *Gender-based persecution: Guidelines for investigation and evaluation of the needs of women for protection* (p. 15). https://www.refworld.org/pdfid/3f8c1a654.pdf

[126] Haenel, F. (2001). Foreign bodies in the soul. In S. Graessner, N. Gurris, & C. Pross (Eds.), *At the side of torture survivors treating a terrible assault on human dignity* (pp. 1–28). Johns Hopkins University Press.

[127] UK Government Home Office. (2018, April 10). *Gender issues in the asylum claim.* https://assets.publishing.service.gov.uk/government/uploads/system/uploads/attachment_data/file/699703/gender-issues-in-the-asylum-claim-v3.pdf

"I Forgot to Tell You I Was Electrocuted": Memory Recall in Torture

Toward the end of our interview, I asked Gulnaz why he had not readily shared the experience of torture. He said, "What happened in Fara-El-Eskani for those 3 months and 3 nights I never shared with a soul. I wanted to tell someone, but I could not because I was scared. I forgot to tell you I was electrocuted."

"It is a dark point in my life. I don't want to come back to Syria again to remember what happened to me. At the same time, every year for the last 14 years, I thought I was in prison. I remember what happened to me. I want to cry alone. It comes to me like a film I have to see. I want to delete it, but I cannot. Whether I want it or not, it is a film I have to see. It is a burden I will carry all my life."

It is natural for torture survivors to wish to forget their torture experiences. Doing so serves many functions: it compartmentalizes overwhelming emotions and can protect survivors from disintegrating; it maintains the prevailing social contract with respect to power, hierarchy, and authority;[128] it supports cultural behaviors and taboos of speaking out on intimate (bodily) matters in public in traditional and conservative groups; and, finally, it reflects how the survivor cannot trust their own recollection of torture.

By far the most potent factor behind forgetting, however, goes beyond survivors' fear of further harm to themselves. For the tortured who have been exposed to the most heinous capacity of another human to inflict pain, their wish to protect the ones they love is among the most important motivator for forgetting. Says Gulnaz:

I was the youngest and favorite son of the family. My mother had asthma, and she was a heart patient. In Syria they (torturers) would say "You are dangerous," they would take every detainee's family also to prison. I didn't want to expose my family. I wanted to keep this secret. I never talked about it for fear that it would expose them to danger. I never shared details of it with my doctor for fear that he might turn into a government informant. I would only say, "I have a problem in my body."

Gulnaz was missing for 3 months plus 3 nights. His family presumed he was in college and busy with his studies and friends. After his detention when he arrived home, his parents never asked him why he spent time alone in his room or why he was walking differently.

---

[128] Herman, J. (1992). *Trauma and recovery*. Basic Books.

Substance Use Disorder

Substance use disorders are high among asylum-seekers with multiple etiologies,[129] but witnessing disasters can increase them,[130,131] and this is considered to be a sign of psychological distress. Thus, in the context of those bearing a disproportionate burden of trauma such as torture survivors, torture can result in a greater susceptibility to increased substance use. But on the other hand, preliminary reports from a Dutch mental health site suggests that, in fact, torture survivors may be more resistant to abusing substances.[132] Scientific research is scarce and documentation limited in the context of survivors exposed to political persecution with regimes that routinely employ torture and harsh interrogation tactics, resulting in custodial deaths.[133,134] Further, there is limited information on the use of substances even among the group most vulnerable to it, such as young men.[135]

Sexual Torture

Sexual violence is widely employed as a weapon of war, taking different forms for men and women. Injuries are severe and long-lasting with physical, psychological, familial, social, and economic impacts. Physical injuries include genital and

---

[129] Asylum-seekers' substance-abuse usage is affected by host country's positive or lenient attitude to alcohol and drug use than the motherland: D'Avanzo, C. E. (1997). Southeast Asians: Asian-Pacific Americans at risk for substance misuse. *Substance Use and Misuse*, 32(7–8), 829–848; Vega, W. A., Kolody, B., Aguilar-Gaxiola, S., Alderete, E., Catalano, R., & Caraveo-Anduaga, J. (1998). Lifetime prevalence of DSM-III-R psychiatric disorders among urban and rural Mexican Americans in California. *Archives of General Psychiatry*, 55(9), 771–778. Substance abuse is used as a coping mechanism for adapting to a new or hostile environment: Yee, B. W. K., & Thu, N. D. (1987). Correlates of drug use and abuse among Indochinese refugees: Mental health implications. *Journal of Psychoactive Drugs*, 19, 17–83.

[130] Berah, E. F., Jones, H. L., & Valent, P. (1984). The experience of a mental health team involved in early phase of a disaster. *Australian and New Zealand Journal of Psychiatry*, 18, 354–358.

[131] Madakasira, S., & O'Brian, K. (1987). Acute posttraumatic stress in victims of a natural disaster. *Journal of Nervous and Mental Disease*, 175(5), 286–290.

[132] European Union Agency for Fundamental Rights (FRA). (2017, February). *Current migration situation in the EU: Torture, trauma and its possible impact on drug use*. https://fra.europa.eu/sites/default/files/fra_uploads/fra-february-2017-monthly-migration-report-focus-torture-trauma_en.pdf

[133] Rizkalla, N., Bakr, O., Alsamman, S., Sbini, S., Masud, H., & Segal, S. P. (2022). The Syrian regime's apparatus for systemic torture: A qualitative narrative study of testimonies from survivors. *BMC Psychiatry*, 787.

[134] Tayler, L., & Epstein, E. (2022, January 9). *Legacy of the "dark side": The costs of unlawful US detention and interrogations post-9/11* [Report]. Human Rights Watch. https://www.hrw.org/news/2022/01/09/legacy-dark-side#_ftn4

[135] FRA. (2017, February). *Current migration situation in the EU: Torture, trauma and its possible impact on drug use*. https://fra.europa.eu/sites/default/files/fra_uploads/fra-february-2017-monthly-migration-report-focus-torture-trauma_en.pdf

rectal trauma;[136] sexually transmitted infections, including HIV; sexual dysfunction; and problems of urinating, defecating, fistulas, and fissures. Impairment and damage to reproductive capacity or sexual dysfunction also occur.[137,138] Male survivors fear the negative implications of the discovery of their sexual torture: being labeled as homosexual; being blamed; and inviting further torture of their families and significant others. These men may believe that the assaults they endured do not qualify as sexual assault;[139] they fear that what happened to them may not be labeled as a crime; and they fear not being able to marry. In the face of male survivors' overwhelming sense of shame and powerlessness, mental health professionals report a range of challenges: psychological distress, difficulties with intimate relations, social withdrawal, depression, posttraumatic stress, and the need to overcompensate through assertions of masculinity[140] and more. In Chapter 7, we explore how war affects the nature and frequency of traumatic events that female refugees endure and the psychological, medical, and social consequences of gender-based violence on refugee women's experiences of suffering.

Ethnicity, Religion, and the Social Contract of Torture

The Torture of the English Teacher

In 2012 when the Syrian Army started to round up folks for prison, Gulnaz fled to Erbil, capital of Kurdistan, Iraq. He eked a living through teaching English literature at private schools and refugee camps through a modest salary, moving from city to city. He was forced out of teaching altogether when, given the Islamic State's domineering presence in the summer of 2014, the Kurdish government diverted funds away from education. As the Islamic State captured the refugee camp where Gulnaz had been teaching and declared itself the Caliphate, demanding that all Muslims pledge allegiance (bay'ah), Gulnaz felt, "I should go to Europeland. Maybe there I will find a new future. Maybe I will rebuild my life. Iraq had got

---

[136] UNHCR. (2017, October). *"We keep it in our heart": Sexual violence against men and boys in the Syria crisis.* https://www.refworld.org/docid/5a128e814.html

[137] All Survivors Project. (2018, September 6). *Destroyed from within: Sexual violence against men and boys in Syria and Turkey.* https://reliefweb.int/sites/reliefweb.int/files/resources/ASP_Syria_Rep ort.pdf

[138] Van Tienhoven, H. (1993). Sexual dysfunction can have other sources such as malnutrition: It does not always result from sexual assault. "Sexual torture of male victims." *Torture*, 3(4), 133–135.

[139] Ibid.

[140] All Survivors Project. (2018, September 6). *Destroyed from within: Sexual violence against men and boys in Syria and Turkey* (p. 25). https://reliefweb.int/sites/reliefweb.int/files/resources/ASP_S yria_Report.pdfhttps://reliefweb.int/sites/reliefweb.int/files/resources/ASP_Syria_Report.pdf

very dangerous. The Islamic State could have forced men like me into their troops. They could have sent me back to Syria, but I did not want to go back to prison one more time . . . ."

"One more time?" I interrupted Gulnaz, who was barely audible. In his long pause that ensued, I wondered if I had imagined him referencing prison.

"One more time" was an opening in our conversation that Gulnaz was willingly providing to me. I do not view it as a slip but rather as an invitation. That comment buried a transformative moment of his life where he chose to open the door to his past. "Were you in prison before?" I asked. Mention of the prison stirred Gulnaz, and he looked as though an invisible force had just knocked him out. Gulnaz, at first motionless, heaved with remembrances of sufferings, mindful also that no solace could be enough. It was at this moment that Gulnaz decided to take us down to the prison in the sewers. And from that moment on, the interview was punctuated by his heavy breathing.

The year was 2004, the year of the Qamishli riot, an uprising by Syrian Kurds in Qamishli city. The riots had sparked during a football match when Syrian Kurds were angered by guest Arab spectators holding up photographs of Saddam Hussain, oppressor of the Kurdish. Feeling provoked, the Kurds in Qamishli broke down a statue of Hafez Al-Assad, the father of Bashar Al-Assad, escalating into a political conflict. Assad's Syrian army began to crack down on Kurdish men by deploying tanks and an army. Paranoia was in the air.

That morning in Spring, Gulnaz had flung on his backpack and left his student dorm, as usual, to go to class. The fragrance of damask roses hung in the air. It was on his way to class that Assad's regime snatched him off the streets. Gulnaz's capture was part of a campaign of persecution against the Kurds with the broader purpose of weakening the group's resistance and wreaking vengeance for the bomb blast.

It was in this political air that Gulnaz, Kurdish and a minority group of Iranian-ethnicity, was dragged to the interrogation chamber. Late into the night, high-ranking generals from the army, "who was always Arab," from Sweida, Daraa, Idlib cities encircled him. They accused Gulnaz of turning Syria into a "Land of the Kurdish" and that, "You've blasted a bomb."

"I am a student!" At first, Gulnaz had reasoned with his torturers. He had wept, "I didn't do anything. I didn't see anything. I have nothing to say!" He had screamed for hours, "but no one seemed to notice nor care." In his wallet, he had been carrying a photograph of Mustafa Barzani, the widely recognized leader of the Kurdish national party by the Kurdish community. Eventually, the photograph alone was reason enough for him to be imprisoned in a prison meant for traitors; his extremely Kurdish-sounding name and accent invited a greater

fury. "My torturers were waiting to hear when I would recognize their truth and confess."

Ethnicity lent the prisoners a ready-made opposing political agenda, and the 60 boys were all labeled as political prisoners. Most of the electrocutions were in the early morning but some went through the night. "There were five or six torturers each day, always Arab although changed daily. The 'detective,' who was some kind of a supervisor, would command the prison guard to take them to the torture chambers for a half-hour, but instead, they would take us to the chambers for 2 hours, saying, 'You are Kurds. You have to die.'"

Little could anyone have imagined the fate that would befall Gulnaz or that such torture campaigns would eventually trigger the forced displacement of more than 13.5 million Syrians; however, according to other respondents, the systematic bias, devaluation, and disenfranchisement of the Kurdish community laid fertile ground for it. The Kurdish have routinely faced harassment and persecution in Syria, including being banned from speaking, writing, or reading in their language, suppression of ethnic identity, and the undocumented status of children born within mixed marriages.[141] For example, in 1962, 20% of Syria's Kurdish population was stripped of its Syrian citizenship. The bias against ethnic groups like the Kurdish can have the effect of normalizing harrowing behavior that it becomes permissible for Gulnaz and other Kurdish young men and women like him to be detained and subject to human rights violations. Torture through brute force serves to reinforce and remind oppressed minorities of the social contract—their lowly status based on their race, ethnicity, gender, or class (in this case, attributed historically to the Kurdish by the majority Arabs). If it is inequity and bias that enable such tremendous violations of human rights, today we also have the knowledge and skills as a civil society to redress them.

The Asylum Application: The Retelling of Torture

Complex factors can affect the recall of the torture story within the asylum process, which can ultimately affect whether or not refugees will be granted protection status or deported to a place where they are exposed to harm. Asylumseekers' reports include difficulty in remembering because of head trauma, the

---

[141] The silenced Kurds. (1996, October). *Human Rights Watch Publications*, 8(4E). https://www.hrw.org/legacy/summaries/s.syria9610.html

refugee's levels of anxiety, denial of the traumatic event, the interview setting, interviewer's knowledge of torture, and distrust of the interview/interviewer.[142]

Refugees' cases within judicial systems can be presented in a language different from their native ones by interpreters who belong to a different ethnicity, gender, or geographical region and, therefore, may not be entirely knowledgeable of their plight and can miss out on the nuances of their experiences. If interpreters belong to a different ethnicity, this raise issues of trust, confidentiality, and ease of sharing. Refugees can report suspicion of the interpreter being a government agent or being susceptible to blackmail by members of the persecuting regime. The victim could be concerned about impending harm toward themselves or their families who may still live in their native countries, as encountered previously. If the interpreter is a relative, fear of hurting[143,144145] the relative may affect their disclosure. The perception that the interpreter is an independent outsider may facilitate trust-building. Conversely, if interpreters were relatives such as children, shame[146] or discomfort may affect full disclosure of the trauma history.

Prior experience with torture by authority figures can also influence the way that refugees share their private information. Asylum interviews are rife with anxiety as they can carry life-changing outcomes for refugees, and settings can also be reminiscent of those in which their interrogations and imprisonment took place. During interrogations in their home countries, refugees describe attempting to withhold information (in vain) lest they implicate family and friends, who in turn could then be rounded up by paramilitary forces and monitored, detained, or themselves subjected to torture. By evoking reminders of past situations where they may have been mistreated by officials in authority positions, German psychotherapists Graessner, Ahmad, and Merkord argue that the asylum process can have a disorienting influence on refugees' accounts, and "they do not influence the refugee's trauma history towards greater precision." The asylum process does not take into account how the survivor's memory and the retelling of the trauma story are affected by the experiences of complex trauma.

[142] USCIS. (2019, December 20). *Interviewing survivors of torture and other severe trauma* [Training module]. https://www.uscis.gov/sites/default/files/document/foia/Interviewing_-_Survi vors_of_Torture_LP_RAIO.pdf

[143] Iacopino, V., Ozkalipci, O., & Schlar, C. (1999). *Istanbul Protocol: Manual on the effective investigation and documentation of torture and other cruel, inhuman or degrading treatment or punishment.* OHCHR. https://www.ohchr.org/documents/publications/training8rev1en.pdf

[144] Physicians for Human Rights. (2012). *Examining asylum seekers: A clinician's guide to physical and psychological evaluations of torture.* Physicians for Human Rights. https://phr.org/our-work/resources/examining-asylum-seekers/

[145] Randall, G. R., & Lutz, E. L. (1991). *Serving survivors of torture: a practical manual for health professionals and other service providers.* American Association for the Advancement of Science.

[146] Moreno, A., & Grodin, M. (2002). Torture and its neurological sequelae. *Spinal Cord, 40,* 213–223.

In fact, it may be our expectations of precise and unwavering data from a person who has endured horrific tragedies that are excessive and unrealistic. The perception of a refugee offering differing versions[147] of their story during the asylum process and inconsistencies can raise red flags for their asylum eligibility and credibility.[148] Jacqueline Rose offers some statements from investigators to asylum seekers reflecting their suspicion of the embattled refugee: "This is not what you told us before," "What you've told me today does not make a great deal of sense," "Your account makes it difficult to accept that this is a true account of a real event."[149]

Skepticism toward the refugee within the asylum system may be the unfortunate and counterintuitive byproduct of being burdened by terrible things. Unspeakable tragedies may be so stupefying in their brutalities and the instinct to preserve the idea of a benign world so strong that it may result in confronting of the victim.[150] For survivors it can mean a diminishment of their experience, creating a re-enactment of their torture experience. In this way the examiner, without consciously realizing it, may identify with the perpetrator and unknowingly perpetuate a culture of mistrust.

The effects of torture can also be missed by physicians[151] treating survivors. For one, muscles can heal without scarring; imaging studies can prove to be negative, and bone bruises can heal without leaving traces. In Eisenman's study in primary care clinics in the United States of foreign-born Latino torture survivors of political violence, none reported that their physician asked about their history of political violence. Only 3% of the patients reported revealing their torture history to their provider (although some other[152] studies have reported a higher percentage) perhaps doubting they would be believed. In addition, few providers are

[147] Graessner, S., Ahmad, S., & Merkord, F. (2001). Everything forgotten! Memory disorders among refugees who of those who have been tortured (J. M. Reimer, Trans.). In S. Graessner, N. Gurris, & C. Pross (Eds.), *At the side of torture survivors: Treating a terrible assault on human dignity* (pp. 184–197). Johns Hopkins University Press. (Original work published 1996).

[148] Kelly, T. (2012). *This side of silence: Human rights, torture, and the recognition of cruelty.* Pennsylvania University Press.

[149] Rose, J. (2019, October 10). Agents of their own abuse. *London Review of Books, 41*(19).

[150] Graessner, S., Ahmad, S., & Merkord, F. (2001). Everything forgotten! Memory disorders among refugees who have been tortured (J. M. Reimer, Trans.). In S. Graessner, N. Gurris, & C. Pross (Eds.), *At the side of torture survivors: Treating a terrible assault on human dignity* (pp. 184–197). Johns Hopkins University Press. (Originally published 1996).

[151] Eisenman, D. P., Gelberg, L., Liu, H., & Shapiro, M. F. (2003). Mental health and health-related quality of life among adult Latino primary care patients living in the United States with previous exposure to political violence. *Journal of American Medical Association, 290,* 627–634.

[152] Crosby, S. S., Norredam, M., Paasche-Orlow, M. K., Piwowarczyk, L., Heeren, T., & Grodin, M. A. (2006). Prevalence of torture survivors among foreign-born patients presenting to an urban ambulatory care practice. *Journal of General Internal Medicine, 21*(7), 764–768.

prepared[153,154,155,156] for the complexities posed by torture survivors, or are familiar with their physical and psychological sequelae. Despite the best efforts of those tending to the survivors of torture, assessment and treatment may remain inadequate as complex trauma's important clues may go undetected: somatization can be viewed as lethargy; memory may evidence "holes," and dissociation may not be recognized.

For an event so searing, pervasive, and powerful, the tortured refugees may believe they have nothing to show for it even if they could muster the language. "No one is willing to listen to the survivors," says Haenel.[157] "No one wants to have anything to do with torture." The torture story is not readily elicited through the screening questions for asylum-seekers, for example, at US borders. There is no access to counsel at borders[158] during their initial screening. There is no evidence to show whether nonverbal data of fear is gathered during these interviews or whether border officials have access to mental health experts who may have had extensive training in interviewing survivors of torture. If and when refugees might be referred for a "credible fear interview," according to Lindsay Harris, director of the Immigration & Human Rights Clinic at the University of the District of Columbia, they are not entitled to government-paid[159] counsel. When lawyers do offer counsel, they are discouraged[160] or "prevented by the Department of Homeland Security from meaningfully participating in their clients' cases."

Skepticism, silence, stereotyping, and separation from the refugee's story—all of these are some factors fueling the rise of the shadow deportation system. It is riddled with violations, oversights, and punitive actions: absence of supervision by immigration courts, lack of proper mental health training of officials who are unable to recognize mental health conditions or their manifestations,[161] and no

---

[153] Brenner, J. (1996). Human rights education in public health graduate schools: 1996 survey. *Health and Human Rights, 2*, 129–139.

[154] Sonis, J., Gorenflo, D., Jha, P., & Williams, C. (1996). Teaching of human rights in US medical schools. *JAMA, 276*, 1676–1678.

[155] Eisenmann, D., Keller, A., & Kim, G. (2000). Survivors of torture in a general medical setting. *Western Journal of Medicine, 172*, 301–304.

[156] Rafuse, J. (1993). Dealing with a population you weren't quite prepared for. *Canadian Medical Association Journal, 148*(2), 282–285.

[157] Haenel, F. (2001). Foreign bodies in the soul (J. M. Reimer, Trans.). In S. Graessner, N. Gurris, & C. Pross (Eds.), *At the side of torture survivors treating a terrible assault on human dignity* (pp. 1–28). Johns Hopkins University Press. (Originally published 1996).

[158] 8 C.F.R. § 292.5 b (2018).

[159] Harris, L. M. (2019, May 6). Withholding protection. *50.3 Columbia Human Rights Law Review, 1*. SSRN. https://ssrn.com/abstract=3383646

[160] American Immigration Council. (2012, May 1). *Behind closed doors: An overview of DHS restrictions on access to counsel* [Special report]. https://www.americanimmigrationcouncil.org/resea rch/behind-closed-doors-overview-dhs-restrictions-access-counsel

[161] USGAO. (2018, February). *Federal Law Enforcement: DHS and DOJ are working to enhance responses to incidents involving individuals with mental illness* (p. 13). https://www.gao.gov/assets/ 690/689997.pdf

referrals to the "fear interview"[162] or the mandatory documentation of torture under international human rights law by custom and border officials. In both Europe and America, if a refugee refuses to recall his or her torture, given its implications of proven torture for residency status, most likely he or she will not be explicitly asked about it.[163] The onus of torture's revelation, supporting documents and its intricate and repeated recall falls squarely on the embattled refugee victim, who may lack education, literacy skills, language skills, knowledge in navigating the asylum system, and often, documentation (having discarded it at the instructions of traffickers).

Those seeking asylum in the United States, under Congress's 1996 Illegal Immigration Reform and Immigrant Responsibility Act, face a 1-year time-limit for filing their asylum applications.[164] The reason undergirding this deadline is fear that those filing after a year are likelier to file fraudulent claims to gain work authorizations or to get out of trouble. If asylum-seekers fail to file within the year, they can still apply on the grounds of either debilitating extraordinary conditions or changed circumstances. However, filing under these exceptions also increases their burden of proof for the likelihood of future harm, increases applications filed under the Convention Against Torture,[165] and the backlog for torture survivors, in general.[166]

While there is no time limit placed on torture survivors, their mental health challenges such, as avoidance, denial, and inability to revisit traumatic episodes, can prevent them from applying for asylum in a timely manner.[167]

There is also a growth of alternate forms of protection, such as *withholding of removal*[168] as in the United States or the *leave to remain* in the UK,[169] that do

---

[162] A credible fear interview is a screening where the asylum seeker must prove reasonable or credible fear of persecution or torture if returned to their country after which they get to present their asylum case to an immigration judge in the United States.

[163] UNHCR. (2004). *Istanbul protocol: Manual on the effective investigation and documentation of torture and other cruel, inhuman or degrading treatment or punishment* (Professional training series No. 8, Rev. 1). Retrieved on May 4, 2023, from https://www.ohchr.org/sites/default/files/Documents/Publications/training8Rev1en.pdf

[164] Harris, L. (2016). The one-year bar to asylum in the age of the immigration court backlog. *Wisconsin Law Review, 1185,* 1213–1224.

[165] Musalo, K., & Rice, M. (2008). The implementation of the one-year bar to asylum. *Hastings International and Comparative. Law Review, 31*(2), 693, 714–715.

[166] For those seeking asylum under the category of torture, the requirements for a Convention Against Torture protection are more rigorous than those for asylum such as through proving that the abuse was deliberately aimed at the asylum-seeker. The higher burden of proof also increases their chances of being denied refugee status.

[167] Lustig, S. L. (2008). Symptoms of trauma among political asylum applicants: Don't be fooled. *Hastings International and Comparative. Law Review, 31*(2), 725–734.

[168] Under this decree, although an immigration judge has ordered a deportation order, the government cannot execute the order of removal; the removal of persons to their home country is withheld, but the immigrants may not be able to work in the host country. Also, the government can still deport an undesired immigrant to a third country.

[169] Harding, J. (2000, February 3). The uninvited. *London Review of Books, 22*(2). https://www.lrb.co.uk/the-paper/v22/n03/jeremy-harding/the-uninvited

not carry the same benefits as an asylum does, heightening refugees' sense of limbo and insecurity. In over 85% of withholding-only cases, the respondents remained detained[170] throughout their proceedings, curtailing their ability to gather necessary evidence and witnesses.[171] This also results in erroneous and speedy deportations, says Harris. In 2016, 83.6% of removals of asylum-seekers in the United States took place in the form of either expedited removals[172] to their country of origin, or, upon re-entry to the United States, reinstatement of prior removal. Returned deportees face no good options. They can undergo a re-turn journey to an unsafe nation where they may endure persecution, threats to their lives or freedom, or be subjected to human rights violations.[173] Having been denied a lawful way to access host nations, asylum-seekers increasingly subject themselves to greater risks for re-entry. When they may re-enter the country after deportation, they face criminal prosecution for illegal entry, or upon entry, they may be awarded inferior forms of protection.[174] In these ways, the asylum framework in many countries mandated to protect every victim of torture and persecution turns its back on them.

In host nations, refugees who have endured torture fall into another quagmire. On the one hand is the asylum law and on the other is its practice, often ignorant in its knowledge of torture. A refugee's believability is often subject to derision, his oppressors not yet held culpable for their human right violations. Adding to his powerlessness is his private struggle with unpredictable symptoms catalyzed by stressors[175] unfolding over the course of his life. In this space where justice and rehabilitation are elusive and where crippling symptoms pervade his life, he is required to prove their existence and potency.

Recovery and rehabilitation in the aftermath of torture and ill-treatment can be a long-term and continuous process with interventions at several levels

[170] Hausman, D. (2015, April 19). *Withholding-only cases and detention. An analysis based on data obtained through the Freedom of Information Act ("FOIA")* [Fact sheet]. ACLU. https://www.aclu.org/sites/default/files/field_document/withholding_only_fact_sheet_-_final.pdf

[171] Hines, B. (2006). An overview of U.S. immigration law and policy since 9/11. *Texas Hispanic Journal of Law and Policy, 12*(9), 17.

[172] USICE. (2020, October 21). *ICE implements July 23, 2019, expedited removal designation* [Press release]. https://www.ice.gov/news/releases/ice-implements-july-23-2019-expedited-removal-designation

[173] Human Rights Watch. (2022, February 10). *"How can you throw us back?": Asylum seekers abused in the US and deported to harm in Cameroon.* https://www.hrw.org/report/2022/02/10/how-can-you-throw-us-back/asylum-seekers-abused-us-and-deported-harm-cameroon

[174] Reinstatement of Removal Orders. 8 C.F.R. § 1241.8: "An alien who illegally reenters the United States after having been removed, or having departed voluntarily, while under an order of exclusion, deportation, or removal shall be removed from the United States by reinstating the prior order."

[175] Grossman, C. M., Sveaass, N., & Gaer, F. (2018). Rehabilitation in Article 14 of the Convention Against Torture and Other Cruel, Inhuman, or Degrading Treatment or Punishment. *International Lawyer, 51*(1), 2. https://digitalcommons.wcl.american.edu/facsch_lawrev/576/

that need to factor in transmission of parent(s) traumatic experiences to their children,[176,177] presence of impaired memory[178] with recall of central events compared with peripheral details[179] and affected by posttraumatic symptoms,[180] and recognition that reactions of the survivor to adjudicator or interpreter may have a detrimental effect on their asylum application.[181,182] Trust-building, confidentiality, and collaborating with the survivor during rehabilitation is important for a sense of safety.

Remediating torture and rehabilitating survivors would mean addressing existing gaps in its redress in accordance with the guidelines of the Convention. For nations, institutions, and health systems, rehabilitation ought to encompass the educating and training of decision-makers on recognizing signs of torture among asylum-seekers and better implementation of the Istanbul Protocol, a human rights instrument setting international standards on the rights of torture survivors and States' obligations to document and investigate their ill-treatment.[183] Remediation and rehabilitation can also mean improved cultural and scientific knowledge related to torture's assessment and treatment; greater sensitivity in cases of gender and sexual violence (e.g., rape, marital rape, and other sexual violence) to avoid stigma and revictimization; and development of mental health infrastructure with provision of services within asylum structures.

A full rehabilitation that addresses not only trauma's psychological aspects but also its social, community, cultural, legal, and medical aspects can begin to lay bare the violence of the social contract meted to the tortured and a society's refusal to mask it.

[176] Daud, A., Skoglund, E., & Rydelius, P. A. (2005). Children in families of torture victims: Transgenerational transmission of parents' traumatic experiences to their children. *International Journal of Social Welfare, 14*, 23–32.

[177] Children of parents who endured torture report higher levels of depression, anxiety, somatization, attention deficits, and behavioral disorders compared with children whose parents did not endure torture: Ibid.

[178] Kaveh Yaragh Tala v. Sweden, UN Doc. CAT/C/17/D/43/1996 Para. 10.3 (1996).

[179] Herlihy, J., & Turner, S. W. (2007). Asylum claims and memory of trauma: Sharing our knowledge. *British Journal of Psychiatry, 191*(1), 3.

[180] Williams, J. M. G., Barnhofer, T., Crane, C., Hermans, D., Raes, F., Watkins, E., & Dalgleish, T. (2007). Autobiographical memory specificity and emotional disorder. *Psychological Bulletin, 133*(1), 122–148.

[181] UNHCR. (2004). *Istanbul protocol: Manual on the effective investigation and documentation of torture and other cruel, inhuman or degrading treatment or punishment* (Professional training series No. 8, Rev. 1). https://www.ohchr.org/sites/default/files/Documents/Publications/training8Rev 1en.pdf

[182] Australian Administrative Appeals Tribunal, Migration Review Tribunal, & Refugee Review Tribunal. (2017, December 20). *Guidance on the Assessment of Credibility* (para. 4.3).

[183] Scientific literature related to the analysis of the injuries is scarce and not homogeneous as it is based upon case reports: Bianchi, I., Focardi, M., Bugelli, V., Pradella, F., Carlo, G., Francesca, F., & Pinchi, V. (2021). Tortures alleged by migrants in Italy: Compatibility and other medicolegal challenges. *International Journal of Legal Medicine, 135*(6), 2489–2499.

I asked Gulnaz what made him share his story. His face flushed a deep red. His eyes brimmed. He wept through his nose. And he replied with a choked throat:

"I want to share my story. I want to tell the Arabs because I am in Europe now, 'If you think our problems began in 2010, you are wrong. Our problems are more than half a century old. They began with the father of the President. Our problem is old. Our problem is older than you and I.'"

He sighed. It was a long sigh. He replied:

"We saw many deaths. We walked through rivers, crossed seas, countries, through every imaginable danger. We have been transported in fridges, taped to the underside of buses, stuffed into balloon boats in high seas. Our story is that we can do anything. We can do the impossible. I just want to say that we are not here to eat, drink, take money. We are here for a new life, a new future in a safe place. We never saw this in our land. We were oppressed in our country. We want to just have a beautiful life."

Two body bags were thrown out from the prison in the early hours of morning. Gulnaz was in one of them, the only one alive. "I was thrown outside in a nylon body bag with my hand and feet tied behind my back, moments away from suffocating to death." A sheep-herder heard his muffled gasps and released him. "Otherwise, I would have died. I could not believe that I was out."

Then, Gulnaz looked at me and smiled. It was a long, pleasant smile. I said to him, "I am glad you are alive and safe today." He looked away.

5

Enrique Iglesias Goes German
Identity Politics and Identity Repair

Are You *Loco*?: Posing as Enrique at the Gates of Europe

"I must act like a European person. I must act like a Spanish person."

Hamza spent the night repeating these words to himself as he traveled in an air-conditioned bus from Athens to Thessaloniki Airport. Hamza was a frail Syrian refugee, barely five feet three inches, with a slender frame under a mop of hair. In the sizzling heat of the Greek summer, with only four other people on the giant bus, it would have been a good time to stretch out his exhausted limbs on its empty seats. But when the bus arrived at Thessaloniki airport at 6 am, Hamza would face an impossible task: he would have to pose as a Spaniard—Enrique Iglesias, the Latin King of Pop—to match the identity on his fake identity card. Hamza had never before encountered a Spaniard in his life, had never even set foot outside the Middle East. The only Spanish he knew was "Loco" (or crazy) from the real Enrique Iglesias's hit song.

But when the traffickers had asked him, "Whom do you want to be?" Hamza could only think of the world's most famous Spaniard, Enrique Iglesias. "I had spent every last money I had. My phone was dead, and besides my ID I had nothing else." Having spent all his money and gone to great lengths to obtain a fake identity card from human traffickers, he was about to confront the immigration officials who stood between him and his flight to Munich—the last leg of a 2-year odyssey fleeing Syria. "I was at the Gate of Europe," said Hamza "and I was asking myself, 'Can you act like a Europe (an) person?'"

Europeans themselves are asking the same questions: Is it possible for refugees from vastly different places to embrace a new language and culture and become European? Can Muslims in Europe ever become European Muslims?[1,2]

---

[1] Khader, B. (2016). Muslims in Europe or European Muslims? The construction of a problem. *Rivista di Studi Politici Internazionali, 83*(2), 169–187. https://www.jstor.org/stable/44427757

[2] Sargent, C. & Erikson, S. L. (2014). Hospitals as sites of cultural confrontation. In J. R. Bowen, C. Bertossi, J. W. Duyvendak, & M. L. Krook (Eds.), *European states and their Muslim citizens: The impact of institutions on perceptions and boundaries* (pp. 29–53). Cambridge University Press.

Displaced. Shaifali Sandhya, Oxford University Press. © Shaifali Sandhya 2024.
DOI: 10.1093/oso/9780197579886.003.0005

Refugee identity is a fraught affair. It is simultaneously an identity projected onto the refugee, an uncomfortable skin to be shed, a precarious persona to be grasped or grappled with, and a residual personal history whose true details could expose the refugee to danger, a history to be concealed. Similarly, for host countries, refugees' personhood and defining traits can have far-reaching implications. Refugees' cultural identity, for instance, such as their Middle Eastern origins and their Muslim religion, has sparked debates in Western countries about European identity. The concern of "creeping Islamization"[3] of the West for some has galvanized an anti-Other backlash. For, "whether or not it is a component of the person," says the Belgian historian Marcel Detienne,[4] "when it is a question of establishing what we call 'nationality', identity becomes law." A unique national identity as increasingly essential for nations' security. How identity is exploited for governance, assigned to the refugee, and negotiated in the context of trauma symptoms opens a window not only onto globalization and human rights violations but also onto refugee emotional health.

This chapter explores the role of complex trauma on identity development within the context of refugees' transnational milieu, transatlantic ties, and migration. We discussed in the last chapter how torture through brute force can realign a minority's position and community's identity in society. Forced displacement raises two questions for identity development: Can extreme suffering and crises, in fact, nurture certain aspects of identity? And how is cultural trauma that can evoke memories of certain events and situations "accepted and publicly given credence"[5] by one's group affect collective identity?

For the traumatized Middle Eastern refugee, Western host nations offer an array of different forms of relatedness based upon social categories (e.g., ethnicities, social networks, generations, and citizenship), social friction, and suffering. This chapter explores the pragmatic perspective of identity that depicts the refugee as an active agent of self-creation vested in repairing and reinventing their identity. Simultaneously, constructing a refugee identity can also occur through reframing: that is, deploying and negotiating social categories such as ethnicity, religion, nationality, race, and culture within a host nation's organizations. Identity can also be a response to the grievance of one's group and the wish to experience a different relationship with the host nation. Identity is conceptualized as a nonstatic and nonpassive journey in the context of local and transnational ties and organizations. The fluid nature of identity, when it is

---

[3] Landler, M. (2007, July 5). Germans split over a mosque and the role of Islam. *The New York Times.* https://www.nytimes.com/2007/07/05/world/europe/05cologne.html

[4] Detienne, M. (2010). *L'Identité nationale: Une énigme* [National identity: An enigma]. Gallimard.

[5] Smelser, N. (2004). Psychological trauma and cultural trauma. In J. Alexander, R. Eyerman, B. Giesen, & P. Sztompka (Eds.), *Cultural trauma and collective identity* (pp. 31–59). University of California Press.

molded to face challenges in traumatic conditions, may play a positive role for individuals' welfare and their healing from trauma.[6]

Quest for the Self

Throughout history, the quest for the self has evinced a timeless appeal and an unquenchable thirst for individuals and societies alike. It commenced with Classical Greece to the period of Enlightenment with John Locke, and to Rousseau, and it flourished with psychoanalysis. Identity has been referred to in various ways: the unique essence of being who or what a person or thing is; as an authentic inner self or an intrapsychic journey or, of our progression through developmental turning points (or psychosocial conflicts) to be resolved successfully to gain psychological strengths. While Montaigne claims that "each man bears the entire form of human condition," or a degree of sameness in all, the Belgian historian Detienne emphasizes self-awareness in order to create a highly essentialized version of oneself or, in other words, "what it is to be oneself."[7] Rousseau in a somewhat similar vein insists on identity as uniqueness and a personal construct belonging exclusively to the individual. However, Rousseau's "self" is intertwined with memory, for it is only the memory that can aid in tracing and retracing the parts of the self from the past to the present.

Identity has been conceptualized thus as a cultural or cognitive precipitate, but in the context of the forcibly displaced, identity is often a response to the unusual, desperate, and abnormal conditions in which refugees find themselves. Two opposing frameworks can be used to undergird explanations of identity development: cultural and cognitive perspectives. The *cultural* framework views, for example, religion as a discrete system of beliefs and anthropological patterns; it is one that can be mistakenly employed as an explanatory concept for the identity of all refugees, equally. The *cognitive* view explains identity as learned, internalized representations or schemas that assimilate cultural values,[8] interpret and reconstruct experience, and provide culture its motivational striving.[9] Although both views can mutually enrich our understandings of the self, they do not in general investigate the effects of traumatic life experiences on the

---

[6] Sargent, C., & Erikson, S. L. (2014). Hospitals as sites of cultural confrontation. In J. R. Bowen, C. Bertossi, J. W. Duyvendak, & M. L. Krook (Eds.), *European states and their Muslim citizens: The impact of institutions on perceptions and boundaries* (pp. 29–53). Cambridge University Press.

[7] Detienne, M. (2010). *L'identité nationale: Une énigme* [National identity: An enigma]. Gallimard.

[8] Spiro, M. E. (1987). Collective representations and mental representations in religious symbol systems. In B. Kilborne & L. L. Langness (Eds.), *Culture and human nature: Theoretical papers of Melford E. Spiro* (pp. 161–184). University of Chicago Press.

[9] D'Andrade, R. (1992). Schemas and motives. In R. G. D'Andrade & Claudia Strauss (Eds.), *Human motives and cultural models* (pp. 61–89). Cambridge University Press.

developing self-concept nor do they explain how identity may play a role in psychological repair.

Cultural and Cognitive Frameworks of Identity

The view that culture is a socially established and shared structure of symbols and meanings was proposed by Geertz, who outlined *culture* as "a system of inherited conceptions expressed in symbolic forms by means of which men communicate, perpetuate, and develop their knowledge about and attitudes toward life."[10] To understand culture, mental phenomena are not necessary in Geertz's view. Instead, the task is to know the dominant practices and publicly accessible symbols of each culture. Providing an analogy with culture, Geertz argues that what makes Beethoven's quartet music rather than noise is that its meaning is publicly shared,[11] and systems of meanings are what produce culture because they are the collective property of a particular people. Even when no one identifies it with Beethoven's score, the skills and knowledge needed to play it, or with their performers' understanding of it, says Geertz, one instinctively identifies oneself as being part of a shared worldview.[12] If culture is the outcome of shared signs and symbols in an intersubjective space, then religion too constitutes the language and symbol of the social bond.[13,14]

While the culturalist view may afford a glimpse into essentialist notions of national identity, it can also delimit our understanding of newer forms of citizenship forged when individuals may contest dominant cultural ideologies based on their social categories and transformational experiences in a globalizing world. Geertz's outlook would fail to explain how a group of people sharing culture can still ascribe different cultural meanings to any one aspect of it. Refugee families, like other diverse families, can differ from each other across cultures, cohorts,[15]

---

[10]   Geertz, C. (1973). *The interpretation of cultures* (p. 89). Basic Books.

[11]   Geertz, C. (1973). *The interpretation of cultures*. Basic Books. .

[12]   Ibid.

[13]   Geertz, C. (1968). *Islam observed: Religious development in Morocco and Indonesia*. Yale University Press.

[14]   Religion is the fusion of an ethos, according to Geertz, where a person's moral and aesthetic style finds its echo in the cultural form of "religionessess." This is a kind of ethnocentrism that no social group can live without—where ethos resonates in traditional ethnocentrism. Religious crises occur when these two categories are no longer syncretic such as when the ethos searches for meanings and the worldview may have changed because of Westernization. Islamism can be perceived as a failure of the postcolonial state to create religious meanings for its members: Geertz, C. (1973). *The interpretation of cultures*. Basic Books.

[15]   (From MPI) the survey indicates that 19% of refugees who arrived in 2015 were in a job by 2017, and data from the Federal Employment Agency indicate that 40% of working-age individuals who arrived from 2015 onward were in work by September 2019—an accelerating trend. However, their average monthly earnings were about 55% of those of all full-time employees in Germany, mostly because of a disproportional engagement in low-skilled occupations and considerable underemployment in jobs below their skill levels.

experiences,[16] lineage hierarchies, religion, family structure and size, minority status, consanguineous or nonconsanguineous marriages,[17] and their prescription to patriarchal norms.

Geertz's views would also fail to explain how different cultural prescriptions can be internalized[18] to a different extent within the same individual.[19] For example, non-Muslims tend to think that all Muslims are adherents to all cultural values associated with Islam and culture—but this is not so. An overwhelmingly large number of French Arab and African immigrant women who are directly affected by polygamy are opposed to it. In the same vein, Olivier Roy, a French political scientist, draws attention to the transient and uncertain nature of the identity of Muslims in Europe. In Europe Muslims may find themselves in a new transnational milieu that is defined less by ethnic and national cleavages and closer to what an *ummah* is, an "imaginary space created by deterritoriality and transnationalism"[20] affecting their identity. The reason Muslims are no longer foreigners in Europe, according to Roy, is "through the recasting of pristine identities into new variable sets of identity patterns which evade any attempt to substantialize them."[21] Identities then, according to Roy, are forever evolving and overlapping with other identities as they morph with social circumstances and are "less a given fact than an individual choice. . . ." For the refugee in foreign lands, *who* one is can be negotiated not just along with cultural traditions but along multifarious and conflicting paradigms: within the ummah or the universal society of all Muslims in Western societies; institutions of the host nation and their treatment of him or her; new social networks and also those in one's homeland, while also grappling with one's trauma story and symptoms.

Fragmented identity, say Van der Kolk and Van der Hart, results from being unaware of one's traumatic memories or being unable to reconcile with one's traumatic past. In obstructing trauma's assimilation within mental structures, as in the case of dissociation,[22] a traumatic event can result in "unassimilated scraps

[16] Burnett, A., & Peel, M. (2001). Asylum seekers and refugees in Britain: Health needs of asylum seekers and refugees. *British Medical Journal, 322*(7285), 544–547.

[17] El Sabeh, M., Kassir, M. F., Ghanem, P., Saifi, O., El Hadi, D., Khalifeh, Y., Ekkawi, A. R., Ghabach, M., Chaaya, M., Nemer, G., Abbas, O., & Kurban, M. (2021). Consanguinity rates among Syrian refugees in Lebanon: A study on genetic awareness. *Journal of Biosocial Science, 53*(3), 356–366.

[18] Geertz, C. (1973). *The interpretation of cultures*. Basic Books.

[19] Holland, D. C. (1992). How cultural systems become desire: A case study of American romance. In R. G. D'Andrade & C. Strauss (Eds.), *Human motives and cultural models* (pp. 61–89). Cambridge University Press.

[20] Roy, O. (2004). *Globalized Islam: The search for a new ummah* (p. 106). Columbia University Press.

[21] Ibid.

[22] Van der Kolk, B. A. (1994). The body keeps the score: Memory and the evolving psychobiology of posttraumatic stress. *Harvard Review of Psychiatry, 1*, 253–265.

of overwhelming experiences."[23] When traumatic experiences cannot gain access to consciousness individuals can re-experience trauma through physical sensations, nightmares, and other behavioral enactments unless they are able to access prior trauma through language.[24,25] Unclaimed experiences in the form of unconscious emotions can lay buried because of trauma,[26] and can inveigle their way into the victim's mind, resulting in later psychopathology. Rousseau and others' depiction of identity overlooked the role of forcible displacement in identity development and its evolution.

Philosophers like Rousseau or proponents of the culturalist and cognitive views did not examine the effect of complex trauma on identity, how the community may define itself or the cultural values it espouses, and the development of an identity impaired by forcible displacement. Complex trauma with its far-reaching impact can inflict cultural damage on communities in permanent ways. Collective trauma, as described by Alexander is "a blow to the basic tissues of social life that damages the bonds attaching people together and impairs the prevailing sense of communality."[27]

The cultural and cognitive perspectives utilize the assumption that individuals access their own experiences—however, in persecutory conditions, trauma can obstruct access to important aspects of the self or unique experiences or ascribe to their community derogatory cultural traits. Significantly, war-affected refugees face unique fears and persecution resulting from: being on the move; encountering losses of their civil, economic, or human rights; host nations' demands of them, and perception of other ethnic or cultural groups as more valued; and low-wage and risky employment. Survival forces refugees to do unthinkable things that may often lie beyond the templates of their cultural or social norms. Based on the demands of their prevailing circumstances, refugees reinvent attributes and camouflage others. Through vignettes, the pragmatic perspective on identity development illustrates the tremendous shape-shifting and makeshift ability of identity for refugees' survivability, sociability, and welfare. The pragmatic view of refugee identity development enriches our take on the

[23] Van der Kolk, B. A., & van der Hart, O. (1991). The intrusive past: The flexibility of memory and the engraving of trauma. *American Imago, 48*, 447.

[24] Van der Kolk, B. A., & Ducey, C. R. (1989). The psychological processing of traumatic experience: Rorschach patterns in PTSD (p. 271). *Journal of Traumatic Stress, 2*, 259–274.

[25] Freud, S. (1926). Inhibitions, symptoms, and anxiety. In J. Strachey & A. Freud (Eds.), *The standard edition of the complete psychological works of Sigmund Freud* (pp. 77–175). Hogarth Press.

[26] Caruth, C. (1995). The intrusive past: The flexibility of memory and the engraving of trauma. In C. Caruth (Ed.), *Trauma: Explorations in memory* (pp. 158–182). Johns Hopkins University Press.

[27] Alexander, J. C. (2004). *Towards a cultural theory of trauma.* In J. C. Alexander, R. Ayerman, B. Giesen, N. J. Smelser, & P. Sztomka (Eds.), *Cultural trauma and collective identity* (p. 3). University of California Press.

influential roles of cultural and social norms and the belief systems embedded in them.[28]

The Makeshift Identity: The View From Displacement

Defacing Identity

Forced displacement may often present refugees with survival and sustenance dilemmas that may pose a cultural paradox: at times, identity must be either rendered invisible or eradicated to ensure a refugee's survivability and welfare. Since membership in a certain group or identity may thrust asylum-seekers or their loved ones toward more significant trauma, to be a refugee can involve masking, hiding, or delinking identity from one's rightful social and cultural categories. Consider for instance, the concept of a body's sacredness in many religions where bodily integrity is valued and where its dissection, disturbance, or defacement, especially in the Muslim religion, is prohibited. However, when refugees, including Muslim ones, become aware of the Dublin Regulation,[29] they may attempt to mutilate their thumbprints, markers of their personal identities. The Dublin Regulation is a European Union law for tougher border control that establishes the first country of an asylum-seeker's entry as the one to process her application. Asylum-seekers' thumb prints are taken to establish their proof of entry, prevent them from submitting the application to multiple nations, and curtail them from being shuttled between nations.

However, since the border towns where migrants arrive may have poorer welfare provisions, asylum-seekers attempt to deface and damage their fingerprints through razors, acid, fire, or knives, so that their identity cannot be traced as they move to their preferred nation. A Swedish Migration Board identity expert estimated that about 5% of the 26,000 sets[30] of fingerprints the country had taken between January 2003 to April 2004 were not legible for identification. But the mutilation of fingerprints is not the only method that refugees adopt to avoid dangerous situations.

[28] The cognitive view emphasized by psychological anthropologists such as Roy D'Andrade, Dorothy Holland, Naomi Quinn, and Claudia Strauss explain the motivational force undergirding human strivings, situational variance in cultural behaviors, and why in the face of equal potency of two conflicting desires, one of those desires may prevail.

[29] The Dublin Regulation is the European Union's key tool for tougher border controls that returns asylum seekers to their country of first entry.

[30] Swedish refugees mutilate fingers. (2004, April 2). *BBC News.* http://news.bbc.co.uk/2/hi/eur ope/3593895.stm

Disguising Identity

Burundi refugees who fled genocide and self-settled in Kigoma, Tanzania, discovered that the only way to avoid being detected by the police was either by
adopting a fictional identity other than Hutu or Burundi, or by maintaining a low
profile. Violating deep-seated sociocultural mores that discourage contraception, fearing the risk of rape, young female asylum-seekers take contraceptives
before their treacherous flight.[31] Others memorize the Quran and adopt different religious identities in case the Islamic State kidnaps them.[32]

Similarly, in a culture where women are traditionally viewed as factories for
producing babies, South Sudanese refugee women are self-injecting themselves
with contraceptives in opposition to cultural values prohibiting family planning.[33] Rohingya refugees may become pregnant before their flight, believing
that being pregnant saves them from rape.[34] To gain employment, Kurdish
refugees may have to pretend they are not from a particular ethnic group.
Homosexual Afghans routinely pretend they are not lesbian, gay, bisexual, transgender, or queer in the face of social taboos and prosecutions for homosexuality
under Sharia law.[35] Hutu refugees in Kigoma, Tanzania, were unwilling to apply
for identity cards, as they were aware that they did not afford them immunity
against deportation,[36] for the government did not want to regularize their stay.
Their "strategy of invisibility," Kibrear argues, is not as a matter of choice but a
matter of necessity.[37] Many refugees, like Hamza, will do what it takes to survive.

Before Hamza found himself masquerading as Enrique Iglesias, he had been
a student of English literature attending a university. The student community
was on edge with a recent spate of bombings, including one on the university
campus, and the routine smell of burned rubber and gun powder filled the air.
But the televised announcement that the government was going to round up all

[31] Taylor, L. (2016, November 30). Women migrants fearing rape take contraceptives before
journey—rights groups. *Reuters*. https://www.reuters.com/article/us-women-conference-migrant-
rape-idUSKBN13P2BW
[32] Migration from Eritrea slows. (2017, May 25). *The Economist*. https://www.economist.com/mid
dle-east-and-africa/2017/05/25/migration-from-eritrea-slows
[33] Okiror, S. (2020, February 25). "We're not baby factories": The refugees trying injectable
contraceptives. *The Guardian*. https://www.theguardian.com/global-development/2020/feb/25/the-
sel-injectable-contraceptive-helping-refugees-in-uganda-plan-their-families-south-sudan
[34] Aziz, A. (2017, October 29). The real reason so many underage Rohingya girls are getting married (and pregnant). *Scroll*. https://scroll.in/article/855639/the-real-reason-so-many-underage-
rohingya-girls-are-getting-married-and-pregnant
[35] Graham-Harrison, E. (2017, February 26). Deported gay Afghans told to "pretend to be
straight." *The Guardian*. https://www.theguardian.com/uk-news/2017/feb/25/afghanistan-gay-asy
lum-seekers-home-office-illegal-homosexuality
[36] Malkki, L. (1995). *Purity and exile: Violence, memory and national cosmology among the Hutu
refugees in Tanzania*. University of Chicago Press.
[37] Kibrear, G. (1999). Revisiting the debate on people, place, identity and displacement. *Journal of
Refugee Studies, 12*(4), 384–410.

young men to serve in the army sent his parents into a panic. Before the sun went down that day and within a couple of hours of the announcement, they planned Hamza's getaway, although no one in their family had previously ever set foot outside Syria. His mother packed her favorite brown shawl crisscrossed with white lilies, and 13 hundred dollars. His father arranged for a friend of the family to drop him off at the Iraq border. Within the first 3 weeks, Hamza had spent all his money on renting an apartment. Initially in Iraq it had been hard to rent a home as a single man, but he soon chanced upon a shared accommodation with eight other Syrian men in the same position:

> We were eight Syrian men renting a 60 square meter apartment because renting cost is expensive. Everyone was paying $150. But we couldn't get any (police) permission because they think that eight young men together in an apartment are trouble. The Iraqi society does not accept a group of youth living together.
>
> In Iraq even buying some food for myself was difficult as the language is totally different, and when the local people speak with someone from Syria they can tell this person is from Syria. Some say "welcome," but most say "get out"; they think we are dangerous people, and we will do something bad in Iraq. They don't understand that we are only refugees, and we need only work and an apartment.
>
> I lived in Iraq for one year and two months. It was a shock. It was very shocking. Many Iraqis don't know if Kurds from Syria exist in Iraq. They didn't respect us. They said, "You are refugees. Be warned because you are refugees. You shouldn't do this. You shouldn't do that." For example, renting a flat was very difficult. I had to take permission from the police to even look for a flat.

In Search of Identity

Hamza moved from job to job as a cook, server, and worker in a leather goods factory, but was always at the mercy of employers who could fire him without notice or those who worked him in hazardous settings. When he was fired unceremoniously, he would also lose his accommodations (such as they were).

In Iraq Hamza found himself chasing his tail in his hunt to track down an identity card so that he could rent a home. A housing certificate needs to be procured by those who rent or own a home and is a prerequisite for obtaining another primary identity document: the Civil Status ID. However, establishing an identity in Iraq proves to be impossible for refugees despite having housing and employment but also, in turn, lending precariousness to both. When Hamza approached the local Iraqi police for his local identification, he was instead given an unofficial black-and-white photocopied sheet with his photo to serve as his temporary identification. Instead, he was sent to the United Nations High

Commissioner for Refugees (UNHCR) for certification that would also establish his civil identification or unique identity from their registration office. A valid UNHCR certificate confirms the refugee's need for international protection and assistance as an asylum-seeker risks being arbitrarily deported, and subject to immigration laws in Iraq. The UNHCR registration was in a different city and yet, Hamza submitted all his documents diligently, followed by routine visits to the UNHCR office located in a different city each month; he continued to do so for 9 months.

The inability to procure an identification card has many consequences for refugees such as Hamza. They are denied access to public services, health system, food rations, and education; risk arrests;[38] and they may find their freedom of movement curtailed. When they are not identified as refugees, Hamza shares, the neediest are forced to pay high prices for the food rations allocated for humanitarian purposes in the secondary markets. Refugees unable to register with local authorities or to obtain passports find their stay to be riskier as they are subject to being deported or detained.

During his time in Iraq, Hamza worked in hazardous conditions handling toxic chemicals in a factory producing leather goods and earning a fairly good salary, he says, at five hundred dollars a month. Although employers require their employees to have a Civil Status ID to procure employment, in reality it is often overlooked because refugees can be underpaid, health insurance withheld, or be forced into additional hours of work and/or work in perilous settings. Displaced refugees like Hamza are often front-line workers in shadow economies, and their contributions can amount to a large share in the gross domestic product of countries: 34% in sub-Sahara Africa[39] and 16.7% in the Organisation for Economic Cooperation and Development countries,[40] respectively. At the same time, the extent to which they are exploited and excluded from accessing labor markets and benefits[41] implies they can only find work in the black or informal market,[42] lending even greater desperation to their lives.

[38] Anbar IDPs in Baghdad fear for their safety. (2014, May 13). *IRIN*.https://www.refworld.org/docid/5379d6464.html

[39] Adegoke, Y. (2019, December 6). Economists struggle to figure out where Africa's informal economy starts or where it ends. *Quartz*. https://qz.com/africa/1759070/economists-struggle-to-figure-out-where-africas-informal-economy-starts-or-where-it-ends/

[40] Knoema. *Shadow economy in Europe and OECD countries in 2003–2015*. (2018, August 19). https://knoema.com/infographics/jfgjvlg/the-shadow-economy-in-europe-and-oecd-countries-in-2003-2015

[41] Clemens, M., Huang, C., & Graham, J. (2018). *The economic and fiscal effects of granting refugees formal labor market access* (Working Paper 496). Center for Global Development. https://www.cgdev.org/publication/economic-and-fiscal-effects-granting-refugees-formal-labor-market-access

[42] Ibid.

With every challenge posed by displacement, refugees like Hamza attempt to improvise expedient solutions with everything at their disposal as they adapt to their new hardened circumstances.

> At one point, I decided to marry as life is impossible for single men. But then I thought, my children won't have a chance to go to school. Local schools do not accept Kurdish people in their schools. Marriage and children here are difficult. I thought how can I have a family here? That will not be stable. How will a married person live? We need a country where children have the chance to go to school. If someone wants to work, they shouldn't have to worry if their family is safe or not.

After 9 months, Hamza was told his certificate was still being delayed; this time the delay was due to the Iraqi government. "I went from Erbil to Duhok and from Duhok to Zakho to Zhob, and learned the disappointing news that an identification card, even if procured in one city, could not be transferred to another city." A local tout offered to charge him a hundred dollars in order to expedite his application. For many other countless displaced people stranded in Iraq often for more than three years,[43] procuring documents is "lengthy, complex and costly"—but without them they cannot obtain the Civil Status ID.[44,45] Delay or denial of identity documents for asylum-seekers makes it highly likely that they will be either deported or sent to detainment centers while they are in transit.[46] This violates the international agreement of nonrefoulment that forbids refugees from being compelled to return to unsafe nations where they will be endangered. Left to their own devices, however, the absence of identification documents forces refugees to rely on smugglers making their onward travel riskier and the probability of death higher. This is what Hamza was eventually forced to do.

[43] IDMC & NRC. (2020). *Global report on internal displacement 2020*. https://www.internal-displacement.org/sites/default/files/publications/documents/2020-IDMC-GRID.pdf

[44] UNHCR. (2007, August). *UNHCR's eligibility guidelines for assessing the international protection needs of Iraqi asylum seekers* (p. 111). http://www.refworld.org/docid/46deb05557.html

[45] UNHCR. (2012, May 31). UNHCR eligibility guideline for assessing the international protection needs of asylum-seekers from Iraq. UN Doc. HCR/EG/IRQ/12/03.

[46] Countries that are signatory to the 1951 Refugee Convention are required under its Article 28 to assure refugees of procedural safeguards and provisions for refugee identification certificate along with travel documents; however, countries like Iraq and India that are non-signatories to the 1951 Refugee Convention, curiously legitimize their nonratification and absolve themselves of the human right obligations despite their membership in the United Nations and their ratification of many of its core human rights instruments. Even when refugees may not want to stay invisible, economics may suggest exploitative reasons underpinning their invisibility. Refugees are forced to live illegally and in precarious, harsh, and marginalized conditions: Janmyr, M. (2016). Precarity in exile: The legal status of Syrian refugees in Lebanon. *Refugee Survey Quarterly, 35*(4), 58–78.

In the absence of identity card, it was getting impossible to live with the locals, find housing and employment. I decided to start a new journey and a new life. So I escaped again with the help of smugglers.

The Flight: At the Gates of Europe

There was Enrique at the airport.

Despite having paid $100 to smugglers to cross the Syria-Turkey border, Hamza twice failed to cross the border. The first time he narrowly escaped but was hit on his face with an AK47 by an ISIS man "so hard that I did not have any feeling for a month no matter how hard I pinched my right cheek." The second attempt included making his way through a tunnel only two or three feet away from an ISIS camp. After walking for two and a half hours, Hamza succeeded in arriving in Turkey and did his best to sustain himself in several different cities. However, finding no employment, he decided to make the precarious journey across the Aegean Sea from the town of Aliaga to Greece. He nearly died once again when the boat capsized. Others were not so lucky, and several refugees died that day. On his third trip, Hamza made it ashore to Greece, where he was detained and imprisoned for 3 months, after which, he was released by the Greek police.[47]

So with a pounding heart, Enrique made his way to the boarding counter. The agent asked him, "Where are your details?" "Name, address, here's everything— take whatever you wish," Hamza replied. He did, and in perfunctory fashion told him, "Here's your boarding pass. To Gate 5."

Enrique should have known what a gate was and what to do there, but Hamza did not and did not know how to navigate his way through security. As he wandered off, a security guard beckoned him. Breaking into a sweat but trying to maintain his composure, Enrique asked, "Where is Gate 5?" "Go straight then right," he was told.

"I went to the right, but there were still some people coming out of that entrance. I didn't know what a gate is," says Enrique. "I turned around and found the same security officer staring at him and loudly beckoning me, 'Come here.' I thought, 'Oh no. What now?'"

---

[47] Detentions of asylum-seekers, including refugee children, and their enforced disappearance by Greek security officials are a routine occurrence. There are also wide-scale practices that contribute to enforced disappearance, such as secret detentions and asylum-seekers mobile phones being broken or thrown away so they cannot be tracked: Office of the High Commissioner United Nations Human Rights. *UN Committee on Enforced Disappearances publishes findings on Greece and Niger.* (2022, April 12). https://www.ohchr.org/en/press-releases/2022/04/un-committee-enforced-disappearances-publishes-findings-greece-and-niger

Enrique returned and once again was told again, "Go straight and then turn right." Confused, Enrique did not know what to do. But he reminded himself, "I must act like a European person, I must act like a Spanish person."

Before he could determine how to do that, the cop placed his hands on both his shoulders and pointing with an outstretched arm told him, said "this is straight" and "this is right."

Once through security, Enrique to his surprise, found himself seeking out another security guard. This time to find how to charge his phone. A security guard loaned him a phone charger.

As Hamza squatted on the floor charging his phone, he said to himself, "Hey man, what are you doing? You are sitting in front of the police! The kind of thing a European might do. The sort of thing a Syrian will never risk."

Identity for the refugee is thus fluid, constantly influenced but also influencing contexts. The theory of learned helplessness would postulate that the failure to escape painful stimuli creates powerlessness. But the purposeful striving to overcome their conditions by refugees like Hamza affords us a glimpse into their efforts toward repair of their families and communities.

Factors Shaping Identity Formation

Institutional Schemas

As refugees like Hamza strive to reinvent themselves to repair themself or situations, it is through their engagement in the social life of institutions—hospitals, employers, immigration, or schools—that they encounter "the state,"[48] "as a regulator of citizenship, a provider of services, or a source of employment." Institutions and organizations can thus represent and reproduce assumptions concerning identity of the Other.

In a study of West African Malian immigrants residing in France and Turkish immigrants living in Germany, Sargent and Erikson document the role of institutions such as hospitals and their staff in the construction of the cultural Other. Referring to their Turkish patients as a "Typical Turk" is associated with a collection of behaviors that are deemed decidedly "not German."[49] These

[48] Bowen, J. R., Bertossi, C., Duyvendak, J. W., & Krook, M. L. (2003). An institutional approach to framing Muslims in Europe. In J. R. Bowen, C. Bertossi, J. W. Duyvendak, & M. L. Krook (Eds.), *European states and their Muslim citizens: The impact of institutions on perceptions and boundaries* (p. 3, pp. 29–53). Cambridge University Press.

[49] Sargent, C., & Erikson, S. L. (2014). Hospitals as sites of cultural confrontation. In J. R. Bowen, C. Bertossi, J. W. Duyvendak, & M. L. Krook (Eds.), *European states and their Muslim citizens: The impact of institutions on perceptions and boundaries* (p. 43). Cambridge University Press.

behaviors range from being too loud, emotional, and dramatic during labor and delivery, even though they may end up with a healthy woman and infant. "Typical Turk" also includes bringing "smelly," garlicky foods into the hospital rooms, having large groups of visitors come to the hospital room and stay for hours, as well as having "too many children." In contrast, "good" patients are those who are stoic during labor and delivery; are able to contain and manage their pain without making noise; had only one or two children; have few visitors who keep their stays brief; ate bland hospital food without objection and recognized that spicy foods also meant "spicy" breast milk and gassy babies.[50] The beliefs, expectations and routine interactions of German doctors, midwives, and nurses with regard to cultural groups such as the Turks normalize ethnic categories associated with patients. Such institutional beliefs and expectations affect their health outcomes and patient care, and introduce migrants to constructs of what an ideal patient is perceived to be. Construction of the refugee identity can occur through reframing, deploying, and negotiating social categories such as ethnicity, religion, nationality, race, and culture within organizations. Often these dynamics can also propagate the social dynamics and binaries that constitute the Other in the broader society.

Conceptualizing a cultural Other, rooted in colonization practicesor in the deprivation of a diversity of experiences with people different from us, can polarize the differences between the self and the other.[51] "Othering" is likened to a shared dialog[52] and can be framed through legal, media, and contemporary policies of asylum enabling exclusion of those constructed as the margin alized.[53,54] In casting refugees as outsiders, the saliency of their refugee status obfuscates our attention to what is different about them that, if recognized, might create a positive difference in their lives and ours. Consider the "Somali paradox," an entrepreneurial diaspora where economic success is shaped within family and kinship but is not able to materialize in host countries because of ineffective governance. Realizing their human capital by providing them economic autonomy can help host and home nations upon their return. Instead, countries have extended the frame of the other to their needs of securitization by implementing mandatory detention without proper documentation, surveillance, increased border security, and expedited removal of the refugee. Various scholars caution

---

[50] Sargent, C., & Erikson, S. L. (2014). Hospitals as sites of cultural confrontation. In J. R. Bowen, C. Bertossi, J. W. Duyvendak, & M. L. Krook (Eds.), European states and their Muslim citizens: The impact of institutions on perceptions and boundaries (p. 43). Cambridge University Press.

[51] Said, E. (1978). Orientalism: Western conceptions of the Orient. Penguin.

[52] Spivak, G. C. (1985). The Rani of Sirmur: An essay in reading the archives. History and Theory, 24(3), 247–272.

[53] Foucault, M. (1982). The subject and power. Critical Inquiry, 8(4), 777–795.

[54] Foucault, M. (1972). The archaeology of knowledge and the discourse on language. Pantheon.

that[55,56,57,58,59,60,61,62] conflating the Other with securitization amplifies the value of those who are similar to us, makes them worthy of protection, and makes Others those whose lives ought to have less valence and value than ours.

When people's self-worth and identity is devalued, it can result in the formation of involuntary minorities who may reject social norms.[63] The indignity of not being valued can result in groups bonding over feelings of *thymos* ("anger," "pride," and "shame") and lend more acuity to certain grievances, offers the political theorist Fukuyama.[64] Let us examine this with an anecdote.

When Muhannad M. a 25-year-old Syrian refugee, brought a second-hand wardrobe to his new apartment in Minden, Germany, he discovered it contained 150,000 euros in cash. Discovering the 500-euro notes, at first, he thought it was fake money, but soon, his disbelief turned to glee when he realized they were real. "Allah would never allow me to finance my interests with someone else's wealth," he said. "I'm a Muslim," he thought. Keeping all this found money for himself would have been a betrayal of his religion, so he returned it. When other refugees I was interviewing in Bonn heard this, they laughed. Why was Muhammad M. attempting to subvert images of refugees, they asked, by returning the money when refugees were already perceived as "bad?" However, *being good* or *being bad*, reactions of both Muhammad M. and other refugees may serve to be examples of an oppositional identity, identification created in reaction to the social exclusion they may perceive from the dominant group. Widely held schemas about refugees may be internalized and negotiated by the refugees themselves too, in opposition to social expectations of them.

[55] Agamben, G. (2005). *State of exception* (K. Attel, Trans.). University of Chicago Press.

[56] Butler, J. (2006). *Precarious lives: The power of mourning and violence*. Verso.

[57] Butler, J. (1993). *Bodies that matter: On the discursive limits of sex*. Routledge.

[58] Campbell, D. (1998). *Writing security: United States foreign policy and the politics of identity*. University of Minnesota Press.

[59] Doty, R. L. (1996). *Imperial encounters: The politics of representation in North-South relations*. University of Minnesota Press.

[60] Edkins, J., Pin-Fat, V., & Shapiro, M. J. (2004). *Sovereign lives: Power in global politics*. Routledge.

[61] Hansen, L. (2006). *Security as practice: Discourse analysis and the Bosnian war*. Routledge.

[62] Said, E. W. (2003). *Orientalism*. Penguin.

[63] Liebow's 1967 research on "corner street men" shows how idlers and street beggars can adopt behaviors that run contrary both to their group norms and the norms of the dominant majority: Liebow, E. (1967). *Tally's corner: A study of Negro streetcorner men*. Little, Brown.

[64] Fukuyama, F. (2018). *Identity: The demand for dignity and the politics of resentment*. Farrar, Straus and Giroux.

Londonistan and the Other: Emergent Muslim Identity

Many European nations are brimming with the social unrest of their young second-generation Muslims as they grapple with social change, discrimination, ignorance, lower rates of higher education, and higher unemployment relative to the general population.[65] Muslim youth are more likely to face unemployment compared to other faith groups in many European countries: In the UK, unemployment rates are twice that of other communities in the general population.[66] In France, 84% of French Muslims report being either "very worried" or "somewhat concerned" about unemployment among Muslims.[67] The resentment from being excluded from the labor market may be stronger in the second or subsequent generations than among their parents, whose frames of references may be their countries of origin.[68]

For the newly arrived refugees, social indicators such as a decline in well-paid or unskilled or both jobs suggest the presence of either structural barriers or social friction that may forecast poor earnings of one cultural group relative to the dominant majority. Roy likens the unemployed Muslim youth culture to the subculture occupied by African American and Latino youth in America, a phenomenon reflecting a breakdown of integration.[69]

Greater religiosity among European or American Muslims can be understood as a reaction to their rejection, such as "ethnic penalties" in the labor market,[70] and socioeconomic exclusion. Embracing Islam with fervor affords them a respectability, community, and identity in opposition to how they may perceive being treated by society. Mirza, a sociologist, illustrates the adoption of visible religious symbols such as a hijab or headscarf as both a visible symbol of identity flux as well as globalization experienced within European Muslim communities.[71]

---

[65] Fredette, J. (2014). *Constructing Muslims in France: Discourse, public identity, and the politics of citizenship*. Temple University Press.

[66] Fenton, S. (2016, August 11). 6 charts which show the employment barriers faced by British Muslims: Unemployment rates among Muslims are more than double that of any other community in the UK. *The Independent*. https://www.independent.co.uk/news/uk/home-news/muslims-more-likely-to-be-unemployed-than-any-other-social-group-in-the-uk-mps-warn-a7185451.html

[67] Allen, J. T. (2006, August 17). "The French-Muslim connection": Is France doing a better job of integration than its critics? Pew Research Center Publications. http://www.pewresearch.org

[68] Ali, S. & Heath, A. (2013). *Future identities: Changing identities in the UK—the next 10 years* (p. 48). UK Government of Science & Foresight. https://assets.publishing.service.gov.uk/government/uploads/system/uploads/attachment_data/file/275779/13-518-changes-in-national-and-supranatio nal-identities.pdf

[69] Roy, O. (2004). *Globalized Islam: The search for a new ummah*. Columbia University Press.

[70] Ali, S. & Heath, A. (2013). *Future identities: Changing identities in the UK—the next 10 years*. UK Government of Science & Foresight. https://assets.publishing.service.gov.uk/government/uploads/system/uploads/attachment_data/file/275779/13-518-changes-in-national-and-supranational-ide ntities.pdf

[71] Mirza, M. (2009). Multiculturalism, religion, and identity. In V. S. Kalra (Ed.), *Pakistani diasporas: Culture, conflict, and change* (pp. 321–334). Oxford University Press.

Similarly, among the American Muslim youth, there is greater religiosity: about two-thirds of Muslims aged younger than 40 years say religion is very important in their lives, compared to roughly 4 in 10 American millennials.[72] Times of radical social change can usher identity politics, says Fukuyama. In fact, both nationalism and Islam—that is political Islam—can be seen as two sides of the same coin. Both are expressions of a hidden or suppressed group identity that seeks public recognition. Referring to a newer version of their traditional apparel, however, Mirza argues, can reveal the desires of Muslim youth. Identity can be formed thus, in response to social friction and as a response to the grievance of one's group and the wish to experience a different relationship with society. The case of Emini, presented in the next section, exemplifies both how identity is affected when trauma may enter its collectivity and how it creates a cultural crisis in identity.

Collective Suffering in an Age of Globalization

The Man with Winter Eyes: "Did You See Nadia Murad on YouTube?"

One evening I was in an interview with a refugee at a German resettlement camp when the door burst open. With his hand still on the doorknob, Emini, a lanky Yazidi man scanned the room until his dark green winter eyes located me. I was taking notes at a long, white plastic table in the cavernous recreational room in a German resettlement complex filled with old sofas, assorted books, and lots of chairs; I was waiting to interview my last refugee respondent for the day. Emini strode over until he towered over me, brimming with the energy of a caged animal, "I would like to be interviewed," he said. News from other refugees in the settlement who had been interviewed had reached Emini, and he appeared frantic that I would leave without speaking to him.

Emini wanted to be interviewed right then, right away. He agreed to come back in another hour. When Emini returned, he treated me with familiarity and without losing a second, asked "Did you see Nadia Murad on YouTube?" And prodded, "You've seen her on YouTube, yes?" Murad was 21 years old when she was captured along with 6,700 Yazidi women and girls by the Islamic State in 2014 in Iraq, Emini told me. Enslaved in a compound, she was "bought and sold, beaten, burned, and raped again and again and again." Upon finding the house

---

[72] Diamant, J., & Gecewicz, C. (2017, October 26). 5 facts about Muslim millennials in the U.S. *Pew Research Center.* https://www.pewresearch.org/fact-tank/2017/10/26/5-facts-about-muslim-millennials-us/

unlocked one day she escaped. Long before Murad won the Nobel Prize for Peace, there was a WhatsApp video of a gang rape that made its way to Emini. It is unclear to Emini whether the gang rape was Murad's or some other Yazidi woman. The WhatsApp videos kept coming. Each time they were of a different kind each time but equally heinous: "our girls being sold," "our girls being abused," and "our girls being treated worse than animals." Emini's voice was scorching in pain and transported us to that fateful compound in Iraq. It had been two years since Emini made it to a haven like Germany, but his voice like an injured animal exposed his inner torment.

Emini cannot "erase the video from my mind" he says, has "difficulty sleeping," and says he suffers from a searing pain. He identifies with the injury to the womenfolk of his community as though it occurred to him and as though it was still occurring in present time. Cultural trauma is "when members of a collectivity feel they have been subjected to a horrendous event," says the sociologist Jeffrey Alexander, that "leaves indelible marks upon their group consciousness marking their memories forever and changing their future identity in fundamental and irrevocable ways."[73] Individual accounts of trauma can be thus insufficient given trauma's harsh effects on the social relations of groups, says the Salvadoran social psychologist Martín-Baró.[74] Psychosocial trauma, according to Martín-Baró, is evident in the collective and long-term experience of terror, paranoia, or denial of reality experienced by communities.

The is the perception of being made to feel different because their traumas can endure for refugees despite the lapse of more than 1 or 2 decades. In her exploration of newly arrived Serbian refugees into the small town of Ravnica in Serbia from violence-affected Croatia, Bosnia, and Herzegovina, Dragojevic[75] explores how even though they share the same Serbian ethnic identity as the local majority, they are perceived by locals as lacking as strong a sense of Serbian national identity. Despite becoming citizens, the Serbian refugees continued to perceive themselves as outsiders, "connected superficially to both their new place and to their old hometown but profoundly to neither." At first glance, the tendency of the refugees to see themselves as a "different" social group relative to locals may be puzzling; however, at a deeper level, refugees do share everyday

---

[73] Alexander, J. C. (2004). Towards a theory of cultural trauma. In J. C. Alexander, R. Eyerman, B. Giesen, N. J. Smelser, & P. Sztompka (Eds.), *Cultural trauma and collective identity* (p. 1). University of California Press.

[74] Martín-Baró, I. (1988). La violencia politica y la Guerra common causas del trauma psicosocial en El Salvador [Political violence and war common causes of psychosocial trauma in El Salvador]. *Revista de Psicologia de El Salvador, 7*, 123–141.

[75] Dragojevic, M. (2019). "We don't belong anywhere": Everyday life in a Serbian town where immigrants are former refugees. In D. W. Montgomery (Ed.), *Everyday life in the Balkans* (pp. 145–154). Indiana University Press.

experiences of massive trauma, and the resultant personal challenges of depression or posttraumatic stress. Uprooted from their traditional ways of living, and as their identification with their social and religious mores may recede, they may identify with each other through their losses and suffering. Serbian refugees' show greater affinity with other refugees, more than the local Serbians, and Roy's work suggests a unique form of belonging among those affected by trauma—connections forged with others who are perceived to be similarly suffering, victimized, or oppressed.[76]

Refugees are vulnerable to an identity formed as the *Other*. The factors that lend them vulnerability include the presence of their complex trauma, prevalence of stereotypes, their propensity to identify with distant communities or with others who are perceived as similarly afflicted, and the flux within the global Muslim community. For the refugees who might perceive themselves as different from the majority group and, indeed, are treated as such, being embedded in networks of suffering can also mean being interconnected with others like them. In doing so, it is equally likely that for many given their intimate familiarity with violence, refugees evolve a unique culture that may be better able to give meaning to terrible events, negotiate traditional cultures with present needs, and mount ever-challenging circumstances with ingenuity, creativity, and persistence—and in that, lies their resilience.

"Will you marry a German or a Syrian girl?" I asked Hamza.

"My mother would like me to marry a Syrian girl," he said. Hamza's mother spoke to him at least three times a week using WhatsApp and frequently offered advice on his personal life. "Mother told me," Hamza shared, "Try to find Syrian girl. If you can't it's okay." "I have a nice German girlfriend," he said, "Maybe I'll marry a Syrian girl." In the year that followed his arrival to Germany, however, Hamza had some tough luck locating a good Syrian girl to marry.

"Syrians here," he said, "Have no new thinking. They are asking for money, and I can't offer 10,000 euros. This is money that I will need to pay before the wedding, and I also need to buy new furniture. Syrian girl costs very big money. It is about 10,000 euros. That is why many Syrians cannot afford Syrian girls."

One year later, when I asked Hamza the same question, he shared that he was living with his German girlfriend Theresa, but she could not cook to save her life, so he was doing the cooking. I reminded him of his answer a year ago and asked,

[76] Roy, O. (2004). *Globalized Islam: The search for a new ummah*. Columbia University Press. Ali, S. & Heath, A. (2013). *Future identities: Changing identities in the UK—the next 10 years*. UK Government of Science & Foresight. https://assets.publishing.service.gov.uk/government/uploads/system/uploads/attachment_data/file/275779/13-518-changes-in-national-and-supranational-identities.pdf

"Will you marry her?" He replied thoughtfully, "I think so. 80% I think so." At another point in our conversation, his face had softened, and he said, "Theresa you know, is a like a baby. She is totally innocent."

Will you ever consider yourself German? I had asked Hamza this when I had first met him. "I will never belong here even if I have German nationality," Hamza had replied. "I'm Syrian with Kurdish blood," he had said, and "Syria will always be in my heart." Five years later, with his German wife, a good job, fluency in German, and a 6-month-old baby girl, as he was awaiting his shiny, scarlet German passport. I asked Hamza the same question, to which he replied: "I'm German, but I come from Syria."

Culture is a socially established intersubjective space of shared structures of symbols and meanings. Refugee individuals can push back against prevailing cultural discourse as they live with their posttraumatic symptoms. This shows us that while culture is a creation of many stories, identity is an enactment of lived experiences. Beyond the cost of traumatic life experiences, which one of the many selves we value will prevail will depend on the salience of the meanings of trauma, ideas of the *other* as embodied in the host culture, as well as the opportunities for trust and intimacy offered to us in our connections. At the same time, when one's values may not find resonance in the globalized worldview or the collective, suffering and crises ensue.

Identity in contemporary Germany is not static, but instead develops and changes over time, influencing psychological well-being. It is influenced by family in distant locations, perceptions of inclusion and exclusion by others, and the demographic and psychological shifts within its diverse Muslim communities. Through our engagement with refugees, we come to see identity as more than its "identity markers" of gender, caste, class, ethnicity, or religion. Identity is not just who you are, but it is also about who you want to be and with whom you are connected to by social suffering. Identity is about advancement in one's conditions and repair so as not to re-experience the past in its traumatic circumstances. For host nations, creating belonging for refugees will be about providing refugees with opportunities of repair as they forge new families and new communities in Europe. This will also decide outcomes for their health, education, family life, and of their nations.

Trauma is an integral part of the refugee story—but it is not the only one.

6

Culture and Globalization in Postconflict Trauma Care

The Red Suzuki and the Cultural Value of Masculinity

"I fear nothing," said Hosni, 36-year-old, a pale-complexioned and petite Syrian male with a high hairline at the temples and half eyebrows. It was in response to questionnaire items that asked him whether he had experienced terror, panic, or felt scared. Hosni in a sea-green Polo t-shirt wore a silver wedding ring. Hosni had been a wholesaler for potato chips in Syria when the war had begun. After the war, there was a surge in demand for chips and energy drinks, so Hosni would drive his red Suzuki van to the Turkish border and would return with raw materials.

Hosni continued, *"All of a sudden, the war started, and within four months, four of my loved ones were killed by bullets from the Syrian government's forces. First, my wife's father was killed, then a month later, her brother and my twenty-year-old brother-in-law - who was like my best friend - got shot. Shortly after that, my uncle, brother of my mother, was killed - shot in the heart by rebels. Barely a week had gone by, and my 14-year-old cousin was blown to pieces by a bomb. I was with him the hour before his death. One is always thinking: These innocent people have nothing to do with war; why are they dead? Why is my uncle dead? Why are my cousins dead? Why is my friend in the hospital? They have nothing to do with war and politics. I was finding out about their deaths through sifting photographs of the dead on Facebook.*

"How do you describe the feeling when you are leaving someone at home, and you are going out for work, and you don't know whether you will ever see that person again. Sometimes it is not about that one person but about your whole family. You may never see them again. You don't know if you are going to come back again. One day my friend went to the market. He left his wife and three kids at home. Thirty minutes later, he returned to find his home bombed and his wife and kids were buried. Although he was able to give his wife a burial, we were not able to pull out the children's bodies.

"I dreamed of my friend that night. I saw him crying the day his family died. Before the war, when someone died, even if that person was 80 years old, you felt surprised and sad. When you hear of killings nowadays and of people being

Displaced. Shaifali Sandhya, Oxford University Press. © Shaifali Sandhya 2024.
DOI: 10.1093/oso/9780197579886.003.0006

killed here and there, it's not that I am heartless, but I don't feel anything. Syria used to be the Paris of the Middle East. Now my home, shop, neighborhood, and city are destroyed. I had embargoed the car well to ensure that no one could steal chips from it but the fear of being kidnapped was high. With the borders closed, I couldn't even make a dollar selling chips.

"After months of lugging cases of chips, my car was getting tired too. With a heavy heart, I decided to sell my red car. My feelings these days are, I-don't-know-how-I-feel. My feelings are blocked because someone or the other is always dying. Maybe it's going to take me years to forget what has happened.

"Us men, we are all fighting to preserve our life. We are fighting to survive. Just for our families, for our children, for our wives. Some of the dead people leave signs behind—one of my dead friend's left a pregnant wife behind. You can imagine that his son or daughter comes into the world, and he does not know a father. You don't leave people behind like this. You always feel responsible after she lost her husband. I am terrified that my father is still in Syria. But a man has to hide his weakness to save people from dying. You have to be brave. You have to be strong. When you become weak, it makes other people feel weak too.

"The sadness is killing me. I cannot feel. I cannot enjoy life. I am trying to, but I cannot enjoy it because these deaths are still killing me."

The Lens of Culture in Public Mental Health

Worldwide, migration upheavals expose practitioners to myriad groups of displaced persons with a variety of concerns and capacities, compounding the challenge of treatment gap—where sufferers outnumber access to treatment and practitioners.[1,2] Our understanding of trauma as posttraumatic stress disorder (PTSD), long considered to be its universal benchmark, is also being revised.[3,4,5] Suffering is not context free;[6] its expression and experience can manifest variously

[1] World Health Organization. (2022, June 16). *World mental health report: Transforming mental health for all.*

[2] Rayes, D. (2022, July 13). As Ukrainian refugees arrive, EU's public health crisis grows. *New Lines Institute for Strategy and Policy.* https://newlinesinstitute.org/ukraine/as-ukrainian-refugees-arrive-the-eus-public-health-crisis-grows/

[3] Lewis-Fernández, R., & Kirmayer, L. J. (2019). Cultural concepts of distress and psychiatric disorders: Understanding symptom experience and expression in context. *Transcultural Psychiatry,* 56(4), 786–803.

[4] Meyer, C., Kampisiou, C., Triliva, S., Knaevelsrud, C., & Stammel, N. (2022). Lay causal beliefs about PTSD and cultural correlates in five countries. *European Journal of Psychotraumatology,* 13, 1.

[5] Rasmussen, A., Keatley, E., & Joscelyne, A. (2014). Posttraumatic stress in emergency settings outside North America and Europe: A review of the emic literature. *Social Science & Medicine,* 109, 44–54.

[6] Patel, V. (2015). Foreword. In B. Kohrt & E. Mendenhall (Eds.), *Global mental health: Anthropological perspectives.* Routledge.

across cultures and contexts. Together, and along with the increased prevalence of posttraumatic stress in the displaced, these challenges suggest the need for a strengthened, synergistic, and sustainable role of culture-based interventions at the different stages and levels of displacement. Incorporating local concepts of health at the clinic and community levels can engage communities to be partners, improve patient engagement, ameliorate treatment gaps, and enhance public health status through early detection and screening of mental health disorders.[7]

As we saw in the previous chapters, our life-worlds,[8] in the form of ethnic,[9] racial, historical,[10] political, and cultural contexts,[11,12] can penetrate and shape our narratives. The cultural script of masculinity or the response of being unafraid that Hosni displays in the vignette in the preceding section requires men in his society to soldier on in the face of death and despair. At the research level, cultural scripts in places where speaking about emotional topics may be taboo, can assist in opening the door to the participants' subjective world. But in understanding mental health challenges posed by complex trauma, approaches with rare exceptions, neglect to take into account core dimensions of trauma unique to culturally diverse populations,[13,14] illness schemas,[15] cultural schemas associated with their healing,[16] spiritual beliefs, religious practices,[17] or how culture

[7] Kohrt, B. A., Rasmussen, A., Kaiser, B. N., Haroz, E. E., Maharjan, S. M., Mutamba, B. B., de Jong, J. T., & Hinton, D. E. (2014). Cultural concepts of distress and psychiatric disorders: Literature review and research recommendations for global mental health epidemiology. *International Journal of Epidemiology*, 43(2), 365–406.

[8] Jenkins, J. H., & Haas, B. M. (2016). Trauma in the lifeworlds of adolescents: Hard luck and trouble in the land of enchantment. In D. E. Hinton & B. J. Good (Eds.), *Culture and PTSD: Trauma in global and historical perspectives* (pp. 179–201). University of Pennsylvania Press.

[9] Pole, N. (2019). Race and ethnicity. In C. B. Nemeroff & C. R. Marmar (Eds.), *Post-traumatic stress disorder* (pp. 537–559). Oxford University Press.

[10] Ball, T., & O'Nell, T. D. (2016). Historical trauma in two native American communities. In D. E. Hinton and B.J . Good (Eds.), *Culture and PTSD: Trauma in global and historical perspectives* (pp. 334–358). University of Pennsylvania Press.

[11] Chiovenda, A. (2020). *Crafting masculine selves: Culture, war, and psychodynamics in Afghanistan*. Oxford University Press.

[12] Kluckhohn, C., & Murray, H. (1948). Personality formation: The determinants. In C. Kluckhohn & H. Murray (Eds.), *Personality in nature, society and culture* (2nd ed., pp. 53–69). Alfred A. Knopf.

[13] Hinton, D. E., & Lewis-Fernandez, R. L. (2011). The cross-cultural validity of post-traumatic stress disorder: Implications for DSM-5. *Depression and Anxiety*, 29, 148–155.

[14] Alemi, Q., James, S., & Montgomery, S. (2016). Contextualizing Afghan refugee views of depression through narratives of trauma, resettlement stress, and coping. *Transcultural Psychiatry*, 53(5), 630–653.

[15] Gone, J. P., & Kirmayer, L. J. (2010). On the wisdom of considering culture and context in psychopathology. In T. Millon, R. F., Krueger, & E. Simonsen (Eds.), *Contemporary directions in Psychopathology: Scientific foundations of the DSM-V and ICD-11* (pp. 72–96). Guilford.

[16] Fadiman, A. (1997). *The spirit catches you and you fall down: A Hmong child, her American doctors, and the collision of two cultures*. Farrar, Straus and Giroux.

[17] Fernando, G., & Berger, D. (2017). The role of religion in youth exposed to disasters in Sri Lanka. *Journal of Prevention & Intervention in the Community*, 45, 238–249.

may interact with their social world.[18,19] In refugee studies, rarely does research routinely examine the work of culture[20] or the process by which cultural symbols and meanings "get created and recreated through the minds of people." There is a chasm between the purported significance of culture and demonstrating its influence on minority patients' symptoms in practice in the new DSM-5.[21] In making the cultural context relevant to only some types of patients, some scholars critique the DSM-5 for creating an "ethnic dividing line."[22]

Despite the recognition of the paramount role of culture for health, cultural assessment among diverse populations can be a mystifying process. Although progress has been achieved, for instance with the inclusion of the Outline for Cultural Formulation in the DSM-5 (OCF), much remains to be clarified around cultural inquiry and assessment. In other words, how to "adapt the core questions to different settings and types of patients" or how "experts pursue particular lines of inquiry to gain an understanding of patients' symptoms, concerns, and adaptation,"[23] and so on, these feature as prominent concerns. In other fields, such as anthropology and psychology, there exists some resistance to studying the effects of individual factors or broader social and relational factors, respectively.[24] Moreover, cultural-competence approaches in refugee services are deleteriously affected by the insufficient attention afforded to the needs and challenges of refugees.[25,26]

In fact, culture affects every aspect of patient care, from diagnosis[27] to treatment planning. It lends insight into locating the traumatized self through narratives, dreams, and symbols, and socially and culturally mediated indigenous expressions of distress. However, researchers caution that it is only in

[18] Jenkins, J. H., & Haas, B. M. (2016). Trauma in the lifeworlds of adolescents: Hard luck and trouble in the land of enchantment. In D. E. Hinton & B. J. Good (Eds.), *Culture and PTSD: Trauma in global and historical perspectives* (pp. 179–201). University of Pennsylvania Press.

[19] Kirmayer, L. J., & Ramstead, M. J. D. (2017). Embodiment and enactment in cultural psychiatry. In C. Durt, T. Fuchs, & C. Tewes (Eds.), *Embodiment, enaction, and culture: Investigating the constitution of the shared world* (pp. 397–422). MIT Press.

[20] Obeyesekere, G. (1990). *The work of culture: Symbolic transformation in psychoanalysis and anthropology* (p. xix). University of Chicago Press.

[21] Bredström, A. (2019). Culture and context in mental health diagnosing: Scrutinizing the DSM-5 revision. *Journal of Medical Humanities, 40,* 347–363.

[22] Ibid.

[23] Kirmayer, L. J. (2016). The future of cultural formulation. Lewis-Fernández, R., Aggarwal, N. K., Hinton, L., Hinton, D. E., & Kirmayer, L. J. (Eds.), *DSM-5 handbook on the cultural formulation interview* (pp. 267–285). American Psychiatric Publishing.

[24] LeVine, R., & Norman, K. (2001). The infant's acquisition of culture: Early attachment reexamined in anthropological perspective. In C. Moore & H. Mathews (Eds.), *The psychology of cultural experience* (pp. 83–104). Cambridge University Press..

[25] Kirmayer, L. J. (2010). Rethinking cultural competence. *Transcultural Psychiatry, 49,* 149–164.

[26] Lau, L. S., & Rodgers, G. (2021). Cultural competence in refugee service settings: A scoping review. *Health Equity, 5*(1), 124–134.

[27] Kirmayer, L. J., Groleau, D., Guzder, J., Blake, C., & Jarvis, E. (2003). Cultural consultation: A model of mental health service for multicultural societies. *Canadian Journal of Psychiatry, 48*(3), 145–153.

conjunction with the psychological investigation of individual thought processes and emotional reactions that we can gain an insight into personal meanings carried by cultural idioms.[28] Aside from a minority patient population, even with patients belonging to a similar linguistic and racial backgrounds as the clinician, a cultural frame can enable us to parse the various expectations that sufferers may hold. It is only through engaging with culture, as previously discussed in Chapter 5, that cultural models acquire the force to become personal and enact social change.[29,30] Adopting a cultural frame can help us understand how a cultural milieu can be changed by individual actors, thus bringing about social change.

Culture can shape both healing and suffering: patients carry expectations of the nature of acceptable care,[31] its duration, the pattern of their symptoms,[32] and to whom and how they will narrate their experiences of illness.[33,34] Culture thus is also at the heart of clinical encounter and the care for life problems.[35] How culture frames suffering, whether by incorporating local expressions and meaning systems or not, can facilitate either the sufferer's social integration or their ostracism. Investigating the cultural and social meanings attributed to trauma[36] can affect an illness's course and outcome.[37] Over and above, in traumatized and underserved populations, including those with specialized needs (e.g., women, the disabled, lesbian, gay, bisexual, transgender, and queer (LGBTQ),[38,39] the elderly, and children), culturally informed care is a crucial step toward mitigating the treatment gap in mental health.

[28] Chiovenda, A. (2020). *Crafting masculine selves: Culture, war, and psychodynamics in Afghanistan* (pp. 2–3). Oxford University Press.

[29] Geertz, C. (1973). *The interpretation of cultures.* Basic Books.

[30] Hollan, D. (2000). Constructivist models of mind, contemporary psychoanalysis, and the development of culture theory. *American Anthropologist, 102,* 538–550.

[31] Rogler, L. H., & Cortes, D. E. (1993). Help-seeking pathways: A unifying concept in mental health care. *American Journal of Psychiatry, 150,* 554–561.

[32] Kleinman, A. (1977). Depression, somatization and the "new cross-cultural psychiatry. *Social Science and Medicine, 11,* 3–10.

[33] Zhang, A. Y., Snowden, L. R., & Sue, S. (1998). Differences between Asian- and White-Americans' help-seeking and utilization patterns in the Los Angeles area. *Journal of Community Psychology, 26,* 317–326.

[34] Sue, S. (1998). In search of cultural competence in psychotherapy and counseling. *American Psychologist, 53,* 440–448.

[35] Kleinman, A. (1988). *The illness narratives: Suffering, healing and the human condition.* Perseus.

[36] Castillo, R. (1996). *Culture and mental illness: A client-centered approach.* Brooks/Cole.

[37] Kirmayer, L. J., & Swartz, L. (2013). Culture and global mental health. In V. Patel, M. Prince, A. Cohen, & H. Minas (Eds.), *Global mental health: Principles and practice* (pp. 41–62). Oxford University Press.

[38] Bassetti, E. (2019). Integration challenges faced by transgender refugees in Italy. In A. Güler, M. Shevtsova, & D. Venturi (Eds.), *LGBTI asylum seekers and refugees from a legal and political perspective* (pp. 337–348). Springer.

[39] Morales, F. R., Nguyen-Finn, K. L., Haidar, M., & Mercado, A. (2022). Humanitarian crisis on the US-Mexico border: Mental health needs of refugees and asylum seekers. *Current Opinion in Psychology, 9*(48), 101452.

Culturally informed care can increase patient access, engagement, and equity, and assist in building culturally responsive global mental health care. Despite much research on the failures in incorporating cultural competency in mental health delivery and their devastating consequences, the impact of health care providers' cultural misunderstandings continue to be noted in Latinos and Hmong,[40] Native Americans and Alaska Natives,[41] and African Americans.[42] Local categories, even when they may seem aligned with psychiatric categories, are embedded in unique contexts. Incorporating cultural research in complex humanitarian settings or during psychiatric epidemiological surveys can highlight at-risk populations, expand psychiatric categories, and mobilize community resources.[43] The elucidation of local concepts can help in distinguishing between social suffering and mental disorders and, thus, assist in designing effective and sustainable interventions.

Toward this purpose, the chapter explores posttraumatic stress as a cultural entity among refugees shaped by navigating various subcultures or by engaging with local cultural constructs of well-being and distress. The section that follows defines *culture* and *cultural competence*. After this, it utilizes Hollowell's five frames to illustrate how a therapist and the refugee client can together harness cultural knowledge by tapping into a respondent's description of their experiences organized across five parameters of their behavioral sphere (to be discussed later).[44] In doing so, the chapter also highlights the value of utilizing person-centered ethnographies, in line with other research,[45,46,47,48] that integrate subjective experiences.

[40] Park, L., Schwei, R. J., Xiong, P., & Jacobs, E. A. (2018). Addressing cultural determinants of health for Latino and Hmong patients with limited English proficiency: Practical strategies to reduce health disparities. *Journal of Racial and Ethnic Health Disparities, 5*(3), 536–544.

[41] Nahian, A., & Jouk, N. (2022). Cultural competence in caring for American Indians and Alaska Natives: Cultural competence. *StatPearls.* https://www.ncbi.nlm.nih.gov/books/NBK570619/

[42] Dawadi, A., Lucas, T., Drolet, C. E., Thompson, H. S., Key, K., Dailey, R., & Blessman, J. (2021). Healthcare provider cultural competency and receptivity to colorectal cancer screening among African Americans. *Psychology, Health & Medicine.*

[43] Kohrt, B. A., Rasmussen, A., Kaiser, B. N., Haroz, E. E., Maharjan, S. M., Mutamba, B. B., de Jong, J. T., & Hinton, D. E. (2014). Cultural concepts of distress and psychiatric disorders: Literature review and research recommendations for global mental health epidemiology. *International Journal of Epidemiology, 43*(2), 365–406.

[44] Hallowell, I. A. (2010). Psychological leads for ethnological field workers. In R. A. Levine (Ed.), *Psychological anthropology: A reader on self in culture* (pp. 30–52). Blackwell. (Original work published 1937)

[45] Devereaux, G. (1980). *Basic problems of ethnopsychiatry.* University of Chicago Press.

[46] Estroff, S. E. (1989). Self, identity, and subjective experiences of schizophrenia: In search of the subject. *Schizophrenia Bulletin, 15,* 189–197.

[47] Rosaldo, M. (1984). Toward an anthropology of self and feeling. In R. A. Shweder & R. A. LeVine (Eds.), *Culture theory: Essays on mind, self, and emotion* (pp. 137–157). Cambridge University Press.

[48] Pandolfo, S. (2000). The thin line of modernity: Some Moroccan debates on subjectivity. In T. Mitchell (Ed.), *Questions of modernity* (pp. 115–147). University of Minnesota Press.

This chapter also explores the role of local expressions in illustrating refugee well-being and illness, and how aspects of culture are dynamic and evolving: they may be negotiated within and between individuals for purposes of assimilation, building communality, or greater support for their family member challenged by posttraumatic stress. Utilizing data from questionnaires provided to the Middle Eastern refugees in my study, I highlight the five ways in which refugees manifested distress in their current situations: (1) depression, (2) affective distress (terror and sadness), (3) distress in relationships whether with self or others, (4) cognitive, and (5) somatization. Refugees' perception of the etiology[49] and their lived experience of illness can also assist in the development of cultural models of care to improve clinical outcomes.[50] This chapter proposes extending the depth and scope of culture both in the clinic and in the community with an aim to improving, scaling up, and empowering the mental health capacity of host nations through harnessing local sources of understanding and resilience.

First, let us ask: What is culture? And how does harnessing cultural knowledge help us tap into the elusive and ever-changing experience of another person?

Understanding Culture and Cultural Competence

Broadly defined, *culture* is the system of knowledge, concepts, and practices; through a process of enculturation, culture encapsulates the way of life, identity, and traditions of a group of people.[51] It also transmits the social world with its symbols, systems, and social values across generations. Culture affects the social conditions structuring socioeconomic inequities, individuals' course of recovery and outcomes of illness, and the patient-doctor relationship, thus playing a critical role in global health care. Historically, culture has typically been equated with a nation or society or the typical behavior of groups. In the anthropological sciences, individuals and cultures were often seen as identical, and it was assumed that abstract cultural patterns typified all of its people. In recent times, this universal metaphysics of emotional experience has been contested—and rightly so—and culture remains an essential tool for understanding nation-states, groups, and individuals.

Cultural competence as a trait of individuals and organizations in humanitarian emergencies prioritizes diversity, demonstrates capacity for cultural

[49] Watters, C. (2001). Emerging paradigms in the mental health care of refugees. *Social Science & Medicine, 52*(11), 1709–1718.

[50] Bhui, K., & Bhugra, D. (2002). Explanatory models for mental distress: Implications for clinical practice and research. *British Journal of Psychiatry, 181*(1), 6–7.

[51] Kirmayer, L. J., & Swartz, L. (2013). Culture and global mental health. In V. Patel, M. Prince, A. Cohen, & H. Minas (Eds.), *Global mental health: Principles and practice* (pp. 41–62). Oxford University Press.

assessment and for developing cultural knowledge, and, on the basis of acquiring new awareness, adaptability in service delivery.[52] It can be defined as a "set of values, behaviors, attitudes, and practices within a system, organization, program, or among individuals that enables people to work effectively across cultures. It refers to the ability to honor and respect the beliefs, language, interpersonal styles, and behaviors of individuals and families receiving services, as well as staff who are providing such services."[53]

The Cultural Quest for "Experience": A Brief History

The word *experience* derives from its Latin origin experiential, from *"experiential"* or *"to try."* It implies the process of perceiving or possessing knowledge of conscious events that make up an individual or a group's life. The study of "the illness experience" as shaped by culture in diverse societies faces a conundrum and is at an impasse. This conundrum is due, in part, to its history and to methodology. When anthropological investigations were undertaken during the period between the World Wars "to discover something about the psychology of primitive man (they) discovered a 'group mind,' 'pre-logical mentality,' " according to the anthropologist Alfred Irving Hallowell, investigators "came to the conclusion that myths could be equated with dreams, and neurotic compulsions and avoidances with primitive rites and taboos."[54] Generally, neither the individuals' beliefs, individual variability in their psychological traits, how cultural institutions affected their psychology, cultural change in economic and social life, or how cultural negotiation may play a role were seen as significant influences on subjectivity.

The historic neglect of the study of individual experiences most likely perpetuated the idea of homogenous cultures and corresponded to "specious generalizations about the primitive man, primitive mind and primitive culture as unitary entities." Thus, individual experiences, including "the problems connected with variability in individual behavior; the role of the individual as such in different societies, and the extent to which its institutions serve his personal needs have been indifferently treated, if at all," so wrote Hallowell in 1937.[55]

[52] Cross, T. L. (1989). *Towards a culturally competent system of care. Vol. 1. A monograph of effective services for children who are severely emotionally disturbed.* Georgetown University Child Development Center.

[53] U.S. Department of Health and Human Services. (2003). *Developing cultural competence in disaster mental health programs: Guiding principles and recommendations* (DHHS Pub. No. SMA 3828).

[54] Hallowell, I. A. (2010). Psychological leads for ethnological field workers. In R. A. Levine (Ed.), *Psychological anthropology: A reader on self in culture* (p. 31). Blackwell. (Original work published 1937)

[55] Hallowell, I. A. (2010). Psychological leads for ethnological field workers. In R. A. Levine (Ed.), *Psychological anthropology: A reader on self in culture* (pp. 30–52). Blackwell. (Original work published 1937)

Culture, then, is located in the individual and in her social world and it is fluid, forever dynamic and evolving.

Although much research is converging to show that cultural precursors shape and maintain experiences including the posttraumatic experience, Hallowell says, we cannot expect to have concepts of the self-articulated for us. We must adopt a naive approach in which one can articulate the concepts of self, examine them from different angles, and determine how cultural concepts such as *reincarnation*, *karma*, and *moksha* may become psychologically significant. The following section utilizes five frames established to help the therapist gather cultural knowledge, with the collaboration of the client.

The Five Frames of the Posttrauma Experience Psychological Field

According to Hallowell, rather than a pure cultural description, the most critical task of gaining direct insight into the worldview or the psychological field of the individual is by assuming the point of view of the self in its behavioral environment.[56] Hallowell refers to the experiential world that individuals sense, comprehend, and orient themselves to as the *behavioral environment*. The behavioral apparatus, comprising basic orientations, is colored by one's specific culture. As the self develops, these orientations anchor the self with an identity and with self-continuity. Hallowell based this frame on the Ojibwe Native American people, indigenous to southern Canada and the northern Midwestern United States.

Hallowell's orientations are not only the starting point for studying cultural knowledge but also offer a reconsideration of the knowledge we may possess about a culture and its people. For example, references to cosmic dimensions and metaphysical principles within a culture may not be religion but, in fact, may reflect the attitudes, needs, goals, and affective experience of the self, in interaction with objects such as deities, spiritual beings, and ancestors. Tapping into experience for individuals means gleaning cultural knowledge of an individual's behavioral sphere across five parameters: (1) self-orientation, (2) object orientation, (3) spatial orientation, (4) motivational orientation, and (5) normative orientation. However, Hallowell cautions, a knowledge of culture is necessary as the content from the behavioral field may pose subtleties that are often not easily discernible to people outside of the culture.[57]

---

[56] Hallowell, I. A. (2010). Psychological leads for ethnological field workers. In R. A. Levine (Ed.), *Psychological anthropology: A reader on self in culture* (p. 46). Blackwell. (Original work published 1937)

[57] Hallowell, I. A. (2010). Psychological leads for ethnological field workers. In R. A. Levine (Ed.), *Psychological anthropology: A reader on self in culture* (pp. 30–52). Blackwell. (Original work published 1937)

These five basic orientations or conceptual frameworks advanced by Hallowell are embedded with cultural knowledge, and structure the core of an individual's experience. Let us take a closer look at how they structure the individual's experience by examining the story of Manas, a 24-year-old student from Aleppo:

> I remember it was March 1, 2013. It was the first day of my translation exams. We (students) needed to translate texts to English. The time was 10:30 or 10:35 am. We heard an army plane fly over the university. It was so low that we could see and hear it. The glass windows of the classroom were shaking, and thick shards of glass were flying all around us. My first concern was for my five siblings, and my father who was always outside as he was in the construction industry. This second time the plane had returned and attacked the university.[58] The attack occurred between 10:30 and 11:00 am. I also remembered with shock that it was the break period when most students gathered to talk in groups assuring the maximum impact of the bombing on them.

Self-orientation refers to the way that the individuals orient themselves with regard to others. In recalling the traumatic episode, Manas emphasizes the *we* aspect, his concern for his siblings, family, and the students, in his recall of the cumulative devastation of the bombing on the student body. In the face of a life-changing violent event, his primary identities as a son, sibling, and student will later affect his motivation to become a refugee.

Object orientation refers to the individual's orientation to a world of objects that are articulated and culturally constituted. This can assist individuals in interpreting events in the behavioral environment and in forming beliefs regarding the causation of events. Depending on the conceptual framework provided by one's culture, individuals can also have an orientation to a cosmic, religious, or metaphysical worldview and not necessarily because of, as some might be wont to believe, that natural-supernatural categories are the domains of nonliterate people.

Spatial orientation refers to the ability to identify oneself through a physical locus or by naming places and topographical features—in other words, the individual's ability to construct a mental map. Spatial orientation allows individuals to distinguish events from one another and allows the self to evolve by recalling where one was at a particular moment in time and where one expects to be in the future. The particularities of spatial orientation vary across cultures. For example, if a culture does not have names for days of the week, then spatial orientation may come from "moons," and an individual must know his moons.

---

[58] On January 15, 2013, 82 people were killed during the Aleppo University bombings or airstrike as reported by students at the campus.

The ability to remember and sense events through time and one's relationship to those events in time can be identified with an image of oneself and give the self-continuity. Hallowell underscores that this recall need not be true to be psychologically significant for all respondents. In Syria, people's olive farms and historical sites, some of the world heritage sites, were destroyed or plundered. These include the Old City of Damascus, Bosra, Palmyra, and the medieval buildings of Aleppo. These landmarks feature in Manas's recurring nightmares.

> These days I have a nightmare every 2 to 3 weeks. The dream is not the same, but the story is the same. I find myself (in my nightmares) on the dusty corner of our old neighborhood being shot at by a sniper. It is a story of war. Of running from the Syrian Free Army, killings, of destroyed ancient castles, and of Palmyra or Bosra vanishing in rubble. . . . These nightmares also happen during the day. I dream once a day about the destruction I am running away from. I tell myself "I need to run," but why or where I don't know. I realize that I am in a dream being shot at by a sniper, but it feels as if it's happening in reality.

Motivational orientation refers to goal-driven activity toward objects or activities that are valued within the culture. In approaching the needs of the self, we can encounter, identify, and discriminate different motivational patterns of the self. During the war, for instance, as paramilitary forces were rounding up young male students to force them in the government's army, Manas, like many other young male adults of Syria, was forced to flee. His sisters, like many other women, were required to stay behind to tend to the family. Similar to Hosni's case, Manas's narrative can afford us a glimpse of different gender responsibilities valued within the culture, as well as their mutations in times of crisis.

Normative orientation refers to cultural values, goals, and standards. Whether they are explicit or implicit, they are intrinsic components of all cultures, and they affect self-reference, meanings of illness and recovery, and motivational striving of individuals and their relationship to others in society. As individuals judge their own conduct by the standards of one's society, anxiety, guilt, or shame can be evoked if they perceive themselves as falling short. They also judge the conduct of others in and outside of that society.

The behavioral frame discussed above is by no means exhaustive, with much room for it to be tailored according to the unique circumstances of diverse patients. However, it can offer an initial frame for the clinician to solicit crucial elements of culture, organizing information to understand the respondent's life-world. Through the organization of information in this manner, clinicians can obtain tacit understandings of refugees' cultures through the ways they look at the world, in their motivational strivings, in how they describe their reactions to others in their social worlds. At the same time, a competent formulation of respondents' behavioral and, therefore, cultural world will rely on the skillful use of language, clinical expertise, safety of the client-therapist relationship, and proficiency in culture and trauma to draw out the respondent's perspectives and inform what inquiry to pursue.

Cultural Syndromes and Idioms of Distress

Just as culture constructs the individual experience, culture also constructs how we experience illness and recovery.[59,60,61,62,63] Consider, for example, the case of Hosni, the 36-year-old Syrian whose story we read about in the prologue to this chapter:

> I try to bury the sadness, but it comes up as nervousness. One gets aggressive sometimes. My wife used to be a person who used to laugh. Now you can see the sadness on her face all the time. She was happy visiting her family and had a relaxed demeanor about her. She fell unconscious after hearing of her father's death. Some people even slap their spouses as they get aggressive sometimes.
>
> My wife for instance, when she heard about her father, she started to break things in the house, she started to slap me. Those same things unfolded when her brother died. Same thing with my aunt. My aunt was a quiet person. After she lost her children, she could not stay at home. She is leaving the house all the time. When we ask her, "Where are you going?" She replies, "I'm just coming back." Many people have problems with sleeping. They try to bury their sadness, but if it comes up, they can feel nervousness. In the beginning, when I had just moved to Germany, I had nightmares.
>
> But sometimes, when I think very deeply about some persons, I see them in my dreams. I imagine them to be well dressed in heaven. We are believers, and that gives you discipline and hope.

[59] Kleinman, A. (1982). Neurasthenia and depression: A study of somatization and culture in China. *Culture, Medicine, and Psychiatry, 6*, 117–190.

[60] Littlewood, R. (1992). DSM-1V and culture: Is the classification internationally valid? *Psychiatric Bulletin, 16*, 257–261.

[61] Marsella, A. J., Sartorius, N., Jablensky, A., & Fenton, F. R. (1985). Cross-cultural studies of depressive disorders: An overview. In A. Kleinman & B. Good (Eds.), *Culture and depression: Studies in the anthropology and cross-cultural psychiatry of affect and disorder* (pp. 299–324). University of California Press.

[62] Weiss, M. G., & Kleinman, A. (1988). Depression in cross-cultural perspective: Developing a culturally informed model. In P. R. Dasen, J. W. Berry, & N. Sartorius (Eds.), *Health and cross-cultural psychology: Toward applications* (pp. 179–206). Sage.

[63] Obeyesekere, G. (1981). *Medusa's hair: An essay on personal symbols and religious experience.* University of Chicago Press.

As we see, Hosni experiences posttraumatic stress in himself and others in his family in the form of an uptick of aggression, nervousness, and restlessness. Cultural scripts such as masculinity or an awareness of gender have been utilized by researchers such as Chiovenda to investigate the inner life of his Afghani Pashto informants.[64] It is not as though Hosni is unafraid, we realize as the cultural script is pierced, but that the rain of death and losses have deprived him of his ability to be in touch with his emotions, including fear.

In the case of women, Hosni interprets swooning as a symptom of posttraumatic stress. Indeed, fainting in research has been classified as a defensive and dissociative response in the face of proximate danger.[65] Omidian and Miller have alerted us to *khapa*,[66] a construct signifying sadness, annoyance, and anger or intense emotional distress in Afghani women through injury they inflict on themselves, their children, and others. Unlike psychiatric categories in North America and Europe, both fainting and self-directed aggression may be culturally prescribed ways of communicating distress[67,68] among Syrians and Afghanis, respectively.

Prototypical cultural ailments[69] are widely recognized patterned ways or symptoms in which people of a specific cultural setting perceive, experience, and express distress;[70] they coalesce around one or more core cultural symbols.[71] These can include cultural-bound syndromes,[72] where specific and recurrent cognition, behavior, or experience may play a troubling role in a particular geographic setting or culturally distinct people (e.g., *Dhat*, semen loss

[64] Chiovenda, A. (2015). *Crafting masculine selves: Culture, war and psychodynamics among Afghan Pashtuns.* Oxford University Press.

[65] Schauer, M., & Elbert, T. (2010). Dissociation following traumatic stress: Etiology and treatment. *Zeitschrift für Psychologie/Journal of Psychology, 218*(2), 109–127.

[66] Omidian, P., & Miller, K. (2006). Addressing the psychosocial needs of women in Afghanistan. *Critical Half, 4*(1), 17–22.

[67] Kirmayer, L. J., & Bhugra, D. (2009). Culture and mental illness: Social context and explanatory models. In I. M. Salloum & J. E. Mezzich (Eds.), *Psychiatric diagnosis: Patterns and prospects* (pp. 29–37). John Wiley.

[68] Nichter, M. (1981). Idioms of distress: Alternatives in the expression of psychosocial distress; a case study from South India. *Culture, Medicine, and Psychiatry, 5*(4), 379–408.

[69] Rasmussen, A., Ventevogel, P., Sancilio, A., Eggerman, M., & Panter-Brick, C. (2014). Comparing the validity of the self-reporting questionnaire and the Afghan symptom checklist: Dysphoria, aggression, and gender in transcultural assessment of mental health. *BMC Psychiatry, 14*, 206.

[70] Ibid.

[71] Nichter, M. (2010). Idioms of distress revisited. *Culture, Medicine, and Psychiatry, 34*,(2), 401–416.

[72] Researchers like Kohrt and colleagues recommend the use of cultural concepts of distress or idioms of distress or cultural syndrome, instead of culture-bound to reflect limitations associated with it such as the presence of same pattern of distress across cultures, lack of concrete symptoms to characterize a syndrome, and so forth: Kohrt, B. A., Rasmussen, A., Kaiser, B. N., Haroz, E. E., Maharjan, S. M., Mutamba, B. B., de Jong, J. T., & Hinton, D. E. (2014). Cultural concepts of distress and psychiatric disorders: Literature review and research recommendations for global mental health epidemiology. *International Journal of Epidemiology, 43*(2), 365–406.

syndrome[73] in India; *Uppgivenhetssyndrom*, or *Resignation syndrome*, in Sweden; *Taijinkyofusho*, a specific form of social anxiety occurring in Japan; and ghost visitation among Cambodians,[74] and others). Idioms of distress are culturally inflected language and pragmatic communication that can index distress or pathology.[75]

Many respondents in my study spontaneously endorsed the presence of symptoms of posttraumatic stress, as we can also ascertain from the vignettes. They reported recurrent nightmares, feeling startled, avoidance of activities that may remind them of a hurtful past, challenges in concentrating, and others that are similar to the PTSD constellation in the United States. However, in the absence of local terms denoting posttraumatic syndrome for Afghans,[76] some scholars have indicated that depression or sadness, more than PTSD, is more salient to their community.[77,78] Indeed, among resettled Afghan diaspora who had lived in the United States for an average of approximately 17 years, for instance, a study by Alemi and colleagues found that depression is a common sequela of complex trauma.[79] Likewise, depressive symptomatology was also reported within other Afghan communities of the United States resettled in San Diego and among Afghan refugees resettled in Drenthe, Netherlands.[80] Fifty-seven percent of Afghans[81] with secure residential status in Drenthe nevertheless reported moderate-to-high depression. Recently, however, emerging research is illustrating that Afghans have a high exposure to trauma and incidence of PTSD

[73] Rao, T. S. S. (2021). History and mystery of Dhat syndrome: A critical look at the current understanding and future directions. *Indian Journal of Psychiatry*, 63(4), 317–325.

[74] Hinton, D. E., Reis, R., & de Jong, J. (2020). Ghost encounters among traumatized Cambodian refugees: Severity, relationship to PTSD, and phenomenology. *Culture, Medicine, and Psychiatry*, 44(3), 333–359

[75] Kidron, C. A., & Kirmayer, L. J. (2019). Global mental health and idioms of distress: The paradox of culture-sensitive pathologization of distress in Cambodia. *Culture, Medicine, and Psychiatry*, 43(2), 211–235.

[76] In his doctoral dissertation among Afghani respondents, Ventevogel reports his challenge in explaining PTSD as Afghans did not have a word for it and did not refer to it as a constellation of particular symptoms: Ventevogel, P. (2016). *Borderlands of mental health: Explorations in medical anthropology, psychiatric epidemiology and health systems research in Afghanistan and Burundi* [Unpublished doctoral dissertation] (p. 259). University of Amsterdam.

[77] Miller, K. E., Omidian, P., Kulkarni, M., Yaqubi, A., Daudzai, H., & Rasmussen, A. (2009). The validity and clinical utility of post-traumatic stress disorder in Afghanistan. *Transcultural Psychiatry*, 46(2), 219–237.

[78] Miller, K. E., Omidian, P., Rasmussen, A., Yaqubi, A., & Daudzai, H. (2008). Daily stressors, war experiences, and mental health in Afghanistan. *Transcultural Psychiatry*, 45(4), 611–638

[79] Alemi, Q., James, S., & Montgomery, S. (2016). Contextualizing Afghan refugee views of depression through narratives of trauma, resettlement stress, and coping. *Transcultural Psychiatry*, 53(5), 630–653.

[80] Gernaat, H. B., Malwand, A. D., Laban, C. J., Komproe, I., & de Jong, J. T. (2002). Many psychiatric disorders in Afghan refugees with residential status in Drenthe, especially depressive disorder and post-traumatic disorder. *Nederlands Tijdschrift voor Geneeskunde*, 146(24), 127–131.

[81] Ibid.

in contrast to other disorders such as major depression disorders or generalized anxiety.[82,83]

Afghans have a rich cultural vocabulary to describe their experience of illness[84] that manifests itself in the form of depression.[85] In studying depression among Afghans, researchers such Alemi et al.,[86,87] Miller et al.,[88] and Ventevogel,[89] using ethnographic research, delineate various idioms and one cultural syndrome (*jigar khun*)[90] to highlight local forms of understandings and responses to stress:

- *asabi ("irritability")*
- *afsurdagi ("grief, low mood, and restlessness")*
- *fishar ("internal agitation or low motivation")*[91]
- *gham ("sadness")*
- *goshagiry ("self-isolation")*
- *jigar khun ("bloody liver or heart to signify chronic stress")*
- *khapgan ("deep sadness or sorrow")*
- *peyran ("possessed by spirits")*
- *waswasi ("constant worry")*
- *wahmi ("easily frightened")*

[82] National Mental Health Symposium. *Balance: The mutual reinforcement of mental well-being, peace and economic stability.* (2019, March). https://moph.gov.af/sites/default/files/2019-09/Natio nal%20Mental%20Health%20Symposium%20Report%20English%2015May%202019.pdf

[83] Brea, L. D., Sandal, G. M., Guribye, E., Markova, V., & Sam, D. L. (2022). Explanatory models of post-traumatic stress disorder (PTSD) and depression among Afghan refugees in Norway. *BMC Psychology, 10,* 5.

[84] Alemi, Q., James, S., & Montgomery, S. (2016). Contextualizing Afghan refugee views of depression through narratives of trauma, resettlement stress, and coping. *Transcultural Psychiatry, 53*(5), 630–653.

[85] Alemi, Q., James, S., Cruz, R., Zepeda, V., & Racadio, M. (2014). Psychological distress in Afghan refugees: A mixed-method systematic review. *Journal of Immigrant & Minority Health, 16*(1), 1247–1261.

[86] Alemi, Q., James, S., Cruz, R., Zepeda, V., & Racadio, M. (2014). Psychological distress in Afghan refugees: A mixed-method systematic review. *Journal of Immigrant & Minority Health, 16*(1), 1247–1261.

[87] Alemi, Q., Weller, S. C., Montgomery, S., & James, S. (2017). Afghan refugee explanatory models of depression: Exploring core cultural beliefs and gender variations. *Medical Anthropology Quarterly, 31*(2), 177–197. https://doi.org/10.1111/maq.12296

[88] Miller, K. E., Omidian, P., Quraishy, A. S., Quraishy, N., Nasiry, M. N., Nasiry, S., Karyar, N. M., & Yaqubi, A. A. (2006). The Afghan symptom checklist: A culturally grounded approach to mental health assessment in a conflict zone. *American Journal of Orthopsychiatry, 76,* 423–433.

[89] Ventevogel, P. (2016). *Borderlands of mental health: Explorations in medical anthropology, psychiatric epidemiology and health systems research in Afghanistan and Burundi* [Unpublished doctoral dissertation] (p. 258). University of Amsterdam.

[90] Rasmussen, A., Ventevogel, P., Sancilio, A., Eggerman, M., & Panter-Brick, C. (2014). Comparing the validity of the self-reporting questionnaire and the Afghan symptom checklist: Dysphoria, aggression, and gender in transcultural assessment of mental health. *BMC Psychiatry, 14,* 206.

[91] Omidian, P., & Miller, K. (2006). Addressing the psychosocial needs of women in Afghanistan. *Critical Half, 4*(1), 17–22.

The array of local idioms highlighted above may illustrate the complexity of a culture's emotional dictionary; however, it is important to examine how idioms may also be used by individuals in nonclinical contexts. Kidron and Kirmayer caution against medicalizing idioms or equating them with psychiatric disorders and thus pathologizing a culture's adaptive forms of coping.[92] Identifying local categories can unearth meanings and emotions salient in the local context. For instance, utilizing a culturally grounded instrument as opposed to an internationally developed one, enabled Rasmussen and colleagues to discover "*jigar khun*" and aggression, two central elements of Afghan mental health. The capture of subtleties within local explanations by culturally grounded instruments lead researchers to conclude on their effectiveness and imperative to develop culturally relevant measures for long-term programming in countries.[93]

Distress for Afghans living in Afghanistan is also manifested as somatic distress in the form of irritability and anger, lethargy, agitation, chronic fatigue, headaches, and physical malaises.[94] Most Afghans resettled in San Diego for over a decade, and who were mostly Pashtun, Alemi found, expressed their state of depression through bodily malaise such as headaches, abdominal pain, dizziness, insomnia, pale complexion, overeating, tension in the neck and shoulders, low energy, appetite loss, feelings of pins and needles all over the body, and heart/chest pains.[95] Somatic distress in the form of headaches and pain have been reported among other war-affected communities, such as among the young female rape survivors of Kovumi of the Democratic Republic of Congo. Reports Nyata Mwakavuha of her 8-year-old daughter to the journalist Christina Lamb:[96]

> *My daughter is always complaining about headache and back pain. One day she was taunted by a classmate who said, "You were raped," and she fainted. I'm afraid she will have problems in the future.*

Somatic distress may have cultural precursors, but tragically, so does the violence inflicted on female toddlers and children by the Congolese militia. Ripping hymens and the blood obtained from them, the male abusers believe, have

[92] Kidron, C.A., & Kirmayer, L. J. (2019). Global mental health and idioms of distress: The paradox of culture-sensitive pathologization of distress in Cambodia. *Culture, Medicine, and Psychiatry*, 43(2), 211–235.

[93] Rasmussen, A., Ventevogel, P., Sancilio, A., Eggerman, M., & Panter-Brick, C. (2014). Comparing the validity of the self-reporting questionnaire and the Afghan symptom checklist: Dysphoria, aggression, and gender in transcultural assessment of mental health. *BMC Psychiatry, 14*, 206.

[94] Eggerman, M., & Panter-Brick, C. (2010). Suffering, hope, and entrapment: Resilience and cultural values in Afghanistan. *Social Science & Medicine, 71*(1), 71–83.

[95] Alemi, Q. (2013). *Cultural consensus model of depression beliefs among Afghan refugees* [Doctoral dissertation, Loma Linda University]. Loma Linda University Electronic Theses, Dissertations & Projects. http://scholarsrepository.llu.edu/etd/111

[96] Lamb, C. (2020). *Our bodies, their battlefield: What war does to women*. William Collins.

special powers to protect them against bullets on the battlefield. As elucidated by the warped beliefs that underlie this practice, when explanatory mechanisms for both violence and recovery may lie within the culture, in order to systemically change them, integrating cultural brokers or folk healers in treatment planning can be useful.

Although there may be some overlap of the location and attribution of distress across cultures, they can also vary with cultures. Traumatized Yazidi female refugees, for instance, in addition to posttraumatic stress, report pain symptoms, feelings of suffocation, and movement disorders.[97] The role of pain in how illness is represented is associated with their perceptions of personal injury, health, and well-being. The health effects of the violence they have endured are attributed to psychological, physical, religious causes, and supernatural causes. However, female refugees with pain were more likely than those without pain to attribute their symptoms mostly to physical causes. The well-being of formerly enslaved Yazidi female refugees is influenced by the extent of pain that afflicts them.

The Middle Eastern refugees interviewed for the study discussed in this book, as revealed by a principal component factor analysis, tended to manifest distress in five ways: (1) depression, (2) affective distress (terror and sadness), (3) distress in relationships whether with self or others, (4) cognition, thoughts, and beliefs, and (5) somatization. In Factor 1, respondents endorsed items such as "feeling worthless," "hopeless," and having "no interest." In Factor 2, they reported feelings of being "suddenly scared" and "fearful," and "feeling blue" and experiencing their "heart-pounding." In Factor 3, participants reported distress because of relational factors, such as separation, breakup, or ongoing stress. In Factor 4, respondents reported experiences such as "feeling lonely," "blaming oneself," and "crying easily." In Factor 5, respondents reported "headaches" and "feeling tense." Consider two examples of how Factor 5 can manifest itself in the reports of two refugees:

> "I have huge headaches. I feel sad, but I don't cry. . . . I am living with men, and I cannot have them see me cry." Arbaz, aged 23 years, Afghani
> "This illness of the head overcomes me. . . . due to lack of work." Ferooz, aged 32 years, Syrian

Hosni's case study seemed to be exemplifying distress manifested through Factor 2, with high arousal states of terror and sadness. Although the sample by no means is vast, taken together, these factor structures can also represent

[97] Rometsch, C., Denkinger, J. K., Engelhardt, M., Windthorst, P., Graf, J., Gibbons, N., Pham, P., Zipfel, S., & Junne, F. (2020). Pain, somatic complaints, and subjective concepts of illness in traumatized female refugees who experienced extreme violence by the "Islamic State" (IS). *Journal of Psychosomatic Research*, 130. https://doi.org/10.1016/j.jpsychores.2020.109931

the various methods in which memories of trauma may be activated by thought, emotion, and somatic means, as suggested by Hinton and Kirmayer's multiplex model.[98] The presence of these modalities of distress can also suggest they may be interrelated: how everyday worries in the lives of refugees who have endured multiple stressors can result in vicious cycles of symptomatology.

It is important to broaden and deepen our lens on the psychological lives of our patients and explore the situations underpinning their emotions in their daily lives to distinguish between everyday forms of distress and trauma-related ill-ness constructs. More systematic research with Afghans will need to include local expressions of trauma, rely on reports from family members, assess for resilience and so forth to differentiate between their distress and disorder, determine its PTSD's prominence over depression or vice versa, and explore a cross-cultural con-stellation of posttraumatic stress symptoms.

Trauma is steeped in cultural meanings—and stripping it of meaning will make it impossible to formulate the intervention or treat the suffering. However, interventions intended to be culturally competent may paradoxically undermine local understandings if they neglect to examine individual engagement with negotiating or contesting local or cultural constructs. For instance, a Muslim refugee mother embraced the idea of her underage son drinking alcohol with his friends, a behavior in opposition to the cultural/religious dictates, as she was terrified of her teenager's growing posttraumatic stress. The benefits of her son pursuing social relationships to combat depression outweighed the guilt of transgressing against cultural mores and incurring the wrath of her family; this can be seen as individual negotiation of a cul-tural and religious values, and when more members of a community engage in such negotiations, it can be a precursor of social change. Kidron and Kirmayer thus em-phasize the importance of paying attention to the gap between local meanings and individuals' engagement with local and cultural concepts of distress.[99]

In the section that follows, let us consider how cultural negotiation might also extend to providers. When local providers prioritize some clinical symptoms over others, it may in turn trump the use of some diagnoses over others in a particular culture. Similarly, the unique socio-historical conditions of a community[100,101] can influence what its inhabitants perceive trauma to be.

[98] Hinton, D. E., & Lewis-Fernandez, R. (2011). The cross-cultural validity of posttraumatic stress disorder: Implications for DSM-5. *Depression and Anxiety, 28*, 783–801.

[99] Kidron, C. A., & Kirmayer, L. J. (2019). Global mental health and idioms of distress: The par-adox of culture-sensitive pathologization of distress in Cambodia. *Culture, Medicine, and Psychiatry, 43*(2), 211–235.

[100] Jenkins, J. H., & Haas, B. M. (2016). Trauma in the lifeworlds of adolescents: Hard luck and trouble in the land of enchantment. In D. E. Hinton & B. J. Good (Eds.), *Culture and PTSD: Trauma in global and historical perspectives* (pp. 179–201). University of Pennsylvania Press.

[101] Kirmayer, L. J., & Ramstead, M. J. D. (2017). Embodiment and enactment in cultural psychi-atry. In C. Durt, T. Fuchs, & C. Tewes (Eds.), *Embodiment, enaction, and culture: Investigating the constitution of the shared world* (pp. 397–422). MIT Press.

Negotiating Trauma and Healing: Familial, Social, Historical, and Political Contexts

Just as with individual experiences in general, experiences of trauma are shaped by culture and community, diagnoses of mental disorders, assessment of distress, and whether treatment needs to be sought must be negotiated within the family and community context. How understandings of trauma are negotiated is as seminal to its experience as are the discourses of society, culture, and self in shaping it.[102]

Ultimately, the label of mental disorder, levels of distress, and their repair are also dependent on its negotiation within the family and community context. Anthropologist Whitney Duncan's work on Oaxacan women[103] notes that cultural meanings assigned to trauma, whether trauma will be labeled as such, and whether treatment will be pursued for it, is the result of negotiation between the public and providers. In Oaxaca, Mexico, domestic violence is ubiquitous, but the traditional Oaxacan culture discourages females from explicitly attributing suffering to violence perpetrated by their menfolk. In recent times statewide efforts to deter violence have coordinated initiatives from churches, nongovernmental organizations, mental health clinics, and human rights organizations. Such public health initiatives can create a shift, pivoting from the old, routine presence of domestic violence in women's lives and its reluctant acceptance to the realization of the grave dangers of violence, how it "marks you"[104] for the traditional Oaxacan community. Even when the trauma is violent enough to trigger PTSD, the trauma experienced by battered women is often attributed to other mental health problems such as depression and anxiety.

Duncan's research highlights the social negotiation of the PTSD diagnosis by various community therapists to keep women from being stigmatized by it. Despite the emergence of a new sensitivity to the presence of PTSD diagnoses, the primary reason why PTSD is mostly not utilized in attributing suffering to domestic violence is, according to Duncan, a "sense of antipsychiatry" among Oaxacan therapists.[105] Oaxacan therapists can fault psychiatry for pathologizing normal and adaptive emotions and allege that it can misidentify the source of

---

[102] Jenkins, J. H. (1991). The state construction of affect: Political ethos and mental health among Salvadoran refugees. *Culture, Medicine, and Psychiatry, 15,* 139–165.

[103] Duncan, W. L. (2015). Gendered trauma and its effects: Domestic violence and PTSD in Oaxaca. In D. E. Hinton & B. J. Good (Eds.), *Culture and PTSD: Trauma in global and historical perspective* (pp. 202–239). University of Pennsylvania Press.

[104] Duncan, W. L. (2015). Gendered trauma and its effects: Domestic violence and PTSD in Oaxaca. In D. E. Hinton & B. J. Good (Eds.), *Culture and PTSD: Trauma in global and historical perspective* (p. 206). University of Pennsylvania Press.

[105] Duncan, W. L. (2015). Gendered trauma and its effects: Domestic violence and PTSD in Oaxaca. In D. E. Hinton & B. J. Good (Eds.), *Culture and PTSD: Trauma in global and historical perspective* (pp. 202–239). University of Pennsylvania Press.

patients' problems, rather than promoting explicit actions to change the social situations in which Oaxacans live.

Thus, cultural practices of nondiagnoses of PTSD may, in turn, affect Oaxacan women's efforts at denouncing it, the palpable existence of it in their lives, and whether or not they will seek or shun treatment. Survivors may live with a particular constellation of distressing symptoms but without a diagnosis. Duncan's study shows that prevalent patriarchal ideology can sway patient-provider perceptions of the gravity of domestic violence. Mental health professionals can internalize and explicitly promote false beliefs, such as that a culture of violence accustoms people to its traumatic effects. The recognition of mental health or, conversely, downplay of symptoms by their significant others ("It's not as bad as depression." "She must be bipolar." "It's all in your head.") are often a primary reason individuals will either seek or shun treatment. Thus, it is understandable that beliefs held by Oaxacan providers can also inhibit the detection of trauma-related symptoms of domestic abuse.[106] Extending the exploration of the local idioms of distress and well-being to other indigenous healers and treatment providers as per Duncan's lens then can potentially reveal the role of provider and cultural bias in affecting the diagnosis, treatment, and recovery.

"To begin to more fully comprehend experiences of trauma and loss,"[107] we must be more "theoretically attuned to the contexts of psychological development and social-historical structures from which they arise." Jenkins and Haas parse the nature of trauma in the lives of 47 young teenagers of the Southwestern United States.[108] They use the term *psychic trauma* to describe the matrix of unrelenting, recurrent, and inexorable traumatic events endured by adolescents and their families from Albuquerque, New Mexico. Many developmental periods of these youth's lives have been riddled with physical, sexual, and emotional abuse; assault; drug abuse; gang activity; housing instability; frequent contact with police; and involvement in the correctional system. In adopting a broad frame of trauma, Jenkins and Haas's research also urges incorporating social-historical circumstances, such as 5 centuries of political unrest and conflict in the region, to glean an individual or community's lived experiences of trauma. Adolescents' attributions of trauma as a normal way of life, Jenkins and

[106] Duncan, W. L. (2015). Gendered trauma and its effects: Domestic violence and PTSD in Oaxaca. In D. E. Hinton & B. J. Good (Eds.), *Culture and PTSD: Trauma in Global and Historical Perspective* (p. 232).University of Pennsylvania Press.

[107] Jenkins, J. H., & Haas, B. M. (2016). Trauma in the lifeworlds of adolescents: Hard luck and trouble in the land of enchantment. In D. E. Hinton & B. J. Good (Eds.), *Culture and PTSD: Trauma in global and historical perspectives* (pp. 179–201). University of Pennsylvania Press

[108] Jenkins, J. H., & Haas, B. M. (2016). Trauma in the lifeworlds of adolescents: Hard luck and trouble in the land of enchantment. In D. E. Hinton & B. J. Good (Eds.), *Culture and PTSD: Trauma in global and historical perspectives* (p. 198). University of Pennsylvania Press.

Haas argue, are molded by the degree of violence as a result of their historic economic marginalization.

Through the plight of Salvadoran refugees' sufferings in a culture of terror, Jenkins illustrates the importance of analyzing a state's influence on the construction of affect. The influence on Salvadorans' widespread dysthymic ethos must be considered within the political environment in its entirety—State's activities, economic conditions, and domestic environment—that are dimensions of a single political ethos.[109] Both the above insights from Jenkins and Haas's[110] and Jenkins's[111] studies are directly applicable to the case of Akbar, a 17-year-old Afghan refugee, which exemplifies the normalization of violence in the lives of Afghan children.

These Shoes Are Made for Walking

When 17-year-old Akbar, an Afghan, bought the fanciest white shoes in Khorāsān in eastern Iran for his European journey, little did he realize that in some ways, he would be following in the footsteps of his father, Amir Khusro Lodi. Three decades prior, Amir Khusro, a farmer who had never set foot outside his village, had left a violent Afghanistan in search of a safe home in Iran for his family. The sun comes from Khorāsān, a Persian saying goes, and finding that he could make a living as a tailor in one of its fertile valleys, the senior Lodi had beckoned his aging parents and wife there. In the brief crack when the war ended, says Akbar, illegals like us were expected to return to our countries. Amir Khusro once again took another solo return journey to Afghanistan to determine the feasibility of his family's return. But he never came back. Akbar was 1 year old when he lost his father. He was born in a refugee camp and never stepped foot in Afghanistan. "I was really small, so I didn't understand my father's death and had to accept it. Harder to accept was that I couldn't attend school all my life."

"It was a lifetime of hiding in Iran." In July 2015, to help his mother and three younger siblings escape their poor living conditions and illegal statuses, with his new shoes, Akbar set on foot the almost 1,400-mile trek from Iran to Turkey by walking. In a grueling trek, he crossed mountains, gorges, and forests. "Mostly

[109] Jenkins, J. H. (1991). The state construction of affect: Political ethos and mental health among Salvadoran refugees. *Culture, Medicine, and Psychiatry, 15*(2), 139–165. https://doi.org/10.1007/BF0 0119042

[110] Jenkins, J. H., & Haas, B. M. (2016). Trauma in the lifeworlds of adolescents: Hard luck and trouble in the land of enchantment. In D. E. Hinton & B. J. Good (Eds.), *Culture and PTSD: Trauma in global and historical perspectives* (pp. 179–201). University of Pennsylvania Press.

[111] Jenkins, J. H. (1991). The state construction of affect: Political ethos and mental health among Salvadoran refugees. *Culture, Medicine, and Psychiatry, 15*(2), 139–165. https://doi.org/10.1007/BF0 0119042

older people don't make it," says Akbar. "There was one very narrow and precarious path in the gorges," he said, "where oxygen was rare at high altitudes that it caused many elderly people to slip and crash to their deaths. I witnessed one such death. Other fellow walkers just kept walking." In Turkey, Akbar took a bus to its coast, a ship to Greece, walking 10 miles to Athens, a bus to Macedonia, train to Hungary, and finally arrived about four weeks later to Passau in south Germany; he was to move through five other German cities, Munich, Bonn, Kerken, Koblenz, and Hanau.

The entire journey had cost him 5,000 euros. This was his second attempt; in the first aborted attempt, he had been caught by the Greek border police before being handed over to Turkish authorities and imprisoned for 3 months. If I met the German Chancellor Merkel, says Akbar I would tell her, "Of course those people are not satisfied in a country which is destroyed, where there is no work, no infrastructure, no security, education, no health. Of course these people will attempt to enter Europe. If you really care about us Afghan people, help to fix the problem in Afghanistan itself." If my father was alive today, he would tell me, "You did well to come to Germany. If you hadn't come to Germany, your child would have or your child's child would have."

Conditions like posttraumatic stress are psychologically, culturally, and politically constructed. Refugees' perceptions of their favorable socio-political treatment by host nations, as in the case of Akbar, may play an instrumental role in their healing and recovery. Of the respondents in my study, 75% voiced beliefs about geopolitical nexus and the role of other nations in the breakdown of the social contract, and as factors ultimately responsible for their mental health.

Says Manas:

Asad is a toy of Russia, Iran, and Turkey. Iran supports Syria with fighters; Russians support Syria with weapons, and China supports with money. America is supplying weapons to Syria and Iraq. There has been no political solution in Syria for the last 7 years. The only solution is war, weapons, money, and access.

Manas suggests the involvement of many countries in the proxy wars in Syria is ultimately responsible for the condition of his countrymen. Although his proposition may be debatable by some, what is undeniable is the sense of abandonment refugees feel by the global community. Their perception of the role of their host nation's involvement in controlling their native country's resources and in prolonging the war can challenge its exceptionalism and affect repatriation and integration in those nations. Similarly, Nishad, an Afghani refugee, voices the role of his government in his restlessness:

Afghania is my homeland. I love it with my heart. But the way the war is going on in Afghanistan, I view the government very poorly. The ongoing war has filled my heart with restlessness. I also feel that when there is news or on Facebook or email, I cannot stop my worrying.

"By developing further our understanding of the political psychology of traumatic events, we may identify better strategies for preventing or ameliorating the negative effects of such acts."[112] Equally significant to the perspective of psychological reaction to a traumatic political event as in the case of veterans of the Persian Gulf War of 1991 is taking into account aspects of the political/environmental situation survivors were exposed to[113] and exploring the effects of the event on the personal ethos of those who were present and those who may not have been present.

Refugee survivors have often been referred to as a "silent majority."[114] However, when treatments are not culturally relevant, many asylum-seekers may either drop out of therapy or simply not show up. The dearth of contextually sensitive interventions tailored to refugees' unique circumstances makes it challenging to pin their unwillingness to talk as the primary factor undergirding their silence. Diagnostic interpretations made using our own cultural meaning systems—and not our patients',[115,116] "has led to the medicalization of social problems," such as the high rates of substance abuse among refugees.[117,118] Culturally relevant care may also be unavailable because of clinicians' being unprepared to provide it.[119] Increasingly cross-cultural understanding for clinicians requires being multilingual in the dictionaries of other cultures.[120] This would involve an understanding

[112] Koopman, C. (1997). Political psychology as a lens for viewing traumatic events. *Political Psychology, 18*(4), 830–847.

[113] Koopman, C. (1997). Political psychology as a lens for viewing traumatic events. *Political Psychology, 18*(4), 832.

[114] Baker, R. (1992). Psychosocial consequences for tortured refugees seeking asylum and refugee status in Europe. In M. Basoglu (Ed.), *Torture and its consequences: Current treatment approaches* (pp. 83–106). Cambridge University Press.

[115] Loughry, M., & Eyber, C. (2003). *Psychosocial concepts in humanitarian work: A review of the concepts and related literature.* National Academies Press.

[116] Betancourt, T. S., & Williams, T. (2008). Building an evidence base on mental health interventions for children affected by armed conflict. *Intervention, 6*, 39–56.

[117] Frederik, C. J. (1981). Violence and disaster: Immediate and long-term consequences. In (WHO Working Group on the Psychosocial Consequences of Violence, Ed.), *Helping victims of violence* (pp. 32–46). World Health Organization.

[118] Lai, L. (2014). Treating substance abuse as a consequence of conflict and displacement: A call for a more inclusive global mental health *Medicine, Conflict and Survival, 30*(3), 182–189.

[119] BeLue, R., Barnes, A., Manu, S., Luckett, C., & Adam, B. (2021). Culturally responsive psychiatric services for refugee and immigrant adolescents: Are child and adolescent psychiatrists prepared to serve refugee children? A focus on African refugee families. *Health Equity Open Access, 5*(1), 306–309.

[120] Landrine, H. (1992). Clinical implications of cultural differences: The referential versus the indexical self. *Clinical Psychology Review, 12*(4), 401–415.

of their unique explanatory models across different contexts, distinct experiences of wellness and distress, coping behaviors, and pathways to healing.[121]

However, to accommodate the diverse settings where asylum-seekers are today, our cultural lens must be expanded to encompass contextual sensitivity. Consider refugees in extrajudicial settings and in detentions, subject to deterrent immigrant policies. In detention settings, political and legal communications can embody violence and inequity and perpetuate dehumanization. Clinical interventions in such settings mean recognizing the role of political and legal structures in refugees' experiences of illness.[122] Sensitivity to refugee contexts can influence the nature, role, and scope of clinical intervention.

Cultural competence in refugee services, then, means prioritizing a cultural frame for a better understanding of ethnocultural variations in distress to create effective and sustainable interventions with refugee communities. Within individuals and systems, culturally responsive practices are ones that seek to understand how cultural competence is experienced and the influences of class, urban-rural background, literacy, history of racism, and discrimination on its minority communities that can differentially affect the help-seeking behaviors of refugees.

Cultural competence in interventions among refugee communities displaced in different contexts can be enhanced through other ways. Developing culturally valid research instruments can identify meaningful, local categories of well-being or illness using ethnographic data collection. They can also underscore the importance of linguistically appropriate measures with participants representative of the target community (with respect to, e.g., race, ethnicity, language preference, and country of origin). Building a team of cultural consultants that may include cultural experts or traditional healers, bilingual staff, interpreters with frequent staff trainings and conducting regular reviews can improve access to and the availability and knowledge of services. Incorporating a combination of qualitative and quantitative research to design contextually relevant instruments for cultural epidemiology can assist in identifying appropriate interventions.[123] Disseminating educational materials in languages and formats understood by the target communities to outline study goals can ensure transparency, engage prospective participants, and the community. Expanding community-based initiatives to increase synergy between hosts and refugees and promote interdependence between communities can only be possible through culturally competent ways of alleviating their trauma.

[121] Kidron, C. A., & Kirmayer, L. J. (2019). Global mental health and idioms of distress: The paradox of culture-sensitive pathologization of distress in Cambodia. *Culture, Medicine, and Psychiatry*, 43(2), 211–235.

[122] Fennig, M. (2021). Cultural adaptations of evidence-based mental health interventions for refugees: Implications for clinical social work. *British Journal of Social Work*, 51(3), 964–981.

[123] De Jong, J. T. (2014). Challenges of creating synergy between global mental health and cultural psychiatry. *Transcultural Psychiatry*, 51(6), 806–828.

Worldwide, innovative measures by stakeholders around poverty reduction, gender-based violence prevention, child protection, education, substance-abuse treatment, and restoration of livelihoods among displaced communities all contribute toward empowering the displaced.[124],[125] But for professionals who work with refugees in many different settings, much work at the level of culture, community, and mental health remains to be done to lessen the long-term effects of ill-treatment and facilitate growth in conflict-affected communities.

[124] UNHCR. (2021). *UNHCR global strategy for public health: Annex B mental health and psychosocial support.* https://www.unhcr.org/media/40190

[125] Stakeholders range from the World Health Organization (WHO), United Nations Children's Fund (UNICEF), United Nations High Commissioner for Refugees (UNHCR), Norwegian Refugee Council (NRC), International Rescue Committee (IRC), Médecins Sans Frontières (MSF), Amnesty International (AI), and others.

7

What's the Trouble with Mrs. Khaled?

The Mental Health of Refugee Women and Their Communities

The Fire Alarm

One afternoon without so much as a knock, a woman in a trench coat with giant Hollywood-type sunglasses and a floral scarf on her head breezed into the interview room. Outside, spring was melting into summer in the German town of Bonn, and the bough of cherry blossoms was no longer showering blazing pink petals on cobblestone streets. I was wrapping up with another refugee couple who, following their interview, were heading off to get married. My new visitor was a commanding and self-assured figure as she clutched her trench coat to her neck. Unlike other respondents, instead of occupying the spot across the table, she dragged the chair only a few inches away from me, the interviewer.

There she sat, peering at me as a camel would through a needle's eye. When the couple left, she crossed her arms, swirled the chair to face me, and asked, "Why do you think I am here?" As an afterthought, she volunteered, "Call me Mrs. Khaled." Thus, began the interrogation by Mrs. Khaled.

Why do I think you are here? Many a psychologist might have chosen this customary response. But with her Teflon demeanor and pursed lips, I understood Mrs. Khaled would not take too kindly to it. I replied that people had different reasons to speak to me, and I was interested in hearing of her experiences. Mrs. Khaled pursed her lips harder and pinned me with eyes-behind-opaque-frames. Evading, she wanted to know, "Why did you come here to know about the Syrian [sic]?"

Mrs. Khaled is a 43-year-old Kurdish Syrian refugee who had newly arrived in Germany with her five children and husband. After moving around in three or four different German cities and living in three or four refugee camps, unlike other refugees, the government had provided Mrs. Khaled and her family a home. It was a stylish light-green home under a cherry blossom tree in an accessible neighborhood. Despite that, Mrs. Khaled said she has just had enough of it. "I can't sleep. I can't be, with the alarm going off in the middle of the night." A malfunctioning fire alarm would go off a few times each night, its shrill beeps

Displaced. Shaifali Sandhya, Oxford University Press. © Shaifali Sandhya 2024.
DOI: 10.1093/oso/9780197579886.003.0007

sabotaging the sleep of the Khaled household. Without fail, Mrs. Khaled would appear each Thursday at the housing meetings to press her case of the errant fire alarm with local officials. Mrs. Khaled did not speak a word of German and had not even a diploma. Nevertheless, she persuaded German administrators holding the meetings to relent and hire a translator so when she voiced her problems, they could better understand her.

"Is it true," Mrs. Khaled said, and she glared. "If I talk to you, will it injure me more?"

"Some people believe that, although there are others who believe the opposite, that talking helps," I replied. Adding, "You can decide what you choose to share." It was only toward the end of the interview that Mrs. Khaled revealed her real agenda for coming.

In this chapter we explore how forced migration affects refugee women's mental health, and how war affects the nature and frequency of traumatic events female refugees endure and their levels of posttraumatic stress, and the psychological, medical, and social consequences of gender-based violence on refugee women's experiences of suffering. During conflicts, political affiliations, ethnicity, and patriarchal norms can mediate the link between gender and complex trauma.[1] The exploration of gender-specific experiences of war and knowledge of unique social-environmental contexts underscoring women's traumas can allow us an opportunity to investigate their expressions of suffering and paths to recovery.[2]

Given women's influential and supportive roles in their communities, there is a need for strategic social initiatives across displacement settings to empower positive change within families and communities. International policy bodies such as the Directorate-General of Internal Policies at the European Parliament urge legislation implementing gender-specific approaches to guarantee female refugees' integration into the host society.[3] However, in order for nations and policies to offer women meaningful protection, their gender-specific experiences must be made "legible."[4] This chapter addresses a significant gap in scientific literature, namely, how war and female refugees' traumatic experiences can affect their engagement with themselves, their families, and their societies.

[1] Morina, N. (2018). Mental health among adult survivors of war in low- and middle-income countries: Epidemiology and treatment outcome. In N. Morina & A. Nickerson (Eds.), *Mental health of refugee and conflict-affected populations theory, research and clinical practice* (pp. 3–15). Springer.

[2] Kim, J. Y., Kim, H. J., Choi, K., & Nam, B. (2017). Mental health conditions among North Korean female refugee victims of sexual violence. *International Migration, 55*(2), 68–79.

[3] Sansonetti, S. (2016). *Female refugees and asylum seekers: The issue of integration.* European Parliament. https://www.europarl.europa.eu/RegData/etudes/STUD/2016/556929/IPOL_STU(2016)556929_EN.pdf

[4] Pittaway, E., & Bartolomei, L. (1991). Refugees, race, and gender: The multiple discrimination against refugee women. *Refuge, 19*(6), 21–32.

Gendered Nature of Posttraumatic Stress

Scholars, for the most part, agree that posttraumatic stress is gendered:[5] women tend to exhibit a higher propensity[6] for more prolonged and severe complex trauma[7] compared to men.[8] Women are twice as likely as men to meet diagnostic criteria for posttraumatic stress disorder (PTSD)[9,10] and four times as likely to experience posttraumatic stress lasting more than 6 months.[11] The association of gender and complex trauma extends to refugees. Compared to males, female refugees are exposed to more traumatic episodes[12] (although some studies show otherwise[13,14]) and report higher levels of posttraumatic stress[15] for extended periods with more crippling symptoms.[16,17] Belonging to the female sex predicts

[5] Kornfield, S. L., & Epperson, C. N. (2018). PTSD and women. In B. Nemeroff & C. M. Marmar (Eds.), *Post-traumatic stress disorder* (pp. 348–378). Oxford University Press.

[6] Breslau, N., & Davis, G. C. (1992). Post-traumatic stress disorder in an urban population of young adults: Risk factors for chronicity. *American Journal of Psychiatry, 149*(5), 671–675.

[7] Gülşen, C., Knipscheer, J., & Kleber, R. (2010). The impact of forced migration on mental health: A comparative study on post-traumatic stress among internally displaced and externally migrated Kurdish women. *Traumatology, 16*(4), 109–111.

[8] Tolin, D. F., & Foa, E. B. (2006). Sex differences in trauma and post-traumatic stress disorder: A quantitative review of 25 years of research. *Psychological Bulletin, 132*(6), 959–992; ; Irish, L. A., Fischer, B., Fallon, W., Spoonster, E., Sledjeski, E. M., & Delahanty, D. L. (2011). Gender differences in PTSD symptoms: An exploration of peritraumatic mechanisms. *Journal of Anxiety Disorders, 25*(2), 209–216.

[9] Breslau, N., Kessler, R. C., Chilcoat, H. D., Schultz, L. R., Davis, G. C., & Andreski, P. (1998). Trauma and post-traumatic stress disorder in the community: The 1996 Detroit area survey of trauma. *Archives of General Psychiatry, 55*(7), 626–632.

[10] Tolin, D. F., & Foa, E. B. (2006). Sex differences in trauma and posttraumatic stress disorder: A quantitative review of 25 years of research. *Psychological Bulletin 132*, 959–992.

[11] Breslau, N., & Davis, G. C. (1992). Post-traumatic stress disorder in an urban population of young adults: Risk factors for chronicity. *American Journal of Psychiatry, 149*(5), 671–675.

[12] Vallejo-Martín, M., Sánchez Sancha, A., & Canto, J. M. (2021). Refugee women with a history of trauma: Gender vulnerability in relation to post-traumatic stress disorder. *International Journal of Environmental Research and Public Health, 18*(9), 4806.

[13] Ibrahim, H., & Hassan, C. Q. (2017). Post-traumatic stress disorder symptoms resulting from torture and other traumatic events among Syrian Kurdish refugees in Kurdistan region, Iraq. *Frontiers in Psychology, 8*, 241.

[14] Some studies report that compared to women, male refugees suffer from more kinds of traumatic events, more interpersonal traumatic events, and are exposed to more interpersonal traumatic events and torture: Haldane, J., & Nickerson, A. (2016). The impact of interpersonal and noninterpersonal trauma on psychological symptoms in refugees: The moderating role of gender and trauma type. *Journal of Traumatic Stress, 29*(5), 457–465; Morina, N. (2018). Mental health among adult survivors of war in low- and middle-income countries: Epidemiology and treatment outcomes. In N. Morina & A. Nickerson (Eds.), *Mental health of refugee and conflict-affected populations theory, research and clinical practice* (pp. 3–15). Springer.

[15] Ainamani, H. E., Elbert. T., Olema, D. K., & Hecker, T. (2020). Gender differences in response to war-related trauma and posttraumatic stress disorder: A study among the Congolese refugees in Uganda. *BMC Psychiatry, 20*, 17. https://doi.org/10.1186/s12888-019-2420-0

[16] Vallejo-Martín, M., Sánchez Sancha, A., & Canto, J. M. (2021). Refugee women with a history of trauma: Gender vulnerability in relation to post-traumatic stress disorder. *International Journal of Environmental Research and Public Health, 18*(9), 4806.

[17] Vromans, L., Schweitzer, R. D., Brough, M., Kobe, M. A., Ignacio, C., Farrell, L., Murray, C., Lenette, C., & Sagar, V. (2021). Persistent psychological distress in resettled refugee women-at-risk at

mental distress,[18] and the risk is heightened if one is single, divorced, widowed, or living apart from one's spouse. Despite the passage of time and resettlement, severe symptoms continue to strain female refugees.[19] But whether the route to posttraumatic stress is direct or indirect, new scholarship[20] on refugee women concurs that the nature of traumatic events they experience is also instrumental in determining their level of trauma.[21]

Sexual Violence

The scale of sexual violence against refugee women from conflict zones in displacement settings compared to men is widespread, routine, and underscored by pre-existing societal power dynamics. Sexual violence can take many forms and occur in many settings:

- One in five refugee women[22] (21.4%) aged 11-70 years from conflict-torn nations experiences sexual violence.[23] Its form can range from forced sex (i.e., rape), gang rapes of girls as young as 9 years old by up to six

one-year follow-up: Contributions of trauma, post-migration problems, loss, and trust. *Transcultural Psychiatry, 58*(2), 157–171.

[18] Renner, A., Jäckle, D., Nagl, M., Hoffmann, R., Röhr, S., Jung, F., Grochtdreis, T., Dams, J., König, H. H., Riedel-Heller, S., & Kersting, A. (2021). Predictors of psychological distress in Syrian refugees with posttraumatic stress in Germany. *PLOS One, 16*(8), E0254406.

[19] Vojvoda, D., Weine, S. M., McGlashan, T., Becker, D. F., & Southwick, S. M. (2008). Posttraumatic stress disorder symptoms in Bosnian refugees 3 1/2 years after resettlement. *Journal of Rehabilitation Research and Development, 45*(3), 421–426.

[20] Ainamani, H., Elbert, T., Olema, D., & Hecker, T. (2020). Gender differences in response to war-related trauma and post-traumatic stress disorder: A study among the Congolese refugees in Uganda. *BMC Psychiatry, 20*, 17. https://doi.org/10.1186/s12888-019-2420-0

[21] Renner, A., Jäckle, D., Nagl, M., Hoffmann, R., Röhr, S., Jung, F., Grochtdreis, T., Dams, J., König, H. H., Riedel-Heller, S., & Kersting, A. Predictors of psychological distress in Syrian refugees with posttraumatic stress in Germany. *PLOS One, 16*(8), E0254406.

[22] Vu, A., Adam, A., Wirtz, A., Pham, K., Rubenstein, L., Glass, N., Beyrer, C., & Singh, S. (2014). The prevalence of sexual violence among female refugees in complex humanitarian emergencies: A systematic review and meta-analysis. *PLOS Currents, 18*, 6.

[23] *Sexual violence* is defined as a sexual act that is committed or attempted by another person without freely given consent of the victim or against someone who is unable to consent or refuse. It includes forced or alcohol or drug facilitated penetration of a victim; forced or alcohol or drug facilitated incidents in which the victim was made to penetrate a perpetrator or someone else; non-physical pressured unwanted penetration; intentional sexual touching; or noncontact acts of a sexual nature. Sexual violence can also occur when a perpetrator forces or coerces a victim to engage in sexual acts with a third party: UN Economic and Social Council, December 20, 2013, UN Doc. E/CN.6/2014/13. *Gender equality and the empowerment of women in natural disasters* [Report]. https://digitallibrary.un.org/record/764450?ln=en%2522%2520%255Cl%2520%2522record-files-collapse-header

https://www.cdc.gov/violenceprevention/pdf/sv_surveillance_definitionsl-2009-a.pdf

perpetrators,[24] genital mutilation, intimate partner violence,[25] child sexual abuse, dowry-related violence and trafficking that inflict severe pain and suffering.

Although approximately 6,000 women have been raped in Syria since the surge of the crisis, this figure most likely does not include the high rates of sexual assaults, harassment,[26] forced marriages, and polygamy.

- The Nauru files,[27] a cache of 2000 leaked incident reports written by guards, caseworkers and teachers detail the rape of female asylum seekers held in detention with guards demanding sexual favors and engaging in violent assaults and abuse of teenagers and children in Australia's offshore detention facility. In Libya's detention centers male guards subjected detainees including pregnant females, to different forms sexual violence and torture or to sexual intercourse in exchange for clean water, food or their freedom, severely beating those who resisted rape.[28]

For war-affected female refugees, posttraumatic stress is a familiar, chronic, and debilitating long-term health condition,[29] but a lot pertaining to the mental health of female refugees remains unexplored.[30]

[24] UN Human Rights Council, March 8, 2018, UN Doc. A/HRC/37/CRP. "I lost my dignity": Sexual and gender-based violence in the Syrian Arab Republic. https://www.ohchr.org/sites/default/files/Documents/HRBodies/HRCouncil/CoISyria/A-HRC-37-CRP-3.pdf

[25] Araujo, J. O., Souza, F. M., Proença, R., Bastos, M. L., Trajman, A., & Faerstein, E. (2019). Prevalence of sexual violence among refugees: A systematic review. Revista de Saude Publica, 53, 78.

[26] Çöl, M., Bilgili Aykut, N., Usturalı Mut, A. N., Koçak, C., Uzun, S. U., Akın, A., Say, L., & Kobeissi, L. (2020). Sexual and reproductive health of Syrian refugee women in Turkey: A scoping review within the framework of the MISP objectives. Reproductive Health, 17(1), 99.

[27] Evershed, N., Liu, R. Farrell, P. & Davidson, H. (2016). The lives of asylum seekers in detention. The Guardian. https://www.theguardian.com/australia-news/ng-interactive/2016/aug/10/the-nauru-files-the-lives-of-asylum-seekers-in-detention-detailed-in-a-unique-database-interactive

[28] Amnesty International (2021). 'No one will look for you': Forcibly returned from sea to abusive detention in Libya (2021). https://www.amnesty.org/en/documents/mde19/4439/2021/en/

[29] An empirical study of 1,127 displaced Kurdish women living in Turkey or another EU country revealed that although more than 80% had experienced traumatic events more than 5 years ago, almost half were suffering from posttraumatic stress. Three-quarters of women reported traumatic reactions indicative of a PTSD diagnosis. Despite years after living in a safe country, 90.2% reported crippling posttraumatic reactions, such as intrusions, avoidances (80%), and hyperarousal (82.2%), interfering with their life activities: Gülşen, C., Knipscheer, J., & Kleber, R. (2010). The impact of forced migration on mental health: A comparative study on post-traumatic stress among internally displaced and externally migrated Kurdish women. Traumatology, 16(4), 109–116.

[30] Vromans, L., Schweitzer, R. D., Brough, M., Kobe, M. A., Ignacio, C., Farrell, L., Murray, C., Lenette, C., & Sagar, V. (2021). Persistent psychological distress in resettled refugee women-at-risk at one-year follow-up: Contributions of trauma, post-migration problems, loss, and trust. Transcultural Psychiatry, 58(2), 157–171.

Sexual violence[31,32,33] and the threat of it[34] is one such exceptional and traumatic event, widely prevalent among female refugees from Bangladesh to the Democratic Republic of Congo to the Middle East. Armed conflict exerts a disproportionate and unique impact on women and girls.[35] As the case of kidnapped Chibok girls by the Islamic terrorist group Boko Haram illustrates, the battleground can often be women's bodies, wherein the military strategy is heinous sexual violence.[36] Among female Yazidi survivors of severe protracted sexual trauma, those who were captives suffered significantly higher rates of trauma compared to those who were not.[37] Women's biology puts them at greater risk for violence, and gender-based violence intensifies the trauma of forced migration for women.

Sexual violence, irrespective of gender, may be linked to a higher conditional risk for posttraumatic stress. Congolese female refugees from Uganda who are survivors of rape report higher PTSD symptom severity than female refugees and male refugees who had not been raped.[38] At the same time, both male and female refugees in this postconflict community who share similarly horrific violence such as sexual violence or torture report similar[39] and elevated symptomatology.[40] Finally, female refugees who are survivors of rape report higher levels of posttraumatic stress when compared to raped male refugees. In war, gender, by constituting a critical dimension for violence for female refugees,[41] also leads to increased posttraumatic stress.

[31] Carta, M. G., Oumar, F. W., Moro, M. F., Moro, D., Preti, A., Mereu, A., & Bhugra, D. (2013). Trauma and stressor related disorders in the Tuareg refugees of a camp in Burkina Faso. *Clinical Practice & Epidemiology in Mental Health, 9*, 189–195.

[32] Breslau, N., Kessler, R. C., Chilcoat, H. D., Schultz, L. R., Davis, G. C., & Andreski, P. (1998). Trauma and post-traumatic stress disorder in the community: The 1996 Detroit area survey of trauma. *Archives of General Psychiatry, 55*(7), 626–632.

[33] Kessler, R. C., Sonnega, A., Bromet, E., Hughes, M., & Nelson, C. B. (1995). Post-traumatic stress disorder in the National Comorbidity Survey. *Archives of General Psychiatry, 52*, 1048–1060.

[34] Ainamani, H. E., Elbert. T., Olema, D. K., & Hecker, T. (2020). Gender differences in response to war-related trauma and posttraumatic stress disorder—a study among the Congolese refugees in Uganda. *BMC Psychiatry, 20*, 17. https://doi.org/10.1186/s12888-019-2420-0

[35] UN Security Council, October 31, 2000, UN Doc. SC/6942. https://press.un.org/en/2000/20001 031.sc6942.doc.html

[36] Hynes, M., & Lopes, C. B. (2000). Sexual violence against refugee women. *Journal of Women's Health & Gender-Based Medicine, 9*(8), 819–823.

[37] Taha, P. H., & Slewa-Younan, S. (2020). Measures of depression, generalized anxiety, and post-traumatic stress disorders amongst Yazidi female survivors of ISIS slavery and violence. *International Journal of Mental Health Systems, 14*, 80.

[38] Ainamani, H., Elbert, T., Olema, D., & Hecker, T. (2020). Gender differences in response to war-related trauma and post-traumatic stress disorder: A study among the Congolese refugees in Uganda. *BMC Psychiatry, 20*, 17. https://doi.org/10.1186/s12888-019-2420-0

[39] Ibrahim, H., & Hassan, C. Q. (2017). Post-traumatic stress disorder symptoms resulting from torture and other traumatic events among Syrian Kurdish refugees in Kurdistan Region, Iraq. *Frontiers in Psychology, 8*, 241.

[40] Both enhanced levels of PTSD symptom severity and higher PTSD prevalence.

[41] Fiddian-Qasmiyeh, E. (2014). Gender and forced migration. In E. Fiddian-Qasmiyeh, G. Loescher, K. Long, & N. Sigona (Eds.), *The Oxford handbook of refugee and forced migration studies* (pp. 395–408). Oxford University Press.

There is little doubt that sexual violence may trigger and exacerbate posttraumatic stress. When male refugees endorsed rape as their worst traumatic event, their conditional risk of developing posttraumatic stress soared to 100%.[42] Such findings from postconflict communities underscore the importance of paying attention to traumatic events eliciting posttraumatic stress. At the same time, gender differences in the elevated suffering of Congolese female refugees compared to the male refugees cannot be fully explained by the nature of traumatic events they endure.[43] Women are more likely to experience intense affective states of self-blame, dysfunctional appraisals,[44,45] and dissociative symptoms,[46] and these may be rooted in societal factors.

While some have hypothesized that precursors of female refugees' cognitive or behavioral responses may lie within their psyche, the role of families, cultures, and communities in maintaining their distress, with some exceptions, has not been studied. The increased number of victimizations endured by women, according to Tolin and Foa, may be instrumental on the one hand, in increasing the strength of connections between appraisals of danger and impaired interpersonal relatedness, and on the other, in locating the epicenters of their posttraumatic stress within women.[47] Sexual violence can be a tool for discrimination and persecution for extending harm to women in diverse and systematic ways. In the section below, we review sexual violence against refugee women in conflict zones that reveals as much about the politics of pain as about the power relations that are one of the primary sources of posttraumatic stress in war-affected female refugees. While this analysis focuses on sexual violence among females, sexual violence among males exists in forced-displacement settings and has been elaborated in Chapter 4.

[42] Ainamani, H., Elbert, T., Olema, D., & Hecker, T. (2020). Gender differences in response to war-related trauma and post-traumatic stress disorder: A study among the Congolese refugees in Uganda. *BMC Psychiatry, 20*, 17. https://doi.org/10.1186/s12888-019-2420-0

[43] Christiansen, D. M., & Hansen, M. (2015). Accounting for sex differences in PTSD: A multi-variable mediation model. *European Journal of Psychotraumatology, 6*, 26068.

[44] Cromer, L. D., & Smyth, J. M. (2010). Making meaning of trauma: Trauma exposure doesn't tell the whole story. *Journal of Contemporary Psychotherapy, 40*, 65–72.

[45] Tolin, D. F., & Foa, E. B. (2002). Gender and PTSD: A cognitive model. In R. Kimerling, P. Ouimette, & J. Wolfe (Eds.), *Gender and PTSD* (pp. 66–97). Guilford Press.

[46] Schalinski, I., Moran, J., Schauer, M., & Elbert, T. (2014). Rapid emotional processing in relation to trauma-related symptoms as revealed by magnetic source imaging. *BMC Psychiatry, 14*, 193.

[47] Tolin, D. F., & Foa, E. B. (2002). Gender and PTSD: A cognitive model. In R. Kimerling, P. Ouimette, & J. Wolfe (Eds.), *Gender and PTSD* (pp. 76–97). Guilford Press

Power Dynamics, Social Roles, and Sexual Violence

Although there are many purposes of wide-scale sexual aggression against women, such as sexual services for armed combatants, the primary ones are instigating fear and humiliation[48] in society, as we see with the reproductive control of the Rohingya women. The Burmese military in August 2017, it is estimated by the Ontario International Development Agency, burned 34,436 Rohingya by tossing them into a fire and beat 114,872, and women were singled out for systematic gang rape as they fled their hometown for northern Rakhine state (nRS).[49] Decades-old discriminations against the Muslim Rohingya, impoverished, largely illiterate, and viewed as "illegal" by the Buddhist community despite their historical, cultural, and religious ties to Myanmar, have culminated in ethnic cleansing crackdowns against them. Although it is most likely a gross underestimate for this conservative population where topics of sex are taboo, the military reportedly raped and enslaved for sexual exploitation at least 18,000 women and girls.[50]

Mossamet Nasima is a 36-year-old refugee and mother of four daughters and three sons who fled with her family from Myanmar.[51] She lives in a camp in Cox's Bazar, a port city in Bangladesh that houses two government-run refugee camps. She said:

> I was always worried about my daughters . . . girls were raped in my village while their parents were forced to watch. . . . Life is hard for a Rohingya woman in Myanmar. Women, girls, and even infants were tortured, raped and killed by the Myanmar army every day. They would even cut off some women's breasts before killing them. I don't understand why . . . .

An 11-year-old girl who fled her hometown in Yae Khat Chaung Gwa Son, Rakhine State, Myanmar, and who lives in Cox's Bazar,[52] the world's largest refugee camp, provided her testimony:

---

[48] Pittaway, E., & Bartolomei, L. (2001), Refugees, race and gender: The multiple discrimination against Refugee Women. *Refuge, 19*, 6.

[49] Habib, M., Jubb, C., Ahmad, S., Rahman, M., & Pallard, H. (2018). *Forced migration of Rohingya: The untold experience* (1st ed., p. 69). Ontario International Development Agency.

[50] OHCHR. (2017, December 5). *Human Rights Council opens special session on the situation of human rights of the Rohingya and other minorities in Rakhine State in Myanmar*. https://www.ohchr.org/EN/NewsEvents/Pages/DisplayNews.aspx?NewsID=22491&LangID=E

[51] Nasima Mossamet shared her story with Helprekind, a Massachusetts based nonprofit organization that supports refugees: Helprekind [@helprekind]. (2018, June 2). *Mossamet Nasima: #Mother, 36 years old "I have seven children, four daughters and three boys.* [Three people sitting in conversation]. Instagram. https://www.instagram.com/p/BjhVIoUnfrd/

[52] OHCHR. (2017, February 3). *Report of OHCHR mission to Bangladesh: Interviews with Rohingyas fleeing from Myanmar since October 9, 2016.*

After entering our house, the army apprehended us. They pushed my mother on the ground. They removed her clothes, and four officers raped her. They also slaughtered my father, a prayer leader, just before raping my mother. After a few minutes, they burned the house with a rocket, with my mother inside. All this happened before my eyes.

The Human Rights Council report based on 454 interviews with survivors, their relatives, health care practitioners, and medical personnel, lawyers, and other members of the communities, underscores the routine and casual ways sexual violence is inflicted:[53]

In one particularly brutal incident in Branch 62, 4th Division (Damascus), in 2012, a female prisoner did not co-operate throughout her interrogation. A pro-government militia member asked the officer for permission to make her talk and, on receiving it, rammed a metal rod into her anus in the presence of her infant son. She passed out from the pain and sustained severe internal injuries but was not interrogated further after that day.

Consider the abuse and maltreatment of Zahira, who was detained for six months as described by Lawyers and Doctors for Human Rights (LDHR):[54]

Zahira was 45-years-old when she was arrested in 2013 from her work place in the suburbs of Damascus. She was detained in multiple locations for approximately 6 months, including Al Mezzeh Military Airport (15 days), the Palestine Branch (Branch 235)(3 months 22 days), a center in Rukheddeen neighborhood (1 month), another in Kafr Sousa district (1 month) and Adra Prison.

During 15 days at Al Mezzeh Military Airport, Zahira was subjected to multiple rapes and threats of rape and sexual violence. Immediately upon arrival, she was stripped searched, before being taken to another location where she was tied to a bed and gang-raped orally and vaginally by five men. She was later threatened to be raped in front of her husband, who was also detained at Al Mezzeh airport. During one interrogation session, having been beaten and asked to confess, she was then stripped naked and sexually penetrated in "every body cavity." Her interrogator filmed this and threatened to show the people in her community.

---

[53] UN Human Rights Council, March 8, 2018, UN Doc. A/HRC/37/CRP. *"I lost my dignity": Sexual and gender-based violence in the Syrian Arab Republic.* https://www.ohchr.org/sites/default/files/Documents/HRBodies/HRCouncil/CoISyria/A-HRC-37-CRP-3.pdf

[54] Lawyers and Doctors for Human Rights (2017). *Voices from the dark: Torture and sexual violence against women in Assad's detention centers.* https://ldhrights.org/en/wp-content/uploads/2017/07/Voices-from-the-Dark.pdf

Despite being released from detention, Zahira still faces complex medical and psychological concerns: she suffers from headaches and startles easily—symptoms that affect her relationship with her body and mind. In the aftermath of her detention, health concerns ranged from hepatitis to pneumonia and anemia. Given the multiple and violent rapes she had to undergo multiple surgeries to correct fecal-urinary incontinence, blood transfusion, and curettage to "clean out her uterus."

The nature of gender-based crimes that female refugees grapple with can also reveal the embedded plural systems of patriarchy in many contexts. Consider, for instance, the period between 2012 and 2017 when war raged in Syria: 28,405 Syrian females were killed with 91% of the deaths perpetrated by the Syrian regime and its allies.[55] In Syria, the rape of women and girls was perpetrated in 20 Syrian government political and military intelligence branches. The perpetrators include government forces and militias who carry out rapes during ground operations and house searches, while monitoring protestors and securing checkpoints, or when women were detained.[56] Between March 2011 and February 2017, the Syrian Network for Human Rights[57] documented 8,764 women forcibly disappeared by the Syrian government.

When wars break out, power is concentrated among men through their access, vigilance, and aggression of females and their bodies. The ever-present threat of violence skews demands of morality from women more than men. In an incident[58] a woman was hanging out clothes on her balcony in ar-Raqqah city without being fully covered. Members of al-Hisbah on patrol reportedly sighted the woman and used a pincer to bite her breast; the woman died of her injuries.

In many host countries, policies can reflect the assumption that rape is an arbitrary or private act of harm rather than a form of political persecution that annihilates women's positive experiences and punishes them for their perceived transgressions and beliefs. As a consequence of the political and persecutory act of rape or threat of sexual violence, particular beliefs and transgressions of social and religious mores get recalibrated as women may themselves start to believe they are responsible for jeopardizing their safety more than the people who commit heinous acts against them, thus reshaping their encounters with trauma.

---

[55] Syrian Network of Human Rights. (2020, November 25). *On the international day for the elimination of violence against women: Ninth annual report on violations against females in Syria.* https://snhr.org/blog/2020/11/25/55660/

[56] UN Human Rights Council, March 8, 2018, UN Doc. A/HRC/37/CRP. *"I lost my dignity": Sexual and gender-based violence in the Syrian Arab Republic.* https://www.ohchr.org/sites/default/files/Documents/HRBodies/HRCouncil/CoISyria/A-HRC-37-CRP-3.pdf

[57] Syrian Network of Human Rights. (2020, November 25). *On the International Day for the Elimination of Violence against Women: Ninth annual report on violations against females in Syria.*

[58] UN Human Rights Council, March 8, 2018, UN Doc. A/HRC/37/CRP. *"I lost my dignity": Sexual and gender-based violence in the Syrian Arab Republic* (p. 18). https://www.ohchr.org/sites/default/files/Documents/HRBodies/HRCouncil/CoISyria/A-HRC-37-CRP-3.pdf

Sexual violence in conflict and postconflict societies is an enunciation of societal power dynamics. At various stages of women's flight, perpetrators take many forms: traffickers, trusted strangers,[59] fellow refugees, family members, members of UN peacekeeping forces,[60] and humanitarian workers.[61]

Women with a previous history of gender-based violence, impoverished, with disabilities or without family support are at exceptionally high risk for violence.[62] Compared to those without disabilities, female refugees with disabilities can endure rates of violence four to ten times higher.[63] Over 115,000 Syrian children have been born as refugees in five host countries of the region. The personal and social ramifications of being a raped woman or a child without a father are enormous in conservative societies. If sexual abuse occurs early in life, it can amplify the risk to reproductive health[64] during women's lifespans.[65,66]

Health Crises in Female Refugees: Short-Term and Long-Term Effects

The large-scale medical crises generated by damage to women's reproductive health[67] because of sexual violence are stupefying. Health consequences in refugees include high levels of psychological distress[68] manifested through:

[59] Wirtz, A. L., Glass, N., Pham, K., Aberra, A., Rubenstein, L. S., Singh, S., & Vu, A. (2013). Development of a screening tool to identify female survivors of gender-based violence in a humanitarian setting: Qualitative evidence-base from research among refugees in Ethiopia. *Conflict and Health, 7*, 13.

[60] Withnall, A. (2015, April 29). French soldiers accused of raping and abusing refugee children in Central African Republic in exchange for food in "leaked UN report." *The Independent.* https://www.independent.co.uk/news/world/africa/french-soldiers-accused-raping-and-abusing-refugee-child ren-central-african-republic-exchange-food-leaked-un-report-10213197.html

[61] Spencer, R. (2018, February 27). Aid workers demanded sex from Syrians, UN reveals. *The Times.* https://www.thetimes.co.uk/article/women-in-syria-sexually-exploited-in-return-for-aid-df0kxnw20.

[62] UNHCR. (2008). *UNHCR handbook for the protection of women and girls.* http://www.unhcr.org/47cfa9fe2.html

[63] Women's Refugee Commission. (2014). *Refugees with disabilities: Increasing inclusion, building community* (p. 3). https://www.womensrefugeecommission.org/wp-content/uploads/2020/04/Disab ilities-Discussion-Tool-Editable.pdf

[64] Wiersielis, K. R., Wicks, B. Simko, H., Cohen, S. R., Khantsis, S., Baksh, N., Khantsis, S., Baksh, N., Waxler, D. E., & Bagassser, D. A. (2016). Sex differences in corticotropin releasing factor-evoked behavior and activated networks. *Psychoneuroendicronology, 73*, 204–216.

[65] Kornfield, S. L., & Epperson, C. N. (2018). PTSD and women. In C. B. Nemeroff & C. R. Marmar (Eds.), *Post-traumatic stress disorder.* (pp. 209–222). Oxford University Press.

[66] Gülşen, C., Knipscheer, J., & Kleber, R. (2010). The impact of forced migration on mental health: A comparative study on Post-traumatic Stress among internally displaced and externally migrated Kurdish women. *Traumatology, 16*(4), 109–116.

[67] McLean, I., Roberts, S. A., White, C., & Paul, S. (2011). Female genital injuries resulting from consensual and non-consensual vaginal intercourse. *Forensic Science International, 204*(1–3) 27–33; Draughton, J. E. (2012). Sexual assault injuries and increased risk of HIV transmission. *Advanced Emergency Nursing Journal, 34*(1), 82–87.

[68] Médecins Sans Frontières. (2017, May 2017). *Taj makeshift camp: No one should have to live like this Tal makeshift camp; the Rohingya people from Myanmar seeking refuge in Bangladesh* [Briefing paper]. https://www.msf.org/sites/default/files/2018-08/stateless-rohingyas-in-bangladesh.pdf

- Posttraumatic stress disorder
- Depression
- Physical injuries
- Sexually transmitted infections,[69] including HIV[70]
- Fistulas or tears in walls between the vagina and the bladder
- Chronic pain[71]
- Ruptured anuses' and vaginas speared by bayonets and rifles
- Unsafe or unwanted pregnancies[72]
- Suicide[73]

When wars break out, the threat of sexual violence is palpable for women and their families. Given their second-class status in many societies, women are only too aware that the worst will befall them, their gender predisposing them to persecution. Of women in my sample and their family members, 100% reported immense fear when wars broke out. Anticipating sexual violence is commonplace;[74] female refugees fleeing Libya took birth control ahead of their sea journeys.[75] Syrian families in refugee camps rushed to get their girls married: 25% of girls under the age of 18 years are married off[76] to whichever male is willing, able, or interested.

[69] Jina, R., & Thomas, L. S. (2013). Health consequences of sexual violence against women. *Best Practice & Research Clinical Obstetrics & Gynaecology, 27*(1), 15–26.

[70] Olynik, M. G. P., Cannon, M. E., & Lachapelle, G. (2002). *Temporal variability of GPS error sources and their effect on relative positioning accuracy* [Paper presentation]. National Technical Meeting of the Institute of Navigation, San Diego, CA; Campbell, J. C., Lucea, M. B., Stockman, J. K., & Draughon, J. E. (2012). Forced sex and HIV risk in violent relationships. *American Journal of Reproductive Immunology, 69*(1), 41–44.

[71] Djuknic, G. M., & Richton, R. E. (2001). Geolocation and assisted GPS. *Computer, 34*(2), 123–125; Longombe, A. O, Claude, K. M., & Ruminjo, J. (2008). Fistula and traumatic genital injury from sexual violence in a conflict setting in Eastern Congo: Case studies. *Reproductive Health Matters, 16*(31), 132–141.

[72] García-Moreno, C., Jansen, H. M. E., Heise, L., & Watts, C. (2005). *WHO multi-country study on women's health and domestic violence against women: Initial results on prevalence, health outcomes and women's responses.* World Health Organization. https://apps.who.int/iris/handle/10665/43309

[73] Falb, K. L., McCormick, M. C., Hemenway, D., Anfinson, K., & Silverman, J. G. (2013). Suicide ideation and victimization among refugee women along the Thai-Burma border. *Journal of Traumatic Stress, 26*(5), 631–635.

[74] Amnesty International spoke to 90 refugees and migrants in Puglia and Sicily, Italy, in May 2016 and collected 16 accounts of sexual violence from survivors and eyewitnesses: Amnesty International. (2016, July 1). *Refugees and migrants fleeing sexual violence, abuse and exploitation in Libya.* https://www.amnesty.org/en/latest/news/2016/07/refugees-and-migrants-fleeing-sexual-violence-abuse-and-exploitation-in-libya/

[75] Taylor, L. (2017, November 30). Women migrants fearing rape take contraceptives before journey: Rights groups. *World News.* https://www.reuters.com/article/us-women-conference-migrant-rape/women-migrants-fearing-rape-take-contraceptives-before-journey-rights-groups-idUSKBN13P2BW

[76] Save the Children. (2014). *Too young to wed: The growing problem of child marriage among Syrian girls in Jordan.* https://resourcecentre.savethechildren.net/pdf/too_young_to_wed.pdf/

Consequences for female survivors of sexual violence range from threats of divorce and excommunication from one's family, to honor killings and prospects of a future marriage ruined, particularly in more conservative regions. For a minority group believing that chastity is at the same level as worship and God, sexual violence is a life-altering event for women, and it can destroy their community connections. Given rape's powerful additive effects for posttraumatic stress for both male and female refugees, it may be the proverbial "hair on a camel's back," tipping the scales of demoralization and despair and, in turn, affecting financial emancipation and erosion of support from the community. For refugee women, since neither class nor comportment may buffer against sexual violence, it may be more useful to identify not "at-risk" females but specific situations and contexts that are unsafe for different groups of women.

Half a Story: The "Forgotten Majority"

War is waged on women's bodies, but it is seldom portrayed through women's eyes. The impact of complex trauma in women's lives and their roles as mothers, daughters, sisters, and wives needs to be explored. Complex trauma and gender remain inadequately studied.[77,78] When we neglect women's accounts or hear of their accounts as collated by men, we stand to risk hearing only "half the story,"[79] with experiences of posttraumatic stress invalidated and unrecognized. It also risks overlooking the impact of women's experiences on their family members and community. Clutching only half a story results in women's experiences not being woven into the host nations' future stories; it is not only harmful for women but also pose a fraught situation for a nation.

Refugee women are the "forgotten majority." '[80] The neglect of refugee women's experiences happens for at least three primary reasons. One, it is driven by the slanted conception that women are fragile, dependent,[81,82,83] and Madonna-like

[77] Ainamani, H. E., Elbert, T., Olema, D. K., & Hecker, T. (2020). Gender differences in response to war-related trauma and posttraumatic stress disorder: A study among the Congolese refugees in Uganda. *BMC Psychiatry, 20*, 17. https://doi.org/10.1186/s12888-019-2420-0

[78] Vallejo-Martín, M., Sánchez Sancha, A., & Canto, J. M. (2021). Refugee women with a history of trauma: Gender vulnerability in relation to post-traumatic stress disorder. *International Journal of Environmental Research and Public Health, 18*(9), 4806.

[79] Lamb, C. (2020). *Our bodies, their battlefields: War through the lives of women* (p. 14). Scribner.

[80] Camus-Jacques, G. (1989). Refugee women: The forgotten majority. In G. Loescher & L. Monahan (Eds.), *Refugees and international relations* (pp. 141–157). Clarendon Press.

[81] Hyndman, J. (2000). *Managing displacement: Refugees and the politics of humanitarianism.* University of Minnesota.

[82] Szczepanikova, A. (2009). Beyond "helping": Gender and relations of power in nongovernmental assistance to refugees. *Journal of International Women's Studies, 11*(3), 19–33. https://vc.bridgew.edu/cgi/viewcontent.cgi?article=1190&context=jiws

[83] Rajaram, P. K. (2002). Humanitarianism and representations of the refugee. *Journal of Refugee Studies, 15*(3), 247–264.

figures.[84] With their agency suspect and amid a dearth of data, women are categorized alongside children, as "women and children."[85] Two, fearing social reprisals of the burdens they bear, refugee women also view themselves as damaged, dirty and impure.[86] In contrast, there are those like Mrs. Khaled who do not conform to such essentializing stereotypes. Three, forcible migration is also mistakenly associated primarily with men.[87] This is not accurate, for at the end of 2020 women and girls constituted 52% of the internally displaced,[88] and 47% of all displaced across international boundaries.[89] In some regions like Syria, 75%[90] of refugees in neighboring countries are women and children. Challenges in understanding the experiences and their consequences for female refugees can result in their being discounted as routine experiences; gender is misrepresented policy and women are rendered invisible in the refugee determination process.[91] It is important to enhance awareness and capacity building of gendered knowledge in integration programs.

Integration practices of nations' resettlement systems can be improved by including a lifespan perspective on the influence of age and life-stage on women's experiences of displacement. The type of conflict, country of resettlement, quality of relationships, and the familial and social roles women are embedded in can affect psychological well-being and recovery. When women are rooted in traditional structures of power and control, this can reproduce the inequities they face; this knowledge can be taken into consideration in the design of community programs to eliminate gender bias and promote female empowerment and family cohesion.

[84] Malkiki, L. (1992). National Geographic: The rooting of peoples and the territorialization of national identity among scholars and refugees. *Cultural Anthropology, 7*(1), 24–44.

[85] Enloe, C. H. (1991). "Womenandchildren": Propaganda tools of patriarchy. In G. Bates (Ed.), *Mobilising democracy: Changing the US role in the Middle East* (pp. 29–32). Common Courage Press.

[86] Lamb, C. (2020). *Our bodies, their battlefields: War through the lives of women* (p. 116). Scribner..

[87] Sansonetti, S. (2016). *Female refugees and asylum seekers: The issue of integration.* European Parliament. https://www.europarl.europa.eu/RegData/etudes/STUD/2016/556929/IPOL_STU(2016)556929_EN.pdf

[88] UNHCR. (2020). *Global trends forced displacement in 2020* (p. 28). https://www.unhcr.org/60b638e37/unhcr-global-trends-2020

[89] UNHCR. (2020). *Global trends forced displacement in 2020* (p.16). https://www.unhcr.org/60b638e37/unhcr-global-trends-2020

[90] Baker, D. (2014). *Regional situation report for Syria crisis.* United Nations Population Fund.

[91] Valji, N., de la Hunt, L. A., & Moffett, H. (2003). Where are the women? Gender discrimination in refugee policies and practices. *Agenda: Empowering Women for Gender Equity, 55,* 61–72.

Sweet Sister: Affiliation, Persecution, and Depression

I asked Mrs. Khaled about some of her difficult experiences. Her hard demeanor disintegrated as she started to quietly heave and sob, saying, "You're asking to open old stories."

Mrs. Khaled's family was Sunni, large, and spread across many adjacent villages. She was the second oldest and the only sister of six brothers. The Khaleds were a landed, prominent, and politically connected family. For generations, they had exercised control over the region. "But my grandfather was in the opposition for over 30 years, and one day, the regime came and took him. In one day and night, the war came. The war caused us to lose everything." The Khaled's went from riches and reputation to "nothing." "We had everything we wanted," said Mrs. Khaled. "Now we have nothing at all."

It was June 2012, and more was to follow. Shared Mrs. Khaled:

In one day and one night, everything changed. One morning, as usual, Amer, her youngest brother and 16 years old, but one who was more like a son to her, had hugged Mrs. Khaled tightly and said to her, "I am going out with my friends. I will be back soon, my sweet sister." But that evening, she waited and waited, in vain.

Amer was kidnapped by ISIS. When news of his disappearance reached Mrs. Khaled's family, her father, who was the region's chief along with other elders, negotiated in vain for hours for his release. As the hours went by, rumors trickled in that Amer may have been killed. ISIS was refusing to return him. Mrs. Khaled's elder brother threatened, "If you won't give us Amer, we will wage another war."

In the dry heat of that summer, when temperatures touched 60 degrees centigrade and the sun scorched their land, Mrs. Khaled and her family learned that ISIS had returned Amer to the village square. Naked feet they raced down the dusty street and found instead Amer's blood-soaked body wrapped in a blanket with three bullets in his chest.

"It was the worst thing that happened to me," she said.

Political affiliation, kinship, ethnicity, and religion can moderate the relationship between persecutory experiences and complex trauma in refugee women. Amer had been targeted because of his family's political affiliations. Fearing that her sons too would be entrapped in this way, Mrs. Khaled decided to initiate their flight to Germany.

Other research[92] has corroborated the relationship of kinship and ethnicity with complex trauma: consider the Yazidis, a minority community endogenous to Kurdish regions of Iraq, Iran, Syria, and Turkey who have historically faced many persecutions. Although Christians were found to be the most exposed to trauma as compared to Muslims and Yazidis, Yazidis, an ethnic minority, exhibited a higher PTSD rate (70%) compared to Muslims (44%) and to Christians (32%). In one sample, 42.9% of Yazidi women displaced in Turkey met the criteria for posttraumatic stress[93] and reported somatic complaints and pain.[94] Another study found that in a sample of 416 females, more than 80% of girls and women met criteria for a DSM-5 PTSD diagnosis.[95] Almost all formerly sexually enslaved women also met the criteria. Female Yazidis, the authors suggest, might bear a greater brunt of the consequences of trauma due to their ostracism within society. When in Iraq, 2.5% Yazidis were killed[96] within days by the Islamic State, and many women were also kidnapped, forcibly converted to Islam, raped, and tortured in captivity.[97,98]

"Mama, If You Don't Like Germany, How Will We?"

For female refugees like Mrs. Khaled, above and beyond the disadvantages of gender, have others, such as the lack of access to finances and poor professional qualifications,[99] which have further unpleasant effects. On the one hand, women can be targeted because of their family members' political, ethnic, and religious belonging.[100] On the other hand, culturally primed to be caregivers, they find

[92] Richa, S., Herdane, M., Dwaf, A. Khalil, R. B., El Khoury, R., Zarzour, M., Kassab, A., Dagher, R. Brunet, A., & El-Hage, W. (2020). Trauma exposure and PTSD prevalence among Yazidi, Christian and Muslim asylum seekers and refugees displaced to Iraqi Kurdistan. *PLOS One*, *15*(6), E0233681.

[93] Tekin, A., Karadağ, H., Süleymanoğlu, M., Tekin, M., Kayran, Y., Alpak, G., & Sar, V. (2016). Prevalence and gender differences in symptomatology of post-traumatic stress disorder and depression among Iraqi Yazidis displaced into Turkey. *European Journal of Psychotraumatology*, *7*(1), 28556.

[94] Rometsch, C., Denkinger, J. K., Engelhardt, M., Windthorst, P., Graf, J., Gibbons, N., .Pham, P., Zipfel, S., & Junne, F. (2020). Pain, somatic complaints, and subjective concepts of illness in traumatized female refugees who experienced extreme violence by the "Islamic State" (IS). *Journal of Psychosomatic Research*, *130*, 109931.

[95] Ibrahim, H., Ertl, V., Catani, C., Ismail, A. A., & Neuner, F. (2018). Trauma and perceived social rejection among Yazidi women and girls who survived enslavement and genocide. *BMC Medicine*, *16*, 154. https://doi.org/10.1186/s12916-018-1140-5

[96] Cetorelli, V., Sasson, I., Shabila, N., & Burnham, G. (2017). Mortality and kidnapping estimates for the Yazidi population in the area of Mount Sinjar, Iraq, in August 2014: A retrospective household survey. *PLOS Medicine*, *14*(5), E1002297.

[97] Mohammadi, D. (2016). Help for Yazidi survivors of sexual violence. *Lancet Psychiatry*, *3*(5), 409–410.

[98] Ahram, A. I. (2015). Sexual violence and the making of ISIS. *Survival*, *57*(3), 57–78.

[99] Chung, K., Hong, E., & Newbold, B. (2013). Resilience among single adult female refugees in Hamilton, Ontario. *Refuge*, *29*, 1.

[100] Sansonetti, S. (2016). *Female refugees and asylum seekers: The issue of integration.* European Parliament. https://www.europarl.europa.eu/RegData/etudes/STUD/2016/556929/ IPOL_STU(2016)556929_EN.pdf

themselves responsible for repairing the havoc wreaked by war within their families and homes.

Although much research portrays refugee women as lacking agency, it was Mrs. Khaled who decided to move her family to Germany. After her brother's death, Mrs. Khaled said, "my heart broke. I saw him wherever I looked." But, "It was essential that my children not see my weakness." Out of nowhere one day in the predominantly family neighborhood of Houla, to the northwest of the city of Homs in Syria, gunmen massacred 108 people, including 49 children and 34 women, shaking Mrs. Khaled, who was preoccupied with her children's safety. The summary executions of innocent civilians in their homes occurred house by house by militiamen despite the presence of UN monitors, unarmed soldiers trained in peacekeeping. The incident escalated with greater violence, cementing Mrs. Khaled's decision to flee Syria:

> You cannot forget the bombs and rockets that cut people into pieces. Rockets came to us just 50–60 feet away. That's a horrible thing. The Islamic State killed people, and they put them on electricity poles. One day I saw a baby no more than 20 days old hung on those poles. I didn't want my children to see a dead baby. I did not want to see the fear in my children's eyes.

I asked, "How do you hide your sadness from your children?"

> I sit alone in my room a lot, and I keep crying. I feel very bad. I cry a lot. I am breathing, but it feels like I am breathing fire. Our houses are very small here, and I just try to go everywhere, and I cry. I walk around the mall and go to the bathroom and cry. After one hour, I come out and tell myself, "Okay, I am strong and I can survive." And I keep going. But I am not sure how I will stay in that way.

Integration of Female Refugees

Women Are the Fulcrum of Family Success: "If I Am Weak, My Family Will Be Weak"

I asked, "What would happen if your children saw you so sad?"

> It's very hard. I don't want to let my children see my weakness because if they see it, they will blame me. You don't have any choice. We will lose our children, or we will die at the hands of either rebels or regime or ISIS. I didn't raise my children to kill people or be soldiers to kill people. If I had stayed, the army would have taken

them. There were no schools there. I have a dream for my children to continue
their school and to be educated.

A mother takes on tremendous responsibility for the future of her children.
Thus, Mrs. Khaled believed her suffering needed to be a closely guarded secret. Anything less than her unwavering faith in Germany would jeopardize her
children's attachment to their new home. Although she had chosen to move her
family to Germany, Mrs. Khaled wrestled with self-doubt and sadness over the
rightness of her choice and whether she was doing all she could to ensure their
success. Not just for Mrs. Khaled but for other female refugees (like Sabrina,
see the vignette in Chapter 7), self-doubt and concern for family members are
heightened following resettlement.

Self-trust in Cambodian refugees, Marjorie Muecke elaborates, is in itself
gendered. "Being a refugee puts Khmer women at risk of self-mistrust on two
accounts: first, the impossibility, when outside the traditional cultural bounds
of Khmer society, of upholding the womanly ideal of being 'virtuous,' and their
separation from children. Both are breaches of fundamental Khmer ideals for
women."[101] In Germany as a sole decision-maker, leached from her old supports
and faced with the growing responsibility of her children's success, Mrs. Khaled
quickly shed her old role. She took on a new role of problem maker to ensure her
family's success. She was being a trouble-maker and raising hell to channel her
worries into other constructive outlets.

I go to organizations and made a lot of problems at the housing meetings. I told
the employees there, "I made the journey from Syria not to sit idle but so that my
children could attend school and be educated" At one point, Mrs. Khaled says, "I
got so weak I became sick." Her children asked, "Mama if you don't like Germany
how will you accept that we will like Germany?" So, till I die, I will stay strong and
show them that I like Germany.

On the receiving end of a taciturn family member is Sabrina, a 21-year-old Arab
recently arrived in Germany. She is concerned about her twin sister Sana's health
and personality transformation as a consequence of their flight from Syria:

Sana's fainting started with the journey. We saw it first in Turkey . . . in July 2015.
It's hard for her. It's hard for us. For me, if I remember the times she is falling down
fainting, I can't speak about it and it makes me nervous. And my mother too. She's

---

[101] Muecke, M. A. (1995). Trust, abuse of trust, and mistrust among Cambodian refugee: A cultural interpretation. In E. V. Daniel & J. C. Knudson, *Mistrusting Refugees* (p. 44). University of
California.

crying a lot as she is nervous. We call the ambulance a lot and asked doctors about it. But a lot of them didn't give us an answer of what she's going through and what afflicts her. We are upset having to ask and ask, and ask without getting a reason.

Interviewer: She talks about it?

Sana doesn't like to talk about it. Sana is the person who doesn't want to share a lot. When we go to the doctor and he asks her, "What's hurting you?" she replies (only) "My hand." At that time, her health, her body, and her feet may all be suffering and hurting. But she just replies in short answers.

Interviewer: She used to be different?

She's not quiet but she doesn't talk. She was independent, strong, and angry, but she doesn't talk much now. She's nervous and uptight.

Arrival in new displacement contexts can overturn women's social contract with society. In her hometown in Syria, Mrs. Khaled was the doted-upon daughter and sister; she had many a shoulder to cry on. Her children also had access to support and mentorship by many parental figures in their extended family. In Germany, Mrs. Khaled's trustworthiness within her family and her confidence rested on her ability to hide her sadness and shield her family from its weakness. Sabrina and Sana were vibrant, loving, and healthy siblings who turned to each other for support; now, Sabrina finds it hard to recognize her sister, and herself in the caregiver role for a young invalid.

For host countries like Germany, new concerns and unique challenges may arise from their female refugee protectorate. There are many faces of female refugees—single women who traveled alone with or without children, unaccompanied girls, child brides sometimes with newborn babies, adolescent girls, older women, pregnant and lactating women, and women with disabilities. There may also be refugees at the intersection of other identity markers, as in the case of Arthur Britney Joestar, the first nonbinary person granted refugee status in the UK; many[102] will have exceptional needs. Attention to the needs of this refugee protectorate requires knowledge of discriminatory gender practices and persecutions based on gender in their countries of origin, and cultural pressures on them in their host country. If sexual violence might exert its deleterious effect through cumulative trauma and changes the treatment of women by society, then the role of nations who accept resettled refugees becomes even more critical. It would require social and clinical interventions on how to incorporate the knowledge to address female refugees' trauma at every stage of their flight to empower them to change their conditions and, thus, their communities. Nonrecognition

---

[102] Kelly, N. (2020, December 30). "I felt like I was born again": First non-binary person granted UK refugee status. *The Guardian*. https://www.theguardian.com/world/2020/dec/30/i-felt-like-i-was-born-again-first-non-binary-person-granted-uk-refugee-status

or unpreparedness of the needs of female refugees can result in a quagmire of problems for host nations.

Postconflict Reconstruction of the Female Refugee Protectorate

Consider the challenges of Ashwaq Haji Hamid and Mrs. Khaled as they attempt to integrate:

> Ashwaq Haji Hamid is a Yazidi girl resettled in Germany. Ashwaq was sold to an ISIS fighter in Iraq when she was 15 years old and enslaved for 10 weeks in Mosul, Iraq. In Germany, she had hoped to restart her life with her brother and mother, as far away from her tormentor as possible: "I ran away from Iraq so I would not see that ugly face and forget anything that reminds me of it, but I was shocked to see him in Germany," said Ashwaq.[103]
>
> Encountering one's stalker or abuser is already one time too much. But Ashwaq ran into her abuser twice. "The first time was in 2016," she said. "He was chasing me. He was the same person, but the second time, he came close to me and told me he knew everything about me." Although she had notified the police, she was forced to flee Germany when her former abuser confronted her. "If I had not seen him, I would have stayed in Germany. I wanted to complete my studies and get a degree that would give me a decent life," she said.

Shares Mrs. Khaled:

> They say, "You should integrate," But how? asks Mrs. Khaled. Shortly after I arrived in the fourth and final city, I started to feel lightheaded and needed a doctor. I called the hospital, but they refused to pay for translators. They said, "insurers are not ready to pay for translators." So I had to arrange for a friend to go to the hospital with me. I found I got diabetes with the highest level. I am on four insulins and have to measure it [sic] six times a day. I have no one in her family who is a diabetic. I don't eat any sugar. In the meantime, the fire alarm is going on. How shall I integrate when my children and I cannot even sleep?

Conflict-related trauma and the health consequences of forced migration can affect refugee women's engagement with host communities. A majority of

---

[103] Hussein, M. (2018, August 17). Yazidi woman encounters "Islamic State" captor in Germany. *Infomigrants News*. https://www.infomigrants.net/en/post/11368/yazidi-woman-encounters-islamic-state-captor-in-germany

refugees continue to have at least one or more symptoms related to traumas after 3 years and 6 months.[104] At the same time, women's positive mental health can be a positive reservoir impacting host nations. Across many ethnic and cultural communities, female groups share a strong sense of social support, shared identification, and internal solidarity.[105] To lessen the effects of complex trauma, policies aimed at female refugees' integration must incorporate gender-specific experiences through knowledge of their unique social-environmental context and relationships.

International human rights organizations and instruments such as the United Nations Security Council's Resolution 1325[106] and its related resolutions urge adopting a gender-sensitive perspective to consider the unique needs of women and girls during conflicts in aspects of resettlement, rehabilitation, reintegration, repatriation, and postconflict reconstruction. Guidelines on Gender-Related Persecution and the Guidelines on Membership of a Particular Social Group within the Context of Article 1A(2) of the 1951 Convention and its 1967 Protocol relating to the Status of Refugees promote a gender-sensitive interpretation of the Convention and of the Refugee Status Determination procedures to prevent marginalizing gender-based experiences of persecution.[107] But consistent programming is not always available for female refugees from conflict-affected countries[108] and application of its key recognitions for instance, that sexual violence can be a form of persecution in policy or law remain largely, inconsistent or elusive.

To empower females, we would require knowledge and assessment of their social and cultural roles and gender mores within their countries of origin,[109] experiences during migration, competencies such as language or education,[110]

[104] Vallejo-Martín, M., Sánchez, A. S., & Canto, J. M. (2021). Refugee women with a history of trauma: Gender vulnerability in relation to post-traumatic stress disorder. *International Journal of Environmental Research and Public Health, 18*(9), 4806.

[105] Berruti, D., Doru, E., Erle, E., Gianfelici, F., & Khayati, K. (2002). *Kurds in Europe—from asylum right to social rights.* Marsico.

[106] UN Security Council, October 31, 2000, UN Doc. SC/6942. Retrieved on November 20, 2019, from https://press.un.org/en/2000/20001031.sc6942.doc.html.

[107] Martin, S. (2011). Refugee and displaced women: 60 years of progress and setbacks. *Amsterdam Law Forum, 3*(2), 72–91.

[108] Ward, J., & Vann, B. (2002). Gender-based violence in refugee settings. *Lancet, 360*(Suppl.), s13–s14.

[109] Florian, S. (2010), Lo stato di salute delle rifugiate somale in America: Alcuni studi recenti, in DEP. *Deportate, Esuli, Profughe, 12,* 207–221.

[110] Jesuthasan, J., Sönmez, E., Abels, I., Kurmeyer, C., Gutermann, J., Kimbel, R., Krüger, A., Niklewski, G., Richter K., Stangier, U., Wollny, A., Zier, U., Oertelt-Prigione, S., Shouler-Ocak, M. (2018). Near-death experiences, attacks by family members, and absence of health care in their home countries affect the quality of life of refugee women in Germany: A multi-region, cross-sectional, gender-sensitive study. *BMC Medicine, 16,* 15.

and challenges experienced by their family members.[111] At the Refugee Status Determination level some measures could prove useful: asylum decisions broken down by the gender; understanding of cultural differences in female asylum seekers' demeanors as reflected in asylum procedures; consideration of gender and the consequences of trauma in asylum provisions such as interviews.

Given the influence of women's roles for their children and communities, strategic social initiatives with them across displacement settings can also mean empowering their families and communities. Gender-empowering policies could include, among others, expedient and effective resolution of complaints of sexual harassment or assaults, reducing women's isolation to increase the reporting gender-based crimes,[112] enhancing a shared sense of safety through increasing community-building efforts, addressing their needs for sanitation and hygiene in safe situations,[113] and ways to recognize their prior credentials so their prior skills training can be utilized in host nations. Gender-sensitive policies include an awareness of, and psychoeducation within, community programming to prevent the reproducing of social dynamics such as social rejection that may occur with severely abused women. Unfamiliarity with the host-nation's language can increase women's vulnerability to the persistence of the effects of trauma. Thus, the availability of trained translators, mediators, interpreters, childcare, and cultural mediators to assist refugee women in accessing social services can also increase their independence, gain employment, and improve the outcomes of their children in host societies.

The interview with Mrs. Khaled wrapped up. She reminded the interviewer, "Remember, I said at the beginning of the interview that I was here for a reason? You still don't know that reason."

Let us find out in the next chapter.

---

[111] In pregnant Somali refugees a provider's cultural knowledge of their dilemmas quelled their fears and hesitations and increased their receptivity toward medical procedures: Njenga, A. (2022). Somali refugee women's cultural beliefs and practices around pregnancy and childbirth. *Journal of Transcultural Nursing, 33*(4), 484–490.

[112] Sansonetti, S. (2016). *Female refugees and asylum seekers: The issue of integration.* European Parliament. https://www.europarl.europa.eu/RegData/etudes/STUD/2016/556929/IPOL_STU(2016)556929_EN.pdf

[113] Sansonetti, S. (2016). *Female refugees and asylum seekers: The issue of integration.* European Parliament. https://www.europarl.europa.eu/RegData/etudes/STUD/2016/556929/IPOL_STU(2016)556929_EN.pdf

8

Family Trauma

The Psychological Legacy of War

"My Boy Cannot Forget"

"Remember the 10-year-old boy whose uncle was killed?" said Mrs. Khaled, nudging the memory of her son, Tommy. "He loved his uncle a lot and often trailed his favorite uncle like a shadow."

On the day his uncle was kidnapped by ISIS, Tommy had spent the day with him in the city. His uncle had bought him a pair of shoes and they had hung out with his friends. But at sunset, his uncle, likely sensing impending danger, dispatched Tommy on the pretext of running an errand to another location. It was to keep Tommy out of harm's way.

Since then, says Mrs. Khaled, "Tommy has a fixed idea in his head that if he were with his uncle, his uncle would not have died." She wrings her hands. "He lost his uncle. He tries to forget but cannot. I hear him talk to his uncle saying, 'I want to be near you.'" Her own memories are unbearable, but her son's concerns keep her up at night. "But my boy cannot forget. My boy doesn't forget. And that is why I'm here today."

War-Affected Families and Trauma

The family holds a powerful influence as a socializing agent for its members, in making meaning of adversity, moderating trauma,[1,2] lending hope, initiative, spirituality and resilience[3] to its members. Key adaptational processes strengthen a family's capacity to withstand

---

[1] Kaplin, D., Parente, K., & Santacroce, F. (2019). A review of the use of trauma systems therapy to treat refugee children, adolescents, and families. *Journal of Infant Child and Adolescent Psychotherapy*, *18*, 417–431.

[2] Ozer, E. J., Best, S. R., Lipsey, T. L., & Weiss, D. S. (2003). Predictors of posttraumatic stress disorder and symptoms in adults: A meta-analysis. *Psychology Bulletin*, *129*, 52–73.

[3] Walsh, F. (1998). Beliefs, spirituality, and transcendence: Keys to family resilience. In M. McGoldrick (Ed.), *Revisioning family therapy* (pp. 465–484). Guilford.

adversity and buffer stress,[4] but humanitarian emergencies and complex trauma can often strain a refugee family's resources, coping abilities, and ability to serve as a protective support during resettlement. In clinical work with families, identifying its strengths and resources, is critical to enable its positive growth from serious life challenges. In the case of refugee families, it is also important to go beyond. Understanding of the flow of trauma is critical in designing family focused care to address relational and family trauma and for enabling healthy individuals and refugee communities.

To understand how forcible displacement can affect posttraumatic stress, we look within the Khaled family. In doing so, we ask, in turn, five important questions about families affected by war and displacement in order to gain short-term and long-term perspectives on trauma transmission within:

1. Does the emotional functioning of one or more affected family members affect others' mental health?
2. What can we learn from these five pathways of family functioning with reciprocal effects on trauma within refugee families—maternal posttraumatic stress, marital relations, child mental health, paternal posttraumatic stress, and parental psychopathology?
3. How does trauma affect marital relations and happiness within couples?
4. What are the mental health consequences of war on children?
5. What do longitudinal studies of trauma in the offspring of the traumatized reveal to us of trauma transmission within families?

Little is known[5] about the experience of family disruption from the vantage point of family members, such as how children's experience of the violence of war may affect their parents. Solid scholarship on traumatized non-Western families, identification of dysfunctional family dynamics, and pertinent multigenerational processes of trauma transmission within families[6] is sparse yet critical.[7]

[4] Walsh, F. (2016). Family resilience: A developmental systems perspective. *European Journal of Developmental Psychology*, 13(3), 313–324.

[5] McCormack, L., & Sly, R. (2013). Distress and growth: The subjective "lived" experiences of being the child of a Vietnam veteran. *Traumatology*, 19(4), 303–312.

[6] Sagi-Schwartz, A., van IJzendoorn, M. H., & Bakermans-Kranenburg, M. J. (2008). Does intergenerational transmission of trauma skip a generation? No meta-analytic evidence for tertiary traumatization with third generation of Holocaust survivors. *Attachment and Human Development*, 10, 205–221.

[7] Schick, M., Morina, N., Klaghofer, R., Schnyder, U., & Müller, J. (2013). Trauma, mental health, and intergenerational associations in Kosovar families 11 years after the war. *European Journal of Psychotraumatology*, 4, http://doi.org/10.3402/ejpt.v4i0.21060

As a result there is a paucity of effective and methodologically rigorous family interventions for traumatized refugee families.

Besides the broader socioeconomic effects of war and violence, trauma's psychological legacy is its pernicious after-effects on the person, family, and future generations. Survivors of mass trauma can re-experience the trauma in broad and derivative ways, sometimes as many as 4 or 5 decades after exposure.[8,9] Despite the duration of time, posttraumatic stress or other mental health concerns in war-affected families, fail to fall to the levels of a comparable civilian population level[10] or those who have never been exposed to war. Second- and third-generation offspring[11] can show poor mental health symptoms related to their parents' and grandparents' trauma.

War can change the very notion of what it means to be a family, one's cultural role within one's family, and who comprises one's family. Psychological shifts within the family are precipitated by social and demographic changes brought on by war such as the arrival of stateless children, women forced into roles of survivors due to food insecurity, and other such changes. Wars and conflict can bring about great flux within the family by shifting control of women's sexuality to a militia or to the community giving rise to greater sexual violence against them,[12,13] and other male, transgender, and nonbinary family members.[14] Militarization

[8] Bramsen, I., & van der Ploeg, H. M. (1999). Fifty years later: The long-term psychological adjustment of aging World War II survivors. *Acta Psychiatrica Scandinavica, 100*(5), 350–358.

[9] Castro-Vale, I., Severo, M., Carvalho, D., & Mota-Cardoso, R. (2019). Intergenerational transmission of war-related trauma assessed 40 years after exposure. *Annals of General Psychiatry, 18*, 14.

[10] Schick, M., Morina, N., Klaghofer, R., Schnyder, U., & Müller, J. (2013). Trauma, mental health, and intergenerational associations in Kosovar families 11 years after the war. *European Journal of Psychotraumatology, 4*, http://doi.org/10.3402/ejpt.v4i0.21060

[11] Maffini, C. S., & Pham, A. N. (2016). Overcoming a legacy of conflict: The repercussive effects of stress and intergenerational transmission of trauma among Vietnamese Americans. *Journal of Aggression, Maltreatment & Trauma, 25*(6), 580–597.

[12] UN Human Rights Council, March 15, 2023, UN Doc. A/HRC/52/62. https://www.ohchr.org/sites/default/files/documents/hrbodies/hrcouncil/coiukraine/A_HRC_52_62_AUV_EN.pdf. The Independent International Commission of Inquiry on Ukraine determined that there was widespread rape and sexual violence involving women, men, and girls from 4 to 82 years of age by Russian armed forces committed on the pretext of house-to-house searches and unlawful confinement and through imposing forced nudity for prolonged periods in detention and at checkpoints.

[13] The Islamic State of Syria and Iraq (ISIS), a militant group, engaged in forcible marriage, selling women as sex slaves, rapes, beatings, sexual exploitation of children, and enforced veiling: International Federation for Human Rights. (2013, April 9). *Violence against women in Syria: Breaking the silence.* https://www.fidh.org/en/region/north-africa-middle-east/syria/13134-violence-against-women-in-syria-breaking-the-silence; UN Security Council, June 15, 2016, UN Doc. A/HRC/32/CRP.2; US Department of State. (2020). https://www.state.gov/wp-content/uploads/2021/03/SYRIA-2020-HUMAN-RIGHTS-REPORT.pdf; Marcus, J. (2014, October 3). UN report reveals ISIS abuse of women and children. *The New York Times.* http://www.nytimes.com/2014/10/04/world/middleeast/un-report-isis-abuse-women-children.html?_r=0

[14] Human Rights Watch. (2023). *Syria: Events of 2022.* https://www.hrw.org/world-report/2023/country-chapters/syria

reproduces the oppressive systems through gendered forms of dominance, and can amplify existing forms of violence, including child marriages;[15] plummeting rates of labor-participation of women;[16,17] and increased number of widows, including teenage widows[18,19] in Syria, Afghanistan, and Uganda.[20] For instance, there are 2.5 million widows in Afghanistan with 50,000 living in Kabul[21] itself. Volatility is the most salient feature of war-affected families of the Middle East, and it is marked by short lifespans, higher mortality rates, separations, and fewer family supports. The burdens of war and humanitarian emergencies are often borne by the family.

The mental health ramifications of wars have generally been gathered through select mass traumas or the individual accounts of veterans of war,[22,23] such as those of Holocaust survivors and their offspring,[24,25] and war veterans in other

[15] Although prevalent in preconflict Syria, child marriage occurred mostly among poor and/or rural families. During 2014–2018, children forced into marriages rose from 15% to 36% as families secured protection for their daughters by marrying them to older men. In repressive regimes, child marriages exacerbate children's vulnerabilities to physical and sexual violence in the absence of critical sexual and reproductive health services, such as emergency contraception. Chakraborty, R. (2019). Child, not bride. *Harvard International Review, 40*, 1; US Department of State. (2020). https://www.state.gov/wp-content/uploads/2021/03/SYRIA-2020-HUMAN-RIGHTS-REPORT. pdf; Child marriage on the rise among Syrian refugee girls in Jordan. (2018, April 18). *Al Jazeera.* https://www.aljazeera.com/videos/2018/4/18/child-marriage-on-the-rise-among-syrian-refugee-girls-in-jordan

[16] Between 2001 and 2010, in the absence of state protections, women's participation rates in labor declined more rapidly than men's, from 21% to 12.9%. Although marital and educational status prior to the war, were key determinants of their labor force participation, married Syrian women abandoned the labor force in droves with greater negative consequences for slum-dwellers, and agricultural women: Nasser, R., & Mehchy, Z. (2012, July). Determinants of labour force participation in Syria (2001–2010) (Working Paper No. 698). *Economic Research Forum.* https://erf.org.eg/app/uploads/2014/08/698.pdf

[17] Caldwell, J. C. (2001). The globalization of fertility behavior. In R. Bulatao & H. B. Casterline (Eds.), *Global fertility transition* (pp. 93–115). Population Council.

[18] Khan, H. (2018, February 18). Sorrow and stigma: The double tragedy of Afghanistan's young widows. *The New Humanitarian.* https://deeply.thenewhumanitarian.org/womensadvancement/articles/2018/02/08/sorrow-and-stigma-the-double-tragedy-of-afghanistans-young-widows

[19] Valette, D., & Matei, A. (2022). The women and children of Syria's widow camps: Hardest to reach, most at risk. *World Vision International.* https://www.wvi.org/sites/default/files/2022-04/WVSR%202022%20report_%20widow%20camps%20_%20FINAL16April%202022_0.pdf

[20] Kiconco, A. (2021). *Gender, conflict and reintegration in Uganda: Abducted girls, returning women.* Routledge.

[21] Bronstein, P. (2015, November 5). *War widows of Afghanistan: Struggling to survive.* https://pulitzercenter.org/projects/war-widows-afghanistan-struggling-survive

[22] Although some studies find that findings are comparable to civilians: Southwick, S. M., Morgan, C. A., Nicolaou, A. L., & Charney, D. S. (1997). Consistency of memory for combat-related traumatic events in veterans of Operation Desert Storm. *American Journal of Psychiatry, 154*(2), 173–177.

[23] Priebe, S., Bogic, M., Ajdukovic, D., Franciskovic, T., Galeazzi, G. M., Kucukalic, A., Lecic-Tosevski, D., Morina, N., Popovski, M., Wang, D., & Schützwohl, M. (2010). Mental disorders following war in the Balkans: A study in 5 countries. *Archives of General Psychiatry, 67*(5), 518–528.

[24] Danieli, Y. (Ed.). (1998). *International handbook of multigenerational legacies of trauma.* Plenum.

[25] Sangalang, C. C., & Vang, C. (2017). Intergenerational trauma in refugee families: A systematic review. *Journal of Immigrant and Minority Health, 19*(3), 745–754.

European contexts.[26,27,28,29] Seldom are they explored by investigating their impact on those who may vicariously suffer alongside.[30] A family member's posttraumatic stress can evoke secondary trauma,[31] an emotional syndrome kindled in intimate others as a result of the emotional support required by the traumatized person. Individuals' traumatic events can result in an increase in posttraumatic stress in their significant others,[32,33] such as offspring[34] and partners, who may not have been present during the traumatic encounter.[35] Many researchers conceptualize secondary trauma as "nearly identical to PTSD"[36] and arising out of the knowledge of traumatizing events experienced by someone close. With rare exceptions,[37] family processes of adaptation or disruption of relationships within refugee families are rarely identified or investigated.[38,39]

[26] Santavirta, T., Santavirta, N., & Gillman, S. E. (2017). Association of the World War II Finnish evacuation of children with psychiatric hospitalization in the next generation. *Journal of American Medical Association Psychiatry, 75*(1), 21–27.

[27] Ager, A. (1993). *Mental health issues in refugee populations: A review* (Working Paper). http://fmo.bodleian.ox.ac.uk:8080/fedora/get/fmo:1082/PDF

[28] Steel, Z., Silove, D., Phan, T., & Bauman, A. (2002). The long-term impact of trauma on the mental health of Vietnamese refugees resettled in Australia. *Lancet, 360*(9339), 156–162.

[29] Blair, R. G. (2000). Risk factors associated with PTSD and major depression among Cambodian refugees in Utah. *Health and Social Work, 25*(1), 23–30.

[30] Franciskovic, T., Stevanovic, A., Jelusic, I., Roganovic, B., Klaric, M., & Grkovic, J. (2007). Secondary traumatization of wives of war veterans with post-traumatic stress disorder. *Croatian Medical Journal, 48*, 177–184.

[31] Fullerton, C. S., & Ursano, R. J. (1997). Post-traumatic responses in spouse/significant others of disaster workers. In C. S. Fullerton & R. J. Ursano (Eds.), *Post-traumatic stress disorder: Acute and long-term responses to trauma and disaster* (pp. 59–76). APA.

[32] Nickerson, A., Bryant, R. A., Steel, Z., Silove, D., & Brooks, R. (2010). The impact of fear for family on mental health in a resettled Iraqi refugee community. *Journal of Psychiatric Research, 44*, 229–235.

[33] Schweitzer, R., Melville, F., Steel, Z., & Lacherez, P. (2006). Trauma, post-migration living difficulties, and social support as predictors of psychological adjustment in resettled Sudanese refugees. *Australian and New Zealand Journal of Psychiatry, 40*, 179–188.

[34] Kellerman, N. P. F. (2001). Psychopathology in children of Holocaust survivors: A review of the research literature. *Israel Journal of Psychiatry and Related Sciences, 38*(1), 36–46.

[35] However, one study of Darfuri asylum-seekers showed the reverse, that indirect exposure to others' traumatic events can reduce an individual's emotional distress and increase psychological well-being: Regev, S., & Slonim-Nevo, V. (2019). Sorrow shared is halved? War trauma experienced by others and mental health among Darfuri asylum seekers. *Psychiatric Research, 273*, 475–480.

[36] Renshaw, K. D., Allen, E. S., Rhoades, G. K., Blais, R. K., Markman, H. J., & Stanley, S. M. (2011). Distress in spouses of service members with symptoms of combat-related PTSD: Secondary traumatic stress or general psychological distress? *Journal of Family Psychology, 25*(4), 461–469.

[37] Santavirta, T., Santavirta, N., & Gillman, S. E. (2017). Association of the World War II Finnish evacuation of children with psychiatric hospitalization in the next generation. *Journal of American Medical Association Psychiatry, 75*(1), 21–27.

[38] Karageorge, A., Rhodes, P., Gray, R., & Papadopoulos, R. K. (2017). Refugee and staff experiences of psychosocial services: A qualitative systematic review intervention. *Journal of Mental Health and Psychosocial Support in Conflict Affected Areas, 15*(1), 51–69.

[39] Karageorge, A., Rhodes, P., & Gray, R. (2018). Relationship and family therapy for newly resettled refugees: An interpretive description of staff experiences. *Australian and New Zealand Journal of Family Therapy, 39*, 303–319.

Many international family therapists working with refugee families from Libya[40] to Cyprus[41] assert that a refugee's posttraumatic experience may only be fully appreciated when viewed within the family context.

Families as Sites of Emotional Contagion: Does the Emotional Functioning of One Affect That of the Others?

Families are sites of shared emotions.[42] Parents and children can "catch" each other's emotions from birth, studies show, either explicitly or implicitly; such transmission of emotion along with its synchrony in one's close others is found in all societies.

The phenomenon wherein "an attentional, emotional, and behavioral synchrony"[43] is produced in others is an important feature of emotional contagion and has an evolutionary advantage for social entities such as dyads and families. Emotional contagion is generally conceptualized as a "package"[44] of elements ranging from facial expressions, neurophysiological activity, and instrumental behaviors that are also produced by multiple factors or "multiply determined." Given this feature of emotional contagion in families, in general, and Arab social interconnectivity, the psychological trauma of an affected member will affect family functioning.

The emotions produced as a consequence of the traumatic event(s) on one member can be felt by all members often in multiple ways. The effects of trauma can flow through a family in the form of altered parent-child relationships, child's mental health problems,[45] inadequate infant sensorimotor and language development,[46] high correlations in posttraumatic stress levels of

[40] Giaber, M. B. (2016). Family therapy in global humanitarian contexts: Voices and issues from the field. In L. L. Charlés & G. Samarasinghe (Eds.), (pp. 103–114). AFTA Springer Briefs in Family Therapy.

[41] Killian, K. D. (2016). Time, trauma, and ambiguous loss: Working with families with missing members in postconflict Cyprus. In L. L. Charlés & G. Samarasinghe (Eds.), Family therapy in global humanitarian contexts: Voices and issues from the field (pp. 77–89). AFTA Springer Briefs in Family Therapy.

[42] Thomson, R A. (1987). Empathy and emotional understanding: The early development of empathy. In N. Eisenberg & J. Strayer (Eds.), Empathy and its development (pp. 119–145). Cambridge University Press.

[43] Hatfield, E., Cacioppo, J., & Rapson, R. (1993). Emotional contagion: Studies in emotion and social interaction (p. 5). Cambridge University Press.

[44] Ibid. (p. 4).

[45] Schick, M., Morina, N., Klaghofer, R., Schnyder, U., & Müller, J. (2013). Trauma, mental health, and intergenerational associations in Kosovar families 11 years after the war. European Journal of Psychotraumatology, 4. http://doi.org/10.3402/ejpt.v4i0.21060

[46] Punamaki, R.-L., Diab, S. Y., Isosavi, S., & Kuittinen, S. K. N. (2018). Maternal pre- and postnatal mental health and infant development in war conditions: The Gaza Infant Study. Psychological Trauma: Theory, Research, Practice, and Policy, 10, 144–153.

spouses,[47] detachment of a parent,[48] parent-child role-reversals, and over-protectiveness.[49] Intimate partners of survivors with posttraumatic symptoms report elevated levels of loneliness, somatic ailments, and psychiatric symptoms[50,51] and high incidence of separation[52] or divorce.[53] A traumatic event experienced by one or several members of the family can abort or change the nature of emotion within families. Since systematic studies on trauma transmission within war-affected refugee families and their mental health consequences are rare, some gaps in understanding remain, such as the identification of indirect pathways of trauma[54] through the family, peer group, and community.

Research in the areas of developmental psychology, social psychology, animal studies, and clinical psychology has affirmed the powerful mirroring effect of emotion. Studies document such modeling and mimicry of parental emotions in a variety of ways, and the effects can be long-term: mothers suffering from depression can communicate their depression to their infants[55] and put them at risk for future depression; children who observe angry adults demonstrate aggression against peers,[56] and so forth.

A view of complex trauma[57] can be gained by assessing its effects on family members or a specific developmental family stage. In one study, when offspring

[47] Schick, M., Morina, N., Klaghofer, R., Schnyder, U., & Müller, J. (2013). Trauma, mental health, and intergenerational associations in Kosovar families 11 years after the war. *European Journal of Psychotraumatology*, 4. http://doi.org/10.3402/ejpt.v4i0.21060

[48] Ruscio, A. M., Weathers, F. W., King, L. A., & King, D. W. (2002). Male war-zone veterans' perceived relationships with their children: The importance of emotional numbing. *Journal of Traumatic Stress*, 15(5), E351–E357.

[49] Field, N. P., Muong, S., & Sochanvimean, V. (2013). Parental styles in the intergenerational transmission of trauma stemming from the Khmer Rouge regime in Cambodia. *American Journal of Orthopsychiatry*, 83(4), E483–E494.

[50] Caspi, Y., Slobodin, O., Kammerer, N., Enosh, G., Shorer, S., & Klein, E. (2010). Bedouin wives on the home front: Living with men serving in the Israel defense forces. *Journal of Traumatic Stress*, 23, 682–690.

[51] Lambert, J. E., Engh, R., Hasbun, A., & Holzer, J. (2012). Impact of posttraumatic stress disorder on the relationship quality and psychological distress of intimate partners: A meta-analytic review. *Journal of Family Psychology*, 26, 729–737.

[52] Steel, Z., Silove, D., Phan, T., & Bauman, A. (2002). The long-term impact of trauma on the mental health of Vietnamese refugees resettled in Australia. *Lancet*, 360(9339), 156–162.

[53] Karam, E. G., Mneimneh, Z., Karam, A. N., Fayyad, J. A., Nasser, S. C., Chatterji, S., & Kessler, R. C. (2006). Prevalence and treatment of mental disorders in Lebanon: A national epidemiological survey. *Lancet*, 367(9515), 1000–1006.

[54] Sigvardsdotter, E., Malm, A., Tinghög, P., Vaez, M., & Saboonchi, F. (2016). Refugee trauma measurement: A review of existing checklists. *Public Health Reviews*, 371, 1–9.

[55] Downey, G., & Coyne, J. C. (1990). Children of depressed parents: An integrative review. *Psychological Bulletin*, 108(1), 50–76.

[56] Cummings, E. M. (1987). Coping with background anger in early childhood. *Child Development*, 58, 976–984.

[57] Schick, M., Morina, N., Klaghofer, R., Schnyder, U., & Müller, J. (2013). Trauma, mental health, and intergenerational associations in Kosovar families 11 years after the war. *European Journal of Psychotraumatology*, 4, http://doi.org/10.3402/ejpt.v4i0.21060

of parents with moderate and severe depression were examined at a 20-year follow-up, rates of anxiety disorders, major depression, and substance dependence were approximately three-times higher compared to the offspring of nondepressed parents.[58] The persistence of depression in the offspring suggest the magnitude and continuity of parental emotions on future generations.

Connectivity of emotions within families can also extend to sharing of a subjective state by two or more individuals who may agree on their shared meaning of a particular situation or event or "intersubjectivity." "Experience is thoroughly intersubjective," according to Kleinman, as it involves contestations with others with whom we are connected.[59] Given the absence of the centrality of experience in social theory, experience has not always been conceptualized as interpersonal and intersubjective. Intersubjectivity is the shared experience that can bridge individuals' experiences of trauma with their interpersonal world.[60]

Consider the case of Karam, a 24-year-old Syrian refugee whose guilt heightens his posttraumatic symptoms. His symptoms have escalated between 2017 and 2020:

> I was bad to my family too. I was disappointing them. I was disappointing my girlfriend as I was not working or studying, or attempting to work on my goals. And this thing is the one that fucks me up, disappointing the people. Then I got in another relationship that lasted 8–9 months. When things ended, she said to me, "You're the one that is damaging us."

The trauma experience can also be an intersubjectively created realm of meaning and significance where the subjective experience of the trauma may be available to the participant and to others in his or her intimate or proximate circle. Kleinman frames experience at once as individual and collective, subjective and social. According to Kleinman, the foundations of symbolic meanings within our interaction can be found in the earliest symbols and social interactions gathered by our senses.[61] Our subjectivities can return to those symbols to reshape and reinterpret them and be shaped by our local worlds.[62] Karam's family and girlfriend believe his untruths about his condition and advancement in

[58] Weissman, M. M., Wickramaratne, P., Nomura, Y., Warner, V., Pilowsky, D., & Verdeli, H. (2006). Offspring of depressed parents: 20 years later. *American Journal of Psychiatry, 163*(6), 1001–1008.

[59] Kleinman, A. (1998, April 13–16). *Experience and its moral modes: Culture, human conditions, and disorder* [Lecture]. Tanner Lectures on Human Values, Stanford University, Stanford, CA. https://tannerlectures.utah.edu/_resources/documents/a-to-z/k/Kleinman99.pdf

[60] Jenkins, J. H., & Barrett, J. B. (2003). *Schizophrenia, culture, and subjectivity: The edge of experience.* Cambridge University Press.

[61] Kleinman, A. (1998, April 13–16). *Experience and its moral modes: Culture, human conditions, and disorder* [Lecture]. Tanner Lectures on Human Values, Stanford University, Stanford, CA. https://tannerlectures.utah.edu/_resources/documents/a-to-z/k/Kleinman99.pdf

[62] Biehl, J., Good, B., & Kleinman, A. (2007). Introduction: Rethinking subjectivity. In J. Biehl, B. Good, & A. Kleinman (Eds.), *Subjectivity: Ethnographic investigations* (pp. 1–24). University of California Press.

Germany. Being entwined in his subjective experience of posttraumatic stress in some ways can also amplify negative emotions such as disappointments and the cycle of stress.

Suad Joseph describes the Arab's family's close-knit fabric through the notion of connectivity where people see themselves as inherently linked to another's perceptions and experiences of self.[63] Thus, societal and familial expectations can include reading each other's minds and anticipating the other's needs. It is no wonder then that forced separations from family or close friends and the loss or disappearance of family members and loved ones were experienced as traumatic events by Syrian refugees resettled in Sweden.[64] Among stressful postmigration factors, 50% of respondents reported sadness over not being reunited with family members. Further, this sadness was significantly associated with anxiety, depression, low subjective well-being, and posttraumatic stress. Where the family is the focus and when family relations are deemed significant, the effects of trauma are better seen through a family lens.[65] For scholars of the global family, understanding the broad swathe and diversity of factors that affect the functioning of modern multicultural families, such as refugee and other minority families, is of paramount significance.

Five Pathways of Family Functioning

Let us explore the five pathways of family functioning with reciprocal effect on trauma within refugee families: maternal posttraumatic stress, marital relations, child mental health, paternal posttraumatic stress, and parental psychopathology. Studies[66] have indicated that secondary trauma requires a more rigorous assessment than it has been accorded previously; identifying pathways of secondary trauma can be useful in understanding what sustains trauma for families.

---

[63] Joseph, S. (1993). Connectivity and patriarchy among urban working-class Arab families in Lebanon. *Ethos: Journal of the Society for Psychological Anthropology, 21*(4), 452–484.

[64] Tinghög, P., Malm, A., Arwidson, C., Sigvardsdotter, E., Lundin, A., & Saboonchi, F. (2017). Prevalence of mental ill health, traumas and postmigration stress among refugees from Syria resettled in Sweden after 2011: A population-based survey. *BMJ Open, 7*(12), E018899. https://doi. org/10.1136/bmjopen-2017-018899

[65] Weine, S., Muzurovic, N., Kulauzovic, Y., Besic, S., Lezic, A., Mujagic, A., Muzurovic, J., Spahovic, D., Feetha, S., Ware, N., Knafl, K., & Pavkovic, I. (2004). Family consequences of refugee trauma. *Family Process, 43*, 147–160.

[66] Renshaw, K. D., Allen, E. S., Rhoades, G. K., Blais, R. K., Markman, H. J., & Stanley, S. M. (2011). Distress in spouses of service members with symptoms of combat-related PTSD: Secondary traumatic stress or general psychological distress? *Journal of Family Psychology, 25*(4), 461–469.

Maternal Posttraumatic Stress

Private Investigator and Snitch Mahmoud

The loss of the youngest brother was a traumatic event for the extended Khaled household. But his tragic death had not been brought up with outsiders prior to my interview with Mrs. Khaled. Generally, Middle Eastern people believe that mental health care is only sought in the most urgent of cases. Perhaps viewing people with extreme mental health conditions makes them reluctant to seek care in less extraordinary but significant times of need. Lipson's research found that Afghans in Northern California exhibited distrust of outsiders, were slow to build friendships, and jealously guarded information.[67]

Patriarchal families in general are hierarchically organized: fathers have authority over their sons and women of the household, and the young are subordinate to the old.[68] Thus, communication within the Arab family has been described as hierarchical,[69,70] wherein elders holding authority also guard the privacy of family emotions. This appeared to be breaking down within Mrs. Khaled's family. Mounting concern for her son's well-being overshadowed her need for privacy. This is consistent with findings from other studies:[71] concerns for the child's behavior disorder, problematic grades, anxiety, or depression are often the reasons why refugee parents first broach therapy. In breaking the silence of 4 years, it was Mrs. Khaled who disclosed the family secret and its effect on both her son and her. What is unusual is the connection between trauma and depression that Mrs. Khaled herself had made.

Mrs. Khaled suffers from a pervasive sense of helplessness. On the one hand, she strives to forget her brother's death, and on the other, she is unable to, as the trauma is alive in her son's eyes. "When I see his face," she says, "I cannot forget what happened to us." Her own sorrows, symptoms, and stress levels are sacrificed and stifled in her concerns for her son.

[67] Lipson, J. G. (1991). Afghan refugee health: Some findings and suggestions. *Qualitative Health Research*, 1(3), 349–369.

[68] Barakat, H. (1985). The Arab family and the challenge of social transformation. In E. W. Fernea (Ed.), *Women and the family in the Middle East: New voices of change* (pp. 27–48). University of Texas Press.

[69] Sharabi, H. (1988). *Neopatriarchy: A theory of distorted change in Arab society.* Oxford University Press.

[70] Barakat, H. (1985). The Arab family and the challenge of social transformation. In E. W. Fernea (Ed.), *Women and the family in the Middle East: New voices of change* (pp. 27–48). University of Texas Press.

[71] Shahini, M., Ahmeti, A., & Charlés, L. L. (2016). Family therapy in postwar Kosova: Reforming cultural values in new family dynamics. In L. L. Charlés & G. Samarasinghe (Eds.), *Family therapy in global humanitarian contexts: Voices and issues from the field* (pp. 65–76). AFTA Springer Briefs in Family Therapy.

Three months prior, and fearing that things would get worse, Mrs. Khaled set up an expansive human surveillance system to spy on Tommy. Mahmoud, 10 years old, began to report on his brother's every move on the hour. Although funds were tight, Mrs. Khaled purchased a cell phone for Mahmoud. "If Mahmoud is in school, he would always need to have his phone on him. When at home, he would have to report to me "to say Tommy is going out. Or Tommy is eating. Or Tommy took a bath. . . ." In the evening, little 7-year-old Sophie would let her know if Tommy came out of his room or not. One day little Mahmoud had a change of heart. "Mamma," he asked her, "why do I have to go to school when Tommy doesn't have to go to school?" I did not want the bad state of one to affect the state of another. . . . Mrs. Khaled's cottage industry of espionage fell apart.

Not to be daunted, a desperate Mrs. Khaled began frequenting playgrounds. She would try to befriend other younger people on Tommy's behalf. She would coax them home with promises of her incredible home-brewed coffee with green cardamoms with the hope that Tommy would come out of his room. On one occasion, she got so desperate that she even relaxed her religious prohibition on alcohol consumption, and in fact, beseeched Tommy to go and share a drink to make friends. But to no avail— all her efforts at getting Tommy out of his room had failed. "Yesterday I wanted to go out with him. But Tommy just went to the door, changed his mind, and returned. The problem is becoming worse," she said.

Mrs. Khaled is not alone. In many patriarchal cultures around the world, women internalize and elevate their cultural role of protection and care for their family over their own well-being. According to family therapists in global humanitarian settings, if they cannot protect their children, they are besieged with worry, guilt, and anxiety, and report failing as mothers.[72] Mr. Khaled, Tommy's father, must suffer from his own sorrow. On my visits to their home, and despite attempting to put on a cheerful face, he was often lost, staring blankly into space.

In contrast to the role of paternal posttraumatic stress disorder (PTSD),[73] researchers have found that maternal PTSD was related to an increased risk for PTSD in 211 adult offspring of Holocaust survivors, while PTSD in any parent contributed to the risk for depression, and parental traumatization was associated with increased anxiety disorders. Indicative of heightened vulnerability is low cortisol levels in offspring.[74] A study of Palestinian mothers found

[72] Giaber, M. B. (2016). Family therapy in Libya: Navigating uncharted waters. In L. L. Charlés & G. Samarasinghe (Eds.), *Family therapy in global humanitarian contexts: Voices and issues from the field* (pp. 103–114). AFTA Springer Briefs in Family Therapy.

[73] Yehuda, R., Schmeidler, J., Wainberg, M., Binder-Brynes, K., & Duvdevani, T. (1998). Vulnerability to post-traumatic stress disorder in adult offspring of Holocaust survivors. *American Journal of Psychiatry, 155*(9), 1163–1171.

[74] Yehuda, R., Teicher, M. H., Seckl, J. R., Grossman, R. A., Morris, A., & Bierer, L. M. (2007). Parental post-traumatic stress disorder as a vulnerability factor for low cortisol trait in offspring of Holocaust survivors. *Archives of General Psychiatry, 64,* 1040–1048.

that,[75] more than war exposure, symptoms of posttraumatic stress should be given clinical attention in the prevention of psychological maltreatment of children. Further, self-reported data of 339 mothers and children from a study of parents from Bosnia-Herzegovina[76] revealed high levels of posttraumatic stress symptoms in mothers, and child distress was related to both their level of exposure and to maternal posttraumatic stress reactions. In Schick et al.'s study, however, maternal symptoms did not correlate with their children's in any respect.[77]

Social support can reduce the effects of traumatic stress; however, the foreignness of Mrs. Khaled's new home has accentuated the lack of traditional supports that she previously enjoyed. Additionally, unlike their menfolk, women in many non-Western cultures do not have access to public spaces such as coffee houses or "*kafeneias*," and thus are unable to cultivate community support, conversations, and camaraderie.[78] In Francisković et al., study of 56 married women, those with secondary stress were also unemployed, underscoring their social isolation and their reduced outlets for social support. and independence.[79]

Although individuals' deteriorating conditions affect every member of their family, it does so especially with female members of the family. As the traditional hierarchy in the home disintegrates, women invest much of their energy into solving their husbands' and children's problems, and meeting their needs, and may deny their own posttraumatic symptoms.[80] In this way, they shoulder additional burdens.[81] Mrs. Khaled's efforts toward her children's educational successes and comforts, such as by putting a stop to a malfunctioning fire alarm, are her panacea to her own unresolved trauma.

[75] Palosaari, E., Punamäki, R. L., Qouta, S., & Diab, M. (2013). Intergenerational effects of war trauma among Palestinian families mediated via psychological maltreatment. *Child Abuse and Neglect, 37*(11), 955–968.

[76] Smith, P., Perrin, S., Yule, W., & Rabe-Hesketh, S. (2001). War exposure and maternal reactions in the psychological adjustment of children from Bosnia-Hercegovina. *Journal of Child Psychology and Psychiatry, 42*(3), 395–404.

[77] Schick, M., Morina, N., Klaghofer, R., Schnyder, U., & Müller, J. (2013). Trauma, mental health, and intergenerational associations in Kosovar families 11 years after the war. *European Journal of Psychotraumatology, 4*, http://doi.org/10.3402/ejpt.v4i0.21060

[78] Agathangelou, A. (2003). Envisioning a feminist global society Cypriot women, civil society and social change. *International Feminist Journal of Politics, 5*, 290–299.

[79] Dekel, R., Goldblatt, H., Keider, M., Solomon, Z., & Polliack, M. (2005). Being a wife of a veteran with post-traumatic stress disorder. *Family Relations, 54*, 24–36.

[80] Killian, K. D. (2016). Time, trauma, and ambiguous loss: Working with families with missing members in postconflict Cyprus. In L. L. Charlés & G. Samarasinghe (Eds.), *Family therapy in global humanitarian contexts: Voices and issues from the field* (pp. 77–89). AFTA Springer Briefs in Family Therapy.

[81] Shahini, M. Ahmeti, A., & Charlés, L. L. (2016). Family therapy in postwar Kosova: Reforming cultural values in new family dynamics. In L. L. Charlés & G. Samarasinghe (Eds.), *Family therapy in global humanitarian contexts: Voices and issues from the field* (pp. 65–76). AFTA Springer Briefs in Family Therapy.

Marital Relations

Marital relationships are negatively affected by posttraumatic stress. In one study of the wives of Croatian veterans of war, 30% of the women reported secondary traumatic stress.[82] Wives' secondary trauma may be due to their additionally shouldering responsibility from a change of roles.[83] The aftermath of trauma can witness the unaffected partner becoming the over-functioning partner as they strive to reduce family demands[84] on the traumatized family member(s) in an effort to ease interpersonal conflict and/or promote family harmony.

Living with "That Thing"

Consider the case of 38-year-old Rania, a Syrian refugee who is married with two children. Two bomb explosions close to her children's school precipitated Rania's decision to flee Syria. Her husband, who had a thriving medical practice, had been hesitant to leave Syria. Two years following their resettlement, she suffers from nightmares and reports being woken up by the sound of bombs raining down on her. The most challenging aspect of the flight, she says, is the gradual erosion of her husband's personality.

> *The most difficult thing is for my husband. He is 50 years old. He has to take many exams now as he used to when he was a student. That thing makes him depressed. That thing, depression does not leave us these days. "That thing" is always with us. It is like a normal thing for us to live with this depression. He has changed a lot. These days he is disinterested, always sitting and not doing anything. Before that, he worked a lot, so there was no time to sit and think. He traveled a difficult and long road to reach what he wanted—it was difficult. We are sad and uncomfortable, and that thing impacts our children and the harmony in our house. . . As a refugee, one has to live life in two parts. One cannot live as before.*
>
> *It's hard because one thinks doctors and lawyers, professional folks will be protected. He was always the person who was working very hard. After working so hard for 20 years he lost everything in one moment. That is not an easy thing to deal with and handle. He was always thinking that at the age of 50 everything would be okay. But it is not.*

[82] Renshaw, K. D., Allen, E. S., Rhoades, G. K., Blais, R. K., Markman, H. J., & Stanley, S. M. (2011). Distress in spouses of service members with symptoms of combat-related PTSD: Secondary traumatic stress or general psychological distress? *Journal of Family Psychology, 25*(4), 461–469.

[83] Solomon, Z. (1998). The effect of combat-related PTSD on the family. *Psychiatry, 52,* 323–329.

[84] Rabin, C., & Nardi, C. (1991). Treating post traumatic stress disorder couples: A psychoeducational program. *Community Mental Health Journal, 27*(3), 209–224.

Marital stress caused by a partner's posttraumatic stress may facilitate wives' own sense of vulnerability and depression while also affecting their partner's sense of failure. Lower levels of intimacy and self-disclosure[85] found in combat veterans with higher levels of posttraumatic stress-related avoidance may also affect marital adjustment. Wives may also believe that their love can cure their husbands of the effects of posttraumatic stress, but the "empathy trap" and "caregiver overload,"[86] with the burden of caregiving also leads to psychological distress, dysphoria, and anxiety.[87]

Child Mental Health

Children's exposure to multiple and severe stressors relates to worse psychological outcomes, including higher rates of PTSD and elevated depression, as indicated by a study of 7,920 war-affected children aged 5–17 years.[88] As for children affected by indirect trauma, the evidence is mixed.[89,90] Some studies show that children with lower lifetime trauma exposure may exhibit clinically relevant trauma symptoms, but when compared to their parents, they may be less affected. Some epidemiological studies of mental health problems among Holocaust survivors[91,92] indicate that there are no direct negative intergenerational effects of parental trauma on children's depressive and anxiety disorders.

Broadly, studies investigating the intergenerational effects of war among European children affected by World War II generally show that children who may have witnessed parental psychopathology can be prone to developmental

[85] Solomon, Z., Dekel, R., & Zerach, G. (2008). The relationships between post-traumatic stress symptom clusters and marital intimacy among war veterans. *Journal of Family Psychology, 22,* 659–666.

[86] Franciskovič, T., Stevanović, A., Jelusić, I., Roganović, B., Klarić, M., & Grković, J. (2007). Secondary traumatization of wives of war veterans with post-traumatic stress disorder. *Croatian Medical Journal, 48*(2), 177–184.

[87] Beckham, J. C., Lytle, B. L., & Feldman, M.E. (1996). Caregiver burden in partners of Vietnam War veterans with post-traumatic stress disorder. *Journal of Consulting and Clinical Psychology, 64*(5), 1068–1072.

[88] Attanayake, V., Mckay, R., Joffres, M., Singh, S., Burkle, F., & Mills, E. (2009). Prevalence of mental disorders among children exposed to war: A systematic review of 7,920 children. *Medicine, Conflict, and Survival, 25,* 4–19.

[89] Bean, T., Derluyn, I., Eurelings-Bontekoe, E., Broekaert, E., & Spinhoven, P. (2007). Comparing psychological distress, traumatic stress reactions, and experiences of unaccompanied refugee minors with experiences of adolescents accompanied by parents. *Journal of Nervous and Mental Disease, 195*(4), 288–297.

[90] Betancourt, T. S. (2015). The intergenerational effect of war. *JAMA Psychiatry, 72*(3), 199–200.

[91] Sagi-Schwartz, A., van IJzendoorn, M. H., Grossmann, K. E., Joels, T., Grossmann, K., Scharf, M., Koren-Karie, N., & Alkalay, S. (2003). Attachment and traumatic stress in female holocaust child survivors and their daughters. *American Journal of Psychiatry, 160,* 1086–1092.

[92] van IJzendoorn, M. H., Bakermans-Kranenburg, M. J., & Sagi-Schwartz, A. (2003). Are children of Holocaust survivors less well-adapted? A meta-analytic investigation of secondary traumatization. *Journal of Traumatic Stress, 16,* 459–469.

and mental health problems. Like adult survivors of war who can demonstrate posttraumatic stress for many years afterward, children who may have witnessed parental trauma as a result of war also fare worse as adults.

Female—but not male—offspring of Finnish mothers who were evacuated as children[93] and placed with foster families in Sweden during World War II showed an elevated risk for psychiatric hospitalization[94] compared with their Finnish cousins who had remained with their biological families throughout the war. Upon reaching adulthood and as mothers, they were also twice as likely to be hospitalized for a mood disorder than their nonevacuated sibling.[95] Compared to the Finnish children's placement of 2–5 years, it is anticipated that contemporary refugee children who endure more substantial protracted settings will experience more substantial effects of negative childhood experiences. Disruptions in the form of separations, fostering, disrupted attachment, living in protracted war settings, along with gender and parental mental health can affect child mental health.

Parental psychopathology may exert its adverse effects through diminished family functioning, as a study of Southeast Asian mothers who had been in the United States on an average of almost 14 years concluded. The trauma of their mothers indirectly affected the children's mental health through poor family functioning; it significantly affected their depression, antisocial behavior, and delinquent behavior one year later.[96] If the children were born outside the United States, they were especially vulnerable to their mother's trauma, which contributed to school problems. Reporting school problems to their parents could also increase familial stress. Thus, indirect effects of increased family strain may affect children's performance issues or delinquency more than poor maternal well-being.

Sangalang et al., argue that a "constellation of family characteristics taken together are important for understanding the intergenerational transmission of trauma among foreign-born children in Southeast Asian refugee families."[97]

[93] *However*, the authors note that the study does not fully address the possibility that parental psychopathology contributed to the observed association between evacuation and psychopathology among offspring, as only severe psychiatric disorders receive hospitalization.

[94] Santavirta, T., Santavirta, N., & Gillman, S. E. (2017). Association of the World War II Finnish evacuation of children with psychiatric hospitalization in the next generation. *Journal of American Medical Association Psychiatry*, 75(1), 21–27.

[95] Santavirta, T., Santavirta, N., Betancourt, T. S., & Gilman, S. E. (2015). Long term mental health outcomes of Finnish children evacuated to Swedish families during the second world war and their non-evacuated siblings. *British Medical Journal*, 350, G7753.

[96] Sangalang, C. C., Jager, J., & Harachi, T. W. (2017). Effects of maternal traumatic distress on family functioning and child mental health: An examination of Southeast Asian refugee families in the U.S. *Social Science Medicine*, 184, 178–186.

[97] Sangalang, C. C., Jager, J., & Harachi, T. W. (2017). Effects of maternal traumatic distress on family functioning and child mental health: An examination of Southeast Asian refugee families in the US. *Social Science Medicine*, 184, 178–186.

Factors undergirding children's well-being in host nations thus can include foreign-born status of the child, the status of maternal and paternal mental health, children's linguistic capacity, and familiarity with the host culture.

In the section that follows, we shall discuss other secondary family processes by which trauma gets transmitted within families: from the father to the child and from the extended family that may be based in the war-affected country to family members abroad.

Father's PTSD

Implicating the role of the father's posttraumatic stress, researchers Klaric et al. show that children of war veterans in Bosnia and Herzegovina are more likely to display behavioral issues and[98] developmental[99] and psychiatric issues such as depression,[100] compared to those children with fathers who were not veterans. Findings that offspring of veterans express problems with authority, hyperactivity, and aggression and experience learning challenges have also been corroborated by accounts from partners and spouses of veterans.[101,102,103,104,105,106] Although causation cannot be ascertained, the cascade of events and reciprocal effects of children's behavioral issues can further create dysfunctional family functioning,[107] and problems with future relational attachment patterns.

[98] Dansby, V. S., & Marinelli, R. P. (1999). Adolescent children of Vietnam combat veteran fathers: A population at risk. *Journal of Adolescence, 22,* 329–340.

[99] Klarić, M., Frančišković, T., Klarić, B., Kvesić, A., Kaštelan, A., Graovac, M., & Lisica, D. (2008). Psychological problems in children of war veterans with post-traumatic stress disorder in Bosnia and Herzegovina: Cross-sectional study. *Croatian Medical Journal, 49,* 491–498.

[100] Al-Turkait, F. A., & Ohaeri, J. U. (2008). Psychopathological status, behavior problems, and family adjustment of Kuwaiti children whose fathers were involved in the first gulf war. *Child and Adolescent Psychiatry and Mental Health,* 2(1), 12.

[101] Beckham, J. C., Braxton, L. E., Kudler, H. S., Feldman, M. E., Lytle, B. L., & Palmer, S. (1997). Minnesota Multiphasic Personality Inventory profiles of Vietnam combat veterans with post-traumatic stress disorder and their children. *Journal of Clinical Psychology, 53,* 847–852.

[102] Harkness, L. L. (1991). The effect of combat-related PTSD on children: National Center for PTSD. *Clinical Newsletter, 2,* 12–13.

[103] Ancharoff, M. R., Munroe, J. F., & Fisher, L. M. (1998). The legacy of combat trauma: Clinical implications of intergenerational transmission. In Y. Danieli (Ed.), *International handbook of multigenerational legacies of trauma* (pp. 257–276). Plenum.

[104] Ahmadzadeh, G. H., & Malekian, A. (2004). Aggression, anxiety, and social development in adolescent children of war veterans with PTSD versus those of non-veterans. *Journal of Research in Medical Sciences,* 9(5), 231–234.

[105] Jacobsen, L. K., Sweeney, C. G., & Racusin, G. R. (1993). Group psychotherapy for children of fathers with PTSD: Evidence of psychopathology emerging in the group process. *Journal of Child and Adolescent Group Therapy, 3,* 103–120.

[106] Caselli, L. T., & Motta, R. W. (1995). The effect of PTSD and combat level on Vietnam veterans' perceptions of child behavior and marital adjustment. *Journal of Clinical Psychology, 51,* 4–12.

[107] Westerink, J., & Giarratano, L. (1999). The impact of post-traumatic stress disorder on partners and children of Australian Vietnam veterans. *Australian and New Zealand Journal of Psychiatry, 33,* 841–847.

Building on the idea of posttraumatic stress transmission from one's father, McCormack and Sly investigated the "lived experience" of three sisters living with their father, a Vietnam War veteran with PTSD. They found that shared feelings of emotional neglect, guilt, and unworthiness were signs of vicarious trauma. Further, the sisters also reported experiencing revictimization through their inability to form healthy adult relationships with males and their inability to exit abusive relationships.[108] Several cross-cultural studies have implicated father's trauma though increased psychological suffering in their children in the form of:[109] elevated anxiety and depression as in the case of Kuwaiti children of Gulf war veterans;[110] somatization in the adult children of Portuguese war veterans;[111] and depression in Kosovar children 11 years after the war.[112]

A majority of studies show that a parenting style[113] that is harsh, rejecting, or insensitive, mediates[114] the relationship between parents' traumatic experiences and children's attachment, behavior, and mental health; there are some exceptions. Also, in contrast, it has been found that[115] Vietnam veterans' participation in violence (e.g., torture, killing civilians) during the war predicted their children's behavioral disturbances, but parenting that included physical family violence did not mediate the association. On the other hand, compared to mothers, fathers may also present with more externalizing behaviors,[116] resulting in a higher impact on family members.

The findings of the Kosovar war-affected families—posttraumatic stress symptoms of fathers being significantly related to children's depressive symptoms—can be explained by the privileged position of fathers within the family structure: a

[108] McCormack, L., & Sly, R. (2013). Distress and growth: The subjective "lived" experiences of being the child of a Vietnam veteran. *Traumatology, 19*(4), 303–312.

[109] Palosaari, E., Punamäki, R. L., Qouta, S., & Diab, M. (2013). Intergenerational effects of war trauma among Palestinian families mediated via psychological maltreatment. *Child Abuse and Neglect, 37*(11), 955–968.

[110] Al-Turkait, F. A., & Ohaeri, J. U. (2008). Psychopathological status, behavior problems, and family adjustment of Kuwaiti children whose fathers were involved in the first Gulf war. *Child and Adolescent Psychiatry and Mental Health, 2*(1), 12.

[111] Castro-Vale, I., Severo, M., Carvalho, D., & Mota-Cardoso, R. (2019). Intergenerational transmission of war-related trauma assessed 40 years after exposure. *Annals of General Psychiatry, 18*, 14.

[112] Schick, M., Morina, N., Klaghofer, R., Schnyder, U., & Müller, J. (2013). Trauma, mental health, and intergenerational associations in Kosovar families 11 years after the war. *European Journal of Psychotraumatology, 4*, http://doi.org/10.3402/ejpt.v4i0.21060

[113] Scharf, M. (2007). Long-term effects of trauma: Psychosocial functioning of the second and third generation of holocaust survivors. *Development and Psychopathology, 19*, 603–622.

[114] Yehuda, R., Schmeidler, J., Wainberg, M., Binder-Brynes, K., & Duvdevani, T. (1998). Vulnerability to post-traumatic stress disorder in adult offspring of Holocaust survivors. *American Journal of Psychiatry, 155*(9), 1163–1171.

[115] Rosenheck, R., & Fontana, A. (1998). Transgenerational effects of abusive violence on the children of Vietnam combat veterans. *Journal of Traumatic Stress, 11*, 731–742.

[116] Miller, M. W., Greif, J. L., & Smith, A. A. (2003). Multidimensional personality questionnaire profiles of veterans with traumatic combat exposure: Externalizing and internalizing subtypes. *Psychological Assessment, 15*(2), 205.

large review recently found that perceived paternal rejection, as could be expected in case of fathers with mental disorders, is associated with negative personality development in offspring, that is, in terms of self-esteem and emotional stability.[117] The hypothesis is supported by the correlations of father's symptoms of depression, anxiety, and posttraumatic stress with those of their wives and the negative correlation of paternal education with depression of mothers and children, also indicating higher paternal education as a protective factor.

Parental Psychopathology

A parent's experience with and response to trauma can impact family functioning through a child's attachment style; some studies implicate the role of both parents' mental health on children's mental health.[118] In a study of 100 families, both parents and children from Gaza directly affected by war found that children's posttraumatic symptoms were significantly associated with their parents' emotional responses.[119] Scharf discovered that children whose parents were both Holocaust survivors were more likely to have an insecure-anxious attachment style than if one or neither parent was a so affected.[120] A review of 35 comparative studies on the mental state of offspring of Holocaust survivors indicated that the nonclinical population of children of Holocaust survivors did not show more psychopathological symptoms than people in general, while the clinical population of offspring tended to present a specific profile including a predisposition to PTSD.[121] Children of torture survivors have more symptoms of posttraumatic stress[122,123] and depression than children whose parents were not tortured.[124]

[117] Khaleque, A., & Rohner, R. P. (2012). Transnational relations between perceived parental acceptance and personality dispositions of children and adults: A meta-analytic review. *Personality and Social Psychology Review*, 16(2), 103–115.

[118] Catani, C., Jacob, N., Schauer, E., Kohila, M., & Neuner, F. (2008). Family violence, war, and natural disasters: A study of the effect of extreme stress on children's mental health in Sri Lanka. *BMC Psychiatry*, 8, 33.

[119] Thabet, A., Tawahina, A. A., El Sarraj, E., & Vostanis, P. (2008). Exposure to war trauma and PTSD among parents and children in the Gaza strip. *European Child & Adolescent Psychiatry*, 17(4), 191–199.

[120] Scharf, M. (2007). Long-term effects of trauma: Psychosocial functioning of the second and third generation of Holocaust survivors. *Development and Psychopathology*, 19(2), 603–622.

[121] Kellerman, N. P. F. (2001). Psychopathology in children of Holocaust survivors: A review of the research literature. *Israel Journal of Psychiatry and Related Sciences*, 38(1), 36–46.

[122] Daud, A., Skoglund, E., & Rydelius, P.-A. (2005). Children in families of torture victims: Transgenerational transmission of parents' traumatic experiences to their children. *International Journal of Social Welfare*, 14(1), 23–32.

[123] Montgomery, E. (1998) Refugee children from the Middle East. *Scandinavian Journal of Public Health*, 54, 1–152. https://www.jstor.org/stable/45199799

[124] In the Kosovar study by Schick et al., neither parents' nor children's trauma exposure correlated with children's symptoms: Schick, M., Morina, N., Klaghofer, R., Schnyder, U., & Müller, J. (2013).

Postconflict Environment and Family Functioning

In the foregoing section we have discussed the great complexity, bidirectionality, and variation[125] in the expression of mental health problems in the postconflict family climate and how a family member's mental health challenges can set in motion, either directly or indirectly, adverse mental health processes for other family members. The postconflict refugee family with a trauma-stricken member may experience the effects of trauma from at least five sources: the psychiatric symptoms experienced by the primary trauma survivor, their changed responses and behaviors, their own substitute feelings through empathic identification with the family member, their concern for other members of the family, and the disappointment associated with their loss of potential linked to them. Parental psychopathology thus can enhance the additive effects of stressors faced by resettled refugee families and trigger other dysfunctional family dynamics. In the absence of warmth and affection that are strong predictors of their offspring's mental health, a parent's posttraumatic stress is thought to potentially[126] contribute to a range of offspring behavioral[127] and developmental abnormalities.[128]

At the same time, a child's trauma and dynamics can affect parental dynamics as well. Through the study of Darfuri refugees in Eastern Chad, researchers[129] found that although war-related traumatic events were the initial causes of refugees' distress, stressors related to children could also affect parental trauma. As children acculturated and became proficient in English at a faster rate than their immigrant or refugee parents, they also tended to subvert traditional hierarchical family roles and challenge cultural obligations or parental

Trauma, mental health, and intergenerational associations in Kosovar families 11 years after the war. *European Journal of Psychotraumatology, 4*, http://doi.org/10.3402/ejpt.v4i0.21060

[125] Santavirta, T., Santavirta, N., & Gillman, S. E. (2017). Association of the World War II Finnish evacuation of children with psychiatric hospitalization in the next generation. *Journal of American Medical Association Psychiatry, 75*(1), 21–27.

[126] Schick, M., Morina, N., Klaghofer, R., Schnyder, U., & Müller, J. (2013). Trauma, mental health, and intergenerational associations in Kosovar families 11 years after the war. *European Journal of Psychotraumatology, 4*, http://doi.org/10.3402/ejpt.v4i0.21060

[127] Dekel, R., & Goldblatt, H. (2008). Is there intergenerational transmission of trauma? The case of combat veterans' children. *American Journal of Orthopsychiatry, 78*(3), 281–289.

[128] Galovski, T., & Lyons, J. A. (2004). Psychological sequelae of combat violence: A review of the impact of PTSD on the veteran's family and possible interventions. *Aggression and Violent Behavior, 9*, 477–501.

[129] Rasmussen, A., Nguyen, L., Wilkinson, J., Vundla, S., Raghavan, S., Miller, K. E., & Keller, A. S. (2010). Rates and impact of trauma and current stressors among Darfuri refugees in Eastern Chad. *American Journal of Orthopsychiatry, 80*, 227–236.

expectations.[130,131,132] For example, language gaps between parents and their children can cause anger outbursts toward family members that, in turn, can trigger traumatic memories.[133]

Intergenerational Impact of Trauma

In taking a broad and long view of posttraumatic stress, using cross-sectional research, we can discover a nuanced and deeper understanding of complex trauma. We can also investigate differential risks in the consequent development of the disorder (i.e., being female, older, under- or uneducated, unemployed, and having been exposed to more potentially traumatic experiences during and after the war), which can tend to increase the probability of experiencing posttraumatic stress. A cross-sectional study was conducted of 586 Cambodian adults[134] aged between 35 and 75 years, with an average age of 52, who resettled in Long Beach, California, and who had lived in Cambodia during the Khmer Rouge reign and immigrated to the United States prior to 1993. Before immigration, 99% of those surveyed experienced near-death because of starvation; 96% reported forced labor; 90% had a family member or friend murdered; and 70% experienced violence after immigration to the United States, such as seeing a dead body in their neighborhood or being robbed. The study found 62% and 51% of refugees can continue to be challenged by high rates of posttraumatic stress and depression, respectively, 20 years later. Cambodian refugees[135] exhibit a dose-dependent relationship between posttraumatic stress and depression, as well as a high comorbidity between both, suggesting a greater understanding of the interrelationship between posttraumatic stress and depression.

The finding that a greater number of potentially traumatic experiences during and after the war can tend to increase the probability of experiencing posttraumatic stress is corroborated across other settings and historical conte

---

[130] Renzaho, A. M. N., Dhingra, N., & Georgeou, N. (2017). Youth as contested sites of culture: The intergenerational acculturation gap amongst new migrant communities—Parental and young adult perspectives. PLoS ONE, 12(2), e0170700.

[131] Ying, Y. W., & Han, M. (2007). The longitudinal effect of intergenerational gap in acculturation on conflict and mental health in Southeast Asian American adolescents. American Journal of Orthopsychiatry, 77, 61–66.

[132] Abi-Hashem, N. (2011). Working with Middle Eastern immigrant families. In A. Zagelbaum & J. Carlson (Eds.), Working with immigrant families: A practical guide for counsellors (pp. 151–180). Taylor & Francis.

[133] Hinton, D. E., Rasmussen, A., Nou, L., Pollack, M. H., & Good, M. J. (2009). Anger, PTSD, and the nuclear family: A study of Cambodian refugees. Social Science and Medicine, 69(9), 1387–1394.

[134] Marshall, G. N., Schell, T. L., Elliott, M. N., Berthold, S. M., & Chun, C. (2005). Mental health of Cambodian refugees 2 decades after resettlement in the United States. JAMA, 294(5), 571–579.

[135] Marshall, G. N., Schell, T. L., Elliott, M. N., Berthold, S. M., & Chun, C. (2005). Mental health of Cambodian refugees 2 decades after resettlement in the United States. JAMA, 294(5), 571–579.

xts.[136,137,138,139,140,141] A large community study conducted across five Balkan countries found that more than 5 years after the Balkan war,[142] the 3,313 participants who were still living in the area of conflict exhibited high prevalence rates of posttraumatic stress, anxiety, and mood disorders: 10.6% to 35.4% posttraumatic stress; 12.1% to 35.9% mood disorders; and 15.6% to 41.8% anxiety disorders.

Correlational and multivariate studies of posttraumatic stress across generations can investigate comorbidities as they evolve, identify risk factors contributing to the strong dose-response[143] relationship with trauma, and illuminate the nature of intergenerational conflicts, one of the top-seven postmigration stressors[144] for displaced families. However, drawbacks in design can include the cross-sectional nature of investigation, the use of participants from clinical samples,[145] the use of self-report measures that can risk reporting bias, and the use of nonrandom sampling methods.[146] Cross-sectional research can restrict us from inferring the causality of observed associations. Together, both cross-sectional and longitudinal approaches to clinical research can elucidate different aspects of the sequelae of distress and family functioning in refugee families. These approaches raise critical research and clinical issues for future exploration.

[136] Marshall, G. N., Schell, T. L., Elliott, M. N., Berthold, S. M., & Chun, C. A. (2005). Mental health of Cambodian refugees 2 decades after resettlement in the United States. JAMA, 294(5), 571–579.

[137] Nicholson, B. L. (1997). The influence of pre-emigration and postemigration stressors on mental health: A study of Southeast Asian refugees. Social Work Research, 21(1), 19–31.

[138] Hinton, L., Jenkins, C. N., McPhee, S., Wong, C., Lai, K. Q., Le, A., Du, N., & Fordham, D. (1998). A survey of depressive symptoms among Vietnamese-American men in three locales: Prevalence and correlates. Journal of Nervous and Mental Diseases, 186(11), 677–683.

[139] Gerritsen, A. A., Bramsen, I., Deville, W., van Willigen, L. H., Hovens, J. E., & van der Ploeg, H. M. (2006). Physical and mental health of Afghan, Iranian and Somali asylum seekers and refugees living in the Netherlands. Social Psychiatry and Psychiatric Epidemiology, 41(1), 18–26.

[140] Chung, R. C., & Kagawa-Singer, M. (1993). Predictors of psychological distress among Southeast Asian refugees. Social Science and Medicine, 36(5), 631–639.

[141] Karam, E. G., Mneimneh, Z., Karam, A. N., Fayyad, J. A., Nasser, S. C., Chatterji, S., & Kessler, R. C. (2006). Prevalence and treatment of mental disorders in Lebanon: A national epidemiological survey. Lancet, 367(9515), 1000–1006.

[142] Priebe, S., Bogic, M., Ajdukovic, D., Franciskovic, T., Galeazzi, G. M., Kucukalic, A., Lecic-Tosevski, D., Morina, N., Popovski, M., Wang D., & Schützwohl, M. (2010). Mental disorders following war in the Balkans: A study in 5 countries. Archives of General Psychiatry, 67(5), 518–528.

[143] Marshall, G. N., Schell, T. L., Elliott, M. N., Berthold, S. M., & Chun, C. (2005). Mental health of Cambodian refugees 2 decades after resettlement in the United States. JAMA, 294(5), 571–579.

[144] Tinghög, P., Malm, A., Arwidson, C., Sigvardsdotter, E., Lundin, A., & Saboonchi, F. (2017). Prevalence of mental ill health, traumas and postmigration stress among refugees from Syria resettled in Sweden after 2011: A population-based survey. BMJ Open, 7, 12.

[145] Broers, T., Hodgetts, G., Batic´-Mujanovic, O., Petrovic, V., Hasanagic, M., & Godwin, M. (2006). Prevalence of mental and social disorders in adults attending primary care centres in Bosnia and Herzegovina. Croatian Medical Journal, 47(3), 478–484.

[146] Basoglu, M., Livanou, M., Crnobaric, C., Franciskovic, T., Suljic, E., Duric, D., & Vranesic, M. (2005). Psychiatric and cognitive effects of war in former Yugoslavia: Association of lack of redress for trauma and post-traumatic stress reactions. JAMA, 294(5), 580–590.

Further, the severity of posttraumatic stress alone may not immediately help us discern the impact of trauma on war-affected families at a specific developmental moment of refugee families. Loss of family members' subjective well-being, emotional spillover of poor mental health to other members, chaos or apathy in interpersonal relationships, concerns about children's behavior (e.g., hyperactivity, problems with authority, and learning challenges), and integration challenges in life's essential domains can offer subtle clues to the serious after-effects of trauma in families. In such a scenario, reliance on the improvement of PTSD symptoms in family members risks overlooking the complex picture of traumatic reactions and, consequently, the inclusion of effective trauma treatments for the refugee family.

Incorporating longitudinal and long-term studies can reveal additional aspects about complex trauma in refugee families. For example, although 30% of Cambodian refugee families in Long Beach, California, may lack any major disorders, they nevertheless suffer from a high degree of chaos owing to living challenges and unresolved trauma, and for some, even 25 years after resettlement in America. Further, most in the Cambodian refugee community spoke little or no English, were at income levels below poverty, and relied on public assistance. In the sample, 69% had household incomes of less than 100% of the federal poverty level, and 72% were reliant on government assistance. Such persistent psychosocial challenges and difficulties in psychological functioning and social and cultural adaptation of refugee families lend focus to the complex pathways of impact and the need for longitudinal follow-up on various types of family functioning, not just psychiatric symptoms.

Longitudinal Studies

Longitudinal studies systematically follow subjects over time with repeated monitoring of risk factors and/or health outcomes. Additional investigations into trauma's impact on refugee families should systematically assess families' level of subjective well-being. In the section that follows, we review some empirical studies that elaborate on long-term and longitudinal perspectives on mostly war-affected families; although the studies are not without methodological shortcomings that make extrapolation challenging, they are helpful in affording insights on trauma transmission across different generations of war-affected families. They can also alert us to the possible mental health needs of war-affected displaced families in the decades following their exodus.

Additional insights on trauma's transmission and mental health trajectories of displaced families can be assessed using longitudinal studies; this involves systematic follow-up on the same subjects or groups over time, with repeated monitoring of risk factors or health outcomes. That posttraumatic stress can ebb and flow within individuals, and family members can manifest effects after prolonged periods, underscores the potential utility of tracking mental health disorders and subjective well-being over time. At the same time, the inherent limitation of longitudinal studies among vulnerable, war-affected, and displaced people with a high probability of mortality can make it impossible to render comparable control groups and establish causality of an intergenerational transfer of posttraumatic symptoms from parents to children. We can also see that relationships between parents and children manifest differently in the presence of the same trauma, based on personal and interpersonal factors, rather than based on the actual existence of trauma.[147] Thus, the mediating factor between parent PTSD and child anxiety is the parent-child relationship as determined by the parenting style. This is an important connection because it gives a mechanism or link for this intergenerational dynamic of trauma transmission, which is missing from many studies.

Nevertheless, wherever possible, more comprehensive research with more checkpoints along the life-cycle of children and their families would be beneficial to verify conclusions. Some longitudinal studies can shed valuable insights and lacunae in trauma transmission across generations. A longitudinal study[148] carried out over 23 years on family triads (mother-father-child) reveals the prolonged impact of war trauma on offspring through its flow between parents. Posttraumatic stress levels in Israeli ex-prisoner-of-war (ex-POW) fathers at two points in time (2003 and 2008) and their wives' posttraumatic stress in 2004, for instance, predicted their offspring's posttraumatic stress in 2014. The presence of posttraumatic stress in offspring underscores the importance of assessing direct and indirect pathways of both parents' posttraumatic stress levels. A parent's trajectory and struggles with posttraumatic stress can independently affect their offspring's posttraumatic stress years later, and impact how their partner's posttraumatic stress affects their offspring's posttraumatic stress many years later.

With regard to third generations, some researchers contend that if the transmission of trauma occurs, its intensity may be less. In a longitudinal study of three generations, grandparent, parent, and grandchildren, to assess the intergenerational transference of PTSD from parents with PTSD to their children, researchers[149] found that third-generation Holocaust survivors are more likely

[147] Field, N. P., Muong, S., & Sochanvimean, V. (2013). Parental styles in the intergenerational transmission of trauma stemming from the Khmer Rouge regime in Cambodia. *American Journal of Orthopsychiatry, 83*(4), 483–494.
[148] Zerach, G., Levin, Y., Aloni, R., & Solomon, Z. (2017). Intergenerational transmission of captivity trauma and post-traumatic stress symptoms: A twenty three-year longitudinal triadic study. *Psychological Trauma: Theory, Research, Practice, and Policy, 9*(1, Suppl.), 114–121.
[149] Zerach, G., & Solomon, Z. (2016). Low levels of post-traumatic stress symptoms and psychiatric symptomatology among third-generation Holocaust survivors whose fathers were war veterans. *Journal of Psychiatric Research, 73*, 25–33.

than non-third-generation Holocaust victim offspring of ex-POWs and veterans to show lower anxiety and symptoms of anxiety disorders. This might be because third-generation families can develop better coping mechanisms and strategies to deal with anxiety and other psychosomatic disorders, although mechanisms of adaptations are not illuminated.

Even though traumas may differ in intensity across generations, or the burden of trauma may be less for third-generation families, families are likely to experience traumas collectively. In a study[150] of two generations of Cambodian refugees living in the western United States, 209 Khmer adolescent-parent pairs were interviewed on affective disorders and posttraumatic stress, and posttraumatic stress was found to be significantly related across parent-child generations. Feelings of communal solidarity may reflect the shared posttraumatic distress in offspring as one study shows,[151] in which of 689 older, second-generation Armenians, especially those having had a close relative killed during wartime events while living in Greece or Cyprus, participants were divided into two groups: (1) those with a clinical or subclinical expression of a traumatic reaction for (at least) 1 month during their lifetime and (2) those without such (clinical or subclinical) characteristics. The group in which clinical and subclinical expressions of a traumatic response have not only the negative characteristics that come with posttraumatic stress but also positive characteristics such as a stronger connection to the Armenian community; however, they report more guilt and shame as compared to the other group. They demonstrate higher than group averages for "national pride," "prosocial attitudes," and "endurance," but also higher "helplessness" and "persistent distress."

Conversely, when posttraumatic stress does not show up as posttraumatic stress in offspring, researchers conclude that it may still translate into other indicators of poor mental health of the children, such as poor school performance. Consider this study that was part of a larger project investigating the psychological and physical long-term consequences of flight and expulsion at the end of World War II: The authors studied 50 refugees (25 with diagnosed PTSD symptoms and 25 without) who were severely traumatized as children at the end of World War II and their offspring. Although offspring of refugee parents with chronic posttraumatic stress did not differ from offspring of refugee parents without posttraumatic stress in terms of quality of life and mental health, the

[150] Sack, W. H., Clarke, G. N., & Seeley, J. (1995). Post-traumatic stress disorder across two generations of Cambodian refugees. *Journal of the American Academy of Child & Adolescent Psychiatry*, 34(9), 1160–1166.
[151] Karenian, H., Livaditis, M., Karenian, S., Zafiriadis, K., Bochtsou, V., & Xenitidis, K. (2011). Collective trauma transmission and traumatic reactions among descendants of Armenian refugees. *International Journal of Social Psychiatry*, 57(4), 327–337.

authors suggest that "the experienced burden of parental refugee history affects current mental well-being and quality of life of offspring."[152]

War-affected displaced families are one of the most disenfranchised populations. Refugee families have a significant need for mental health services. Refugee children and adults face ongoing challenges at different displacement phases, and as a result, their stressors can be of many types, related to acculturation, complex trauma, or resettlement. These can manifest as concerns about family reunification, behavioral challenges in school, fears of deportation, safety, or those related to struggles of a family member with posttraumatic stress. A systems view of treatment in refugee families must take into account what "family" means in the context of refugee families; effectiveness of trauma treatments on family communication, family pathways, and resilience; and identifying community and culture-specific resilience. Some refugee populations, such as unaccompanied children, may not obtain psychotherapy relevant to their unique circumstances, as Western psychotherapy is based on assumptions of a nuclear family rather than on considerations of these children's larger collectives, such as clans or villages.[153]

In times of war and conflict, with homes and communities destroyed, the family can be an important source of resilience for the displaced. Family interventions with the forcibly displaced must include family therapists who are skilled within international humanitarian contexts with knowledge of sociocultural contexts and political allegiances of ethnic factions of its population. A system-based approach to family therapy must also integrate culturally sensitive interventions with evidence-based ones to minimize the impact of conflict's ramifications on future generations. Family therapy interventions for war-affected children also should be both trauma-informed and strength- and resilience-oriented.[154]

The following considerations can aid in strengthening the provision of family therapy with refugee families: building in intergenerational assessments or genograms to understand patterns of losses, family trauma, and resilience within the family and community; a parent-level intervention for effective

[152] Muhtz, C., Wittekind, C., Godemann, K., Von Alm, C., Jelinek, L., Yassouridis, A., & Kellner, M. (2016). Mental health in offspring of traumatized refugees with and without post-traumatic stress disorder. *Stress Health*, 32(4):367–373.

[153] Hart, J. (2014). Children and forced migration. In E. Fiddian-Qasmiyeh, G. Loescher, K. Long, & N. Sigona (Eds.), *The Oxford handbook of refugee and forced migration studies* (pp. 648–667). Oxford University Press.

[154] Bürgin, D., Anagnostopoulos, D., the Board and Policy Division of ESCAP, Vitiello, B., Sukale, T., Schmid, M., & Fegert, J. M. (2022). Impact of war and forced displacement on children's mental health—multilevel, needs-oriented, and trauma-informed approaches. *European Child & Adolescent Psychiatry*, 31, 845–853.

parenting practices; incorporating community understandings and values of healing through family or group therapy;[155] and school-based mental health approaches to address the stigma of seeking mental health and to increase the likelihood of refugee families seeking mental health services. Family therapy can help to strengthen and extend support for vulnerable and displaced individuals at multiple levels by including home-based clinicians, school therapists, clinical supervisors, and cultural experts,[156] thus, helping to create sturdier families.

[155] Der Sarkissian, A., & Sharkey, J. D. (2021). Transgenerational trauma and mental health needs among Armenian genocide descendants. *International Journal of Environmental Research and Public Health*, *18*(19), 10554.

[156] Kaplin, D., Parente, K., & Santacroce, F. (2019). A review of the use of trauma systems therapy to treat refugee children, adolescents, and families. *Journal of Infant Child and Adolescent Psychotherapy*, *18*, 417–431.

9

Mental Health and Integration
Structuring Refuge for Resettled Refugees

"Everyone Is Having Depression"

Each time I was drinking, I was hurting myself. Bad things came up for me when I was drinking. I did bad stuff to myself, like jumping from balcony to balcony or breaking mirrors and punching walls. I started jumping at the beginning of Covid. It went on for a few months. Once I fell from the roof and then a tree and . . . it was a wake-up call for me . . . I got hurt but not that bad. Both times I fell on my chest (Laughs). But it's fine now.

I got scared. I called the hotline for Corona (virus). They transferred me to a psychologist. She said, "How is your family?" (quick laugh) and I started to weep. Somehow, I don't know, I was too honest with her. I don't know she asked me one question and then I started to cry . . . So stupid. I told her "I'm very sorry I don't know why I am crying." She said, "You need immediate treatment." She said, "Sorry, I can only see you for the first session because I already have a lot of patients." She didn't have a place for me.

But she described me as "anxious-depression," someone who is afraid and depressed, together. She told me, "I will give you a few numbers, and maybe they'll have a place for you." I went to another doctor. I thought maybe she would have a place for me, but she also didn't. I wanted to get out of my situation. When I talked to them, I felt good.

I gave up after 1–2 weeks. I thought, because of Corona, everyone has depression. Their weren't any appointments. I gave up after some time. But now I am back in the whirlpool. I feel I am disappointing everyone.

Karam, a 22-year-old refugee, belonged to a highly educated and wealthy Syrian family. He was a student of architecture at the University of Aleppo when he had to flee. In Germany, as he took a series of low-paid jobs, working as a janitor and as a restaurant worker, and he began consuming alcohol. His escalating depression and suicide attempts affected his attendance at work, ability to gain fluency in German, and, consequently, his education and integration.

Displaced. Shaifali Sandhya, Oxford University Press. © Shaifali Sandhya 2024.
DOI: 10.1093/oso/9780197579886.003.0009

Who is a good immigrant? What ought to be the right path for these unin-vited guests who show up at our doorstep? How quickly will they learn our cul-ture? Worldwide, such questions about the palatability of foreigners animate debates, elections, and popular imagination. In countries as diverse as Italy, India, South Africa, Japan, and others, deep hostilities toward immigrants are fanning the fires of nationalism. The idea of a foreign *Other*, especially those who differ racially, ethnically, and on religious grounds from the mainstream pop-ulation, is congealing toward one of greater polarity.In an era of increasing se-curitization from the threat migrants pose, there is no shortage of immigration policies for nations,[1] but immigration policies are seldom *immigrant* policies.[2] Rarely do nations' integration policies recognize asylum seekers' unique socio-cultural contexts such as gender, religion, or family structure and its own role in facilitating their personal agency, reconstructing their lives, and enabling their integration with host communities. The socio-economic climate of countries as much as the ethnicity of refugees can affect refugees' dynamics with the local pop-ulation,[3] whether they will adapt to its institutions, how much public provisions they will be afforded, and their daily experiences. Consider, for instance, coun-tries like Zimbabwe and several others in Africa like Burkina Faso, Chad, Mali, and Sudan where integration efforts may either not be possible or may fall short of obligations for the full economic, social, and cultural participation of its ref-ugee communities, given ongoing economic and political volatility.[4] Or coun-tries like Denmark, where the preferential treatment of Ukrainians is threatening the security of already settled Syrian refugees[5] and risks implementing a harmful hierarchical social system with deleterious long-term outcomes.

It is no wonder, then, that although the foreign-born in many countries exhibit the "healthy-migrant effect," this story is reversed for refugees.[6,7] Although the 1951 Convention includes provisions related to refugees' rights to work, access to health, and schools, and freedom to move in host communities, its non-binding

---

[1] Immigration laws determine the selection process, the visa status they will get accorded, and the resources they will be awarded.

[2] Geddes, A. (2005). *The politics of migration and immigration in Europe.* Sage.

[3] Ager, A., & Strang, A. (2008). Understanding integration: A conceptual framework. *Journal of Refugee Studies, 21,* 166–191.

[4] Wamara, C. K., Muchacha, M., Ogwok, B., & Dudzai, C. (2022). Refugee integration and glob-alization: Ugandan and Zimbabwean perspectives. *Journal of Human Rights and Social Work, 7,* 168–177.

[5] Rauhala, E. (2023, April 6). How progressive Denmark became the face of the anti-migration left. *The Washington Post.* https://www.washingtonpost.com/world/2023/04/06/denmark-zero-asy lum-refugees/

[6] Ruiz, I., & Vargas-Silva, C. (2017). Are refugees' labour market outcomes different from those of other migrants? Evidence from the United Kingdom 2005–2007. *Population Space and Place, 23*(6), E2049.

[7] Ruiz, I., & Vargas-Silva, C. (2018). Differences in labour market outcomes between natives, refugees and other migrants in the UK. *Journal of Economic Geography, 18,* 855–885.

nature creates a gap between its aspirations and its practice for the refugees themselves. Sixty-six to seventy percent of asylum seekers may face restrictions on their freedom to move and right to work[8] and many others may lack adequate access to food, water, health, or mental health care.[9,10]

Good mental health actualizes active engagement.[11] Chronic deficits in refugees' mental health further, impedes refugee integration,[12,13] performance, and engagement in their new homes. Forced displacement exacts a psychological toll on refugees fleeing war and conflict. Unaddressed mental illness and collective trauma faced by a refugee community compromises their well-being and affects whether they will cope effectively with postmigration challenges[14] (e.g., humiliation, exclusion, loneliness, and challenges in mastering a language) in their host nations. The integration practices of a nation's resettlement system are a refugee's range of rights, as per the Refugee Convention and ought to be equal to those accorded to members of its society.[15] Integration practices if implemented, have the power to counteract the marginalization and exclusion of the displaced. In this chapter, we ask: What are the pressures that mental health challenges pose and place on the integration processes of a country's resettlement system? And how do national integration practices and policies (or lack thereof) affect refugees' opportunities for relatedness, functioning, and reconstruction in their host society? If integration can be conceptualized at individual, community, and national levels, in the light of limitations such as poverty, recession, and climate-related displacements how do host nations reimagine and reorganize refugee engagement in their society?

Successful integration of refugees, emerging research suggests, can endow a well-being advantage for host nations and is considered vital for a

[8] *Livelihoods and economic inclusion* (n.d.) UNHCR. Retrieved on June 27, 2023, from https://www.unhcr.org/what-we-do/build-better-futures/livelihoods-and-economic-inclusion

[9] Afkhami, A. A., & Gorentz, K. (2019). Addressing the invisible affliction: An assessment of behavioral health services for newly resettled refugees in the United States. *Journal of International Migration and Integration, 20*, 247–259.

[10] Morales, F. R., Nguyen-Finn, K. L., Haidar, M., & Mercado, A. (2022). Humanitarian crisis on the US-Mexico border: Mental health needs of refugees and asylum seekers. *Current Opinion in Psychology, 9*(48), 101452.

[11] Feinstein, S., Poleacovschi, C., Drake, R., & Winters, L. A. (2022). States and refugee integration: A comparative analysis of France, Germany, and Switzerland. *International Migration & Integration, 23*, 2167–2194.

[12] Aoe, T., Shetty, A., Sivilli, T., Blanton, S., Ellis, H., Geltman, P., Cochran, J., Taylor, J., Lankau, J., & Cardozo, B. L. (2015). Suicidal ideation and mental health of Bhutanese refugees in the United States. *Journal of Immigrant and Minority Health, 18*(5), 828–835.

[13] Meyerhoff, J., Rohan, K. J., & Fondacaro, K. M. (2018). Suicide and suicide-related behavior among Bhutanese refugees resettled in the United States. *Asian American Journal of Psychology, 9*(4), 270–283.

[14] Tsegay, S. M. (2022). Hope springs eternal: Exploring the early settlement experiences of highly educated Eritrean refugees in the UK. *International Migration and Integration, 23*, 1235–1255.

[15] Article 34 of the Refugee Convention and its 1967 Protocol urges states to facilitate the assimilation and naturalization of refugees.

well-functioning migration management system.[16] Inclusive integration policies can lead to a positive perception of refugees[17] in host communities, better relations between refugees and host communities, and their better assimilation. With a growing number of displaced in host countries, especially those in the Global South, there is a new urgency to prioritize effective integration through conceptualizing it as a complex,[18] context-specific,[19] multifaceted,[20] dynamic,[21] and inclusive process that factors in the context of receiving communities as well as refugee experiences.[22,23]

This chapter explores the role of receiving nations in designing better opportunities for access and belonging for their refugee communities. Toward this purpose, the chapter proposes a comprehensive definition of integration and one that has the scope to include refugee experiences within multicultural societies. It also explores the role of some exigent factors such as refugee's untreated mental illness, the number of refugees, the history of settlement of the particular refugee group, host nations' reactions to refugees, type of host country (transit or target), colonial pasts, present political and economic climate, humanitarian traditions[24] relating to the treatment of refugees, and the political will of the elite.[25] Using different national resettlement frameworks, the chapter also explores how integration processes, or the economic, legal, social, cultural,

[16] European Commission. (2020, November 24). *Action plan on integration and inclusion 2021–2027*. https://home-affairs.ec.europa.eu/system/files_en?file=2020-11/action_plan_on_integration_and_inclusion_2021-2027.pdf

[17] Callens, M. S., & Meuleman, B. (2017). Do integration policies relate to economic and cultural threat perceptions? A comparative study in Europe. *International Journal of Comparative Sociology*, 58(5), 367–391.

[18] Sigona, N. (2005). Refugee integration: Policy and practice in the European Nation. *Refugee Survey Quarterly*, 24(4), 115–122.

[19] Ndofor-Tah, C., Strang, A., Phillimore, J., Morrice, L., Michael, L., Wood, P., & Simmons, J. (2019). *Home Office indicators of integration framework 2019*. https://assets.publishing.service.gov.uk/government/uploads/system/uploads/ attachment_data/file/805870/home-office-indicators-of-integration-framework-2019-horr109.pdf

[20] Penninx, R. (2004, January 12–14). *Integration of migrants: Economic, social, cultural and political dimensions* [Paper presentation]. European population forum: Population challenges and policy responses. UN Economic Commission for Europe. https://unece.org/fileadmin/DAM/pau/_docs/pau/2004/PAU_2004_EPF_BgDocPenninx.pdf

[21] Robinson, V. (1998). Defining and measuring successful refugee integration. In *Proceedings of ECRE International Conference on Integration of Refugees*. European Council on Refugees and Exiles. https://ecre.org/wp-content/uploads/2016/07/ECRE-Position-on-the-Integration-of-Refugees-in-Europe_December-2002.pdf

[22] Korac, M. (2003). Integration and how we facilitate it: A comparative study of the settlement experiences of refugees in Italy and the Netherlands. *Sociology*, 37(1), 51–68.

[23] Wamara, C. K., Muchacha, M., Ogwok, B., & Dudzai, C. (2022). Refugee integration and globalization: Ugandan and Zimbabwean perspectives. *Journal of Human Rights and Social Work*, 7(2), 168–177.

[24] Loescher, G., & Scanlan, J. A. (1986). *Calculated kindness: Refugees and America's half-open door, 1945 to the present*. Free Press.

[25] Brown, E. L., & Krasteva, A. (2013). *Migrants and refugees: Equitable education for displaced populations* (p. 5). Information Age.

educational, and political aspects of policies,[26] affect refugees' participation, self-sufficiency, and empowerment in host societies.

The study of integration is constrained, however, by the absence of policy-relevant research on specific vulnerable segments such as refugee children and others,[27] absence of reliable measures on refugee integration outcomes, knowledge gaps in communities' adjustment over the critical initial period and its association with interventions[28] and a lack of tracking of outcomes over time. Thus, although new groups of refugees may differ with each other in educational profiles, language proficiency, and occupation upon arrival, despite the passage of time, some may outperform others on socioeconomic outcomes. Integration schemes or obstacles within them, such as limited cash assistance in the United States, nonrecognition of prior refugee degrees and bureaucratic delays in Germany,[29] challenges in accessing language programs in France, or uncertainty in acquiring residency permits in Switzerland[30] can erase society's human capital.[31,32] The loss of recognition of one's abilities, delays in work placements, and the denial of resources necessary for achieving integration could, in fact, increase the anguish of refugee families.

Integration, if it is envisioned as and implemented toward greater inclusivity for the immigrant in the host society, can serve to have parallel but positive effects—akin to clinical treatment—on the mental health of refugees. Some nations such as Colombia, Brazil, and Ecuador in the case of Venezuelan refugees are championing for inclusive development through their greater access to national health, education, and the labor market.[33,34] Integration gaps or nonrecognition of successful integration components in contrast, given migrants' unique ethnic,

[26] Wamara, C. K., Muchacha, M., Ogwok, B., & Dudzai, C. (2002). Refugee integration and globalization: Ugandan and Zimbabwean perspectives. *Journal of Human Rights and Social Work, 7*(2), 168–177.

[27] Pastoor, L. (2016), Rethinking refugee education: Principles, policies and practice from a European perspective. *Annual Review of Comparative and International Education, 30,* 107–116.

[28] International Rescue Committee. (2017). *Financial capability for new Americans: Lessons from early interventions with refugees.* https://www.rescue.org/sites/default/files/document/1591/lg01jp mwhitepaperdigitalfinal.pdf

[29] Pearlman, W. (2020). Aspiration, appreciation and frustration: Syrian asylum seekers and bureaucracy in Germany. In Abdelhady, D., Gren, N., & Joormann, M. (Eds.), *Refugees and the violence of welfare bureaucracies in Northern Europe* (pp. 180–194). Manchester University Press.

[30] Feinstein, S., Poleacovschi, C., Drake, R., & Winters, L. A. (2022). States and refugee integration: A comparative analysis of France, Germany, and Switzerland. *International Migration and Integration, 23,* 2167–2194.

[31] Tran, V. C., & Lara-García, F. (2020). A new beginning: Early refugee integration in the United States. *RSF: The Russell Sage Foundation Journal of the Social Sciences, 6*(3), 117–149.

[32] Gowayed, H. (2022). *Refuge: How the state shapes human potential.* Princeton University.

[33] Treisman, R. (2021, February, 9). Colombia offers temporary legal status to nearly 1 million Venezuelan migrants. *NPR.* https://www.npr.org/2021/02/09/965853031/colombia-offers-temporary-legal-status-to-nearly-1-million-venezuelan-migrants

[34] Cortes, G. (2023, March 9). Regularization brings hope and stability to Venezuelan migrants in Ecuador. *IOM.* https://storyteller.iom.int/stories/regularization-brings-hope-and-stability-venezuelan-migrants-ecuador

educational, religious, and cultural backgrounds, may negatively affect refugee experiences as well as host populations. The multiple domains of integration also suggest the potential utility for empowering refugee communities through innovative integration schemes and leveraging partnerships at local and international levels.

Revisiting Integration for the Mental Health of Minorities: Taking the Long View

Integration has recently been heralded as core to the "(European) way of life" and central to the longer-term well-being of its communities and economies, by the European Commission's Action Plan on Integration and Inclusion (2021–2027).[35] But nations' integration strategies have been criticized for being top-down,[36,37] culture-blind, and ethnically neutral,[38] seldom perceiving refugees as social actors with differentiated needs[39] who may contest and negotiate dominant cultures. With some exceptions,[40] in reality the integration strategies of many nations do not focus on the constellation of unique and dynamic interactions between host nations and the displaced.[41] Integration practices and plans, for instance, do not take into account how the mental illness of its refugee populations can affect their ability to participate or, in turn, how prejudice, exclusion, or discounting of their capacities during the postmigration period can affect their mental health. Although nations like the United States at the federal level may "embrace the full participation of the newest Americans,"[42] they do not have a national integration policy and are debilitated by an outmoded, random,[43] and fragmented resettlement system.

[35] European Commission. (2020, November 24). *Action plan on integration and inclusion 2021–2027.* https://home-affairs.ec.europa.eu/system/files_en?file=2020-11/action_plan_on_integration _and_inclusion_2021-2027.pdf

[36] Indra, D. (1993). *Some feminist contributions to refugee studies* [Paper presentation] (p. 7). (1993, May 9–11). Development Implications Conference on Gender Issues and Refugees, York University, Toronto, Canada.

[37] Watters, C., & Ingleby, D. (2004). Locations of care: Meeting the mental health and social care needs of refugees in Europe. *International Journal of Law and Psychiatry, 27*(6), 549–570.

[38] Brown, E. L., & Krasteva, A. (2013). *Migrants and refugees: Equitable education for displaced populations* (p. 5). Information Age.

[39] Korac, M. (2003). Integration and how we facilitate It: A comparative study of the settlement experiences of refugees in Italy and the Netherlands. *Sociology, 37*(1), 51–68.

[40] Hynie, M., Korn, A., & Tao, D. (2016). Social context and social integration for Government Assisted Refugees in Ontario, Canada. In M. Poteet & S. Nourpanah (Eds.), *After the flight: The dynamics of refugee settlement and integration* (pp. 183–227). Cambridge Scholars.

[41] Gowayed, H. (2022). *Refuge: How the state shapes human potential.* Princeton University Press.

[42] Exec. Order No. 14012, 86 C.F.R. 8277 (2021, February 5). https://www.federalregister.gov/d/2021-02563

[43] Tran, V. C., & Lara-García, F. (2020). A new beginning: Early refugee integration in the United States. *RSF: The Russell Sage Foundation Journal of the Social Sciences, 6*(3), 117–149.

Whether a nation has a formal integration policy or not, integration of new immigrant groups can be affected by any number of factors: the receiving communities' attitudes toward the displaced group; the receiving community's perception of the scarcity of resources and economic emaciation because of the arrival of the refugees; partnerships between their governmental, nongovernmental, and private sectors; collaboration within the different agencies within its resettlement system, and so forth. Successful integration can be facilitated through integration initiatives promoting social harmony and government policies that balance favors to refugees with host populations, global partnerships, and community dialogs and engagement.[44] Knowledge gaps in implementing integration plans tailored to specific refugee groups (e.g., lesbian, gay, bisexual, transgender, and queer persons; women, children; the disabled; and the elderly), poor socioeconomic resources, and political will can result in the warehousing of the displaced or their placement in desolate settings with restricted mobility for long durations.[45]

Underscoring the knowledge gap in how integration practices affect immigrants is the term *integration* itself. Integration has variously been labeled as complex, chaotic,[46] nebulous,[47] and with diverging meanings,[48] and nations worldwide have struggled with conceptualizing it. Integration, in its practice, as ascertained by how long nations extend integration measures to its refugees, has also been conceptualized in a time-limited way. The European Council on Refugees and Exiles (ECRE) definition of *integration* is an exception to the challenges that a definition of integration poses. It describes *integration* to be a process of change, time, and dimensionality:[49] It urges our attention to the dynamicity and mutuality of demands, placed on both receiving societies and individuals and communities. Expectations of societies toward greater inclusion of their newcomers can range from: their willingness to adapt public institutions

[44] Wamara, C. K., Muchacha, M., Ogwok, B., & Dudzai, C. (2022). Refugee integration and globalization: Ugandan and Zimbabwean perspectives. *Journal of Human Rights and Social Work, 7*(2), 168–177.

[45] Smith, M. (2004). Warehousing refugees: A denial of rights, a waste of humanity. *World Refugee Survey,* 38–56. *World Refugee Survey.* US Committee for Refugees. https://www.refugees.org/wp-content/uploads/2021/06/Warehousing_Refugees_A_Denial_of_Rights-English.pdf

[46] Robinson, V. (1998, November 12–14). *Defining and measuring successful refugee integration* [Paper presentation] (p. 118). European Council on Refugees and Exiles Conference on Integration of Refugees in Europe, Antwerp, Belgium.

[47] UK Ministry of Housing. (2016, December 5). *The Casey Review: A review into integration and opportunity* (p. 20). https://www.gov.uk/government/publications/the-casey-review-a-review-into-opportunity-and-integration

[48] Ager, A., & Strang, A. (2008). Understanding integration: A conceptual framework. *Journal of Refugee Studies, 21,* 166–191. http://dx.doi.org/10.1093/jrs/fen016

[49] European Council on Refugees and Exiles. (1999, September). *Position on the integration of refugees in Europe* (p. 4). https://www.refworld.org/docid/3df4d3874.html

to refugee population profiles, accept refugees as part of the mainstream community, and facilitate their access to resources and decision-making processes. Integration expectations from refugees can include a preparedness to adapt to the host society's lifestyle without losing their cultural identity.

Integration thus is generally conceptualized as the extent, quality, and degree of mutuality in refugees' participation in the various socioeconomic, health, language, education, political, and cultural domains of host societies. The quality and degree of refugees' mutuality across various social domains will determine their enjoyment, access to educational and employment opportunities,[50] and assimilation of the host country's values and norms, irrespective of their religion, sexuality, ethnicity, or gender,[51] and alongside benefits to their hosts. As for the duration of integration measures, both the ECRE and the European Commission (EC) recommend taking a broader approach to migrant adaptation with a long-term investment in them until they become knowledgeable in navigating the host society.[52] Formalizing a national integration policy could have a number of benefits for nations: it would allow for collection of data on integration challenges at the local and integration level; tracking and monitoring of integration outcomes to understand the impact of informal policies of their nations' diverse refugee groups across time and regions; and the development of refugee competencies and resilience over time.

Integration Challenges

Refugee Factors: Mental Health and Socioeconomic Integration

Refugees of humanitarian crises often arrive in host communities bearing complex health scars that are exacerbated by postdisplacement living challenges[53] that sustain their psychological distress.[54] Although the mental health

[50] Bevelander, P., & Irastorza, N. (n.d.). The labor market integration of refugees in Sweden. *Nordregio*.Retrieved on June 28, 2023 from, https://nordregio.org/nordregio-magazine/issues/migration-and-integration/the-labour-market-integration-of-refugees-in-sweden/

[51] The UK government's report defines integration broadly as social mixing: "Integration is the extent to which people from all backgrounds can get on with each other and [enjoy] and respecting the benefits that the United Kingdom has to offer.": UK Ministry of Housing. (2016, December 5). *The Casey Review: A review into integration and opportunity* (pp. 19–20). https://www.gov.uk/government/publications/the-casey-review-a-review-into-opportunity-and-integration

[52] European Commission. (2020, November 24). *Action plan on integration and inclusion 2021–2027* (p. 7). https://home-affairs.ec.europa.eu/system/files_en?file=2020-11/action_plan_on_integration_and_inclusion_2021-2027.pdf

[53] Laban, C. J., Gernaat, H. B., Komproe, I. H., Van der Tweel, I., & De Jong, J. T. (2005). Postmigration living problems and common psychiatric disorders in Iraqi asylum seekers in the Netherlands. *Journal of Nervous and Mental Disease*, 193(12), 825832.

[54] Porter, M., & Haslam, N. (2005). Predisplacement and postdisplacement factors associated with mental health of refugees and internally displaced persons: A meta-analysis. *Journal of the American Medical Association*, 294(5), 602–612.

impairments of refugees and asylum-seekers are well-established, generally little
is known about their needs and limitations regarding integration in the presence of psychological impairments. Issues such as posttraumatic stress disorder,
traumatic brain injury, depression, and anxiety can impede social integration,[55]
and can exacerbate the difficulties in staying employed, learning a language,
maintaining relationships, regulating motions, and adapting to the lifestyle of
the host country. Notions of integration of host nations in general fail to factor
in how poor mental health can make the tasks of integration hard to achieve or
how integration difficulties can have an additive effect on refugee mental health.

National integration plans fail to recognize the myriad manifestations of complex trauma and how to plan for and treat myriad health concerns in their diverse
refugee newcomers. When refugees' mental health challenges go unrecognized
or are misattributed to a lack of interest in adopting a host nation's values, the
troubled are also likely to be perceived as troublesome. Also, migration scholars
can misrepresent supports available to refugees by relying on domestic programs
of integration.[56,57]

Integration policies of nations may also fail to identify specific factors aiding
positive integration. At the same time, improving mental health infrastructure
in a way that prioritizes and plans for the mental health needs of its diverse refugee communities is likely to be advantageous to host nations. For instance, it
can aid in greater social integration that may, in turn, lead to an embrace of and
access to a country's care models and health networks. Although Norway has
universal health care coverage, researchers found that when Syrian refugees in
Norway perceived stronger feelings of connectedness to the majority of the host
country, it not only led to greater help-seeking behaviors from their medical
community but also a greater probability of building durable relationships such
as marriage within a society.[58] In the context of a community that harbors taboos
against help-seeking from Western professionals, seeking instead health advice
from partners, parents, and religious leaders or from faith,[59] integration's role in
fostering more inclusivity in the national health systems is valuable.

[55] Trong, A., Shetty, S., Sivilli, T., Blanton, C., Ellis, H., Geltman, P., Cochran, J., Taylor, E., Lankau,
E., & Cardozo, B. (2015). Suicidal ideation and mental health of Bhutanese refugees in the United
States. *Journal of Immigrant and Minority Health*, *18*(5), 828–835.

[56] Bloemraad, I. (2006). *Becoming a citizen*. University of California Press.

[57] Jimenez, T. R. (2011). Immigration in the United States: How well are they integrating into society? *Migration Policy Institute*. http://www.migrationpolicy.org/sites/default/files/publications/inte
gration-Jimenez.pdf

[58] Markova, V., Sandal, G. M., & Pallesen, S. (2020). Immigration, acculturation, and preferred
help-seeking sources for depression: Comparison of five ethnic groups. *BMC Health Services
Research*, *20*, 648.

[59] Sandal, G. M., Bye, H. H., Palinkas, L. A., & Binder, P. (2021). Integration is correlated with
mental health help-seeking from the general practitioner: Syrian refugees' preferences and perceived
barriers. *Frontiers in Public Health*, *9*, 777582.

Emerging research such as Ruiz and Vargas-Silva's[60] highlights how individuals' mental health challenges can be intertwined with their integration success or failure. On the one hand, integration difficulties can be strongly associated with trauma symptoms and depression: they can compound its effect[61] beyond the number of traumatic events impacting a refugee. The adverse effects of trauma and poor mental health, emerging research shows, can also overshadow the beneficial effects of demographic resources.[62] On the other hand, research from host nations like Germany shows that there may be qualitative differences in refugees' ability to integrate across host nations[63] that may, in turn, influence refugees' well-being. There may be many reasons we could expect refugees to have worse outcomes and many reasons we could expect better outcomes. But undeniably it is the mental health challenges that underscore the socioeconomic disparity between refugees and other migrants and native workers from countries such as the UK[64,65,66,67] and Sweden.[68] Some promising measures in the form of counselling, networking opportunities, work placements and training of Ukrainian refugee women are positively affecting their socio-economic integration in some European countries, and it remains to be seen if such gains will be sustainable. Examining refugees' mental health challenges and the gains in it they acquire from favorable policies as they integrate can also benefit host nations.

A closer examination of refugees in the UK can indicate how in contrast, chronic deficits in social or health domains may play a role in participation in the

[60] Ruiz, I., & Vargas-Silva, C. (2018). Differences in labour market outcomes between natives, refugees and other migrants in the UK. *Journal of Economic Geography, 18*(4), 855–885.

[61] Schick, M., Zumwald, A., Knöpfli, B., Nickerson, A., Bryant, R. A., Schnyder, U., Müller, J., & Morina, N. (2016). Challenging future, challenging past: The relationship of social integration and psychological impairment in traumatized refugees. *European Journal of Psychotraumatology, 7*, 28057.

[62] Ibid.

[63] Brücker, H., Jaschke, P., & Kosyakova, Y. (2019, December). *Integrating refugees and asylum seekers into the German economy and society: Empirical evidence and policy objectives.* Migration Policy Institute. https://www.migrationpolicy.org/sites/default/files/publications/TCM_2019_Germany-FINAL.pdf

[64] Ruiz, I., & Vargas-Silva, C. (2018). Differences in labour market outcomes between natives, refugees and other migrants in the UK. *Journal of Economic Geography, 18*, 855–885.

[65] Kone, Z., Ruiz, I., & Vargas-Silva, C. (2019). *Refugees and the UK labor market.* Nuffield Foundation.

[66] Ruiz, I., & Vargas-Silva, C. (2017). Are refugees' labour market outcomes different from those of other migrants? Evidence from the United Kingdom in the 2005–2007 period. *Population Space and Place, 23*(6), E2049.

[67] Ruiz, I., & Vargas-Silva, C. (2017). Differences in labour market outcomes between natives, refugees and other migrants in the UK. *Journal of Economic Geography, 18*(4), 855–885.

[68] Bevelander, P., & Irastorza, N. (n.d.). The labor market integration of refugees in Sweden. *Nordregio.* https://nordregio.org/nordregio-magazine/issues/migration-and-integration/the-labour-market-integration-of-refugees-in-sweden/

labor market and functioning and assimilation in other domains. Compared to the UK-born, refugees have a lower employment rate (51% versus 73%), are less likely to work full-time, earn less per hour when they work for others, and work for fewer hours, earn less overall, and are less likely to be in professional or managerial positions.[69]

Compared to other migrants and the UK-born, 25% of refugees with a health condition reported mental health problems.[70] After controlling for sociodemographic factors, refugees in comparison to the UK-born are 3% more likely to report a mental health condition, and 9% more likely to report long-lasting health problems with arms, legs, the back, and/or neck; cardiovascular problems; and mental health issues, and report that this impedes their ability to work or stay engaged in work.[71]

The health patterns of refugees to the UK depict different patterns compared to migrants and locals and are a critical factor in creating their labor market disadvantage.[72,73] Close to 50% reported being debilitated by a health problem to the extent that it limited the number of hours they could work (33% for UK natives) and the type of work that they could undertake (37% of UK natives) in comparison to other foreign-born populations (28–30%). The study concluded that those reporting a long-term health problem are 19% less likely to be in employment and earn 9% less per week. This trend of socioeconomic exclusion was reported among highly educated and recent Eritrean refugees to the UK. The long and complicated asylum process is as important of an obstacle along with refugees' growing disappointment and anxiety in their economic integration.[74] Could the socioeconomic lag witnessed in the refugee groups in Sweden, the United States, and the UK then be the tip of the iceberg reflecting their struggles with integration and yet masking their full extent?

How could a system intended to facilitate refugees' entry into the labor market in fact thwart this process? In countries such as the United States, the UK, and

[69] Kone, Z., Ruiz, I., & Vargas-Silva, C. (2019). *Refugees and the UK labor market*. Centre on Migration, Policy and Society. https://www.nuffieldfoundation.org/wp-content/uploads/2019/04/ECONREF-Refugees-and-the-UK-Labour-Market-report.pdf

[70] Kone, Z., Ruiz, I., & Vargas-Silva, C. (2019). *Refugees and the UK labor market* (p. 3). Centre on Migration, Policy and Society. https://www.nuffieldfoundation.org/wp-content/uploads/2019/04/ECONREF-Refugees-and-the-UK-Labour-Market-report.pdf

[71] Kone, Z., Ruiz, I., & Vargas-Silva, C. (2019). *Refugees and the UK labor market* (p. 37). Centre on Migration, Policy and Society. https://www.nuffieldfoundation.org/wp-content/uploads/2019/04/ECONREF-Refugees-and-the-UK-Labour-Market-report.pdf

[72] Ruiz, I., & Vargas-Silva, C. (2017). Are refugees' labour market outcomes different from those of other migrants? Evidence from the United Kingdom in the 2005–2007 period. *Population Space and Place*, *23*(6), E2049.

[73] Ruiz, I., & Vargas-Silva, C. (2017). Differences in labour market outcomes between natives, refugees and other migrants in the UK. *Journal of Economic Geography*, *18*(4), 855–885.

[74] Tsegay, S. M. (2022). Hope springs eternal: Exploring the early settlement experiences of highly educated Eritrean refugees in the UK. *International Migration and Integration*, *23*, 1235–1255.

Sweden,[75] refugee groups relative to migrants and the native-born populations lag on socioeconomic metrics, such as the probability of being employed and wages, several years after arrival. Health factors, in particular, mental health, affect their socioeconomic mobility.[76] The advantage of expanding both our long-term examination of refugee lives, according to some scholars, also lies in implementing individualized integration plans with attention to refugees' experiences and mental health needs.[77]

Refugees' Religion, Ethnicity, and Race

Religion may affect the pace and probability of integration. Research[78] indicates that Muslims have a different rate of integration compared to non-Muslims, and religion influences the ability and willingness to integrate into Western communities. Let us examine whether a relationship between the strength of ethnic identity and rates of integration exists. Using the UK's Fourth National Survey of Ethnic Minorities data (FNSEM) and a sample of 5,963 ethnic minorities (3,594 non-Muslims and 2,369 Muslims), researchers argue that ethnic identity impacts the level and pace of integration.[79] Researchers defined "ethnic identity" as very specific markers: the importance of religion in one's life; the extent of negative attitudes one held toward the possible marriage of a close relative with a White partner, and one's preference for similar ethnic composition in schools for their children. Based on this, the researchers concluded that the percentage of Muslims having an intense religious identity was twice that of non-Muslims. The ethnic identity of Muslims as defined by the "importance of religion" according to the research, played a pivotal role in determining their integration rate. A Muslim born in the UK and one who has lived in the UK for 50 years will have "on an average the same probability of a strong religious identity as compared to a first-generation non-Muslim who has been in the U.K. for less than twenty years."[80]

The finding that the longer one lives in a host culture, the more attenuated is one's attachment to one's native culture or culture of birth is counterintuitive

[75] Gren, N. (2020). Living bureaucratisation: Young Palestinian men encountering a Swedish introductory programme for refugees. In D. Abdelhady, N. Gren, & M. Joormann (Eds.), *Refugees and the violence of welfare bureaucracies in Northern Europe* (pp. 161–179). Manchester University.

[76] Ruiz, I., & Vargas-Silva, C. (2018). Differences in labour market outcomes between natives, refugees and other migrants in the UK. *Journal of Economic Geography, 18*, 855–885.

[77] Tsegay, S. M. (2022). Hope springs eternal: Exploring the early settlement experiences of highly educated Eritrean refugees in the UK. *International Migration and Integration, 23*, 1235–1255.

[78] Bisin, A., Patacchini, E., Verdier, T., & Zenou, Y. (2008). Are Muslim immigrants different in terms of cultural integration? *Journal of the European Economic Association, 6*(2–3), 445–456.

[79] Ibid.

[80] Ibid.

to what we might expect. However, when integration was measured using this particular definition of identity (religious attenuation), it was concluded that UK Muslims integrated less and more slowly compared to non-Muslims. Ethnic identity thus trumps the time a person has spent in the country as both first and second-generation Muslims continued to exhibit a far stronger religious identity despite spending decades in the UK. The non-Muslim second generation, in turn, seemed to lose its attachment to culture-of-origin more rapidly than the Muslim second generation. Further, it is suggested that second-generation Muslims compared to second-generation non-Muslims never achieve lower levels of religious identity at any point in time.

Let us revisit the conceptualization of ethnic identity in the study by Bisin et al., in order to see how and why it may be problematic. *Ethnic identity* was defined as a combination of the importance of faith in one's life, negative preference toward the intermarriage of a close relative with a White partner, and a preference for similar ethnic composition in schools for their children. A preference for one's native language at home may signal comfort for a family in a foreign land, and religious identity could serve a protective function. Secure family composition through marriage alliances within one's tribe could also be a response to the circumstances a refugee family has faced in the UK, a nation embroiled with accusations of racism and hostilities toward its refugees and migrants. Instead, it may be that society's expectations that refugees give up their religion to signal their integration in host nations that may be more problematic.[81] Further, although it considers predominantly Pakistanis and Bangladeshis who have exhibited unique immigration patterns in the UK, the study generalizes its results to all Muslims.[82] The Muslim population in the study is, on average, less educated and has a lower household income compared to the mainstream population, is likely to be unemployed, and cannot be representative of all Muslims, in general.

At the same time, Bisen et al.'s research is illuminating in showing that integration can consist of sets of overlapping processes that can occur in different ways in the various domains of receiving societies, and that have various outcomes.[83] For instance, preferences for one's marriage partner may be more resistant to change than educational aspirations that could be more aligned to the ones exhibited by the mainstream population. Consider the practice of cross-cousin marriage even in British Pakistanis. This transnational marriage between

---

[81] Ibid. The authors' metrics for cultural integration are very narrow: they range from speaking English at home or with friends and having their marriage arranged by their parents as a signal of attachment to cultural and religious traditions.

[82] Ibid.

[83] Ibid.

a fourth- or fifth-generation British Pakistani involves marrying a cousin or relative in Pakistan for opportunities for a better life, and suggests more socioeconomic, psychological, and emotional drivers[84] than simply those of insularity or resistance to assimilation within a host culture. However, the task of identifying multiple integration domains and implementing multipronged integration strategies would be a mammoth enterprise for any host nation.

The refugee's family background,[85] disrupted family networks, insecure housing, and whether or not they share the receiving culture's religion, can also affect their integration.[86] Integration outcomes for refugees can also diverge based on their gender, duration in the host country, country of origin, education levels, whether their family resides with them or not, whether they are resettled refugees or asylum-seekers who became refugees when they showed up at the border,[87] or whether they are on permanent or temporary visas.[88] "There is no single or best integration model," says the OECD.[89]

Host Societies: Xenophobia and Intergroup Relations

Receiving societies are also not monolithic entities,[90] and the host nation's demographic composition and domestic politics can also affect the implementation and adoption of integration strategies. Consider the case of Turkey, which has absorbed more than 3.4 million refugees over the past 6 years. Low-income communities in Turkey, such as the marginalized Kurds and the Alevis, the heterodox Shiites that comprise 15%–20% of Turkish society, tend to be resentful of the Syrian refugees they perceive as vying for the same jobs, especially in the informal economy. In some cases, there may be reverse discrimination—discrimination occurring against an existing ethnic community when refugees

---

[84] Shaw, A. (2014). Drivers of cousin marriage among British Pakistanis. *Human Heredity, 77*(1–4), 26–36.

[85] Koehler, C., & Schneider, J. (2019). Young refugees in education: The particular challenges of school systems in Europe. *Comparative Migration Studies, 7*, 28.

[86] Crul, M., Schneider, J., & Lelie, F. (2012). *The European second generation compared: Does the integration context matter?* Amsterdam University Press.

[87] Bevelander, P. (2011). The employment integration of resettled refugees, asylum claimants, and family reunion migrants in Sweden. *Refugee Survey Quarterly, 30*, 22–43.

[88] Hainmueller, J., Hangartner, D., & Lawrence, D. (2016). When lives are put on hold, lengthy asylum processes decrease employment among refugees. *Science Advances, 2*, 1–7.

[89] Cerna, L. (2019, May 13). *Refugee education: Integration models and practices in OECD countries* (OECD Education Working Paper No. 203, UN Doc. OECD EDU/WKP(2019)11, p. 23). https://one.oecd.org/document/EDU/WKP(2019)11/En/pdf

[90] Castles, S., Korac, M., Vasta, E., & Vertovec, S. (2002, December). *Integration: Mapping the field* [Home Office online report by the University of Oxford Centre for Migration and Policy Research and Refugee Studies Centre, Immigration Research, and Statistics Service].

arrive. An employer[91] in the city of Izmir, Turkey, for example, appears to favor Syrians as they are considered "obedient" compared to the "hard-to-manage" Turkish Kurdish. Since the Syrians often also speak adequate Turkish, hiring locals does not necessarily bring with it a language advantage:

> "If you ask me whether I prefer a Syrian or a local Kurd, I would say Syrian, because they are really respectful," said the manager of a shoemaking workshop. "Kurds usually behave in an unmannerly way. . . . They pick fights quickly."

The influx of economic investment into Turkey has also created the perception that the hosts are second-class citizens, as echoed by a middle-class man[92] in Ankara, Turkey:

> It is as if all these distributors of aid and the state only realized that this neighborhood had a poverty problem after the Syrians settled here. Suddenly they opened shiny offices and started distributing aid. As if before Syrians came, our neighborhood was a bed of roses. Nobody ever cared about us as we struggled for years to sustain ourselves. After the Syrians arrived, suddenly everyone came here to help them.

As a result of antipathy toward Syrians, intercommunal violence increased three-fold in the second half of 2017 in Turkey, compared to the same period in 2016, resulting in the deaths of 24 Syrians. The estimated 750,000–950,000 Syrians who currently work in the informal sector in Turkey tend to have little education and fewer skills than those who tend to migrate to Europe. Fearing that there would be a public backlash at accepting Syrians permanently, local integration for the displaced may be elusive.

Almost 60% of European respondents expressed concerns that refugees increase the likelihood of terrorism, and half believed that refugees imposed an economic burden by usurping social benefits.[93] Others have been concerned with highly concentrated monoreligious and/or monoethnic communities becoming separated from the existing or wider community. In countries like Germany, however, overwhelmingly positive attitudes toward refugees have generally existed, as has been discussed previously in Chapter 2. Public perceptions of refugees affect whether or not integration will take place.

[91] International Crisis Group. (2018, January 29). *Turkey's Syrian refugees: Defusing metropolitan tensions* (Europe Report No. 248). https://www.crisisgroup.org/europe-central-asia/western-euro pemediterranean/turkey/248-turkeys-syrian-refugees-defusing-metropolitan-tensions
[92] Ibid.
[93] Wike, R., Stokes, B., & Simmons, K. (2016, July 11). Europeans fear wave of refugees will mean more terrorism, fewer jobs. *Pew Research Center*. https://www.pewresearch.org/global/2016/07/11/europeans-fear-wave-of-refugees-will-mean-more-terrorism-fewer-jobs/

Host Nations' Resettlement Systems

Nations vary in their policies and treatments, historically and contemporaneously, toward asylum-seekers, immigrants, and refugees. Specifically, such differences can emanate or be reflected through refugee programs that allow their entry (government assisted, privately sponsored, or shared), policies related to refugee intake, the levels (federal, state, or municipal) at which policies are coordinated, the duration and kinds of support provided to the refugee, and how they may determine the success of their refugees. A host nation's resettlement system will determine whether its concept of integration is articulated and has political visibility; the intake of its refugees, provision, and delivery of its specific services; who it envisions as its stakeholders; and interdependence between its various agencies.

Four nations' resettlement frameworks, for instance, provide varying examples of models used to manage migrants' ethno-cultural diversity and contexts that regulate their intake, arrival, how they will be treated and the quality of their stay in host nations. Assessing refugees' levels of integration across nations may not be an entirely valid or practical exercise.[94] The US refugee program is a complex, hierarchical, and bureaucratic system consisting of state actors, voluntary organizations, voluntary agency councils, and assorted public and private departments and bodies, as well as refugee self-help organizations.[95] In the UK, the Refugee Council, an umbrella organization, receives funds from the Home Office to coordinate UK-based voluntary agencies who work with refugees.[96] In Sweden, the municipality is the main agent of refugee intake; although politics, interests (e.g., unions, proimmigration groups), and geographical location dictate whether a municipality will participate or not.[97] Canada's private sponsorship program (Private Sponsorship of Refugees, PSR) that complements the Government Assisted Refugee (GAR) program and the

---

[94] For instance, the previous waves of refugees in Sweden between 1980 and 1999 were Bosnian, Chilean, and Iranian. In the United States roughly during that period, refugee arrival was mostly from the former Soviet Union, Southeast Asia, and the Balkans, primarily Serbs from Bosnia and Croatia.

[95] Darrow, J. (2015). The (re)construction of the U.S. Department of State's Reception and Placement Program by refugee resettlement agencies. *Journal of the Society for Social Work and Research, 6*, 91–119.

[96] Majka, L. (1991). Assessing refugee assistance organizations in the United States and the United Kingdom. *Journal of Refugee Studies, 4*, 267–283.

[97] Lidén, G., & Nyhlén, J. (2014). Explaining local Swedish refugee policy. *Journal of International Migration and Integration, 15*(3), 547–565.

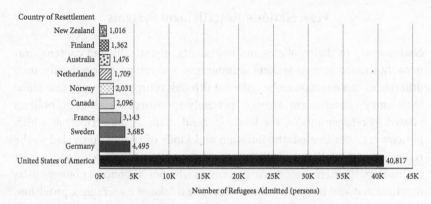

Figure 9.1   Countries of Refugee Resettlement (by September 1, 2022)
Source: UNCHR, https://rsq.unchr.org/en/#p7Zj

Blended Visa-Office Referred (BVOR) program has shown to have more promising results[98] in resettling refugees.[99]

Although it may be challenging to assess the best integration model in the absence of data, and most countries might engage in a bricolage of practices, what
may be more valuable is examining refugee competencies with time, across various integration domains, and relative to the native population. It may also be
useful to comparatively explore and assess examples of countries that may approach the ideal parameter in the context of their unique refugee groups. Using
the case study of the United States, let us take a closer look at the relationship
between mental health and integration through the lens of resettlement policy,
often considered the starting point for integration.

Resettlement: Conceptualizing the Individual and Public Expressions of Culture

Resettlement is the transfer of refugees from an asylum country to another State
that has agreed to grant them permanent residency. Figure 9.1 illustrates the

---

[98]   Private sponsorship of refugees exhibited an advantage compared to the Canadian government's
refugee assisted program even among the less educated. After controlling for education, official
language ability, and some other sociodemographic characteristics, privately sponsored refugees
demonstrated higher employment rates and earnings particularly during the initial settlement period: Kaida, L., Hou, F., & Stick, M. (2020). The long-term economic outcomes of refugee private
sponsorship [Analytical studies branch research paper series]. *Statistics Canada.* https://www150.
statcan.gc.ca/n1/pub/11f0019m/11f0019m2019021-eng.htm

[99]   Government of Canada. (2019, November 27). *How Canada's refugee system works.* https://
www.canada.ca/en/immigration-refugees-citizenship/services/refugees/canada-role.html

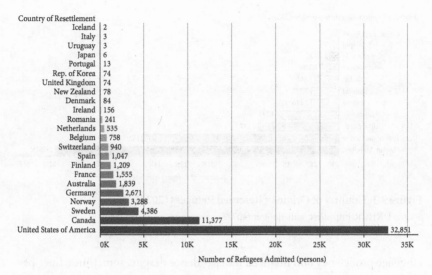

Figure 9.2 Countries of Resettlement (2021)
Source: UNHCR, https://rsq.unhcr.org/en/#H0Hp

top ten countries where asylum seekers resettled, and Figures 9.2 and 9.3 depict their countries of origin. Although there are projected to be 2 million refugees requiring resettlement in 2023, a miniscule fraction of the displaced, only 1% or less refugees will be resettled.[100] In small communities in far-flung locales such as Glasgow,[101] Brittany, and Istanbul, the sudden influx of refugees has overtaxed communities that were already previously under-resourced.

In their implementation, nations' resettlement strategies tend to be unilateral and focused on the asylum-seekers' rapid attainment of economic independence. Although some studies such as one in the Netherlands[102] report that "host-country-specific education, work experience, language proficiency and contacts with natives were positively related to the likelihood of obtaining employment and occupational status," the mutuality aspect of integration or the sharing of a relationship between two or more parties with a high degree of mutuality of respect for each other's expertise is not taken into account. Instead, refugees are legally obliged to rapidly[103] gain self-sufficiency in Western host nations through

[100] UNHCR. (2023). *Projected resettlement needs 2023.* https://www.unhcr.org/sites/default/files/2023-01/62b18e714.pdf
[101] Glasgow "second top in UK" for asylum seekers per head of population. (2016, June 1). *BBC.* http://www.bbc.co.uk/news/uk-scotland-glasgow-west-36429041
[102] De Vroome, T., & van Tubergen, F. (2010). The employment experience of refugees in the Netherlands. *International Migration Review, 44*(2), 376–403.
[103] Schick, M., Zumwald, A., Knöpfli, B., Nickerson, A., Bryant, R. A., Schnyder, U., Müller, J., & Morina, N. (2016). Challenging future, challenging past: The relationship of social integration

Resettled Refugees: Countries of Origin (2022)

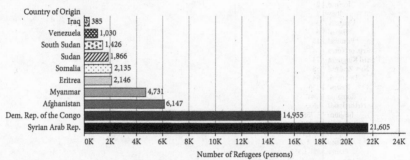

Number of Refugees (persons)

Figure 9.3 Country of Origin of Resettled Refugees (2022)
Source: UNHCR, https://rsq.unhcr.org/en/#p7Zj

language proficiency and financial independence despite, sometimes, their psychological impairments.

Case Study: United States Resettlement Program (USRAP)—Broken Integration and Its Effects on Mental Health

The US resettlement program focuses on immediate employment of the incoming refugee at the expense of identifying and alleviating mental health barriers among refugees whose past trauma experiences may obstruct their path to economic self-sufficiency. The United States resettlement program emphasizes speed more than efficiency[104] and presses refugees to find jobs "as fast as possible."[105] Refugees are provided food, housing, clothing, and support for employment guidance and language training[106] for the first 30 days of their arrival by resettlement agencies funded by the USRAP. The US resettlement policy is not

and psychological impairment in traumatized refugees. *European Journal of Psychotraumatology*, 7, 28057.

[104] "In providing assistance under this section, the Director shall, to the extent of available appropriations, (i) make available sufficient resources for employment training and placement in order to achieve economic self-sufficiency among refugees as quickly as possible." Immigration and Nationality Act, Pub. L. No. 89–236, 82nd Cong (1952) 66 Stat § 412 (a)(1)(A).

[105] Capps, R., Newland, K., Fratzke, S. Groves, S., Fix, M. McHugh, M., & Auclair, G. (2015). *The integration outcomes of U.S. refugees: Successes and challenges*. Migration Policy Institute. https://www.migrationpolicy.org/sites/default/files/publications/UsRefugeeOutcomes-FINALWEB.pdf

[106] Ibid.

unlike other nations like Japan, who select only those for resettlement who can be employed full-time within 6 months.[107]

Other barriers within the resettlement structure include inability to locate higher-skilled and better-paid employment commensurate with refugees' skills,[108] inability to articulate which types of employment might be feasible for various refugee communities and across genders, and absence of training or skill development programs. Health insurance coverage for refugees in the United States has also plummeted from 36 months to 8 months in the past 2 decades.[109]

Within its resettlement framework, not dissimilar from other nations', there is limited understanding in the United States of how increasing depressive symptom severity may also increase absenteeism among refugees,[110] and reciprocally, the effect of lack of work on mental health. Research from UK asylum-seekers indicates that those with long-lasting health problems report limited working hours and the type of employment they can undertake.[111] UK asylum-seekers, relative to natives and other migrants, are less likely to be in employment, have lower weekly earnings, earn less per hour, and work fewer hours than natives and those who migrated for work reasons.[112] Since work and productivity may be related more strongly to self-esteem in men than in women,[113] absenteeism from work may result in more severe symptoms of depression in refugee men. Despite the emphases on labor market integration, in general, refugees in the United States, as compared to native populations, can exhibit a slower pace of labor market integration,[114] remain reliant on public benefit programs, and sustain lower household incomes.[115]

---

[107] Phillimore, J., Morrice, L., Kabe, K., Hashimoto, N., Hassan, S., & Reyes, M. (2021). Economic self-reliance or social relations? What works in refugee integration? Learning from resettlement programmes in Japan and the UK. *Comparative Migration Studies, 9,* 17.

[108] US Government Accountability Office (GAO). (2012, July). *Refugee resettlement: Greater consultation with community stakeholders.* https://www.gao.gov/assets/600/592975.pdf

[109] US Department of Health and Human Services & Office of Refugee Resettlement. (2019, February 12). *Beyond the first eight months.* https://www.acf.hhs.gov/orr/programs/refugees/health

[110] Eßl-Maurer, R., Flamm, M., Hösl, K., Osterbrink, J., & van der Zee-Neuen, A. (2021). Absenteeism and associated labour costs according to depressive symptom severity in the German general population: Why preventive strategies matter. *International Archives of Occupational and Environmental Health, 95*(2), 409–418.

[111] The health of refugees in the UK. (2017, June 16). *ECONREF Research Note, 1,* 1–5. https://www.nuffieldfoundation.org/wp-content/uploads/2019/11/PB-2017-ECONREF-Health_Refugees_UK-1.pdf

[112] Ruiz, I., & Vargas-Silva, C. (2018). Differences in labour market outcomes between natives, refugees and other migrants in the UK. *Journal of Economic Geography, 18,* 855–885.

[113] Alvaro, J. L., Garrido, A., Pereira, C. R., Torres, A. R., & Barros, S. C. (2019). Unemployment, self-esteem, and depression: Differences between men and women. *Spanish Journal of Psychology, 22,* E1.

[114] Chambers, S. (2017). *Somalis in the twin cities and Columbus: Immigrant incorporation in new destinations.* Temple University Press.

[115] Data from 2009 to 2011.

The structure of USRAP, with its overemphasis on oversight through documentation, affects feelings of precariousness among caseworkers with respect to their jobs. It also affects case workers' ability to be critical resources for refugees[116] in helping refugees to achieve their benchmarks in the areas of integration (finding jobs to achieve self-sufficiency, gaining language proficiency, and other critical skills for navigating society). Further, the decentralized nature of the US resettlement system and refugees' placement across different states or local communities can also affect refugees' access to public services, the content and mode of delivery of services received,[117] and the level of public assistance they receive.[118,119] The limited assistance refugees receive in the United States, say scholars, does the reverse to self-sufficiency, it hinders their socioeconomic integration and financial independence.[120] Emerging scholarship by migration scholars is also revealing that outsourcing integration-related tasks to private organizations rather than public ones increased barriers to integration.[121]

USRAP lacks a systematic, consistent, and reliable[122] means of evaluating or routine tracking of the incidence and prevalence of disease of its various refugee populations. Researchers have suggested that the low utilization of health services by refugees[123] indicates communication challenges with their health providers (and not missed appointments) that in turn, can have implications for inadequacies of health education/health promotion.

[116] Fee, M. (2019). Paper integration: The structural constraints and consequences of the US refugee resettlement program. *Migration Studies*, 7(4), 477–495.

[117] US Department of Health and Human Services & Office of Planning, Research and Evaluation. (n.d.). *Understanding the intersection between temporary assistance for needy families (TANF) and refugee cash assistance service*. https://www.acf.hhs.gov/opre/project/understanding-intersection-between-tanf-and-refugee-cash-assistance-services-2014-2018

[118] Brick, K., Cushing-Savvi, A., Elshafie, S., Krill, A., McGlynn Scanlon, M., & Stone, M. (2010). *Refugee resettlement in the United States: An examination of challenges and proposed solutions* (p. 12–13). Columbia University School of International and Public Affairs.

[119] Fix, M., Hooper, K., & Zong, J. (2017). *How are refugees faring? Integration at U.S. and state levels*. Migration Policy Institute.

[120] Tran, V. C., & Lara-García, F. (2020). A new beginning: Early refugee integration in the United States. *RSF: The Russell Sage Foundation Journal of the Social Sciences*, 6(3), 117–149.

[121] Feinstein, S., Poleacovschi, C., Drake, R., & Winters, L. A. (2022). States and refugee integration: A comparative analysis of France, Germany, and Switzerland. *International Migration and Integration*, 23, 2167–2194.

[122] Weinstein, H. M., Sarnoff, R. H., Gladstone, E., & Lipson, J. G. (2000). Physical and psychological health issues of resettled refugees in the United States. *Journal of Refugee Studies*, 13(3), 303–327.

[123] Ibid.

Integration Dimensions: Challenges of Some Refugee Communities

Integration is generally conceived as refugees' participation in multiple domains such as economic, cultural, social, legal, health, and political, and others. *Economic integration* refers to participating in the economy through employment or cultivating skills that are valuable in market interactions, such as education or skill development. *Cultural integration* pertains to learning of the language, host nations' cultural habits, and values and beliefs. *Social integration* refers to forging of social bonds with people who share a sense of identity, connections or social bridges with people with different backgrounds, and links to institutions.[124] Social integration for the Somalis of Minnesota can be considered through the lens of discriminatory experiences based on race and religion[125] that result in extremely low wages. Poor social integration can also be ascertained when financial support is sent to the birth country, suggesting weaker ties to the host country. *Legal integration* involves navigating the legal system to acquire knowledge and finesse with different visas and their implications. *Political integration* refers to participation and interest in voting and public decision-making in the host communities and country. Recent research demonstrates the significant role of high ethnic composition and neighborhood or residential context on the likelihood of minorities' political representation.[126]

Language is considered to be "embodied cultural capital,"[127] and *language integration* refers to competence in the host country's official language. For instance, when English language proficiency is lower among the Burmese, it has been seen as a contributing factor in their poorer socioeconomic integration, with a third living below the US poverty line. Recent research on Syrian refugees in Canada shows how gender can affect language integration, with unavailability of affordable childcare and long waitlists hampering women's participation in language-learning classes.[128]

[124] Lindgren, K., Nicholson, M., & Oskarsson, S. (2022). Immigrant political representation and local ethnic concentration: Evidence from a Swedish refugee placement program. *British Journal of Political Science*, 52(3), 997–1012.

[125] Chambers, S. (2017). *Somalis in the twin cities and Columbus: Immigrant incorporation in new destinations*. Temple University Press.

[126] Lindgren, K., Nicholson, M., & Oskarsson, S. (2022). Immigrant political representation and local ethnic concentration: Evidence from a Swedish refugee placement program. *British Journal of Political Science*, 52(3), 997–1012.

[127] Abdelhady, D., & Al Ariss, A. (2022). How capital shapes refugees' access to the labour market: The case of Syrians in Sweden. *International Journal of Human Resource Management*. https://doi.org/10.1080/09585192.2022.2110845

[128] Ives, N., Oda, A., Bridekirk, J., Hynie, M., McGrath, S., Mohammad, R., Awwad, R., Sherrell, Mahi Khalaf, M., & Diaz, M. (2022). Syrian refugees participation in language classes: Motivators and barriers. *Refuge: Canada's Journal on Refugees*, 38(2), 1–19.

Health integration can be assessed in the context of the Bhutanese community, which sustains high rates of suicide.[129] Iraqi refugee children in Detroit, Michigan, struggle with *educational integration* as they suffer gaps in their educational history.[130]

The multiple domains through which integration into host societies is achieved also illustrates the interdependence of the domains. Exclusion in the area of education perceived by refugees in Michigan also illustrates how strong communal solidarity within refugee communities can also create obstacles to successful integration. The segregation or partial segregation of school-going children in Norway, Denmark, and Sweden demonstrates that 70% or so of immigrant/refugee pupils cluster in schools within refugee neighborhoods, making it challenging for them to learn the local language.[131] At the same time, limitations in local language proficiency also poses obstacles in other meaningful life tasks for refugees, such as developing social networks, sustaining employment, and educational goals.[132,133]

Nonrecognition of Integration Gaps

Many resettlement programs, including those in Sweden, the United Kingdom, and the United States, have been criticized for their myopic vision, as reflected in sparse and basic economic support to refugees. Financial support for refugees remains sparse; concentrated in the first 28[134] to 30[135] days or 12 months after their arrival,[136] the period of eligibility of cash and medical assistance can remain

[129] The Bhutanese have high suicide rates in refugee camps even prior to arrival in the United States: Meyerhoff, J., Rohan, K. J., & Fondacaro, K. M. (2018). Suicide and suicide-related behavior among Bhutanese refugees resettled in the United States. *Asian American Journal of Psychology, 9*(4), 270–283.

[130] Bang, H., & Collet, B. A. (2018). Educational gaps and their impact on Iraqi refugee students' secondary schooling in the greater Detroit, Michigan Area. *Research in Comparative and International Education, 13*(2), 299–318.

[131] Learning the hard way: Educating refugees. (2016, January 2). *The Economist.* https://www.economist.com/europe/2016/01/02/learning-the-hard-way

[132] Morrice, L., Tip, L. K., Collyer, M., & Brown, R. (2021). You can't have a good integration when you don't have a good communication: English-language learning among resettled refugees in England. *Journal of Refugee Studies, 34*(1), 681–699.

[133] Ives, N., Oda, A., Bridekirk, J., Hynie, M., McGrath, S., Mohammad, R., Awwad, M., Sherrell, K., Khalaf, M., & Diaz, M. (2022). Syrian refugees participation in language classes: Motivators and barriers. *Refuge: Canada's Journal on Refugees, 38*(2), 1–19. https://doi.org/10.25071/1920-7336.40799

[134] After you get refugee status. (n.d.). Citizens Advice. Retrieved on May 6, 2023, from https://www.citizensadvice.org.uk/immigration/asylum-and-refugees/after-you-get-refugee-status/

[135] Swedish Migration Agency. (n.d.). *Financial support for asylum seekers.* Retrieved on May 6, 2023, from https://www.migrationsverket.se/English/Private-individuals/Protection-and-asylum-in-Sweden/While-you-are-waiting-for-a-decision/Financial-support.html

[136] US Department of State. (2011, October 17). *Refugee admissions, reception and placement program* [Fact sheet]. https://2009-2017.state.gov/j/prm/releases/factsheets/2011/181029.htm

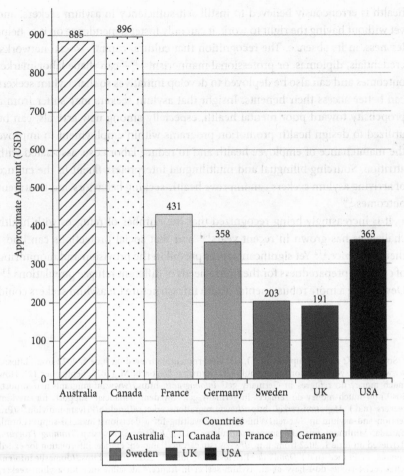

Figure 9.4 Approximate Amount of Cash Assistance Provided to Refugees Upon Arrival (2022)

static for decades despite inflation,[137] offering them only meagre means of support (Figure 9.4).[138] This inadequate system of support in accessing basic public

[137] The Refugee Act of 1980, 8 U.S.C. 1522(e)(1) provided refugees with cash and medical assistance for their first 36 months after arrival, although the eligibility period dropped to 8 months in 1992 until recently, when it was extended to 12 months: Extending refugee cash assistance and refugee medical assistance from 8 months to 12 months, 87 C.F.R. § 59 (2022, pp. 17312–17313), Doc. No. ORR. 87 FR 17312. https://www.federalregister.gov/documents/2022/03/28/2022-06356/extending-refugee-cash-assistance-and-refugee-medical-assistance-from-8-months-to-12-months

[138] UK: =40.85(weekly cash support)* 4(weeks a month)* 1.1683(exchange rate)
Sweden: =71(daily cash support)*30(days a month)*0.095342(exchange rate)
France: =14.2(daily cash support)*30(days a month)*1.0122(exchange rate)
Australia: =642.7(every two weeks)*2(2 payments a month)*0.6888(exchange rate)

health is erroneously believed to instill self-sufficiency in asylum seekers, and yet without having the right to work, it can only foster dependence on it or help-lessness, in its absence. The recognition that cultural capital—social networks, credentials, diplomas, or professional mannerisms[139]—can shape labor-market outcomes and can also be deployed to develop initiatives so that asylum seekers can better access their benefits. Insight that asylum seekers may suffer from a propensity toward poor mental health, especially among new arrivals, can be utilized to design health-promotion programs within employment to improve the maintenance of employee health and to reduce labor costs associated with attrition. Sourcing bilingual and multilingual interpreters fluent in the culture of arriving asylum seekers can improve health-seeking behaviors and treatment outcomes.[140]

It is increasingly being recognized that the number of refugees with health challenges has grown in recent years[141] and that social protections can boost their resilience.[142] Yet significant lapses prevail in the provision and monitoring of care and preparedness for the future needs of different refugee populations.[143] Developing a more robust mental health infrastructure for asylum seekers could

Sources: UK: Asylum support (n.d.). UK Government. Retrieved on June 1, 2022 from, https://www.gov.uk/asylum-support/what-youll-get; Germany: Bierbach, M. (2017, September 12). How much money do refugees in Germany get? Infomigrants. https://www.infomigrants.net/en/post/5049/how-much-money-do-refugees-in-germany-get; Sweden: Financial support for asylum seekers (n.d.) Migrationsverket. https://www.migrationsverket.se/English/Private-individuals/Protection-and-asylum-in-Sweden/While-you-are-waiting-for-a-decision/Financial-support.html; Canada: Minimum financial support calculator (n.d.). Refugee Sponsorship Training Program. Retrieved on June 1, 2022 from, https://www.rstp.ca/calc/?lang=en; France: Information for exiled persons in France (n.d.) Dom'Asile. Retrieved on June 1, 2022 from, https://domasile.info/en/what-social-rights-do-i-have-as-an-asylum-seeker-in-france/#ada-allowance-for-asylum-seeker; USA: Refugee cash assistance (n.d.). Washington State Department of Social and Health Services. Retrieved on June 1, 2022 from, https://www.dshs.wa.gov/esa/community-services-offices/refugee-cash-assistance; Australia: How much you can get (n.d.). Services Australia. Retrieved on June 1, 2022 from, https://www.servicesaustralia.gov.au/how-much-jobseeker-payment-you-can-get?context=51411

[139] Bourdieu, P. (1986). Forms of capital. In J. G. Richardson (Eds.), Handbook of theory and research for the sociology of capital (pp. 241–258). Greenwood Press.
[140] Olani, A. B., Olani, A. B., Muleta, T. B., Rikitu, D. H., & Disassa, K. G. (2023) Impacts of language barriers on healthcare access and quality among Afaan Oromoo-speaking patients in Addis Ababa, Ethiopia. BMC Health Services Research, 23, 39.
[141] US GAO. (2011, March). Refugee assistance: Little is known about the effectiveness of different approaches for improving refugees' employment outcomes [Report to congressional committees]. https://www.gao.gov/assets/gao-11-369.pdf
[142] Malik, S. (2022, October, 27). Social protection and humanitarian systems must work together to boost resilience and meet the needs of the forcibly displaced. UNHCR. https://www.unhcr.org/blogs/social-protection-and-humanitarian-systems-must-work-together-to-boost-resilience-and-meet-the-needs-of-the-forcibly-displaced/
[143] Unaccompanied children: HHS can improve monitoring of their care, 115th Cong. (2016) (testimony of Kay E. Brown). https://www.gao.gov/assets/gao-16-429t.pdf

involve a tailored[144] and segmented approach that takes into account their professional qualifications, formal education, physical limitations, mental-health status, and so forth to create relevant integration programs.

Although studies document how postmigration stressors can affect mental health and hinder refugees' socioeconomic integration,[145] few nations invest in investigating how mental health shortfalls may impact integration gaps. The inability of national programs to tailor support for refugees in relevant and effective ways may result in the persistence of significant gaps in refugees' integration relative to native-born populations.[146] Let us dive a bit deeper into some international refugee communities to understand how poor mental health may obstruct integration.

Case Studies of the UK and Switzerland: Social and Cultural Integration and Mental Health

Social integration is the process during which newcomers or minorities blend into the social structure of the host society. A study of the elderly Alevi Kurdish refugees from Turkey living in the UK, aged 55–98, documents how poor mental health may prime refugees for not venturing out to create social linkages outside of their community; at the same time, a poor quality of social ties may also enhance the perception of alienation and isolation.

In another study, the Kurdish Alevis of London had four to eight children, many of them born in the UK after their parents' arrival almost 2 decades prior. But despite their large families born in the UK and long residence in the UK, they mostly survived on either minimum levels of pension credits or disability allowance with an average income of approximately £100 per week. Their social engagement was within their ethnic enclaves and community centers. Their daily routine centered around watching cable television, chatting in their native language, and eating familiar native foods. An overwhelming 97% of them did not engage in social outreach to the wider society in the form of volunteering in both formal or informal ways, nor did they pursue outside hobbies. They lived in high poverty and demonstrated poor health, low levels of education, and high

[144] *What are the integration challenges of Ukrainian refugee women* (2023, May 30). OECD. https://www.oecd.org/ukraine-hub/policy-responses/what-are-the-integration-challenges-of-ukrainian-refugee-women-bb17dc64/
[145] Bakker, L., Dagevos, J., & Engbersen, G. (2014). The importance of resources and security in the socio-economic integration of refugees: A study on the impact of length of stay in asylum accommodation and residence status on socio-economic integration for the four largest refugee groups in the Netherlands. *International Migration and Integration, 15*, 431–448.
[146] Report uses 2010–2017 data from the UK labour force survey (LFS).

isolation, and generally, exhibited poor mental health, despite living in London for over 2 decades.[147]

The majority of the Alevi Kurds lacked proficiency in the English language, with approximately 74% being illiterate with no formal education from either Turkey or the UK, and almost none of them knew how to use a computer. Approximately 80% of the participants reported having at least two chronic illnesses, which included depression, diabetes, hypertension, high cholesterol, heart disease, and rheumatic and joint disease.

Using the host language,[148] especially among older refugees, positively influences health, well-being, empowerment, and social inclusion. Instead, language barriers can lead to additional[149,150,151] challenges for refugees in host societies, including poor health education and lower quality of care with prolonged stay in hospitals when sick. Lack of language proficiency makes it more challenging to use social and health services,[152] and instead forces refugees to rely on other community members. In the same vein, in the United States, it is notable that "even after two decades, the majority of this community (Cambodians) speak little or no English, are at income levels below poverty, and rely on public assistance."[153] Of those surveyed, 69% had household incomes of less than 100% of the federal poverty level, and 72% currently received government assistance.

Cultural integration can be defined as one's transnational ties, subscribing to cultural beliefs, preservation of cultural values, and a sense of solidarity with one's ethnic identity. Alevi Kurds participants aged older than 60 years who believed they were either too old to be physically and socially active or that seeking mental health treatment would result in a loss of their reputation also evidenced poor integration. The burden of isolation cumulatively experienced by the older first-generation Alevi Kurds contributed to their lack of integration.

The socioeconomic and cultural fragility of the Alevi Kurds, despite their living in a major economic center of the world, highlights how a minority group's

[147] Oglak, S., & Hussein, S. (2016). Active aging: Social and cultural integration of older Turkish Alevi refugees in London. *Journal of Muslim Minority Affairs, 36*(1), 74–87.

[148]. Enneli, P., Modood, T., & Bradley, H. (2005). *Young Turks and Kurds: A set of 'invisible' disadvantaged groups.* Joseph Rowntree Foundation. http://www.tariqmodood.com/uploads/1/2/3/9/12392325/young_turks.pdf

[149] Divi, C., Koss, R. G., Schmaltz, S. P., & Loeb, J. M. (2007). Language proficiency and adverse events in US hospitals: A pilot study. *International Journal for Quality in Health Care, 19*(2), 60–67.

[150] Lindholm, M., Hargraves, J. L., Ferguson, W. J., & Reed, G. (2012). Professional language interpretation and inpatient length of stay and readmission rates. *Journal of General Internal Medicine, 27*(10), 1294–1299.

[151] Ribera, J. M., Hausmann-Muela, S., Grietens, K. P., & Toomer, E. (2008, March). *Is the use of interpreters in medical consultations justified? A critical review of the literature* [Report]. PASS-International. https://doi.org/10.1016/j.amjmed.2019.12.008

[152] Cummings, S., Sull, L., Davis, C., & Worley, N. (2011). Correlates of depression among older Kurdish refugees. *Social Work, 56*(2), 159–168.

[153] Marshall, G. N., Schell, T. L., Elliott, M. N., Berthold, S. M., & Chun, C. (2005). Mental health of Cambodian refugees 2 decades after resettlement in the United States. *JAMA, 294*(5), 571–579.

exclusive reliance on ethnic enclaves may facilitate, maintain, and mask mental health problems and can also disadvantage multicultural societies. When a displaced and persecuted refugee group faces prejudice, they may perceive investment in relationships with the host community as a continuing liability and, thus, they may choose to establish trust along ethnic lines rather than with host communities. At the same time, the lack of close ties with the host community, as is the case of Bosnian war refugees in Amsterdam, can create shaky beginnings by solidifying a sense of insecurity regarding refugees' legal status.[154] The Alevi Kurds' early settlement into their community, Oglak and Hussein emphasize, may have isolated them from the wider society, leading to more significant stresses both individually and for the community, as they aged.

Generally, when refugee efforts at establishing connections are unsuccessful, a sense of detachment with the refugees may result, with refugees giving up on trying to forge relationships of trust outside of their ethnic group. In a study of refugees of the Bosnian war newly settled in Amsterdam and Rome, a researcher describes the early efforts of a 51-year-old, unemployed, Bosnian[155] man who tried to make new friends in Amsterdam:

> I did try in my neighbourhood to break the ice and make friendships. The first Christmas after I moved in, in 1994, I dropped a card to all my new neighbours. They seemed to like it, because I got cards from them next year, for Christmas. By the third year, they learned that I was a Muslim, and sent me cards for the New Year. They are nice people, I can't say that they are not, but our contacts don't go much further than that.

Social integration across eleven domains in 104 refugees seeking treatment with high exposures of torture who had been resettled in Switzerland for over 10 years documented serious challenges. However, almost 88% of the sample enjoyed a secure visa status and higher education[156] as they adapted to their new life in Swiss society. Most of them experienced trouble gaining employment, with only 22% having part-time or full-time employment; they also experienced challenges in paying for food, clothes, rent, or appropriate housing; they felt isolated, bored, and lonely, and perceived discrimination. The Swiss refugees had worries about receiving specialized health care and waited almost 8 years on average before receiving treatment; in this we see how poor mental health can be a barrier to

---

[154] Korac, M. (2003). Integration and how we facilitate it: A comparative study of the settlement experiences of refugees in Italy and the Netherlands. *Sociology*, 37(1), 51–68.

[155] Korac, M. (2003). Integration and how we facilitate it: A comparative study of the settlement experiences of refugees in Italy and the Netherlands. *Sociology*, 37(1), 57.

[156] Schick, M., Zumwald, A., Knöpfli, B., Nickerson, A., Bryant, R. A., Schnyder, U., Müller, J., & Morina, N. (2016). Challenging future, challenging past: The relationship of social integration and psychological impairment in traumatized refugees. *European Journal of Psychotraumatology*, 7, 1.

gaining essential skills for adaptation in their new society. This study shows how refugees' poor mental health can undermine the effectiveness of public resources available to them.

Both cases of the refugees in Switzerland and Britain elucidate that a delay in mental health treatment for this vulnerable community and, thus, an absence of tailor-made social interventions to combat poor mental health proactively and preemptively may also have a role in maintaining insular communities.

When social integration is low, mental health challenges may be unrecognized or misattributed to refugees' lack of interest in abiding by the host nation's values. In Turkey, for example, a study found that refugees' lack of interaction with their hosts reinforced their mistaken conviction that Syrians cannot conform to Turkish social norms: 63% of Turkish[157]reported that they felt "far" or "very far" from Syrians, while 72% of Syrians felt "close" or "very close" to Turkish society. In countries like Turkey this has resulted in an empathy gap between host and guests and inter-ethnic rivalries and urban violence. The chronic ennui in the Turkish Alevi and refugees of trauma from Switzerland, both long resettled, is often the result of brief, sporadic one-way interventions at many levels of the host community rather than mutual and collaborative engagements.

Successful Integration

Despite the refugee disadvantage, in many nations such as Canada, refugees narrow their earnings gap with other immigrant communities,[158,159] sometimes achieving a rate of increase even higher than that of all immigrant groups.[160] In the United States, in contrast, recent refugees generally take longer to become economically self-sufficient, are concentrated in low-wage sectors, and take longer to develop a sense of belonging in their new communities.[161] Only a fraction pursue schooling.[162]

[157] Erdogan, M. M. (2017, June 6). *Syrian barometer: A framework for achieving social coherence with Syrians.* https://mmuraterdogan.files.wordpress.com/2016/06/syrians-barometer-executive-summary.pdf

[158] Bevelander, P., & Luik, M. (2020). Refugee employment integration heterogeneity in Sweden: Evidence from a cohort analysis. *Frontiers in Sociology, 5,* 44.

[159] De Vroome, T., & van Tubergen, F. (2010). The employment experience of refugees in the Netherlands. *International Migration Review, 44,* 376–403.

[160] Abbot, M. G., & Beach, C. M. (2011). *Do admission criteria and economic recessions affect immigrant earnings?* (Study No. 22). Institute for Research on Public Policy.

[161] Fix, M., Hooper, K., & Zong, J. (2017). *How are refugees faring? Integration at U.S. and state levels.* Migration Policy Institute.

[162] Tran, V., & Lara-Garcia, F. (2020). A new beginning: Early refugee integration in the United States. RSF: The Russell Sage Foundation Journal of the Social Sciences, 6(3), 117–149.

Recent waves of refugees in Germany, compared to refugees in America and arrivals of prior years, some data suggest, have integrated better socioeconomically and socially. Approximately 43% found their first job accessing personal networks[163] within the host community, including friends, family, and acquaintances, and acquired the German language more proficiently; those who completed integration programs found employment within approximately 1.5–2 years.

Expanding our lens of mental health to assess its interplay in integration domains (i.e., language education, social, educational, cultural, health, and housing) can assist in crafting sustainable and tailored support for the many refugee communities in our midst. If nations' integration efforts fail to be tailored to a specific group's struggles, or fail to plan for their children's challenges, a nation's future second generation, it can have economic, social, and political consequences. The social and cultural dynamics of diverse groups and their behavioral norms can further shape the provision of public goods and fiscal transfers, and thus, market outcomes.[164] The efficacious and timely treatment of mental health conditions could enhance the successful integration of traumatized refugees in the host society.[165] Conceptualizing integration and its challenges in refugees' voices and needs[166] through its effect on their mental health can provide a valuable framework to view integration challenges for a particular refugee group.

Positive mental health, motivation, and resilience of the displaced can be significant factors in overcoming integration barriers and driving the development of host nations. Integration in the form of—national laws, local and international support, and frameworks—can offer the displaced opportunities to harness their human capacity and skills for immediate and long-term benefits.

We may believe that more than policy itself, "the main engine for their successful integration . . . [is] committed and active persons with intercultural sensitivity, ready to innovate, experiment, build bridges of understanding and

[163] Brücker, H., Croisier, J., Kosyakova, Y., Kröger, H., Pietrantuono, G., Rother, N., & Schupp, J. (2019, March). *Second wave of the IAB-BAMF-SOEP survey: Refugees are making progress in language and employment*. Institute for Employment Research.

[164] Algan, Y., Bisin, A., & Verdier, T. Introduction: Perspectives on cultural integration of immigrants. In Y. Algan, A. Bisin, A. Manning, & T. Verdier (Eds.), *Cultural integration of immigrants in Europe* (pp. 1–48). Oxford University Press.

[165] Schick, M., Zumwald, A., Knöpfli, B., Nickerson, A., Bryant, R. A., Schnyder, U., Müller, J., & Morina, N. (2016). Challenging future, challenging past: The relationship of social integration and psychological impairment in traumatized refugees. *European Journal of Psychotraumatology, 7*, 1.

[166] Brown, A., & Scribner, T. (2014). Unfulfilled promises, future possibilities: The refugee resettlement System in the United States. *Journal on Migration and Human Security, 2*(2), 101–120.

intercultural dialog."[167] But Karam's challenges with his mental health introduced at the start of the chapter and how hopelessness impacted his employment, income, socioeconomic mobility, and the global economy shows the value of early intervention for positive mental health.

To harness refugee resilience at the individual and community levels, as a society we need to go beyond. It is imperative that host nations embark on mental health assessments that are systematic, segmented, tailored, comprehensive, long-term, and not simply limited to initial and cursory mental health screenings of asylum-seekers. For many Western nations, health screenings take place only at ports of entry or at the time of refugees' initial placement. They are not consistent or in-depth enough to track the mental health and health parameters of a refugee population over time. When refugees are grouped with "foreign-born" populations or in larger groups by ethnicity, they are seen as having a "common identity." If their refugee status is unknown, monitoring and tracking of refugees' challenges is nearly impossible. Policymakers, researchers, and clinicians must collaborate to improve the availability of health data as well as the health status of refugees by providing tailored, multimodal, and psychosocial interventions for better management of refugees' traumatic stress. Host nations ought to also tailor their preexisting policies created with different demographic profiles to adjust to the specific profile of their incoming asylum seekers.

Refugee women, compared to men, face far more acute obstacles to their socio-economic integration. By translating refugee experiences into facilitative policies, integration practices, and institutional processes can leverage the power of refugee inclusion and refugee-centered integration. Ways of enhancing refugees' social and cultural capital can include a variety of ways such as: improved access to tuition-free education, vocational training, apprenticeship opportunities, recognition of their prior qualifications, access to multilingual and multicultural case-workers, access to child-care, provision of micro-credits, technical assistance to refugee entrepreneurs, mental health support, and matching refugee skills with local jobs.

Many countries, such as Turkey, Iraq, Lebanon, Japan, and others, conflate the availability of low-skilled labor with the resettlement of refugees, thus undermining refugee rights and the purpose of resettlement programs. Public relations education[168] on refugee rights, including that to counter misinformation, can engender greater reciprocity between resettlement agencies and stakeholders. "In many countries displaced communities' access to labor markets is limited to the informal

---

[167] Brown, E. L., & Krasteva, A. (2013). *Migrants and refugees: Equitable education for displaced populations* (p. 4). Information Age.

[168] Brown, A., & Scribner, T. (2014). Unfulfilled promises, future possibilities: The refugee resettlement system in the United States. *Journal on Migration and Human Security, 2*(2), 101–120.

market,"[169] and the displaced comprise a majority of its shadow workers. Governments should conduct more frequent inspections of unregistered workplaces so that refugees are not trapped as shadow workers in informal economies.

More innovative initiatives in emergency humanitarian contexts utilizing the support of the public, private corporations, civil society, faith-based organizations, and the forcibly displaced themselves are urgent today to galvanize necessary reforms that will improve the lives of the forcibly displaced.

A transformation in the way we implement integration can only begin with whether we think of the mental health of society's marginalized, and that will be our first step.

---

[169] Shaifali, S. (2020, May 19). COVID-19 crisis: Why we must prioritise mental health of the world's displaced. *OECD Development Matters*. https://oecd-development-matters.org/2020/05/19/covid-19-crisis-why-we-must-prioritise-mental-health-of-the-worlds-displaced/; Clemens, M. Huang, C., & Graham, J. (2018, October). *The economic and fiscal effects of granting refugees formal labor market access* (Working Paper 496). Center for Global Development. https://www.cgdev.org/sites/default/files/economic-and-fiscal-effects-granting-refugees-formal-labor-market-access.pdf

10
Best Practices in Treating Trauma and Refugee Care

The Ecology of Trauma-Informed and Cultural Health Interventions

The Rape of Rumi

Rumi, a 15-year-old Yazidi girl from Iraq's religious minority and a family of shepherds, was granted refugee status in Canada 2 years ago. At an outpatient psychiatric clinic recently, Rumi recounts her crippling symptoms: insomnia, fainting spells, and recurrent flashbacks where she re-experiences being savagely raped over and over and over again. The flashbacks occur during the day and envelope her at night. They have intensified since her resettlement.

Rumi was taken hostage by ISIS on August 31, 2014, when she was 8 years old, and kidnapped from her hometown in Sinjar, Iraq. Sixteen other male family members were burned alive in the fields. During the ISIS siege of Sinjar, an estimated 3,100 Yazidis were killed, and 6,800 captured.[1] Nearly half of the executed were either shot, beheaded, or burned alive, while the rest died from starvation or dehydration. But 2,893 remain missing,[2] and because of the close structure of their community and the shame around sexual assault, no one really knows how many young men and women have, in reality, been raped.

Shortly after her kidnapping, Rumi was transported to the city of Palmyra, Syria, where she was caged along with hundreds of other little girls waiting to be sold as slaves. Rumi has been sold from one man to another 16 times, enslaved by various Islamic State officials, traded, caged, whipped, and raped hundreds of times, often multiple times during the course of day or night. Over the years, she has witnessed many other young, enslaved Yazidi girls commit suicide by slashing their wrists or pouring gasoline over themselves. When she was 12 years old, Rumi

---

[1] Cetorelli, V., Sasson, I., Shabila, N., & Burnham, G. (2017). Mortality and kidnapping estimates for the Yazidi population in the area of Mount Sinjar, Iraq, in August 2014: A retrospective household survey. *PLOS Medicine, 14*(5), E1002297.

[2] UN Iraq Office of the Special Representative of the Secretary-General. (2020). *Sexual violence in conflict.* https://www.un.org/sexualviolenceinconflict/wp-content/uploads/2020/07/report/conflict-related-sexual-violence-report-of-the-united-nations-secretary-general/2019-SG-Report.pdf.

Displaced. Shaifali Sandhya, Oxford University Press. © Shaifali Sandhya 2024.
DOI: 10.1093/oso/9780197579886.003.0010

became pregnant by one of her abusers. On a visit to procure an abortion in town, Rumi was able to escape her abuser and found her way to a refugee camp. Although she had wanted to keep her baby since it belonged to a non-Yazidi man, she had to eventually give up her baby to be accepted into her community.

The Triple Trauma of the Silent Majority

In the morass of mass displacement, contemporary refugees can experience catastrophic violence that is prolonged and repetitive. Posttraumatic stress in postconflict communities presents a high and routine burden, although not every refugee may be traumatized. Among the war-affected, large-scale studies estimate those affected by posttraumatic stress to be in the range of 15%[3] to 30.6%;[4,5,6] although this is considered by some researchers[7] to be an underestimate, as for many internally displaced populations, prevalence data on mental health disorders are largely unavailable.[8] Nevertheless, refugee trauma outpaces its occurrence in the general population of the United States[9] (6% at some point in their lives) and in many nonrefugee populations,[10] by a wide margin.

[3] Priebe, S., Giacco, D., & El-Nagib, R. (2016). *Public health aspects of mental health among migrants and refugees: A review of the evidence on mental health care for refugees, asylum seekers and irregular migrants in the WHO European region.* WHO Regional Office for Europe. https://apps.who.int/iris/bitstream/handle/10665/326308/9789289051651-eng.pdf?sequence=3&isAllowed=y

[4] Steel, Z., Chey, T., Silove, D., Marnane, C., Bryant, R. A., & van Ommeren, M.(2009). Association of torture and other potentially traumatic events with mental health outcomes among populations exposed to mass conflict and displacement. *JAMA, 302*(5), 537–549.

[5] Hoell, A., Kourmpeli, E., Salize, H. J., Heinz, A., Padberg, F., Habel, U., Kamp-Becker, I., Höhne, E., Böge, K., & Bajbouj, M. (2021). Prevalence of depressive symptoms and symptoms of posttraumatic stress disorder among newly arrived refugees and asylum seekers in Germany: Systematic review and meta-analysis. *BJPsych Open, 7*(3), E93.

[6] It is estimated that approximately one in five persons in postconflict settings suffers from depression, anxiety, bipolar disorder, or schizophrenia: Charlson, F., van Ommeren, M., Flaxman, A., Cornett, J., Whiteford, H., & Saxena, S. (2019). New WHO prevalence estimates of mental disorders in conflict settings: A systematic review and meta-analysis. *Lancet, 394*(10194), 240–248.

[7] Kinzie, J. D. (2016). Medical approach to the management of traumatized refugees. *Journal of Psychiatric Practice, 22*(2), 76–83.

[8] Gammouh, O. S., Al-Smadi, A. M., Tawalbeh, L. I., & Khoury, L. S. (2015). Chronic diseases, lack of medications, and depression among Syrian Refugees in Jordan, 2013–2014. *Preventing Chronic Disease, 12*, E10.

[9] How common is PTSD in adults? (n.d.). *National Center for PTSD. US Department of Veterans Affairs.* Retrieved on January 12, 2023, from https://www.ptsd.va.gov/understand/common/common_adults.asp

[10] Karam, E. G., Friedman, M. J., Hill, E. D., Kessler, R. C., McLaughlin, K. A., Petukhova, M., Sampson, L., Shahly, V., Angermeyer, M.C., Bromet, E. J., de Girolamo, G., de Graaf, R., Demyttenaere, K., Ferry, F., Florescu, S. E., Haro, J. M., He, Y., Karam, A. N., Kawakami, N., Kovess-Masfety, V., Medina-Mora, M. E., Browne, M. A., Posada-Villa, J. A., Shalev, A. Y., Stein, D. J., Viana, M. C., & Zarkov, Z.,(2014). Cumulative traumas and risk thresholds: 12-month PTSD in the World Mental Health (WMH) surveys. *Depression and Anxiety, 31*(2), 130–142.

In this chapter, using an ecological and multidisciplinary lens, we examine important considerations in treating traumatized refugees. The chapter discusses two axes, often at odds—culture-based and evidence-based research—to design clinically relevant, culturally sensitive, and sustainable interventions for refugees. It discusses five levels, or settings, in which to increase culturally competent clinical work that will promote refugees' healthy integration into host societies. It progresses to discuss ways in which evidence-based practice can incorporate cultural factors and ethnographic considerations. The attention to cultural factors and evidence-based care is critical, and it can play out along a continuum across the cross-sectoral and diverse domains of interventions—psychopharmacologic, psychotherapeutic, social-environmental, trauma-informed community, and somatic—in refugee care.

The refugee's distinctive conditions pose a triple trauma paradigm—the condition of trauma and stressors at pre- and postmigratory asylum-seeking stages—according to Ron Baker, a researcher with the European Consultation on Refugees and Exiles. For refugees like Badam (discussed a little later in this chapter), the symptoms of blast-related head trauma can be mistaken for posttraumatic stress; at the same time, treatment needs to focus on the mutually exacerbating conditions of traumatic brain injury (TBI) and posttraumatic stress,[11] where cognitive impairment can worsen posttraumatic stress and vice versa.

Overwhelmingly from low-resource non-Western nations, refugees can present with myriad and complex physical, neurological,[12] and medical[13,14] injuries and concerns such as head trauma,[15] chronic pain,[16] infectious diseases, female-genital mutilation,[17] physical disabilities,[18] and illness syndromes. For

[11] King, N. S. (2008). PTSD and traumatic brain injury: Folklore and fact? *Brain Injury*, 22(1), 1–5.

[12] Weisleder, P., & Rublee, C. (2018). The neuropsychological consequences of armed conflicts and torture. *Current Neurology and Neuroscience Reports*, 18(3), 9.

[13] Doocy, S., Sirois, A., Tileva, M., Storey, J. D., & Burnham, G. (2013). Chronic disease and disability among Iraqi populations displaced in Jordan and Syria. *International Journal of Health Planning and Management*, 28(1), E1–E12.

[14] Yanni, E. A., Naoum, M., Odeh, N., Han, P., Coleman, M., & Burke, H. (2013). The health profile and chronic diseases comorbidities of US-bound Iraqi refugees screened by the International Organization for Migration in Jordan: 2007–2009. *Journal of Immigrant and Minority Health*, 15(1), 1–9.

[15] McMurry, H. S., Tsang, D. C., Lin, N., Symes, S. N., & Dong, C. (2020). Head injury and neuropsychiatric sequelae in asylum seekers. *Neurology*, 95(19), E2605–E260910.

[16] Rometsch-Ogioun El Sount, C., Windthorst, P., & Denkinger, J., Ziser, K., Nikendei, C., Kindermann, D., Ringwald, J., Renner, V., Zipfel, S., & Junne, F. (2019). Chronic pain in refugees with posttraumatic stress disorder (PTSD): A systematic review on patients' characteristics and specific interventions. *Journal of Psychosomatic Research*, 118, 83–97.

[17] Lever, H., Ottenheimer, D., Teysir, J., Singer, E., & Atkinson, H. G. (2019). Depression, anxiety, post-traumatic stress disorder and a history of pervasive gender-based violence among women asylum seekers who have undergone female genital mutilation/cutting: A retrospective case review. *Journal of Immigrant and Minority Health*, 21(3), 483–489.

[18] Buhmann, C., Nordentoft, M., Ekstroem, M., Carlsson, J., & Mortensen, E. (2016). The effect of flexible cognitive–behavioural therapy and medical treatment, including antidepressants

many refugees being caught in the maelstrom of camps and clinics means not having access to clinicians and, if they do gain access, electing to keep their traumas from their practitioners, as cultural norms may require deference to the doctor.[19]

In the landscape of conflict and postconflict settings, complex trauma presents itself in many forms of mental health responses at the individual, family, and community levels. These can range from substance abuse, psychosis,[20] lack of parent-child engagement, fatigue,[21] nightmares, trichotillomania,[22] enuresis,[23] depression, anxiety, sleep problems,[24] interpersonal violence,[25] or other protest responses, such as organized political movements of the traumatized community.[26] Whether they may find themselves in camps or poor or rich host nations, these injuries may go untreated for a variety of reasons. Not only is there a chronic shortage of mental health providers, but also practitioners may lack expert knowledge of trauma, like not knowing how or when to ask about torture history.[27] Most conflict-affected communities on most continents face challenges such as a wide gap between their afflicted who need care and those who receive it; absence of a rapid, phase-based, effective, coordinated care for the

on post-traumatic stress disorder and depression in traumatised refugees: Pragmatic randomised controlled clinical trial. *British Journal of Psychiatry*, 208(3), 252–259.

[19] Shannon, P., O'Dougherty, M., & Mehta, E. (2012). Refugees' perspectives on barriers to communication about trauma histories in primary care. *Mental Health in Family Medicine*, 9(1), 47–55.

[20] Hjern, A., Palacios, J., & Vinnerljung, B. (2021). Early childhood adversity and non-affective psychosis: A study of refugees and international adoptees in Sweden. *Psychological Medicine*, 53(5), 1–10.

[21] Hassan, G., Kirmayer, L. J., Mekki-Berrada, A., Quosh, C., el Chammay, R., Deville-Stoetzel, J. B., Youssef, A., Jefee-Bahloul, H., Barkeel-Oteo, A., Coutts, A., Song, S., & Ventevogel, P. (2015). *Culture, context and the mental health and psychosocial wellbeing of Syrians: A review for mental health and psychosocial support staff working with Syrians affected by armed conflict*. UNHCR.

[22] Lingering psychological trauma three years after Libya's uprising. (2014, May 6). *The New Humanitarian*. https://www.ecoi.net/en/document/1203242.html

[23] Jurković, M., Tomašković, I., Tomašković, M., Smital Zore, B., Pavić, I., & Roić, A. C. (2019). Refugee status as a possible risk factor for childhood enuresis. *International Journal of Environmental Research and Public Health*, 16(7), 1293.

[24] International Medical Corps. (2017). *Understanding the mental health and psychosocial needs, and service utilization of Syrian refugees and Jordanian nationals: A qualitative & quantitative analysis in the Kingdom of Jordan*. https://reliefweb.int/report/jordan/understanding-mental-health-and-psychosocial-needs-and-service-utilization-syrian

[25] Brooks, M. A., Meinhart, M., Samawi, L., Mukherjee, T. Jaber, R. Alhomsh, H. Kaushal, N. Al Qutob, R. Khadra, M. El-Bassel, N. & Dasgupta, A. (2022). Mental health of clinic-attending Syrian refugee women in Jordan: Associations between social ecological risks factors and mental health symptoms. *BMC Women's Health*, 22, 4.

[26] Edkins, J. (2003). *Trauma and the memory of politics*. Cambridge University Press.

[27] Ostergaard, L. S., Wallach-Kildemoes, H., Thøgersen, M. H., Dragsted, U.B., Oxholm, A., Hartling, O., & Norredam, M. (2020). Prevalence of torture and trauma history among immigrants in primary care in Denmark: Do general practitioners ask? *European Journal of Public Health*, 30(6), 1163–1168.

recovery of community; and disconnecting trauma from its contexts of history, geography, and social position.

Intervention Contexts

Intervention contexts, from refugee camps to the clinics of resettled nations, are volatile, under-resourced, overstretched, and imbued with feelings of hopelessness and helplessness of refugee patients and often of practitioners.[28]

In refugee camps, "mental health is not a priority for anyone," shares the former United Nations High Commissioner for Refugees official Kilian Kleinschmidt, who served as a director of the Zaatari refugee camp in Jordan. During Kleinschmidt's tenure (2013–2014), Zaatari was home to roughly 85,000 people.[29] Yet there were "a maximum of 4–5 psychologists or mental health counselors," shares Kleinschmidt. This woeful shortage of critical mental health professionals is in line with Jordan's frail public mental health infrastructure, in which there are an estimated two psychiatrists for every 100,000 citizens.[30] It is also consistent with reports from other humanitarian camp managers and workers from some major global refugee camps.[31]

Conflicts and wars can dismantle public health infrastructure,[32,33] resulting in an acute shortage of formally trained healthcare professionals[34] and besieged health workers,[35,36] compounding health system strain. Female humanitarian

[28] Steel, Z., Mares, S., Newman, L. K., Blick, B., & Dudley, M. (2004). The politics of asylum and immigration detention: Advocacy, ethics, and the professional role of the therapist. In J. P. Wilson & B. Drozdek (Eds.), *Broken spirits: The treatment of traumatized asylum seekers, refugees, war and torture victims* (pp. 659–688). Brunner-Routledge.

[29] Kimmelman, M. (2015, July 5). Refugee camp for Syrians in Jordan evolves as a do-it-yourself city. *The New York Times.* https://www.nytimes.com/2014/07/05/world/middleeast/zaatari-refugee-camp-in-jordan-evolves-as-a-do-it-yourself-city.html

[30] International Medical Corps. (2017). *Understanding the mental health and psychosocial needs and service utilization of Syrian refugees and Jordanian nationals: A qualitative and quantitative analysis in the Kingdom of Jordan* [Report] (p. 11). https://reliefweb.int/sites/reliefweb.int/files/resources/JordanAssessmentReport-UnderstandingtheMentalHealthandPsychosocialNeedsandServiceUtilizationofSyrianRefugeesandJordanianNationals.pdf

[31] Humanitarian workers working in four major refugee camps around the world (personal communication, n.d.).

[32] Cook, J. (2016, December 12). Syrian medical facilities were attacked more than 250 times this year. *Huffington Post.* http://www.huffingtonpost.com/entry/syria-hospital-attacks_us_56c330f0e4b0c3c550528d2e

[33] Heisler, M., Baker, E., & McKay, D. (2015). Attacks on health care in Syria—normalizing violations of medical neutrality? *New England Journal of Medicine, 373,* 2489–2491.

[34] World Bank. *Physicians (per 1,000 people)—Syrian Arab Republic.* Retrieved on May 6, 2023, from https://data.worldbank.org/indicator/SH.MED.PHYS.ZS?locations=SY

[35] Heisler, M., Baker, E., & McKay, D. (2015). Attacks on health care in Syria—normalizing violations of medical neutrality? *New England Journal of Medicine, 373,* 2489–2491.

[36] Fouad, F. M., Sparrow, A., Tarakji, A., Alameddine, M., El-Jardali, F., Coutts, A.P., El Arnaout, N., Karroum, L. B., Jawad, M., Roborgh, S., Abbara, A., Alhalabi, F., AlMasri, I., & Jabbour, S. (2017).

workers "face threats to their personal safety from both local militia and police," as a humanitarian aid officer shared with me.[37] At the height of the Syrian crisis, for instance, according to Eyad Zanes, a psychiatrist and mental health officer for the World Health Organization in Syria (WHO-Syria), there are only 60 psychiatrists in all of Syria, with two-thirds concentrated in the major cities of Damascus and Aleppo.[38] For many other impoverished regions and people, it could mean no access to a psychiatrist,[39] forgoing medications, reliance on extended family, or in the event of psychological illnesses, exclusion from the community. Rising cases of suicides and attempted suicides, for instance, among the South Sudanese living in Ugandan settlements, illustrate the dire need for mental health care. "Mental health and the chronic diseases" (e.g., heart disease, cancer, and diabetes) "ought to be priorities but seldom are," says Kleinschmidt.

The true picture of mental health needs in conflict and postconflict settings may be more sprawling than it appears at first glance. Consider the case of Badam:

> Badam, 24 years old, Hajara, and son of a metalworker from Bamiya, Afghanistan, is an asylum-seeker in Norway. He arrived in the primary care clinic of Bergen, Norway, by way of displacements in Shamshato camp, Pakistan, and a refugee camp near Iran's southeastern Sistan and Baluchistan province. He has been in Norway for 2 years. Barely able to sleep more than 3 hours a night and with persistent nightmares when he did manage to fall asleep, he sought psychotropic relief for his sleepless nights. He has tried unsuccessfully in the past to cure his insomnia through the use of alcohol and illegally obtained amphetamines. During the day, Badam worked odd jobs, with grueling shifts as a stevedore loading, unloading, and stacking cargo, or in the construction industry. A follow-up conversation reveals anxiety, problems in concentration, difficulty making decisions, distractibility, persistent headaches, ringing in his ears, sensitivity to light, and memory lapses lasting anything from 3 to 24 hours. Badam also reports multiple head trauma at the hands of the Taliban where he lost consciousness for 5 to 15 minutes. During the last 9-years, he has endured multiple life-threatening migrations and separation from his family, who are in Iran, and he suffered other abuses. At 16 years of age, he and his younger brother hid in a shipping container of tea leaves that brought them to Salerno, Italy. A brain MRI showed considerable

Health workers and the weaponisation of health care in Syria: A preliminary inquiry for the *Lancet*-American University of Beirut Commission on Syria. *Lancet, 390*, 2516–2526.

[37] Humanitarian officer (personal communication, September 8, 2021).
[38] Eyad Yanes (personal communication, April 12, 2017). Yanes is a Syrian psychiatrist; Assalman, I., Alkhalil, M., & Curtice, M. (2008). Mental health in the Syrian Arab Republic. *International Psychiatry, 5*(3), 64–66.
[39] World Health Organization. (2019, September 13). *2 psychiatrists for more than 3 million people.* https://reliefweb.int/report/syrian-arab-republic/2-psychiatrists-almost-4-million-people

encephalomalacia or softening of brain tissue and gliosis in the bilateral frontal lobes, atrophy, and neurodegenerative changes consistent with moderate traumatic brain injury.

When clinicians are available, they often treat multiple co-occurring diagnoses,[40] as refugees are at an increased risk for psychoses[41] and schizophrenia compared to other immigrants and host populations.[42] They may confront the specialized needs of subpopulations of refugees such as unaccompanied young refugees, child soldiers, the disabled, the elderly, and women considered "spoils of war," with histories of systematic rape. For therapists in postconflict settings, especially in the age of the pandemic, providing services for refugees can mean offering support and holding space when they themselves may be experiencing burnout, losses, and risk to their safety.

The volatile and challenging scenarios posed by refugee mental health issues make salient the pressing need to design clinically relevant, culturally sensitive treatments that are also scalable for low- and middle-income host nations. But there is disagreement on how to best understand refugees' clinical and social-environmental needs.[43,44,45,46] Also, although there is a profusion of research exploring psychological therapies for vulnerable populations,[47] very little evidence exists on how to treat posttraumatic stress effectively in refugees or what successful intervention components may be.[48,49,50] When interventions are

[40] Kinzie, J. D. (2016). Medical approach to the management of traumatized refugees. *Journal of Psychiatric Practice, 22*(2), 76–83.

[41] Parrett, N. S., & Mason, O. J. (2010). Refugees and psychosis: A review of the literature. *Psychosis, 2*(2), 111–121.

[42] Hollander, A., Dal, H., Lewis, G., Magnusson, C., Kirkbride, J. B., Dale, B., & Dalman, C. (2016). Refugee migration and risk of schizophrenia and other non-affective psychoses: Cohort study of 1.3 million people in Sweden. *British Medical Journal, 352,* I1030.

[43] Miller, K. E., Jordans, M. J. D., Tol, W. A., & Galappatti, A. (2021). A call for greater conceptual clarity in the field of mental health and psychosocial support in humanitarian settings. *Epidemiology and Psychiatric Sciences, 8*(30), E5.

[44] Ibid.

[45] Tol, W. A., Purgato, M., Bass, J., Galappatti, A., & Eaton, W. (2015). Mental health and psychosocial support in humanitarian settings: A public mental health perspective. *Epidemiology and Psychiatric Sciences, 24*(6), 484–494.

[46] Ventevogel, P. (2018). Interventions for mental health and psychosocial support in complex humanitarian emergencies: Moving towards consensus in policy and action? In N. Morina & A. Nickerson (Eds.), *Mental health of refugee and conflict-affected populations* (pp. 155–180). Springer.

[47] Brady, F., Katona, C., Walsh, E., & Robjant, K. (2021). Psychotherapy and refugees. In D. Bhugra (Ed.), *Oxford textbook of migrant psychiatry* (pp. 493–502). Oxford University Press.

[48] Buhmann, C. B., Nordentoft, M., Ekstroem, M., Carlsson, J., & Mortensen, E. L. (2016). The effect of flexible cognitive-behavioural therapy and medical treatment, including antidepressants on post-traumatic stress disorder and depression in traumatised refugees: Pragmatic randomised controlled clinical trial. *British Journal of Psychiatry, 208*(3), 252–259.

[49] Nickerson, A., Bryant, R. A., Silove, D., & Steel, Z. (2010). A critical review of psychological treatments of posttraumatic stress disorder in refugees. *Clinical Psychology Review, 31*(3), 399–417.

[50] Koch, T., Ehring, T., & Liedl, A. (2020). Effectiveness of a transdiagnostic group intervention to enhance emotion regulation in young Afghan refugees: A pilot randomized controlled study. *Behaviour Research and Therapy, 132,* 103689.

implemented, either specified outcomes may not correspond to the intervention's goals or the lack of conceptual clarity in an intervention may misattribute the outcome to a different causal factor.[51] Questions of clinical significance (e.g., Is this treatment going to benefit my family and me?), effectiveness or clinical utility (e.g., Which patients and under what circumstances is this treatment going to be beneficial?), efficiency or cost-effectiveness (e.g., Is it going to be affordable?") and scalability, impact refugees' health and their integration. Such questions are useful for practitioners, researchers, and patients alike, as they aid in clinical decision-making, assessing needs, and determining whether or not a patient will seek help and stay engaged in treatment during its duration. In the case of the persecuted who have been forced to surrender and sublimate their identities, therapy must extend beyond its usual clinical role to the community level: restoring the identity of the traumatized must also mean rebuilding family and community.

Exploring these different domains also acquaints us with critical clinical factors in refugee care, such as the roles played by interpreters,[52,53] multiple pathways of healing created by providing practical and logistical help for refugees in a camp setting, and integrating interventions such as body-based ones to soothe distressing symptoms. Therapeutic care is often optimal when it is structured and not necessarily sequentially, within a three-phase approach:[54] stabilization, trauma-focused, and reintegration[55,56] or integration. Given the multiple stressors in refugees' lives, the authors emphasize the importance of flexibility in altering treatment plans to attend to refugees' fluctuating needs.

[51] Miller, K. E., Jordans, M. J. D., Tol, W. A., & Galappatti, A. (2021). A call for greater conceptual clarity in the field of mental health and psychosocial support in humanitarian settings. *Epidemiology and Psychiatric Sciences, 8*(30), E5.

[52] The therapeutic relationship is also influenced by the availability of interpreters for refugee patients: Codrington, R., Iqbal, A., & Segal, J. (2011). Lost in translation? Embracing the challenges of working with families from a refugee background: Australian and New Zealand. *Journal of Family Therapy, 32*(2), 129–143; Mirdal, G. M., Ryding, E., & Essendrop Sondej, M. (2012). Traumatized refugees, their therapists, and their interpreters: Three perspectives on psychological treatment. *Psychology and Psychotherapy: Theory, Research and Practice, 85*(4), 436–455; Puvimanasinghe, T., Denson, L., Augoustinos, M., & Somasundaram, D. (2015). Vicarious resilience and vicarious traumatisation: Experiences of working with refugees and asylum seekers in South Australia. *Transcultural Psychiatry, 52*(6), 743–765.

[53] Miller et al., observed, for example, that interpreters had an impact on the therapeutic alliance, as well as on complex emotional reactions within the therapy triad, which may sometimes result in therapists feeling excluded from the bond forming between interpreters and patients: Miller, K., Martell, Z., Pazdirek, L., Caruth, M., & Lopez, D. (2005). The role of interpreters in psychotherapy with refugees. *American Journal of Orthopsychiatry, 75*(1), 1.

[54] Brady, F., Katona, C., Walsh, E., & Robjant, K. (2021). Psychotherapy and refugees. In D. Bhugra (Ed.), *Oxford textbook of migrant psychiatry* (pp. 493–502). Oxford University Press.

[55] Herman, J. (1992). *Trauma and recovery*. Basic Books.

[56] Cloitre, M., Courtois, C. A., Charuvastra, A., Carapezza, R., Stolbach, B. C., & Green, B. L. (2011). Treatment of complex PTSD: Results of the ISTSS expert clinician survey on best practices. *Journal of Traumatic Stress, 24*(6), 615–627.

With the refugee as a patient in different conflict settings, myriad treatment challenges abound for clinical and humanitarian practitioners. Refugee healing, consensus supports,[57],[58] is grounded not only in emotions but also in the unique ecological and structural contexts and life-worlds of the person seeking treatment. Healing does not happen in the clinic alone, and the clinical context extends to the social and political conditions in society.[59] For effective refugee care, we need evidence-based and culturally driven multilevel (e.g., individual, family, and community levels) approaches and multiple programs (e.g., psychosocial, somatic, or psychodynamic).

Treatment Planning in Conflict-Affected Refugees: The Two Axes of Refugee Care—Culture- and Evidence-Based Care

An ecological scope, one that blends psychotherapeutic and social-environmental interventions to explore the dual but interconnected influences of pre- and postmigratory factors, as well as trauma and resilience at multiple levels, holds good utility for refugee mental health.

The Clinician in Different Contextually Embedded Practices

Our contexts, cultures, and settings can present as our "unwritten social and psychiatric dictionary," says Peter Elsass,[60] an expert in the treatment of survivors of torture. Clients belonging to the same culture as the clinician can provide a shared canvas of understanding the world or, some would counter, a short-hand or self-confirmation of any diagnostic activity.[61] Conversely, settings with ongoing stressors can threaten to constrain the clinical roles of practitioners[62] and can render intervention meaningless. Health professionals working in a variety of settings with refugees (e.g., detention centers, border camps, medical settings,

[57] Kleinman, A. (1988). *The illness narratives: Suffering, healing, and the human condition.* Basic Books.

[58] Kirmayer, L. J. (2005). Culture, context and experience in psychiatric diagnosis. *Psychopathology, 38*(4), 192–196.

[59] Duden, G. S., & Martins-Borges, L. (2021). Psychotherapy with refugees—supportive and hindering elements, *Psychotherapy Research, 31*(3), 402–417.

[60] Elsass, P. (1997). The cultural psychology of the torture syndrome: A distinction between what is universal and what is culture-bound. In P. Elsass (Ed.), *Treating victims of torture and violence, theoretical, cross-cultural, and clinical implications* (J. Andersen & H. Fuglsang, Trans., p. 91–112). NYU Press.

[61] Kleinman, A. (1988). *The illness narratives: Suffering, healing, and the human condition.* Basic Books.

[62] Fennig, M. (2021). Cultural adaptations of evidence-based mental health interventions for refugees: Implications for clinical social work. *British Journal of Social Work, 51,* 964–981.

outpatient clinics, nurseries, schools, and colleges, and within communities) must take into account how social, political, and legal factors can affect a refugee's agency, consent, perception of duress, and ability to either share their trauma story or, in turn, to have it heard.[63]

Clinically relevant treatments respect the refugee's cultural-psychological world-view. Take, for example, the story of Mr. Ben.

The Pharmacist Who Is Unable to Dispense of His Pain

"I am Mr. Ben," said the 55-year-old unshaven pharmacist with neat and tidy hair. He was father to five children from the town of Daraa in Syria, residing in Germany for 1.5 years. Three deep worry lines etched his forehead as he spoke of his present-life circumstances. "Daraa was everything to me—it was my future, my past, my stability, my everything. Especially at my age." In Daraa he had started his pharmacy business, had an apartment, and a car. The son of an impoverished farmer, Mr. Ben had painstakingly built his life over 25 years. "I had everything planned," says Mr. Ben. But in Germany, "for people of my generation, middle-aged but who are not as-yet retired," he said, "We can't start. We can't stop."

While Mr. Ben's passage to Germany was expedient and efficient as his brother, an official in the German government, had sponsored him, I learned that for an overwhelming number of refugees, this is not so. The collared striped black and white shirt he wore underneath a nurses' scrub-blue sweater escaped the waist of his black pants. Caught in the nether zone due to his refugee status, Mr. Ben feels helpless to start life anew. For, he feels, "I have no real power. Nothing is in my hands." He wrings his hands. "In my culture, fathers do everything for their children. But I have lost everything. I feel nearly dead because I have no opportunity to be useful."

Emotional attunement and a sense of safety for individuals like Mr. Ben can be elicited in therapy through exploring the role of fathers in the client's culture, as well as his expectations of himself and his children. Patients may worry about losing the entirety and lifelong meanings[64] embedded in their cultures, and about their worries being undermined[65,66] when their providers may not share

[63] Fletcher, K. (2005, March 17). A minimum of charity. *London Review of Books, 27,* 6.

[64] Danieli, Y., & Engdahl, B. (2018). In multigenerational legacies of trauma. In C. B. Nemeroff & C. Marmar (Eds.), *Post-traumatic stress disorder* (p. 497–512). Oxford University Press.

[65] Steel, Z., Silove, D., Chey, T., Bauman, A., Phan, T., & Phan, T. (2005). Mental disorders, disability and health service use amongst Vietnamese refugees and the host Australian population. *Acta Psychiatry Scandinavia, 111*(4), 300–309.

[66] Steel, Z., Silove, D., Phan, T., & Bauman, A. (2002). Long-term effect of psychological trauma on the mental health of Vietnamese refugees resettled in Australia: A population-based study. *Lancet, 360*(9339), 1056–1062.

their race or ethnicity. Incorporating culturally and contextually relevant information in intervention is an important way to facilitate patient-centered care by identifying outcomes important to refugee clients.

Emphasizing the importance of contextual knowledge and the dilemmas it can pose, researchers[67] assert that survivors of torture should not be classified as psychiatric patients since medicalizing the sequelae of torture can shift the focus away from the violation of their human rights. Consider the case of John Otieno, detailed by American Civil Liberties Union and Physicians for Human Rights Research (PHR),[68] an asylum-seeker held in US Immigration and Customs Enforcement detention who, in the summer of 2020, went on a 12-day hunger strike: .

> *After some time, the medical staff began to force-feed John Otieno.* * *"They put me on a bed and handcuffed me to an emergency medical stretcher," he said. "[They] strap you on the chest, waist, legs, [with] hard restraints . . . there is no point in fighting back because you are there with six male, strong officers, and three nurses, and there is nothing you can do." The doctor claimed to have a judicial order but declined to show it to him. Mr. Otieno saw two other hunger strikers who were also force-fed.*

Detention settings from America to Australia[69] can subject asylum-seekers to cruel, inhumane, and degrading treatment and punitive measures like solitary confinement, force-feeding, forced hydration, forced urinary catheterization, involuntary blood draws, use of restraints, and use of chemical constraints to manage behavior, including the incarceration of children. In detention settings, asylum-seekers are subject to immigration policies that can increase future health risks, prolong postmigration stresses, impact their mental health, and in many cases, prove fatal.

Rendering treatment in detention settings or politically charged contexts can pose any number of ethical dilemmas for clinicians,[70] who may become

---

[67] Hastrup, K., & Elsass, P. (1990). Anthropological advocacy: A contradiction in terms? *Current Anthropology, 31*(3), 301–311.

[68] American Civil Liberties Union & Physicians for Human Rights Research. (2021). *Behind closed doors: Abuse and retaliation against hunger strikers in US immigration detention.* https://www.aclu.org/report/report-behind-closed-doors-abuse-retaliation-against-hunger-strikers-us-immigration-detention

[69] Briskman, B., Zion, D., & Loff, B. (2010). Challenge and collusion: Health professionals and immigration detention in Australia. *International Journal of Human Rights, 14*(7), 1092–1106.

[70] Steel, Z., Mares, S., Newman, L. K., Blick, B., & Dudley, M. (2004). The politics of asylum and immigration detention: Advocacy, ethics, and the professional role of the therapist. In J. P. Wilson & B. Drozdek (Eds.), *Broken spirits: The treatment of traumatized asylum seekers, refugees, war and torture victims* (1st ed., pp. 659–688). Brunner-Routledge.

"privileged witnesses of abuse."[71] Health professionals can experience dual-loyalty conflicts where their obligation to their patients conflicts with the demands of the detention setting. They can face other risks and pressures relating to violating their ethical obligations[72] by colluding with abuses by loaning their names and credibility to medical declarations associated with nonconsensual medical procedures. This can involve disregarding the core ethical values of respecting consent and autonomy, as in the case of identifying a detainee in their care who may be at risk for self-harm for isolation rather than factoring in the instrumental role of the detention environment.[73] Practice in these settings can also lead to a gradual moral disengagement that makes it increasingly hard for clinicians to distinguish between active and passive collusion.[74]

Contextual knowledge can offer the potential to revitalize areas for patient advocacy[75,76] by moving beyond the individual to domains of social responsibility and political action. A roadmap for multicultural societies to address refugee mental health in a culturally competent manner requires attention to contextual, collaborative, and multidisciplinary approaches at every stage of the displacement process.

Five Recommendations to Promote Cultural Competence for Healthy Integration

Cultural competence has been described in various ways, from a system's ability to provide care to its diverse patient population with its diverse values and

[71] World Medical Association (WMA). (2020, October). *WMA resolution on the responsibility of physicians in the documentation and denunciation of acts of torture or cruel or inhuman or degrading treatment.* https://www.wma.net/policies-post/wma-resolution-on-the-responsibility-of-physicians-in-the-documentation-and-denunciation-of-acts-of-torture-or-cruel-or-inhuman-or-degrading-treatment/

[72] WMA. (1991, November). *Competent patients who refuse to eat should not be fed artificially: WMA Declaration of Malta on hunger strikers.* https://www.wma.net/policies-post/wma-declaration-of-malta-on-hunger-strikers/; WMA. (2006). Declaration of Malta, a background paper on the ethical management of hunger strikes. *World Medical Journal, 52*(2), 36–43.

[73] Maylea, C., & Hirsch, A. (2018). Social workers as collaborators? The ethics of working within Australia's asylum system. *Ethics and Social Welfare, 12*(2), 160–178.

[74] Gready, P. (2007). Medical complicity in human rights abuses: A case study of district surgeons in apartheid South Africa. *Journal of Human Rights, 6,* 417.

[75] Baranowski, K. A., Moses, M. H., & Sundri, J. (2018). Supporting asylum seekers: Clinician experiences of documenting human rights violations through forensic psychological evaluation. *Journal of Traumatic Stress, 31*(3), 391–400.

[76] Başoğlu, M. (1993). Prevention of torture and care of survivors: An integrated approach. *Journal of the American Medical Association, 270*(5), 606–611.

social, cultural and linguistic needs,[77] to cultural safety,[78,79] to concrete skills and practices,[80] to cultural humility,[81] and as an enduring process of commitment to cultural knowledge.[82] To provide culturally competent interventions in refugee mental health, it is essential to build cultural knowledge, skills, and awareness[83] at five levels: provider and treatment, humanitarian, detention or extrajudicial, institutional, and community of host countries. These can range from:

- Culturally sensitive interventions delivered in refugee settlements that effectively reduce refugees' psychological distress[84] and promotion of mental health service delivery within communities.[85]
- Behavioral health organizations' efforts to expand capacity by providing training sessions on refugee trauma, and on cultural expressions of distress in the refugee communities.[86] Organizations can champion cultural competence through increasing staff diversity, lowering workload expectations (as lower caseloads may assist providers to engage better with their refugee clients' needs),[87] and partnering with refugee communities.

[77] Betancourt, J. R., Green, A. R., & Carrillo, J. E. (2002, October). Cultural competence in health care: Emerging frameworks and practical approaches [Field report]. *The Commonwealth Fund.* https://www.commonwealthfund.org/sites/default/files/documents/___media_files_publications_fund_report_2002_oct_cultural_competence_in_health_care__emerging_frameworks_and_practical_approaches_betancourt_culturalcompetence_576_pdf.pdf

[78] Papps, E., & Ramsden, I. (1996). Cultural safety in nursing: The New Zealand experience. *International Journal for Quality in Health Care, 8*(5), 491–497.

[79] Curtis, E., Jones, R., Tipene-Leach, D., Walker, C., Loring, B., Pain, S.-J., & Reid, P. (2019). Why cultural safety rather than cultural competency is required to achieve health equity: A literature review and recommended definition. *International Journal for Equity in Health, 18,* 174. https://doi.org/10.1186/s12939-019-1082-3

[80] Whitley, R. (2007). Cultural competence, evidence-based medicine, and evidence-based practices. *Psychiatric Services, 58*(12), 1588–1590.

[81] Tervalon, M., & Murray-García, J. (1998). Cultural humility versus cultural competence: A critical distinction in defining physician training outcomes in multicultural education. *Journal of Health Care for the Poor and the Underserved, 9*(2), 117–125.

[82] Lau, L. S., & Rodgers, G. (2021). Cultural competence in refugee service settings: A scoping review. *Health Equity, 5*(1), 124–134.

[83] Sue, D. W., Bernier, J. E., Durran, A., Feinberg, L., Pedersen, P. Smith, E. J., & Vasquez-Nuttall, E. (1982). Position paper: Cross-cultural counseling competencies. *Counseling Psychologist, 10,* 45–52.

[84] Goninon, E. J., Kannis-Dymand, L., Sonderegger, R., Mugisha, D., & Lovell, G. P. (2021). Successfully treating refugees' post-traumatic stress symptoms in a Ugandan settlement with group cognitive behaviour therapy. *Behavioural and Cognitive Psychotherapy, 49*(1), 35–49.

[85] Aktar, B., Ahmed, R., Hassan, R., Farnaz, N., Ray, P., Awal, A., Bin Shafique, S., Hasan, M. Quayyum, Z., Jafarovna, M., Kobeissi, L., Tahir, K., Chawla, B., & Rashid, S. (2020). Ethics and methods for collecting sensitive data: Examining sexual and reproductive health needs and services for Rohingya refugees at Cox's Bazar, Bangladesh. *International Journal of Information, Diversity, & Inclusion, 4,* 68–86.

[86] Im, H., Rodriguez, C., & Grumbine, J. M. (2021). A multitier model of refugee mental health and psychosocial support in resettlement: Toward trauma-informed and culture-informed systems of care. *Psychological Services, 18*(3), 345–364.

[87] Lau, L. S., & Rodgers, G. (2021). Cultural competence in refugee service settings: A scoping Review. *Health Equity, 5,* 124–134.

- Incorporating culturally sensitive assessment methods at different stages of refugee displacement to foster trust and begin repair of self, family, and community.
- Involve cultural brokers who may be linguistically able to help refugees navigate available resources.
- Knowledge of cultural and structural barriers that may impede refugees' access, utilization, and effectiveness of services.[88,89]
- Seeking continued self-education by professionals of their own culture, ethnicity, race, religion, and class, and how they might interact with clinical work. Practitioners' engagement with the refugee community may build up knowledge of refugee cultures, journeys, and experiences and establish trauma-informed communities.

Evidence-Based Practice

Evidence-based practice requires that the treatment of refugees is guided by scientifically validated methods and clinical expertise for appropriate and effective patient care. Although researchers and clinicians agree that a solid evidence base informs effective psychological and psychosocial interventions, there may be differing ideas about whether an intervention effectively reduces distress and what constitutes evidence.[90] Some researchers are of the view that randomized control trials (RCTs) and efficacy trials represent the gold standard of experimental design. RCTs are clinical trials where participants are randomly allocated to two or more groups to reduce selection bias, with one group receiving the intervention and the other receiving a placebo, or no intervention for the same condition. Later, the groups are compared to determine whether the benefits observed are due to the treatment and not any confounding factors. Following trauma-focused treatment in refugees, some RCTs have reported large effect sizes in their symptomatic reduction in posttraumatic stress.[91,92,93]

[88] Paniagua, F. A. (2005). *Assessing and treating culturally diverse clients: Practical guide.* Sage.

[89] Sue, S., Zane, N., Nagayama, Hall, G. C., & Berger, L. K. (2008). The case for cultural competency in psychotherapeutic interventions. *Annual Review of Psychology, 60,* 10.1–10.24.

[90] Martini, C. (2021). What "evidence" in evidence-based medicine? *Topoi 40,* 299–305.

[91] Crumlish, N., & O'Rourke, K. (2010). A systematic review of treatments for post-traumatic stress disorder among refugees and asylum-seekers. *Journal of Nervous and Mental Disease, 198*(4), 237–251.

[92] Palic, S., & Elklit, A. (2011). Psychosocial treatment of posttraumatic stress disorder in adult refugees: A systematic review of prospective treatment outcome studies and a critique. *Journal of Affective Disorders, 131*(1), 8–23.

[93] Nickerson, A., Bryant, R. A., Silove, D., & Steel, Z. (2011). A critical review of psychological treatments of posttraumatic stress disorder in refugees. *Clinical Psychology Review, 31*(3), 399–417.

On the other hand, RCTs have challenges,[94] and researchers underscore methodological and ethical shortcomings when applied to non-Western, culturally diverse, conflict-affected populations.[95,96] One, the evidence base regarding the use of empirically supported treatments with non-Western refugees is sparse, and only a small number of RCTs have been conducted with refugees. Two, the relevance of the posttraumatic stress disorder (PTSD) diagnosis to non-Western populations is questionable. As a result, the generalizability of findings from RCTs to diverse populations with complex traumas profile is uncertain.[97] Three, randomization, some researchers assert,[98,99] can undermine the clinical realism of the naturalistic settings and thus also the relevance of the findings to those settings. Four, clinicians encounter many complex situations in their treatment of refugee patients, and studies conducted in highly controlled settings may only provide us with partial solutions for treating our diverse clients. Findings from RCTs, researchers caution, ought to be interpreted with circumspection.

Merging Evidence-Based and Cultural Practice

Some new culturally sensitive adaptations of trauma-focused cognitive behavioral therapy (TF-CBT) programs among refugees appear promising.[100,101,102] A study of 174 Congolese refugees living in a Ugandan settlement found a

[94] Whitley, R., Rousseau, C., Carpenter-Song, E., & Kirmayer, L. J. (2011). Evidence-based medicine: Opportunities and challenges in a diverse society. *Canadian Journal of Psychiatry, 56*(9), 514–522.

[95] Slobodin, O., & de Jong, J. T. V. M. (2015). Family interventions in traumatized immigrants and refugees: A systematic review. *Transcultural Psychiatry, 52*(6), 723–742.

[96] Tol, W. A., Barbui, C., Galappatti, A., Silove, D., Betancourt, T. S., Souza, R., Golaz, A., & van Ommeren, M. (2011). Mental health and psychosocial support in humanitarian settings: Linking practice and research. *Lancet, 378*, 1581–1591.

[97] Whitley, R., Rousseau, C., Carpenter-Song, E., & Kirmayer, L. J. (2011). Evidence-based medicine: Opportunities and challenges in a diverse society. *Canadian Journal of Psychiatry, 56*(9), 514–522.

[98] Seligman, M. E. P. (1995). The effectiveness of psychotherapy: The Consumer Reports study. *American Psychologist, 50*, 965–974.

[99] Chambless, D. L., & Hollon, S. D. (1998). Defining empirically supported therapies. *Journal of Consulting and Clinical Psychology, 66*, 7–18.

[100] Durbeej, N., McDiarmid, S., Sarkadi, A., Feldman, I., Punamäki, R., Kankaanpää, R. Andersen, A., Hilden, P. K., Verelst, A., Derluyn, I., & Osman, F. (2021). Evaluation of a school-based intervention to promote mental health of refugee youth in Sweden (the Refugees Well School Trial): Study protocol for a cluster randomized controlled trial. *Trials, 22*, 98.

[101] Barhoma, M., Sonne, C., Lommen, M. J. J., Mortensen, E. L., & Carlsson, J. (2021). Stress management versus cognitive restructuring in trauma-affected refugees: A follow-up study on a pragmatic randomised trial. *Journal of Affective Disorders, 294*, 628–637.

[102] Young, K. Chessell, Z. J., Chisholm, A., Brady, F., Akbar, S. Vann, M., Rouf, K., & Dixon, L. (2021). A cognitive behavioural therapy (CBT) approach for working with strong feelings of guilt after traumatic events. *Cognitive Behavior Therapist, 14*, E26.

culturally sensitive CBT program reduced refugees' posttraumatic stress.[103] Incorporating cultural adaptations with culturally diverse populations, as prior research demonstrates,[104,105] may boost treatment efficacy. In the past 2 decades, readily standardized CBT and brief trauma therapies have been the most widely studied treatment method among refugee populations.[106,107] Let us examine them.

Cognitive Therapies

Cognitive therapies of PTSD in postconflict settings focus on repairing maladaptive meanings of traumatic memories and generating new meanings through new memory associations. Although they can differ in the protocols used, and a brand of "third-generation CBT"[108,109] is on the rise, their methodology typically draws upon disconfirming negative appraisals, psychoeducation of trauma and its effects, and motivation to reconnect with life's meaningful activities. Specifically, Anke Ehlers, a German psychologist, breaks down the cognitive therapies into five components: collaboration between the practitioner and patient to derive an individualized case formulation, updating trauma memories (through access, updating meanings, and linking new memories to the traumatic events), discrimination training where the patient learns to distinguish between present and past cues of the traumatic events; discarding unhelpful cognitions that are counterproductive to the patient's recovery with experimentation, and reclaiming or reengaging with life activities and connections.

[103] Goninon, E. J., Kannis-Dymand, L., Sonderegger, R., Mugisha, D., & Lovell, G. P. (2021). Successfully treating refugees' post-traumatic stress symptoms in a Ugandan settlement with group cognitive behaviour therapy. *Behavioural and Cognitive Psychotherapy, 49*(1), 35–49.

[104] Hinton, D. E., Chhean, D., Pich, V., Safren, S. A., Hofmann, S. G., & Pollack, M. H. (2005). A randomized controlled trial of cognitive-behavior therapy for Cambodian refugees with treatment-resistant PTSD and panic attacks: A cross-over design. *Journal of Traumatic Stress, 18*(6), 617–629.

[105] Hinton, D. E., Pham, T., Tran, M., Safren, S. A., Otto, M. W., & Pollack, M. H. (2004). CBT for Vietnamese refugees with treatment-resistant PTSD and panic attacks: A pilot study. *Journal of Traumatic Stress, 17*(5), 429–433.

[106] Silove, D., Ventevogel, P., & Rees, S. (2017). The contemporary refugee crisis: An overview of mental health challenges. *World Psychiatry, 16*(2), 130–139.

[107] Herman, J. L. (1992). *Trauma and recovery* (p. 251). Basic Books.

[108] Third-generation PTSD focused CBT can conflate all of the following as CBT versions: art therapy, mindfulness, eclectic psychotherapy, acceptance, meditation, narrative exposure, extinction, relationship, value training, suicide therapy, and meta-cognition: Tolin, D. F. (2010). Is cognitive-behavioral therapy more effective than other therapies? A meta-analytic review. *Clinical Psychology Review, 30*(6), 710–720.

[109] Prolonged exposure, EMDR, and imagery rehearsal therapy are all sometimes referred to as forms of CBT: Pagel, J. F. (2021). Classic cognitive behavioral therapy. *Post-traumatic stress disorder: A guide for primary care clinicians and therapists* (pp. 83–90). Springer.

Other forms of cognitive therapies can range from TF-CBT, cognitive processing therapy (CPT),[110] brief manual-based trauma therapies (BTT), and prolonged exposure therapy (PET). TF-CBT is a variant of CBT that can assist refugee children in overcoming their trauma by actively focusing on thoughts and behaviors related to traumatic experiences. BTTs are conducted in 20–30-minute sessions drawing on the principles, strategies, and components of CBT, such as prolonged exposure, cognitive restructuring, behavioral strategies, stress management, and mindfulness. The benefits of such programs can include their low cost, short duration, and amenability to task-shifting by community workers (and thus wider dissemination).[111]

Through restructuring negative cognitive appraisals common in refugee populations, such as those involving guilt and shame, cognitive therapies can be useful. But newer studies critique the efficacy of CBT therapies in treating refugees who are severely sick[112] or depressed,[113] or who present with a multiple comorbidities or a complex profile of trauma.[114] For instance, severely traumatized refugees exposed to torture[115] and living in Denmark for an average of 14 years were treated in a controlled trial with antidepressants, and weekly manualized psychotherapy sessions (with CBT techniques such as acceptance and commitment therapy, mindfulness, and visualized exposure). This trial found no effect of CBT and antidepressants on self-reported PTSD. Although another study found high baseline levels of PTSD symptoms were unchanged after a one-year follow-up, they also made some interesting observations.[116] The chronic condition of their participants and prior unsuccessful treatments may have rendered these refugees treatment resistant; as such their dosage of CBT (average of 12 sessions) may have been too short. The typical trauma-informed CBT course with refugees generally is between 12 and 28 treatment sessions,

[110] Resick, P. A., & Schnicke, M. K. (1993). *Cognitive processing therapy for rape victims: A treatment manual.* Sage.

[111] Silove, D., Ventevogel, P., & Rees S. (2017). The contemporary refugee crisis: an overview of mental health challenges. *World Psychiatry, 16*(2), 130–139.

[112] Jeon, S., Lee, J., Jun, J. Y., Park, Y. S., Cho, J., Choi, J., Jeon, Y., & Kim, S. J. (2020). The effectiveness of cognitive behavioral therapy on depressive symptoms in North Korean refugees. *Psychiatry Investigation, 17*(7), 681–687.

[113] Hinton, D. E., Pich, V., Hofmann, S. G., & Otto, M. W. (2013). Acceptance and mindfulness techniques as applied to refugee and ethnic minority populations with PTSD: Examples from culturally adapted CBT. *Cognitive and Behavioral Practice, 20*(1), 33–46.

[114] Brady, F., Katona, C., Walsh, E., & Robjant, K. (2021). Psychotherapy and refugees. In D. Bhugra (Ed.), *Oxford textbook of migrant psychiatry* (pp. 493–502). Oxford University Press.

[115] Buhmann, C. B., Nordentoft, M., Ekstroem, M., Carlsson, J., & Mortensen, E. L. (2016). The effect of flexible cognitive-behavioural therapy and medical treatment, including antidepressants on post-traumatic stress disorder and depression in traumatised refugees: Pragmatic randomised controlled clinical trial. *British Journal of Psychiatry, 208*(3), 252–259.

[116] Buhmann, C. B., Nordentoft, M., Ekstroem, M., Carlsson, J., & Mortensen, E. L. (2016). The effect of flexible cognitive-behavioural therapy and medical treatment, including antidepressants on post-traumatic stress disorder and depression in traumatised refugees: Pragmatic randomised controlled clinical trial. *British Journal of Psychiatry, 208*(3), 252–259.

each lasting between 60 and 100 minutes,[117] to exert substantial positive effects for survivors of multiple and protracted traumas. The relevance and success of a particular treatment with trauma-affected refugees centers on its ability to factor in a refugee patient's language, cultural context, trauma, and level of functioning, a limitation of this study and many other CBT studies.

Cultural emphases of certain types of evidence-based practices, such as CBT, can mirror the dominance of Euro-American perspectives and reinforce mainstream cultural values such as rational thought, logic, and verbal skills over others like spirituality.[118] This can affect the growth of our knowledge-base of interventions with refugees, asylum-seekers, and ethnocultural communities and what may be accepted as clinical tools. When treated with CBT, refugees with low literacy rates, those unfamiliar with "talk therapy,"[119,120] and those with high posttraumatic stress or living in fear of repatriation, may demonstrate ambivalence[121] or simply drop out of therapy. At the same time, there are a substantial number of diverse treatments classified as TF-CBT in meta-analyses,[122] which make it challenging to determine efficacy. Further, the inconsistent groupings of treatment-protocols within TF-CBT can also mean that the evidence base was inflated.[123,124] As a clinical intervention with traumatized refugees and one without cultural adaptations, there seems to a general consensus that TF-CBT shows limited evidence for improvement in refugees' health-related quality of life[125,126] and in those whose citizenship status is

---

[117] Chipalo, E. (2021). Is trauma focused-cognitive behavioral therapy (TF-CBT) effective in reducing trauma symptoms among traumatized refugee children? A systematic review. *Journal of Child and Adolescent Trauma, 14*(4), 545–558.

[118] Hays, P. A. (2006). Introduction. In P. A. Hayes & G. Y. Iwamasa (Eds.), *Culturally responsive cognitive-behavioral therapy: Assessment, practice, and supervision* (p. 6). American Psychological Association.

[119] Kinzie, J. D. (2016). Medical approach to the management of traumatized refugees. *Journal of Psychiatric Practice, 22*(2), 76–83.

[120] Fung, K., & Lo, T. (2017). An integrative clinical approach to cultural competent psychotherapy. *Journal of Contemporary Psychotherapy, 47*(2), 65–73.

[121] Vincent, F., Jenkins, H., Larkin, M., & Clohessy, S. (2013). Asylum-seekers' experiences of trauma-focused CBT. *Behavioural & Cognitive Psychotherapy, 41*(5), 579–593.

[122] Thompson, C. T., Vidgen, A., & Roberts, N. P. (2018). Psychological interventions for posttraumatic stress disorder in refugees and asylum seekers: A systematic review and meta-analysis. *Clinical Psychology Review, 63*, 66–79.

[123] Brady, F., Katona, C., Walsh, E., & Robjant, K. (2021). Psychotherapy and refugees. In D. Bhugra (Ed.), *Oxford textbook of migrant psychiatry* (pp. 493–502). Oxford University Press.

[124] On the other hand, the varying ways in which trauma severity manifests itself in individuals— discrete trauma, multiple forms of trauma, complex presentations, or those exhibiting dissociation— necessitates their inconsistent use. According to Brady et al., TF-CBT approaches are effective with individuals who have experienced a small number of discrete traumas but not necessarily for more complex presentations following prolonged or multiple traumas: Ibid.

[125] Carlsson, J. M., Mortensen, E. L., & Kastrup, M. A. (2005). Follow-up study of mental health and health-related quality of life in tortured refugees in multidisciplinary treatment. *Journal of Nervous and Mental Disease, 193*, 651–657.

[126] Palic, S., & Elklit, A. (2009). An explorative outcome study of CBT-based multidisciplinary treatment in a diverse group of refugees from a Danish treatment centre for rehabilitation of traumatized refugees. *Torture, 19*, 248–270.

uncertain,[127] and it may not be adequate for the forcibly displaced with complex presentations, history of multiple traumas, significant dissociative symptoms, and difficulties with emotional regulation.[128] In order to better represent the realities of refugees' lives, researchers[129,130,131,132] propose that adapting TF-CBT, including tailoring interventions to a specific cultural group, can improve the relevance and efficacy of treatments.[133,134] When providing therapy to refugees and asylum-seekers, the cultural adaptation of CBT is generally accepted, with its systematic modification through incorporating the cultural worldviews, context, traditional methods of resilience and healing, and language of the reference cultural group.[135,136,137,138] Researchers[139] aspire to reconcile the disconnect between ethnographic and evidence-based research so that "cultural competency becomes more evidence-based, and evidence-based medicine becomes more culturally competent" to bring about more effective patient-centered care. One such promising pilot study of 16 traumatized Tamil refugees and asylum-seekers clients in the UK adapted the CBT framework using a cultural framework.[140] It anchored core CBT components using Tamil metaphors, stories, and culturally relevant emotional regulation techniques and harnessed community knowledge.

[127] Bowley, J. (2006). Working with asylum seekers. In N. Tarrier (Ed.), *Case formulation in cognitive behaviour therapy: The treatment of challenging and complex cases* (pp. 330–348). Routledge.

[128] Brady, F., Katona, C., Walsh, E., & Robjant, K. (2021). Psychotherapy and refugees. In D. Bhugra (Ed.), *Oxford textbook of migrant psychiatry* (pp. 493–502). Oxford University Press.

[129] Grey, N., & Young, K. (2008). Cognitive behaviour therapy with refugees and asylum seekers experiencing traumatic stress symptoms. *Behavioral & Cognitive Psychotherapy, 36,* 3–19.

[130] Hinton, D. E., & Patel, A. (2017). Cultural adaptations of cognitive behavioral therapy. *Psychiatric Clinics of North America, 40*(4), 701–714.

[131] Hinton, D. E., & Jalal, B. (2019). Dimensions of culturally sensitive CBT: Application to Southeast Asian populations. *American Journal of Orthopsychiatry, 89*(4), 493–507.

[132] Naeem, F. (2019). Cultural adaptations of CBT: A summary and discussion of the Special Issue on Cultural Adaptation of CBT. *Cognitive Behaviour Therapist, 12,* E40.

[133] Griner, D., & Smith, T. B. (2006). Culturally adapted mental health interventions: A meta-analytic review. *Psychotherapy: Theory, Research, Practice, Training, 43,* 531–548.

[134] Hinton, D. E., Chhean, D., Pich, V., Safren, S. A., Hofmann, S. G., & Pollack, M. H. (2005). A randomized controlled trial of cognitive-behavior therapy for Cambodian refugees with treatment-resistant PTSD and panic attacks: A cross-over design. *Journal of Traumatic Stress, 18,* 617–629.

[135] Naeem, F. (2012). *Adaptation of cognitive behaviour therapy for depression in Pakistan: Adaptation of cognitive behaviour therapy for depression in Pakistan.* Lambert Academic Publishing.

[136] Bernal, G., Jiménez-Chafey, M. I., & Domenech Rodríguez, M. D. (2009). Cultural adaptation of treatments: A resource for considering culture in evidence-based practice. *Professional Psychology: Ressearch and Practice, 40,* 361–368.

[137] De Jong, J. T. V. M., & van Ommeren, M. (2009). Toward a culture-informed epidemiology: Combining qualitative and quantitative research in transcultural contexts. *Transcultural Psychiatry, 39,* 422–433.

[138] Dossa, P. (2009). *Racialized bodies, disabling worlds: Storied lives of immigrant Muslim women.* University of Toronto Press.

[139] Whitley, R. (2007). Cultural competence, evidence-based medicine, and evidence-based practices. *Psychiatric Services, 58*(12), 1588–1590.

[140] Bahu, M. (2019). War, trauma and culture: Working with Tamil refugees and asylum seekers using culturally adapted CBT. *Cognitive Behaviour Therapist, 12,* E46.

Outcome measures suggested significant improvements in mood and anxiety, with 50% making significant improvements in PTSD symptoms. Studies like this lend momentum to prior research that the more specific the adaptation to the target culture, the more effective therapy can be.[141,142] Overall, a critique for culturally adapting CBT may appear to be appropriating an existing measure or obstructing the design of bottom-up cultural interventions, and there is a need for evidence-driven cultural research with traumatized refugees.[143]

Engaging cultural and evidence-based discourses so that they can mutually enrich each other can be done through:

- Incorporating these two core paradigms in designing assessments.
- Enhancing the evidence base of refugee mental health by conducting high-quality relational, longitudinal,[144,145] and culturally sensitive empirical research.
- Blending cultural competence and empirically supported findings in interventions ranging from social-environmental to somatic treatments.
- Developing "bottom-up" research agendas in conflict-affected communities to boost the body of evidence-based literature, test intervention efficacy in various minority populations, and identify unique efficacious cultural variables.

Narrative Exposure Therapy

In 4–12 90-minute sessions,[146] narrative exposure therapy (NET)[147] focuses on the patient's recollection of the trauma, prioritizing memories and making

[141] Benish, S. G., Quintana, S., & Wampold, B. E. (2011). Culturally adapted psycho- therapy and the legitimacy of myth: A direct-comparison meta-analysis. *Journal of Counseling Psychology, 58,* 279–289.

[142] La Roche, M. J., D'Angelo, E., Gualdron, L., & Leavell, J. (2006). Culturally sensitive guided imagery for allocentric Latinos: A pilot study. *Psychotherapy: Theory, Research, Practice, Training, 43,* 555–560.

[143] Mueser, K. T., & Drake, R. E. (2005). How does a practice become evidence-based? In R. E. Drake, M. R., Merrens, & D. W. Lynde (Eds.), *Evidence-based mental health practice: A textbook* (pp. 217–241). Norton.

[144] Hauff, E., & Vaglum, P. (1995). Organised violence and the stress of exile: Predictors of mental health in a community cohort of Vietnamese refugees three years after resettlement. *British Journal of Psychiatry, 166,* 360–367.

[145] Beiser, M., & Hou, F. (2001). Language acquisition, unemployment and depressive disorder among Southeast Asian refugees: A 10-year study. *Social Science & Medicine, 53,* 1321–1334.

[146] Schauer, M., Neuner, F., & Elbert, T. (2011). *Narrative exposure therapy: A short-term intervention for traumatic stress disorders after war, terror or torture* (2nd ed.). Hogrefe & Huber.

[147] Ibid.

meaning of those memories that evoke the strongest responses.[148] The practitioner assists the patient in reliving traumatic memories by embedding traumatic memories and emotional responses in one's autobiographical story. The therapist also encourages the patient to recall positive memories, and in this way, cognitive associations of particular trauma memories are reorganized, and positive resources mobilized.

NET includes in its scope the role of the social environment, recognition of the patient's trauma, social status, and emotions on attrition or the failure of a patient to respond to treatment. The patient receives the written narrative as a documented testimony at the end of therapy. In furthering its scope to include acts that break social norms and addressing consequent emotions, such as guilt or shame, NET extends the recovery space to excombatants, former militia members, perpetrators, and others who may have fallen victim to social rejection. It reports reductions in trauma-related symptoms and comorbidities and improvements in psychosocial functioning and physical health[149] across diverse, war-affected populations. Patients also reported low dropout rates from therapy.[150] Older age predicted better PTSD and depression outcomes. Exposure therapy in trauma that includes several exposures or repetitions may carry additional advantages of building cognitive coherence and self-reflection and restoring meaning.[151]

Eye Movement Desensitization and Reprocessing

Eye movement desensitization and reprocessing (EMDR) processing of a traumatic event requires the patient to repetitively move their eyes during short sequential exposures while recalling the traumatic memory. It posits that traumatic life events can lead to unprocessed memories, emotions, and physical sensations experienced at the time of the trauma. Maladaptive information processing networks link present distressing symptoms to past events and can be triggered by external and internal stimuli. It is proposed that eye movements unblock the networks. Thus, in response to the therapeutic stimulus, EMDR realizes new physiological responses and reconnects the adverse and frozen

[148] Schnyder, U., Ehlers, A., Elbert, T., Foa, E., Gersons, B., Resick, P., Shapiro, F., & Cloitre, M. (2015). Psychotherapy for PTSD: What do they have in common? *European Journal of Psychotraumatology, 6*, 28186.

[149] Stenmark, H., Catani, C., Neuner, F., Elbert, T., & Holen, A. (2013). Treating PTSD in refugees and asylum seekers within the general health care system: A randomized controlled multicenter study. *Behaviour Research and Therapy, 51*(10), 641–647.

[150] Lely, J. C. G., Smid, G. E., Jongedijk, R. A., Knipscheer, W. J., & Kleber, R. J. (2019). The effectiveness of narrative exposure therapy: A review, meta-analysis and meta-regression analysis. *European Journal of Psychotraumatology, 10*(1), 1550344.

[151] Ibid.

experiences. Three elements underlie a patient's adaptive functioning: a sense of stabilization in the face of traumatic memories, processing memories and triggers, and gaining skills. In a systematic review of evidence RCTs examining the efficacy of EMDR therapy, researchers concluded that EMDR improved PTSD, depression, and anxiety, including with refugees.[152] Studies report the successful use of EMDR with refugees with a reduction in depression, distressful memories, anxiety, nightmares, severe fatigue, and phobias using 2–12 EMDR sessions. Although EMDR was found to be more effective than other trauma treatments and control groups,[153] its efficacy was greater when delivered by trained therapists[154] and when sessions were longer than 60 minutes.[155] Since EMDR also does not address trauma associations and physiological habituation, its utility with refugees of complex trauma has largely been called into question. Although some EMDR therapies have shown some positive effects in refugees, effectiveness is small when compared to other clinical populations. Much of the current evidence relies on small sample sizes with limited longitudinal research. More research is needed to determine its theoretical basis, the role of eye movements in improvement of symptoms, and whether it can maintain its positive effects long-term with refugee patients.

Although methodological weaknesses prevail and it is unclear which treatment strategies work best with survivors of complex trauma given the diversity of their circumstances, in general, NET and culturally adapted CBT are considered to be more effective interventions for refugee populations.[156,157,158] Seven common elements of evidence-driven treatments include psychoeducation, emotion regulation and skills training, imaginal exposure, cognitive processing, restructuring cognitions, emotional processing, and reorganizing

[152] Gattinara, P. C., & Pallini, S. (2017). The use of EMDR with refugees and asylum seekers: A review of research studies. *Clinical Neuropsychiatry, 14*(5), 341–344.

[153] Wilson, G., Farrell, D., Barron, I., Hutchins, J., Whybrow, D., & Kiernan, M. D. (2018). The use of eye-movement desensitization reprocessing (EMDR) therapy in treating post-traumatic stress disorder: A systematic narrative review. *Frontiers in Psychology, 6*(9), 923.

[154] Chen, Y. R., Hung, K. W., Tsai, J. C., Chu, H., Chung, M. H., Chen, S. R., Liao, Y. M., Ou, K. L., Chang, Y. C., & Chou, K. R. (2014). Efficacy of eye-movement desensitization and reprocessing for patients with posttraumatic-stress disorder: A meta-analysis of randomized controlled trials. *PLOS One, 9*(8), E103676.

[155] Chen, L., Zhang, G., Hu, M., & Liang, X. (2015). Eye movement desensitization and reprocessing versus cognitive-behavioral therapy for adult posttraumatic stress disorder: Systematic review and meta-analysis. *Jouranl of Nervous and Mental Disease, 203*, 443–451.

[156] Crumlish, N., & O'Rourke, K. (2010). A systematic review of treatments for post-traumatic stress disorder among refugees and asylum-seekers. *Journal of Nervous and Mental Disease, 198*, 237–251.

[157] Nosè, M., Ballette, F., Bighelli, I., Turrini, G., Purgato, M., Tol, W., Priebe, S., & Barbui C. (2017). Psychosocial interventions for post-traumatic stress disorder in refugees and asylum seekers resettled in high-income countries: Systematic review and meta-analysis. *PLOS One, 12*(2), E0171030.

[158] Slobodin, O., & de Jong, J. T. (2015). Mental health interventions for traumatized asylum seekers and refugees: What do we know about their efficacy? *International Journal of Social Psychiatry, 61*, 17–26.

memory functions.[159] However, effective treatment interventions for refugee families with multiple and protracted traumas must also take into account the role of relational dynamics within families, patient-practitioner relationships, or relationships within communities. With some exceptions,[160,161,162] there is generally a dearth of family focused theories concerning refugees. Some family rese archers[163,164] underscore the importance of investigating not only psychological deficits but also family and community violence or strengths to better grasp environmental resources and barriers to an intervention's efficacy.

The conditions under which therapy is provided to refugees and the war-affected thus, is important. Concerns about legal security and stability as a pre-requisite for therapy are not only inconsistent with the evidence base but can cause delay and denial of necessary services. "Where there is an imminent risk that a vulnerable migrant might be removed from the UK or detained," "this should not necessarily mean that trauma-focused therapy is not offered. Rather, the client should still be offered an evidence-based trauma-focused therapy, and the therapist and client can discuss the possible advantages or disadvantages of such an approach."[165]

Equally important to evidence-driven treatments is the clinical judgment, competence, and experience of the practitioner[166,167] who will need to utilize qualitative studies[168,169] and tailor it to the client's settings and needs. Treatment is more than the change that has occurred under controlled conditions.[170] Experimental settings of interventions can fail to factor in the roles played

[159] Schnyder, U., Ehlers, A., Elbert, T., Foa, E., Gersons, B., Resick, P., Shapiro, F., & Cloitre, M. (2015). Psychotherapy for PTSD: What do they have in common? *European Journal of Psychotraumatology*, 6, 28186.

[160] Weine, S., Muzurovic, N., Kulauzovic, Y., Besic, S., Lezic, A., Mujagic, A., Muzurovic, J., Spahovic, D., Feetham, S., Ware, N., Knafl, K., & Pavkovic, I. (2004). Family consequences of refugee trauma. *Family Process*, 43(2), 147–160.

[161] Slobodin, O., & de Jong, J. T. (2015). Family interventions in traumatized immigrants and refugees: A systematic review. *Transcultural Psychiatry*, 52(6), 723–742.

[162] Ee, E. V. (2018). Multi-family therapy for veteran and refugee families: A Delphi study. *Military Medical Research*, 5(1), 25.

[163] Rolland, J. S. (1994). *Families, illness, and disability: An integrative treatment model*. Basic Books.

[164] Walsh, F. (1998). *Strengthening family resilience*. Guilford Press.

[165] Brady, F., Katona, C., Walsh, E., & Robjant, K. (2021). Psychotherapy and refugees. In D. Bhugra (Ed.), *Oxford textbook of migrant psychiatry* (pp. 493–502). Oxford University Press.

[166] Bonisteel, P. (2009). The tyranny of evidence based medicine. *Canadian Family Physician*, 55(10), 979.

[167] Anjum, R. L., Kerry, R., & Mumford, S. D. (2015). Evidence based on what? *Journal of Evaluation in Clinical Practice*, 21, E11–E12

[168] Thorne, S. (2008). The role of qualitative research within an evidence-based context: Can metasynthesis be the answer? *International Journal of Nursing Studies*, 46(4), 569–575.

[169] Reece, M. J., & Rubin, S. (2021). Qualitative pilot study: Challenges for primary healthcare providers caring for refugees in northeast Ohio. *Cureus*, 13(1), E12572.

[170] American Psychological Association Task Force on Psychological Intervention Guidelines. (1995). *Template for developing guidelines: Interventions/or mental disorders and psychological aspects of physical disorders*. American Psychological Association.

by patient and practitioner or investigator variables for treatment success. Practitioner experience can drive robustness in the patient-practitioner relationship, securing therapeutic success.[171,172,173,174,175]

Systemic Interventions

This section presents a critical examination of the cross-sectoral and diverse domains of interventions in refugee care—psychopharmacological, psychotherapeutic, social-environmental, trauma-informed community, and somatic. Some research recommends[176] that treatment planning may be structured with different interventions deployed in an integrative rather than sequential manner, in consideration of multiple interactions between interventions on different levels.

Mental health and psychosocial support (MHPSS), adopted by the Interagency Standing Committee (IASC), an interagency forum of United Nations and non-UN humanitarian partners, is an umbrella term that encapsulates both social-environmental intervention methods and clinical or biological ones, across a variety of humanitarian sectors. These methods include school-based supports,[177] resettlement assistance (e.g., assistance with residency status, housing, family reunion, and access to employment), somatic psychoeducation of mind-body connection,[178] caregiver support,[179] physical

[171] Schlechter, P., Hellmann, J. H., Wingbermuhle, P., & Morina, N. (2021). Which psychological characteristics influence therapists' readiness to work with refugees? *Clinical Psychology and Psychotherapy*, 28(2), 334–344.

[172] Briere, J. N., & Scott, C. (2013). *Principles of trauma therapy: A guide to symptoms, evaluation, and treatment* (2nd ed.). Sage.

[173] Isakson, B. L., Legerski, J. P., & Layne, C. M. (2015). Adapting and implementing evidence-based interventions for trauma-exposed refugee youth and families. *Journal of Contemporary Psychotherapy: On the Cutting Edge of Modern Developments in Psychotherapy*, 45(4), 245–253.

[174] Duden, G. S., & Borges, L. M. (2021). Psychotherapy with refugees—supportive and hindering elements, *Psychotherapy Research*, 31(3), 402–417.

[175] Hanft-Robert, S., Pohontsch, N. J., Uhr, C., Redlich, A., & Metzner, F. (2020). Therapeutic alliance in interpreter-supported psychotherapy from the perspective of refugee patients: Results of qualitative interviews. *Verhaltenstherapie*, 30(3), 200–291.

[176] IASC. (2007). *IASC guidelines on mental health and psychosocial support in emergency settings* [Report]. https://interagencystandingcommittee.org/system/files/2020-11/IASC%20Guideli nes%20on%20Mental%20Health%20and%20Psychosocial%20Support%20in%20Emergency%20S ettings%20%28English%29.pdf.

[177] Jordans, M. J., Komproe, I. H., Tol, W. A., Kohrt, B. A., Luitel, N. P., Macy, R. D., & deJong, J. V. T. M. (2010). Evaluation of a classroom based psychosocial intervention in conflict-affected Nepal: A cluster randomized controlled trial. *Journal of Child Psychology and Psychiatry*, 51(7), 818–826.

[178] Gordon, J. S., Staples, J. K., Blyta, A., Bytyqi, M., & Wilson, A. T. (2008). Treatment of posttraumatic stress disorder in postwar Kosovar adolescents using mindbody skills groups: A randomized controlled trial. *Journal of Clinical Psychiatry*, 69(9), 1469–1467.

[179] Miller, K. E., Koppenol-Gonzalez, G. V., Arnous, M., Tossyeh, F., Chen, A., Nahas, N., & Jordans, M. J. D. (2020). Supporting Syrian families displaced by armed conflict: A pilot randomized controlled trial of the caregiver support intervention. *Child Abuse and Neglect*, 106, 104512.

activity,[180] and oral health,[181] among others. Social programs can be built around a community's specific psychosocial stressors, and they can include assisting families in income generation, increasing awareness of gender issues, reducing poverty and violence, and procuring volunteers for childcare; they can also help in reducing refugees' postconflict stress.

Although psychosocial measures in postconflict settings can have the benefit[182] of fostering community engagement and health, social and cultural adaptation, self-help, and reviving fragmented social networks, it is unclear whether ameliorating stressors impacts refugees' mental health. While psychosocial interventions are extensively used in postconflict settings, evidence does not support that psychosocial stabilization measures reduce posttraumatic stress.[183] Thus, although complementary in stabilizing efforts toward refugee health, it is critical that psychosocial interventions are not utilized as a substitute for treatment. An analysis of 11 RCT studies with 3,143 child and adolescent participants showed that reductions in children's symptoms of depression and anxiety were not as significant compared to the control group.[184] Although reductions in posttraumatic symptoms were found among 15–18 year olds,[185] researchers estimate their conditions are not equivalent to asylum-seekers during humanitarian emergencies. Not prioritizing psychosocial measures over others, such as some psychotherapeutic ones with documented efficacy, can thus stall research on effective interventions targeting specific mental health issues in postconflict settings. It is for these reasons that researchers[186] recommend targeted mental health interventions; this includes those discussed next.

[180] Richards, J., Foster, C., Townsend, N., & Bauman, A. (2014). Physical fitness and mental health impact of a sport for development intervention in a postconflict setting: Randomised controlled trial nested within an observational study of adolescents in Gulu, Uganda. *BMC Public Health*, 14, 619.

[181] Hamid, S., Dashash, M., & Latifeh, Y. (2021). A short-term approach for promoting oral health of internally displaced children with PTSD: The key is improving mental health—results from a quasi-randomized trial. *BMC Oral Health*, 21, 58.

[182] Silove, D., Ventevogel, P., & Rees, S. (2017). The contemporary refugee crisis: An overview of mental health challenges. *World Psychiatry*, 16(2), 130–139.

[183] Neuner, F. (2010). Assisting war-torn populations—should we prioritize reducing daily stressors to improve mental health? *Social Science and Medicine*, 71(8), 1381–1384.

[184] Purgato, M., Tedeschi, F., Betancourt, T. S., Bolton, P., Bonetto, C., Gastaldon, C., Gordon, J., O'Callaghan, P., Papola, D., Peltonen, K., Punamaki, R. L., Richards, J., Staples, J. K., Unterhitzenberger, J., de Jong, J., Jordans, M. J. D., Gross, A. L., Tol, W. A., & Barbui, C. (2020). Mediators of focused psychosocial support interventions for children in low-resource humanitarian settings: Analysis from an individual participant dataset with 3,143 participants. *Journal of Child Psychology and Psychiatry*, 61(5), 584–593.

[185] Kohrt, B. A., & Song, S. J. (2018). Who benefits from psychosocial support interventions in humanitarian settings? *Lancet Global Health*, 6, E354–E356.

[186] World Health Organization. (2010). *mhGAP intervention guide for mental, neurological and substance use disorders in non-specialized health settings*. https://www.who.int/publications/i/item/9789241549790

Community-Centered Trauma Interventions

Some culturally focused trauma-informed community work also highlights cultural adaptation of trauma treatments. The repair of trauma must extend to communities, social groups, families, and interpersonal connections for healing to occur. Trauma-informed interventions must factor in historic disinvestments, distrust, and power dynamics that may be at the root of forced displacements. Community-centered efforts such as training providers can afford opportunities for healing and reframe community narratives, peer-support networks, and outlets for community members to express and heal from their collective trauma. Community-based mental health can be cost-effective and have large-scale impact on the affected population.

"Building safety and healing within communities requires a multi-layered approach," advocates Ilya Yacevich, Founding Director of Global Trauma Project (GTP), based in East Africa. Its community engagement is multitiered; it includes first empowering local providers affected by secondary trauma to "identify, be aware, and have a language for our experiences." Following this, providers such as religious leaders, teachers, police, and government/military leaders can facilitate such support within their community. The GTP's program is structured, says Yacevich, through consultations with strategic community partners or stalwarts and focus groups using "language and concepts that normalize aspects of mental health and wellbeing."

"We normally start the conversation by using an analogy of a 'Market Basket,'" says Yacevich, pulling out a hand-painted illustration of a large woven basket, filled with fruits and vegetables. "Here, it is common to use a woven basket to carry grocery items. It is ideal to have a good, strong basket, to carry the load well. But sometimes, we could end up with a basket with small tears or larger holes." She shows a second image of the basket, which is now torn, with fruits falling through the holes. "The basket is used to talk about things like 'Adverse Childhood Experiences,' and the impacts of compounded stress—when more weight is added to the small tears, it can create bigger holes, unless mended. If this was the only basket you could ever get, could anything be done to strengthen the basket?" As people talk about stitching, patching, and having more people to help carry the load, the trainer speaks about "resilience."

Culturally relevant and familiar analogies such as the market basket can serve to normalize experiences and introduce concepts of compounded stress, trauma, and healing. Some of the goals of trauma-informed community mental health work can include growing resources for organizing support; working with community partners to better understand the context, stereotypes, fears, and needs of the community; and better supports to manage burnout and effects of secondary trauma.

Pharmacotherapy: The Medical Management
of Mental Health Issues

Psychopharmacology, as a complement to psychotherapy, is recommended for refugees with complex trauma for relief from disruptive symptoms such as sleep disturbances,[187] nightmares, irritability, or psychoses,[188] and to prevent the onset and progression of chronic diseases.[189]

In the absence of a specific pharmacological treatment for complex trauma in refugees,[190] in low-income countries, typical antipsychotic medications—in contrast to atypical antipsychotics with broader advantages[191] and fewer side effects,[192] such as haloperidol and chlorpromazine—are used to treat psychotic breakdowns.[193] Tricyclic drugs and antidepressants such as selective serotonin reuptake inhibitors (e.g., SSRIs including sertraline, paroxetine), are used for major depression and anxiety. However, SSRIs may be contraindicated in elderly patients;[194] they also may not be effective in treating those with multiple symptoms.[195] Although tricyclic antidepressants (TCAs) are useful in treating insomnia, migraines,[196] and chronic back pain, the evidence base for their effectiveness in treating posttraumatic stress is poor. An analysis of prescriptions among Syrian refugees in the Azaatari camp in Jordan reveals the complexity of pharmacological treatment refugees can receive: 59% of patients received neuroleptics; 22% benzodiazepines; 17% hypnotics; and 10% antidepressants.[197]

---

[187] Sandahl, H., Vindbjerg, E., & Carlsson, J. (2017). Treatment of sleep disturbances in refugees suffering from post-traumatic stress disorder. *Transcultural Psychiatry. 54*(5–6), 806–823.

[188] Kinzie, J. D. (2016). Medical approach to the management of traumatized refugees. *Journal of Psychiatric Practice, 22*(2), 76–83.

[189] Gammouh, O. S., Al-Smadi, A. M., Tawalbeh, L. I., & Khoury, L. S. (2015). Chronic diseases, lack of medications, and depression among Syrian refugees in Jordan, 2013–2014. *Preventing Chronic Disease, 12*, E10.

[190] Sonne, C., Carlsson, J., Bech, P., & Mortensen, E. L. (2017). Pharmacological treatment of refugees with trauma-related disorders: What do we know today? *Transcultural Psychiatry, 54*(2), 260–280.

[191] Meltzer, H. Y., & Gadaleta, E. (2021). *Contrasting typical and atypical antipsychotic drugs.* https://focus.psychiatryonline.org/doi/full/10.1176/appi.focus.20200051

[192] First versus second generation. (2020, October 15). *NeuRA.* https://library.neura.edu.au/schizo phrenia/treatments/physical/pharmaceutical/second-generation-antipsychotics/first-versus-sec ond-generation/

[193] Silove, D., Ventevogel, P., & Rees, S. (2017). The contemporary refugee crisis: An overview of mental health challenges. *World Psychiatry, 16*(2), 130–139.

[194] Wilson, K., & Mottran, P. (2004). A comparison of side effects of selective serotonin reuptake inhibitors and tricyclic antidepressants in older depressed patients: A meta- analysis. *International Journal of Geriatric Psychiatry, 19*(8), 754–762.

[195] Kinzie, J. D. (2016). Medical approach to the management of traumatized refugees. *Journal of Psychiatric Practice, 22*(2), 76–83.

[196] Jackson, J. L., Shimeall, W., Sessums, L., Dezee, K. J., Becher, D., Diemer, M., Berbano, E., & O'Malley, P. G. (2010). Tricyclic antidepressants and headache: Systematic review and meta-analysis. *BMJ, 341*, C5222.

[197] Moutaouakkil, Y., Gartoum, M., Tadlaoui, Y., Bennana, A., Cherrah, Y., Lamsaouri, J., & Bousliman, Y. (2017). The prescription of psychotropic drugs in the Syrian refugee camp of Azaatari. *Medecine Therapeutique, 23*(6), 403–408.

But sparse research on psychopharmacological use and delivery[198] among the refugee and internally displaced populations calls into question the direct transferability of results from nonrefugee populations to refugee ones.

Some other challenges encountered in psychopharmacological management of mental health concerns in various refugee settings are maintaining a continuous supply of medications, training of community health workers in overseeing prescriptions, managing side effects, and interaction with ongoing health conditions prevalent in refugees, such as diabetes and hypertension. Also consider the questionable ethics and sustainability of prescribing an antipsychotic to which a person may not have continued access. Although optimal treatment planning is achieved with collaborations between primary care physicians and psychiatrists, clinicians may find themselves overwhelmed in some refugee settings.[199]

As a possible result of the limitations of pharmacotherapy with those with mass trauma experiences, substance use increases among displaced populations, presumably in part to assuage emotional suffering. Stigma associated with pharmacological treatment can result in self-medication, using indigenous stimulants such as coca, Khat, and betel leaf, by traumatized populations including refugees. Among 33 male Somali refugees in Kenya, traumatic experiences were associated with the use of Khat—a plant-based psychoactive substance that is a natural amphetamine.[200] More refugees who were Khat chewers had PTSD diagnoses compared to nonchewers. Of the Somali refugees, 85% reported that Khat use helped them to forget their painful memories.[201]

Ethnopsychopharmacology suggests medications and doses need to be individually titrated across ethnic and racial groups.[202] Ethnicity significantly influences response to psychotropic drugs,[203] prescription adherence, side effects, frequency of prescription usage, and outcome of treatment.[204]

[198] Kay, M., Wijayanayaka, S., Cook, H., & Hollingworth, S. (2016). Understanding quality use of medicines in refugee communities in Australian primary care: A qualitative study. *British Journal of General Practice: Journal of the Royal College of General Practitioners, 66*(647), E397–E409.

[199] Rousseau, C. (2018). Addressing mental health needs of refugees. *La Revue Canadienne de Psychiatrie, 63*(5), 287–289.

[200] Tol, W. A., Komproe, I. H., Susanty, D., Jordans, M. J., Macy, R. D., & de Jong, J. T. (2008). School-based mental health intervention for children affected by political violence in Indonesia: A cluster randomized trial. *JAMA, 300*(6), 655–662.

[201] Widmann, M., Warsame, A. H., Mikulica, J., von Beust, J., Isse, M. M., Ndetei, D., al'Absi, M., & Odenwald, M. G. (2014). Khat use, PTSD and psychotic symptoms among Somali refugees in Nairobi: A pilot study. *Frontiers in Public Health, 2,* 71.

[202] Henderson, D. C. (2021). Psychopharmacology and refugees, asylum seekers and migrants. In D. Bhugra (Ed.), *Oxford textbook of migrant psychiatry* (pp. 483–492). Oxford University Press.

[203] Marazziti, D., Stahl, S. M., Simoncini, M., Baroni, S., Mucci, F., Palego, L., Betti, L., Massimetti, G., Giannaccini, G., & Dell'Osso, L. (2020). Psychopharmacology and ethnicity: A comparative study on Senegalese and Italian men. *World Journal of Biological Psychiatry, 21*(4), 300–307.

[204] Marazziti, D., Mucci, F., Avella, M. T., Palagini, L., Simoncini, M., & Dell'Osso, L. (2021). The increasing challenge of the possible impact of ethnicity on psychopharmacology. *CNS Spectrums, 26*(3), 222–231.

Well-designed clinical trials to investigate drug effects, and the effect of ethnicity on use, compliance, and side effects, are needed to strengthen the use of pharmacotherapy as a complement to psychotherapy. Effective treatment planning must go beyond immediate symptoms. Associated and pre-existing medical conditions must also be addressed, necessitating a robust practitioner-patient relationship and culturally acceptable treatment approaches.[205] Emphasizing the importance of an empathic alliance in the uptake and continuation of medication, any dichotomy between pharmacology and the use of talk therapy may, in essence, be a false polarity.[206]

Rape and Maternal Health: Somatic Interventions

Rape and mass rape have been regularly employed in war to brutalize women and intimidate, subjugate, and punish entire communities, as Rumi's vignette at the start of this chapter reveals. Sexual enslavement can involve holding women (and men) captive for months or years while they are being raped violently by scores of victimizers, as in the case of Yazidi, Chibok, and Democratic Republic of Congo[207] young women. Major bleeding in females aged 15–45 years, usually related to pregnancy, is the leading cause of their death in refugee camps.[208]

This highlights four issues for treatment:

- Somatic concerns, such as vaginismus and pain disorder, are *gateway concerns* to exploring women's history of violence, as they are highly correlated with sexual and gender-based violence (SGVB survivors),[209] even among children and adolescents.[210]

[205] Kinzie, J. D., Tran, K. A., Breckenridge, A., & Bloom, J. D. (1980). An Indochinese refugee psychiatric clinic: Culturally accepted treatment approaches. *American Journal Psychiatry, 137*(11), 1429–1432.

[206] McWilliams, N. (2003). The educative aspects of psychoanalysis. *Psychoanalytic Psychology, 20*(2), 245–260.

[207] Kelly, A. (2014, July 23). Sexual slavery rife in Democratic Republic of the Congo, says MSF. *The Guardian.* https://www.theguardian.com/global-development/2014/jul/23/sexual-slavery-democratic-republic-congo-msf

[208] Van Boekholt, T. A., Moturi, E., Hölscher, H., Schulte-Hillen, C., Tappis, H., & Burton, A. (2023). Review of maternal death audits in refugee camps in UNHCR East and Horn of Africa and Great Lakes Region, 2017–2019. *International Journal of Gynecology & Obstetrics, 160*(2), 483–491.

[209] Ciocca, G., Limoncin, E., Di Tommaso, S., Gravina, G. L., Di Sante, S., Carosa, E., Tullii, A., Marcozzi, A., Lenzi, A., & Jannini, E. A. (2013). Alexithymia and vaginismus: A preliminary correlation perspective. *International Journal of Impotence Research, 25*(3), 113–116.

[210] Pichel, A. N., & Suryadi, D. (2021). Somatic symptoms in young adult women who experienced sexual violence throughout life development: A systematic review. In S. Tiatri & L. C. Seong (Eds.), *Proceedings of the International Conference on Economics, Business, Social, and Humanities: Advances in social science, education and humanities research* (pp. 533–539).

- Prioritizing treatment for those who have been sexually enslaved while being mindful that their acute trauma stage may overlap with their resettlement within host nations.
- Treatment planning needs to incorporate healers from within communities, thus ameliorating the stigma of being sullied through rape.
- Expediting care and bridging capacity gaps must be provided for emergency obstetric care, family planning, and adolescent sexual and reproductive health services.

Somatization, the unconscious process wherein psychological distress is expressed through physical discomfort, is an important aspect of concurrent or previous trauma.[211,212,213,214] Somatic symptoms can range from sleep distu rbances,[215,216] pain, headaches,[217] stomach pain, insomnia, vaginismus, fatigue, tinnitus, and so forth, and can feature prominently among traumatized, diverse populations. Indeed, as discussed in Chapter 4, unexplained somatization is higher across the lifespan in refugees than in the general Western population.[218] The chief complaints of the Yazidi women of northern Iraq are pain symptoms and chronic pain being comorbid with posttraumatic stress. Besides the nature of trauma, somatization can be affected by age, education, language proficiency, and culture. Other groups that can express distress through somatization include the elderly, the tortured,[219] and those of low socioeconomic status, those with

[211] Jongedijk, R. A., Eising, D. D., van der Aa, N., Kleber, R. J., & Boelen, P. A. (2020). Severity profiles of posttraumatic stress, depression, anxiety, and somatization symptoms in treatment seeking traumatized refugees. *Journal of Affective Disorders, 266*, 71–81.

[212] Mölsä, M., Punamäki, R. L., Saarni, S. I., Tiilikainen, M., Kuittinen, S., & Honkasalo, M. L. (2014). Mental and somatic health and pre- and post-migration factors among older Somali refugees in Finland. *Transcultural Psychiatry, 51*(4), 499–525.

[213] Laban, C. J., Gernaat, H. B., Komproe, I. H., Schreuders, B. A., & de Jong, J. T. (2004). Impact of a long asylum procedure on the prevalence of psychiatric disorders in Iraqi asylum seekers in the Netherlands. *Journal of Nervous and Mental Disease, 192*(12), 843–851.

[214] Spiller, T. R., Schick, M., Schnyder, U., Bryant, R. A., Nickerson, A., & Morina, N. (2016). Somatisation and anger are associated with symptom severity of posttraumatic stress disorder in severely traumatised refugees and asylum seekers. *Swiss Medical Weekly, 146*, W14311.

[215] Ashina, H., Al-Khazali, H. M., Iljazi, A., Ashina, S., Amin, F. M., Lipton, R. B., & Schytz, H. W. (2021). Psychiatric and cognitive comorbidities of persistent post-traumatic headache attributed to mild traumatic brain injury. *Journal of Headache and Pain, 22*(1), 83.

[216] Lee, S., Lee, J., Jeon, S., Kim, S., Seo, Y., Park, J., Lee, Y. J., & Kim, S. J. (2021). Nightmares and alexithymia in traumatized North Korean refugees. *Sleep Medicine, 86*, 75–80.

[217] Headache can also be a sequela of mild traumatic brain injury: Nampiaparampil, D. E. (2008). Prevalence of chronic pain after traumatic brain injury: A systematic review. *JAMA, 300*(6), 711–719; Ashina, H., Porreca, F., Anderson, T., Amin, F. M., Ashina, M., Schytz, H. W., & Dodick, D. W. (2019). Post-traumatic headache: Epidemiology and pathophysiological insights. *Nature Reviews Neurology, 15*(10), 607–617; Ashina, H., Eigenbrodt, A. K., Seifert, T., Sinclair, A. J., Scher, A. I., Schytz, H. W., Lee, M. J., de Icco, R., Finkel, A. G., & Ashina, M. (2021). Post-traumatic headache attributed to traumatic brain injury: Classification, clinical characteristics, and treatment. *Lancet Neurology, 20*(6), 460–469.

[218] Rohlof, H. G., Knipscheer, J. W., & Kleber, R. J. (2014). Somatization in refugees: A review. *Social Psychiatry and Psychiatric Epidemiology, 49*(11), 1793–1804.

[219] Ibid.

poor language proficiency or education, such as displaced females from non-Western countries such as Iraq, Chechnya, Afghanistan, and West Africa,[220] as well as those with high postmigration stress.[221]

The body can thus be a repository of trauma, where trauma memories can be encoded,[222] thwarting other self-protective functions such as regulation, interoception (the body's ability to sense and represent sensations in its internal and external world is referred to as *interoception*), or their interrelationship. Interoception is a critical barometer for discerning emotions and for emotional regulation and shaping cognitions.[223] Psychological disturbances such as PTSD can accompany deficits in interoception, such as the inability to identify, express, and regulate emotions or alexithymia[224] and dysfunctionality in the sense of self. Since the core of our sense of self, self-awareness, and social awareness is the body, therapeutic processes should aim at improving interoceptive processes.[225]

Other researchers too underscore the presence of embodied trauma in physical distress and suggest body-based movements,[226,227] such as art and theater to activate group belonging;[228] building awareness of the body through body psychotherapy;[229] bonding and building trust and self-esteem through equine-assisted therapy;[230] promoting improved sleep and physical health[231] and so

[220] Taha, P. H., & Sijbrandij M. (2021). Gender differences in traumatic experiences, PTSD, and relevant symptoms among the Iraqi internally displaced persons. *International Journal of Environmental Research and Public Health, 18*(18), 9779.

[221] Renner, W., & Salem, I. (2009). Post-traumatic stress in asylum seekers and refugees from Chechnya, Afghanistan, and West Africa: Gender differences in symptomatology and coping. *International Journal of Social Psychiatry, 55*(2), 99–108.

[222] Van Der Kolk, B. A. (2014). *The body keeps the score: Brain, mind, and body in the healing of trauma.* Viking.

[223] Pollotos, O., & Herbert, B. M. (2018). Introception: Definitions, dimensions, neural substrates. In G. Hauke & A. Kritikos (Eds.), *Embodiment in psychotherapy: A practitioner's guide* (pp. 15–28). Springer International.

[224] Sifneos, P. E. (1976). The prevalence of "alexithymic" characteristics in psychosomatic patients. *Psychotherapy and Psychosomatics, 22*(2), 255–262.

[225] Pollotos, O., & Herbert, B. M. (2018). Introception: Definitions, dimensions, neural substrates. In G. Hauke & A. Kritikos (Eds.), *Embodiment in psychotherapy: A practitioner's guide* (p.15–28). Springer.

[226] Schaeffer, A. J., & Cornelius-White, H. D. (2021). Qualitative studies on body-based interventions for refugees: A meta-synthesis. *Body, Movement and Dance in Psychotherapy, 16*(4), 267–285.

[227] Aranda, E., De Zárate, M. H., & Panhofer, H. (2020). Transformed ground, transformed body: Clinical implications for dance movement therapy with forced migrants. *Body, Movement and Dance in Psychotherapy, 15*(3), 156–170.

[228] Apergi, A. (2014). Working with liminality: A dramatherapeutic intervention with immigrants in a day care centre in Greece. *Dramatherapy, 36*(2–3), 121–134.

[229] Çesko, E. (2020). Body oriented work with refugees. *Body, Movement and Dance in Psychotherapy, 15*(3), 142–155.

[230] Shelef, A., Brafman, D., Rosing, T., Weizman, A., Stryjer, R., & Barak, Y. (2019). Equine assisted therapy for patients with post traumatic stress disorder: A case series study. *Military Medicine, 184*(9–10), 394–399.

[231] Nilsson, H., Gustavsson, C., Gottvall, M., & Saboonchi, F. (2021). Physical activity, post-traumatic stress disorder, and exposure to torture among asylum seekers in Sweden: A cross-sectional study. *BMC Psychiatry, 21*, 452.

forth. Yoga treatments, especially of an extended duration with homework adherence, can result in significant reductions of symptoms of posttraumatic stress, dissociation,[232] tension, and depression in females with chronic treatment-resistant PTSD.[233]

In body-based interventions with refugees between 2014 and 2020, researchers identified some key intervention elements: attunement (e.g., being empathetic and gentle, treating the patient according to the patient's needs), safety (e.g., choice of a familiar location for therapy), increased bodily awareness, improved physical health, and improved emotional experiencing. This study also demonstrated that sleep symptoms have an indirect and long-term impact on mental health among refugees.[234]

Sexual and somatic health is deeply interwoven with mental health in female refugees. Trauma-focused care with displaced women must incorporate a deep yet nuanced knowledge of somatization and interpersonal violence. Psychoeducation can be provided in venues such as religious organizations, language programs, group therapy, and vocational guidance. However, since women can face ostracization and further violence by their community given the stigmas surrounding sexual violence, utmost care must be taken to ensure that mobile clinics or other spaces where health workers interact with them are confidential, sound-proof, and secure. Tailoring interventions around resilience themes may also help women integrate mental health awareness for the benefit of their families who may be reluctant to engage in mental health care.

These therapies show that a number of treatment components in a multiphase and multitiered mental health system can assist refugees.

Other Vulnerable Populations

LGBTQI+: Fear and Forced Concealment

Lesbian, gay, bisexual, transgender, queer, and intersex life (LGBTQI+) asylum-seekers[235] experience high levels of distress through confronting unique barriers to integration. For many experiences of homo-bi-transphobia can interact with

[232] Price, M., Spinazzola, J., Musicaro, R., Turner, J., Suvak, M., Emerson, D., & van der Kolk, B. (2017). Effectiveness of an extended yoga treatment for women with chronic posttraumatic stress disorder. *Journal of Alternate and Complementary Medicine, 23*(4), 300–309.

[233] Van der Kolk, B., West, J., Rhodes, A., Emerson, D., Suvak, M., & Spinazzola, J. (2014). Yoga as an adjunctive treatment for posttraumatic stress disorder: A randomized controlled trial. *Journal of Clinical Psychiatry, 75*(6), E559–E565.

[234] Lies, J., Drummond, S. P. A., & Jobson, L. (2020). Longitudinal investigation of the relationships between trauma exposure, post-migration stress, sleep disturbance, and mental health in Syrian refugees. *European Journal of Psychotraumatology, 11*(1), 1825166.

[235] Estimates of the size of this population are not known.

experiences of racism,[236] and amplify their safety concerns and marginalization in host nations. They may face challenges integrating and accessing housing and employment. It is critical, for example, that housing facilities collaborate with grass-roots organizations to ensure trans asylum-seekers' needs for physical and psychological safety to support integration.[237]

Many LGBTQI+ asylum-seekers, especially transgender and gender nonconforming individuals, may decline support out of fear, shame, and forced concealment of their gender identity or sexual orientation because of family pressures. A case study of the *buddy system* adopted by the Netherlands illustrates the importance of proactive steps in establishing mentors and peer-support in the LGBTQI+ community to assist in early steps toward integration. There is a need to address barriers such as language, as well as the potential for randomized surveys to facilitate a greater understanding of the needs of the transgender asylum population.[238] Besides the approaches highlighted in previous sections, other considerations for improving well-being and integration include the availability of mental health resources to those awaiting asylum determinations and to those who are not proficient in English.[239] Group support and tele-health may be useful to scale-up supportive interactions and reduce social isolation for those without health insurance or who may not have access to a therapist proficient in their language.[240] Mental health provisions to this population must be sensitized to systems of oppression because of social norms of cisnormativity and heteronormativity, their interaction with race, and their postmigration stressors.

[236] Mulé, N. J., & Gamble, K. (2018). Haven or precarity? The mental health of LGBT asylum seekers and refugees in Canada. In N. Nicol, A. Jjuuko, R. Lusimbo, N. J. Mulé, S. Ursel, A. Wahab, & P. Waugh (Eds.), *Envisioning global LGBT human rights: (Neo)colonialism, neoliberalism, resistance and hope* (pp. 205–220). Human Rights Consortium & University of London.

[237] Bassetti, E. (2019). Integration challenges faced by transgender refugees in Italy. In A. Güler, M. Shevtsova, & D. Venturi (Eds.), *LGBTI asylum seekers and refugees from a legal and political perspective* (pp. 337–354). Springer.

[238] Munir, L. P. (2019). Fleeing gender: Reasons for displacement in Pakistan's transgender community: Persecution, asylum and integration. In A. Güler, M. Shevtsova, & D. Venturi (Eds.), *LGBTI asylum seekers and refugees from a legal and political perspective: Persecution, asylum and integration* (pp. 49–69). Springer.

[239] Fox, S. D., Griffin, R. H., & Pachankis, J. E. (2020). Minority stress, social integration, and the mental health needs of LGBTQ asylum seekers in North America. *Social Science and Medicine, 246,* 112727.

[240] Logie, C. H., Lacombe-Duncan, A., Lee-Foon, N., Ryan, S., & Ramsay, H. (2016). "It's for us—newcomers, LGBTQ persons, and HIV-positive persons. You feel free to be": A qualitative study exploring social support group participation among African and Caribbean lesbian, gay, bisexual and transgender newcomers and refugees in Toronto, Canada. *BMC International Health and Human Rights, 16,* 18.

Older Refugees and Languishing in Place

Older refugees, typically defined as those aged 60 years and older, make up 4% of the displaced internationally,[241] although this is likely an underestimate owing to older refugees' illiteracy, lack of knowledge of their birth date, or barriers in the registration process for asylum-seekers.[242] In a refugee crisis, most older refugees are either unable to or unwilling to leave their homes because of the arduous flight to safety. Often, the deaths of younger male relatives may leave them unable to fend for themselves, and, thus, there is a greater likelihood of older refugees finding themselves in long-term camps, as compared with younger asylum-seekers.[243] In addition to economic challenges, the displaced elderly experience high mortality rates in the earlier phase of humanitarian emergencies.[244] They are challenged by a host of chronic health problems such as hypertension, diabetes, heart disease,[245] and other such as vision and mobility issues[246] or diarrheal diseases, measles, and acute respiratory infections.[247] Although a majority of older refugees are preoccupied about their physical health[248] and perceived their health to have worsened in host nations,[249] they also face considerable challenges in accessing basic healthcare and medications.

The health and palliative needs of older refugees are under-represented in research. On one hand, challenges such as their older age, erosion of their social support, poor physical health status, food insecurity, and insufficient healthcare facilities in camps may lend a precarity to the lives of the elderly.[250] On the other hand, their resilience may derive from their experiences in life and their

[241] UNHCR. (2020). *Global trends: Forced displacement in 2019*. https://www.unhcr.org/5ee200 e37.pdf

[242] UNHCR. (2021). *Working with older people in forced displacement*. https://www.refworld.org/ pdfid/4ee72aaf2.pdf

[243] Crisp, J. (2010). Forced displacement in Africa: Dimensions, difficulties, and policy directions. *Refugee Survey Quarterly, 29*(3), 1–27.

[244] Toole, M. J., & Waldman, R. J. (1997). The public health aspects of complex emergencies and refugee situations. *Annual Review of Public Health, 18*, 283–312.

[245] Coutts, A., Fouad, F. M., Abbara, A., Sibai, A. M., Sahloul, Z., & Blanchet, K. (2015). Responding to the Syrian health crisis: The need for data and research. *Lancet, 3*(3), 8–9.

[246] Strong, J., Varady, C., Chahda, N., Doocey, S., & Burnham, G. (2015). Health status and health needs of older refugees from Syria in Lebanon. *Conflict and Health, 9*, 12.

[247] Toole, M. J., & Waldman, R. J. (1997). The public health aspects of complex emergencies and refugee situations. *Annual Review of Public Health, 18*, 283–312.

[248] Tippens, J. A. (2020). Generational perceptions of support among Congolese refugees in urban Tanzania. *Global Social Welfare, 7*(1), 69–80.

[249] Strong, J., Varady, C., Chahda, N., Doocey, S., & Burnham, G. (2015). Health status and health needs of older refugees from Syria in Lebanon. *Conflict and Health, 9*, 12.

[250] Böcker, A., & Hunter, A. (2022). Older refugees and internally displaced people in African countries: Findings from a scoping review of literature. *Journal of Refugee Studies*, feac023. https:// doi.org/10.1093/jrs/feac023

social status within their families and communities.[251] Some recommendations for improving the health of older refugees are attention to age-specific health-related needs, inclusion in programming for psychosocial support, and prioritizing research on the lived experiences of displaced elders. Eliminating food insecurity and improving dietary diversity[252] can also prevent a build-up of comorbid conditions and enhance their daily functionality.[253] Displacement can also affect mourning, bereavement, and whether or not families have access to their cultural rituals and practices during the death of their significant others.[254] In resource-strapped environments, as we witnessed especially during Covid-19, significant disparities exist in the quality of healthcare received by the elderly, heightening their pain and suffering as that of their families. The older forcibly displaced face unique challenges that require targeted resources and community services to identify their mental health needs and access to necessary health care.

Prioritizing the vision, strategy, and development of mental health services in marginalized refugee communities can rebuild capacity for refugee mental health. Combining research insights either cross-sectorally or developmentally across the lifespan can boost treatment efforts, develop graduated rehabilitation, and build on our advances.[255]

A culturally fluent mental health system for rehabilitating[256] severely traumatized refugees unresponsive to treatment[257] requires different recovery trajectories. Treatments need to be flexible with targeted interventions for specific

[251] Hampshire, K., Porter, G., Kilpatrick, K., Kyei, P., Adjaloo, M., & Oppong, G. (2008). Liminal spaces: Changing inter-generational relations among long-term Liberian refugees in Ghana. *Human Organization, 67*(1), 25–36.

[252] Gichunge, C., Mutiso, D., & Brynjarsdottir, J. (2020). Predictors of social support, physical health and mental health among food insecure internally displaced persons in Turkana, Kenya. *Conflict and Health, 14,* 58.

[253] Frost, C. J., Morgan, N. J., Allkhenfr, H., Dearden, S., Ess, R., Albalawi, W. F., Berri, A., Benson, L. S., & Gren, L. H. (2019). Determining physical and mental health conditions present in older adult refugees: A mini-review. *Gerontology, 65*(3), 209–215.

[254] Madi, F., Ismail, H., Fouad, F. M., Kerbage, H., Zaman, S., Jayawickrama, J., & Sibai, A. M. (2019). Death, dying, and end-of-life experiences among refugees: A scoping review. *Journal of Palliative Care, 34*(2), 139–144.

[255] Silove, D., Tay, A., & Rees, S. (2019). Psychotherapy for refugees and other populations exposed to conflict. In D. Stein, J. Bass, & S. Hofmann (Eds.), *Global mental health and psychotherapy: Adapting psychotherapy for low- and middle-income countries* (pp. 341–362). Academic Press.

[256] Silove, D., Ventevogel, P., & Rees, S. (2017). The contemporary refugee crisis: An overview of mental health challenges. *World Psychiatry, 16*(2), 130–139.

[257] Buhmann, C. B., Nordentoft, M., Ekstroem, M., Carlsson, J., & Mortensen, E. L. (2016). The effect of flexible cognitive-behavioural therapy and medical treatment, including antidepressants on post-traumatic stress disorder and depression in traumatised refugees: Pragmatic randomised controlled clinical trial. *British Journal of Psychiatry, 208*(3), 252–259.

difficulties,[258] and take into account unique constellations of comorbidities, circumstances, and settings. Since most refugees generally reside in resource-impoverished settings, knowledge of evidence-based, trauma-informed, and culturally sensitive psychotherapeutic interventions can promote better mental health outcomes and improve health access.

In coordinating culturally sensitive assessment with evidence-based intervention through different displacement contexts, wherever possible, the field of refugee intervention science can benefit from a cohesive intervention system. It will also form the bedrock for healthier integration of refugees in host nations.

[258] World Health Organization. (2010). *mhGAP intervention guide for mental, neurological and substance use disorders in non-specialized health settings.* https://www.who.int/publications/i/item/9789241549790

Epilogue

The Forcibly Displaced: Looking Ahead

In December 2022, I visited Ukraine and Poland and celebrated the displaced Ukrainians' first Christmas since the Russian invasion of their nation.

Since February 24 2022, Przemyśl, a sleepy town of approximately 60,000 on the Polish-Ukraine border, has witnessed a steady influx of distraught Ukrainian mothers, grandmothers, and children fleeing the Russian invasion of their home. The menfolk accompanying them stayed just long enough at the razor-wire fence to hand over the children, then turned back to serve in the military. On that first day of the war, approximately 800 Ukrainians poured into Przemyśl in about 5-degree centigrade weather: "On the second day the line of people seeking entry had grown to 18 km. It was the first wave of refugees that would swell to 50,000–60,000 people per day for a few days," says Mayor Wojciech Bakun. Like other inhabitants of Przemyśl, he too felt "embattled," but at the same time, he said, "We couldn't move our city to another place."

As Ukrainians flooded in, Przemyśl's railway stations were converted into reception centers offering refugees sandwiches, tea, and coffee; schools were converted into dorms, and the town hospital doubled up to provide emergency services to the hungry, fatigued, dehydrated, sick, and pregnant. In those initial days, an inexperienced township transformed itself into a rapid responder. Until international assistance in the form of Red Cross and the World Central Kitchen arrived, Bakun's 67-year-old mother sheltered refugees in her home, and its citizens—including its elderly—worked 24/7 spearheading the most gargantuan volunteer effort in its history. "Whatever happens," Bakun remembers thinking, "we have to think about the people. *Nothing* else matters. We have to save each person trying to run out of Ukraine."

"You know," a Ukrainian mother with a toddler told me, "they showed up with diapers and baby strollers." Following bomb attacks on her hometown, she had hidden in her basement for weeks, waited at the railway station for days, and then boarded a train crammed with others not knowing where it would take her. When she finally arrived utterly exhausted at the border, like other Ukrainians, she was overwhelmed to find diapers, wheelchairs, pet carriers, and fully equipped strollers left for their use by Polish mothers. In Poland, as in Germany in 2015, ordinary citizens have organized themselves and their communities

Displaced. Shaifali Sandhya, Oxford University Press. © Shaifali Sandhya 2024.
DOI: 10.1093/oso/9780197579886.003.0011

into powerful grassroots movements to feed, teach, find employment, direct donations, understand through translators, console, and house refugees and sometimes their pets and children, often for months.

This moment in Poland, of citizen-led hospitality, private sector-refugee partnerships, and the cultural closeness it engenders between hosts and refugees, is also our moment of promise to seize upon to address proactively the trauma of refugees. One in five people in postconflict settings and among specific refugee groups one in three, has depression, anxiety disorder, posttraumatic stress disorder (PTSD), bipolar disorder, or schizophrenia.[1] Refugees resettled in safe havens, as my study established, continue to report high levels of posttraumatic stress, depression, and crippling anxiety for several years far beyond their initial settlement. War-affected families suffer not just from PTSD, "the most dangerous of psychiatric diseases,"[2] but undergo complex trauma when trauma presents more than it *ordinarily* would—with severity, chronicity, multiple influences - with enduring effects on individuals, communities, nations, and their future generations. Becoming a refugee poses the single biggest risk to one's morbidity and mortality and is the turning point that can change the trajectory of one's life forever.

Strengthening the resilience of the displaced by tackling their poor mental health to facilitate their integration into work, education, housing, legal, and social domains ought to be a key priority for the global community.

The toll of failing to elevate refugees' mental health, at the personal, communal, and international levels, is sprawling and growing. With the number of displaced projected to increase to 130.8 million and 94 million children estimated to be impacted by humanitarian crises in 2024, their scope of need is immense. If their plight is not alleviated, the forcibly displaced will lose many valuable years of their lives trapped in grinding poverty, and persecution alongside bearing the significant burden of disease If their plight is not alleviated, the forcibly displaced will lose many valuable years of their lives trapped in grinding poverty, persecution alongside bearing the significant burden of disease. They will experience educational, cultural, and linguistic emaciation in the absence of access to schools, family rituals, medical assistance, and a thriving community life. Generations of children will reel under the effects of being deprived of education, health, and safety, thus widening social inequality and pushing them into generational poverty.

[1] Charlson, F., van Ommeren, M., Flaxman, A., Cornett, J., Whiteford, H., & Saxena, S. (2019). New WHO prevalence estimates of mental disorders in conflict settings: A systematic review and meta-analysis. *Lancet, 394*(10194), 240–248.
[2] Pagel, J. F. (2017). Post Freudian PTSD: Breath, the protector of dreams [Commentary]. *Journal of Clinical Sleep Medicine, 13*(10), 1121–1122.

The odds are stacked against the refugees. The forcibly displaced will jeopardize their lives as they repeatedly attempt to escape their languishment in long-term camps or when they are ordered back to their countries by hostile nations.[3] In many parts of the world it is exceptionally difficult to be a woman or a child; displacement exacerbates their challenges. A strong connection exists between social pathologies like poverty in refugee camps and domestic violence and child abuse that can heighten trauma. Displaced children in camps are routinely abused through child-hawking,[4] child marriage, neglect, sexual assaults, and other forms of verbal and physical violence,[5] with perpetrators ranging from their parents to traffickers to UN aid workers.[6] With insecurities created by food, fuel or fertilizers and other deprivations a majority of the world's displaced live in regions that are like time bombs. Vulnerable civilians are becoming displaced at an alarming rate today.

The stakes could not be higher for the world's refugees—and for us, the global community. Within the United States, the total economic burden of PTSD was estimated at $232.2 billion for 2018 or $19,630 per individual.[7] During 2020 and 2021, as human distress has soared, more than 90% of countries reversed their progress on human development according to the United Nations Development Program (UNDP).[8]

Unaddressed trauma is costly for the world. But much more must be initiated at individual, regional, and international levels to stem the unbearable costs to human suffering.

[3] Mexican asylum-seekers who were turned away from the United States under Title 42 have suffered at least 8,705 violent attacks and kidnappings since January 2021: Human Rights First. (2021). *Human Rights First Tracker of reported attacks during the Biden administration against asylum seekers and migrants who are stranded in and/or expelled to Mexico.* https://humanrightsfirst.org/wp-content/uploads/2021/08/AttacksonAsylumSeekersStrandedinMexicoDuringBidenAdministration.6.17.21.pdf

[4] *9000 DR Congo refugee children hawking in Angola.* (2018, June 13). The East African. https://www.theeastafrican.co.ke/tea/news/rest-of-africa/9-000-dr-congo-children-hawking-in-angola-1396008

[5] Dickson, C., & Danjuma, J. (2020). An appraisal of the incidences of child abuse among the internally displaced persons (IDPs) in Benue state, Nigeria. *The New Humanitarian.*

[6] Mednick, S. (2022, September 22). Alleged sex abuse by aid workers unchecked for years in UN-run South Sudan camp. *The New Humanitarian.* https://www.thenewhumanitarian.org/2022/09/22/exclusive-alleged-sex-abuse-aid-workers-unchecked-years-un-run-south-sudan-camp

[7] The costs encompass those beyond direct health care to include nondirect health care costs (e.g., substance-use disorder, homelessness, and disability benefits), and indirect costs of unemployment (e.g., disability, premature mortality, costs of being a caregiver to someone who suffers from it, and from productivity loss at work): Davis, L., Schein, J., Cloutier, M., Gagnon-Sanschagrin, P., Maitland, J. Urganus, A., Lefebvre, P., & Houle, C. R. (2022). *The economic burden of posttraumatic stress disorder in the United States from a societal perspective.* https://www.psychiatrist.com/jcp/trauma/ptsd/economic-burden-posttraumatic-stress-disorder-united-states-societal-perspective/

[8] UNDP. (2022, September 8). *Multiple crises halt progress as 9 out of 10 countries fall backwards in human development, UNDP report warns.* https://www.undp.org/press-releases/multiple-crises-halt-progress-9-out-10-countries-fall-backwards-human-development-undp-report-warns

Contemporary multicultural health care is a significant tool to address the critical role of culture, race, religion, gender, stigma, sexual orientation, and social status, and remedy their prejudicial and racialized treatment. For the effective recovery[9] of the trauma of the displaced, it must be implemented and tailored at all stages of displacement and resettlement through multiple sectors. First, let us address a promising new area in refugee mental health:

Citizen-led efforts in the area of refugee integration and humanitarian assistance offers a promising vibrant arena for mainstreaming the public as stakeholders in supporting refugees. The citizen-refugee collaborations can help us explore how interpersonal connections may mitigate refugee trauma and how community-based interventions can boost their physical and mental health. Assisting the displaced today is also a labyrinthian network of engaged and invested supporters in the form of nongovernmental organizations, the private sector, religious leadership, sports organizations, donors, and academics. Worldwide, strident efforts to improve the living conditions of the refugees (through, e.g., distributing food, building camps, educating children, and treating traumas from accidents) are spearheaded by an army of tireless humanitarian and health workers working around the clock. Unexpected donors like the secret Bansky Boat that rescued the lives of 89 migrants in the Mediterranean highlight the efforts of human rights defenders and nongovernmental organizations conducting rescue operations on the sea.

The commitment of multiple stakeholders, represented by the Global Refugee Forum 2023, also marks a significant opportunity to catalyze our partnerships, innovate synergistic solutions with the communities that need our help, craft new stories of what we value, and reinvigorate a new leadership around refugee mental health.

But some stumbling blocks to refugee well-being and integration are myths about the refugees. Misconceptions abound concerning who constitutes a refugee; valid ways of entry into the country for asylum applications; why certain types of refugees cannot adhere to state rules, and the fast versus slow rate of integration of some asylum-seekers versus others, and more. The prominence of the immigration issue in US politics, for instance, gives the impression that the United States is awash with refugees, but the truth is quite different. In 2022 for instance, the United States admitted only 10,000 refugees, the fewest in almost half a century. Worldwide, only about 0.13% of registered refugees deemed to require protection in 2020 were relocated to a new country. 2021 witnessed an increase of 71% in refugees (429,300) from the year prior who were returned to their countries of origin from the previous year. In practice, the number of

[9] Ingleby, D. (2005). Editor's introduction. In D. Ingleby (Ed.), *Forced migration and mental health: Rethinking the care of refugees and displaced persons* (pp. 1–27). Utrecht University Press.

rejected applications and forced returns of migrants to their home countries is far higher than those who are admitted. A recent universal trend is that refugee admissions to the Global North and its most affluent nations are plummeting.[10]

The prejudicial treatment of asylum seekers' can amplify their experience of danger and posttraumatic stress. The world's reception of Ukrainian refugees offers a striking contrast,[11] with the differential treatment of asylum-seekers of color and those from the Global South. The clandestine removal of asylum-seekers by coast guards prevents refugees from arriving at a host nation or pushbacks and their detention in secret prisons[12] is a widespread phenomenon today that is occurring at an all-time high.[13] Despite Poland's welcome of the Ukrainians, it engaged in unlawful pushbacks and detention of asylum-seekers from other countries at the Belarussian border. In the United States, migrants at its border towns are being transported unannounced by the governors of Texas and Florida to cities and towns in the northern United States, further politicizing the issue of immigration and treating migrants as political pawns. A public health order called Title 42[14] is being used to return asylum-seekers across the southern US-Mexico border to their countries without consideration of their fears of persecution.

[10] FitzGerald, D. S. (2019). *Refuge beyond reach: How rich democracies repel asylum seekers*. Oxford University Press.

[11] Ukrainians were provided free connectivity (i.e., free smart phones, data, and phone cards) by telephone operators in many European countries, and they could access their banks and continue to use their credit cards. In Poland, they were eligible for the same health insurance, child allowance, and education as Polish citize Compared to 2020, when 9,798 asylum seekers after landing in their destinations were illegally sent back to their points of departure or left adrift in dinghies at sea, pushbacks of refugee seekers have increased, in violation of international, European, and national laws. In 2022, 8,720 pushbacks in the central Mediterranean to Libyan detention centers and 40,000 by Greek authorities were re- corded in the Evros region: Euromed Rights (2022, June 20). *World Refugee Day 2022: Pushbacks, Frontex and the EU's responsibility*. https://euromedrights.org/publ ication/world-refugee-day-2022- pushbacks-frontex-and-the-eus-responsibility/; Mare Liberum. (2021). *Pushback back report 2020*. https://daten.mare-liberum.org/s/4HdxAPACaPsqzEx ns. Poland also provided work permits for Ukrainian refugees and their partners and guaranteed them access to the labor market.

[12] Urbina, I. (2021, November 28). The secretive prisons that keep migrants out of Europe. *The New Yorker*. https://www.newyorker.com/magazine/2021/12/06/the-secretive-libyan-pris ons-that- keep-migrants-out-of-europe

[13] Compared to 2020, when 9,798 asylum seekers after landing in their destinations were illegally sent back to their points of departure or left adrift in dinghies at sea, pushbacks of refugee seekers have increased, in violation of international, European, and national laws. In 2022, 8,720 pushbacks in the central Mediterranean to Libyan detention centers and 40,000 by Greek authorities were re- corded in the Evros region: Euromed Rights (2022, June 20). *World Refugee Day 2022: Pushbacks, Frontex and the EU's responsibility*. https://euromedrights.org/publication/world-refugee-day-2022- pushbacks-frontex-and-the-eus-responsibility/; Mare Liberum. (2021). *Pushback back report 2020*. https://daten.mare-liberum.org/s/4HdxAPACaPsqzEx

[14] American Immigration Council. (2021, October 15). A guide to Title 42 expulsions at the border. https://www.americanimmigrationcouncil.org/research/guide-title-42-expulsions-border

The risk of privileging one minority group over another is inherently dangerous as it fosters social inequality and exclusion. Furthermore, the treatment of all members of the prioritized group alike can exclude its needy from mental health literacy and other public assistance. For any nation to be regarded as a safe haven country, the safety and the human rights of all of its marginalized groups must be ensured equally, and *all* groups (including LGBTQI+, elderly, women, and people of different ethnicities) ought to be able to access equally their health, legal, education, employment and asylum systems without discrimination.

Equitable, inclusive, and culturally competent healthcare systems can be critical in eliminating social disparities and alleviating posttraumatic stress among the displaced. Equity in health care is anchored by twin capacities: knowledge of one's cultural systems (and the power inherent in them) and cultural competency. Cultural competence is a dynamic and developmental process that requires not just clinicians but also systems to acknowledge and incorporate the importance of culture; invest time and resources and commitment to learning the skills, knowledge, and attitudes for service delivery to culturally diverse patient groups; and implement practices and policies for their responsive and tailored treatment.[15] Cultural competency can contribute to reducing trauma through a greater awareness of cultures of privilege, social inequality, and how multiple marginalized identities can intersect with complex trauma. In contrast, when cultural knowledge is insufficient or de-emphasized in favor of rapid assessments of their situation,[16] it can erode interpersonal trust, distance marginalized communities from institutions,[17] [18]and result in other well-documented consequences of social exclusion.

Although most displaced individuals are in developing nations, most mental health professionals train and reside in developed, geographically distant nations. To be culturally competent with the displaced in low-income nations, mental health services must be integrated within primary health,[19] be embedded in a multisectoral approach, and extend beyond the clinic into the various communities where a majority of the world's displaced reside. For host countries in general, an improved understanding of how sociocultural-religious contexts can interact with trauma in war-affected refugee families can translate

---

[15] U.S. Department of Health and Human Services. (2003). *Developing cultural competence in disaster mental health programs: Guiding principles and recommendations* [DHHS Pub. No. SMA 3828]. Center for Mental Health Services, Substance Abuse and Mental Health Services Administration.

[16] Ibid.

[17] Banfield, E. (1958). *The moral basis of a backward society*. Free Press.

[18] Easton, D. (1966). *A Systems analysis of political life*. Wiley.

[19] Rasco, L. M., & Miller, K. E. (2004). Innovations, challenges, and critical issues in the development of ecological mental health interventions with refugees. In K. E. Miller & L. M. Rasco (Eds.), *The mental health of refugees: Ecological approaches to healing and adaptation* (pp. 375–416). Lawrence Erlbaum Associates.

to improving health delivery, eliminating health disparities, and enhancing access to cross-cultural medicine for minority communities,[20] while also building the capacity of their own health systems.[21]

In summary, there is a global need to address consciously and proactively the fallout from trauma or posttraumatic stress in displaced populations, including other groups afflicted with trauma such as war veterans. To improve the health outcomes of the displaced at all levels, maximize the impact of public health resources, and encourage stability and prosperity for all, the section below outlines ten initiatives:

1. Dismantling the perception of the refugee as either a bogus migrant or dangerous Other that justifies their exclusion from public concern and resources

   Media coverage of refugee policy can shape the public's misperceptions of refugees and attitudes. Journalists' coverage clarifying what it means to be a refugee (versus economic migrants), asylum seekers' legal rights, the circumstances of their exodus, and our human rights obligations towards them can help cast asylum seekers in a more humanizing light, disrupt harmful stereotypes, and preferential treatment of some groups over others.

2. Developing the cultural competence of institutions and health professionals providing trauma-informed services to asylum-seekers and affected others for their tailored care and recovery

   For health institutions, improving cultural competence can mean expanding their mental health capacity by building a team of cultural consultants to include cultural experts, traditional healers, bilingual staff, and interpreters with regular staff training and reviews to improve access of marginalized communities to services. For educators, psychologists in correctional facilities, humanitarian workers, and clinicians who work with veterans affected by posttraumatic stress, it can mean crafting cultural, structural, and legal dimensions into the treatment plan or teaching, partnering with affected communities, training on human rights and multicultural competencies at every level, and supervision/monitoring for vicarious trauma.

3. Implementing evidence-based family and community-based interventions, and partnerships with regular government intercession to promote asylum-seekers' rehabilitation, recovery, and resilience

---

[20] Fadiman, A. (1997). *The spirit catches you and you fall down: A Hmong child, her American doctors and the collision of two cultures.* Farrar, Straus and Giroux.

[21] According to the Health Inclusivity Index, although 93% of countries may recognize health as a right, 20% have policies of health exclusion, restricting access of certain groups from health care: The Economist Group. (2022). *The health inclusivity index: Measuring progress towards good health for everyone. Economist Impact.* https://impact.economist.com/projects/health-inclusivity-index/documents/EI-Haleon_Report_A4.pdf

The sustainability and success of community-based initiatives such as the availability of education to children or skill development in its support staff by nonprofit groups and humanitarian agencies can be enhanced by tracking mental health outcomes with women, LGBTQI+, and older members, investing in early education programs for children, and advocacy with government bodies, thus also broadening the resilience agenda for displaced families.

4. Addressing knowledge gaps and prioritizing research into the mental health effects of torture and other sequelae over the refugee life-span
Rehabilitating survivors of torture for the international community can mean addressing existing gaps in its redress by the guidelines of the Convention against Torture, banning the trade of equipment used in torture, prosecuting torturers, and repudiating reliance on information obtained from third countries through torture to improve accountability and reduce complicity in crimes of torture. For asylum systems, it can also include educating and training decision-makers such as immigration attorneys, judges, and law enforcement on recognizing signs of torture and greater sensitivity in cases of sexual violence in both men and women to avoid stigma and re-victimization.

5. Empowering robust public mental health infrastructures in host nations through integrating mental health awareness into national health and social policy; mental health delivery with primary care; and, scaling up of services through disseminating cost-effective interventions for asylum-seekers and refugees
In poor-resource countries, international agencies such as the WHO can provide consistent messaging to prioritize mental health care and stronger advocacy to increase financial allocations to mental health services through international donors. To ensure that a greater number of people are provided a wider range of services, host nations must adapt psychological support to specific communities, improve the skills of their health workers, and develop relevant mental health policies and legislation to improve prioritization and access of displaced communities to psychological treatments.

6. Educating for the gender-sensitive interpretation of Refugee Status Determination procedures to prevent marginalizing the experiences of female refugees from conflict-affected countries during resettlement, rehabilitation, reintegration, repatriation, and post-conflict reconstruction *Gender-responsiveness by border management personnel, UN staff, and community members can include a focus on the unique experiences of trafficking victims to increase their capacity for identification, timely data collection, and international collaboration. Gender-empowering policies by host societies can include expedient and effective resolution of complaints of sexual harassment or assaults, reducing women's isolation to increase the reporting of gender-based crimes, enhancing a shared sense of safety through*

increasing community-building efforts, addressing their needs for sanitation and hygiene, and ways to recognize their prior credentials so their prior skills training can be utilized.

7. Prioritizing effective integration of refugees through conceptualizing it as a complex dynamic that factors in social determinants of health, and business-government-and technology partnerships

   Through innovative initiatives like tuition-free education, vocational training, apprenticeship opportunities, recognition of asylum seekers' prior qualifications, and provision of micro-credits or technical assistance to refugee entrepreneurs, private-public partnerships can enhance refugees' social and cultural capital. Greater involvement with strong monitoring mechanisms by international agencies like the World Bank, European Investment Bank, and the African Development Bank can assist in their housing, healthcare, improvement of their environmental conditions, ways to mitigate intergenerational poverty, and support for infrastructure projects can extend the private sector's innovations across conflict contexts.

8. Data collection and research on mental health for expanding knowledge on migration and refugees, and on outreach of its services

   Generate disaggregated and high-quality data on the nature of mental health needs, and the availability and accessibility of services for policy and programming decisions concerning migrants and refugees. A comprehensive assessment of the mental health services and quality of care afforded to the forcibly displaced within nations and the barriers to accessing them is essential in developing mental health services that are equitable and culturally appropriate.

9. Cultivating global solidarity to engage governments for more effective regional responses to internal displacement

   Regional institutions can benefit through improved collaborations with UN inter-agency platforms to improve the protection environment of the forcibly displaced and stateless people, expediting identification cards and access to public services, and providing psychological first aid in inclusive and non-discriminatory ways. Cultivating governments' support can be useful for more effective support to internal displacement, addressing the drivers of internal displacement, and improving resettlement processing capacity.

10. Anchoring host nations' development and economic indicators with asylum-seekers and refugee well-being metrics, and their regular monitoring by autonomous bodies.

    Dissemination of psychological research to explore how marginalization can affect both the quality of employment and who gets employed, and how national policies supporting employment in asylum seekers' can be related to improving their health while precarious work can instead, be associated with a host of negative outcomes.

It is time to stretch ourselves at the individual, national, intergovernmental, and international levels.

At a macro level, systemic, comprehensive, and sustainable solutions will rest with host communities in the form of greater financial investments in their health systems, mobilization of community resources, and improving the health of the displaced through scaling up their mental health services. This can be achieved by initiatives such as, but not limited to, boosting task-sharing of mental health services through which shortages in human resources are addressed by training non-specialist providers for routine interventions to close the treatment gap; building an infrastructure of trauma-informed and culturally sensitive task forces across multiple sectors comprising of specialists, local healers, and caseworkers so they can triage serious mental health concerns; and designing community-based therapy for groups.

To build on the vision to better the condition of the forcibly displaced, host nations will need to calibrate refugees' psychological well-being with their long-term self-sufficiency, integration, and national prosperity. National initiatives toward reducing trauma and promoting psychological well-being in refugees can include centering antiracism and racial equity in public health campaigns to dismantle structural racism and to build positive national narratives about refugee hosting; incorporating cultural competency objectives and strategies in pedagogy and practice within refugee mental health and developing allyships to build the internal capacity and cultural knowledge of its health systems; teaching the refugee psychology in higher education accreditation of refugee mental health in required curricula; exploring new trends in technology that have the potential to positively impact refugee mental health and can be used to bridge inequities and the digital divide; and collaborating and aligning international objectives at the governmental and community levels. Public health initiatives to address discrimination and racism and to demystify the refugee can include conferences, advocacy, publications, and integrating knowledge of asylum-seekers in syllabi of higher education to promote shared experiences, intercultural respect, and inclusive societies.

At intergovernmental levels, adopting the betterment of the forcibly displaced can also be expanded with implications for regional development, through the enactment of a domestic law for refugees; improving the conditions of the people displaced within a nation's borders; creating legal pathways for asylum-seekers or those perceived to be irregular migrants; placing pressure on more countries to ratify the Convention; and enhancing more coordination and information- sharing between different nations on refugees' mental health conditions. Innovative measures could include creating partnerships with private sponsors that may go beyond funding, such as by envisioning and creating hygienic and safe homes for the displaced with proper sanitation, water, and electricity, which could with time, ease their sense of disempowerment.

At the international level, the support of refugees has shown much vitality and progress with advocates championing their human rights and international organizations who have facilitated the inclusion of the displaced in regional economies through development financing and other innovative deals of burden-sharing. International agreements such as the Global Compact on Refugees (2018), its follow-up Global Refugee Forum (2019), and regional cooperative relationships have enabled temporary protections for forcibly displaced Syrians and Venezuelans. Concessional financing by the World Bank to countries such as Jordan and Lebanon, in turn, has led to the education of Syrian refugees. In Colombia it has led to efforts to regularize 260,000 Venezuelans and facilitate their access to jobs and basic social services.[22]

While in Belo Tsiribihana, a village in northern Madagascar I traveled to in 2022, I witnessed waves of climate-change migrants escaping hunger and drought from Southern Madagascar pouring in. Belo Tsiribihana is one of the most impoverished places in the world. The chief of the ancient Sakalava people who lived there told me that immigration is their biggest problem. "These people," he said of the displaced, wringing his hands, "are destroying our village, burning our forests, and our climate is getting hotter and hotter." The profound effects of the refugee crisis on the development and economies are not the experience of Western and wealthy host nations alone. It is posing new dilemmas and quandaries alike, for far-flung, small, and impoverished communities like Belo.

Much more effort from the global community is required for the developing nations hosting 83% of the world's displaced. There is much scope for innovative burden-sharing international agreements to promote host nations' progressive stance with refugees, with tangible commitments and accountability to refugees' psychological well-being. Such international agreements must be reliant on listening to those proximate to the problems, the displaced, and their communities who have the power to revitalize aging economies. As all agreements can involve hidden incentives, it is critical that burden-sharing deals regarding refugees are regularly monitored to ensure they remain mutually beneficial and their success is linked with outcome measures such as refugee well-being. Otherwise, it may just result in a lost opportunity for the forcibly displaced and the integration policies and programs designed for them.

The well-being of refugees needs to be paramount. To empower symbiotic collaborations with host nations, solutions can lie in prioritizing practical and

---

[22] Global Concessional Financing Facility. (2021). *Global concessional financing facility: 2020–2021 annual report.* https://globalcff.org/wp-content/uploads/2021/10/FINAL_WBG-GCFF-2021-Annual-ReportPage.pdf

innovative solutions for improving the health of asylum seekers, returnees, internally displaced, and the stateless, as well as improving the processes and frameworks of humanitarian aid. These can range from improving food security and nutritional diversity through educating the cultivation of climate-smart home gardens; and, empowering women refugees through mental health support in addition to child-care support, microfinance, vocational training, and mentorship to promote their economic inclusion.

Other interventions that can ease the pressure on host nations and enhance refugees' self-reliance can include: grassroots mental health support through non-specialist female peers who are trained and supervised by specialists, to assist single mothers, survivors of violence and human trafficking, female-headed households, or those ostracized from their communities, and others; and the management of menstrual hygiene, sanitation and waste disposal to reduce its associated stress, stigma, and insecurity for displaced women in humanitarian contexts. Within the humanitarian landscape, other interventions may lie in the improvement of internal processes within relief agencies such as investigations of bias in discourses and independent oversight to maintain a noncoercive partnership with host nations and improve accountability to the populations they are mandated to protect. Aid workers, personnel, and regional care specialists in humanitarian settings can often report vicarious trauma, burnout, and attrition. Provisions of expedient and continuous mental health support, training, and onsite personal safety to humanitarian officers is critical in improving their capacity to support the displaced communities. It is essential that psychologists and counselors providing support in humanitarian spaces are trained in trauma therapy, intimate partner violence, relational counseling, and have competence in navigating cross-cultural spaces.

Promoting the resilience of refugees is the key to building global resilience, a critical goal of the Refugee Employment and Employability Initiative of the World Economic Forum. It is only through the well-being of refugees can we build a global resilience to buffer against future refugee crises.

Ukraine's and the Israel-Gaza humanitarian crises are proximate and, hence, visible, but let us not forget they are not the only ones producing refugees today. Many other regions in the Global South (e.g., Afghanistan, Eritrea, Central Sahel, Sudan, South Sudan, Democratic Republic of Congo, Mozambique, Haiti, Venezuela, and Bangladesh) remain cradles for wars and conflict, and where the plight of the forcibly displaced will also remain unfortunately, invisible.

Leaders of the world face a choice: either heal the wounds of refugees and find ways to better integrate them into their societies, or deal with political, economic, and social fragmentation and the resultant stresses. Healing the wounds of refugees will require rebuilding their trust in the world. That can only occur within a systemic frame of treatment that validates their experiences and recognizes the political conditions that produced and perpetuated their oppression. This is the wisest choice, as well as the most humane.

With timely and strategic investments in their mental health, refugees are more likely to become not just stronger individuals, but also stronger nation-building partners, workers, residents, and citizens. As a global community, through uplifting the conditions of refugees, we are reminded of the standards by which human beings ought to treat other human beings, the very affirmation of humanity that was once snatched from them.

Quantitative Data on Anxiety and Depression Subscales

Table A.1 Hopkins Symptom Checklist-25: Means, Frequencies, and Standard Deviation

Symptom	Frequency Endorsed	Mean	Standard Deviation
Anxiety subscale			
Suddenly scared	89%	2.33	0.84
Feeling fearful	65%	2.10	1.12
Faintness, dizziness, or weakness	40%	1.85	1.23
Nervousness or shakiness inside	50%	2.00	1.26
Heart pounding or racing	35%	1.45	0.76
Trembling	15%	1.25	0.72
Feeling tense or keyed up	90%	2.95	1.10
Headaches	42%	1.95	1.27
Spell of terror or panic	70%	2.55	1.32
Feeling restless or cannot sit still	90%	3.25	1.12
Depression subscale			
Feeling low in energy, slowed down	55%	2.25	1.33
Blaming self for things	60%	2.25	1.25
Crying easily	60%	2.40	1.35
Loss of sexual interest or pleasure	28%	1.50	0.99
Poor appetite	33%	1.33	0.49
Difficulty falling asleep or staying asleep	70%	2.80	1.32
Feeling hopeless about the future	65%	2.50	1.36
Feeling blue	37%	1.63	1.01
Feeling lonely	65%	2.85	1.42
Thoughts of ending own life	39%	1.50	0.79
Feeling of being trapped or caught	70%	2.75	1.33
Worry too much about things	100%	3.80	0.52
Feeling no interest in things	70%	2.55	1.32
Feeling everything is an effort	85%	2.90	1.21
Feeling worthless	68%	2.53	1.31

Table A.2 Correlation Matrix: Hopkins Symptom Checklist (Depression + Anxiety)

Variables	(1)	(2)	(3)	(4)	(5)	(6)	(7)	(8)	(9)	(10)	(11)	(12)	(13)	(14)	(15)	(16)	(17)	(18)	(19)	(20)	(21)	(22)	(23)	(24)	(25)
(1) Suddenly scared	1.000																								
(2) Feeling fearful	0.694	1.000																							
(3) Faintness, dizziness, or weakness	0.127	0.482	1.000																						
(4) Nervousness or shakiness inside	0.152	0.256	0.431	1.000																					
(5) Heart pounding or racing	0.194	0.044	0.283	0.250	1.000																				
(6) Trembling	−0.124	−0.251	−0.131	−0.194	−0.174	1.000																			
(7) Feeling tense or keyed up	0.160	−0.259	−0.145	0.100	0.135	−0.258	1.000																		
(8) Headaches	−0.257	−0.312	−0.149	0.218	0.031	0.059	0.229	1.000																	
(9) Spell of terror or panic	0.265	0.266	0.161	0.585	0.185	−0.085	0.095	−0.054	1.000																
(10) Feeling restless or cannot sit still	0.044	0.230	0.162	0.046	−0.155	−0.240	−0.055	0.213	0.106	1.000															

	(1)	(2)	(3)	(4)	(5)	(6)	(7)	(8)	(9)	(10)	(11)	(12)	(13)	(14)	(15)	(16)	(17)	(18)	(19)	(20)
(11) Feeling low in energy, slowed down	0.252	0.065	0.266	0.050	-0.161	-0.062	0.143	-0.033	0.174	0.279	1.000									
(12) Blaming self for things	0.121	0.010	0.216	0.129	0.225	-0.039	0.202	-0.244	-0.050	0.345	0.311	1.000								
(13) Crying easily	0.040	-0.049	0.380	0.283	0.506	-0.220	0.200	-0.172	-0.092	-0.003	0.256	0.762	1.000							
(14) Loss of sexual interest or pleasure	-0.195	-0.142	0.077	-0.110	-0.274	-0.105	-0.326	-0.131	-0.073	0.333	0.338	0.202	0.110	1.000						
(15) Poor appetite	-0.497	-0.235	-0.029	-0.398	-0.164	0.383	-0.135	0.031	-0.631	0.081	-0.470	0.225	0.074	-0.099	1.000					
(16) Difficulty falling asleep or staying asleep	0.008	0.192	0.186	0.148	-0.426	0.239	-0.194	-0.301	0.085	0.178	0.443	0.376	0.085	0.313	-0.007	1.000				
(17) Feeling hopeless about the future	0.154	-0.021	0.109	0.130	-0.080	0.271	0.183	0.388	0.106	0.177	0.635	0.233	0.126	0.249	-0.179	0.309	1.000			
(18) Feeling blue	0.406	0.033	0.246	0.315	0.439	0.168	0.289	-0.083	-0.003	-0.407	0.211	0.274	0.438	-0.206	-0.185	-0.039	0.426	1.000		
(19) Feeling lonely	-0.191	-0.432	-0.304	-0.193	0.018	0.263	-0.133	0.213	-0.199	0.210	0.412	0.441	0.193	0.356	0.018	0.333	0.451	0.054	1.000	
(20) Thoughts of ending own life	-0.165	-0.210	-0.189	-0.203	0.345	0.184	0.159	0.564	0.356	0.316	0.231	0.237	0.099	0.084	-0.032	0.143	0.467	-0.189	0.340	1.000

(continued)

Table A.2 Continued

Variables	(1)	(2)	(3)	(4)	(5)	(6)	(7)	(8)	(9)	(10)	(11)	(12)	(13)	(14)	(15)	(16)	(17)	(18)	(19)	(20)	(21)	(22)	(23)	(24)	(25)
(21) Feeling of being trapped or caught	0.505	0.310	0.162	0.240	0.117	0.271	-0.228	0.052	0.210	0.057	0.530	0.344	0.236	0.249	-0.376	0.380	0.633	0.374	0.515	0.351	1.000				
(22) Worry too much about things	0.358	0.202	-0.291	0.067	0.060	0.115	0.000	0.000	0.487	0.415	-0.149	0.068	-0.246	0.182	-0.181	0.022	0.102	-0.162	0.020	0.248	0.184	1.000			
(23) Feeling no interest in things	-0.015	0.068	0.240	-0.062	-0.090	-0.074	0.285	0.065	0.301	0.275	0.439	0.226	0.138	0.378	-0.090	0.226	0.542	-0.144	0.021	0.384	0.195	0.212	1.000		
(24) Feeling everything is an effort	0.088	0.152	0.199	0.118	-0.074	0.220	-0.050	0.172	0.623	0.353	0.203	-0.114	-0.238	0.216	-0.182	-0.085	0.350	-0.206	-0.157	0.472	0.204	0.515	0.622	1.000	
(25) Feeling worthless	0.047	0.070	0.192	0.015	-0.093	0.127	0.197	0.249	0.350	0.415	0.456	0.234	0.025	0.393	-0.093	0.273	0.707	-0.093	0.196	0.524	0.383	0.397	0.926	0.725	1.000

Author Index

For the benefit of digital users, indexed terms that span two pages (e.g., 52–53) may, on occasion, appear on only one of those pages.

Abbara, A., 236n.36, 265n.245
Abbas, O., 111n.17
Abbot, M. G., 228n.160
Abdallah, F. B., 38n.290
Abdelhady, D., 204n.29, 221n.127
Abels, I., 89n.81, 172n.110
Aberra, A., 162n.59
Abi-Hasham, N., 193n.132
Aborghetti, H. P., 38n.289, 39n.293
Adam, A., 155n.22
Adam, B., 149n.119
Adegoke, Y., 116n.39
Adeoye, A., 5n.23
Adhikari, S. B., 33n.255
Adjaloo, M., 266n.251
Afkhami, A. A., 202n.9
Agamben, G., 121n.55
Agathangelou, A., 185n.78
Ager, A., 59n.53, 59n.56, 178n.27, 201n.3, 206n.48
Aggarwal, N. K., 130n.23
Agrò, F., 32n.245
Agrawal, R., 8n.40
Aguilar-Gaxiola, S., 96n.129
Ahmad, S., 23n.163, 38n.286, 101n.147, 101n.150, 159n.49
Ahmadzadeh, G. H., 189n.104
Ahmed, R., 244n.85
Ahmeti, A., 183n.71, 185n.81
Ahram, A. I., 167n.98
Ainamani, H. E., 154n.15, 155n.20, 157n.34, 157n.38, 158n.42, 164n.77
Ajdukovic, D., 177n.23, 194n.142
Akbar, S., 246n.102
Akin, A., 156n.26
Aktar, B., 244n.85
al'Absi, M., 259n.201
Aladjem, A., 20n.146
Alameddine, M., 236–37n.36
Al Ariss, A., 221n.127
Albalawi, W. F., 266n.253

Albert, L., 54n.23
Alderete, E., 96n.129
Alemi, Q., 20n.142, 129n.14, 140n.79, 141n.84, 142n.95
Alexander, J. C., 61n.59, 62n.69, 63n.72, 108n.5, 112n.27, 124n.73
Alferez, M. G., 25n.169
Algan, Y., 42nn.323–24, 54n.26, 229n.164
Alhalabi, F., 236–37n.36
AlHeresh, R., 41n.322
Alhomsh, H., 235n.25
Ali, S., 122n.68, 122n.70, 125n.76
Aljunid, S. M., 19n.131
Alkalay, S., 187n.91
Alkhalil, M., 237n.38
Al-Khazali, H. M., 88n.72, 261n.215
Allden, K., 27n.199, 34n.267
Allebeck, P., 12n.72
Allen, E. S., 178n.36, 182n.66, 186n.82
Allen, J. T., 122n.67
Allkhenfr, H., 266n.253
Alloy, L. B., 65n.76
AlMasri, I., 236–37n.36
Aloni, R., 196n.148
Alpak, G., 167n.93
Al Qutob, R., 235n.25
Al-Rousan, T., 41n.322
Alsamman, S., 96n.133
Al-Smadi, A. M., 233n.8, 258n.189
Al-Turkait, F. A., 189n.100, 190n.110
Alvaro, J. L., 219n.113
Alzuhairi, B., 41n.320
Amann, J., 43n.331
Amara, A. H., 19n.131
Amarasena, L., 8n.40
Amin, F. M., 88n.72, 261n.215, 261n.217
Amon, J. J., 19n.127
Amris, K., 92n.108
Anagnostopoulos, D., 8n.38, 198n.154
Anastasiou, A. I., 89–90n.83
Anastasiou, I. P., 89–90n.83

Ancharoff, M. R., 189n.103
Andersen, A., 246n.100
Andersen, J., 240n.60
Anderson, T., 261n.217
Andersson, A. C., 40n.306
Andrade, S. M., 92n.105
Andreski, P., 154n.9, 157n.32
Anfinson, K., 163n.73
Angell, R. H., 26n.180
Angermeyer, M. C., 233n.10
Anjum, R. L., 254n.167
Annan, J. K., 51n.8
Annas, G. J., 94n.124
Anzolin, A. P., 26–27n.183
Aoe, T., 202n.12
Aptekar, L., 15n.94
Aragona, M., 32n.245
Aranda, E., 262n.227
Araujo, J. O., 156n.25
Araujo, P. C. A., 92n.105
Araya, R., 29n.214
Archibald, H. C., 27n.185
Arendt, H., 61n.58
Arieli, A., 32n.254
Arnous, M., 255n.179
Aron, A., 28n.205
Arrighi, J., 5n.29
Arwidson, C., 182n.64, 194n.144
Ashbaugh, C., 12n.72
Ashina, H. , 88n.72, 261n.215, 261n.217
Ashina, M., 261n.217
Ashina, S. , 88n.72, 261n.215
Asic Kobe, M., 65n.84
Aspergi, A., 262n.228
Assalman, I., 237n.38
Assayag, J., 38n.288
Atkinson, H. G., 234n.17
Attanayake, V., 187n.88
Aub, M., 20n.148
Auclair, G., 32n.246, 218n.105
Auerbach, A., 69n.3
Augoustinos, M., 239n.52
Austin, K., 54n.20
Avella, M. T., 259n.204
Awal, A., 244n.85
Awwad, M., 222n.133
Awwad, R., 221n.128
Aycheh, S., 32n.254
Ayerman, R., 112n.27
Aziz, A., 114n.34

Bagasser, D. A., 162n.64
Baglio, G., 32n.245

Bahu, M., 250n.140
Bailey, C., 62n.68
Baingana, F., 33n.265
Bajbouj, M. , 43n.331, 233n.5
Baker, D., 165n.90
Baker, E., 236n.33, 236n.35
Baker, R., 21n.155, 85n.39, 85n.45, 149n.114
Bakermans-Kranenburg, M. J., 175n.6, 187n.92
Bakker, L., 225n.145
Bakr, O., 96n.133
Baksh, N., 162n.64
Baldoumas, A., 16n.97
Ball, T., 27n.198, 129n.10
Ballette, F., 253n.157
Banfield, E., 273n.17
Bang, H., 222n.130
Barak, Y., 262n.230
Barakat, H., 183n.68, 183n.70
Baranowski, K. A., 243n.75
Baranowsky, A. B., 23n.165
Barash, J. A., 52n.15
Barbui, C., 246n.96, 253n.157, 256n.184
Barhoma, M., 246n.101
Barimalala, R., 5n.29
Barkeel-Oteo, A., 235n.21
Barnes, A., 149n.119
Barnhofer, T., 94n.120, 105n.180
Baron, A., 30n.224
Baroni, S., 259n.203
Barrett, J. B., 181n.60
Barrett, R. J., 40n.307
Barron, K., 253n.153
Barros, S. C., 219n.113
Barry, E., 53n.17
Barry, T. J., 93n.110, 93n.114
Bartolomei, L. , 153n.4, 159n.48
Basabe, N., 30n.225
Basetti, E., 131n.38
Basoğlu, M., 85n.38, 87n.68, 194n.146, 243n.76
Bass, J., 238n.45, 266n.255
Bass, J. K., 31n.227
Bassetti, E., 15n.91, 264n.237
Bastos, M. L., 19n.125, 156n.25
Batic-Mujanovic, O., 194n.145
Bauer-Babef, C., 17n.109
Bauman, A., 31n.238, 32n.252, 41n.318,
      178n.28, 180n.52, 241n.65, 241n.66,
      256n.180
Baumgartner, S., 17n.104
Beach, C. M., 228n.160
Bean, T., 187n.89
Becher, D., 258n.196
Bech. P., 258n.190

Becker, D. F., 65n.83, 155n.19
Beckham, J. C., 187n.87, 189n.101
Behrman, S., 7n.34
Beiser, M., 65n.80, 251n.145
BeLue, R., 149n.119
Benish, S. G., 251n.141
Benjet, C., 12n.72
Bennana, A., 258n.197
Benson, L. S., 266n.253
Ben-Ze'ev, E., 39n.299
Benzmiller, H. L., 82n.27, 82–83n.28
Berah, E. F., 96n.130
Berbano, E., 258n.196
Berger, D., 27n.196, 129n.17
Berger, L. K., 245n.89
Bernal, G., 250n.136
Bernier, J. E., 244n.83
Berri, A., 266n.253
Berruti, D., 172n.105
Berry, J. W., 46n.354, 138n.62
Berryman, P., 91n.94
Berthold, S. M., 32n.247, 193nn.134–35,
    194n.136, 194n.143, 226n.153
Bertossi, C. , 107n.2, 109n.6, 119n.48, 119n.49,
    120n.50
Besic, S., 182n.65, 254n.160
Best, S. R., 174n.2
Betancourt, J. R., 244n.77
Betancourt, T. S. 34n.267, 149n.116, 187n.90,
    188n.95, 246n.96, 256n.184
Betti, L., 259n.203
Betts, A., 12n.66, 43n.337, 44n.347
Bevelander, P., 43n.335, 207n.50, 209n.68,
    213n.87, 228n.158
Beyrer, C., 155n.22
Bharadwaj, B., 51n.8
Bhatia, M., 82n.24, 83n.32
Bhatta, D. N., 33n.255
Bhattacharyya, P., 40n.310
Bhugra, D., 20n.145, 27n.191, 31n.241, 133n.50,
    139n.67, 157n.31, 249n.123, 259n.202
Bhui, K., 20n.145, 27n.191, 31n.241, 47n.358,
    133n.50
Bianchi, I., 86n.53, 105n.183
Bibby, C., 5n.30
Biehl, J., 181n.62
Bierer, L. M., 184n.74
Bighelli, I., 253n.157
Bilgili, Ö, 45n.349
Bilgili Aykut, N., 156n.26
Binder, P., 43n.332, 208n.59
Binder-Brynes, K., 184n.73, 190n.114
Bin Shafique, S., 244n.85

Bishop, D., 51n.8
Bisin, A., 42nn.323–24, 54n.26, 211n.78,
    229n.164
Blair, R. G., 178n.29
Blais, R. K., 178n.36, 182n.66, 186n.82
Blake, C., 130n.27
Blanchet, K., 265n.245
Blanton, C., 208n.55
Blanton, S., 202n.12
Blendon, R. J., 90n.90, 92n.107
Blessman, J., 132n.42
Blick, B., 236n.28, 242n.70
Bloemraad, I., 208n.56
Blondin, C., 44n.341
Bloom, J. D., 260n.205
Blow, A. J., xviiin.4, 28nn.204–206
Blyta, A., 255n.178
Bochtsou, V., 197n.151
Böcker, A., 265n.250
Boelen, P. A., 261n.211
Böge, K., 233n.5
Bogic, M., 21n.154, 177n.23, 194n.142
Böhm, A., 56–57nn.41–42
Bolton, P., 34n.267, 256n.184
Bonetto, C., 256n.184
Bonisteel, P., 254n.166
Bonnet, R., 5n.29
Boochani, Behrouz, 83n.32
Borges, L. M., 255n.174
Börjesson, U., 40n.306
Bosen, R., 62n.71
Boubtane, E., 44n.343, 45n.348
Bou Khalil, R., 20n.140, 20n.150
Bourdieu, P., 224n.139
Bousliman, Y., 258n.197
Bowen, J. R., 107n.2, 109n.6, 119n.48, 119n.49,
    120n.50
Bowley, J., 250n.127
Bradley, H., 226n.148
Brady, F., 238n.47, 239n.54, 246n.102, 248n.114,
    249nn.123–24, 250n.128, 254n.165
Brady, K., 55n.32
Brafman, D., 262n.230
Braga, J. U., 19n.125
Bramsen, I., 176n.8, 194n.139
Brand, L. A., 9n.52, 53n.18
Brandt, L., 65n.77
Brandt, Willy, 62n.71
Braxton, L. E., 189n.101
Brea, L. D., 141n.83
Breckenridge, A., 260n.205
Bredström, A., 130n.21
Breitborde, N. J. K., 12n.72

Brenner, J., 102n.153
Brenzel, H., 56–57n.42
Breslau, N., 154n.6, 154n.9, 154n.11, 157n.32
Brick, K., 220n.118
Bridekirk, J., 221n.128, 222n.133
Briere, J. N., 255n.172
Briskman, B., 242n.69
Brockmann, S., 61n.60
Broekaert, E., 187n.89
Broer, P. N., 43n.333
Broers, T., 194n.145
Bromet, E., 157n.33
Bromet, E. J., 233n.10
Bronstein, P., 177n.21
Brooks, M. A., 235n.25
Brooks, R., 41n.320, 178n.32
Brough, M., 65n.84, 154–55n.17, 156n.30
Brown, A., 36n.281, 229n.166, 230n.168
Brown, A. D., 93n.111, 93n.114
Brown, E. L., 203n.25, 205n.38, 230n.167
Brown, Kay E., 224n.143
Brown, R., 222n.132
Browne, M. A., 233n.10
Bruce-Jones, E., 82n.24, 83n.32
Brücker, H., 44n.345, 56n.41, 56–57n.42,
    57n.45, 57n.48, 57n.49, 209n.63, 229n.163
Brugha, T., 12n.72
Brunet, A., 20n.140, 20n.150, 167n.92
Brunoni, A. R., 26–27n.183
Bryant, R. A., 47n.357, 87n.65, 93n.114,
    178n.32, 209n.61, 217–18n.103, 227n.156,
    229n.165, 233n.4, 238n.49, 245n.93,
    261n.214
Bryant. R. A., 93n.111
Brynjarsdottir, J., 266n.252
Buckley, C., 4n.15
Bugelli, M., 86n.53
Bugelli, V., 105n.183
Buhmann, C., 234–35n.18
Buhmann, C. B., 238n.48, 248nn.115–16,
    266n.257
Bulatao, R., 177n.17
Bullock, M., 72n.10
Bürgin, D., 8n.38, 198n.154
Burgos, J. L., 61n.57
Burke, A. L., 92n.104
Burke, H., 234n.14
Burkle, F., 187n.88
Burnett, A., 111n.16
Burnham, G., 167n.96, 232n.1, 234n.13,
    265n.246, 265n.249
Burra, S., 54n.23
Burton, A., 260n.208

Busby, Scott, 4n.14
Butcher, J., 85n.42
Butler, J., 121nn.56–57
Bye, H. H., 43n.332, 208n.59
Bytyqi, M., 255n.178

Cabrera, M. A. S., 92n.105
Cacioppo, J., 179n.43
Caetano, R., 19n.125
Cahn, N., 30n.223
Calderon, A. J., 90n.87
Caldwell, J. C., 177n.17
Callens, M. S., 203n.17
Campanini, M. Z., 92n.105
Campbell, D., 121n.58
Campbell, J. C., 163n.70
Camus-Jacques, G., 164n.80
Canning, V., 85n.47
Cannon, M. E., 163n.70
Canto, J. M., 154n.12, 154n.16, 164n.78,
    172n.104
Capps, R., 32n.246, 218n.105
Carapezza, R., 239n.56
Caraveo-Anduaga, J., 96n.129
Cardeña, E., 87n.66
Cardozo, B., 202n.12, 208n.55
Carlo, G., 105n.183
Carlsson, J., 234–35n.18, 238n.48, 246n.101,
    248nn.115–16, 258n.187, 258n.190,
    266n.257
Carlsson, J. M., 88n.75, 249n.125
Carosa, E., 260n.209
Carpenter-Song, E., 246n.94, 246n.97
Carrillo, J. E., 244n.77
Carta, M. G., 157n.31
Carter, D. J., 82n.27, 82–83n.28
Caruth, C., 26n.177, 112n.26
Caruth, M., 239n.53
Carvalho, D., 176n.9, 190n.111
Caselli, L. T., 189n.106
Casey, D. L., 47n.360
Caspi, Y., 180n.50
Castaldo, M., 32n.245
Castaneda, A. E., 39n.295
Casterline, H. B., 177n.17
Castillo, R., 27n.194, 131n.36
Castle, S., 17n.114
Castles, S., 59n.51, 213n.90
Castro-Vale, I., 176n.9, 190n.111
Catalano, A., 19n.129
Catalano, R., 96n.129
Catani, C., 167n.95, 191n.118, 252n.149
Cecco, L., 41n.314

Cerna, L., 22n.160, 213n.89
Cernovsky, Z. Z., 42n.326
Çesko, E., 262n.229
Cetorelli, V., 167n.96, 232n.1
Chaaya, M., 111n.17
Chahda, N., 265n.246, 265n.249
Chakraborty, R., 177n.15
Chambers, S., 219n.114, 221n.125
Chambless, D. L., 246n.99
Chang, A., 19n.128
Chang, L. J., 93n.111, 93n.114
Chang, Y. C., 253n.154
Chappell, B., 82n.25
Charlés, L. L., 179nn.40–41, 183n.71,
    185nn.80–81
Charles, S., 10n.60
Charlier, P., 38n.289, 38n.290, 39n.293
Charlson, F., 269n.1
Charlson, F. J., 12n.72
Charney, D. S., 177n.22
Charuvastra, A., 239n.56
Chaskel, R., 29n.214
Chatterji, S., 180n.53, 194n.141
Chawla, B., 244n.85
Chen, A., 255n.179
Chen, L., 253n.155
Chen, S. R., 253n.154
Chen, Y. R., 253n.154
Cherian, S., 8n.40
Chernoff, M., 21n.152
Cherrah, Y., 258n.197
Chessell, Z. J., 246n.102
Chetty, D., 25nn.174–75
Cheung, S. Y., 19n.136
Chey, T., 32n.252, 87n.65, 233n.4, 241n.65
Chhean, D., 94n.118, 247n.104, 250n.134
Chilcoat, H. D., 154n.9, 157n.32
Chiovenda, A., 129n.11, 131n.28
Chipalo, E., 249n.117
Chisholm, A., 246n.102
Cho, J., 248n.112
Choi, J., 248n.112
Choi, K., 153n.2
Choivenda, A., 139n.64
Chou, K. R., 253n.154
Christiansen, D. M., 158n.43
Chu, H., 253n.154
Chun, C., 193nn.134–35, 194n.143, 226n.153
Chun, C. A., 32n.247, 194n.136
Chung, K., 167n.99
Chung, M. H., 253n.154
Chung, R. C., 65n.79, 194n.140
Chynoweth, S., 79n.1

Ciocca, G., 260n.209
Clarke, G. N., 197n.150
Claude, K. M., 163n.71
Clemens, M., 116n.41, 231n.169
Clohessy, S., 249n.121
Cloitre, M., 239n.56, 252n.148, 254n.159
Cloutier, M., 270n.7
Cochran, J., 202n.12, 208n.55
Codrington, R., 239n.52
Coenders, M. T. L., 56n.37
Cohen, A., 131n.37, 133n.51
Cohen, I., 20n.146
Cohen, R., 53n.16
Cohen, S. R., 162n.64
Çöl, M., 156n.26
Coleman, J., 8n.40
Coleman, M., 234n.14
Collet, B. A., 222n.130
Collin, S. M., 38n.289, 39n.293
Collins, S. R., 29n.215
Collyer, M., 222n.132
Combs, S., 90n.87
Cook, H., 259n.198
Cook, J., 236n.32
Cooper, H., 17n.106
Cordesman, A. J., 10n.59
Corne, S., 28n.205, 30n.224
Cornelius-White, H. D., 262n.226
Cornett, J., 269n.1
Correa-Salazar, C., 19n.127
Correa-Velez, I., 65n.84
Cortes, D. E., 131n.31
Cortes, G., 204n.34
Cossu, G., 19n.129
Coulibaly, D., 44n.343, 45n.348
Coulter, S., 28n.207
Courtois, C. A., 239n.56
Coutts, A., 235n.21, 265n.245
Coutts, A. P., 236–37n.36
Coyne, J. C., 180n.55
Craig, T., 20n.145, 31n.241
Craig. D. C., 82n.27, 82–83n.28
Crane, C., 94n.120, 105n.180
Crimmins, E. M., 31n.229
Crisp, J., 265n.243
Cristina Tumiati, M., 32n.245
Crnobaric, C., 194n.146
Crock, M., 15n.90
Croisier, J., 44n.345, 57n.49, 229n.163
Cromer, L. D., 158n.44
Crosby, S. S., 101n.152
Cross, T. L., 134n.52
Crul, M., 213n.86

Crumlish, N., 245n.91, 253n.156
Cruz, R., 141nn.85–86
Cueto, R. M., 55n.30
Cummings, C. A., 27n.192
Cummings, E. M., 180n.56
Cummings, S., 226n.152
Curtice, M., 237n.38
Curtis, E., 244n.79
Cushing-Savvi, A., 220n.118

Dagawal, S., 20n.148
Dagevos, J., 225n.145
Dagher, R., 20n.140, 20n.150, 167n.92
Dai, X., 12n.72
Dailey, R., 132n.42
Dal, H., 238n.42
D'Albis, H., 44n.343, 45n.348
Dale, B., 238n.42
Dalgleish, T., 94n.120, 94n.123, 105n.180
Dalman, C., 238n.42
Dal Secco, A., 32n.245
Dams, J., 155n.18, 155n.21
Dandona, R., 12n.72
D'Andrade, R., 109n.9, 111n.19, 113n.28
Danesh, J., 31n.234
D'Angelo, E., 251n.142
Daniel, E. V., 9n.46, 169n.101
Danieli, Y., 26n.179, 28n.201, 177n.24, 241n.64
Danielsen, L., 90n.88
Daniulaityte, R., 33n.255
Danjuma, J., 270n.5
Dannon, Z., 29n.215
Dansby, V. S., 189n.98
Dansky, L., 85n.46, 88n.71
Dansky, L,, 88n.74
Darrow, J., 215n.95
Das, Ram, xxiv–xxv
Dasen, P. R., 46n.354, 138n.62
Dasgupta, A., 235n.25
Dashash, M., 256n.181
Daud, A., 105n.176, 191n.122
Daudzai, H., 140n.77, 140n.78
Dauvergne, C., 30n.221
D'Avanzo, C. E., 96n.129
Davidov, E., 56n.38
Davidson, H., 156n.27
Davies, Michele, xxi
Davis, C., 226n.152
Davis, G. C., 154n.6, 154n.9, 154n.11, 157n.32
Davis, L., 270n.7
Dawadi, A., 132n.42
De, S., 42n.328
Dean, K. E., 69n.6

Dearden, S., 266n.253
de Assis, M. V., 94n.121
Degenhardt, L., 12n.72
de Girolamo, G., 233n.10
de Graaf, R., 233n.10
Dehos, F. T., 55–56n.34
de Icco, R., 261n.217
de Jong, J., 89n.79, 140n.74, 256n.184
de Jong, J. T., 129n.7, 132n.43, 139n.72, 140n.80,
    150n.123, 207n.53, 253n.158, 254n.161,
    259n.200, 261n.213
De Jong, J. T. V., 87n.66
De Jong, J. T. V. M., 65n.82, 246n.95, 250n.137
De Jong, J. V. T. M., 27n.191, 255n.177
Dekel, R., 27n.186, 28nn.206–8, 185n.79,
    187n.85, 192n.127
Delahanty, D. L., 154n.8
de la Hunt, L. A., 165n.91
DeLoach, Chante, xxi
Del'Osso, L., 259nn.203–4
Demyttenaere, K., 233n.10
Deng, Francis M., 3n.7
Denkinger, J. K., 91n.98, 92n.101, 92n.103,
    143n.97, 167n.94, 234n.16
den Otter, Joost, xxiv–xxv
Denson, L., 239n.52
Denson, L. A., 92n.104
Deo, S., 38n.290
Deps, P., 38n.289, 39n.293
Derluyn, I., 187n.89, 246n.100
Derrick, P., 91n.92
der Sarkissian, A., 199n.155
Destefanis, C., 19n.129
Detienne, M., 108n.4, 109n.7
Devereaux, G., 132n.45
Deville, W., 194n.139
Deville-Stoetzel, J. B., 235n.21
De Vroome, T., 47n.359, 217n.102, 228n.159
de Zárate, M. H., 262n.227
Dezee, K. J., 258n.196
Diab, M., 185n.75, 190n.109
Diab, S. Y., 179n.46
Diamant, J., 123n.72
Diaz, M., 221n.128, 222n.133
Dickson, C., 270n.5
Diemer, M., 258n.196
Di Sante, S., 260n.209
Disassa, K. G., 224n.140
Di Tommaso, S., 260n.209
Divi, C., 226n.149
Dixon, L., 246n.102
Djuknic, G. M., 163n.71
Dodick, D. W., 261n.217

Dogra, N., 20n.145, 31n.241
Doherty, B., 21n.159
Domenech Rodriguez, M. D., 250n.136
Donelan, K., 90n.90, 92n.107
Dong, C., 234n.15
Donnelly, F., 27n.195
Doocey, S., 265n.246, 265n.249
Doocy, S., 234n.13
Doru, E., 172n.105
Dossa, P., 250n.138
Doty, R. L., 121n.59
Downey, D. L., 33n.256
Downey, G., 180n.55
Dragojevic, M., 124n.75
Dragsted, U. B., 85n.44, 235n.27
Drake, R., 202n.11, 204n.30, 220n.121
Drake. R. E., 251n.143
Draughton, J. E., 162n.67, 163n.70
Drolet, C. F., 132n.42
Drozdek, B., 26n.182, 236n.28, 242n.70
Drummond, S. P. A., 263n.234
Du, N., 194n.138
Ducey, C. R., 112n.24
Duden, G. S., 23n.162, 240n.59, 255n.174
Dudley, M., 236n.28, 242n.70
Dudzai, C., 201n.4, 203n.23, 204n.26, 206n.44
Dudzai, G., 48n.361
Dulac, Y. M., 38n.290
Dumper, M., 18n.119
Duncan, W. L., 145nn.103–4, 145n.105, 146n.106
Dunlavy, A. C., 11n.63, 20n.143, 31n.237, 31n.239
Durand, J., 52n.11
Duranton, G., 44n.340
Durbeej, N., 246n.100
Duric, D., 194n.146
Durran, A., 244n.83
Durt, C., 130n.19, 144n.101
Duvdevani, T., 184n.73, 190n.114
Duyvendak, J. W., 107n.2, 109n.6, 119n.48, 119n.49, 120n.50
Dwaf, A., 20n.140, 20n.150, 167n.92

Easton, D., 273n.17
Eaton, W., 238n.45
Eßl-Maurer, R., 219n.110
Edkins, J., 27n.200, 121n.60, 235n.26
Edston, E., 39n.294, 39n.296, 88n.70, 88n.73
Edwards, A., 80n.7
Edwards, B., 10n.58
Ee, E. V., 254n.162
Eggerman, M., 46n.355, 139n.69, 141n.90, 142n.93, 142n.94

Ehlers, A., 252n.148, 254n.159
Ehring, T., 238n.50
Ehrkamp, P., 32n.243
Eigenbrodt, A. K., 261n.217
Eisenberg, N., 179n.42
Eisenman, D. P., 55n.29, 85n.41, 101n.151
Eisenmann, D., 102n.155
Eising, D. D., 261n.211
Ekkawi, A. R., 111n.17
Ekström, E., 40n.306
Ekstroem, M., 234–35n.18, 238n.48, 248nn.115–16, 266n.257
El Arnaout, N., 236–37n.36
El-Bassel, N., 235n.25
Elbert, T., 139n.65, 154n.15, 155n.20, 157n.34, 157n.38, 158n.42, 158n.46, 164n.77, 251n.146, 252n.148, 252n.149, 254n.159
el Chammay, R., 235n.21
El Hadi, D., 111n.17
El-Hage, W., 20n.140, 20n.150, 167n.92
Elias, C., 90n.90, 92n.107
El-Jardali, F., 236–37n.36
El Khoury, R., 20n.140, 20n.150, 167n.92
Elklit, A., 245n.92, 249n.126
Elliott, M. N., 32n.247, 193nn.134–35, 194n.136, 194n.143, 226n.153
Elliott, R., 69n.4
Ellis, H., 202n.12, 208n.55
Ellman, L. M., 65n.76
Elmira, R., xviin.2
El-Nagib, R., 233n.3
El Sabeh, M., 111n.17
El Sarraj, E, 191n.119
Elsass, P., 240n.60, 242n.67
Elshafie, S., 220n.118
Emerson, D., 263n.232, 263n.233
Emile, Mahajano Tsitozoe, xxiv
Emmanuel, E. R., 89–90n.83
Engbersen, G., 225n.145
Engdahl, B., 26n.179, 28n.201, 241n.64
Engel, G. L., 27n.187
Engelhardt, M., 91n.98, 92n.101, 92n.103, 143n.97, 167n.94
Engh, R., 180n.51
Enloe, C. H., 165n.85
Enneli, P., 226n.148
Enosh, G., 180n.50
Epperson, C. N., 154n.5, 162n.65
Epstein, E., 96n.134
Equihua Martinez, G., 19n.130
Erdogan, M. M., 228n.157
Eriksen, J., 91n.97
Erikson, S. L., 107n.2, 109n.6, 119n.49, 120n.50

Erle, E., 172n.105
Ernst, C., 15n.90
Erskine, H. E., 12n.72
Ertl, V., 167n.95
Espinel, Z., 29n.214
Espinola, M., 29n.214
Espinosa, A., 55n.30
Ess, R., 266n.253
Essam, M., 76n.17
Essendrop Sondej, M., 239n.52
Estroff, S. E., 132n.46
Eurelings-Bontekoe, E., 187n.89
Evans, W. N., 10n.57
Evershed, N., 156n.27
Eyber, C., 149n.115
Eyerman, R., 61n.59, 62n.69, 63n.72, 108n.5,
　　124n.73

Fabre, C., 10n.60
Fadiman, A., 129n.16, 274n.20
Faerstein, E., 19n.125, 156n.25
Fahmi, E., 76n.17
Fajth, V., 45n.349
Falb, K. L., 163n.73
Fallon, W., 154n.8
Farmer, P., 27n.184, 84n.33
Farnaz, N., 244n.85
Farrell, D., 253n.153
Farrell, L., 65n.84, 154–55n.17, 156n.30
Farrell, P., 156n.27
Fayyad, J. A., 180n.53, 194n.141
Fazel, M., 31n.234
Febert, J. M., 198n.154
Fee, M., 38n.283, 38n.285, 220n.116
Feetha, S., 182n.65
Feetham, S., 254n.160
Fegert, J. M., 8n.38
Feinberg, L., 244n.83
Feinstein, S., 202n.11, 204n.30, 220n.121
Feldman, I., 246n.100
Feldman, M. E., 187n.87, 189n.101
Fendel, T., 56n.41
Fennig, M., 150n.122, 240n.62
Fenton, F. R., 138n.61
Fenton, S., 122n.66
Fenton-Kreuger, Annabel, xxv
Fenton-Kreuger, Jens, xxv
Fenton-Kreuger, Nina, xxv
Ferguson, W. J., 226n.150
Fernando, G., 27n.196, 129n.17
Ferrari, A. J., 12n.72
Ferry, F., 233n.10

Fiddian-Qasmiyeh, E., 47n.356, 157n.41,
　　198n.152
Field, J., 54n.23
Field, N. P., 180n.49, 196n.147
Fink, J. W., 89–90n.83
Finkel, A. G., 261n.217
Fischer, B., 154n.8
Fischer, F., 12n.72
Fisher, L. M., 189n.103
Fitzgerald, D., 10n.57
FitzGerald, D. S., 272n.10
Fitzpatrick, S., 33n.258
Fix, M., 32n.246, 218n.105, 220n.119, 228n.161
Flamm, M., 219n.110
Flaxman, A., 269n.1
Fletcher, K., 241n.63
Flick, U., 43n.331
Florescu, S. E., 233n.10
Florian, S., 172n.109
Foa, E., 252n.148, 254n.159
Foa, E. B., 154n.8, 154n.10, 158n.45, 158n.47
Focardi, M., 86n.53, 105n.183
Foldspang, A., 80n.9, 85n.40
Fondacaro, K. M., 33n.257, 202n.13, 222n.129
Fontana, A., 21n.151, 190n.115
Fordham, D., 194n.138
Forese, A., 32n.245
Forrester, A. C., 44n.341
Forster, Michael, xxiv
Foster, C., 256n.180
Fouad, F. M., 236–37n.36, 265n.245, 266n.254
Foucault, M., 120nn.53–54
Fox, S. D., 264n.239
Fraihat, I., 13n.79, 16n.102
Francesca, F., 105n.183
Francis, J. R., 8n.40
Franciskovic, T., 177n.23, 178n.30, 187n.86,
　　189n.99, 194n.142, 194n.146
Franco, P., 33n.264
Frank, T., 83n.31
Frankel, M., 90n.90, 92n.107
Fratzke, S., 32n.246, 218n.105
Frederik, C. J., 149n.117
Fredette, J., 122n.65
Freeman, M., 12n.70
Freire, P., 84n.34
Freud, A., 112n.25
Freud, S., 38n.287, 112n.25
Friani, F., 86n.53
Friedman, M. J., 233n.10
Friedrich, M., 56n.41
Fromkin, David, 10n.62

Frost, C. J., 266n.253
Fuchs, T., , 130n.19, 144n.101
Fuglsang, H., 240n.60
Führer, A., 64n.74
Fukuyama, F., 121n.64
Fullerton, C. S., 178n.31
Fung, K., 249n.120

Gabel, D., 65n.77
Gadaleta, E., 258n.191
Gaer, F., 84n.36, 104n.175
Gagnon-Sanschagrin, P., 270n.7
Galappatti, A., 34n.267, 238n.43, 238n.45,
    239n.51, 246n.96
Galeazzi, G. M., 177n.23, 194n.142
Galovski, T., 192n.128
Gamble, K., 264n.236
Gammouh, O. S., 233n.8, 258n.189
Garcia-Barcena, Y., 29n.214
Garcia-Moreno, C., 163n.72
Garfin, D. R., 29n.214
Garoff, F., 39n.295
Garrido, A., 219n.113
Gartoum, M., 258n.197
Gastaldon, C., 256n.184
Gatrell, P., 8n.45
Gattinara, P. C., 253n.152
Gaviria, S. L., 29n.214
Gaynor, T., 8n.43
Gebhardt, M., 40n.301, 40n.302,
    61n.61, 61n.63
Gecewicz, C., 123n.72
Geddes, A., 201n.2
Geertz, C., 110nn.10–11, 110nn.13–14,
    111n.18, 131n.29
Gega, L., 12n.69, 15n.93
Geissler, W., 35n.275
Gelberg, L., 55n.29, 101n.151
Gelep, Sophie, xxiv
Geltman, P., 202n.12, 208n.55
Gerdle, B., 88n.77
Gernaat, H., 65n.82
Gernaat, H. B., 140n.80, 207n.53, 261n.213
Gerritsen, A. A., 194n.139
Gersons, B., 252n.148, 254n.159
Gerth, H. H., 9n.47
Gertler, M., 19n.130
Ghabach, M., 111n.17
Ghanem, P., 111n.17
Ghufran, N., 20n.138
Giaber, M. B., 179n.40, 184n.72
Giacco, D., 233n.3

Giammarinaro, M. G., 51n.7
Gianfelici, F., 172n.105
Giannaccini, G., 259n.203
Giarratano, L., 189n.107
Gibbons, N., 91n.98, 92n.101, 92n.103, 143n.97,
    167n.94
Gibson, L. E., 65n.76
Gichunge, C., 266n.252
Giesen, B., 61n.59, 62n.69, 63n.72, 108n.5,
    112n.27, 124n.73
Giesen, N. J., 61n.59
Giesselmann, M., 56n.41
Gijsberts, M. I. L., 56n.37
Gilat, I., 32n.254
Gillman, S. E., 178n.26, 178n.37, 188nn.94–95,
    192n.125
Ginio, R., 39n.299
Giolli, C., 86n.53
Girotto, E., 92n.105
Gladstone, E., 220n.122
Glass, N., 155n.22, 162n.59
Gnavi, R., 19n.129
Gnielka, V., 26–27n.183
Godwin, M., 194n.145
Goff, B. S. N., 28nn.206–8
Golaz, A., 246n.96
Goldberg, D., 33n.262
Goldblatt, H., 27n.186, 185n.79, 192n.127
Gomaa, H. I. M., 8n.41
Gómez Ceballos, A. M., 29n.214
Gone, J. P., 129n.15
Goninon, E. J., 244n.84, 247n.103
González, A. D., 92n.105
Gonzalez, J. L., 30n.225
Good, B., 181n.62
Good, B. J., 9n.49, 27n.198, 73–74n.15, 129n.8,
    130n.18, 145n.103, 145n.104, 145n.105,
    146n.106, 146nn.107–8, 147n.110
Good, M. J., 193n.133
Goodson, L., 59n.55
Goosen, S., 19n.135
Gorczynski, P., 12n.69, 15n.93
Gordon, J., 256n.184
Gordon, J. S., 255n.178
Gorenflo, D., 102n.154
Gorentz, K., 202n.9
Gostomski, C., 56n.41
Gottvall, M., 262n.231
Gough, K., 10n.60
Gowayed, H., 44n.339, 204n.32, 205n.41
Graessner, S., 23n.163, 38n.286, 94n.126,
    101n.147, 101n.150, 102n.157

Graf, J., 91n.98, 92n.101, 92n.103, 143n.97,
    167n.94
Graham, J., 116n.41, 231n.169
Graham-Harrison, E., 114n.35
Granstein, J., 33n.262
Graovac, M., 189n.99
Grasser, L. R., 19n.132, 35n.276
Gravina, G. L., 260n.209
Gray, R., 178nn.38–39
Gready, P., 243n.74
Green, A. R., 244n.77
Green, B. L., 239n.56
Greenber, L. S., 69n.4
Greif, J. L., 190n.116
Gren, L. H., 266n.253
Gren, N., 204n.29, 211n.75
Grey, N., 250n.129
Grietens, K. P., 226n.151
Griffin, R. H., 264n.239
Griffith, J. W., 93n.110, 93n.114
Griner, D., 250n.133
Grkovic, J., 178n.30, 187n.86
Grochtdreis, T., 155n.18, 155n.21
Grodin, M., 86n.52, 91n.93, 94n.124, 100n.146,
    101n.152
Groleau, D., 130n.27
Gross, A., 17n.108
Gross, A. L., 256n.184
Grossman, C. M., 84n.36, 104n.175
Grossman, R. A., 184n.74
Grossmann, A., 40n.302
Grossmann, K., 187n.91
Grossmann, K. E., 187n.91
Groves, S., 32n.246, 218n.105
Grumbine, J. M., 34n.269, 35n.272, 244n.86
Gualdron, L., 251n.142
Guidoni, C. M., 92n.105
Güler, A., 15n.91, 16n.95, 131n.38, 264n.237,
    264n.238
Gülşen, C., 154n.7, 156n.29, 162n.66
Gunasekera, H., 8n.40
Guo, A. V. Esq., 82n.27, 82–83n.28
Gupta, S., 20n.145, 31n.241
Guribye, E., 141n.83
Gurris, N., 23n.163, 38n.286, 94n.126,
    101n.147, 101n.150, 102n.157
Gustavsson, C., 262n.231
Gutermann, J., 89n.81, 172n.110
Güven, S., 43n.329
Guzder, J., 130n.27

Haagsma, J. A., 12n.72
Haar, R. J., 94n.121

Haas, B. M., 73–74n.15, 129n.8, 130n.18,
    144n.100, 146nn.107–8, 147n.110
Habbach, H., 94n.121
Habel, U., 233n.5
Habib, M., 159n.49
Haddad, F., 20n.140, 20n.150
Haenel, F., 89n.82, 91n.95, 94n.126, 102n.157
Hagendoorn, A. J. M., 56n.37
Hahn, E., 43n.331
Haidar, M., 131n.39, 202n.10
Hainmueller, J., 213n.88
Hajjar, L., 81n.13
Halcon, L., 85n.42
Haldane, J., 154n.14
Hall, G. C., 245n.89
Hallowell, I. A., 132n.44, 134n.54, 134n.55,
    135n.56, 135n.57
Hamid, S., 256n.181
Hampshire, K., 266n.251
Hampton, K., 94n.121
Han, P., 234n.14
Hanft-Robert, S., 255n.175
Hangartner, D., 213n.88
Hannes, K., 57n.49
Hansen, L., 121n.61
Hansen, M., 158n.43
Haq, S., 93n.112
Haque, S., 4n.13, 93n.113
Harachi, T. W., 188n.96, 188n.97
Harding, C. E., 11n.63, 20n.143, 31n.237,
    31n.239
Harding, L., 103n.169
Harding, S., 47n.358
Hargraves, J. L., 226n.150
Harioon, A., 20n.148
Harling, O., 85n.44, 235n.27
Harms, G., 19n.130
Harness, L. L., 189n.102
Haro, J. M., 12n.72, 233n.10
Haroz, E. E., 129n.7, 132n.43, 139n.72
Harrington, L. J., 5n.29
Harrington, Sarah, xxv
Harris, L., 103n.164
Harris, L. M., 23n.164, 89n.78, 102n.159
Harris, S. M., 43n.332
Hart, J., 198n.152
Hasan, M., 244n.85
Hasanagic, M., 194n.145
Hasbun, A., 180n.51
Hashimoto, N., 219n.107
Haslam, N., 207n.54
Hassan, C. Q., 91n.99, 154n.13, 157n.39
Hassan, G., 235n.21

Hassan, R., 41n.316, 244n.85
Hassan, S., 219n.107
Hastrup, K., 242n.67
Hatfield, E., 179n.43
Hatton, T. J., 50n.1
Hauff, E., 88n.76, 251n.144
Hauke, G., 262n.223, 262n.225
Hausman, D., 104n.170
Hausmann-Muela, S., 226n.151
Hawley, C., 38n.292
Haynes, D. F., 30n.223
Hays, P. A., 249n.118
Hazra, S., 51n.8
He, Y., 233n.10
Heath, A., 122n.68, 122n.70, 125n.76
Hecker, T., 154n.15, 155n.20, 157n.34, 157n.38,
    158n.42, 164n.77
Hedman, A. R., 86n.51
Heeren, T., 101n.152
Heinrich, D., 5n.29
Heinz, A., 65n.77, 233n.5
Heise, L., 163n.72
Heisler, M., 236n.33, 236n.35
Hellmann, J. H., 255n.171
Hemenway, D., 163n.73
Henderson, D. C., 259n.202
Henssler, J., 65n.77
Herbert, B. M., 262n.223, 262n.225
Herdane, M., 20n.140, 20n.150, 167n.92
Herlihy, J., 93n.116, 94n.119, 94n.123, 105n.179
Herman, D., 94n.120
Herman, J., 95n.128, 239n.55
Herman, J. L., 247n.107
Hermans, D., 93n.110, 93n.114, 105n.180
Hermansson, A. C., 88n.77
Hernán, D. G., 24n.167, 25n.169
Herren, Jaime, xxiv
Herrera, A. M. M., 12n.72
Hervé, C., 38n.290
Hickie, J., 89–90n.83, 90n.84
Higgins, A., 21n.157
Higham, S., 83n.29
Hijazi, Z., 34n.267
Hilden, P. K., 246n.100
Hill, E. D., 233n.10
Hille, P., 62n.71
Hines, B., 104n.171
Hinton, A. L., 27n.193
Hinton, D., 27n.191, 94n.118
Hinton, D. E., 9n.49, 27n.193, 27n.198,
    73–74n.15, 129n.7, 129n.8, 129n.13,
    130n.18, 130n.23, 132n.43, 139n.72,
    140n.74, 144n.98, 145nn.103–4, 145n.105,

146n.106, 146nn.107–8, 147n.110,
    193n.133, 247n.104, 247n.105, 248n.113,
    250nn.130–31, 250n.134
Hinton, L., 130n.23, 194n.138
Hirsch, A., 243n.73
Hirshfield, L. E., 69n.1
Hirst, W., 93n.111, 93n.114
Hitchcock, W., 61n.65
Hjern, A., 235n.20
Hock, A., 55n.33
Hodgetts, G., 194n.145
Hodzic, E., 65n.83
Hoell, A., 233n.5
Hoffman, D., 82n.27, 82–83n.28
Hoffmann, R., 155n.18, 155n.21
Hofmann, S., 266n.255
Hofmann, S. G., 247n.104, 248n.113, 250n.134
Høgh, T. M., 32n.244
Höhne, E., 233n.5
Holen, A., 252n.149
Hollan, D., 131n.30
Holland, D. C., 111n.19, 113n.28
Hollander, A., 238n.42
Hollingworth, S., 259n.198
Hollon, S. D., 246n.99
Hölscher, H., 260n.208
Holst, E., 56n.41
Holt, E., 19n.126
Holzer, J., 180n.51
Hong, E., 167n.99
Honkasalo, M. L., 261n.212
Hooper, K., 220n.119, 228n.161
Hösl, K., 219n.110
Hou, F., 216n.98, 251n.145
Hougen, H. P., 86n.54
Houle, C. R., 270n.7
Hovens, J. E., 73n.12, 194n.139
Hu, M., 253n.155
Hu, N., 8n.40
Huang, C., 10n.60, 116n.41, 231n.169
Hughes, M., 157n.33
Hung, K. W., 253n.154
Hunter, A., 265n.250
Hussain, A., 88n.76
Hussain, Z., 54n.22
Hussein, M., 171n.103
Hussein, S., 32n.242, 226n.147
Hutchins, J., 253n.153
Huxman, S. A. J., 28nn.206–8
Hvidtfeldt, C., 19n.133
Hyman, L., 65n.83
Hyndman, J., 164n.81
Hynes, M., 157n.36

Hynie, M., 59n.54, 205n.40, 221n.128, 222n.133

Iacopino, V., 85n.46, 88n.71, 88n.74, 100n.143
Ibrahim, H., 91n.99, 154n.13, 157n.39, 167n.95
Ignacio, C., 154–55n.17, 156n.30
Iljazi, A., 88n.72, 261n.215
Im, H., 34n.269, 35n.272, 244n.86
Inalo, Sherihan, xxiv
Indra, D., 205n.36
Ingleby, D., 205n.37, 271n.9
Ingleby, J. D., 20n.145, 31n.241
Ingram, J., 33n.258
Iqbal, A., 239n.52
Irastorza, N., 207n.50, 209n.68
Irastorza, P., 43n.335
Irfan, M., 12n.69, 15n.93
Irish, L. A., 154n.8
Isaacs, D., 8n.40
Isakson, B. L., 255n.173
Ismail, A. A., 167n.95
Ismail, H., 266n.254
Isosavi, S., 179n.46
Isse, M.M., 259n.201
Ives, N., 221n.128, 222n.133
Iwamasa, G. Y., 249n.118

Jabbour, S., 236–37n.36
Jaber, R., 235n.25
Jablensky, A., 138n.61
Jäckle, D., 155n.18, 155n.21
Jackson, J. L., 258n.196
Jacob, N., 191n.118
Jacobs, E. A., 132n.40
Jacobsen, J., 56–57n.42, 77n.19
Jacobsen, L. K., 189n.105
Jacqueline, S. L. B., 38n.290
Jafarovna, M., 244n.85
Jager, J., 188n.96, 188n.97
Jalal, B., 250n.131
James, S., 20n.142, 129n.14, 140n.79, 141nn.84–87
Janmyr, M., 117n.46
Jannini, E. A., 260n.209
Jansen, H. M. E., 163n.72
Jaranson, J. M., 85n.42
Jarason, J., 87n.67
Jarvis, E., 130n.27
Jaschke, P., 57n.45, 57n.48, 209n.63
Javanbakht, A., 19n.132, 35n.276
Jave, I., 55n.30
Jawad, M., 236–37n.36
Jayawickrama, J., 266n.254
Jefee-Bahloul, H., 235n.21

Jelusic, I., 178n.30, 187n.86
Jenkins, C. N., 194n.138
Jenkins, H., 249n.121
Jenkins, J. H., 40n.307, 73–74n.15, 129n.8, 130n.18, 144n.100, 145n.102, 146nn.107–8, 147nn.109–11, 181n.60
Jensen, T. K., 94n.122
Jeon, S., 248n.112, 261n.216
Jeon, Y., 248n.112
Jesuthasan, J., 89n.81, 172n.110
Jha, P., 102n.154
Jiménez-Chafey, M. I., 250n.136
Jiménez-Molina, A., 33n.264
Jimenez, T. R., 208n.57
Jina, R., 163n.69
Jjuuko, A., 264n.236
Jobson, L., 263n.234
Joels, T., 187n.91
Joffres, M., 187n.88
John, S., 20n.141
John, T., 17n.107
Johnson, D. R., 85n.42
Johnson, K., 34n.267
Johnson-Douglas, S., 23n.165
Jones, E., 38n.287
Jones, H. L., 96n.130
Jones, L., 34n.267
Jones, R., 244n.79
Jongedijk, R. A., 252n.150, 261n.211
Joormann, M., 204n.29
Jordans, M. J., 255n.177, 259n.200
Jordans, M. J. D., 238n.43, 239n.51, 255n.179, 256n.184
Joscelyne, A., 128n.5
Joseph, S., 182n.63
Jotheeswaran, A. T., 20n.141
Jouk, N., 132n.41
Jubb, C., 159n.49
Julian, Paul, xxi
Jun, J. Y., 248n.112
Jung, F., 155n.18, 155n.21
Junne, F., 91n.98, 92n.101, 92n.103, 143n.97, 167n.94, 234n.16
Juran, S., 43n.333
Jurkovic, M., 235n.23
Juszczyk, G., 8n.39

Kabe, K., 219n.107
Kadis, L., 34n.267
Kadkoy, O., 43n.329
Kagawa, S., 65n.79
Kagawa-Singer, M., 194n.140
Kahn, M., 40n.304

Kaida, L., 216n.98
Kaiser, A. P., 82n.19
Kaiser, B. N., 129n.7, 132n.43, 139n.72
Kaiser, R., 41n.315
Kalfa, V., 64n.74
Kalra, V. S., 122n.71
Kalume, A. K., 31n.228
Kammerer, N., 180n.50
Kamp-Becker, I., 233n.5
Kampisiou, C., 128n.4
Kane, J. C., 31n.227
Kankaanpää, R., 246n.100
Kannis-Dymand, L., 244n.84, 247n.103
Kanyangara, P., 30n.226
Kapczinski, F., 26–27n.183
Kaplan, C., 89n.79
Kaplin, C., 174n.1
Kaplin, D., 199n.156
Käppeli, A., 43n.336
Karadağ, H., 167n.93
Karageorge, A., 178nn.38–39
Karam, A. N., 180n.53, 194n.141, 233n.10
Karam, E. G., 180n.53, 194n.141, 233n.10
Karenian, H., 197n.151
Karenian, S., 197n.151
Kareth, M., 9n.48
Karroum, L. B., 236–37n.36
Karyar, N. M., 141n.88
Kassab, A., 20n.140, 20n.150, 167n.92
Kassir, M. F., 111n.17
Kastelan, A., 189n.99
Kastrup, M., 88n.75
Kastrup, M. A., 249n.125
Katona, C., 41n.316, 238n.47, 239n.54,
      248n.114, 249n.123, 250n.128, 254n.165
Kaushal, N., 235n.25
Kawakami, N., 233n.10
Kay, M., 259n.198
Kayran, Y., 167n.93
Keatley, E., 128n.5
Keller, A., 20n.146, 102n.155
Keller, A. S., 85n.41, 192n.129
Kellerman, N. P. F., 178n.34, 191n.121
Kelly, A., 260n.207
Kelly, K. M., 89–90n.83
Kelly, N., 170n.102
Kelly, T., 101n.148
Kelly, Timothy, xxiv–xxv
Kelstrup, J., 86n.54
Kemei, J., 8n.41
Kenanoğlu, M., 43n.329
Kent, A., 7n.34
Kerbage, H., 266n.254

Kerkhof, A., 19n.135
Kernberg, O., 69n.8
Kerry, R., 254n.167
Kersting, A., 155n.21
Kersting. A., 155n.18
Kerwin, D., 36n.282, 43n.338
Kessler, R. C., 154n.9, 157n.32, 157n.33,
      180n.53, 194n.141, 233n.10
Kew, S., 5n.29
Key, K., 132n.42
Khader, B., 107n.1
Khadra, M., 235n.25
Khalaf, M., 221n.128, 222n.133
Khaleque, A., 191n.117
Khalifeh, Y., 111n.17
Khalil, R. B., 167n.92
Khalil, S. A., 20n.139
Khan, H., 177n.18
Khan, S., 4n.13, 93n.112, 93n.113
Khantsis, S., 162n.64
Khaw, F. M., 8n.39
Khayati, K., 172n.105
Khoury, L. S., 233n.8, 258n.189
Khudsen, J. C., 9n.46
Kibrear, G., 114n.37
Kiconco, A., 177n.20
Kidron, C. A., 140n.75, 142n.92, 144n.99,
      150n.121
Kienzler, H., 34n.266, 82n.21
Kiernan, M. D., 253n.153
Kilborne, B., 109n.8
Killian, K. D., 179n.41, 185n.80
Kilpatrick, K., 266n.251
Kim, E., 42n.328
Kim, G., 85n.41, 102n.155
Kim, H. J., 153n.2
Kim, J. Y., 153n.2
Kim, S., 261n.216
Kim, S. J., 248n.112, 261n.216
Kimbel, R., 89n.81, 172n.110
Kimerling, R., 158n.47
Kimmelman, M., 236n.29
Kindermann, D., 234n.16
King, D. W., 82n.19, 180n.48
King, L. A., 82n.19, 180n.48
King, N. S., 234n.11
Kingdom, D., 20n.148
King-Smith, Alastair, xxi
Kinzie, D., 258n.195
Kinzie, J. D., 26n.180, 85n.43, 233n.7, 238n.40,
      249n.119, 258n.188, 260n.205
Kinzie, J. M., 85n.43
Kirkbride, J., 20n.145, 31n.241

Kirkbride, J. B., 238n.42
Kirmayer, L. J., 27n.188, 27nn.192–93, 128n.3,
    129n.15, 130n.19, 130n.23, 130n.25,
    130n.27, 131n.37, 133n.51, 139n.67,
    140n.75, 142n.92, 144n.99, 144n.101,
    150n.121, 235n.21, 240n.58, 246n.94,
    246n.97
Kitoko, G. M. B., 31n.228
Kitroeff, N., 5n.28
Kizilhan, J. I., 92n.102
Klaghofer, R., 175n.7, 176n.10, 179n.45,
    180n.47, 180n.57, 185n.77, 190n.112, 191–
    92n.124, 192n.126
Klaric, B., 189n.99
Klaric, M., 178n.30, 187n.86, 189n.99
Kleber, R., 154n.7, 156n.29, 162n.66
Kleber, R. J. , 20n.149, 91n.96, 252n.150,
    261n.211, 261n.218
Kleijn, W. C., 73n.12
Klein, E., 180n.50
Kleinman, A., 46n.354, 131n.32, 131n.35,
    138n.59, 138n.62, 181n.59, 181nn.61–62,
    240n.57, 240n.61
Kleinschmidt, Kilian, xxiv–xxv
Klemettilä, A., 39n.295
Kluckhohn, C., 129n.12
Knaevelsrud, C., 128n.4
Knafl, K., 182n.65, 254n.160
Knapp, A., 19n.128
Knipscheer, J., 154n.7, 156n.29, 162n.66
Knipscheer, J. W., 91n.96, 261n.218
Knipscheer, W. J., 252n.150
Knöpfli, B. 47n.357, 209n.61, 217–18n.103,
    227n.156, 229n.165
Knudsen, J. C., 65n.85
Knudson, J. C., 169n.101
Kobe, M. A., 154–55n.17, 156n.30
Kobeissi, L., 156n.26, 244n.85
Koçak, C., 156n.26
Koch, T., 238n.50
Koch-Schulte, S., 41n.312
Koehler, C., 213n.85
Kofman, E., 16n.100
Kohila, M., 191n.118
Kohmann, A. M., 26–27n.183
Kohrt, B. A., 129n.7, 132n.43, 139n.72,
    255n.177, 256n.185
Kolody, B., 96n.129
Komproe, I., 87n.66, 140n.80
Komproe, I. H., 65n.82, 207n.53, 255n.177,
    259n.200, 261n.213
Kone, Z., 209n.65, 210n.69, 210nn.70–71
König, H. H., 155n.18, 155n.21

Kontoangelos, K., 89–90n.83
Koopman, C., 40–41n.311, 149nn.112–13
Kopinak, J. K., 33n.263
Koppenol-Gonzalez, G. V., 255n.179
Korac, M., 59n.51, 203n.22, 205n.39, 213n.90,
    227n.154, 227n.155
Koren-Karie, N., 187n.91
Korn, A., 59n.54, 205n.40
Korn, M., 69n.2
Kornfield, S. L., 154n.5, 162n.65
Koss, R. G., 226n.149
Kosyakova, Y., 44n.345, 56n.41, 56–57n.42,
    57n.45, 57n.48, 57n.49, 209n.63, 229n.163
Koulouvaris, P., 89–90n.83
Kourmeli, E., 233n.5
Kovess-Masfety, V., 233n.10
Krasteva, A., 203n.25, 205n.38, 230n.167
Krill, A., 220n.118
Kritikos, A., 262n.223, 262n.225
Kröger, H., 44n.345, 229n.163
Kroh, M., 56n.41, 56–57n.42
Krook, M. L., 107n.2, 109n.6, 119n.48, 119n.49,
    120n.50
Krueger, R. F., 129n.15
Krüger, A., 89n.81, 172n.110
Krystal, H., 26n.178
Kucukalic, A., 177n.23, 194n.142
Kudler, H. S., 189n.101
Kuhn, S. K., 93n.113
Kühne, S., 56–57n.42
Kuittinen, S., 261n.212
Kuittinen, S. K. N., 179n.46
Kulauzovic, Y., 182n.65, 254n.160
Kulkarni, M., 140n.77
Kunst, A. E., 19n.135
Kurban, M., 111n.17
Kurmeyer, C., 89n.81, 172n.110
Kurt, T., 43n.329
Kvesic, A., 189n.99
Kyei, P., 266n.251

Laban, C. J., 65n.82, 140n.80, 207n.53,
    261n.213
Labate, Robert, xxiv
Lachapelle, G., 163n.70
Lacherez, P., 41n.321, 178n.33
Lacombe-Duncan, A., 264n.240
Lai, K. Q., 194n.138
Lai, L., 149n.118
Lal, Nikhil, xxv
Lal, Ranjan, xxv
Lal, Rocky, xxv
Lal, Sohan, xxv

Lal, Sunita, xxv
Lamb, C., 142n.96, 164n.79, 165n.86
Lambert, J. E., 180n.51
Lamsaouri, J., 258n.197
Landler, M., 108n.3
Landrine, H., 149n.120
Langer, L., 94n.117
Langness, L. L., 109n.8
Lankau, E., 208n.55
Lankau, J., 202n.12
Lara-Garcia, F., 204n.31, 205n.43, 220n.120,
    228n.162
Larcombe, P., 8n.40
Larkin, M., 249n.121
La Roche, M. J., 251n.142
Latifeh, Y., 256n.181
Latifi, S. Y., 82n.27, 82–83n.28
Lau, L. S., 40n.308, 42n.325, 130n.26, 244n.82,
    244n.87
Laub, D., 65n.83
Lavell, J., 92n.107
Lavelle, J., 20n.147, 21n.152, 90n.90
Lavin, T., 8n.41
Lawless, M., 86n.59
Lawrence, D., 213n.88
Layne, C. M., 255n.173
Lazrove, S., 65n.83
Le, A., 194n.138
Le, T. N., 32n.251
Leary, K., 34n.267
Leavell, J., 251n.142
Lecic-Tosevski, D., 177n.23, 194n.142
Lee, A. C. K., 8n.39
Lee, J., 248n.112, 261n.216
Lee, M. J., 261n.217
Lee, R. C., 89–90n.83
Lee, S., 261n.216
Lee, Y. J., 261n.216
Lee-Foon, N., 264n.240
Lefebvre, P., 270n.7
Legerski, J. P., 255n.173
Lelie, F., 213n.86
Lely, J. C. G., 252n.150
Lemelson, R., 27n.192
Lenaert, B., 93n.110, 93n.114
Lenette, C., 65n.84, 154–55n.17, 156n.30
Lenguerrand, E., 47n.358
Lenzi, A., 260n.209
Leustean, L. N., 9n.55
Lever, H., 234n.17
Levi, P., 39n.297
Levin, Y., 196n.148
LeVine, R., 130n.24

Levine, R. A., 132n.44, 134n.54, 134n.55,
    135n.56, 135n.57
Levitt, D., 8n.40
Lewis, G., 238n.42
Lewis-Fernández, R., 128n.3, 130n.23, 144n.98
Lewis-Fernandez, R. L., 129n.13
Lezic, A., 182n.65, 254n.160
Lhewa, D., 20n.146
Li, S., 5n.29
Liang, X., 253n.155
Liao, Y. M., 253n.154
Lidén, G., 215n.97
Lie, B., 21n.153, 65n.81
Liebau, E., 56n.41, 56–57n.42
Liebow, E., 121n.63
Liedl, A., 238n.50
Lies, J., 263n.234
Lifton, R. J., 46n.351
Lilja, E., 39n.295
Limoncin, E., 260n.209
Lin, N., 234n.15
Lindgren, K., 43n.334, 221n.124, 221n.126
Lindholm, M., 226n.150
Lindman, A. E. S., 8n.39
Lindner, A. K., 19n.130
Lindstrøm, J. C., 88n.76
Lingam, R., 8n.40
Linke, U., 35n.277
Lipsey, T. L., 174n.2
Lipson, J. G., 183n.67, 220n.122
Lipton, R. B., 88n.72, 261n.215
Lisica, D., 189n.99
Littlewood, J., 46n.353
Littlewood, R., 138n.60
Liu, H., 55n.29, 101n.151
Liu, R., 156n.27
Livaditis, M., 197n.151
Livanou, M., 194n.146
Lo, T., 249n.120
Löbel, L., 77n.19
Loeb, J. M., 226n.149
Loescher, G., 9n.51, 18n.117, 18n.119, 157n.41,
    164n.80, 198n.152, 203n.24
Loescher, K., 47n.356
Loff, B., 242n.69
Logie, C. H., 264n.240
Loi, A., 4n.20
Loizides, N., 16n.101
Lommen, M. J. J., 246n.101
Long, D. M., 27n.185
Long, K., 47n.356, 157n.41, 198n.152
Longman, T., 91n.100
Longombe, A. O., 163n.71

Lopes, C. B., 157n.36
Lopes Cardozo, B., 41n.315
Lopez, C. R. V., 82n.27, 82–83n.28
Lopez, D., 239n.53
Lorenzon, V. R., 26–27n.183
Loring, B., 244n.79
Loschmann, C., 45n.349
Loughry, M., 149n.115
Lovell, G. P., 244n.84, 247n.103
Luban, D., 89n.80
Luborsky, L., 69n.3
Lucas, T., 132n.42
Lucea, M. B., 163n.70
Luci, M., 27n.190, 28n.203, 40n.304
Luckett, C., 149n.119
Lui, K., 16n.103
Luik, M., 228n.158
Luitel, N. P., 255n.177
Lunde, I., 86n.55
Lundin, A., 182n.64, 194n.144
Lusimbo, R., 264n.236
Lustig, S. L., 103n.167
Lütkefun, T., 13n.74
Lutz, C., 73–74n.15
Lutz, E. L., 100n.145
Lyford, B., 33n.258
Lynch, Jake, xxv
Lynch, John, xxv
Lynch, Kasia, xxv
Lynch, Sophie, xxv
Lynde, D. W., 251n.143
Lyons, J. A., 192n.128
Lytle, B. L., 187n.87, 189n.101

MacArthur, J. R., 35n.277
McAtamney, A., 33n.258
McCallum, R., 15n.90
McCarrey, M., 23n.165
Macciotta, A., 19n.129
McCormack, L., 175n.5, 190n.108
McCormick, M. C., 163n.73
McDiarmid, S., 246n.100
McDougall, A., 62n.66
McFarlane, A., 32n.252
McFarlane, C., 93n.115
McGlashan, D. F., 65n.83
McGlashan, T., 155n.19
McGlashan, T. H., 65n.83
McGlynn Scanlon, M., 220n.118
McGoldrick, M., 174n.3
McGrath, J. J., 12n.72
McGrath, S., 221n.128, 222n.133
McHugh, M., 32n.246, 218n.105
McInnes, K., 20n.147

McKay, D., 236n.33, 236n.35
Mackay, N., 86n.57
Mckay, R., 187n.88
McKinney, K., 40n.305
McLaughlin, K. A., 233n.10
McLean, I., 162n.67
McLellan, A. T., 69n.3
McMurry, H. S., 234n.15
McNally, R., 87n.68
McPhee, S., 194n.138
McSpadden, L. A., 35n.277
McWey, L. M., xviiin.4, 28nn.204–206
McWilliams, N., 260n.206
Macy, R. D., 255n.177, 259n.200
Madakasira, S., 96n.131
Madge, C., 8n.44
Madi, F., 266n.254
Maffini, C. S., 176n.11
Magana, C., 61n.57
Magnusson, C., 238n.42
Maharjan, S. M., 129n.7, 132n.43, 139n.72
Maitland, J., 270n.7
Majka, L., 215n.96
Major, E. F., 23n.165
Malekian, A., 189n.104
Malik, S., 224n.142
Malkki, L., 114n.36, 165n.84
Malkki, L. H., 41n.313
Malm, A., 180n.54, 182n.64, 194n.144
Malwand, A. D., 140n.80
Man, J., 4n.20
Manfredi, L., 19n.129
Manicavasagar, V., 41n.319
Manning, A., 42nn.323–24, 54n.26, 229n.164
Manson, S. M., 26n.180
Manu, S., 149n.119
Mao, F., 18n.116
Marazziti, D., 259nn.203–4
Marcozzi, A., 260n.209
Marcus, J., 176n.13
Mares, S., 8n.40, 236n.28, 242n.70
Marfleet, P., 25n.175
Marin, A. S., 26–27n.183
Marinelli, R. P., 189n.98
Markman, H. J., 178n.36, 182n.66, 186n.82
Markova, V., 141n.83, 208n.58
Marmar, C., 241n.64
Marmar, C. M., 154n.5
Marmar, C. R., 27n.197, 28n.201, 129n.9,
    162n.65
Marnane, C., 87n.65, 233n.4
Marsella, A. J., 138n.61
Marshall, G. N., 32n.247, 193nn.134–35,
    194n.136, 194n.143, 226n.153

Martell, Z., 239n.53
Martin, S., 172n.107
Martín-Baró, I., 28n.205, 30n.224, 124n.74
Martínez, P., 33n.264
Martínez, V., 33n.264
Martini, C., 245n.90
Martins-Borges, L., 23n.162, 240n.59
Masika, Y. D., 31n.228
Mason, O. J., 238n.41
Massagli, M. P., 20n.147, 21n.152
Massey, D. S., 52n.11
Massimetti, G., 259n.203
Masterson, D., 56n.40
Masud, H., 96n.133
Matei, A., 177n.19
Mathews, H., 130n.24
Mathias, J. L., 92n.104
Mattner, M., 9n.56
Maylea, C., 243n.73
Maynard, M. J., 47n.358
Mayne, C., 5n.22
Maystadt, J., 44n.340
Mbeva, J. K., 31n.228
Medina-Mora, M. E., 233n.10
Mednick, S., n.6
Mehchy, Z., 177n.16
Mehta, E., 235n.19
Meinhart, M., 235n.25
Mekki-Berrada, A., 235n.21
Mellinger, H., 23n.164
Meltzer, H. Y., 258n.191
Melville, F., 41n.321, 178n.33
Mercado, A., 131n.39, 202n.10
Mereu, A., 157n.31
Merkord, F., 23n.163, 38n.286, 101n.147, 101n.150
Merrens, M. R., 251n.143
Mesas, A. E., 92n.105
Metzner, F., 255n.175
Meyer, C., 128n.4
Meyerhoff, J., 33n.257, 202n.13, 222n.129
Mezzich, J. E., 139n.67
Michael, L., 203n.19
Mikulica, J., 259n.201
Millbank, J., 30n.221
Miller, C., 27n.185
Miller, K., 27n.189, 139n.66, 141n.91
Miller, K. E., 140n.77, 140n.78, 141n.88, 192n.129, 238n.43, 239n.51, 239n.53, 255n.179, 273n.19
Miller, M. W., 190n.116
Miller, R. B., xviiin.4, 28nn.204–206
Millon, T., 129n.15
Mills, E., 187n.88

Milner, J., 9n.51, 18n.117, 18n.119
Minas, H., 131n.37, 133n.51
Mirdal, G. M., 239n.52
Mirisola, C., 32n.245
Mirza, M., 122n.71
Mishori, R., 94n.121
Mitchell, T., 132n.48
Mneimneh, Z., 180n.53, 194n.141
Modood, T., 226n.148
Moeller, R. G., 40n.302
Moffett, H., 165n.91
Mohamed, H., 85n.43
Mohammad, R., 221n.128, 222n.133
Mohammadi, D., 167n.97
Moisander, P. A., 39n.294, 39n.296, 88n.70, 88n.73
Mollica, R., 20n.147, 92n.107
Mollica, R. F., 21n.152, 90n.90
Mölsä, M., 261n.212
Momartin, S., 41n.319, 41n.320
Monahan, L., 164n.80
Montgomery, D. W., 124n.75
Montgomery, E., 80n.9, 85n.40, 191n.123
Montgomery, S., 20n.142, 129n.14, 140n.79, 141n.84, 141n.87
Moore, C., 130n.24
Moradi, A. R., 94n.123
Morales, F. R., 131n.39, 202n.10
Moran, J., 158n.46
Moreno, A., 86n.52, 91n.93, 100n.146
Morgan, C. A., 177n.22
Morgan, N. J., 266n.253
Morina, N., 47n.357, 153n.1, 154n.14, 175n.7, 176n.10, 177n.23, 179n.45, 180n.47, 180n.57, 185n.77, 190n.112, 191–92n.124, 192n.126, 194n.142, 209n.61, 217–18n.103, 227n.156, 229n.165, 238n.46, 255n.171, 261n.214
Morland, P., 21n.156
Moro, D., 157n.31
Moro, M. F., 157n.31
Morrice, L., 203n.19, 219n.107, 222n.132
Morris, A., 184n.74
Morrison, L. L., 33n.256
Mortensen, E., 234–35n.18
Mortensen, E. L., 88n.75, 238n.48, 246n.101, 248nn.115–16, 249n.125, 258n.190, 266n.257
Moses, M. H., 243n.75
Mossamet, Nasima, 159n.51
Mota-Cardoso, R., 176n.9, 190n.111
Motta, R. W., 189n.106
Mottran, P., 258n.194
Moturi, E., 260n.208

Motz, A., 29n.217
Moussaoui, D., 20n.145, 31n.241
Moutaouakkil, Y., 258n.197
Mucci, F., 259nn.203–4
Muchacha, M., 48n.361, 201n.4, 203n.23,
    204n.26, 206n.44
Muecke, M. A., 169n.101
Mueser, K. T., 251n.143
Muftim, K. A., 20n.148
Mugisha, D., 244n.84, 247n.103
Mujagic, A., 182n.65, 254n.160
Mukherjee, T., 235n.25
Mulé, N. J., 264n.236
Muleta, T. B., 224n.140
Müller, J., 47n.357, 175n.7, 176n.10, 179n.45,
    180n.47, 180n.57, 185n.77, 190n.112, 191–
    92n.124, 192n.126, 209n.61, 217–18n.103,
    227n.156, 229n.165
Müller, K., 19n.130
Müller, M., 65n.77
Mumford, S. D., 254n.167
Muñoz García, N., 29n.214
Munir, L. P., 16n.95, 264n.238
Munk-Andersen, E., 19n.134
Munroe, J. F., 189n.103
Muong, S., 180n.49, 196n.147
Murakami, N., 27n.199
Murray, C., 154–55n.17, 156n.30
Murray, H., 129n.12
Murray, K., 65n.84
Murray-García, J., 244n.81
Musalo, K., 103n.165
Musicaro, R., 263n.232
Mutamba, B. B., 129n.7, 132n.43, 139n.72
Mutiso, D., 266n.252
Muzurovic, J., 182n.65, 254n.160
Muzurovic, N., 182n.65, 254n.160

Nackerud, L., 41n.315
Naeem, F., 12n.69, 15n.93, 20n.148, 250n.132,
    250n.135
Nagata, D. K., 23n.165
Nagayama, 245n.89
Nagl, M., 155n.18, 155n.21
Nahas, N., 255n.179
Nahian, A., 132n.41
Naimark, N. M., 61n.64
Nam, B., 153n.2
Naoum, M., 234n.14
Narayan, D., 41n.312
Nardi, C., 186n.84
Nasiry, M. N., 141n.88
Nasiry, S., 141n.88

Nasser, R., 177n.16
Nasser, S. C., 180n.53, 194n.141
Nazroo, J., 20n.145, 31n.241
Ndetei, D., 259n.201
Ndofor-Tah, C., 203n.19
Negash, S., 64n.74
Nelson, C. B., 157n.33
Nemer, G., 111n.17
Nemeroff, B., 154n.5
Nemeroff, C. B., 27n.197, 28n.201, 129n.9,
    162n.65, 241n.64
Neria, Y., 29n.214
Neuner, F., 35n.271, 167n.95, 191n.118,
    251n.146, 252n.149, 256n.183
Newbold, B., 167n.99
Newell, K. S., 89n.80
Newland, K., 32n.246, 218n.105
Newman, E., 9n.51, 18n.117, 18n.119
Newman, L. K., 236n.28, 242n.70
Nguyen, L., 192n.129
Nguyen-Finn, K. L., 131n.39, 202n.10
Ní Aoláin, F., 30n.223
Nicholson, B. L., 194n.137
Nicholson, M., 43n.334, 221n.124, 221n.126
Nichter, M., 139n.68, 139n.71
Nickerson, A., 47n.357, 153n.1, 154n.14,
    178n.32, 209n.61, 217–18n.103, 227n.156,
    229n.165, 238n.46, 238n.49, 245n.93,
    261n.214
Nicol, N., 264n.236
Nicolaou, A. L., 177n.22
Nikendei, C., 234n.16
Nikewski, G., 89n.81
Niklewski, G., 172n.110
Nikolaus, M., 19n.130
Nilsson, H., 262n.231
Njenga, A., 173n.111
Njoku, A., 21n.154
Noll-Hussong, M., 92n.102
Nomura, Y., 181n.58
Nordentoft, M., 234–35n.18, 238n.48,
    248nn.115–16, 266n.257
Norman, K., 130n.24
Norredam, M., 19n.133, 85n.44, 101n.152,
    235n.27
Nosè, M., 253n.157
Nou, L., 193n.133
Nourpanah, S., 59n.54, 205n.40
Nowrasteh, A., 44n.341
Nyhlén, J., 215n.97

Obeyesekere, G., 46n.352, 130n.20, 138n.63
O'Brian, K., 96n.131

O'Brien, C. P., 69n.3
O'Brien, M. M., 90n.87
O'Callaghan, P., 256n.184
Oda, A., 221n.128, 222n.133
Odeh, N., 234n.14
Odenwald, M. G., 259n.201
O'Dougherty, M., 235n.19
Oertelt-Prigione, A., 89n.81
Oertelt-Prigione, S., 172n.110
Oglak, S., 32n.242, 226n.147
Ogwok, B., 48n.361, 201n.4, 203n.23, 204n.26, 206n.44
Ohaeri, J. U., 189n.100, 190n.110
Ohmar, K., 27n.199
Ojeda, V. D., 61n.57
O'Kane, M., 27n.199
Okeke-Ihejirika, P., 8n.41
Okenwa-Emegwa, L., 15n.88
Okiror, S., 114n.33
Olani, A. B., 224n.140
Olema, D., 155n.20, 157n.38, 158n.42
Olema, D. K., 154n.15, 157n.34, 164n.77
Olsen, D. R., 88n.75
Olynik, M. G. P., 163n.70
O'Malley, P. G., 258n.196
Omar, A. A. H., 39n.295
Omidian, P., 139n.66, 140n.77, 140n.78, 141n.88, 141n.91
O'Nell, T. D., 27n.198, 129n.10
Oosterveld, V., 30n.223
Oppong, G., 266n.251
Oquendo, M. A., 29n.214
Orange, D. M., 69n.5
Ordóñez, A. E., 29n.214
O'Rourke, K., 245n.91, 253n.156
Oskarsson, S., 43n.334, 221n.124, 221n.126
Osman, F., 246n.100
Osterbrink, J., 219n.110
Ostergaard, L. S., 85n.44, 235n.27
Ottenheimer, D., 234n.17
Otto, F. E. L., 5n.29
Otto, M. W., 247n.105, 248n.113
Ou, K. L., 253n.154
Ouimette, P., 158n.47
Oumar, F. W., 157n.31
Oxholm, A., 85n.44, 235n.27
Ozaltin, D., 16n.101
Ozer, E. J., 174n.2
Ozkalipci, O., 100n.143

Paasche-Orlow, M. K., 101n.152
Pachankis, J. E., 264n.239
Padberg, F., 233n.5

Páez, D., 30n.225, 55n.30
Pagel, J. F., 247n.109, 269n.2
Pagel, L., 56–57n.42
Pain, S.-J., 244n.79
Palacios, J., 235n.20
Palagini, L., 259n.204
Palego, L., 259n.203
Palic, S., 245n.92, 249n.126
Palinkas, L. A., 43n.332, 208n.59
Pallard, H., 159n.49
Pallesen, S., 208n.58
Pallini, S., 253n.152
Palmer, S., 189n.101
Palosaari, E., 185n.75, 190n.109
Pan, Ruochan, xxiv
Pandolfo, S., 132n.48
Panhofer, H., 262n.227
Paniagua, F. A., 245n.88
Panter-Brick, C., 46n.355, 139n.69, 141n.90, 142n.93, 142n.94
Papadopoulos, R. K., 178n.38
Papagiannis, G. I., 89–90n.83
Papola, D., 256n.184
Papps, E., 244n.78
Parente, K., 174n.1, 199n.156
Park, C. L., 82n.19
Park, J., 261n.216
Park, L., 132n.40
Park, Y. S., 248n.112
Parker, R., 33n.265
Parrett, N. S., 238n.41
Passos, I. C., 26–27n.183
Pastoor, L., 204n.27
Patacchini, E., 211n.78
Patel, A., 250n.130
Patel, N., 31n.230
Patel, P. P., 34n.267
Patel, R., 41n.312
Patel, V., 128n.6, 131n.37, 133n.51
Paul, S., 162n.67
Pavic, I., 235n.23
Pavkovic, I., 182n.65, 254n.160
Pazdirek, L., 239n.53
Pearlman, W., 204n.29
Peconga, E. K., 32n.244
Pedersen, P., 244n.83
Peel, M., 111n.16
Peltonen, K., 256n.184
Pennebaker, J. W., 30n.225
Penninx, R., 203n.20
Pepe, R. R., 19n.129
Pereira, C. R., 219n.113
Perrin, S., 185n.76

Peruzzolo, T. L., 26–27n.183
Petersen, H. D., 86n.54
Petersen, J. H., 19n.133
Petrovic, V., 194n.145
Petukhova, M., 233n.10
Pezzini, Mario, xxiv
Pfaltz, M. C., 20n.144
Pham, A. N., 176n.11
Pham, K., 155n.22, 162n.59
Pham, P., 91n.98, 92n.101, 92n.103, 143n.97,
    167n.94, 241n.65, 241n.66
Pham, P. N., 91n.100
Pham, T., 247n.105
Phan, T., 41n.318, 178n.28, 180n.52
Philip, S., 5n.29
Philippot, P., 30n.226
Philips, J., 52n.12
Phillimore, J., 19n.136, 59n.55, 203n.19, 219n.107
Pich, V., 94n.118, 247n.104, 248n.113, 250n.134
Pichel, A. N., 260n.210
Pietrantuono, G., 44n.345, 57n.49, 229n.163
Pilling, D., 5n.30
Pilowsky, D., 181n.58
Pinchi, V., 86n.53, 105n.183
Pin-Fat, V., 121n.60
Pinninti, N., 12n.69, 15n.93
Pinto, I., 5n.29
Pinto, J. V., 26–27n.183
Piripiri, A. L., 31n.228
Pittaway, E., 153n.4, 159n.48
Piwowarczyk, L., 101n.152
Plaza, S., 42n.328
Pliskin, N. H., 89–90n.83
Pohontsch, N. J., 255n.175
Pole, N., 27n.197, 129n.9
Poleacovschi, C., 202n.11, 204n.30, 220n.121
Pollack, M., 94n.118
Pollack, M. H., 193n.133, 247nn.104–5,
    250n.134
Polliack, M., 185n.79
Pollotos, O., 262n.223, 262n.225
Pool, R., 35n.275
Popkin, M., 87n.67
Popovski, M., 177n.23, 194n.142
Porreca, F., 261n.217
Porter, G., 266n.251
Porter, M., 207n.54
Porterfield, K., 20n.146
Posada-Villa, J. A., 233n.10
Post, L., 10n.60
Poteet, M., 59n.54, 205n.40
Pradella, F., 86n.53, 105n.183
Pren, K. A., 52n.11

Preti, A., 157n.31
Price, M., 263n.232
Priebe, S., 21n.154, 177n.23, 194n.142, 233n.3,
    253n.157
Prince, M., 131n.37, 133n.51
Prisecaru, M., 19n.129
Procter, N., 33n.259
Proença, R., 19n.125, 156n.25
Pross, C., 23n.163, 38n.286, 94n.126, 101n.147,
    101n.150, 102n.157
Puell de la Villa, F., 24n.167, 25n.169
Pufaa, E., 51n.8
Punamäki, R. L., 88n.69, 179n.46, 185n.75,
    190n.109, 246n.100, 256n.184, 261n.212
Purgato, M., 238n.45, 253n.157, 256n.184
Puvimanasinghe, T., 239n.52

Qouta, S., 185n.75, 190n.109
Quayyum, Z., 244n.85
Quinn, Naomi, 113n.28
Quintana, S., 251n.141
Quosh, C., 235n.21
Quraishy, A. S., 141n.88
Quraishy, N., 141n.88
Qureshi, A., 20n.145, 31n.241

Rabe-Hesketh, S., 185n.76
Rabin, C., 186n.84
Rabin, M., 86n.59
Racadio, M., 141nn.85–86
Racusin, G. R., 189n.105
Rademacher, A., 41n.312
Raes, F., 93n.110, 93n.114, 94n.120, 105n.180
Rafuse, J., 102n.156
Raghavan, S., 192n.129
Rahman, M., 159n.49
Rajaram, P., 40n.309, 55n.27
Rajaram, P. K., 164n.83
Raju, E., 5n.29
Raman, S., 8n.40
Ramarosandratana, A. M., 5n.29
Ramsay, H., 264n.240
Ramsden, I., 244n.78
Ramstead, M. J. D., 130n.19, 144n.101
Ramzy, A., 4n.15
Rana, M. S., 9n.54
Randall, G. R., 100n.145
Rao, T. S. S., 140n.73
Rapson, R., 179n.43
Rasco, L. M., 273n.19
Rashid, S., 244n.85
Rasmussen, A., 27n.189, 46n.355, 128n.5,
    129n.7, 132n.43, 139n.69, 139n.72,

140nn.77–78, 141n.90, 142n.93, 192n.129, 193n.133
Rasmussen, O., 92n.109
Rasmussen, O. V., 86n.54, 86n.55, 90n.89, 91n.91
Rastogi, M., xviiin.4, 28nn.204–206
Rath, B., 26n.180
Ratha, D., 42n.328
Rathod, P., 12n.69, 15n.93
Rathod, S., 12n.69
Ratnayake, B., 89–90n.83
Rauhala, E., 201n.5
Ray, M., 13n.75
Ray, P., 244n.85
Rayes, D., 43n.331, 128n.2
Reátegui, F., 55n.30
Redlich, A., 255n.175
Reece, M. J., 254n.169
Reed, G., 226n.150
Rees, S., 9n.48, 35n.270, 247n.106, 248n.111, 256n.182, 258n.193, 266n.255, 266n.256
Regev, S., 178n.35
Rehmus, W., 19n.128
Reid, P., 244n.79
Reis, R., 140n.74
Renner, A., 155n.18, 155n.21
Renner, V., 234n.16
Renner, W., 262n.221
Renshaw, K. D., 178n.36, 182n.66, 186n.82
Resick, P., 252n.148, 254n.159
Resick, P. A., 248n.110
Reyes, M., 219n.107
Rhoades, G. K., 178n.36, 182n.66, 186n.82
Rhodes, A., 263n.233
Rhodes, P., 178nn.38–39
Riaz, A., 9n.54
Ribera, J. M., 226n.151
Ricceri, F., 19n.129
Rice, M., 103n.165
Richa, S., 20n.140, 20n.150, 167n.92
Richards, J., 256n.180, 256n.184
Richardson, J. G., 224n.139
Richter, D., 56n.41, 56–57n.42
Richter, J., 19n.130
Richter, K., 172n.110
Richton, R. E., 163n.71
Riedel-Heller, S., 155n.18, 155n.21
Rikitu, D. H., 224n.140
Riley, C., 85n.43
Rimé, B., 30n.225, 30n.226
Ringwald, J., 234n.16
Riquelme, H. U., 92n.106
Rizkalla, N., 96n.133

Roberts, J., 69n.7
Roberts, N. P., 249n.122
Roberts, S. A., 162n.67
Robertson, C., 85n.42
Robinson, L., 43n.336
Robinson, V., 203n.21, 206n.46
Robjant, K., 41n.316, 238n.47, 239n.54, 248n.114, 249n.123, 250n.128, 254n.165
Roborgh, S., 236–37n.36
Rodenburg, J. J., 73n.12
Rodgers, G., 40n.308, 42n.325, 130n.26, 244n.82, 244n.87
Rodriguez, C., 34n.269, 35n.272, 244n.86
Roganovic, B., 178n.30, 187n.86
Rogler, L. H., 131n.31
Rohan, K. J., 33n.257, 202n.13, 222n.129
Rohart, A. C., 69n.4
Rohlof, H. G., 91n.96, 261n.218
Rohner, R. P., 191n.117
Röhr, S., 155n.18, 155n.21
Roic, A. C., 235n.23
Rojas, G., 33n.264
Rolland, J. S., 254n.163
Rollin, T., 38n.291
Romaniec, R., 62n.71
Romano, T. A., 93n.111, 93n.114
Rometsch, C., 91n.98, 92n.101, 92n.103, 143n.97, 167n.94, 234n.16
Romiti, A., 56n.41
Root, J. C., 93n.111, 93n.114
Rosaldo, M., 132n.47
Rose, J., 101n.149
Rosenfeld, B., 20n.146
Rosenheck, R., 21n.151, 190n.115
Rosenow, Laurie, xxv
Rosenow, Lindy, xxv
Rosenow, Penny, xxv
Rosenow, Theo, xxv
Rosing, T., 262n.230
Rostami, M. R., 8n.40
Rother, N., 44n.345, 56–57nn.41–42, 57n.49, 229n.163
Rothod, S., 15n.93
Rouf, K., 246n.102
Rousseau, C., 246n.94, 246n.97, 259n.199
Roy, D., 17n.104
Roy, O., 111n.20, 122n.69, 125n.76
Roza, T. H., 26–27n.183
Rubenstein, L., 155n.22
Rubenstein, L. S., 162n.59
Rubin, S., 254n.169
Rublee, C., 234n.12
Ruggeri, M., 33n.262

Ruhlmann, L. M., 28nn.206–8
Ruiz, I., 201nn.6–7, 209n.60, 209nn.64–65, 209nn.66–67, 210n.69, 210nn.70–71, 210nn.72–73, 211n.76, 219n.112
Ruminjo, J., 163n.71
Ruscio, A. M., 180n.48
Ruspini, P., 31n.232
Russell, J., 34n.267
Ryan, S., 264n.240
Rydelius, P. A., 105n.176, 191n.122
Rydholm Hedman, A. M., 86n.60
Ryding, E., 239n.52
Rzanakoto, T., 5n.29

Saadi, A., 41n.322, 94n.121
Saarni, S. I., 261n.212
Sabin, M., 41n.315
Saboonchi, F., 15n.88, 86n.51, 86n.60, 180n.54, 182n.64, 194n.144, 262n.231
Sacerdote, C., 19n.129
Sachs, E., 20n.146
Sack, W. H., 26n.180, 197n.150
Safi, M., 86n.62
Safren, S. A., 247n.104, 247n.105, 250n.134
Sagar, V., 65n.84, 154–55n.17, 156n.30
Sagi-Schwartz, A., 175n.6, 187nn.91–92
Sahloul, Z., 265n.245
Said, E., 120n.51
Said, E. W., 121n.62
Saifi, F., 20n.148
Saifi, O., 111n.17
Salami, B., 8n.41
Salem, I., 262n.221
Salize, H. J., 233n.5
Salloum, I. M., 139n.67
Sam, D. L., 141n.83
Samarasinghe, G., 179nn.40–41, 183n.71, 185nn.80–81
Samawi, L., 235n.25
Samir, N., 8n.40
Sampson, L., 233n.10
Sanahuja, M. M., 24n.167
Sanchez, A. S., 172n.104
Sánchez Sancha, A., 154n.12, 154n.16, 164n.78
Sancilio, A., 46n.355, 139n.69, 141n.90, 142n.93
Sandahl, H., 258n.187
Sandal, G. M., 43n.332, 141n.83, 208nn.58–59
Sander, H., 40n.303, 62n.70
Sandhya, S., xviiinn.3–4
Sandhya, Shipra, xxv
Sandoval, S., 55n.30
Sangalang, C. C., 177n.25, 188n.96, 188n.97

Sansonetti, S., 153n.3, 165n.87, 167n.100, 173nn.112–13
Santacroce, F., 174n.1, 199n.156
Santavirta, N., 178n.26, 178n.37, 188nn.94–95, 192n.125
Santavirta, T., 178n.26, 178n.37, 188nn.94–95, 192n.125
Santomauro, D. F., 12n.72
Santora, M., 21n.157
Sapkota, R. P., 82n.21
Sar, V., 167n.93
Saraceno, B., 33n.262
Sarajlic, I., 20n.147
Sarajlic, I. V., 21n.152
Sarajlic, N., 20n.147, 21n.152
Sargent, C., 107n.2, 109n.6, 119n.49, 120n.50
Sarkadi, A., 246n.100
Sarnoff, R. H., 220n.122
Sartorius, N., 46n.354, 138nn.61–62
Sasson, I., 167n.96, 232n.1
Saucedo, Alfred, xxi
Saucedo, Linda, xxi
Savik, K., 85n.42
Sawyer, M., 65n.83
Saxena, S., 33n.262, 269n.1
Say, L., 156n.26
Sbini, S., 96n.133
Scanlan, J. A., 203n.24
Schacht, D., 56–57nn.41–42
Schaeffer, A. J., 262n.226
Schafft, K., 41n.312
Schalinski, I., 158n.46
Scharf, M., 187n.91, 190n.113, 191n.120
Schauer, E., 191n.118
Schauer, M., 139n.65, 158n.46, 251n.146
Scheepers, P. L. H., 56n.37
Scheible, J. A., 56–57nn.41–42
Schein, J., 270n.7
Schell, T. L., 32n.247, 193nn.134–35, 194n.136, 194n.143, 226n.153
Scher, A. I., 261n.217
Schick, M., 47n.357, 175n.7, 176n.10, 179n.45, 180n.47, 180n.57, 185n.77, 190n.112, 191–92n.124, 192n.126, 209n.61, 217–18n.103, 227n.156, 229n.165, 261n.214
Schillirò, C., 32n.245
Schlar, C., 100n.143
Schlechter, P., 255n.171
Schmaltz, S. P., 226n.149
Schmeidler, J., 184n.73, 190n.114
Schmelzer, P., 56n.41
Schmid, M., 8n.38, 198n.154
Schmitt, E., 17n.106

Schneider, J., 213nn.85–86
Schneider, T., 13n.74
Schnicke, M. K., 248n.110
Schnyder, U., 20n.144, 47n.357, 175n.7,
    176n.10, 179n.45, 180n.47, 180n.57,
    185n.77, 190n.112, 191–92n.124,
    192n.126, 209n.61, 217–18n.103,
    227n.156, 229n.165, 252n.148, 254n.159,
    261n.214
Schreuders, B. A., 65n.82, 261n.213
Schubert, C. C., 88n.69
Schulte-Hillen, C., 260n.208
Schultz, L. R., 154n.9, 157n.32
Schupp, J., 44n.345, 56n.41, 56–57n.42, 57n.49,
    229n.163
Schützwohl, M., 177n.23, 194n.142
Schwart, T., 73–74n.15
Schwei, R. J., 132n.40
Schweitzer, R., 41n.321, 178n.33
Schweitzer, R. D., 65n.84, 154–55n.17, 156n.30
Schyte, H. W., 261n.215
Schytz, H. W., 88n.72, 261n.217
Sciannameo, V., 19n.129
Scott, C., 255n.172
Scott, J. G., 12n.72
Scragg, P., 94n.119
Scribner, T., 36n.281, 229n.166, 230n.168
Sealy, L., 8n.40
Seckl, J. R., 184n.74
Sedighi, B., 85n.43
Seedall, R. B., xviiin.4, 28nn.204–206
Seeley, J., 197n.150
Segal, J., 239n.52
Segal, S. P., 96n.133
Seifert, T., 261n.217
Seligman, M. E. P., 246n.98
Seminario, E., 55n.30
Semyonov, M., 56n.38
Seo, Y., 261n.216
Seong, L. C., 260n.210
Seshan, G., 42n.328
Sessums, L., 258n.196
Severo, M., 176n.9, 190n.111
Shabila, N., 167n.96, 232n.1
Shadid, J., 12n.72
Shahini, M., 183n.71, 185n.81
Shahly, V., 233n.10
Shahraray, M., 94n.123
Shaifali, S., 231n.169
Shakir, E., 16n.101
Shalev, A. Y., 233n.10
Shannon, P., 235n.19
Shapiro, F., 252n.148, 254n.159

Shapiro, M. F., 55n.29, 101n.151
Shapiro, M. J., 121n.60
Sharabi, H., 183n.69
Sharkey, J. D., 199n.155
Sharma, B., 87n.66
Sharma, G. K., 87n.66
Shaw, A., 213n.84
Shelef, A., 262n.230
Sherman, C., 3n.5
Sherrell, K., 222n.133
Sherrell, Mahi, 221n.128
Shetty, A., 202n.12
Shetty, S., 208n.55
Shevtsova, M., 15n.91, 16n.95, 131n.38,
    264n.237, 264n.238
Shimeall, W., 258n.196
Shintani, A. O., 26–27n.183
Shorer, S., 180n.50
Shouler-Ocak, M., 89n.81, 172n.110
Shultz, J. M., 29n.214
Sibai, A. M., 265n.245, 266n.254
Siegel, M., 45n.349
Siegert, M., 56–57nn.41–42
Sifneos, P. E., 262n.224
Sigona, N., 47n.356, 157n.41, 198n.152, 203n.18
Sigvardsdotter, E., 86n.51, 86n.60, 180n.54,
    182n.64, 194n.144
Sijbrandij, M., 262n.220
Silove, D., 31n.238, 32n.252, 35n.270, 41n.318,
    41n.319, 41n.320, 87n.65, 178n.28,
    178n.32, 180n.52, 233n.4, 238n.49,
    241nn.65–66, 245n.93, 246n.96, 247n.106,
    248n.111, 256n.182, 258n.193, 266n.255,
    266n.256
Silove, D. M., 9n.48
Silove, S., 41n.317
Silverman, J. G., 163n.73
Simko, H., 162n.64
Simmons, J., 203n.19
Simmons, K., 214n.93
Simoncini, M., 259nn.203–4
Simonsen, E., 129n.15
Sinclair, A. J., 261n.217
Singer, E., 234n.17
Singh, D. K., 18n.120
Singh, R., xviiin.4, 5n.29, 28nn.204–206
Singh, S., 155n.22, 162n.59, 187n.88
Siqveland, J., 88n.76
Sirois, A., 234n.13
Sirries, S., 56n.41
Sivilli, T., 208n.55
Skardalsmo Bjorgo, E. M., 94n.122
Skogberg, N., 39n.295

Skoglund, E., 105n.176, 191n.122
Sledjeski, E. M., 154n.8
Slewa-Younan, S., 157n.37
Slobodin, O., 180n.50, 246n.95, 253n.158, 254n.161
Slonim-Nevo, V., 178n.35
Sly, R., 175n.5, 190n.108
Smelser, N., 108n.5
Smelser, N. J., 61n.59, 62n.69, 63n.72, 112n.27, 124n.73
Smid, G. E., 252n.150
Smidt-Nielsen, K., 91n.97
Smital Zore, B., 235n.23
Smith, A. A., 190n.116
Smith, D. T., 35n.277
Smith, E. J., 244n.83
Smith, H., 20n.146
Smith, M., 206n.45
Smith, P., 185n.76
Smith, T. B., 250n.133
Smyth, J. M., 158n.44
Snellman, O., 39n.295
Snowden, L. R., 131n.33
Soboka, M., 8n.41
Sochanvimean, V., 180n.49, 196n.147
Sole-Auro, A., 31n.229
Solomon, Z., 185n.79, 186n.83, 187n.85, 196n.148, 196n.149
Somasundaram, D., 239n.52
Sommer, M., 33n.265
Sonderegger, R., 244n.84
Sonderegger. R., 247n.103
Song, S., 235n.21
Song, S. J., 89n.79, 256n.185
Songose, L., 40n.310
Songur, W., 31n.231
Sonis, J., 102n.154
Sönmez, E., 89n.81, 172n.110
Sonne, C., 246n.101, 258n.190
Sonnega, A., 157n.33
Sorensen, M. S., 53n.17
Southwick, S. M., 155n.19, 177n.22
Souza, F. M., 19n.125, 156n.25
Souza, R., 246n.96
Spahovic, D., 182n.65, 254n.160
Sparrow, A., 236–37n.36
Spencer, J. H., 32n.251
Spencer, R., 162n.61
Spiegel, P., 31n.227
Spiller, T. R., 261n.214
Spinazzola, J., 263nn.232–33
Spinhoven, P., 187n.89
Spiro, A., 82n.19

Spiro, M. E., 109n.8
Spivak, G. C., 120n.52
Spoonster, E., 154n.8
Spring, M., 85n.42
Staehr, M. A., 19n.134
Stahl, S. M., 259n.203
Stammel, N., 128n.4
Stangier, U., 89n.81, 172n.110
Stanley, S. M., 178n.36, 182n.66, 186n.82
Stansfeld, S. A., 47n.358
Stanwood, O., 25n.176
Staples, J. K., 255n.178, 256n.184
Steel, J. L., 11n.63, 20n.143, 31n.237, 31n.239
Steel, Z., 31n.238, 32n.252, 41n.317, 41n.318, 41nn.319–21, 87n.65, 178n.28, 178nn.32–33, 180n.52, 233n.4, 236n.28, 238n.49, 241n.65, 241n.66, 242n.70, 245n.93
Stein, D., 266n.255
Stein, D. J., 233n.10
Stenmark, H., 252n.149
Stephens, J., 83n.29
Stevanovic, A., 178n.30, 187n.86
Stick, M., 216n.98
Stockman, J. K., 163n.70
Stokes, B., 214n.93
Stolbach, B. C., 239n.56
Stompe, T., 20n.145, 31n.241
Stone, M., 220n.118
Storey, J. D., 234n.13
Story, B., 54n.24
Strachey, J., 112n.25
Strang, A., 59n.53, 59n.56, 201n.3, 203n.19, 206n.48
Strauss, C., 111n.19
Strauss, Claudia, 109n.9, 113n.28
Strayer, J., 179n.42
Stroebe, M. S., 20n.149
Strong, J., 265n.246, 265n.249
Stronks, K., 19n.135
Stryjer, R., 262n.230
Stump, Todd, xxiv
Subica, A., 89n.79
Sue, D. W., 244n.83
Sue, S., 131n.33, 131n.34, 245n.89
Suhaiban, H. A., 19n.132, 35n.276
Sukale, T., 8n.38, 198n.154
Süleymanoğlu, M., 167n.93
Suljic, E., 194n.146
Sull, L., 226n.152
Sulmont, D., 55n.31
Sundri, J., 243n.75
Suryadi, D., 260n.210
Susanty, D., 259n.200

Susljik, I., 41n.320
Sutton, T., 82n.18
Suvak, M., 263nn.232–33
Sveaass, N., 84n.36, 104n.175
Swartz, L., 131n.37, 133n.51
Sweeney, C. G., 189n.105
Symes, S. N., 234n.15
Szczepanikova, A., 164n.82
Sztompka, P., 61n.59, 62n.69, 63n.72, 108n.5,
    112n.27, 124n.73

Ta, T. M. T., 43n.331
Tadlaoui, Y., 258n.197
Taha, P. H., 157n.37, 262n.220
Tahir, K., 244n.85
Tamblyn, J. M., 90n.87
Tang, C. S.-K., 31n.238
Tao, D., 59n.54, 205n.40
Tappis, H., 260n.208
Tarakji, A., 236–37n.36
Tarrier, N., 250n.127
Tawahina, A. A., 191n.119
Tawalbeh, L. I., 233n.8, 258n.189
Tay, A., 266n.255
Tay, A. K., 8n.42
Tay, K., 9n.48
Tayler, L., 96n.134
Taylor, E., 208n.55
Taylor, J., 202n.12
Taylor, L., 114n.31, 163n.75
Taylor, T., 94n.124
Tedeschi, F., 256n.184
Teicher, M. H., 184n.74
Tekin, A., 167n.93
Tekin, M., 167n.93
Teo, H.-M., 61n.62
Terheggen, M. A., 20n.149
Tervalon, M., 244n.81
Tewes, C., 130n.19, 144n.101
Teysir, J., 234n.17
Thabet, A., 191n.119
Thalheimer, L., 5n.29
Theorell, T., 11n.63, 20n.143, 31n.237, 31n.239
Thøgersen, M. H., 85n.44, 235n.27
Thomas, E., 49n.362
Thomas, L. S., 163n.69
Thompson, C. T., 249n.122
Thompson, H. S., 132n.42
Thomsen, A., 91n.97
Thomson, R. A., 179n.42
Thorne, S., 254n.168
Thornicroft, G., 33n.262
Thu, N. D., 96n.129

Thyberg, M., 88n.77
Tiatri, S., 260n.210
Tiilikainen, M., 261n.212
Tileva, M., 234n.13
Timka, T., 88n.77
Tinghög, P., 15n.88, 180n.54, 182n.64,
    194n.144
Tip, L. K., 222n.132
Tipene-Leach, D., 244n.79
Tippens, J. A., 265n.248
Tkachenko, T. A., 89–90n.83
Tofighian, Omid, 83n.32
Tol, W. A., 31n.227, 89n.79, 238n.43, 238n.45,
    239n.51, 246n.96, 253n.157, 255n.177,
    256n.184, 259n.200
Tolin, D. F., 154n.8, 154n.10, 158n.45, 158n.47,
    247n.108
Tomaskovic, I., 235n.23
Tomaskovic, M., 235n.23
Toole, M. J., 265n.244, 265n.247
Toomer, E., 226n.151
Tor, S., 90n.90
Torleif, R., 88n.76
Torres, A. R., 219n.113
Tors, S., 92n.107
Tosi, M., 32n.245
Tossyeh, F., 255n.179
Townsend, M., 86n.58
Townsend, N., 256n.180
Trajman, A., 19n.125, 156n.25
Tran, K. A., 260n.205
Tran, M., 247n.105
Tran, V., 228n.162
Tran, V. C., 204n.31, 205n.43, 220n.120
Treisman, R., 204n.33
Tribe, R., 20n.145, 31n.241
Triantafyllou, A. I., 89–90n.83
Triliva, S., 128n.4
Troeller, G., 9n.51, 18n.117, 18n.119
Trohl, U., 64n.74
Trong, A., 208n.55
Trübswetter, P., 56–57nn.41–42
Truscott, M., 16n.97
Tsai, J. C., 253n.154
Tsang, D. C., 234n.15
Tsegay, S. M., 202n.14, 210n.74, 211n.77
Tuddenham, R. D., 27n.185
Tullii, A., 260n.209
Tung, C., 4n.20
Turkel, Nury, 4nn.16–17
Turner, J., 263n.232
Turner, S., 93n.116, 94n.119
Turner, S. W., 94n.123, 105n.179

Turrini, G., 253n.157

Uhr, C., 255n.175
Uitenbroek, D. G., 19n.135
Underman, K., 69n.1
Üngör, U. Ü, 25n.168
Unterhitzenberger, J., 256n.184
Urbina, I., 272n.12
Urganus, A., 270n.7
Ursano, R. J., 178n.31
Ursel, S., 264n.236
Usturali Mut, A. N., 156n.26
Uzun, S. U., 156n.26

Vaez, M., 15n.88, 86n.51, 86n.60, 180n.54
Vagheni, M. M., 31n.228
Vaglum, P., 251n.144
Valent, P., 96n.130
Valette, D., 177n.19
Valji, N., 30n.223, 165n.91
Vallejo-Martín, M., 154n.12, 154n.16, 164n.78,
    172n.104
Vallizadeh, E., 56n.41
van Aalst, M., 5n.29
Van Boekholt, T. A., 260n.208
van Dam, Nikolaos, xxiv–xxv, 10n.62
van der Aa, N., 261n.211
van der Hart, O., 28n.204, 112n.23
Van der Kolk, B. A., 28n.204, 93n.115, 111–
    12nn.22–24, 262n.222, 263nn.232–33
van der Ploeg, H. M., 176n.8, 194n.139
Van der Tweel, I., 207n.53
van der Zee-Neuen, A., 219n.110
Van Eijk, E., 65n.75
Vang, C., 177n.25
van IJzendoorn, M. H., 175n.6, 187nn.91–92
Vann, B., 172n.108
Vann, M., 246n.102
van Oldenborgh, G. J., 5n.29
van Ommeren, M., 31n.227, 87n.65, 87n.66,
    233n.4, 246n.96, 250n.137, 269n.1
van Oostrum, I. E. A., 19n.135
van Roemburg, E., 16n.97
Van Tienhoven, H., 97n.138
van Tubergen, F., 47n.359, 217n.102, 228n.159
van Willigen, L. H., 194n.139
Varady, C., 265n.246, 265n.249
Varese, L., 41n.315
Vargas-Ojeda, A. C., 61n.57
Vargas-Silva, C., 201nn.6–7, 209n.60, 209n.64,
    209nn.66–67, 210n.69, 210nn.70–71,
    210nn.72–73, 211n.76, 219n.112
Vasquez-Nuttall, E., 244n.83

Vasta, E., 59n.51
Vasta, F., 213n.90
Vautard, R., 5n.29
Vega, W. A., 96n.129
Velázquez, T., 55n.30
Ventevogel, P., 31n.227, 35n.270, 35n.273,
    46n.355, 139n.69, 140n.76, 141nn.89–90,
    142n.93, 235n.21, 238n.46, 247n.106,
    248n.111, 256n.182, 258n.193, 266n.256
Venturi, D., 15n.91, 16n.95, 131n.38, 264n.237,
    264n.238
Verdeli, H., 29n.214, 181n.58
Verdier, T., 42nn.323–24, 54n.26, 211n.78,
    229n.164
Verelst, A., 246n.100
Vertovec, S., 59n.51, 213n.90
Veselinovic, M., 17n.107
Viana, M. C., 233n.10
Vidgen, A., 249n.122
Vijaya, R., 44n.342
Vijayakumar, L., 20n.141
Villalba, C. S., 84n.37
Vincent, F., 249n.121
Vindbjerg, E., 258n.187
Vinnerljung, B., 235n.20
Vitiello, B., 8n.38, 198n.154
Vivalya, B. M. N., 31n.228
Vojvoda, D., 65n.83, 155n.19
Volpe, D., 5n.28
von Beust, J., 259n.201
von Gruenberg, Felix, xxi
Vostanis, P., 191n.119
Vranesic, M., 194n.146
Vromans, L., 65n.84, 154–55n.17, 156n.30
Vu, A., 155n.22, 162n.59
Vundla, S., 192n.129
Vutegha, J. M., 31n.228

Wade, F., 4n.18
Wade, N. J., 90n.86
Wagner, K., 64n.74
Wahab, A., 264n.236
Wainberg, M., 184n.73, 190n.114
Wainberg, M. L., 29n.214
Waldman, R. J., 265n.244, 265n.247
Walker, C., 244n.79
Walker, C. C., 89–90n.83
Wall, S., 65n.77
Wallach-Kildemoes, H., 85n.44, 235n.27
Wallen, J., 81n.16
Walsh, E., 238n.47, 239n.54, 248n.114,
    249n.123, 250n.128, 254n.165
Walsh, F., 174n.3, 175n.4, 254n.164

Walther, L., 43n.331
Wamara, C. K., 48n.361, 203n.23, 204n.26, 206n.44
Wampler, K. S., xviiin.4, 28nn.204–206
Wampold, B. E., 251n.141
Wang, D., 177n.23, 194n.142
Ward, Carrington, xxiv
Ward, J., 172n.108
Ware, N., 182n.65, 254n.160
Warner, V., 181n.58
Warrick, J., 2n.1
Warsame, A. H., 259n.201
Watkins, E., 94n.120, 105n.180
Watson, J. C., 69n.4
Watters, C., 133n.49, 205n.37
Watters, C. P., 41n.317
Watters, E., 73–74n.15
Watts, C., 163n.72
Waugaman, R. M., 69n.2
Waugh, P., 264n.236
Waxler, D. E., 162n.64
Weathers, F. W., 180n.48
Weber, M., 9n.47
Weine, S., 182n.65, 254n.160
Weine, S. M., 65n.83, 155n.19
Weiner, S., 12n.71
Weinstein, H., 85n.46, 88n.71, 88n.74
Weinstein, H. M., 91n.100, 220n.122
Weisleder, P., 234n.12
Weiss, D. S., 174n.2
Weiss, M. G., 46n.354, 138n.62
Weissman, M. M., 181n.58
Weizman, A., 262n.230
Weller, S. C., 141n.87
Wesner, M. L., 89–90nn.83–84
West, J., 263n.233
Westerink, J., 189n.107
Westermeyer, J., 65n.78, 85n.42, 87n.67
Wheeler, J., 31n.234
White, C., 162n.67
White, G., 73–74n.15
Whiteford, H., 269n.1
Whiteford, H. A., 12n.72
Whitley, R., 244n.80, 246n.94, 246n.97, 250n.139
Whittaker, D., 18n.123
Whybrow, D., 253n.153
Wickramaratne, P., 181n.58
Wicks, B., 162n.64
Widmann, M., 259n.201
Wienke, A., 64n.74
Wiersielis, K. R., 162n.64
Wijayanayaka, S., 259n.198

Wike, R., 214n.93
Wilkinson, J., 192n.129
Wilkinson, L., 40n.310
Willard, C. L., 86n.59
Williams, A. C. de C., 92n.108
Williams, C., 102n.154
Williams, J. M., 94n.120
Williams, J. M. G., 105n.180
Williams, M., 87n.67
Williams, T., 149n.116
Williams-Keeler, L., 23n.165
Williamson, J. G., 50n.1
Wilson, A. T., 255n.178
Wilson, F. E., 29n.214
Wilson, G., 253n.153
Wilson, J. P., 31n.238, 236n.28, 242n.70
Wilson, K., 258n.194
Windthorst, P., 91n.98, 92n.101, 92n.103, 143n.97, 167n.94, 234n.16
Wingbermuhle, P., 255n.171
Winicki, Chantal, xxiv
Winter, J., 39n.299
Winters, L. A., 202n.11, 204n.30, 220n.121
Wirtz, A., 155n.22
Wirtz, A. L., 162n.59
Wisaeth, L., 93n.115
Withnall, A., 162n.60
Wolfe, J., 158n.47
Wollny, A., 89n.81, 172n.110
Wolski, P., 5n.29
Wong, C., 194n.138
Wood, P., 203n.19
Woody, G. E., 69n.3
Worley, N., 226n.152
Woticha, A., 85n.43
Wren, C. S., 50n.1
Wright, R., 17n.108
Wright Mills, C., 9n.47
WSamara, C. K., 201n.4
Wylegala, A., 94n.122

Xenitidis, K., 197n.151
Xiong, P., 132n.40

Yameogo, N. D., 42n.328
Yanes, Eyad, 237n.38
Yang, W., 5n.29
Yanni, E. A., 234n.14
Yaqubi, A., 140nn.77–78
Yaqubi, A. A., 141n.88
Yasenov, V., 56n.40
Yasseri, G., 94n.123
Yee, B. W. K., 96n.129

Yehuda, R., 184nn.73–74, 190n.114
Yiannopoulou, K. G., 89–90n.83
Young, H., 8n.40
Young, K., 246n.102, 250n.129
Young, M., 23n.165
Yousafzai, S., 3n.6
Yule, W., 185n.76
Yzerbyt, V., 30n.226

Zafiriadis, K., 197n.151
Zakowski, S. G., 72n.10
Zaman, S., 266n.254
Zane, N., 245n.89
Zannettino, L., 32n.249
Zarkov, Z., 233n.10
Zarzour, M., 20n.140, 20n.150, 167n.92

Zenou, Y., 211n.78
Zepeda, V., 141nn.85–86
Zerach, G., 187n.85, 196n.148, 196n.149
Zhang, A. Y., 131n.33
Zhang, G., 253n.155
Zier, U., 89n.81, 172n.110
Zion, D., 242n.69
Zipfel, S., 20n.144, 91n.98, 92n.101, 92n.103,
    143n.97, 167n.94, 234n.16
Ziser, K., 234n.16
Zoe, O., 9n.53
Zoline, Susan, xxiv
Zong, J., 220n.119, 228n.161
Zumwald, A., 47n.357, 209n.61, 217–18n.103,
    227n.156, 229n.165
Zwi, K., 8n.40

Subject Index

For the benefit of digital users, indexed terms that span two pages (e.g., 52–53) may, on occasion, appear on only one of those pages.

Tables and figures are indicated by an italic *t*, and *f* following the page number.

Action Plan on Integration and Inclusion, European Commission, 205
Afghanistan
 Akbar's story, 147–48
 conflict-related internal displacement (2021-2022), 6*f*
 distress for Afghans, 142
 khapa and Afghani women, 139
 refugees, 13
 refugees (2021), 14*f*
 resettled refugees (2022), 218*f*
 stigma of disabilities, 29–30
Afghans
 Arbaz (refugee) in Germany, 50–51, 66, 74–75
 Battle of Kunduz, 13n.76
 conflict and violence, 4–5
 depression in, 141
 homosexuals from, 114
 posttraumatic syndrome for, 140–41
Al-Assad, Bashar, 98
Al-Assad, Hafez, 98
al-Bashir, Omar, Darfur genocide, 18n.122
alcoholism, 60
Aleppo University bombings, 136, 136n.58
Alevi Kurdish refugees
 cultural integration, 226–27
 in United Kingdom (UK), 225–26
Alexander, Jeffrey, 112, 124
Alexander von Humboldt Foundation, xviii
American Civil Liberties Union, 242
American Institutional Review Board (IRB), 70–71, 70n.9
American Muslims, identity, 122–23
American Psychological Association (APA), 82–84, 82n.25, 82–83n.28, 254n.170
Amnesty International, 163n.74
amphetamine, natural, 259
animal studies, emotion, 180
antidepressants, 258–59
antipsychotics, 258–59

anxiety, post-conflict settings, 233n.6
anxiety subscale
 correlation matrix, 282*t*
 Hopkins Symptom Checklist-25, 281*t*
Arab family, 64–65
Arabic
 language, 75
 proverb, 76
Argentina, complex intergroup dynamics, 30–31
Armenian people
 close relatives of wartime events, 197
 genocide of, 24–25
Assayag, Jackie, 38–39
asylum application, retelling of torture, 99–106
asylum seekers
 affect and language, 54–56
 conflict-related displacements, xv*f*
 detention by Greek officials, 118, 118n.47
 hostile territories for, 51–52
 integration, 201
 LGBTQI+, 263–64
 Mexican, and Title 42, 270n.3
 most dangerous routes, 16–17
 most fatal crossings for 2022, xiii*f*
 retelling of torture, 99–106
 skepticism toward, 101, 102–3
 South-Asian and Middle-Eastern, xix
 study of (2016-2021), 70–56
 widespread phenomenon, 272, 272n.13
Aufgeschlossenheit
 frameworks of, 52
 sense of, in Germany, 58–59
Australia
 approximate cash assistance to refugees upon arrival (2022), 223*f*
 refugee resettlement, 216*f*
 resettlement (2021), 217*f*

Baker, Ron, 234
Bakun, Wojciech, 268

Bangladesh, 3–4
behavioral environment, orientations, 135–38
Belarus-Poland border, 18
Belgium, resettlement (2021), 217f
Bhutanese communities, suicide
     ideation, 32–33
bipolar disorder
     post-conflict settings, 233n.6
     refugees in Poland, 269
Blended Visa-Office Referred (BVOR)
     program, 215–16
Blessin, Christoph, German Red Cross, 58–59
Boko Haram, Chibok girls and, 157
Bonn University, xviii
Boochani, Behrouz, 82–84
border crossings, illegal, 51–52
Bosnia-Herzegovina
     children of war veterans in, 189
     posttraumatic stress symptoms in
          mothers, 184–85
Brazil, heat stress in, 8
Brexit, UK, 53
British Pakistanis, cross-cousin
     marriage, 212–13
Buddhist Chakmas, East Pakistan
     (Bangladesh), 18
buddy system, case study of, 264
Burmese military, Rohingya women and, 159

Caesar, Syrian military photographer, 86–87
Cambodia
     intergenerational impact of trauma, 193
     refugee families in California, 193, 195, 197
     resettled Cambodians in U.S., 32–33
Cambridge University, xvii
Canada
     approximate cash assistance to refugees upon
          arrival (2022), 223f
     language integration in, 221
     Private Sponsorship of Refugees
          (PSR), 215–16
     refugee resettlement, 216f
     resettlement (2021), 217f
     story of rape of Rumi, 232–33
cancer, 18–19
Cartegena Declaration, 15n.85
Central Intelligence Agency (CIA), 81–83
Chad, 3–4
chemical attack, Syrian civilians, 1–2
children
     child-hawking, 270, 270n.4
     conflict-related displacements seeking
          asylum, xvf

educational exclusion and integration, 8n.35,
     204–5, 207
educational exclusion of refugee, 222
mental health, 187–89
school drop-out rates, 8n.35
suicide attempts, 7–8, 74, 200
Chile, complex intergroup dynamics, 30–31
China
     disaster-related internal displacement
          (2021), 7f
     refugee populations, 54
chlorpromazine, 258–59
cholera, 18–19
chronic pain, traumatic brain injury (TBI),
     261n.217
chronic pain syndrome, torture, 91–92
Civil Status ID, 115–16, 117
climate change, 3
     disasters, global internal displacements,
          6nn.31–32, 7f
     displacement and, 8
     famine induced by, 5n.29
     migrants, 278
     vulnerable countries/communities
          (2022), xiif
climate refugees, term, 7–8
     in Europe, xvii
clinical practice, xviii
     minority patients, xvii
     survivors of childhood abuse, captivity,
          sexual abuse or incest, torture, terrorism,
          and ethnic cleansing, xviii
clinical psychology, emotion, 180
cognitive-behavioral therapy (CBT)
     third-generation, 247, 247n.108
     trauma-focused CBT (TF-CBT), 246–47,
          248, 249–51
cognitive frameworks, identity, 109, 110
cognitive therapies, 247–63
     brief manual-based trauma therapies
          (BTT), 248
     cognitive processing therapy (CPT), 248
     community-centered trauma
          interventions, 257
     eye movement desensitization and
          reprocessing (EMDR), 252–55,
          253nn.153–54
     narrative exposure therapy (NET), 251–52
     pharmacotherapy, 258–60
     prolonged exposure therapy (PET), 248
     PTSD in post-conflict settings, 247
     rape and maternal health, 260–63
     somatic interventions, 260–63

systemic interventions, 255–56
see also treatment planning
Colombia, conflict-related internal
    displacement (2021-2022), 6*f*
Community-centered trauma
    interventions, 257
complex posttraumatic stress disorder (CPTSD)
    polyvictimization, 26n.181
    repeated, sustained and multiple trauma,
        26n.181
    term, 26, 26n.181
complex trauma
    assessing family members, 180–81
    forced migration, 41–42
    identity development, 108
    integration of refugees, 60–63
    pharmacological treatment for, 258–59
    refugees of, 39n.297
    refugees' well-being and, 45
    role of gender in development of, 46–47
conflict-related displacements
    child asylum seekers, xv*f*
    top seven countries with, 5, 6*f*
conflict-related sexual violence, term, 79n.2
Congolese female refugees, from
    Uganda, 157–58
Convention Against Torture, 84, 103, 103n.166
Convention related to Status of Refugees
    (1951), 15n.83
corner street men, 121n.63
Covid-19, 3–4
    older refugees, 265–66
    refugee mental health and, 19–21
Cox Bazaar, Bangladesh, 3–4
creeping Islamization, concern of, 108
cultural competence
    definition, 132
    health care, 275
    promoting healthy integration, 243–45
    refugee services, 150
    understanding, 133–34
cultural framework, identity, 109, 110
cultural integration, 221
    Alevi Kurdish refugees, 226–27
    definition, 226
cultural syndrome, *jigar khun*, 141, 142
cultural themes, integration system, 64–65
cultural trauma, description of, 124
culture
    definition of, 132, 133
    description of, 110
    public mental health, 128–33
    Salvadoran refugees' sufferings, 147

shared structures of symbols and
    meanings, 126
syndromes and idioms of distress, 138–44,
    139n.72
understanding, 133–34
Cyclone Amphan, 3–4

Danieli, Yael, 28
Darfur genocide, 18n.122
Darien Gap, 16–17
Democratic Republic of the Congo, 3–4
    conflict-related internal displacement (2021-
        2022), 6*f*
    disaster-related internal displacement
        (2021), 7*f*
    female refugees from Bangladesh to, 157
    female victimization, 260
    rape survivors of Kovumi, 142
    refugees, 13
    resettled refugees (2022), 218*f*
Denmark
    resettlement (2021), 217*f*
    segregation in education, 222
    treatment of Ukrainians in, 201
depression
    Afghans, 140–41
    child mental health, 188
    family members, 180–81
    post-conflict settings, 233n.6
    refugee experiences, 200–5
    refugee population in Germany, 56–57
    refugees in Poland, 269
depression subscale
    correlation matrix, 282*t*
    Hopkins Symptom Checklist-25, 281*t*
Destroying a Nation (van Dam), 10n.62
detention centers, 82–83, 240–41
    human rights abuses, 3n.7, 9, 21n.159
    Libya's, 156, 272n.13
    mental health crisis of child refugees,
        21n.159
    UK, 86
    women and children in U.S., 242–43
Detienne, Marcel, 108, 109
developmental psychology, emotion, 180
diabetes, 18–19, 259
disabled, 29–30, 61–62, 131, 206, 238
    men and boys with disabilities, 16n.99
    nature of disability, 15–16, 15n.89
    older refugees, 15–16, 31–32
disaster-related internal displacement (2021),
        top seven countries with, 5–6, 7*f*
discrimination, Muslim women, xviin.2

displaced populations
    child-hawking, 270, 270n.4
    initiatives for dealing with trauma in, 274–76
    least developed countries, 3–4, 3n.10
    map, xi*f*
    Palestinian, 13
    total, 3n.2
    Ukrainian, 3n.2, 4–5, 268
    Venezuelan, 3n.2
displacement
    mental health effects of, 7–8
    refugees, protection gap, and
        protracted, 13–19
    statistic of 112.6 million, 3n.2
    weather-related events and, 8
distress, idioms of, 138–44
Dublin Regulation, 113, 113n.29
Duncan, Whitney, 145–46

École Normale Supérieure, France, xviii
economic assimilation, 41–42
economic integration, 221
Edict of Nantes (1598), 25
educational integration, 222
Ehlers, Anke, 247
electrocution
    memory recall in torture, 95
    torture, 89–90, 89–90n.83
El Salvador
    complex intergroup dynamics, 30–31
    massacre, 82n.22
Elsass, Peter, 240–41
emotional contagion, families as sites of, 179–82
empathy, therapists', 69–70
English Channel, 16–17
Eritrea, resettled refugees (2022), 218*f*
Ethiopia, 3–4
    conflict-related internal displacement (2021-
        2022), 6*f*
    heat stress in, 8
ethnic cleansing, xviii, 24–25, 159
ethnic identity
    definition of, 211, 212
    Muslims, 211
    Serbian, 124–25
ethnicity, refugees, 211–13
ethnopsychopharmacology, 259–60
Europe
    climate refugees in, xvii
    identity of Muslims in, 111, 122–23
    terrorism and refugees, 214
    Ukrainian refugee women in, 209
European Commission (EC), 205, 207

European Consultation of Refugees and
    Exiles, 234
European Council on Refugees and Exiles
    (ECRE), 206–7
European Union Agency for Fundamental
    Rights, 55–56
evidence-based practices (EBPs)
    cognitive-behavioral therapy (CBT), 246–51
    merging cultural practice and, 246–47
    refugees, 245–46
experience
    cultural quest for, 134–38
    cultural syndromes and idioms of
        distress, 138–44
    frames of post-trauma, 135–38
    motivational orientation, 137
    negotiating trauma and healing, 145–51
    normative orientation, 137
    object orientation, 136
    self-orientation, 136
    spatial orientation, 136–37
    word, 134
experiences of the vulnerable
    ecological balance, 234, 240
    economic progress and, 96–97
    human development, 270
    social cohesion, 33–34, 44–45
eye movement desensitization and reprocessing
    (EMDR), 252–55, 253nn.153–54

family trauma
    child mental health, 187–89
    father's PTSD, 189–91
    five pathways of functioning, 182–91
    intergenerational impact of, 193–95
    longitudinal studies, 195–99
    marital relations, 186–87
    maternal posttraumatic stress, 183–85
    parental psychopathology, 191
    post-conflict environment and, 192–93
    as sites of emotional contagion, 179–82
    war-affected, 174–79, 198
fatal journeys, refugees in host nations, 50–52
fear interview, 102–3, 103n.162
Federal Chamber of Psychotherapists in
    Germany (BPtK), 56–57
Federal Employment Agency, refugees, 110n.15
female refugees
    affiliation, persecution, and
        depression, 166–67
    as forgotten majority, 164–68
    gender-sensitive policies, 173
    health crisis in, 162–64

integration of, 168–71
international human rights
    organizations, 172–73
international policy bodies, 153
interview of Ashwaq Haji Hamid, 171
mental health, 153
Mrs. Khaled as Kurdish Syrian refugee in
    Germany, 152–53, 166, 167–68, 171
nature of posttraumatic stress, 154–58
post-conflict reconstruction of, 171–73
power dynamics, social roles and sexual
    violence, 159–62
rape and maternal health, 260–63
remembering sadness of, 167–68
sexual violence, 155–58
socioeconomic integration, 230
Yazidis, 167
see also refugees
Finland
    refugee resettlement, 216*f*
    resettlement (2021), 217*f*
First Persian Empire, 24
fixity, 28
forced displacement
    cultural competency and health
        care, 273–74
    definition, 3n.7
    history of, 24–25
    identity development, 108
    makeshift identity for, 113–18
    mental illness and, 202
    Ukrainians in Poland, 268–69, 272
Forster, Michael, xviii
France
    approximate cash assistance to refugees upon
        arrival (2022), 223*f*
    identity of French Muslims, 122
    integration, 204
    refugee resettlement, 216*f*
    resettlement (2021), 217*f*
Freire, Paul, 84

Gebhardt, Miriam, 61–62, 61n.61
gender
    complex trauma and, 46–47
    see also female refugees
geopolitics
    displacement and, 9
    refugee mental health, 19–21
German Democratic Republic, 62n.67
German Red Cross, Blessin of, 58–59
Germany
    applying for asylum, 2

approximate cash assistance to refugees upon
    arrival (2022), 223*f*
Arbaz (Afghan) refugee in, 50–51, 66
case study, 45
crime by refugees in, 55n.32, 55–56n.34
female refugees in, 167–68
focus on self-help (*Selbsthilfe*), 59
identity of refugees, 126
integration, 204
integration of female refugees, 169–71
integration system, 64
interview of Ashwaq Haji Hamid, 171
Mrs. Khaled as Kurdish Syrian refugee in,
    152–53, 166, 167–68, 171
philosophy of help, 63
refugee interviews, 11
refugee population in, 56–58
refugee resettlement, 216*f*
refugees from Middle East (2016-
    2021), 45–46
refugees in, 43–44, 55n.32
refugees' integration in, 209
resettlement (2021), 217*f*
Sabrina and Sana (twin sisters) in, 169–70
sense of Aufgeschlossenheit, 58–59
study of asylum seekers (2016-2021),
    70–77
successful integration, 229
trauma as basis for preventing
    deportations, 63–64
violence against refugees, 55–56
"ghettos" and "ghetto children,"
    Denmark, 53
Ghouta chemical attack, Sabris family, 1–
    2, 48–49
Giesen, Bernhard, 61–63
gigantic Auschwitz, 18–19
Global Burden of Diseases, Injuries, and Risk
    Factors Study (2019), mental disorders,
    leading cause, 12n.72
Global Compact on Refugees, 278
Globalization, collective suffering in age
    of, 123–12
Global North, 275
Global Refugee Forum, 278
Global South, xix, 19–21, 279
Global Trauma Project (GTP), 257
Government Assisted Refugee (GAR)
    program, 215–16
Greece, detection of asylum-seekers, 118,
    118n.47
Greek Coast Guard, South-Asian and Middle-
    Eastern asylum-seekers, xix

Gudamalulgal Nation, refugees from indigenous cultures of, 5–6
Guiding Principles on Internal Displacement (1998), 13n.80
Gulf War veterans, Kuwaiti children of, 190

Halimi, Sarah, murder of, 52–53
Hallowell, Alfred Irving, 134–37
haloperidol, 258–59
Hamza (Syrian refugee), identity, 107, 115, 118–19, 125–26
Handbook on Procedures and Criteria for Determining Refugee Status and Guidelines on International Protection, 14–15
Harris, Lindsay, 102, 103–4
haste makes waste, proverb, 76
headache, traumatic brain injury (TBI), 261n.217
head trauma, traumatic brain injury (TBI), 234
health care
    obstacles for refugees, 33
    shortage of workers, 64, 235–37, 274n.21
    social exclusion in, 273
health crises
    female refugees, 162–64
    shortage of workers, 64, 235–37, 274n.21
    women's reproductive health, 162–63
Health Inclusivity Index, 274n.21
health integration, 222
healthy-migrant effect, refugees, 201–2
helplessness, refugees with feelings of, 48
Hindu nationalist party, India, 53
history, forced displacement in, 24–25
Hoffman, David, 82–83
Holocaust, 61–63
    children of survivors, 191
    mental health among survivors, 187
    PTSD for offspring of survivors, 184–85, 196–97
    survivors and offspring, 177–79
hopelessness, refugees with feelings of, 48
Hopkins Checklist (HSCL-25), 72–73, 73n.12
    Anxiety and Depression subscales, 73–74
Hopkins Symptom Checklist-25, 281t
host nations
    complex trauma of refugees, 60–63
    fatal journeys for refugees in, 50–52
    health professionals assisting refugees, 63–66

high social cost of stereotyping refugees, 54–56
reception of refugees, 52–66
resettlement systems, 215–16
xenophobia and intergroup relations, 213–14
human immunodeficiency virus, 18–19
humanitarian emergencies, refugee mental health care, 34–36
humanitarian professionals, readership for refugee crisis, 23–24
Human Rights Council, 160
Human Rights Institute, 36–38
Hutu refugees, Tanzania, 114
hypertension, 18–19, 259

Iceland, resettlement (2021), 217f
identity
    collective suffering in age of globalization, 123–12
    cultural and cognitive frameworks of, 110–13
    defacing, 113
    disguising, 114–15
    emergent Muslim, 122–23
    factors shaping formation of, 119–23
    flight experience of refugee, 118–19
    German refugees, 126
    institutional schemas, 119–21
    makeshift, 113–18
    oppositional, 121
    quest for the self, 109–10
    refugees, 108–9
    in search of, 115–18
    view from displacement, 113–18
idioms, 141–42
Iglesias, Enrique
    experience at airport, 118–19
    Hamza (Syrian refugee) identity as, 107
Illegal Immigration Reform and Immigrant Responsibility Act (1996), United States, 103
illegal migrants, distinction between refugees and, 55
illness experience, 134
immigrant policies, 201
Immigration & Human Rights Clinic, University of the District of Columbia, 102
immigration issue, United States politics, 271–72
India
    Bengalis in Assam, 4–5

disaster-related internal displacement
(2021), 7*f*
heat stress in, 8
refugee populations, 54
India-Pakistan Partition, 24
Indonesia, disaster-related internal
displacement (2021), 7*f*
infectious diseases, 18–19
insecurity, 3
Institute for Employment Research (IEB),
Germany, 44n.344
Institutional Review Board (IRB), 70–71, 70n.9
integration
case studies of UK and Switzerland, 225–28
case study of US Resettlement Program
(USRAP), 218–20
challenges of, 207–11
concept of, 207
cultural, 221, 226
definition of, 206–7
economic, 221
educational, 222
female refugees, 168–71
health, 222
immigrant in host society, 204–5
immigrant policies, 201
language, 221
legal, 221
mental health and socioeconomic, 207–11
mental health of minorities, 205–7
nonrecognition of, gaps, 222–28
political, 221
recommendations promoting cultural
competence for healthy, 243–45
refugee communities, 221–22
social, 221, 225
social mixing, 207n.51
study of, 204
successful, of refugees, 202–3, 228–31
term, 206–7
unemployed Muslim youth as breakdown
of, 122
xenophobia and intergroup relations of host
societies, 213–14
integration (*Selbsthilfe*), 52
integration policies
cultural themes and, 64–65
Germany, 64
host countries, 47
refugees well-being, 47–48
Interagency Standing Committee
(IASC), 255–56

intergroup relations, host societies, 213–14
International Center for Philosophy, Bonn
University, xviii
International Classification of Diseases (ICD-
11), 26
International Covenant on Civil and Political
Rights, 80nn.5–6
International Organization for Migration
(IOM), 13n.77
international refugee organizations, refugee
crisis readers, 23–24
interoception, 262
intersubjectivity, connectivity of emotions, 181
internally-displaced, 3
difference between, and refugees, 3n.2,
13n.80, 15–16, 15n.92, 207n.54, 258–59
Guiding Principles on Internal Displacement
(1998), 13n.80
southern Madagascar, 5n.29, 278
UNHCR's mandate, 3n.2
interventions, 234, 236–40
community-centered trauma, 257
refugees, 236–40
intervention science, refugee, 48
interviews/stories
Afghan man Arbaz, 50
Akbar (Afghan) as refugee, 147–48
Arwa's story, 67–69
Ashwaq Haji Hamid (Yazidi girl), 171
Badam as asylum-seeker in
Norway, 237–38
depression of refugee, 200
Emini, Yazidi man, 123–24
Gulnaz and torture in Syria, 78–79, 89–90,
89–90n.83, 93, 95, 97–99, 106
Hamza, Syrian refugee, and identity, 107, 115,
118–19, 125–26
Hosni Syrian refugee, 127–28, 138–
39, 143–44
miracle method for interviewing, 74n.16
Mossamet Nasima in Bangladesh, 159
Mrs. Khaled as Kurdish Syrian refugee, 152–
53, 166, 167–68, 171, 183–85
Nishad as Afghani refugee, 148–49
pharmacist Mr. Ben, refugee in
Germany, 241–42
posttraumatic symptoms of Syrian
refugee, 181
qualitative, with primary sources, 72n.11
qualitative methodology, 73–74nn.14–15
refugee crisis, 11–12
refugee Rumi's rape in Canada, 232–33

interviews/stories (*cont.*)
  refugees in Germany, 71, 72–73
  Sabrina and Sana (twin sisters) in
      Germany, 169–70
  Sabris (Johnny, Sara, and Faisal) of Syria,
      1–2, 48–49
  Zahira on her detention, 160–61
Iran, Covid-19, 19–21
Iranian King Khosrow, 24
Iraq
  resettled Iraqis in U.S., 32–33
  resettled refugees (2022), 218*f*
  resettlement of refugees, 230–31
Iraqi-Kurdish women, self-immolation, 29–30,
      30n.219
Ireland, resettlement (2021), 217*f*
irregular migrants, 13n.77, 277–78
Islamic State of Iraq and Syria (ISIS), 91–
      92, 114, 118, 166, 168–69, 171, 174,
      176n.13, 232
Islegias, Enrique, Hamza masquerading
      as, 114–15
Israel
  collective punishment of civilians, 2
  creation of, in 1948, 24–25
  displaced Palestinians of 1948 Arab and, 13
  posttraumatic stress in ex-prisoner of
      war, 196
  traumatized children, 196
Italy, resettlement (2021), 217*f*

Japan
  resettlement (2021), 217*f*
  resettlement of refugees, 230–31
Jews
  emigration from Nazi Germany, 24–25
  Holocaust and, 61–62
jigar khun, cultural syndrome, 141, 142
Joestar, Arthur Britney, 170–71
Jordan
  assimilation process as Jordanization, 53–54
  Covid-19, 19–21
  refugee surge in, 44
  Syrian refugees in, 258–59
Joseph, Suad, 182
jus cogens, prohibition against torture, 79–80

Kalobeyei Settlement, 44
Kampala Convention, 15n.92
karma, concept of, 135
Kenya, Somali refugees in, 259

Khan, Majid, 81–82
khapa, Afghani women, 139
Khat, 259
Khmer Rouge reign, Cambodia, 193, 197
khwaja siras, protection gaps for, 15–16
Kleinschmidt, Kilian, 236
Kosovar war, affected families, 190–91

Lamb, Christina, 142
language integration, 221
Lawyers and Doctors for Human Rights
      (LDHR), 160
Lebanon, resettlement of refugees, 230–31
legal integration, 221
leishmaniasis, 18–19
lesbian, gay, bisexual, transgender, and queer
      (LGBTQ), 131, 270, 275
lesbian, gay, bisexual, transgender, queer, and
      intersex life (LGBTQI+) asylum seekers,
      vulnerable population, 263–64
Lhotshampa, Nepal, 24–25
lice, 18–19
lifetime trauma, refugees, 19–21
listening, White Heart (empathic) and White
      Coat (detached), 70
lived experiences, vulnerable
      communities, 38–42
Locke, John, 109
Louis XIV (King), Protestant Huguenots fleeing
      religious persecution, 25
low- and middle-income countries, internally
      displaced, 3–4, 10n.60

Madagascar, migrants in, 276
malaria, 18–19
maps
  child asylum seekers, xv*f*
  conflict-related displacements, xv*f*
  countries/communities vulnerable to
      extreme climate events (2022), xii*f*
  displaced (2022), xi*f*
  fatal crossings for asylum seekers
      (2022), xiii*f*
  protection gap (2021), xiv*f*
  top ten countries/communities with climate-
      related internal displacement, xii*f*
marital relationships, posttraumatic stress
      in, 186–87
masculinity
  cultural script of, 129–30
  cultural value of, 127–28

massive trauma, 26
  systems view of, 26–28
  World War II, 40
Mayflower, Protestants sailing aboard, 24–25
memory
  recall in torture, 95
  trauma and, 93–94
mental health
  active engagement, 202
  case study of US Resettlement Program
    (USRAP), 218–20
  children, 187–89
  complex trauma of refugees, 33–34
  culture in public, 128–33
  displacement, 7–8
  integration for, of minorities, 205–7
  intervention contexts, 236–40
  limitations of refugee, in humanitarian
    settings, 34–36
  medical management of, 258–60
  multicultural societies addressing, 22
  obstacles for refugees, 33
  older refugees, 265–67
  picture of, in conflict and post-conflict
    settings, 237–38
  posttraumatic stress disorder (PTSD),
    73–74n.15
  ramifications of wars, 177–79
  refugee, 19–21
  refugee interviews, 12
  refugees' well-being, 45
  social and cultural integration and,
    225–28
  socioeconomic integration and,
    207–11
  specialized needs of asylum seekers, 65
  see also treatment planning
mental health and psychosocial support
  (MHPSS), 255–56
mental health services, readership for refugee
  crisis, 22–24
Merkel, Angela, 148
Mexico, PTSD diagnosis by Oaxacan
  therapists, 145–46
Middle East
  distress in refugees, 133
  distress manifested as, 143
  prevalence of torture, 86–87
migration, *hijrah*, flight to mark Muslim
  calendar, 25, 25n.170
Missing Migrant Project, 52n.13

modern society, refugee crisis and, 9–11
moksha, concept of, 135
motivational orientation, 137
Muecke, Marjorie, 169
Muslims
  discrimination of women, xviin.2
  emergent identity, 122–23
  ethnic identity of, 211, 212
  identity in youth culture, 122
  identity of, 111
  refugee crisis, 9
mutuality, 63
Mwakavuha, Nyata, 142
Myanmar
  refugees, 13
  refugees (2021), 14*f*
  resettled refugees (2022), 218*f*

narrative exposure therapy (NET), 251–
  52, 253–54
Nasima, Mossamet, 159
nationalism, integration, 201
Nazi Germany, 24–25
Nepal, Lhotshampa eviction, 24–25
Netherlands
  case of buddy system, 264
  integration in, 217–18, 225n.145
  refugee resettlement, 216*f*
  resettlement (2021), 217*f*
New Zealand
  refugee resettlement, 216*f*
  resettlement (2021), 217*f*
Nez Percé of Pacific Northwest, violence
  endured by, 25
nonrefoulement, principle of, 15n.86
normative orientation, 137
Norway
  Badam as asylum-seeker in, 237–38
  refugee resettlement, 216*f*
  resettlement (2021), 217*f*
  segregation in education, 222
  Syrian refugees' integration, 208

object orientation, 136
Okwurime, Oscar Lucky, 86
older refugees, vulnerable population,
  265–67
Ontario International Development
  Agency, 159
oppositional identity, 121
Orange, Donna, 69–70

Organisation for Economic Cooperation and Development (OECD), 22, 116
Organisation of African Unity (OAU), 15n.84
Other(s)
    creation of, 53–54
    crimes against, 55–56
    cultural, 119–20
    idea of a foreign, 201
    "otherness" as, 45n.350
    refugee as subversive, 53
    refugees vulnerable to identity, 125
Othering, 120–21
Otieno, John, 242
Outline for Cultural Formulation (OCF), DSM-5, 130

Pakistan, Covid-19, 19–21
Palestine
    displaced Palestinians of 1948 Arab-Israeli war, 13
    multigenerational displacement, 18
    partition, 24–25
    refugees, 3n.2
    word, 53–54
pandemic, 3
parental psychopathology
    dysfunctional family dynamics, 192
    family functioning, 188
patriarchy, 30–31
Persian Gulf War (1991), 149
Peru, internal armed conflict in, 55
pharmacotherapy
    ethnopsychopharmacology, 259–60
    medical management of mental health, 258–60
    psychopharmacology, 258
Philippines, disaster-related internal displacement (2021), 7f
Physicians for Human Rights Research (PHR), 242
Pinheiro, Paulo, 87
Poland
    mental health practitioners, 274n.21
    refugee interviews, 11
    Ukrainian refugees in, 65–66, 268–69, 272, 272n.11
political integration, 221
Portugal, resettlement (2021), 217f

post-conflict communities
    family functioning, 192–93
    trauma in, 29–34
posttraumatic stress
    frames of experience in psychological field, 135–38
    intergenerational impact of trauma, 193–95
    Israeli ex-prisoner-of-war (ex-POW), 196
    maternal, 183–85
    refugee interviews, 12
    refugee mental health care, 34–35
    refugees, 19–21
    silent majority, 233–36
posttraumatic stress disorder (PTSD), 73–74n.15
    biological bases, 26–27n.183
    child mental health, 187
    diagnosis of, 246
    displaced Kurdish women in Turkey, 156n.29
    economic burden of, 270, 270n.7
    father's, 175
    gendered nature of, 154–58
    health care costs, 270n.7
    inflammatory markers, 26–27n.183
    Khat chewers and, 259
    longitudinal studies of refugee families, 195–99
    Oaxacan women in Mexico, 145–46
    paternal and maternal, 184–85
    refugee population in Germany, 56–57
    refugees in Poland, 269
    substance abuse and, 60
    third generation PTSD focused CBT, 247n.108
    trauma memories, 262–63
    understanding trauma, 128–29
    United States, 140–41
posttraumatic stress syndrome, 87n.65
poverty, 3
practitioners, readership for refugee crisis, 22–23
principle of nonrefoulement, 15n.86
Private Sponsorship of Refugees (PSR), 215–16
protection, withholding of removal, 103–4, 103n.168
protection gap
    map (2021), xivf
    refugees, and protracted displacement, 13–19
    special populations, 15–16
proverbs, 76

psychic trauma, term, 146–47
psychological health, social-political
    conditions, xviii, 18–19
psychopharmacology, 258
Psychosocial Center for Refugees in Düsseldorf
    (PSZ), 60
psychosocial trauma, 124
public health, conflicts and wars, 236–37
pushbacks of refugees, xviii–xix, 272, 272n.13

Qamishli riot, 98
Quran, 114

race, refugees, 211–13
randomized control trials (RCTs), treatment of
    refugees, 245–46
rape, maternal health and, 260–63
readership, refugee crisis, 22–24
Red Cross, 70–71, 268
refugee(s)
    approximate cash assistance upon arrival in
        countries (2022), 223f
    benefits of social inclusion, 42–45
    complex trauma of refugees, 60–63
    consequences of delayed treatment 40,
        40–41n.311
    by country of origin (2021), 14f
    culture competence in services for, 150
    depression in, 200–5
    evidence-based practice in treatment
        of, 245–46
    high social cost of stereotyping, 54–56
    host countries framing of, 52–66
    identity, 108–9
    international and interdisciplinary
        research, 22
    intervention contexts, 236–40
    older, 265–67
    parents, 32n.248, 183, 192–93, 197–98
    post-traumatic stress, 261–62, 262n.221
    pushbacks of, xviii–xix, 272, 272n.13
    religion, ethnicity and race, 211–13
    silent majority, 149–50
    substance abuse, 59–60
    successful flight is survival, 17–18
    successful integration, 202–3, 228–31
    survivors vs. victims, 39n.297
    term, 15–16
    treatment planning in conflict-
        affected, 240–45

weaponizing, in hybrid wars, 21
White Heart (empathic) and White Coat
    (detached), 70
word, 25
see also family trauma; female refugees
Refugee Act (1980), 223n.137
Refugee Convention (1951). 15n.83, 54,
    117n.46, 202
refugee crisis
    approach of book, 22
    benefits of social inclusion of
        refugees, 42–45
    conflict-affected and untreated
        trauma, 26–34
    experiences of social exclusion and
        integration, 34–42
    forced displacement in history, 24–25
    interviews, 11–12
    mental health, 19–21
    Muslims at Europe's door, 9
    protection gap and protracted
        displacement, 13–19
    Sabris (Johnny, Sara, and Faisal), 1–2
    setting of, 3–11
    Ukraine, 9–11
refugee protection, legal instruments
    Cartegena Declaration on Refugees, 15n.85
    Geneva Convention, 15n.83
    1951 Refugee Convention, 15n.84
    Organisation of African Unity Convention
        Governing the Specific Aspects of Refugee
        Problems in Africa, 15n.84
refugees experiences
    importance of lived experiences of vulnerable
        communities, 38–42
    limitations of mental health care, 34–36
    one-size-fits-all national resettlement
        framework, 36–38
    social exclusion and integration, 34–42
    US resettlement system, 37f
Refugee Status Determination, 172–73,
    275–76
refugee women
    access to care, 30–31
    see also female refugees
reincarnation, concept of, 135
religion
    as fusion of ethos, 110n.14
    Muslim communities, 122–23
    refugees, 211–13

Republic of Korea, resettlement (2021), 217*f*
Research Centre on Migration, Integration, and Asylum of the Federal Office of Migration and Refugees (BAMF-FZ), 44n.344
resettled refugee communities
  as disadvantaged groups, 31–32
  resettled to third countries, 16n.98
  trauma in, 29–34
  under UNHCR protection, 16n.97
resettlement
  case study of US Resettlement Program (USRAP), 218–20
  countries of (2021), 217*f*
  definition of, 216–17
  individual and public expressions of culture, 216–20
  refugee rights and, 230–31
resettlement framework, one-size-fits-all national, 36–38
resettlement programs, professionals assisting refugees, 63–66
resettlement systems, host nations, 215–16
resignation syndrome, Sweden, 139–40
Rio Grande/US border, 18
Rohingya refugees, 244n.85
Rohingya women, Burmese military and, 159
Romania, resettlement (2021), 217*f*
Rometsch, Caroline, 91–92
Rose, Jacqueline, 101
Rousseau, Jean-Jacques, 111–12
Roy, Olivier, 111
Russia, invasion of Ukraine, 4–5
Rwanda, complex intergroup dynamics, 30–31

Sabris (Johnny, Sara, and Faisal)
  chemical attack on, 1–2, 48–49
  refugee crisis of, 1–2
  setting of conflict, 3
Sahara Desert, 16–17
Salvadoran refugees, culture of terror, 147
scabies, 18–19
schizophrenia, 233n.6, 238, 238n.42, 269
selective serotonin reuptake inhibitors (SSRIs), 258–59
self, Other and, 120–21
self-help, 63
self-help (*Sittenverständnis*), 52
self-orientation, 136
self-trust, Cambodian refugees, 169

semen loss syndrome, India, 139–40
Serbian refugees, traumas, 124–25
sexual violence
  child marriages, 176–77, 177nn.15–16
  conflict-related, 79n.2
  definition, 155n.23
  female refugees, 155–58
  female, *Trümmerfrau* (Germany's "rubble women"), 40n.303, 62
  male, in childhood, 79n.1
  male, in detention, 85–86
  power dynamics, social roles and, 159–62
  rape and maternal health of women, 260–63
  torture and, 96–97
  women's reproductive health, 162–63
Sharia law, 114
silent majority
  refugee survivors as, 149–50
  triple trauma of, 233–36
Sittenverständnis, framework of, 60
skin conditions, 18–19
social construction, refugees, 54–55
social exclusion, cultural competency, 273
social inclusion, benefits of, of refugees, 42–45
social integration, 221, 225
  definition, 225
  refugees resettling in Switzerland, 227–28
  Syrian refugees in Turkey, 228
social psychology, emotion, 180
Socio-Economic Panel (SOEP), German Institute for Economic Research, 44n.344
Somalia
  refugees (2021), 14*f*
  refugees in Kenya, 259
  resettled refugees (2022), 218*f*
  social integration in Minnesota, 221
Somali paradox, 120–21
Somatization, definition of, 261–62
South Sudan
  alleged sex abuse by UN aid workers, 270n.6
  refugees, 13
  refugees (2021), 14*f*
  refugee women, 114
  resettled refugees (2022), 218*f*
Spain, resettlement (2021), 217*f*
spatial orientation, 136–37
special populations, protection gaps for, 15–16
spoils of war, 238
statelessness, 3–4, 176–77
  displaced and backlash, 3n.3, 4–5

hierarchy of human life, 95, 185
migrant-management policies, xix
Syrian refugees in Turkey, 213–14, 228
stateless person
definition, 4n.11
displaced El Salvadoreans, 4n.20
displaced Guatemalan, 4n.20
displaced Hondurans, 4n.20
displaced Hong Kong residents, 4n.20
stories. See interviews/stories
substance abuse, refugees and, 59–60
substance use disorders, torture and, 96
Sudan
refugees, 13
refugees (2021), 14f
resettled refugees (2022), 218f
Sudanese fleeing violence, 4–5
suicidal ideation, Bhutanese communities in
U.S., 32–33
suicide, refugees, 32–33
Sunni Muslims, Palestinian refugees, 53–54
survivors, refugees of complex trauma, 39n.297
Sweden
approximate cash assistance to refugees upon
arrival (2022), 223f
Finnish children in, 188
refugee groups relative to migrants and native
population, 210–11
refugee resettlement, 216f
refugees in, 43–44
resettlement (2021), 217f
segregation in education, 222
sub-Saharan refugees in, 31–32
Syrian refugees resettled in, 182
tortured refugees in, 88
Swedish Migration Board, identity expert, 113
Switzerland
case studies for integration and mental
health, 225–28
integration, 204
resettlement (2021), 217f
social integration in, 227–28
Sykes-Picot agreement, 10n.62
Syria
chemical attack on, 1–2, 2n.1
child marriages, 176–77, 177nn.15–16
conflict-related internal displacement (2021-
2022), 6f
conflict and Sykes-Picot agreement, 10n.62
experience of Manas (student), 136
Ghouta chemical attack, 1–2, 48–49

Gulnaz and torture in, 78–79, 89–90, 89–
90n.83, 93, 95, 97–99, 106
Hosni as refugee of, 127–28, 138–39,
143–44
marital relations of refugees from, 186–87
Mrs. Khaled as Kurdish refugee from, 152–
53, 166, 167–68, 171
posttraumatic symptoms of refugee
from, 181
refugees, 13
refugees (2021), 14f
suicide of children, 29–30
torture of English Teacher, 97–99
typical refugee experience, 29
Syrian Arab Rep., resettled refugees
(2022), 218f
Syrian Network for Human Rights, 161
systemic gender-based abuses, 30–31
systemic interventions, 255–56

Taijinkyofusho, Japan, 139–40
Tanzania
Burundi refugees to, 114
Hutu refugees in, 114
testimonies, 159–60, 252
Canadian residential schools, 41n.314
refugees' mutilated bodies as, 38–39
trauma of Indigenous children, 41n.314
therapy
self-awareness in, 69–70
White Heart (empathic) approach and White
Coat (detached), 70
thymos, group bonding over feelings of, 121
"Tisniy Svit," world is small, 9–11
Tokyo Declaration, 80–81, 80–81n.10
torture, 79–84
asylum process and, 46
chronic pain syndrome, 91–92
definition of, 79–80, 85
electrocution, 89–90, 89–90n.83
of English teacher, 97–99
Gulnaz as survivor of, 39–40
high voltage of, 87–97
international treaties, 80n.5
male sexual violence and, 79n.1
memory recall in, 95
prevalence of, 81–84
prohibition against, as jus cogens, 79–80
recovery and rehabilitation, 104–5
refugees and, 85–87
refugees enduring, 21

torture (*cont.*)
    retelling, for asylum application, 99–106
    sexual, 96–97
    silent epidemic, 88
    somatic maelstrom, 89–91
    substance use disorder, 96
    trauma and memory, 93–94
    treatment of survivors of, 240–41
transnational marriage, British
        Pakistanis, 212–13
trauma
    community-centered interventions, 257
    cultural meanings, 144
    demands of present vs. past, 64
    displacement in the self, 28
    experience of, 46
    fixity, 28
    hands-on experience with patients'
        complex, xviii
    initiatives for displaced populations, 274
    integration initiatives, 45
    intergenerational impact of, 193–95
    massive, 26
    memory and, 93–94
    multiple forms of, 249n.124
    negotiating healing and, 145–51
    oppressive social relations, 28n.205
    parental psychopathology, 191
    positive circular feedback loop, 28
    post-conflict and resettled
        communities, 29–34
    refugee mental health, 33–34
    sexual and somatic health, 263
    somatization, 261–62
    triple, of silent majority, 233–36
    war-affected families and, 174–79
    wide-angle systems approach, 28
    word, 26
    see also family trauma
traumatic brain injury (TBI), 234, 261n.217
treatment planning
    cognitive therapies, 247–63
    conflict-affected refugees, 240–45
    evidence-based practice, 245–46
    merging evidence-based and cultural
        practice, 246–47
    see also cognitive therapies
tricyclic antidepressants (TCAs), 258–59
Trinity College, xvii
Troare, Kobili
    murder of Sarah Halimi, 52–53
    verdict, 53

"Trümmerfrau," Germany's 'rubble
        woman', 62
tuberculosis, 18–19
Turkey
    Alevi Kurdish refugees from, 225–26
    antipathy toward Syrians in, 214
    displaced Kurdish women in, 156n.29
    economic investment into, 214
    resettlement of refugees, 230–31
    social inclusion of Syrian refugees, 42–43
    xenophobia and intergroup relations of,
        213–14

Uganda, female refugees from, 157
Ukraine
    conflict-related internal displacement
        (2021–2022), 6f
    first Christmas after Russian invasion, 268
    refugee crisis, 9–11
    refugee interviews, 9–11
    refugees, 13
    refugees (2021), 14f
    refugees in Poland from, 268–69, 272,
        272n.11
    Russian invasion of, 4–5
    surrogacy of war, 9n.50
Ukrainians, 3n.2
United for Intercultural Action, 52n.14
United Kingdom (UK)
    approximate cash assistance to refugees upon
        arrival (2022), 223f
    case studies for integration and mental
        health, 225–28
    examination of refugees in, 209–10
    Fourth National Survey of Ethnic Minorities
        (FNSEM), 211
    health patterns of refugees, 210
    mental health of refugees, 210
    Meteorological Office, 8
    Refugee Council, 215–16
    refugee groups relative to migrants and native
        population, 210–11
    resettlement (2021), 217f
United Nations, 255–56
    responsibilities, 15n.83
United Nations Commission of Inquiry, 87
United Nations Convention Against
        Torture and Other Cruel, Inhuman
        or Degrading Treatment or
        Punishment, 79–80
United Nations Development Program
        (UNDP), 270

United Nations High Commissioner for
    Refugees (UNHCR), 115–16, 236
United Nations Security Council, Resolution
    1325, 29n.216, 172
United States
    APA members colluding with CIA, 82–83,
        82n.25, 82–83n.28
    approximate cash assistance to refugees upon
        arrival (2022), 223f
    case study of US Resettlement Program
        (USRAP), 218–20
    child mental health, 188
    Covid-19, 19–21
    crime and refugees, 55–56, 56n.40
    disaster-related internal displacement
        (2021), 7f
    Illegal Immigration Reform and Immigrant
        Responsibility Act (1996), 103
    immigration issue in US politics,
        271–72
    income status of refugees in, 32–33
    integration, 204
    Mexican asylum-seekers, 270n.3
    Nez Percé of Pacific Northwest, 25
    polarization of politics in, 53
    posttraumatic stress disorder (PTSD)
        in, 140–41
    refugee groups relative to migrants and native
        population, 210–11
    refugee program, 215–16
    refugee resettlement, 216f
    refugees in 2022, 17–18
    resettled Iraqis in, 32–33
    resettlement (2021), 217f
    resettlement system, 36–38, 37f
    Somalis of Minnesota, 221
    State Department, 23
    structure of USRAP, 220
    successful integration, 228, 229
    survivors of police brutality, 81–82
    Title 42, 270n.3, 272, 272n.14
    transportation of migrants
        around, 272
    US Immigration and Customs
        Enforcement, 242
    US Refugee Admissions Program (USRAP),
        36–38, 37f
Universal Declaration of Human Rights,
    80nn.5–6
University of Chicago, xvii
Uppgivenhetssyndrom, Sweden, 139–40
Uruguay, resettlement (2021), 217f

Uyghur, no mercy in China, 3–4

varicella, 18–19
Venezuela
    refugees, 13
    resettled refugees (2022), 218f
Venezuelans, 3n.2
Viet Nam, disaster-related internal
    displacement (2021), 7f
Vietnamese, refugees in U.S., 32–33
Vietnam War veterans
    participation in violence, 190
    posttraumatic stress disorder
        (PTSD), 190
vulnerable populations
    importance of lived experiences of,
        38–42
    LGBTQI+ asylum seekers, 263–64
    older refugees, 265–67
    see also experiences of the vulnerable

war
    children and family suffering from, 47
    families affected by, 174–79
    public health and, 236–37
    refugees as witness, 21
    secondary trauma as emotional
        syndrome, 177–79
    treatment planning in conflict-affected
        refugees, 240–45
    violence on refugees, 29–30
    weaponizing refugees in hybrid, 21
    see also family trauma
weather-related disasters, common, 7–8
well-being
    refugee population in Germany, 56–58
    refugees integration boosting, 47–48
    refugees mental health and, 45
wide-angle systems approach, trauma, 28
Windgasse, Annette, 60–61, 63–64
withholding of removal, protection, 103–4,
    103n.168
World Central Kitchen, 268
World Economic Forum, Refugee Employment
    and Employability Initiative of, 279
World Health Organization, complex
    posttraumatic stress disorder (CPTSD),
    26, 26n.181
World Health Organization in Syria
    (WHO-Syria), 236–37
World Medical Association (WMA), 79–80n.3,
    243n.71

World War II, 24, 40
    child mental health, 187–88
    Holocaust and, 61–62
    offspring of refugee parents, 197–98
World Weather Attribution
        Report, 5n.29

xenophobia, host societies, 213–14
xerosis cutis, 18–19

Yacevich, Ilya, 257

Yazidis
    complex trauma of, 167
    German resettled females, 91–92
    interview of Ashwaq Haji Hamid, 171
    rape and maternal health of women, 260, 261–62
yellow jacket, France, 53
Yemen, conflict-related internal displacement
        (2021-2022), 6f

Zanes, Eyad, 236–37
zones of anguish, 18–19